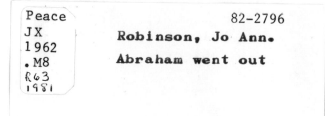
DATE			

Abraham Went Out

A Biography of A. J. Muste

Abraham Went Out

A Biography of A. J. Muste

Jo Ann Ooiman Robinson

Shambaugh Library

Temple University Press

Philadelphia

Temple University Press, Philadelphia 19122
© 1981 by Temple University. All rights reserved
Published 1981
Printed in the United States of America

Library of Congress Cataloging in Publication Data

Robinson, Jo Ann.
  Abraham went out.

  Bibliography: p.
  Includes index.
  1. Muste, Abraham John, 1885–1967. 2. Pacifists—United States—Biography. I. Title.
JX1962.M8R63   327.1′72′0924 [B]   81-14492
ISBN 0-87722-231-2   AACR2

To Joseph and Eleanor

If a man sets himself a goal for his endeavor here
in this life, and he fails to reach it,
then, in the judgment of eternity,
it is quite possible that he may be blameless.

Yes, he may even be worthy of praise.

He might have been prevented by death,
or by an adversity that is beyond his control;
in which case he is entirely without blame.

He might even have been prevented from reaching the goal
just by being unwilling to use any other means
than those which the judgment of eternity permits.

In which case by his very renunciation of
the impatience of passion and the inventions of cleverness,
he is even worthy of praise. . . .

He whose means are invariably just as important as the end,
never comes too late. Eternity is not curious and impatient
as to what the outcome in this world of time will be.

It is just because of this that the means
are without exception as important as the end.
To earthly and worldly passion, this observation
must seem shocking and paralyzing.

To it conscience must seem the most paralyzing thing of all.

For conscience is indeed "a blushing innocent spirit
that sets up a tumult in a man's breast and fills him
with difficulties" just because to conscience the means
are without exception as important as the end.

Soren Kierkegaard, 1950

Acknowledgments

Over the years that I have worked on this book I have acquired a huge debt to the many people who have helped me. Not all of them can be named here, though the names of some appear in the Bibliography under "Oral and Living Sources" and others—librarians and archivists—are indirectly acknowledged in the listing of their libraries under the designation "Manuscript Sources." To staff from the four libraries where I spent the most time—the Eisenhower Library at the Johns Hopkins University, the Swarthmore College Peace Collection, the Haverford College Library, and the Walter Reuther Archives at Wayne State University—and to the Reference Service of the Enoch Pratt Free Library in Baltimore, I am especially indebted. A graduate fellowship from Johns Hopkins, a faculty research grant and sabbatical leave from Morgan State University, and a T. Wistar Brown Fellowship from Haverford College supported important parts of my research. I am grateful to each of these institutions.

To those who read all or parts of the manuscript and shared their advice and reactions, I owe thanks. Charles A. Barker, my graduate advisor and mentor, tops this list, which also includes John Howard Yoder, president of Goshen College; Benjamin Quarles, Emeritus Professor of History at Morgan State University; Frank A. Warren, Professor of History at Queens College; Muste's daughter and son, Nancy Muste Baker and John Muste; his comrades Cara Cook, Barbara Deming, Bill Sutherland, and John Swomley; and my friends Bruce R. Conard, Mary Kovner, and Joseph Kovner.

For leavening my research and interview experiences with hospitality, I thank Dr. and Mrs. Kenneth Bernard in Newtonville, Massachusetts, Dr. and Mrs. Victor Paschkis in Pottstown, Pennsylvania, and numerous friends in and around Haverford College. Thanks are due also to Kenneth Arnold, Editor-in-Chief at Temple University Press, for the patience and good advice that encouraged me to transform an unwieldy manuscript into a book. I am indebted to Jane

Sellman and Deborah Kohl for editorial and research assistance and to Shirley A. Patterson and Melanie Many for expert typing.

Some kinds of help go beyond the actual work on a manuscript. In this regard I am grateful to William Robinson for bearing the many pressures that having an author in the household placed on him. I am also thankful for the support of my parents, Albert W. Ooiman and Zillah M. Ooiman; for the inspiration of two Denver public school teachers, Vernice Van Duzer and the late Ernest D. Ramstetter; and for three special friendships that date from the years that I spent at Knox College in Galesburg, Illinois, and that have been a source of enrichment ever since—the friendships of my teacher and guide, Professor Emeritus John L. Stipp, Cleo M. Stipp, and Audrey Conard. Final thanks are reserved for yet another friend, Gertrude S. Williams, Principal par excellence of Barclay Elementary School in Baltimore; her caring and assistance helped our family over the rough spots in the last stages of this undertaking.

Contents

Introduction

Who is this A. J. Muste?" asked the editors of *The World Tomorrow* on their front cover in June 1929. That question was destined to crop up again and again in the next thirty-odd years and is no doubt in the minds of some readers now.

In 1929—when Muste was forty-four years old—the American Federation of Labor said he was a communist; the American Communist Party said he was a reactionary tool of the capitalists; the magazine that posed the question portrayed him as "a square shooter . . . fighting for a different sort of labor movement from what there is in America today."[1]

Estimates before then—based on his work as pastor in Dutch Reformed and Congregationalist parishes—had marked him as "a spiritual power" and "a man of unusual genius and consecration." The latter estimate, however, came from the same parishioners who, being unable in 1918 to accept his pacifism, had accepted his resignation instead.[2]

In the 1930s—with a sizeable following of workers committed to broad-based and industrial (as opposed to limited and craft) union organizing—Muste was widely discussed in terms of "Musteism," a phenomenon that Stalinists and American Federation of Laborites found threatening while writers and social critics such as Edmund Wilson, Sinclair Lewis, and John Dos Passos noted it with favor. Musteism was also the subject of satire; in the *Saturday Review* a cartoon portrayed the society matron–hostess introducing her guest of honor: "Mr. Pixley, our very foremost authority on Socialism, Musteism, Lovestoneism and Mickey Mouse."[3]

In later years a photograph of Muste appeared in *Time Magazine* over the caption "The Number One U.S. Pacifist." J. Edgar Hoover denounced him as a "long-time communist fronter." A Senate chaplain cited him as a prime example of "moral flabbiness." Martin Luther King, Jr., claimed that without

Muste, "the American Negro might never have caught the meaning of nonviolence." Historian Oscar Handlin saw increasing public interest in Muste in the 1960s as part of "a revival of infantile leftism." Without a doubt the individual who took the safest approach to describing A. J. Muste was the clergyman who had written in 1914, "We cannot but feel that he will develop into a very unusual man."[4]

To examine the full, complex eighty-two years of A. J. Muste's life is the purpose of this biography. The focus is on the central objectives and activities that he pursued. For purposes of coherent description these have been defined as religion, labor, civil rights, civil liberties, and pacifism.

Part One describes Muste's progress from the intellectually orthodox and politically conservative surroundings of his boyhood to the unorthodox and radical activities that he later embraced. It stresses the central role that religious training and personal religious experience played in shaping his character and patterns of behavior and underlines the religious nature of his adult career.

As a man of religion Muste was deeply influenced by the Old Testament prophets, the teachings of Jesus, the example of the earliest Christians, and certain mystics, including George Fox, founder of the Quakers. By emulating the spirit of these figures and by commending that spirit to modern religious institutions, Muste helped maintain the vitality and viability of that often disparaged but historically influential tradition of the social gospel. He did none of the things that bring the better-known social gospel figures to the immediate attention of historians—maintaining long tenure in a famous pulpit, or engaging in systematic religious scholarship, or publishing a social gospel newspaper, or climbing the ladder within a denominational hierarchy. But one historian who has attempted to probe to the heart of the social gospel tradition—Donald B. Meyer in *The Protestant Search for Political Realism*—has found in Muste "the most perfect exemplar of the pure, unmixed, unadulterated social-gospel soul." "In Muste," Meyer writes, "we see in one of its striking forms what politics looks like when it is eternal."[5]

Muste's work in the labor movement is also described and documented here. As noted above, in the 1920s and early thirties, Musteite unions among miners and steelworkers defied A.F. of L. insistence on organizing along craft lines. Musteite concern for black workers, women workers, and young workers stood in stark contrast to the discriminatory values of establishment unions. Musteite unemployed leagues addressed the sufferings of jobless masses, in whom most labor leaders took scant interest. Two developments ultimately undermined Musteism. First, the principle of industrial unionism won support in New Deal legislation and was incorporated, albeit in often watered-down or distorted form, into the policies of the Congress of Industrial Organizations. Second, Muste entered an alliance with the American followers of Leon Trotsky, which ended in the destruction of Muste's own organizational base and the erosion of his position as a labor leader. This eclipse of Musteism at the very moment when the star of John L. Lewis was so dramatically rising helps explain why American history books talk so much of Lewis and usually not at all of Muste.

Part Two of this biography examines Muste's achievements in the areas of civil rights, civil liberties, and anti-war action. Muste did not achieve fame as a civil libertarian. Yet it is difficult to name a major civil liberties case in the United States after World War I to which he did not devote some energy—Mooney-Billings; Sacco-Vanzetti; the Scottsboro Boys; the Rosenbergs; the Smith Act defendants; Morton Sobell. Beyond making his voice heard in these notable cases, Muste was concerned to protect the rights of conscience as guaranteed in the First Amendment, for dissenters of all kinds. Testifying before the House Committee on Un-American Activities, the Senate Subcommittee on Internal Security, the Federal Bureau of Investigation, and various other self-appointed guardians of American security, he defended cohorts and opponents alike in their right to question establishment policies and voice anti-establishment alternatives. When J. Edgar Hoover tried to discredit him, Muste's answer was simple: "In insisting that all views should be publicly heard I am true to one of the most basic of American traditions."[6]

Action on behalf of civil rights was for Muste another part of holding the country to its own basic traditions. As a personal friend of major black leaders—A. Philip Randolph, Martin Luther King, Jr., James Farmer, Bayard Rustin, James Lawson—Muste supported and advised the nonviolent civil rights movement from its shaky inception in the 1940s to the trying and turbulent campaigns of the 1960s, when his steady pacifist voice lent firmness to the always besieged and sometimes wavering forces of nonviolent direct action.

These four categories—religion, labor, civil liberties, and civil rights—are subsumed by the fifth and major classification of Muste's concerns, that of pacifism. He first identified himself with the pacifist movement during World War I and successfully applied nonviolent tactics to the first labor strike he ever led—in the textile mills of Lawrence, Massachusetts, in 1919; but gradually, through the twenties and early thirties, Muste drifted toward acceptance of violent strategies and formally acknowledged that acceptance in uniting with the Trotskyists.

A religious experience in the summer of 1936 led to his return to pacifism. From this experience he emerged with the unshakeable conviction that "love is the basic reality of the universe" and that violence in any form—injustice, deception, exploitation, greed, oppression, war—flies in the face of reality.[7]

Muste was fifty-one years old when this experience occurred. The basic convictions he affirmed then inspired and guided him for the following thirty-one years, until he died in 1967 at the age of eighty-two. In the course of those years Muste worked devotedly for the causes of racial equality, economic justice, free speech, and political liberty. But repeatedly he told his comrades in these struggles that they would never realize their objectives as long as U.S. foreign policy remained insensitive to the aspirations of Third World peoples, military spending held priority over spending for human needs, the Cold War against communism continued, and the stockpiling of arms brought disaster ever nearer. Indeed, he predicted that should nuclear war occur, such goals as racial equality and jobs for all would become irrelevant.

Muste labored, then, to resist, and if possible clog, the machinery of the militarized, arms-stockpiling, war-making modern nation state. To this end he organized campaigns against payment of taxes, against conscription, against nuclear testing, against civil defense, against the building of newer and more devastating weaponry, and, of course, against wars.

He resisted and supported others in resistance to World War II. "If I can't love Hitler I can't love at all," he observed. He resisted the Cold War and worked to create what for a time was discussed as a "Third Camp," a political force that would reject the policies of both sides in the Cold War and concentrate on alleviating the gross maldistribution of resources among the peoples of the earth. He resisted the Korean War; it was, he said, "a spark" that could "set the world afire."[8] And, literally, to his last breath he resisted the war in Vietnam, a war whose destructiveness he had seen first hand, having travelled to Saigon in 1966 and to Hanoi where, just a few days before his death in 1967, he met with Ho Chi Minh.

In resisting these manifestations of violence, Muste looked to a variety of constituencies for support—fellow pacifists, minorities who appreciated nonviolence as a tactic if not a way of life, and youthful leftists whose numbers burgeoned in the 1960s. He also was anxious to tap the intellectual and technical resources of the academic and scientific communities. His influence on each of these groups will be examined in the pages to follow. But he will not appear as a figure who wielded wide influence or enjoyed popular success. In the conventional sense of the term, A. J. Muste was "a loser."

In an article for the *New York Times Book Review* in 1977, Stanford Professor Peter Stansky wrote that "we now seem much more interested in the losers than the winners . . . , in those who offer alternatives, who seem to be on the margins of history but nevertheless have a far firmer grasp on what really matters than those who embody a flashy, meretricious and very often transient success. This change," he concluded, "is based on a profound disillusion with what the state can do."[9] Exactly such an outlook informs the writing of this book. In the era of Vietnam, James Wechsler told readers of the *New York Post* that "on the basis of the record as of this moment, poor A. J. Muste, a lonely, abused iconoclast, has offered sounder counsel to our country than so skilled a product of our diplomatic system as [Secretary of State] Dean Rusk."[10]

In retrospect Muste's counsel on many of the major political, social, and economic issues of this century seems more sound than the policies that actually prevailed. The alternatives that he represents—freedom of conscience over coercion by the state; nonviolent innovations over violent force; courageous disarmament initiatives over fearful stockpiling of weapons; economic justice over the greed and brutality bred by economic imbalance—increase in attractiveness as the consequences of their opposites become more dire.

Columnist Wechsler was not alone in the sixties in feeling that there was something terribly wrong with the definitions of practicality and realism used by Dean Rusk and his associates. That feeling continued to haunt many concerned and thoughtful citizens even after the Vietnam debacle ceased to be a front page issue. But concerned Americans remained perplexed over alternative definitions and even more perplexed over how any alternatives might be realized. Muste's response to this perplexity was to urge a break with the habit of "starting from the existing institutions and political situation . . . [and fixing] upon what the Administration and/or the American people . . . can be expected to buy." Rather, he asserted, individuals should "examine the profound changes that would necessarily be implied in the achievement of [a] world without war." Ask first what is the image of a sane and humane future, advised Muste; then ask "how it is to be translated into political reality."[11]

Abraham Muste was an immigrant whose entire life was spent *en voyage* toward a better world. At various points along the way he had the companionship of others who were also keeping alive in their time the values of peace and justice. Kirby Page, Norman Thomas, A. Philip Randolph, Dorothy Day, and most other figures whose names are woven into the history of twentieth-century dissent and reform were numbered among his associates. But while part of the same historical tradition as they, Muste was unique. No other life was shaped by a range of influences so vast as to include the orthodoxy of Reformed theology, the radicalism of Marxist thought, and the perfectionist ethic of Christian pacifism. And no other reformer remained so consistently open to experimentation and new ideas. Muste turned often to the story of the biblical Abraham who " 'went out not knowing whither he went,' " who, he said, "went out looking for a city which existed—and yet had to be brought into existence."[12] His biography will have most appeal to those who share his vision of that "city which is to be." But his arguments for abandoning the present city are cogent and compelling enough to challenge even those who might discount his vision as unrealistic.

A. J. Muste spent a lifetime tugging at hearts, awakening consciences, and challenging minds. While he did not develop a blueprint for escape from the perils and dilemmas of our age, his life does demonstrate the principle that must, he believed, govern humankind if we are to survive: "There is no way to peace; peace is the way."[13]

Part One
Religion and Labor:
"Not in Certainty, but in Search"

If we lived in a State where virtue was profitable,
common sense would make us good,
and greed would make us saintly. . . .
But since in fact we see that avarice, anger,
envy, pride, sloth, lust and stupidity commonly profit . . .
why then perhaps we *must* stand fast a little
—even at the risk of being heroes.

Sir Thomas Moore in
A Man for All Seasons

Chapter I

The Traveler
from Zierikzee

Zierikzee is an obscure shipping port in the Dutch province of Zeeland. There, on January 8, 1885, a son was born to Adriana and Martin Muste. The child was the second in their marriage; the first, Abraham Johannes, had died in early infancy. The new boy was given the same name, after his paternal grandfather and a paternal uncle.[1] Adriana Jonker and Martin Muste had come from poor and large families. Their education had been minimal. She read only falteringly and could not write. Her husband, though he had completed only the fourth grade, read and wrote proficiently. He was employed as a coachman by a minor noble in Zierikzee, a job that was considered a cut above the more common work in the fields or on the sea, but that still provided only a meager living. There was a "vague tradition" in the Muste family that their origins could be traced back to a Napoleonic soldier who deserted the French army, married a Dutch woman, and remained in Holland when Napoleon withdrew from the Netherlands near the end of his career.[2] When, after many years, Abraham Johannes reached the pacifism of his adulthood, he half-jokingly suspected that he was manifesting an inheritance from this "first member of the Muste tribe . . . [who] evidently had a negative reaction toward war."[3]

Although the Martin Mustes were quite poor, an aura of contentment hovered over Abraham's memories of his first six years, during which two sisters and a brother joined the household.[4] Watching ice-skaters and drinking chocolate, taking family walks, sailing paper boats on the canals in front of his home, and celebrating St. Nicholas Day with parents and siblings were experiences that he associated with Zierikzee. He also retained vivid memories of moments when, as a four or five year old, he was shaken by sensations of beauty, awe, horror, and "a sort of revelation" about the otherness and yet the loveliness of fellow human beings.[5]

Formal instruction that might have given some shape to these early, nearly mystical sensations was apparently absent. "If I went to school," he wrote, "or was taken to church or taught to say my prayers I don't remember it."[6] The religion of Abraham's parents was nonetheless an influence in their family life. They belonged to the *Hereformde Kerk*, the Reformed Church. This established religion of the Netherlands taught that, as he recalled, "God had assigned you your place in life and you were to be contented with that place."[7]

Abraham remembered that he began to learn his place when he was "commandeered at the age of five, or possibly earlier, to fetch the porridge" for his father's employer. This porridge was cooked at a municipal kitchen and enjoyed only by those who could afford it. According to his autobiography, every day, "in the morning twilight," he carried the container of steaming cereal "to the back door of what seemed a palace." His own home had "really only one room to live in, with alcoves off that room for sleeping purposes." He sensed his parents' regret that their children could not have the advantages that children of the nobility possessed.[8] When word arrived from relatives who had recently moved to the United States that opportunity was greater there, the Mustes were receptive to the suggestion that they also emigrate. The journey which followed from their decision stood as "a seminal experience" for Abraham.[9]

The family sailed from Rotterdam in January 1891, booking passage "on an old Holland-American Line steamer named Obdam." They endured the difficulties of travelling in steerage and of having to spend almost a month on an island in New York Harbor, where Adriana Muste was hospitalized with an illness incurred during the voyage. During the island stay a hospital attendant, learning Abraham's first name, took to calling him "Abraham Lincoln" and thereby sparked an historical interest which Muste would always maintain.

When Mrs. Muste was well enough to leave the island, the family set out on the last part of their adventure, the long train ride from New York to Grand Rapids, where they were warmly greeted by waiting uncles and cousins. The family had faced the risks of leaving loved and familiar surroundings, going into permanent indebtedness, and struggling in an environment where the language and all else promised to be strange. Now the journey ended, Muste recalled, "in a warm, brightly lighted room at the uncle's home. . . . My mother laughs happily at her brother's jokes, . . . [and] cousins told me the English words for 'table,' 'chair,' and so on, and were delighted when I imitated them precisely. They made me feel that I was the Traveler they had been waiting for."[10]

The traveler metaphor had lasting significance for Abraham Johannes, who, as an adult, would conclude that "the crucial thing about men, or societies, is not where they come from but where they are going," and who empathized with the biblical Abraham who "went out, not knowing whither he went," demonstrating that "his destiny and his God are not ties which bind and confine him. They are ahead of him and drawing him outward and onward."[11]

Since 1613, Dutch immigrants had been drawn outward and onward to the New World, where "New Netherlanders" took up residence in the Hudson and Delaware River valleys.[12] But the Netherlander immigrants who had most significance for the Mustes were a band of secessionists from the state Dutch Reformed Church who established the settlement of Holland, Michigan, in 1847.[13] In large measure they were seeking freedom of worship. Deteriorating economic conditions and the potato blight which struck Holland in 1845 added economic pressures to their movement. Although the first years of pioneering were extremely difficult for the Dutch Michiganers, their settlements were prospering by the end of the nineteenth century, and their people became the largest single immigrant group in the western part of the state. The Mustes made their journey near the end of a peak of immigration which had begun in 1880, a year in which Holland was beset by economic crisis.[14]

A Dutch scholar has asserted, "Religion and religious education were a primary concern with Dutch immigrants. . . . Only if this fact is grasped can the pattern of Dutch immigrant settlement be understood."[15] One of the issues that had agitated the settlers of the 1840s was the relationship between their new churches springing up in the Midwest and the Reformed Church in America (RCA) on the east coast, which was an offshoot of the state church of the Netherlands—the church from which they had seceded. In 1850 official union between the midwestern congregations and the Reformed Church of America was achieved.[16] But not all recent immigrants approved it. In the eyes of some the Reformed Church was impure. In 1857 the critics seceded and established the True Dutch Reformed Church, which took its present name—the Christian Reformed Church—in 1890.[17]

Historian Harold Lucas has noted that the immigrants who remained with the Reformed Church of America "experienced the infiltration of American ideas earlier and with greater effect than did their brethren in the Christian Reformed Church," which had "no such connection with any American ecclesiastical body [and] remained more closely wedded to Dutch customs and ways of thinking."[18]

In 1891 in Grand Rapids, each church was represented by seven or eight congregations.[19] One of the first crucial decisions that Martin and Adriana Muste had to make upon their arrival concerned church affiliation. Adriana's brothers, who had encouraged and financed their sister and brother-in-law's move to the United States belonged to a Christian Reformed congregation. But when Christian Reformed authorities would not receive the Mustes by transfer of membership from the *Hereformde Kerk*, requiring instead that they make a renewed confession of faith, Mrs. Muste refused and her family turned to the Fourth Reformed Church, which accepted their membership. "The Martin Mustes" a relative later observed, "were the only branch of the family who belonged to the RCA."[20]

Abraham attached some importance to this difference between his parents and his uncles, suggesting that to "choose a church which was more middle of the road with a little more sense of freedom" signified a spirit of moderation in his parents and his home environment. Perhaps, he indicated, his parents' choice of church explained why he never experienced the feelings of terror about eternal damnation which were common among children in that community. He also suspected that the Mustes may have been establishing their emotional independence from Adriana's brothers.[21] Possibly Mrs. Muste simply did not want to be put to any more tests than the long journey and the process of resettlement had already put her.

Had the Mustes chosen otherwise, Abraham's biographers would not be faced with the perplexing problem of tracing his evolution from an extremely conservative and politically quiescent community to a career in the forefront of every major social movement of his time. For the very Dutch-centeredness of the Christian Reformed Church made it susceptible in the 1890s to influences from a movement of social consciousness and action originating in Christian Reformed circles in Holland, under the leadership of Abraham Kuyper, who visited the United States near the end of the nineties. Employing battle language reminiscent of the Old Testament prophets, the Dutch theologian inspired efforts at political organization within American Christian Reformed circles, including some activity in Grand Rapids. Muste remained unaware of these efforts, however.[22] And his family's inclination to keep Christian Reformed influences at a distance was reinforced by a brief and unsatisfactory experience with Christian Reformed schools.

One of Adriana's nephews was headmaster of such a school, where for a short time Muste and his sisters were enrolled. Reading, writing, arithmetic, and Bible study, presented tediously and without imagination, constituted the curriculum. Although put off by such a sterile learning environment, Muste did carry away from the school a thorough familiarity with the Dutch metrical psalms which he loved ever after and which were one source of his abiding enjoyment of poetry.[23]

His stint in the school ended when his parents transferred all of their children to public schools. Tuition had become prohibitive and they were fed up with the schoolmaster who appears in family lore as a "stuffed shirt," excessively untidy and too strict.[24] The Mustes may also have been affected by a controversy in the Dutch-American community of the 1890s regarding church schools, which, one side argued, were unnecessary and perhaps unpatriotic. To Martin Muste, who had taken out his "first papers [for naturalization] as soon as he was eligible and became a citizen at the earliest opportunity," such a suggestion would have been particularly bothersome.[25]

Whatever the reasons for the transfer, Abraham greatly enjoyed his days at Plainfield Public School. "My impression of my public school teachers," he later wrote, "is that they knew their business; their classrooms were orderly; they knew how to handle children. They certainly inspired me."[26] His enthusiasm for learning was avid. His younger brother could not remember a time when Abraham "did not have a book in his hand." By the age of eight or nine he had access to the library of a neighbor family, the Quimbys, who owned the factory where his father worked. In their "shelves upon shelves of books" the richest treasures which he found were bound volumes of *Harper's* and *Century* with a series of articles on the Civil War.[27]

This reading, combined with occasional encounters which he had with Civil War veterans from the nearby Old Soldiers Home, quickened his historical sense of "the days of John Brown, the Emancipation Proclamation, the Martyred President."[28] School assignments (his seventh grade class read *Man Without a Country* and the poetry of James Whitcomb Riley) and his parents' strong sense of identification with their new land encouraged this growing involvement with the mythology of America.[29]

Along with history and patriotism, the immigrant boy was constantly exposed to the customs and values of the Dutch Reformed Church. Based upon the doctrines of predestination, original sin, and salvation by "special grace alone," Reformed teachings were also concerned with the maintenance of the proper Christian home.[30] The parents of Abraham Muste kept, he remembered, "a religious and pious . . . home. We used the religious language and practices of the Dutch families of several decades ago." He recalled Sundays as great days, especially important in family life. They were "different from other days. . . . You had a sense that something very important was happening." He was thrilled by the peal of church bells, "all the people pouring into the church, the music, . . . the solemnity, the prayers, the preaching. . . . All this gave me a feeling of having entered another world, . . . that one had come 'to Mount Zion, the city of the living God, the heavenly Jerusalem.' "[31]

However, it was not sufficient in that Grand Rapids community for deep religious response to remain in the realm of feeling only. According to church law parents were to "require their children to give an account of the sermons they hear, . . . assign them some chapters of Scripture to read, . . . and then impress and illustrate the truths contained in them." Abraham's father—who was first deacon and later an elder in the Fourth Reformed Church—undoubtedly fulfilled this obligation.[32]

Such practices left Abraham Muste "soaked in the Bible and the language of the Bible" and, therefore, with access to religious experience which he came to feel later generations had lost. To this early training, he also attributed the abiding conviction that "you live your life in the sight of God and there is no respecter of persons in Him, and pretension is a low and despicable thing."[33]

In retrospect Muste concluded that these teachings undergirded his adult pacifism. He recalled an experience from seventh grade which seemed to illustrate an early inclination on his part toward nonviolence. The affair began when Abraham tripped the class bully who was on his way to the teacher's desk to receive a reprimand for misconduct. The teacher did not see Muste stick out his foot and was not inclined anyway to suspect an act of that sort from such a good student. She concluded, instead, that the bully's sudden lurch was "some more 'monkey business' " on his part and therefore gave him double punishment. After school the two boys confronted one another. "For some unfathomable reason," Muste recalled, "I no longer felt afraid or nervous, as I had up to that moment. [The bully] said in a belligerent tone, 'You tripped me.' I looked him in the eye and quietly said, 'Yes, I did.' " This response "took him off his guard. He hesitated, shifted his weight to the other leg, hitched one of his shoulders, then turned and walked away without saying a word. His pals followed him. . . . I have no recollection of what my own thoughts were as I walked home," Muste wrote. "It was not until about 1940 . . . that it came home to me that the [episode] illustrated several aspects of the pacifist philosophy. . . . But they were probably a part of me before my mind apprehended them."[34]

Another part of him, ingrained by parents and church, was the expectation that he would grow up to become a minister. "I don't remember a time when to some extent I didn't feel that I was destined for the ministry," he wrote.[35] Therefore, when he was about twelve years old, he began to write and deliver "sermons." His first addressed the meaning of Christmas; another focused on "Jesus as Prophet, Priest and King."[36] His sermonizing was not limited to church audiences. In the eighth grade Muste entered an essay contest sponsored by the Trades and Labor Council of Grand Rapids on the topic of "Child Labor." His piece was, by his later description, "essentially moralistic and religious," emphasizing "the evils of forcing children to work." Although the future labor organizer and labor college director was not beginning his involvement in this area at a very scholarly level, he won the contest, and his prize was "$15 worth of books and publication of the prize essay in the souvenir book issued by the Council on Labor Day." Escorted by the matriarch of the Quimby family and a representative of the Trades and Labor Council, the contest winner went to a downtown bookstore to reap his reward. The harvest included an anthology of poems edited by Agnes Repplier, J. B. Green's *Short History of England*, and—of most value in Muste's eyes—Emerson's *Essays*. Perhaps the philosopher of Concord spoke to the traveler in Abraham, confirming his positive attitude toward venturing.[37]

Whatever Emerson's influence, Abraham's religion was most important to him in this period. He later remembered "the experience of the Good Friday and the Easter services" of his thirteenth year as "something that could be called mystical experiences." On that Easter Sunday afternoon, he was walking out of doors by himself when suddenly "the world took on new brightness and 'Christ is risen indeed' " was spoken within him. "From that day," he later maintained, "God was real to me."[38] Shortly after this experience, Abraham recalled presenting himself before the consistory of the church as a candidate for full membership. His youthfulness is worthy of note, since confirmation in that church at that time usually involved individuals who were at least seventeen or eighteen years old. To the thirteen year old the event was one to be remembered as "an intellectual experience and an emotional and spiritual adventure."[39]

Intensifying the adventure was the fact that plans were being made by his parents—under the active urging of the minister of Fourth Church, Rev. John H. Warnshuis—to send him to Hope Preparatory School, thirty miles away in

Holland, Michigan. The factor of separation from home and family does not seem to have disturbed Abraham. He was thrilled at the thought of "going away to school and being on one's own."[40] Delight in moving outward and onward was already a natural response for him to make.

Hope Preparatory School, which began without campus or buildings in 1851, was operating within the conceptual framework of its ancestral supporters when Muste enrolled there in September 1898. His autobiography reports that the course of studies it offered was "heavily loaded on the side of Greek and Latin and Bible study."[41] The schedule it imposed included twenty minutes of compulsory chapel every morning, a two-hour prayer meeting every Wednesday evening, and three required church services on Sundays.[42]

Muste, pale, sharp-featured, and growing tall, was the youngest scholar in the school and probably one of the most impoverished. His home church provided a small sum for his education. But to support himself he had to work—in the school library, in a restaurant in Holland, and in the college dining hall.[43] These jobs did not interfere with his studies, which he found to be easy. In addition to the classical languages and religious instruction, the school curriculum led him through basic mathematics, algebra, geometry, English literature, and history.[44] He always completed his assignments in time for sports activities every afternoon—football in the fall, basketball in the winter, and his lifelong love, baseball in the spring.[45]

Muste's main intellectual stimulation came from clandestine reading in the library, where his job provided access to "certain books which only college upper classmen could use," some of which discussed Charles Darwin's theory of evolution.[46] Although by the 1880s "an increasing number of Protestant leaders were finding Darwinism compatible with theism," in Dutch Reformed circles this was generally not the case.[47] One exposition of Darwinism that interested Abraham was authored by Joseph Le Conte, professor of geology and natural history at the University of California at Berkeley, who was adamant that scientific explanations of creation had been undeniably proven and that "scripture ought now to be interpreted in accordance with these facts." An older student discovered that Abraham was reading these declarations and threatened to call his parents. But the threat was not carried out and the surreptitious reading continued.[48]

Another source of excitement was a book entitled *The Intellectual Life*, written by Philip Gilbert Hamerton and published in Boston in 1882. Hammerton argued for free inquiry and disparaged dogma.[49] As he read such materials Muste did not feel defiant. "For whatever reason," he mused, "the idea that you shouldn't read something that you wanted to know about was something that I didn't entertain."[50]

Completing his preparatory work in June 1902, Muste enrolled in Hope College as a sophomore the following September. He was eighteen years old and would complete the four-year college degree in only three years. The college curriculum continued the Bible and ancient language studies, probed deeper into history and literature, and introduced the physical sciences. While he estimated that most of the faculty were mediocre at best, he was inspired by three figures.

Samuel Ottmar Mast was the most exciting. Muste reported that the youthful professor of biology and botany "almost forbade us to read books and made us get out our microscopes and dissect and do things ourselves." The Latin teacher, James G. Sutphen, provided a model of intellectual rigor and discipline, and Muste's Greek professor, Edward Dimnent (who later became president of Hope College), appeared as "young" and "somewhat innovative," allowing students in his senior course to act out *Antigone*. Abraham played the role of Haimon (the son of King Creon and an exponent of the position that it is sometimes necessary to defy established authority). Dimnent cultivated in the students a high regard for discipline. "When we recited in Greek class and started to reply, 'I think . . .' he [Dimnent] would say, 'don't think, know.' "[51]

Abraham's only other major exposure to the literature of drama at this time seems to have been through the study of the tragedies of Shakespeare in his English courses. The comedies were forbidden, and Hope students did not attempt to act out any of his works. In fact, public theater was sinful according to Dutch Reformed values. The first visit Abraham ever made to a dramatic performance was made without the knowledge of family or college authorities. He went sometime during his Hope career to a Grand Rapids theater to see the great Richard Mansfield in a play called *Heidelberg*. The production was thrilling, but the fear that his mother might learn of his presence in the theater ("The top would blow off of the theater and the bottom would fall out of it") distracted Muste throughout.[52]

Life at Hope was not all as earnest as proscriptions on theater, dancing, and games of chance might suggest. Abraham enjoyed an active social life of parties and sleighrides. He participated in debate and oratory contests, winning several top prizes and considerable admiration from the college coeds. He also played on the Hope basketball team, which won two Michigan championships while he was its captain.[53]

Hope students were not above pranksterism. One tradition of misbehavior consisted of carrying all the books in the library stacks to the chapel. Muste was always glad when this happened because he earned extra money reshelving the books.[54] He could enjoy jokes at the expense of others, as an underclassman, G. J. Van Zoren, long after remembered: "On one occasion, I came to the window [of the library stacks] and asked for a copy of *Bacon Lights of History* and you asked me if I wanted it served with eggs."[55] Young Muste helped at least once to tie a cow to the college flag pole.[56]

Vacations away from campus were passed in earning money for the next school year. One summer he sold Bibles. During another he worked briefly in a department store and then at the Quimby furniture factory.[57]

The summer job that he liked the most was assistant to a Holland physician who was also the local coroner. The coroner, as Muste remembered him, was "like many doctors in small communities of that time, more liberal than others." He and his young assistant examined the victims of alcoholism, suicide, shootings, and fatal accidents. Abraham could not remember feeling any great compassion for these victims. After all, he had been raised in a community which lived in "black ignorance of heredity, contagious disease, germs and so on and regarded sickness [and poverty] as a cause for punishment."[58]

Asked by an interviewer in the 1950s whether he could recall discussing new experiences and ideas with his family during his college days, Muste replied that he did not initiate or take part in such discussions then. (It is even possible that they did not realize the nature of his work with the coroner since his sisters have no recollection of it.) As far as he could recall, any uneasiness which he might have felt about the difference between the information he was acquiring and the thought patterns of the Dutch Reformed community simply did not raise doubts "serious enough so that I had to get them out into the open."[59]

Although Muste's adolescent years seemed free of serious rebellion, he was, in a variety of ways, consciously challenging the values, customs, and expectations of his community. Certain memories and incidents reveal a degree of tension—his experience at the Richard Mansfield performance, for example, and his inclination at the end of his sophomore year to transfer to the University of Kansas as a literature major. Muste reversed this decision only after the president of Hope College intervened with the contention that his "duty as a Dutchman was to the college."[60]

More than anything else Muste's college essays and orations reveal how his respect for authority was pulling him one way while his inquiring mind was tugging in the opposite direction. In an October 1904 issue of the Hope *Anchor*, Editor-in-Chief Muste (a senior) asserted that "it is well to abide by the simple faith of the fathers." But in the valedictory address which he delivered in June 1905 he reached the opposite conclusion. Speaking on "The Problem of Discontent," he paid his respects to the church fathers but then exclaimed that "the soul is powerless against its own discontent. . . . By some relentless law thought begets doubt." And doubt could produce "utter anguish." But there was no excuse, he declared, for suppressing skepticism.

There was a recurring metaphor in "The Problem of Discontent" of a plant and "its constant struggle with the earth that would hold it forever in bonds of darkness." Because of and through that struggle the plant "grows at last into the princely sentinel of the forest stream." The plant is dependent upon the very soil against which it must struggle. Abraham Muste was being maintained and strengthened by the very traditions which his mind and spirit were beginning to resist. And the defenders of those traditions must have admired the heartiness and obvious power of that mind and spirit which had developed under their care. Their pride in Abraham and their hopes for his future may have blurred the meaning of his oration for many of them and provided sanction for others to let it pass without censure. On his part, the youth seems to have been justifying to himself as well as to his community his imperative need to begin growing away from the soil that bound him to them.[61]

Yet the time had not come for reckoning with the full implications of what he was saying. He remained within the fold and took employment at a church-related junior college after he left Hope. The September after graduation he began teaching at Northwestern Classical Academy in Orange City, Iowa. Regarded as an instrument of Dutch Reformed "missionary work in the Far West," the Academy served "the sons and daughters of devout Iowa corn growers." Muste taught Greek and English, served as librarian, sat on the Athletics Committee and "the Committee on Advertising," and found time to do "a lot of reading," including Gibbon's *Decline and Fall* and some parts of Kant.[62]

But the most important aspect of the job was its proximity to Rock Valley, Iowa, where the Huizenga family resided. Muste and their youngest daughter, Anna, were in love. The pair met at Hope College, where she had transferred in Abraham's senior year, after attending Northwestern Academy. Their meeting, he always maintained, had been a matter of love at first sight. "Fun loving and venturesome," Anna was also intelligent and attractive. Every Friday at noon during the academic year 1905–1906, Muste could be seen "dashing out of class . . . [and] walking three miles to a railroad station to catch a freight for the heavenly regions." His pupils knew of his extra-curricular interests and missed no opportunity to tease him.[63] His weekends with the Huizengas allowed him not only to court Anna but also to come to know her interesting, prosperous, and well-educated family. Mr. Huizenga was a Reformed minister and a successful farmer who had provided college educations to three sons and four daughters and had seen the two eldest sons go on to Rush Medical School at the University of Chicago and eventually become doctors. At four o'clock every Monday morning one of these "obliging brothers" would drive Abraham in horse and buggy to catch a train back to Orange City.

Anna and Abraham reached an understanding that they would be married as soon as he completed his ministerial education.[64]

In September 1906, Muste took "the old train from Grand Rapids to New York, ferried over on the old Pennsylvania ferry," and then travelled by train to New Brunswick, New Jersey, site of the New Brunswick Theological Seminary. He was accompanied by his "closest friend," Benjamin Bush.[65] The seminary in which they enrolled possessed the same kind of started-from-scratch history which characterized their prep school and college. Muste soon discovered that the church's highest academic institution placed more emphasis upon indoctrination than upon learning and valued fidelity more than intellectual growth.[66]

He was most critical of the president of the seminary, John Preston Searle, who held the professorship of systematic theology and taught from a simplified version of Calvin's *Institutes*, which was "almost for kindergarten use. It was terrible." There were, Muste reported, only two good scholars on the faculty, the professor of New Testament Greek, John Gillespie, and the professor of Hebrew, John Raven. Even their instruction was "fairly routine," Muste noted, but at least they could make passages of the original biblical texts come alive and from them one learned the difference between original versions and translations. For the professor of homiletics and preaching Abraham also had kind words. Ferdinand S. Schenck, a graduate of Princeton and of Albany Law School, was an experienced preacher and a prolific author. He insisted that young preachers write out every sermon, word for word. Abraham followed that practice during his first five years in the pulpit and always felt indebted to the New Brunswick instructor "for having developed my vocabulary in that way."[67]

To have his learning experiences limited to vocabulary building and Greek and Hebrew translation was "devastating." Muste wondered if he would have "survived" the seminary education, or "what it would have done to" him, if opportunities for study had not been available in nearby New York City.[68] In his first year at New Brunswick he enrolled for classes at New York University and remembered best a course taught by Charles Gray Shaw, who lectured on ethics, championed humanism, and covered a wide range of philosophical ideas, from Eastern and Western, ancient and contemporary sources.[69]

In his second and final years at New Brunswick, Muste supplemented his seminary work with courses at Columbia University. There he found a lively department of philosophy, boasting such names as William Pepperell Montague, Wendell T. Bush, John Dewey, and Frederick J. E. Woodbridge. Muste remembered, as well, the influence of William James, who had delivered a series of guest lectures at Columbia in January 1907 and whose ideas were the basis for a course which he took the following year. From the Columbia philosophers, he later recalled, he learned "to know my way around in philosophy books, . . . to think in terms of metaphysics. . . . [These teachers] took me very definitely beyond where I had been and beyond where theology had taken me, because that had been too much a cut and dried thing."[70] Of all the influences converging upon Muste at Columbia, that of Frederick Woodbridge "made the deepest impression." Woodbridge fused critical inquiry with toleration and respect and suggested a way of pursuing truth without totally denying and defying one's origins.[71]

In addition to this classroom work Muste was also learning from "on the job training." During the summer after his first year at New Brunswick, he was assigned for eight weeks to a church in Albany, New York, where the congregation expected sermons in Dutch and the practice-minister complied.[72] His second assignment as a supply preacher came the following summer (1908), when he was placed at the Middle Collegiate Church at Second Avenue and Seventh Street in New York City. This "seething" East Side setting, . . . with "Italians, Poles, Jews, recently arrived immigrants, children, babies all over the streets, . . . a babel of tongues," was a revelation. Muste was himself an immigrant who had been raised in a kind of poverty, although, in the Midwest, "you had your own house . . . with a yard. . . . It was clean." Poverty New York style, on the other hand, meant tenements where Muste visited the sick and old parishioners and was struck by "the darkness and filthiness of a great many of the halls."

At the same time, some members of the Middle Collegiate congregation were quite wealthy, including a Wall Street lawyer and an executive in a major drug company. This was also the first time that Muste encountered "people like that" and had an opportunity to "see a Wall Street office from the inside." The contrast between that office and the tenement dwellings did not immediately create a social consciousness for Muste.[73] But his thinking about religion and its relation to life was undergoing a transition. About this time, as he later remembered, "I passed definitely from what you might say was an Old Testament religion to a New Testament religion and from the idea that you begin with a body of doctrine to the idea that you begin with a life, a kind of life. And I was also moving away from the idea that you have a God of Judgment and so on to a concept of a God of love."[74]

He was by then attending lectures on the social gospel by such figures as the noted Presbyterian clergyman, G. Campbell Morgan,[75] and must have been aware of such radical groups as the socialists (Eugene Debs was conducting his third campaign for the presidency in 1908) and the anarchists (Emma Goldman's *Mother Earth* was gaining significant circulation while its editor had no little notoriety). However, in the late spring of 1909, Abraham Muste took steps which would have permanently insulated most lives against such forces. He completed his work at New Brunswick, took Anna Huizenga as his wife, became an ordained minister, and accepted a call to a prosperous church at a salary quite above the average pay offered to new clergymen. Yet these steps were not taken without some noteworthy signs that the young clergyman was not inclined toward a life of conventional security.

As graduation speaker for the 1909 class of the New Brunswick Theological Seminary, Muste proceeded to "go to town on the low intellectual standards of the seminary and to plead that the seminary should not be an institution in which only the most mediocre kind of parish ministers are trained." Applauded by some, resented by others, and long remembered by all at the Seminary, Muste's remarks did not jeopardize his immediate plans.[76] The seminary graduated him. He then returned to Michigan and presented himself before the Classis, under whose official care he still lived as a member of the Fourth Reformed Church in Grand Rapids. Passing their examination, he was granted a license that enabled him to preach but not to administer the sacraments or represent any congregation at an official ecclesiastical assembly.[77]

Muste then made the long awaited journey to Rock Valley, Iowa, where he and Anna were married at her home on June 21, 1909.[78] Mr. and Mrs. Muste then hurried east for his ordination by the Classis of New York. The experience inspired him. "I felt," he said "a very strong call to the ministry and a very strong urge to preach and a feeling that I had something to give."[79]

His first parishioners were the congregation of the Fort Washington Collegiate Church on Washington Heights in New York City. His starting salary was a handsome $2,000 a year. The location of the church was another advantage. "It was only," Muste happily recalled, "a few blocks north of where the Yankee ballpark was then located."[80]

The Fort Washington congregation included figures who were prominent in law, politics, social research, and community welfare work. That such
persons "were expecting to be ministered to by me," Muste reflected later, was a
little awesome. It was also an opportunity to continue to learn and explore. He
heard first-hand accounts of pressing social crises from such parishioners as
John A. Fitch and Raymond Fosdick. Fitch, trained by John Commons at the
University of Wisconsin, was an associate of the Russel Sage Foundation and
economics professor in the New York School of Social Work. He had recently
been engaged in an intensive study of conditions among coal miners in Allegheny County, Pennsylvania. Fosdick (brother of the well-known divine, Harry
Emerson Fosdick) had once foregone graduate school to live in Lillian Wald's
Henry Street Settlement in the slums of New York City and was now top aide to
the commissioner of accounts in that city. Very soon he became the commissioner and launched an all-out attack on municipal corruption.[81]

At the same time unrest among the poor of New York City was becoming
an increasingly public issue. During Muste's tenure at Fort Washington, garment workers began the strikes which led to the founding of the International
Ladies Garment Workers Union. He recalled feeling their "impact to some
extent" and also indicated an awareness of the tragic Triangle Fire in the garment section of New York in 1911 and of the struggles of the Industrial
Workers of the World in the textile mills of Paterson, New Jersey, and Lawrence, Massachusetts.[82]

National politics also began to interest Muste. The same people in his
congregation who were active in socially conscious professions were aligned as
well with national political movements. Initially Muste was intrigued by the
various versions of reformism which the three leading politicians of the Progressive Era—Theodore Roosevelt, Woodrow Wilson, and Robert LaFollette—espoused. By the end of the summer of 1912, however, after reading a
number of socialist tracts, Muste had become a supporter of the Socialist Party
candidate, Eugene Debs. The shift, as he assessed it later, represented more the
taking of "an advanced Progressive position rather than [the] embracing [of]
Marxist philosophy. . . . Debs in a way was also part of the Progressive
tradition."[83]

In retrospect Muste's attraction to the socialist candidate fits the pattern
which he would repeatedly follow. Once his mind went to work on a certain
issue or complex of issues, it did not rest until all possible conclusions had been
considered. Very frequently he would find the least conventional conclusion to
be the most satisfying, or the one, as he said of the socialist viewpoint, that
seemed to "go deeper" than others. On November 5, 1912, in any case, the
Reverend Abraham Muste voted for a socialist for president.[84]

As the young preacher moved politically leftward he also continued in the
direction of theological liberalism. His progress toward a modern religious outlook was hastened in the Fort Washington years by studies at Union Theological Seminary, where in 1912 he earned a Bachelor of Divinity degree, magna
cum laude.[85] At Union, Muste worked with James Everett Frame, George William Knox, William Adams Brown, and Arthur Cushman McGiffert, Sr. Frame

and Knox both emphasized the minds and feelings of religious figures, including Jesus, contributing, perhaps, to that passage Muste was making from "the idea that you begin with a body of doctrine to the idea that you begin with a life." They also stressed the continuity between the Old and New Testaments, a theme that fitted well with their image of a socially conscious and lower class Jesus, who, like the Old Testament prophets, was conscious of social ills and concerned with the common people.[86]

These prophets, Muste later said, "really [came] alive for me at Union." He began to see them as "fellows who preached politics, got into the actual struggle and cursed those who were grinding the faces of the poor."[87] Another of his teachers, William Adams Brown, was helping to make that prophetic tradition relevant to contemporary times. Chairman of the Home Missions Committee of the Presbytery of New York, Brown oversaw the work of two pioneering efforts by the Presbyterian Church to address itself to people living in slums and poverty—the American Parish in East Harlem and the Labor Temple at Second Avenue and East Fourteenth Streets.[88] As Muste was introduced, through Union, to these social gospel influences, he became more familiar with the work of Walter Rauschenbusch and, according to later recollections, thought of himself as a kind of follower of Rauschenbusch's social gospel.[89] But he did not translate that image into action. Instead he gave attention to problems of doctrine that increasingly troubled him.

The Fort Washington congregation may have reinforced his troubled reflections on doctrine by presenting Muste with a gift of "Tolstoy's work on religious and philosophical themes." At the time that he read this Russian writer, who frequently attacked institutional religion and the orthodoxy of his national church, Muste was becoming impatient with the orthodoxy of his own native faith.[90] Along with Tolstoy's work, that of another Union teacher, Arthur Cushman McGiffert, was having a profound impact on him.

McGiffert, soon to become president of Union Seminary, lectured on the history of Christian doctrine. He stressed that outlooks and traditions held sacrosanct in various theological circles could be attributed to human influences and temporary conditions and could be reexamined and replaced. The theologian's lectures, Muste wrote in his reminiscences, "were far and away the most brilliant I have ever experienced. . . . They opened a new approach to the study of religion, and new historical vistas, eventually forcing an 'agonizing reappraisal' of the beliefs in which I had been reared." Something in the manner of McGiffert, as well as in his lectures, moved the young pastor. Muste felt sure that McGiffert "was a very, very skeptical person in his own inside."[91]

As for himself, Abraham Muste was toying with the idea of leaving the ministry. It became impossible, he later recalled, to "tell people that I believed in the Virgin birth if I didn't, . . . and to make people believe that I believed in the literal inspiration of Scripture when I didn't."[92] He confronted more than a need to reassess doctrine. For a period, "it . . . seemed impossible to hold on to any religious faith at all." He turned to McGiffert for counsel and was advised to leave the pulpit and "try religious journalism or something of that sort."[93]

At the end of the academic year of 1912, the professor of history at Hope College died and Muste applied for the vacant position. The Michigan Reformed community seems to have been anxious to have their son return. A year earlier the Dutch Reformed Church at Holland had been disappointed when he turned down their call to fill an open pastorate there. Now the college offered him the history post. But Muste rejected the offer. He later suggested that he had recognized his application for what it really was, an effort to run away from the questions that were hounding him. Another pattern becomes discernible; just as he had not fled before his angry seventh-grade classmate, nor avoided expressing disagreement before his college and seminary elders, he now opted not to retreat from the conflicts that challenged him in the ministry. Also, it was reported that the Fort Washington people "rose up in a body and objected and raised [Muste's] salary to keep him."[94]

So Muste spent two more years at Fort Washington. He recalled that the Fitches and Fosdicks of the church encouraged him to preach as he wished. Contemporary comment indicates that even older, very conservative members of the congregation were "more interested in avoiding a heresy hunt" than in questioning the minister's orthodoxy.[95] Nonetheless, Muste remained unsettled. When in 1914 the Classis of New York addressed its annual query to ministers under its care, regarding their faithfulness to church doctrine, Muste, according to later remembrance, said to himself, "I don't believe in the inerrancy of scripture and I guess that I'll tell the boys that's it. I'm going to a freer denomination." He sent the Classis a statement to that effect, and the church body met several times to consider it. According to an unidentified source, "it was found that many of the consistory agreed with Dr. Muste, but . . . it is said that a majority of the board was opposed. While they loved the pastor, they decided that their duty to the church outweighed personal feelings. . . . Before they were ready for a final vote his resignation was before them. . . . They would recommend that it be accepted." His one-sentence resignation, dated November 22, 1914, took effect on the twenty-eighth of the following month.[96]

According to a Sunday New York Herald report of the time, some church leaders reacted to Muste's action with anger. The senior pastor of the Collegiate Reformed Church, Dr. David J. Burrell, blamed Union Theological Seminary "for the whole trouble," telling the Herald reporter that he was "quite satisfied that this institution was the direct cause of Mr. Muste's loss of faith." On the other hand, the eminent Henry E. Cobb, senior pastor of the West End Collegiate Church, did not accept this view. While he mourned the loss of Muste from Dutch Reformed life, he acknowledged that the dissident "would work more happily . . . in a body freer theologically than our Reformed Church," and wrote on his behalf to friends in the Congregational ministry. Very shortly Muste received two job offers, one of which led, in early 1915, to his installation as minister of Central Congregational Church in Newtonville, Massachusetts.[97]

The mechanics of transition into Congregationalism were facilitated smoothly. But the fact remains that a major upheaval had occurred. Muste had torn away from not only a church but also the community that had loved, educated, admired, and put great faith in him. The stress which severance caused may have been partly responsible for a serious illness that Anna Muste suffered sometime near the end of the Fort Washington assignment. Some family members have speculated that Anna was incapacitated by the "strain and tension and inner conflict" stemming from "the sharp contrast between her girlhood and her early married life." It is also possible that she experienced a miscarriage at this time.[98]

That tension and turmoil had also seriously affected her husband is indicated by mystical encounters associated with this period of his life. The Sunday *New York Herald* report of his separation from Fort Washington included references to Muste's having had a "vision. . . . I have now arrived," Muste was quoted as saying, "at a perfect religious certainty, a peace of mind after a long period of doubt."[99] While he did not later recall the decision to leave the Dutch denomination in mystical terms, Muste did recount the story of a religious experience after the break had been made and the contract with the Newtonville church signed. By this account, Anna and he were staying briefly in a hotel in New Jersey before assuming their duties at Newtonville. She was recovering satisfactorily from her illness. He was no longer consciously thinking about the recent break with his past. At just that point the mystical event broke over him. "I was walking late one morning down the corridor of [the] hotel," he wrote. "Suddenly came again that experience of a great light flooding in upon the world making things stand forth 'in sunny outline brave and clear' and of God being truly present and all-sufficient."[100] The event as Muste recorded it has the air of a celebration.

From the encounter came assurance, he later said, "that I had not the same Gospel as ever to preach but a much greater Gospel, in the sense that my understanding of it was enriched and my personal hold on God firmer." The constricting tie between his faith and what he now called "certain mere opinions or doctrines or dogmas" had been broken. He was a liberated man. His ministry in the future could work to liberate others. When he told Anna of his mystical insight they both rejoiced and shared "a deep sense of . . . the ultimate rightness of things."[101]

When Muste put on the clerical cloth five years before, he had not, he later said, "had a feeling really inside me of having arrived at a place where [I was] going to stay."[102] Perhaps—as he always believed—the immigrant impulse was so much a part of him that he was bound to venture far beyond his origins. He did not realize in 1914—nor, presumably, did his wife—just how far he would be drawn in the future. But the philosophy that would ultimately characterize his life—"the crucial thing about men or societies is not where they come from but where they are going"—was clearly in the making.

Chapter II

The Preacher, the Gospel, and World War I

A. J. Muste was called to Central Congregational Church in Newton-ville, Massachusetts, after a committee of laymen, chaired by the clerk of the congregation, Wallace C. Boyden, investigated his background and qualifica-tions. All of his references were favorable. They pictured Muste as a skilled preacher, "most tender and sympathetic with those who are in trouble," pos-sessed of "a keen sense of humor" and adept at sports. "We cannot but feel," wrote a fellow clergyman, "that in an environment in which he feels a little less restraint theologically [Muste] will develop into a very unusual man."[1]

The opportunity to serve in Newtonville was, Muste later recorded, "a wonderful further opening." He was now "seeing the places that Thoreau and Emerson had looked upon, breathing the air they had breathed, . . . getting saturated with the thought of New England and the whole background of Con-gregationalism."[2] Furthermore, his parishioners were "a really grand lot." Drawn largely from many of the cultural centers of the area, the majority of the congregation were professionals with comfortable incomes. "They [had] very high standards [and lived] cultivated lives but were unpretentious about it." The Mustes' first year among them was rewarding beyond measure. His pas-toral efforts were warmly received, church coffers expanded, and good friend-ships grew for Anna and him. Also, as the second year began in January 1916, their first child, Anne Dorothy (always to be called Nancy), was born.[3]

The Newtonville job brought A. J. Muste into contact with scholars and other clergy in the area. A club of eminent preachers invited him to join their monthly discussion sessions. Some of these individuals (for example, George A. Gordon and J. Edgar Park) were models of high achievement within the de-nominational framework. Others (Willard Sperry of Harvard Theological Sem-inary and Bliss Perry of the *Atlantic Monthly*) were identified more closely with the unconventional and dissenting strain of New England's history. Through them and in other ways Muste learned about "the old Boston non-conformity, going out and carrying the torch on issues."[4]

But the Mustes' happiness in this new setting was threatened even before it began. In the summer before their move to Massachusetts, World War I had erupted. Americans generally thought that it would be a short war, in which they would play only spectator roles. But by April of the following year—two months after Muste's installation at Newtonville, and the month in which one hundred and twenty-eight Americans lost their lives on the *Lusitania*—pressures were mounting for United States intervention. As the slaughter on European battlefields continued, Americans realized that they might be called to sacrifice their sons to the war. Muste reflected more and more that perhaps such sacrifice was futile and un-Christian.

What first tended him toward these pacifist conclusions is not entirely clear. He later stressed the effect of having read Tolstoy during the Fort Washington days. But that effect was not apparent even as late as 1914, when he preached at a memorial service for Spanish-American War veterans and took the "expected, conventional" position that when "democracy and religion are in danger, . . . as good Christians, we must go bravely, though reluctantly, into battle."⁵

Soon after transferring to Newtonville, he began "serious reading of the Christian mystics," and of Quaker scholar Rufus Jones, an historian and interpreter of their thought. The pacifist theme within Christian mysticism struck Muste with most force. Its impact on him derived not only from its content but perhaps even more from its history of having been obscured, if not suppressed, by official church teachings. For the rest of his life Muste was irritated that Christian pacifism had not been accorded a place in the mainstream of religious education.⁶

Besides the work of Rufus Jones, other influences encouraged Muste's interest in pacifism, including acquaintance with Unitarian Charles F. Dole, a founder of the Association to Abolish War, and a meeting, in 1915, with pacifist missionaries Dr. and Mrs. Sherwood Eddy. In 1916, friends drew Muste into personal participation in anti-war work. With Willard Sperry, J. Edgar Park, and others, he helped to create a Boston chapter of the pacifist Fellowship of Reconciliation. Founded in the last days of 1914 at Cambridge University in London, the FOR identified its goals as the promotion of reconciliation among the warring peoples of the world and the creation of a new "world order based on Love." Begun in the United States by British founding member Henry T. Hodgkin, the American FOR eventually attracted one thousand members in the World War I period. No small part of the attraction, as historian Charles Chatfield has pointed out, was "the inspiration [which the FOR] gave to its members. It had been born of the increasing isolation felt by those who sought to apply Christianity totally even to war."⁷

In the pre-Easter season that same year, Muste, while addressing his congregation on "The Opportunity of Lent," revealed his preoccupation with the war. Reminding his audience that citizens of the United States were practically alone in their safety from tragedy and suffering, he challenged them to make some sacrifice and issued his own rather startling personal declaration: "I find myself at the point where I must feel myself doing something that costs and hurts, something for humanity, and God, or go stark mad."[8] A curious outburst, "The Opportunity of Lent" contained some vague allusions to pacifism (including a passing kudos to Henry Ford, who had recently chartered an ocean liner to carry a delegation of American Pacifists to Europe), but primarily it expressed Muste's yearning to leave the edge and enter the eye of the storm, to experience directly the major catastrophe that had overcome half the world. The sermon was an exercise in self-realization.

But his thinking and feelings were not yet clear. In his utterances over the next few months he vacillated, trying the anti-war position and then stepping back to a more conventional patriotism, as if to see which felt best. For the December 14, 1916, *Congregationalist* he wrote an article calling on readers to "Do Your Bit for Belgium."[9] Though denying that he was "pro-Ally and anti-German in the ordinary sense," he wrote here in language that most preparedness advocates could approve. Fifteen days after diplomatic relations between Germany and the United States were severed, however, Muste preached in Central Church on "The Conscientious Objector" and took a moderately pacifist stand.[10] In April 1917, when the Emergency Peace Federation called an anti-war rally in Washington, Muste attended.[11] But then, on the second Sunday after war was declared—April 15, 1917—he led his parishioners in a nationalistic ceremony in the church auditorium, which was filled to capacity. Complete with patriotic hymns and twenty boy scouts bearing state and national flags up the central aisle, the service included a paean by Muste to "the best flag in the world" and to the Pilgrim Fathers, the pioneers, George Washington, Abraham Lincoln, "freedom . . . heroism . . . equal laws . . . opportunity . . . Christianity . . . noble American achievements of the past and still nobler American ideals."[12] The attitude which informed Muste's much later autobiographical comment on the "shocking and horrible" practice of placing national flags in Christian churches had not yet solidified.[13] But his pro-war actions were nearing an end.

On the second Sunday following the flag service, Muste called upon his congregation to speak out on behalf of "national Prohibition" as a "war emergency measure." This is his last recorded pro-war pronouncement.[14] By the first summer of United States involvement, A. J. Muste had ceased oscillating between conventional patriotism and opposition to the war. His ties to the national war effort snapped.

The congregation of Central Church could only have been bewildered by the erratic course which Muste followed in 1916 and 1917. A few members withdrew shortly after he joined the FOR and a small incident occurred on his return from the April 1917 rally in Washington, when a neighboring minister—a preparedness advocate—refused to carry on a scheduled joint service between their two congregations. But, for the most part, parishioners continued to attend church as long as the pastor continued to intersperse his ventures into the anti-war camp with such nationalistic gestures as the flag ceremony. After he became head of the League for Democratic Control (a local

Boston group with a clear anti-war position),[15] however, Muste's relationship with his church began to deteriorate. Although he believed that he held the respect of the young men in the congregation who entered the armed forces, when the casualty reports began to appear, he was unable "to adequately comfort" their parents.[16]

Gradually the Mustes fell into disgrace. Acquaintances "stopped speaking to us on the street. There were telephone callers some of whom suggested I be strung up on a pole," Muste remembered. "I'd ask them to come over and talk about it with me, but none ever did." In the autumn of 1917, Central Church's casualty list included a fatality, the son of Muste's closest neighbor. "His mother," Muste long recalled, "was not able to regard me as anything but a traitor after his death, and she asked that I not come to the funeral."[17] Beginning in November, a series of conferences took place between the minister and officers of the congregation. They offered him a six months' leave of absence with the understanding that he would devote the time to service in some war-relief agency. Unwilling to participate in any phase of the war effort, Muste declined the offer.[18] On December 9, 1917, he delivered his resignation statement in lieu of a regular sermon.

With humility and sorrow he asked forgiveness for personal inadequacies which he felt he had exhibited. Acknowledging that he had been "indeed a wretched and trying pastor," Muste pleaded that, nonetheless, his position be clearly understood. "I won't have it said," he declared, "that I have been untrue to the boys in the service." Those who were sending them to war were the ones who failed to show proper concern. Nor would he have it said that he was a traitor. He asserted that Jesus was a pacifist and that the followers of Jesus could be nothing else. Christians ought not delude themselves, he warned, that they were fulfilling their obligations by supporting war-relief work. "The real task of the church," he insisted, "is to create the spiritual conditions that should stop the war and render all wars unthinkable." Muste added that his own dedication to that task had recently been sanctioned by "a mystical experience of God" which had come on the preceding day, "for the second time in my life," and left him "happy and at rest in God. The war no longer has me by the throat," he said. Muste let his otherwise clear statement end in ambiguity. He told the congregation that if they accepted his resignation, he would leave "without the least feeling of bitterness," but he would also be "humbly and deeply thankful" if they chose to keep him "in spite of our differences as to the war."[19]

In a meeting on December 28, which filled the chapel "to the doors," church officers declared their "honor, respect and love" for the Reverend A. J. Muste, passed a resolution supporting the United States war effort as "a noble purpose," and offered their pastor a three months' leave of absence with partial salary "to investigate the war situation."[20] He accepted the leave but decided at the end of it upon permanent separation from the Newtonville pastorate. The Standing Committee of the church accepted his resignation in March 1918, but voted to continue his salary until May 1. "We feel," they concluded, that "we have been led these three years by a man of unusual genius and consecration.

. . . His life among us has been marked by gentleness and unfailing Christian courtesy." On April 16, a Church Council was called that dissolved relations between Muste and Central Congregational Church, with full recognition of "the fine and disinterested sincerity of the pastor."[21]

What is to be made of this episode in Muste's life and of the recurring "mystical experiences of God" to which he was prone? It is tempting to suspect that Muste habitually justified unconventional behavior by attributing it to divine guidance and that he was given to a self-righteousness which verged on fanaticism. Within the context of his upbringing and of his recent reading in Jones and the Christian mystics, however, he need not be viewed as suffering from messianic delusions. He had grown up believing that literal Christ-likeness was the essence of Christianity. Rufus Jones and other mystical pacifists made similar assumptions about practicing the faith. Muste's conversion to pacifism was the product of nearly three years of emotional and intellectual struggle against the bewildering complexity of unprecedented modern global war and against the failure of his own Christian education to prepare him to meet such a crisis. When he at last managed to bring the war into focus and to find the perspective from which, as a Christian apostle, he might judge it, his conclusions were shaped by an ingrained need for perfect consistency between profession and deed. When such consistency was at long last achieved, Muste experienced the same "Real Presence" that came to him before when his self, once divided, had become whole again.[22] Through the experience of 1917, Muste celebrated relief from inner tension and gained courage to face the dangers and conflicts that lay ahead.

Sometime within two months after drawing their final salary from Central Church, the Mustes travelled in the time-honored direction of earlier dissidents from Massachusetts—to Rhode Island. But that state, in 1918, was not the haven of tolerance that its founder had intended. Providence, where the Mustes were to settle for several months, was later recalled by the Dutch preacher as an "ultra patriotic town," where the state secretary of the Socialist Party had recently been convicted under the Espionage Act for speaking out against the imprisonment of conscientious objectors.[23] One island of free expression did remain, however—a Meeting of the Society of Friends.

When Muste visited the Providence Friends' Meeting in January 1918, its members were touched by his "courageous and difficult decision to devote thy life to the cause of peace." They must have been moved as well by the jobless and homeless status of the preacher and his family. Determining that "thee needed us and we needed thee," they enrolled Muste as their minister. Anna, Nancy, and he were given a home and a small salary in exchange for his teaching a Bible course at the nearby Friends' school, helping to form adult discussion groups, and maintaining a reading room in the basement of the meeting house. Also, he was "encouraged to speak in Sunday morning meetings."[24]

"The Quaker theme," as British Friend Harold Loukes has defined it, is that "true religion consists not in certainty but in search, not old conviction but 'new doubtfulness.' " What definition of religion could be better tailored to a traveler possessed of a soul powerless against its own discontent? And what spiritual mentor could appeal more to an adherent of scrupulous honesty than George Fox, the founder of Quakerism, who, as Rufus Jones has said, "was resolved that if he was going to live at all he would live a sincere life."

The religion established by Fox was wedded, from the beginning, to social action. Quakers "were concerned to be gathered up and used." That very concern followed Muste for years and had come to dominate his consciousness since the advent of the war. The fusion of activist promptings with religious principles—which he had been attempting since adolescence—at last became fully possible. Although he would later renew his clerical credentials within the mainstream of Protestant Christianity, the Society of Friends remained Muste's real spiritual home for the rest of his life.[25]

While this transition clearly benefited Muste, its impact on his partner in marriage was problematical. Anna Muste had to put aside her original expectations of a secure and conventional life as the wife of a promising young minister. Yet she genuinely loved "Bramie," as she called her husband. "She never complained," Muste observed. "She was not particularly an intellectual but she was interested in my ideas." He recalled a summer evening in 1918, when they were lying in bed and his wife pleaded with him: "Please just keep telling me about these things in which you believe and why you believe them."[26] Perhaps as Erik Erikson said of another reformer's wife, Kasturbai Gandhi, Anna Muste "managed gradually to assent to a life of sacrifice which she could not escape." Muste was aware that the trouble his ideas caused could not have been pleasant for his wife, and that she did not "always go along with my positions." Nonetheless, he recalled with satisfaction, "she stood by me."[27]

Muste's beliefs had not entirely crystallized in 1918. He advanced toward anti-war work with some lingering ambivalence. Uncertainty was evident in an article he wrote in the January 10, 1918, issue of the *Congregationalist.* "The Present Status of Conscientious Objectors" was based, Muste explained, on his visit to "one of the camps where the draft army is being trained,"—probably Fort Devens, Massachusetts, where he held biweekly conference and counselling sessions with conscientious objectors. Written before the brutal treatment of war resisters became part of the historical record, Muste's article was a curious mixture of sympathy and near-contempt for the men he described. He praised their courage and sincerity while suggesting that they might be "mistaken," and that War Department officials were justified in maintaining strict controls over draft exemptions so that a "host of slackers" did not "develop consciences over night." In this piece were few indications of the veteran pacifist who, in later times, heartily assented to the proposition that "there is that of the conscientious objector in every person."[28]

Though unclear in his published thoughts, Muste continued to involve himself with the opponents of war. The reading room, which he opened in the basement of Providence Meeting, featured not only literature about Christian pacifism but also socialism, Trotskyism, and other forms of radicalism. According to his autobiography, it became a gathering place of the "unorthodox and persecuted individuals of the city."[29] Muste also maintained a working relationship with anti-war activists in Boston. His acquaintance with Roger Nash Baldwin dates from this period. Baldwin, in 1917, assisted by Muste's Union classmate, Norman Thomas, had founded the National Civil Liberties Bureau (soon to be known as the American Civil Liberties Union). Muste remembered meeting Baldwin through the latter's relatives and soon became "sort of a New England representative of the Civil Liberties Union." At the same time Muste continued to work with the Boston FOR. As the war wound down in the fall of 1918, he moved his family to a "Fellowship House" in Boston.

The Muste's new home, which they shared with two other families, was financed partly by two members of Boston's social elite, Elizabeth Glendower Evans and Ann N. Davis. It became the meeting place of a group who called themselves "the Comradeship" and included Harold Rotzel, a Methodist minister who had lost his pulpit during the war; Cedric Long, a Congregationalist minister whose pacifism had prevented him from ever obtaining a pulpit; Bill Simpson, a younger man whose occupation was trying "literally to live without money and without compromising his convictions"; Ann N. Davis; and another eminent Bostonian, Ethel Paine.

The comrades sought to live " in the way of truth, nonviolence and love." They talked of establishing urban and rural cooperatives from which they could carry on the struggle against war and for economic justice and racial equality.[30] For several weeks during the winter of 1918–1919, Muste and Rotzel sought guidance in these matters by rising daily at five in the morning. "Bundled in overcoats" in an unheated room of the Fellowship House, they poured over the New Testament, "especially the Sermon on the Mount." "Together," as Muste later described their exercises, we "analyzed the passages, meditated on each phrase, even each word, prayed and asked ourselves what obedience to those precepts meant for us, then and there."[31] The influence of these daybreak sessions is obvious in a prospectus which Muste drew up at the very end of 1918.

In his "Suggestions for a Proposed New 'Preaching Order' to Disseminate Fellowship of Reconciliation Principles," Muste envisioned the formation of a band of evangels, patterned partly after the original Christians and partly after the earliest exponents of his adopted faith—who saw themselves as returning to Christian origins. Like Jesus' first followers, the "preachers" described by Muste would "cut loose . . . from the existing order." Like the pioneer Quakers, they would engage in mass propagandizing and "might in groups go voluntarily to jail . . . whenever a flagrant case of oppression arises." Like both antecedents, members of the new order would cultivate the role of a peculiar people, dressing uniformly (though not "too much like a military uniform or clerical dress") to symbolize their internal unity and their repudiation of "the world," and incidentally to provide "protection to the women of the order as they go about." The major goal of the preaching order Muste defined as that of carrying "the message" to both rich and poor that the time had arrived to "rebuke the old order and . . . enter upon a new." All materials used to back up the message would be thoroughly researched, factual, and up-to-date.[32]

This proposal of 1918 provides an index to the basic assumptions and impulses of its author at the end of his thirty-third year. Christian evangelism remained a strong motive force and the mind stimulated by that force was continuing its persistent drive for intellectual integrity. Youthful allegiance to "discontent" still burned strong in the maturing man. And it seemed as if his quite recently adopted pacifist convictions had taken permanent root. "Love or Good Will," the prospectus stated, is "the central fact of the universe." It is "the *method* by which the new order must be achieved."[33]

The atmosphere in which Muste's "Suggestions" were written was, he later stressed, "tense and feverish. . . . The Russian Revolution was less than two years old. Thrones toppled in Europe. . . . 'General strikes' were taking place in cities of Canada and the United States." In early 1919, a "Red Week" was held in Boston. James Larkin, pugnacious labor leader from Ireland, brought the radical celebration to a climax in Boston's Grand Opera House with a speech proclaiming Russia "the only place where men and women can be free." In this same period Larkin addressed a meeting at the Back Bay Fellowship House. The Irishman, Muste recalled in his autobiography, had a "voice like thunder. His speech was red hot." Residents of the house feared (unnecessarily as it turned out) that "the next day the police or men from Army intelligence would come around to shut the place up."[34]

Such episodes were placing a strain on Muste's relationship with the Quakers. A member of the Yearly Meeting of Friends wrote to Muste on February 4, 1919, that "quite a number of people up here are afraid of thy work. They still remember the time thee had here last summer and do not think thee a safe man. At least they do not think it would be wise to have the dogs of war turned loose again." The incident alluded to was Muste's address in June 1918, at the Yearly Meeting in Vassalboro, Maine, which was ill-received by a local Baptist minister in the audience who summoned the sheriff at its conclusion. Muste was hastily driven to his train by some Friends as others stayed and reportedly persuaded the sheriff that the Baptist's charges were unfounded. "However," Muste observed, "if I had been on the grounds, the chances are he would have arrested me, rather than run the risk of being accused of lacking patriotic zeal; and in the atmosphere of the time a conviction on a basis of my writings and general activities would have been almost a foregone conclusion."[35]

While Muste's increasingly radical ideas alarmed the Friends, the plunge he was about to make into radical labor action would end his career as a Quaker minister.

In January 1919, "rumors began to fly," Muste recorded, of an impending textile strike in the mills of Lawrence, Massachusetts. Lawrence in the 1910s was inhabited by approximately 86,000 people; 60,000 worked for the woolen company, half of them, mostly foreign-born, in the "grim mills."[36] Since the earliest days of this settlement, investigators had repeatedly found laboring and housing conditions deplorable. But, while strikes protesting these conditions had occurred in 1882, 1894, 1902, and 1912, unified protest was always difficult to consolidate. At least twenty-five different nationalities worked at Lawrence.[37] Such ethnic variety made union organizing difficult. Compounding the task, as historian Donald Cole has shown, was the gap which developed between generations of foreign workers.[38]

When severe wage cuts created the strike situation of 1912 at Lawrence, the United Textile Workers, dominated by old-stock immigrants and affiliated with the American Federation of Labor, had refused to participate in the protest. "Italians became the backbone of the strike," which was led by the Industrial Workers of the World. The stirring rhetoric of Wobbly leaders and the brutality of police and militia, culminating in a dramatic evacuation of the children of Lawrence to the homes of sympathizers throughout New England, imparted an aura of romance to this chapter of labor history. But "the leaders of the I.W.W. greatly overestimated the results of the strike." Soon after, IWW membership at Lawrence fell off and previous conditions returned.[39]

In the first weeks of 1919, a small AFL affiliate, the United Textile Workers, with about 200 members, called for a forty-eight hour work week, as opposed to fifty-four. Their call was answered when the Lawrence employers inserted slips in all workers' pay envelopes "asking whether they wanted six hours less pay." The UTW, "probably because they felt a strike at that time to be inexpedient because of the dullness of the season,"[40] acceded to the pay cut. But tens of thousands of workers felt otherwise. *Survey Magazine* reported that half of the adult male wage earners at Lawrence were already making less than $1,000 a year, at a time when the federal minimum living wage estimate for a family of five was $1,500 a year. A further salary decrease seemed intolerable, especially when it was known that the mill owners were offering an extra dividend of ten dollars per share to their stockholders.[41]

On February 3, a strike call went out, demanding "Forty-eight/Fifty-four"—the shorter work week without a wage reduction. John Fitch, A. J. Muste's friend from the days of the Fort Washington pastorate in New York, reported for *Survey* in April 1919 that the initial walkout included about 17,000 to 30,000 workers and, two months later, approximately 15,000 remained on strike.[42]

In the dead of winter, with the AFL denouncing the walkout as a "revolutionary movement," the struggle to hold the unorganized protest together was desperate. Sitting in on early strike committee meetings as "mostly silent observers" were three members of the Boston Comradeship—Cedric Long, Harold Rotzel, and A. J. Muste.[43]

When these comrades visited Lawrence their purpose was to see for themselves what conditions were like in the mill town. The "very specific and painful actualities" they found soon led them to promise to "do all [they] could to raise relief money in case of a strike." During the first week of the strike they accordingly sought to interpret the event to the wider public with an eye to arousing sympathy and calling forth aid for the workers. To this end they established the Boston Defense Committee for the Lawrence Strike and set about addressing envelopes, translating relief appeals, distributing leaflets, and talking to reporters. At the close of the first week—which had been marked by numerous clubbings of picketers by police—the strike committee appealed to Muste to accept the position of executive head, with Rotzel and Long to become voting members. The hope, Muste later explained, was that people who had "education and contacts" could more successfully achieve a good press for the strikers and give learned counsel regarding strategy. "When the proposition was made, we clearly either had to undertake the ominous responsibility or else to leave Lawrence altogether."[44]

Muste assumed the leadership position and asked to be relieved from his work in Rhode Island. "The Textile Strike has me in its grip far more securely than I have supposed possible," he wrote Providence Friends. Muste stressed that this was "a unique opportunity to try out in the industrial realm one's moral and spiritual ideals. There are," he admitted, "things about it that I do not like, that I even dread." Yet, he concluded, "I must come back to the position that it is God's will that I should remain with the workers. So . . . I ask Providence Meeting to let me go." The Rhode Island Quakers concluded that, "as there seemed to be nothing else that could be done in the matter, his withdrawal was accepted with regret."[45] This withdrawal did not spell the end of Muste's involvement with Quakerism but the form that involvement would take in the future would be much less traditional.

The depth of the changes occurring in Muste's life during this period may be gauged by comparing his commitment to labor, in 1919, with a speech he had given at a Young Friends' Meeting in Westown, Pennsylvania, less than a year before. Then he assured his listeners that "Jesus did not tell [workers] to organize, strike, fight to obtain food and their rights," and he speculated that, even if the masses did achieve economic restitution, "they will not be satisfied." However, direct experience in the strike situation completely altered this view.[46]

Such experience was bound to affect his family, whose material prospects were permanently diminished by his decision to cease cultivation of ties with prominent professionals and members of the social elite and to identify with the lowest ranking laborers in America's working class. In the most extreme view this meant that Anna Muste faced the possibility that her husband could be jailed, maimed, or killed. She may have derived some comfort from an understanding among the Boston comrades that, as Muste put it, "our families would be taken care of if any of us were injured or jailed." But even with such assurance the strain must have been great.[47]

Muste's training as preacher and pastoral counselor were of limited use in this new endeavor. Ministerial patterns of life—which had centered around words and ideas—had to be subordinated to the activism of the organizer, the strategist, and the battle captain. Muste and his Boston colleagues joined the picket lines. They expected at best to allay police violence by their presence and at least to reassure the strikers that their leaders were not asking more than they themselves were willing to risk. Muste and Long were soon beaten and jailed for "disturbing the peace." They were released on bond after several hours and the following week were acquitted. But the episode was the first in a series of dangerous events.[48]

During the sixteen weeks of the strike, February 1 to May 23, 1919, the comrades were introduced to most of the hard facts of life surrounding labor struggles at that time. These included the plotting of labor spies, which, on one occasion, nearly led to Muste's being charged with a murder unrelated to the strike, and outbreaks of violence from among the workers, often encouraged by *provocateurs*. The *provocateur* menace became deadly when the police set up machine gun lines and the workers had to choose between encouragement to "seize the machine guns" and the nonviolent counsel of their leaders. Muste's persuasiveness seems to have averted a massacre in that case. On another occasion sheer luck allowed him to be out of town when thugs invaded the Lawrence apartments he shared with another key union man, Anthony Capraro. Capraro, who had been loaned to the Lawrence endeavor by the Amalgamated Clothing Workers, was seized and severely beaten.[49]

However, in the context of that era, the 1919 event was not excessively violent. The historian of its 1912 predecessor has written that the latter, which took at least two lives, "was a placid affair" compared with Homestead, Pennsylvania, and other such landmarks: By this kind of reckoning, Lawrence in Muste's time—where no strike-related deaths were recorded—was also a relatively mild episode. John Fitch assured *Survey* readers in April that "the streets of Lawrence are not running with blood. . . . There is nothing even remotely suggesting a state of siege."[50]

If the violence facing Muste and other Lawrence leaders was not unusually massive by U.S. standards, two additional problems were critical. As in all earlier efforts, the strikers had to surmount their ethnic disparateness. Muste's talent for being able to weld dissimilar factions into at least temporary unity was useful here. The problem of sustaining morale was more difficult. The mill operators showed no signs of giving in. According to Harold Rotzel, "during the last three terrible weeks no regular relief could be issued for lack of funds."[51] Only the most stirring encouragement could keep the strike alive under these conditions.

In one instance Muste helped arrange such encouragement. Carlo Tresca, the Italian anarchist whose presence had added romance and inspiration to the 1912 strike, and who was deeply hated by the Lawrence establishment, was daringly smuggled into town.

At another time worker morale soared when Elizabeth Glendower Evans walked openly into Lawrence. This Boston supporter seems to have been a stockholder in the textile mills. She contributed substantially to the strikers' relief fund and then decided, at a moment, Muste later claimed, "when it seemed we could not hold out a day longer," to visit the town and "take a walk." As the sixty-three-year-old matron strolled along streets where picketing was forbidden, "one by one strikers appeared and walked quietly behind." Before her constitutional was over, according to Muste, "a great human chain" of "thousands" of workers was thrown around the mills and the determination to carry on was rekindled.[52]

But such moments could not inspire the workers forever. In the sixteenth week of the strike, leaders "held a long conference and decided that we had no right to call . . . for further sacrifices." Ironically, management was feeling equally depressed. On the very day that Muste was preparing to declare the strike ended, the textile executives called for a conference. The outcome yielded the strikers a forty-eight hour week with the equivalent of fifty-five hours pay, according to their old salary scale. The salary increase was more than had been demanded.[53]

Even so, the impact of the event proved less momentous than its leaders had anticipated. At the outset they had insisted to reporters that they were revolutionaries seeking to replace the old order. In reality, however, the workers' margin of victory was exceedingly narrow and seems to bear out Donald Cole's judgment that the Lawrence strike gains of 1919 were less decisive than those won by the IWW in 1912.

In the wake of a depression that struck the textile industry in 1920, management concessions proved even more transitory. In addition, Cole has documented a "wave of Americanism" that swept the immigrant city after 1919, and resulted in a denunciation by a group of Italian workers (the very nationality that had contributed some of the staunchest support to the strike) of Muste and others for having tried to "de-Americanize" them.[54]

On the other hand, this event, by which Muste was initiated into labor action, did kindle the kind of rebellion against older unions that would eventually flame into industrial union policies of the sort made famous by the early Congress of Industrial Organizations. A pioneering spark was struck at Lawrence when workers revolted against the AFL's United Textile Workers, and a rival organization, the Amalgamated Textile Workers, came into being.

An "outlaw union" in the eyes of the AFL, the ATW emerged from the independent Lawrence strike and other rebel movements among New England textile workers. It was founded in April 1919 by a convention in New York of seventy to eighty delegates, representing workers from Lawrence and the New Jersey mill towns of Paterson, Passaic, Hackensack, and Hoboken. At a follow-up convention in October 1919, Muste was chosen as general secretary and given additional responsibilities as treasurer and editor of the ATW organ, the *New Textile Worker*. At the convention which elected him general secretary, Muste sounded a militant note with his declaration that ATW members were "not interested merely in shorter hours and higher wages but looked far ahead to a future reorganization of the system of production." There was, however, a gap between his call for an overhauling of the socio-economic system and the policies which he actually sanctioned. For example, the union endeavored to prevent confrontations by early agreements with employers. One such pact, recorded by contemporary labor researchers as "the first of its kind ever made in any branch of the textile industries," was that between workers and bosses in the silk ribbon factories of New York.[55]

For some time the ATW seemed to flourish. In the Rand School's *Labor Year Book* for 1921–1922, its record was set down as one of "extraordinary progress." But no sooner had it been registered than the record began to crumble. Worker apathy was one cause. In addition, the textile industry was hit by a depression in 1920–1922. Even before the depression textile unionism had been in a precarious state. At the peak of ATW success (when other textile unions were also growing) no more than a quarter of the mill workers had been unionized. After the slump set in, unionization sagged to include only between 12 and 15 percent of the workers. Muste looked back later on his two year stint with the ATW as an "unremitting desperate effort to establish a beachhead . . . of unionism in a chaotic industry." When opportunity came for him to take other employment which would keep him in the labor movement but relieve him of some of the desperation and chaos which characterized his current efforts, he took it. In October 1921, he resigned as Amalgamated general secretary. Shortly thereafter, the union ceased to exist.[56]

The direction in which he now turned was foreshadowed in certain programs of the ATW, notably experiments with worker cooperatives at Lawrence and worker education classes in Passaic.[57] The spirit of the former and an ambitious extension of the latter were combined in 1921 at Brookwood Labor College in Katonah, New York. There, as director of the school, Muste would reside with his family for the next twelve years.

Chapter III

From Lawrence to Katonah

Two miles out of Katonah, up a winding road through overhanging woods arose a house like Mt. Vernon," wrote poet Sarah Cleghorn describing Brookwood. Helen and William Fincke had purchased the building and its ample, verdant grounds at the end of World War I. It answered perfectly their pacifist longing for a place "where we could live the kind of life that was the most opposite thing we could think of to war." They began an enterprise which later generations would have called a "free school."[1] In 1921, they decided to change the institution from a preparatory school to a college for working-class adults and invited the backing of organized labor.

The plan received an enthusiastic welcome from those labor leaders and educators whom the Finckes invited to Brookwood for a three-day spring conference. Social scientists following in the path of John R. Commons, progressive schoolmen led by John Dewey, and militant trade unionists, of the sort A. J. Muste had become, pledged their support.[2] The Finckes set about recruiting teachers and asked Muste to become chairman of the faculty.

Although the future of Brookwood was by no means guaranteed, the offer was attractive. The location offered a safe and healthy environment for Nancy and her sister, Constance (called Connie), who was born in August of 1920. The job would remove Muste from the gruelling and essentially hopeless ATW battles and allow something of a return to a reflective mode of life. He had begun to feel, he said, that he was "running out of ammunition [and] needed the sort of stimulus you'd get from serious reading."[3]

Religious motives also inclined Muste toward Brookwood, which he viewed as "a spiritual child of the Comradeship." His concern with spiritual values was readily apparent to Sarah Cleghorn, who taught English there and who recalled an evening of poetry reading shortly after the labor college began. Muste read from Henry Vaughn:

I saw Eternity the other night
Like a great ring of pure and endless light
All calm as it was bright.

"Those who were listening seemed all to feel the deep experience that must lie back of such words," wrote Cleghorn. She was certain that Muste possessed "a mystic realization of infinity" and was "deeply, irrevocably aware of the presence of God."[4]

With the confidence that Cleghorn observed, Muste took up his new task. The original expectation that William Fincke and he would work in close partnership ended when the Finckes departed from Brookwood, leaving Muste on his own to shape the new venture.[5] An able faculty was gathered, including labor historian David J. Saposs and sociologist Arthur W. Calhoun. A carryover from the prep school, Sarah Cleghorn assumed the role of English instructor, but was replaced in mid-year by an organizer of teachers' unions, Josephine Colby. A variety of shorter-term teachers and visiting lecturers completed the instructional staff. A dietician, a superintendent of buildings and grounds, and secretarial employees were also hired.[6]

Students were drawn to the college primarily by their desire to improve their effectiveness as labor organizers. But they were also attracted by the welcome contrast between Brookwood surroundings and their usual existence. As Len DeCaux has written: "To the miner, Brookwood was green, clean, all above ground—no coaldust, no cricks in the back. To the machinist, Brookwood was greaseless days far from the grinding roar of metal against metal. To makers of suits, dresses, hats, Brookwood was fairytale country," in sharp contrast to "the trash-strewn cement valleys of Manhattan or Chicago. To those who had known poverty, Brookwood offered ease, security, the fresh-air pleasures of the well-to-do."[7] The students who matriculated in 1921 numbered roughly twenty and ranged in age from the late teens to the early forties. The sexes were fairly represented. A quota system of selection insured that culturally and occupationally the student body would present a variegated picture, though "throughout the 1920's . . . the vast majority of Brookwood students were trade unionists and they came particularly from the needle trades and coal-miners' unions."[8] Within half a decade enrollment doubled, taking in about fourteen "nationalities," under which heading Negro students were listed beside Scots, Norwegians, and Hungarians. The school received official endorsement from thirteen national and international unions. Also within that time the college was incorporated, and a board of directors which represented trade unionism, the faculty, and alumni and students was established to oversee general policies. Pennsylvania socialist and labor leader James Maurer—remembered by Muste for, among other things, his fine aim with chewing tobacco—was its first chairman.[9]

Shortly after incorporation an ambitious fund drive began to create a permanent endowment for the college. Leading progressive intellectuals, including Jane Addams, John Commons, Herbert Croly, Stuart Chase, and Freda

Kirchwey, lent their names to its support. The college expanded structurally as well, with students pitching in to construct a dormitory, garages, faculty housing, volleyball and tennis courts, and a swimming pool.[10] These were but the outer signs of the vivid inner life of Brookwood Labor College.

The school made no claim to being a communal enterprise, but in large measure it was. A "manual-work schedule," which made campus upkeep and expansion a community concern, was included in the daily routine of both students and faculty. Meals were taken in common. College policies were arrived at by consultation among all residents.[11] Naturally enough, these practices were not friction-free. In one of her rare appearances in the historical record, Anna Muste resigned from her job of overseeing "the kitchen department" because of the constant bickering among those under her supervision. "I do not care to give all my strength to trying to settle difficulties that could easily be avoided if people were a little more lenient towards each other," she asserted.[12]

Social regulations were minimal and expressed the director's faith that individuals would be guided by "their own self-respect and their desire to keep Brookwood above the reach of harmful social criticism." Since suspicion was rife in nearby Katonah that the school was a hothouse of "free love," concern about sexual mores was inescapable. Cara Cook, librarian and tutor, recalled that students "would yell pointedly after a couple starting off to hike around the meadow path, 'remember now—above the reach of harmful social criticism.' "[13]

The personal lives of campus residents were often closely entwined. When romances flourished their vicissitudes were sympathetically followed. The college head, it has been said, furthered a number and "saw that they were corrected or consummated." He heard the marriage vows of Cara Cook and the promising young mine worker Cal Bellaver, and those of faculty members Mark Starr and Helen Norton. His pastoral training proved useful in other ways, providing what modern institutions would call Brookwood's counselling service, and what has been more precisely described as "the head of the court of appeals and a fantasy father for . . . students and faculty members."[14] But such was the nature of Brookwood unity that individual joys and sorrows were shared. Tragedy—from the death of a campus canine to the accidental drowning of a visiting alumnus in the new swimming pool—were mourned by the entire body. Triumphs, such as the birth of John Martin Muste in January 1927, were celebrated by everyone.[15]

Brookwooders prided themselves on being able to devise entertainment "without benefit of movies and such." They wrote and acted their own skits, which sometimes included the whole Muste family. Nancy Muste Baker long remembered the Brookwood Saturday night "when our family was up on the stage, huddled around some mechanical parts, while we sang a song about [how] 'the Anarchist Family threw the bomb-bomb-bomb.' " Muste had his own renditions of Milt Gross' "Nize Baby," Shakespeare's "To be or not to be" soliloquy, and an impersonation of John D. Rockefeller, complete with knickers, cap, and golf stick. For more serious moods he had another repertoire, including readings from Housman's *Shropshire Lad* and Benét's *John Brown's Body*.[16]

Another cherished Brookwood activity was singing. "We sang on every occasion," Cara Cook recalled. While Brookwooders joined in choruses of "Not one cent shall be spent for a capitalistic war!" their music took on a more martial cast in reference to the struggles of labor—as in "We Came" by Brookwood student Edith Berkowitz. "They've refused to heed our suffering," her stanzas read. "But they'll hear our marching feet! We have the workers' Red Flag unfurled. We come to take back our world."[17] Muste's passion for baseball found outlet as he acquired a reputation for "wild heaves from first base." Brookwood residents also played volleyball, tennis, an exotic variation thereof called quoit tennis, and horseshoes.[18]

The college curriculum, Muste explained, was designed on the assumption that while in regular schools, students "did not know anything but knew how to say it," at Brookwood they "knew a great deal but did not know how to say it." Classroom work ranged from highly sophisticated sharing of insights into the psychology, sociology, and politics of labor organizing, to rudimentary exercises in speaking and writing. For a number of students English had to be taught as a foreign language. Teaching methods were traditional or innovative, according to the subject matter. Muste conducted an old-fashioned speech course. Josephine Colby, who was said to have "had something approaching genius in teaching . . . English to workers," employed dramatics. Plays authored and enacted by Brookwooders sometimes achieved sufficient polish to be publicly performed. Under the supervision of another English teacher, Helen Norton, students began publishing the *Brookwood Review* in the spring of 1923. The product of this "exercise in labor journalism" soon became "the official organ of Brookwood Labor College."[19] Social science instruction emphasized economics, sociology, and history. Arthur Calhoun lectured from openly avowed Marxist premises. David Saposs stressed the history of working people. Muste conducted a course in the history of civilization.[20]

Along with this course work Brookwood residents were stimulated by a wealth of visiting lecturers from the field of political and union activism and the academic and professional spheres, including novelist Sinclair Lewis, who visited the campus in 1929 with an eye-witness account of the brutal suppression of the textile strike in Marion, North Carolina.[21] Most visitors to Brookwood leaned decidedly leftward in their social thought and included an occasional communist. All of Brookwood's offerings, its director repeatedly insisted, were meant to stimulate free and open discussion. College policy maintained that no point of view should be suppressed but that opinions based on prejudice would not be tolerated.[22]

In some ways, however, Brookwood Labor College had strong biases built into it. An insistence on "relevance" quickly alienated Sarah Cleghorn. Her students, she commented, "were what I called Labor Puritans. They wanted literary feeling and personal expression, not for life in general but for the labor movement alone. To this they were consecrated like Cromwell's Ironsides. It was wonderful, it was sacrificial, but it was altogether different from what I conceived." The college director supported such consecration when he assured readers of the *Brookwood Review* that in its pages no space would be wasted on "polite presentations of remote or academic issues." He took care to warn candidates for Brookwood faculty positions about the practical goals of the college. Muste turned down an application from V. F. Calverton on the grounds that the writer's interests were "primarily cultural or scholarly" and would not meet the expectations of the "practical people" enrolled in the labor school.[23]

Behind the fact that grades and diplomas were not given was a telling rationale. It was the intention to leave students "in a situation where the only way in which their schooling . . . would tell would be in the actual work they did in unions."[24] So practical application of knowledge and activism were integral to the philosophy of workers' education that gave the school its identity. In keeping with this thinking labor educators stressed the importance of helping workers identify their place in the general scheme of things. "The two most important forces in the world today," Muste declared, "are modern science and the organized labor and farm movements." Through the former, man commands his environment. Through the latter the world's producers guarantee that science would work to their benefit.[25]

In the early twenties a full-fledged international movement for workers' education seemed to be under way. In the summer of 1922, Muste returned from Brussels and the First International Conference on Workers' Education with a report on "an imposing movement that is evidently full of vitality." In the United States labor classes and colleges were multiplying. A clearing house, the Workers' Education Bureau (WEB), was established and received the endorsement of the AFL. These developments, Muste said, as he reviewed them a few years later, "came in with a flourish of trumpets. . . . Many labor organizers were enthusiastic. All the intellectuals were in a glow, feeling that once more the world was going to be saved. It was one of those golden dawns."[26] But morning mists obscured critical divisions within the new movement.

By carving out a sphere of influence within the existing socio-political system, the AFL had become the country's most powerful labor organization. Talk of radical alterations in that system found no place in its platform and programs. The militant ideals of labor education defined by Muste and seconded by such figures as James Maurer, president of the WEB, were anathema to the hierarchy of the labor federation. A move by labor chieftains to wrest control of workers' education from the radicals was soon under way. Muste resisted it. While cultivating an image of impartial reconciler within labor ranks, he was in fact directing a partisan offensive on behalf of radically oriented labor education, using the Brookwood campus as his base.

Beginning about 1924, invitations were issued periodically, asking various segments of the labor movement to gather on the hill above Katonah and thresh out their feelings about union organizing. These institutes singled out minority groups within American labor for special notice. Conferences for both youth and Negroes were called. In 1927, "the first institute for women's trade union auxiliaries ever held in the United States" took place on the college campus. The inclusion of these minorities in Brookwood's programs differed pointedly from the subordination and, often, outright discrimination to which many segments of the labor movement subjected them. Also, in marked contrast to the AFL's elitist administration, Brookwood assemblies were structured open-endedly, calculated to appeal to the most restive and disenchanted elements under AFL sway as well as to those whom the organization would not embrace.[27]

Muste used another channel, the Labor Publication Society, to make the same appeal. In the same year that Brookwood Labor College opened, the LPS was established forty miles away in New York City where its socialist founders launched *Labor Age* under the editorship of Louis Budenz. In 1922, Muste joined the editorial board and his writings soon began to appear regularly. Under his increasing influence the magazine became, by 1926, "an outlet for the public expression of the thought and activities of labor progressives," of, that is, those who were growing ever more critical of the AFL.[28]

A series of commemorative assemblies which occurred on the Brookwood campus between 1924 and 1928 further widened the gulf between Muste and union establishment. In 1924, Brookwooders took note of the deaths of Samuel Gompers, who had led the AFL for over forty years, and Arthur Gleason, a British labor expert who had given support to the college. Muste announced that a memorial scholarship fund was being established in Gleason's name and added that the same sort of memorial should have been set up for Gompers, rather than the statue which union officials were reportedly planning to erect. While that remark may have escaped the attention of AFL officialdom, it is unlikely that Brookwood's response to a third death in 1924 went unnoticed. The expiration of Russian Bolshevik chief, Nicolai Lenin, occasioned a special meeting on the campus in the spring of 1925. There an unidentified speaker proclaimed that "Lenin the man is dead. But Leninism still lives." The following year the great socialist Eugene Debs passed from the American scene. His demise stirred little grief in the top leadership ranks of the AFL, where his criticisms had been directed for years. But at Brookwood, Muste presided over a deeply moving commemoration. He stressed the fallen leader's radicalism and called for the labor movement to emulate it.[29]

In 1927, another memorial event provided an opportunity for censure of the labor establishment. That fall Muste charged the American labor movement (along with the "textile autocracy of New England" and "the . . . legal system of Massachusetts") with the "murders" of Sacco and Vanzetti. The tragedy could have been averted, he maintained, if labor organizations had been effective and workers not "too easily misled by talk of 'anarchists and foreigners.'" According to Cara Cook, two carloads of Brookwood people drove to Boston on the night of the execution of the anarchists, "arriving there in time to stand in silent protest outside the Charlestown prison at midnight."[30]

Muste carried his criticism of mainstream labor further during a May Day celebration at Brookwood in 1928, where he described conditions within the AFL as "stagnant" and "reactionary," and singled out William Green for special condemnation.[31] His comments speedily travelled back to Green. The AFL president, as a matter of fact, had been keeping tabs on Brookwood affairs for several years.

Word reached Muste in the fall of 1924 that a debate was in progress in the executive council of the AFL over whether Brookwood was "allright." Thereafter, he received recurring warnings that the college was under suspicion for being too radical.[32] In May 1926, Green initiated a quiet inquiry into the politics of Brookwood's resident Marxist, Arthur Calhoun. The following year he asked Spencer Miller, Jr., secretary of the WEB, to investigate Brookwood's annual celebrations of May Day. Miller, who had been rankled by criticisms directed against the WEB during an American Federation of Teachers conference at Brookwood in 1926, reported back that the college was perpetrating radical doctrines, that Muste had taken no clear stand against them, and that Calhoun was "a most destructive influence" at the school. The WEB secretary also expressed alarm over the popularity of Brookwood institutes and suggested that his own bureau should begin holding rival ones.

Brookwood-AFL relations were further muddied when Muste took a position against an agreement highly touted in official union circles between W. D. Mahone, president of the Amalgamated Association of State and Electric Railway Employees and the Mitten Management Corporation, which operated the streetcar system of Philadelphia. Decrying the Mitten-Mahone accord as a step toward company unionism and Mussolini-type fascism, Muste followed up his published criticism by organizing a conference about the agreement at Brookwood in August 1928. Mahone and representatives of Mitten were invited but did not appear. Meanwhile two representatives of the Mahone union who were students at Brookwood became involved in fifth column activities. As soon as Muste made public his opposition to the agreement, the two railway carmen and three other students requested the elimination of May Day celebrations on the campus. When voted down by the student body they promptly wrote to William Green, were commended for their efforts, and encouraged to send further information. The students complied.[33]

By mid-summer the AFL was ready with an announcement that an investigating committee, chaired by Vice-President Matthew Woll, had looked into conditions at Brookwood and found them tainted with communism and atheism, and with infidelity to the American Federation of Labor. After receiving the report the AFL executive committee recommended that all its unions withdraw financial support from the college and cease sending students. At its fall convention in New Orleans, delegates from the general membership, on a motion made by W. D. Mahone, debated the recommendation and, after intense controversy, ratified it.[34]

The Woll report played heavily on the communist specter and identified four instructors—Arthur Calhoun, David Saposs, Josephine Colby, and Tom Tippett—as "communist influences." The report also charged Brookwood with perfidy, claiming that members of the college community had been involved in the effort of John Brophy to displace John L. Lewis as leader of the United Mine Workers.[35]

The battle of Brookwood still raged in 1929, and spilled over into both the Workers' Education Bureau and the Labor Publication Society, where half of the board of directors walked out when Society leaders insisted on backing Muste and the Workers' Education Bureau. At the annual WEB convention in April 1929, AFL partisans carried a vote to dissolve Brookwood's membership in the Bureau and declared vacant Muste's position on the executive committee.[36] Despite such defections, Brookwood continued to function. While a number of unions disaffiliated themselves from the college, many others rallied to its support, along with about two hundred individuals, including such prominent figures as John Dewey, John Fitch, and labor historian Broadus Mitchell.

Justification could be found on both sides in the controversy. Certainly, some of the programs and proclamations that had originated at Brookwood were provocative and insulting to the AFL. On the other hand the clandestine methods employed by Green and Woll to investigate the college—campus residents, except for student informers, did not know an investigation had occurred until it was announced in the *New York Times*—smacked of foul play.[38]

Neither party in the dispute can be absolved of the charge that it slanted its arguments. Muste chose to ignore Green's allegations about Brookwood participants in the Brophy meeting and was too glib in discounting the influence of communist beliefs among his faculty. Less than a year after Arthur Calhoun had been singled out in the Woll report, he was dismissed by unanimous vote of the Brookwood board of directors, on the grounds that college aims were incompatible with his contention "that Brookwood should adopt a policy of communism and that those who take a contrary position are betrayers of labor." Sometime later, Josephine Colby, another instructor cited by Green, left the United States to take up permanent residence in Russia, where she died in 1938.[39]

Nonetheless, the AFL attacked these teachers with innuendo rather than evidence. Furthermore, Green and his associates completely overlooked the hostility which existed between Brookwood and the Communist Party U.S.A. Had Woll really done his homework, he would have found in Muste's public statements as much criticism of CP policy as of the AFL. The Woll committee relied heavily on the testimony of the two Brookwood students, one of whom, Muste suspected, had been "sent for the express purpose" of spying.[40] The conclusions drawn by contemporaries who supported Brookwood were validated later in the work of historians who assessed the controversy. John Dewey's belief that "the condemnation of Brookwood . . . is a part of the policy to eliminate from the labor movement the schools and influences that endeavor to develop independent leaders of organized labor who are interested in a less passive . . . social policy than now carried on by the American Federation of Labor" was echoed by scholars who have found that the attack on Brookwood was part of an AFL effort to eradicate the threat it had come to perceive in the workers' education movement,[41] and that "the agitation of such progressive forces as the Brookwood College kept the question of industrial unionism alive" in the 1920s.[42]

Evaluation of Muste's role in the episode does not lend itself to quite such a clear verdict. His practice of cultivating ties with the AFL while speaking and writing as its severe critic suggests some measure of either naiveté or duplicity. The argument can be (and has been) made that he simply was caught in the dilemma which so often plagues the radical labor activist in the United States: he must be associated with the established organization where most organized workers are to be found—in the case at hand, the AFL; at the same time, by virtue of his commitment to radical change he must actively oppose the moderation and accommodation upon which the program and leadership of the group depend. While this view may explain the conflict in retrospect, Muste at the time did not seem to understand it in those terms. He was so entangled in the exchange of charges and counter-charges that he failed to develop a clear perspective. In addition, and in the light of his previous history, Muste seemed again to reveal a predilection for trying to ride two horses at once—a conservative steed and a radical charger. As the mounts drew further apart, one or the other was bound to unseat him. The parting kick he received as he left the AFL was delivered with none of the politeness that had cushioned major transitions in his ministerial career.

Its sting told in his remarks to the graduating class of 1928, when he advised its members that "it is only after we have learned that there isn't anything shameful and sordid and bitter of which human beings are not capable that we can get real value . . . out of our human experience."[43] He confided to Fannia Cohn, a Brookwood trustee, the personal hurt which he was experiencing. "I have . . . to encounter on every hand rumors about being dishonest, weak, a conspirator, another irresponsible intellectual, about withdrawing of financial support from Brookwood, etc. . . . They seem to just grow in the air," he sighed. The toll of these pressures, combined with family responsibilities, was beginning to tell. "I have never in my life been in such poor shape," he added. "I do not know frankly what the outcome will be."[44]

Part of the outcome soon became clear. This bitter experience with the labor establishment reinforced negative conclusions which he had drawn from several experiences with other more or less traditional or mainstream reform organizations in the 1920s. Having affiliated briefly with the Fellowship for a Christian Social Order, which turned out to be no more than a discussion group on social ethics, the Conference for Progressive Political Action and its unsuccessful campaign for presidential candidate Robert LaFollette in 1924, and the socialists and liberals who coalesced in 1929 in the League for Independent Political Action but proved ineffective, Muste was finished with liberal alignments.[45] He moved rapidly to the left of such friends and former allies as those who, in 1931, sponsored a testimonial dinner for him in New York City. The occasion was the tenth birthday of Brookwood Labor College. The sponsors included Norman Thomas, Roger Baldwin, Rabbi Stephen Wise, Oswald Garrison Villard, Jane Addams, and W. E. B. Du Bois. James Maurer was the master of ceremonies. He had expected to preside over 200 seated guests but found a crowd of 310, many of whom stood the entire evening. Brookwood alumni eulogized Muste for most of the night until finally the guest of honor "unfolded his lanky frame to address the audience" and met with a prolonged standing ovation. He accepted it, he said, for himself ("I won't be hypocritical enough to say I don't like it") but also for "the institution and the movement which I for the moment symbolize." He predicted that within the next decade that movement would either flower into "a labor movement that is clean, vigorous, militant, intelligent [and] committed to building a [new] social order," or it would be exterminated by "a black and bloody Fascist reaction." To insure the former alternative was "the one job supremely worth doing," he asserted. According to the reporter from the *Brookwood Review*, Muste's voice was "deep with emotion."[46]

The idealism and comradeship which had inspired Muste to enter the labor movement in 1919 had become scarce by 1931. His opportunity to help fashion "workers' control" from within the labor establishment was gone for good, if indeed it had ever existed. His best hope now for maintaining Brookwood as an independent entity was to tie into a firmly structured alliance of individuals and organizations that shared disenchantment with the AFL and believed in the necessity of a new social order.

In February 1929, through the pages of *Labor Age*, Muste issued a call for reorganization and rededication among those who paid lip service to the creation of a better society. His sixteen point "Challenge to Progressives" called for organizing the unorganized, ending discrimination in union membership, and opposing union-management cooperation. Some of its appeals were time-honored planks in American labor history: social insurance, shorter hours, higher wages, and better working conditions. Less conventional was a demand for U.S. recognition of the Soviet Union and labor opposition to imperialist and militarist foreign policies. But the main rationale behind such a program—defiance of the conservative policies embodied in the AFL—was not made explicit.[47]

In the same month that the "Challenge" was published, the annual workers' education conference at Brookwood was given over to assessing the position of progressive laborites who advocated industrial unions and opposed William Green and Matthew Woll. Conferees agreed on the need for "a fighting group throughout the country, . . . a group led by Brookwood which will revitalize the labor movement."[48] With this goal in mind all who considered themselves labor progressives were invited to a meeting on May 25 and 26 at the Presbyterian Labor Temple in New York City.

One hundred and fifty people from eighteen states and thirty-one cities appeared at the Temple on May 25. They included trade unionists (mostly AFL members), Socialist Party affiliates, and "friends of organized labor." After establishing the Conference for Progressive Labor Action, they designated *Labor Age* as their official journal and elected an executive committee of twenty-six persons. Officers included A. J. Muste, chairman; James Maurer, first vice-president; and Louis Budenz, executive secretary. Brookwood board member Abraham Lefkowitz sat on the new committee, as did two of the college's graduates and one student.[49]

The CPLA statement of purpose was intriguingly vague. The organization, it read, would "stimulate in the existing and potential organizations a progressive, realistic, militant labor spirit and activity in all its phases—trade union, political, cooperative and educational." Any outright suggestion of engaging in combat with the AFL was omitted. In the first days of the CPLA's existence chairman Muste even declared the fidelity of his organization to the Federation. "We will show our loyalty . . . by fighting for the principles of progressive trade unionism."[50] Not everyone was convinced, especially after one of the first resolutions passed by the CPLA condemned William Green. Conspicuously absent from CPLA rolls was Fannia M. Cohn, who had been involved with Muste's enterprises since the inception of Brookwood but who now denied that a new fighting organization was needed. She warned that progressives would "read themselves out of the labor movement" by such strident tactics. When *Labor Age* was adopted by the new Conference, she resigned from the publication's board. Several other directors of the magazine either followed her or asked not to be reelected when their terms expired. As James Morris has pointed out, these resignations and dropouts signaled the "alienation of important support" from the CPLA at its very birth.[51]

The AFL executive council was equally unimpressed with the new organization. They issued a mandate two months after it was founded: "The Executive Council warns the membership of the American Federation of Labor against this organization. . . . Do not make any financial contribution in response to any appeal this organization may make for help . . . dissenting or dual groups are not clothed with authority to speak for Labor or act for Labor."[52]

Muste made several rebuttals, but by 1931, the national executive committee of the CPLA dropped all pretense of sympathy for the Federation, and published a scathing pamphlet-length commentary on "the mouthy twaddle" of "the AFL in 1931."[53]

If labor progressives did not gather in the CPLA to promote fraternity with the American Federation of Labor, they were nonetheless concerned with the theme of unity. "If factions are a good thing," Muste wrote his benefactress, Elizabeth Glendower Evans, "we have too much of a good thing just now." In January 1932, he predicted "that the next year or so may see a good deal of clarification," as the left-leaning elements of labor were beginning "to act more unitedly than they have in the recent past." The kind of harmony that Muste hoped to create was unity among those advocates of industrial unionism who might offer a middle way for the American labor movement, a way between the reactionary AFL and various Communist forces.[54] Although he remained hopeful about communist prospects in the Soviet Union, Muste opposed Soviet involvement in U.S. labor politics. He charged that the Communist Party injected "remote and irrelevant" issues into the American scene and maintained that American workers needed unions that were capable of responding to their own immediate situations and that were not dictated to from afar. The Party answered Muste's arguments by designating him and his allies as "the deadliest enemies of the working class."[55]

From within the Brookwood faculty Muste also came under attack. Arthur Calhoun reportedly denounced him as a "crook," described other faculty members as "puppets," and called the Brookwood directors "betrayers of labor." Although he did not belong to the Communist Party, Calhoun urged Brookwood to adopt a posture that in all vital respects was identical to that of the CP. His colleagues not only declined his advice but concluded that Brookwood and Calhoun were no longer compatible. Muste concurred.

Calhoun's political philosophy and prickly personality were clearly the major factors in his unhappy departure from Brookwood. Yet aspects of his dismissal presaged problems that would later destroy the school. A tendency on Muste's part to act hotheadedly by broadcasting the firing in the national press was one disturbing factor. Also symptomatic of things to come was Calhoun's claim that he was ousted primarily because he had disparaged the CPLA.[56] This suggested that in touting the CPLA as an alternative to left wing dogmatics and right wing stagnation, Muste had found a way to denounce factional strife while organizing his own faction.

Those who associated with that faction and became members of the CPLA were soon popularly referred to as Musteites. Their Musteism connoted allegiance to the American working class, avoidance of entanglement with abstract ideologies, active antagonism to the standpat temperament of the AFL, and advocacy of widespread industrial unionism. For a time "progressivism" in labor ranks—general dissatisfaction with AFL policies and a general inclination to support labor reform—and Musteism were near synonyms.

As long as Muste engaged the CPLA in reformist programs he was able to keep the support of a fairly wide spectrum of laborites. The championing of unemployment insurance evoked this kind of support. CPLA energies were heavily devoted to the insurance cause during 1930–1931. James Morris has shown that the groundwork laid then helped prepare the way for some features of later state and national legislation, including the federal Social Security Act.[57] But CPLA attacks upon racketeering in the AFL, campaigns to industrialize existing craft unions, and an increasingly passionate commitment to organizing the unorganized soon strained the meaning of the "progressive" label to which the Musteites tried to cling. Their battle against racketeers, launched via the National Committee against Labor Racketeering and Allied Evils, was supported by some liberals, such as Freda Kirchwey and Paul Douglas. But Brookwood faculty saw the campaign as unwarranted interference in the internal affairs of the AFL.[58] The same charge was made regarding CPLA agitation within the textile, coal, and steel industries.

Conference policy with regard to textile unions was not at first uniform. As Lewis Lorwin has noted, "The CPLA at one and the same time aided AF of L unions and helped to form unions against the AF of L." This was largely because AFL programs in this area were in flux. The textile affiliate in Paterson, New Jersey, proved sufficiently "progressive" to work with Musteite organizers. But in Lawrence, Massachusetts, Musteites followed the pattern set by their leader in 1919, supporting an outlaw union.[59]

In southern mill towns CPLA organizers worked with the AFL through three difficult strikes—in Henderson, North Carolina, in 1927; in Elizabethton, Tennessee, in March 1929; and in Marion, North Carolina, a few months later. While all ended in defeat for the workers, the Marion episode was particularly bitter.[60] On the workers' side the battle was waged "with hymn tunes and Negro spirituals for strike songs and a blind faith that God Almighty, working through the new union, would somehow make . . . conditions right again and 'help us to drive the cotton mill devil out of this here village.' " For the operators it was an occasion to unleash massive brutality, at the climax of which thirty-one strikers were shot in the back. Six eventually died. One sixty-five-year-old victim reportedly died on the operating table, still in handcuffs.[61]

For the CPLA the Marion episode was regarded as a major undertaking. Muste, who helped officiate at the open-air funeral for the strikers, called it "the glorious struggle . . . which focused the eyes of labor and of the nation on the southern textile fields."[62] But the challenge which Marion symbolized proved to be too much for Musteites as well as for the AFL. At its annual conference that fall, the Federation voted to launch a full-scale southern organizing campaign, which turned into a program to conciliate employers rather than sustain the simmering revolt of their mill hands. By early in 1931, the AFL had withdrawn from the southern field. The CPLA then proclaimed its intention to stay in the South with those workers whose cause the AFL had deserted. However, the Conference affiliates which organizer Lawrence Hogan reportedly formed soon passed into oblivion. Hogan himself was killed in an automobile accident in 1935.[63]

In the coal industry CPLA policies aimed at displacing the powerful John L. Lewis and the craft unions which he then supported. Mine workers in Illinois and the Kanawha Valley of West Virginia received CPLA backing for their insurgency against "Lewisism" but to no avail. This "100% American non-A.F. of L. radical venture," as social critic Edmund Wilson described it, left no mark on the turf of the indomitable Lewis, who continued to defend old-line unionism until New Deal legislation made the time ripe for his famous industrial campaign.[64]

Among steel workers the Musteites made slightly better inroads. Elmer Cope, CPLA organizer and graduate of Brookwood, established an underground union, the Brotherhood of the Mills, in eastern Ohio. It lasted until at least 1933, periodically issuing a small newsheet, *Hot Saw Sparks*. James Morris has suggested that Cope's work may "have contributed in a small way . . . to the dissatisfaction with Amalgamated leadership which burst into internal revolt in 1934."[65]

The tone of these Musteite campaigns reflected a marked change in the attitude of their leader. Muste had entered the labor movement a pacifist, conducted the Lawrence strike according to principles of nonviolence, and continued to follow the thread of pacifist doctrine which opposed imperialist war.[66] By the late twenties, however, Muste had begun to weaken his ties with the Fellowship of Reconciliation[67] and had adopted a stance of qualified defense of labor violence.

While contending that "almost invariably" violence in labor disputes was provoked by management or their lackeys and that "it is difficult to find any moral ground for objecting to the spontaneous violence that often occurs in strikes," he cautioned workers against following the example of management in hiring "thugs" and warned that the practice of violence can trap its practitioners in a vicious circle. Nonetheless, he declined, in 1932, to sign a statement in support of the Gandhian independence struggle in India. "Nonviolence may be important," he said, but added, "I do not want to discredit the left-wing elements in India that believe in violence."[68] Muste's own name came to be associated with such elements in his own country. The pattern was set by Brookwood graduate Alfred Hoffman. After he was kidnapped during the Elizabethton, Tennessee, strike of 1929, the organizer hired bodyguards to protect him. A photograph of this Musteite, flanked by two menacing rifle-toters, appeared in the *Brookwood Review* with the caption "Judged by His Bodyguard It Won't Happen Again." In this same period Muste wrote enthusiastically to Elmer Cope about the " 'swell' riot" which occurred "in connection with our picketing of Brooklyn Ed [Brooklyn Edison]."[69]

Such attitudes and episodes caused concern at Brookwood. Faculty members registered alarm in 1931, when the CPLA revised its statement of purpose, identifying the Socialist Party as another obstacle to labor progressivism and redefining the CPLA as a "left-wing political group, . . . a disciplined membership."[70] Several months later the college board issued a protective statement of policy: "Brookwood refuses to be diverted from its established educational program and become subordinated to any particular theoretical or political faction."[71] Their later claim that Muste had personally helped draft the statement is interesting in light of his proposal very shortly thereafter that Brookwood be transformed into a training base for "CPLA fighters." He suggested that the Katonah plant be shut down, resident classes cease, and college headquarters be relocated in Newark. The Brookwood staff would devote most of its time to Conference activities and members of the school faculty would be expected to join the CPLA. It was at least implied that they would hold no other political memberships, "without asking Muste's permission."[72]

Muste's proposal triggered a long and nasty sparring match between his supporters and him on the one hand and a growing anti-CPLA faction on the other. His opponents not only resented his move to subordinate the teaching mission of the college to the activism of the CPLA but also charged that Muste, by neglecting his responsibilities, had undermined the financial security of Brookwood.[73] Although the record indicates that he was doing the best he could, in light of the depression, to keep the school afloat,[74] it is understandable that residents of Brookwood were edgy about the fiscal implications of his involvement in the CPLA. It is also understandable that they were angered when Muste's supporters publicly accused "the majority of the Brookwood faculty [with being] primarily concerned with protecting their own safe nest at Brookwood . . . [and being] jealous of money raised for the maintenance of activities mainly of Brookwood graduates in the field."[75]

The controversy came to a head in late February 1933, at an open and acrimonious college meeting, where Muste seems to have generated the most rancor. He was quoted as referring to his faculty opposition as "numbskulls," "traitors," "turn-coats," "academicians," and "reactionaries." His faithful supporter, Cara Cook, later recalled "the angry huskiness of his voice as he indicted his opponents and their policies." Another member of the staff recalled how Muste would "waggle his long finger, his voice would tremble, and that evenness of temperament we'd all thought was an unchangeable characteristic of A. J. was gone." In one instance, probably after Muste approvingly quoted Bernard Shaw—"Those who can do; those who can't teach"—Josephine Colby cried out, "I protest." Muste's response, according to Cook, was "all right go ahead and protest." He said it "with a shrug of his shoulders and a lifting of his eyebrows, as if to imply that the matter was rather beyond that point."[76]

A few days after this meeting the Brookwood board of directors met with Muste. He requested that they enlist the college in the service of "a realistic revolutionary vanguard organization" and declared that those teachers who did not support a merger with the CPLA should be fired. The directors requested that Muste resign his executive position in the CPLA and turn his full time back to Brookwood. Muste instead resigned from the college and with his followers—including nineteen students—prepared to leave. Cara Cook remembered that they "packed up amidst frigid surveillance to see that we did not depart with the mimeograph machine or a set of encyclopedias." The *Brookwood Review* reported that the Musteites were permitted to remain on campus for a time, "because of the banking crisis"—the final showdown had been enacted as President Roosevelt initiated the famous "holiday." The *Review* added that the dissidents used their time to practice "noncooperation" against the remaining school residents and to set up a headquarters for the CPLA in New York City.[77]

Through the spring of 1933, recriminations between Brookwood and the CPLA took up substantial space in both the college paper and *Labor Age*. Muste charged that Brookwood had fallen into the grip of reactionaries and would soon be lining up with Matthew Woll. Abraham Lefkowitz, now chairman of the school's board of directors, denied that Brookwood had moved to the right.

He argued that the college had not abandoned its commitment to workers' education but that Muste had abandoned his.[78]

Both organizations were scrambling to hold onto their financial supporters. Fund appeal letters went out from both sides. Many of their recipients must have shared Elizabeth Glendower Evans' feeling of bewilderment. She wrote to Brookwood in April of 1933: "It is impossible for me to decide between you and Mr. Muste." She in fact chose to "stay with Mr. Muste—for old times sake" and to "mark Brookwood off the map." Others of Muste's good friends seem to have maintained their loyalty to the school. Abraham Lefkowitz claimed that few steady contributors withdrew their support. But in the long-run their loyalty was not enough. A steady decline in enrollment, which had begun in 1932, culminated in the closing of Brookwood for lack of funds in 1937. The struggle for backing was extended to the liberal media, to which the Conference and school presented their respective cases. The *New Republic* reported receiving "30,000 words of official statements" about the rift. Even with so much evidence the magazine could finally conclude only that "it is impossible for outsiders to exercise an accurate judgment about such a quarrel as this."[79]

For everyone involved—even the Mustes, who were veterans of discomfiting departures—this schism was terribly painful, sundering relationships that had been forged in the intensity of communal living and that had lasted in some cases for twelve years. As Muste later said, "The community itself was disintegrating." To what degree was he responsible? His call for new strategies to create a more militant labor movement was in itself justified. But the heavy-handed tactics he used in trying to win approval for these strategies from his Brookwood colleagues were not. Those whose primary vocation was to teach had good grounds upon which to defend Brookwood against Muste's plans to transform it. Those whose commitment to the labor struggle may have been no less genuine than his, but whose interpretation of events suggested strategies other than his, had the right to go their own way without being subject to his invective. When Muste failed to see this, his former allies began to see him in a new light. By their description he became snappish, dogmatic, authoritarian, adept at infighting, and given to messianic illusions. "The trouble with Muste," observed his longtime ally, James Maurer, "is that he sees himself as a great leader, a sort of American Lenin. . . . He is suffering from an exaggerated ego." Fannia Cohn concurred. "A. J. was too busy in running the United States" to meet his obligations to the school, she said. Yet these harsh comments were tempered by sorrow and a lingering fondness for, as Abraham Lefkowitz put it, "the A. J. Muste beside whom we have for years fought."[80]

"The manner of his going was far from what his friends wanted," noted his old comrade Ann Davis.[81] In his own reflections many years later, Muste complained of the inveterate moderateness of the politics of his opposition but also acknowledged that he had behaved badly. According to his autobiography this was the one instance in his life when he failed to emerge from a conflict feeling as if "I were moving ahead on a straight course . . . in the direction in which I should be moving." He was particularly contrite about the speech in which Josephine Colby and he crossed swords. He judged that he had acted with "arrogance" and "malice," adding that it was "the only time I can recall having been consciously malicious in such a situation. . . . It was one of those moments when you sense that . . . it cannot be 'patched up' any more."[82] He described himself, probably quite rightly, as having entered then, at age forty-eight, a kind of "mid-life crisis," magnified by the pressures and uncertainties of the depression.[83]

He moved close in this period to abandoning three principles which had so far guided him through life: (1) open-mindedness, (2) compassion in human relations, and (3) religious faith. The short-temperedness and intolerance which marked his last days at Brookwood illustrate the weakening hold which the first two principles had upon him. His increasing sympathy for labor's resort to violence was directly linked to his departure from the third, for the original basis of Muste's pacifism had been religious and his departure from nonviolence was parallelled by an increasing indifference to matters of faith.[84] Yet the emotional springs which heretofore had fed that faith were far from dry. Ann Davis noted that Muste showed "a sort of mystical prophetic sense of his own mission, which made all else seem secondary." She wondered where that prophetic sense would lead him.[85] Her query was well taken. His previous missions had been launched from a foundation of intellectual and social poise and religious certitude. Standing upon such firm ground had fortified him against risks and setbacks. Now the foundation was crumbling, and what might take its place was not clear.

Chapter IV

The Call of the Left

From "Progressive Labor Action" to Trotskyism

In 1931 journalist Louis Adamic accurately predicted that "the nineteen thirties will probably see the rise of a new general labor-radical movement, split up into Communists, Socialists, reds of all hues, Wobblies, trade unionists, political actionists, direct actionists, and what not, . . . a wild, chaotic, highly emotional, *violent* belly-hunger movement."[1] In this setting the Musteites, driven steadily leftward in their efforts to both combat and exploit depression conditions, contributed their share of emotionalism and violence.

Muste's Conference for Progressive Labor Action was involved in two of the most highly charged civil liberties causes of the era—the Scottsboro case in Alabama in which nine Negro youths were falsely charged with raping two white women and the case of two obscure radicals in San Francisco, Tom Mooney and Warren K. Billings, who had been questionably convicted of the bombing which killed ten persons and wounded forty others during a Preparedness Day Parade in San Francisco in 1916. The call issued by Muste as secretary of the Tom Mooney Pardon Conference of New York—that citizens "do something to strike fear into the hearts of the masters of America"—conveyed the spirit in which the CPLA approached such issues.[2]

Although the Musteites declared the country to be in a state of civil war and warned that nothing less than survival itself was at stake for the American working class,[3] relatively few workers rallied to the revolutionary banner of either the CPLA or other far-left organizations. Those who did answer such battle cries were responding more to conditions than to ideologies or theories. Being unemployed was one such condition, and unions for unemployed workers attracted a considerable membership. In 1933 Musteite representative Elmer Cope noted that "work with the unemployed require [sic] less resources and on the whole bring quicker results; hungry unemployed are far better revolutionary material than workers in the plants who are fighting for wage increases and shorter hours."[4]

Unemployed unions developed under three different auspices. Stalinists organized Unemployed Councils, leading the way in 1930. Musteites created Unemployed Leagues, beginning in 1932. Socialists established Workers' Alliances, beginning about 1935. While estimates of membership in these groups vary dizzyingly, the Musteites alone claimed nearly a million members in seven hundred locals in 1933.[5]

The CPLA put its campaign among the unemployed on a national footing in 1933. On the weekend so frequently chosen by Muste and his associates for their project-launchings, July 1–4, 15,000 people gathered on the state fairgrounds at Columbus, Ohio, to establish the National Unemployed League (NUL). Muste found the Columbus gathering to be "a most exciting and inspiring affair." At times the excitement threatened to outrun the inspiration, as communist hecklers and then opponents from the right attempted to break up the gathering. But Musteite control prevailed.[6]

The Leagues differed from communist and socialist unions mainly in their emphasis on rural organizing. League personnel put pressure on government relief agencies, established "Mother-Save-Your-Child Clubs" for the medical welfare of children, and set up Housing and Eviction Committees, not only to forestall the expulsion of debtors from their homes but also to help the homeless find shelter and to intervene when the gas and electric company suspended services. Members of such committees exhibited no queasiness about violence and sometimes ended up in jail. Musteites in Pittsburgh reported, in May 1934, on "a mass eviction fight. The eviction was stopped by a mass demonstration. When leaving the house 'an accident' occurred to the constable and the landlord. They went to the hospital. 'Who threw the bricks?' Shrugged shoulders was the reply. No more evictions for six months."[7]

Leadership of the NUL claimed to follow a non-exclusionary policy and to be interested in united-front cooperation with other organizations. But in practice they were beset by factional struggles with both socialists and communists. Muste seems to have been more interested in working with the Communist Party than with the socialists. According to critics in the SP he helped, at a convention in Harrisburg, to steam-roll approval of Communist participation in a new state-wide unemployed organization in 1934. Musteites had also gone on record as being favorably inclined toward exploring with the CP "a broad united front of struggle." Years later Muste wrote in his autobiography, "when you looked out on the scene of misery and desperation during the depression, you saw that it was . . . the people who had adopted some form of Marxian philosophy, who were *doing something* about the situation. . . . In many cases these doers and fighters were Communists."[8]

Yet the CPLA remained critical of the Communist Party U.S.A. and continued to criticize its leaders for taking direction from non-American sources. The Musteities prided themselves on being an American organization, responsive to American conditions. They were acknowledged as such by other leftists, including Communist activist John Gates and Trotskyist Max Schactman.[9]

As for Musteite suspicions of Communist Party motives, they were, in fact, well-founded. At the very moment in 1933–1934 when CP and CPLA representatives were discussing united-front possibilities, Earl Browder was assuring his communist colleagues that "the reason why we make the united front with [Musteites] is because we have got to take their followers away from them."

Muste skirted the CP trap. He and his associates backed off from their sparring with the Browder forces and found another means of identifying themselves with that Marxist-Leninist image of action and commitment which so much impressed them. In December 1933, a Musteite gathering at Pittsburgh provisionally established the American Workers' Party, which soon absorbed the CPLA. The Musteites had transformed themselves from a "left-wing political group" into an "American revolutionary party." In the eyes of the communists this move was intended to "halt the radicalized workers midway on their road to the Communist Party and turn them against it."[10] According to the Musteites, a "radically new economic and political situation" had developed in the United States, with massive government intervention on all fronts and Franklin Delano Roosevelt assuming "more power than any President has had in war or peace." The time had come, Muste declared, for "all elements who do not occupy a privileged position in the existing economic and political set up" to take up the cudgels of revolution. Ultimately, he forecast, the non-privileged of the U.S. would unite with the masses of the world, but first the components of a world-wide movement had to establish themselves in their own nation states.

The new revolutionary party, its leader said, would use slogans, salutes, flags, songs, and other instruments of mass psychology to maintain enthusiasm. Party members would intervene in election campaigns to "cut through sham issues and make workers aware of the real issues." They would launch demonstrations, encourage strikes, and attend to the needs of such downtrodden minorities as "the Negro masses" in their effort to build a broad-based movement. Looking to the future, the AWP organizing committee warned that once the workers' movement had triumphed over the old leader, its members would have to "fight with every weapon to establish and to assure their own democracy." In the process of consolidating political power, the victorious government would "issue and enforce stringent revolutionary laws directed against all who attempt to undermine the new regime."[11]

The AWP was obviously intended to be another "third way" between communism and socialism. Its members maintained their on-going critiques of the two opposition parties, while offering themselves as abjurers of factionalism. "Workers sense the need for unity and are tired of divisions," Muste declared. A few months after the CPLA transformed itself, the Musteites were given a perfect opportunity to lay the responsibility for factionalism at the doorstep of the CP and to expound on their own "effective, intelligent and revolutionary party." A Socialist Party rally in Madison Square Garden to protest fascist attacks on Austrian socialism was broken up by communist agitators. Muste, speaking for the AWP, interpreted the incident as "the death knell for false, inadequate leadership." The socialists had been unable to keep control of their own meeting. The communists had betrayed their proclivities for adventurism and sectarianism. Neither group was capable of sound revolutionary activity, the Musteites concluded. They made a special appeal to "American Intellectuals" to cease flirting with such hopeless elements and to join the ranks of the AWP.[12]

Armed with pamphlets espousing this point of view, Muste and two comrades set out on a speaking tour through Illinois shortly after the AWP was established. When they stopped to address pickets at the Knapp-Monarch electrical supply plant in Saint Clair County, they were arrested for vagrancy and subversion. The first charge was dropped but the second, based on the content of party literature, stuck. They sat in jail until bail money could be raised, treated, in the words of the *Nation*, "like dangerous criminal[s]." As Muste later recalled, most of their bail came from "an elderly German American with a radical background in Germany, who had prospered . . . as a junk and scrap dealer." The man stepped forward to post bond, appeared later to get his money back when the case was dropped, "and then returned to the obscurity of an aged junk dealer's life." But the case was not dropped for nearly a year, during which time Muste lived with the possibility of a jail term for treason.[13]

At the same time his followers and he were drawn into other struggles that would carry their party to the peak of its historical significance. Their greatest opportunity came in the Toledo Auto-Lite strike of April 1934.

Toledo, Ohio, as Muste observed, was the "glass and auto parts center" of the United States. To strike a crippling blow against its industrial enterprises would mean injury not only to the rest of automobile manufacturing but to those many industries, such as steel and coal, tied to auto production. On April 13, AFL Local 18384 struck the Electric Auto-Lite Company in that city, demanding union recognition and a variety of other concessions. The strike was promptly ended by a court injunction. But just as dejected workers began to return to their jobs two Musteite organizers, Sam Pollock and Theodore Selender, persuaded the strike committee to defy the injunction. Pollock and Selender were officers of the Lucas County Unemployed League and had acted under the advice of A. J. Muste and Louis Budenz, who were in daily touch from New York. The American Workers' Party people formed the Lucas County Unemployed League Anti-Injunction Committee and reestablished a picket line at the Auto-Lite plant. The first few pickets were arrested, only to be released and to resume their picketing. Gradually, as repeated arrests and repeated defiance of the injunction dramatized the committee's dedication, Auto-Lite workers joined them on the strike line. Muste maintained that picketers jumped in numbers from a half dozen to "thousands" within a few days.[14]

In the beginning the strikers were orderly, but eventually their discipline collapsed and the National Guard was called in. Guardsmen and strikers engaged in hand-to-hand combat, resulting in the deaths of two workers and injury to at least twenty-five others.[15]

Muste arrived in Toledo on the first or second night of the pitched battle between strikers and the Guard. He remembered long after the "eerie spectacle" which greeted him. The sky was lighted by flares which guardsmen sent up to ascertain the position of their opponents; the picketers crouched behind cars, houses, and trees. He and Sam Pollock took cover behind a tree. Pollock sensed that the entire battle scene was "distressing to 'Rev. Muste,' " who began immediately to plan for a return to peaceful tactics. Eventually local authorities acted upon his advice to have the company agree to keep the plant closed, have the guardsmen withdraw, and have the union assume responsibility for a nonviolent picket line.[16] In later descriptions of the Auto-Lite affair, Muste skirted its violent characteristics. Some twenty years later, he assured an interviewer that during this phase of his labor career he had "accepted the idea that . . . struggle had to be violent," but "I never myself got involved to any extent in the violent aspects . . . and can see now that there was a part of me that just didn't accept it."[17]

The Communist Party was also on the scene in Toledo and contributed the suggestion that the Auto-Lite strike be widened into a general strike. The idea was effective. When an estimated 10,000 workers from 100 local unions marched through the streets of Toledo in solidarity with their Auto-Lite comrades, the company hastened to comply with a number of union demands, including union recognition.[18] Thus the strike, which would have died at its inception had it not been for Musteite intervention, ended in victory. Labor historians have described it as an important breakthrough in increasing union consciousness among workers in the early New Deal period and in laying the groundwork for the CIO. The Auto-Lite story also illustrates one of the most significant consequences of the unemployed organizations—their influence on working people and their ability to radicalize them, at least temporarily.[19] In a vein less promising from the point of view of the Musteites, historians have also found that credit for the Toledo victory redounded almost entirely upon the AFL, whose leadership maneuvered the radicals out of the final stages of the settlement negotiations. But Muste and his followers omitted this development from their descriptions and analyses of the Toledo experience, choosing instead to project an image of themselves as having attained far greater influence within the ranks of workers than would ever prove to have been the case.

The experience and confidence which AWP members gained in Toledo in 1934 prepared them to do battle again in the same city a year later. Then the same AFL local which had initiated the Auto-Lite strike closed down the Chevrolet plant. As before, union recognition was a central issue. Although the strike had not been authorized by the national AFL, the Federation agreed to support it and sent Francis Dillon to assist in leading it. Dillon's biggest challenge, as it turned out, was to keep the most militant strike participants, the Musteites, under control. The strike committee was influenced heavily by AWP personnel; its chairman was Workers' Party member James Roland. In the opinion of historian Sidney Fine, Dillon's ability to curtail Roland's influence kept the walkout bloodless and nonviolent—in marked contrast to the Auto-Lite affair. Dillon's efforts also brought the struggle to a close with fewer con-

cessions having been won by the workers. They failed to receive signed contracts and exclusive bargaining rights for their AFL union. But the plant did at
least recognize the union.[20]

To moderate observers the Chevrolet strike was "the greatest single step
forward" up to that time for unionization in the auto industry. In the eyes of the
Musteites, however, the strike had been sold out by the "treachery" of Francis
Dillon. Muste personally entertained the belief that the Chevrolet workers,
even those who had accepted the settlement, were still essentially revolutionary
in their outlook and he looked forward to joining them in "a future battle."[21]
But though he did not yet realize it, his American Workers' Party had recently
and unwittingly forfeited its chance to shape future battles. They had entered
into an alliance with the Communist League of America, whose orientation was
Trotskyist.

A potential affinity for Trotskyism had revealed itself in Muste as early
as 1926, when he favorably reviewed Leon Trotsky's *Whither England* for the
Brookwood newspaper. In the early 1930s Trotsky made an appeal to Marxists
in the United States, which must have aroused favorable interest in Muste and
his followers. The outcast Bolshevik advised American leftists to eschew both
the Stalinism of the Communist Party and the "counter-revolutionary" tendencies of the Socialist Party. In siding with his own followers, Trotsky asserted,
American radicals would be "rooting Marxism in American soil, verifying it
against the events of American history . . . and assimilating the world revolutionary experience under the viewpoint of the tasks of the American revolution."[22] These were precisely the aims announced by the American Workers'
Party only a few months after Trotsky had published his appeal.

In practice, as well as theory, followers of Muste and Trotsky found common ground. The very spring of 1934 in which the AWP achieved its Auto-Lite
triumph was also the period when Communist League organizers were spear-
heading a massive teamsters' strike in Minneapolis. With the Toledo struggle it
shared bloodiness, fight-to-the-finish dedication on the part of its participants,
and the winning of union recognition. Musteites and Trotskyists exchanged
congratulations.[23]

Several months before these strikes, in January of 1934, Communist
League officials had broached the idea of unity between their group and the
Musteites. In March, Leon Trotsky was consulted. The party chief responded to
a query from League Secretary Arne Swabeck that he could not recommend
fusion unequivocally, but he offered encouragement: "If you can accomplish the
fusion, . . . then we will be enriched by an important experiment." During
the weeks following the strikes the AWP held a series of policy-discussion
meetings which were attended by at least three Communist League "plants"—
George Novack, Herbert Solow, and Felix Morrow. The CLA deputies were
instructed to promote the idea of a merger between their league and the
Workers' Party. They carried out their job successfully.[24]

Soon after the meetings Muste wrote an article in which he paired the CLA and AWP as creators of "the outstanding contributions of the year in Toledo and Minneapolis," and edged up to the notion of the two groups uniting.[25] About the time that this article appeared League Chief James Cannon was in France conferring again with Leon Trotsky. The Russian exile was, Cannon later recalled, "greatly interested in the personality of Muste . . . and entertained some hopes that Muste would develop into a real Bolshevik later." Cannon was likewise attracted to Muste the individual. He was, the League leader said, "a remarkable man . . . for whom I always had the most friendly feelings." But these feelings were qualified. Cannon feared that "the terrible background of the church [had] marred [Muste] in his formative years." Nonetheless the American Trotskyist leader shared his mentor's hope that A. J. Muste could be salvaged from the grips of religion and shaped into a "real revolutionary." Aside from his personal appeal, the former preacher led a movement many of whose members would make valuable recruits to the CLA. A Communist League report on the Musteites listed as the latter's chief assets: "widespread mass contacts, active participation in the class struggle, practical achievements and a general leftward direction." The AWP, the Trotskyists concluded, was "the most important single organization besides the League standing for a new party, an agreement with whom would make the actual launching of the new party possible." In addition, Muste had personal contacts with potentially big financial contributors. All in all, if the Trotskyists could pull Muste into their camp they could hope that he would help "administer the organization more efficiently and tap new sources of financial support."[26]

The two sides settled down to serious negotiations. James Cannon, his close associate Max Schactman, and League Secretary Arne Swabeck spoke for the CLA. Muste, Louis Budenz, J. B. S. Hardman, V. F. Calverton, Sidney Hook, and James Burnham represented the AWP. A protracted argument over language ensued. To the Musteites, Marxian rhetoric—"the dictatorship of the proletariat," for example—was ambiguous and nearly meaningless in an American context. The Trotskyists denied this and asserted that Musteite phrases such as "workers' democracy" were duplicitous. "Under the guise of American terminology" the AWP "pretended to meet the demands of the revolutionists while also allowing the social democrats to satisfactorily construe their own interpretation" of party principles. The debate was not resolved, but as the talks proceeded the Trotskyists felt that the other side was making "certain important concessions."

Musteites joined them in opposing "social reformism" and "Stalinist Centrism"; they agreed to support the Fourth International and assented to the dictum that a party must have "full authority and control of its members" in order to effectively organize the masses. The Musteites also gave in to Cannon's forces on the issue of a name for the new party. Hoping to retain "American Workers' Party" for the new group, they finally agreed to the designation of the Workers' Party of the United States.[27]

At Stuyvesant Casino on the Lower East Side of Manhattan a unity convention was held in December of 1934. From it was born the Workers' Party of the United States, hailed by leaders on both sides with, in George Novack's word, "elation."[28] The terms of merger put Muste in the position of national secretary and made Cannon editor-in-chief of the party organ, the *Militant*. Seasoned radicals who witnessed the fusion and analysts who later evaluated it are in general accord that the Musteites were duped. Philip Selznick, in a work devoted to examining Bolshevik strategies, wrote that CLA leaders gave Muste the secretaryship knowing that their membership would remain united within the new party and would limit his power. Cannon took the editorship, by this account, because the struggle to win followers was seen as basically an ideological one in which the guardians of the press would have a decided advantage. Selznick concluded that "the real point of merger [for the CLA] was to win new cadres . . . and not to wield the practically non-existent power of this splinter organization." Cannon all but admitted that this was the case in his *History of American Trotskyism*, where he emphasized the ideological advantages of controlling the *Militant* and commented that Musteite concern with "purely organizational matters" made the secretaryship very attractive because, "theoretically at least," it would control the party.[29]

The Workers' Party U.S.A. opened headquarters in New York at Fifth Avenue and Fifteenth Street and drafted a "Declaration of Principles" and a "Constitution." These made clear that the party intended to organize a network of local workers' councils, patterned after Russian soviets. The main goal of the party, according to its constitution, was a totally socialized state, controlled by a workers' government. Collectivization of small farmers and businessmen would be arranged without terror, for such middling elements would quickly realize the advantages of socialization. All "socially useless and parasitic classes and groups" on the other hand would have to be "eliminated." Party documents proclaimed solidarity with other revolutionary movements in the world and a strong allegiance to internationalism. This allegiance included opposition to all capitalist-inspired wars, but the Workers' Party promised to support "wars of the oppressed against the oppressor, wars of workers states against capitalist states and wars of enslaved peoples against imperialist exploiters." So, in heading up the WP-U.S.A., Muste broke with the pacifism from which he had been straying over the past decade. The Party constitution made this clear: "The policy of folded arms, passive resistance, 'conscientious objection' etc. is completely futile as a means of struggle against imperialist war, regardless of the sincerity and courage of those who resort to it."[30]

Yet despite the flair and verve with which he now preached Marxism according to Trotsky, Muste seems not to have internalized that dogma completely. His writings and speeches in this period were violently anti-establishment in their overall effect and yet always bore some trace of a less violent disposition. For example, in April 1935, he reduced the party's principles to plain language which the common worker could understand, in a pamphlet titled *Which Party for the American Worker?* The tone was authoritarian and strident. To all those who were tired of unfulfilled promises from representatives of the establishment ("Hoover with his chicken in every pot, . . . Roosevelt with his New Deal, . . . Hooey [sic] Long with a house, automobile and radio for everybody"), Muste offered a simple solution: "Smash the capitalist state and put the workers' state in its place." One could not do this alone, he warned. "A revolutionist cannot be an individualist. He cannot work as an irresponsible free lancer. He must work in an organized and disciplined way. He must belong to the organized vanguard of the working class."

Yet surfacing in and around these declarations were faint traces of other ideals. He promised, for example, that those who did not join WP ranks would not be called "Fascist . . . if you really think you are doing revolutionary work," and asserted that no revolutionary party ought to take away its members' "right to think."[31] Involved in that generous assertion was a doctrinaire attack on Stalinists and various other WP competitors, while he put the new party forward as a "new unifying force" for American workers. This theme of unity, recurring side by side with sectarian allegiations, is perhaps another sign that values which governed Muste in previous periods were not completely submerged in the 1930s. Concerns rooted in his religious past were still operating at some level in the Marxist-Leninist milieu. When, in *Which Party*, Muste designated "comradeship" as one of the primary offerings of the WP, the word may have carried a double connotation—drawing upon the war imagery of revolutionary ideology but harking back as well to the fellowship in Boston in 1919 and its preoccupation with the ethics of the New Testament.

Comradeship of any kind proved hard to sustain in the Trotskyist setting. For a while Muste and Cannon worked well together. They travelled across the country speaking to crowds of enthusiastic supporters, and when they reached Minneapolis high-spirited workers took them on a tour of the clothier and haberdashery factories, outfitting them both with new togs from head to foot.[32] But the honeymoon was short-lived. Soon they were at odds over proper procedures for securing obedience from party cadres. Muste resisted Cannon's heavy-handed methods of discipline. He kept stepping in, Cannon later complained, to "protect people on the grounds of friendship."[33]

Muste also resisted Cannon's decision to infiltrate the Socialist Party. Their differences over this issue ultimately destroyed the WP-U.S.A.. The so-called "French Turn" (the name derived from Leon Trotsky's orders to French followers in 1934 to join the French SP) was a tactic which, in Muste's view, was both underhanded and unworkable. He thought that he had exacted a promise from Cannon that it would not be attempted in the United States. But, in June 1935, Cannon and Schactman began to promote the "Turn" as policy for their party.[34] Muste fought them. On October 2, 1935, the first showdown between pro- and anti-French Turn advocates took place. Muste's position was that the radical wing of the Socialist Party was neither large enough nor influential enough to substantiate the claim that alliance with the SP was crucial to the Workers' Party. He had lined up his allies, but just before the meeting was called to order, the ground was knocked out from under him. "The Old Man," as Trotsky was called, had wired his opinion that the WP should enter the SP. "To true-blue Trotskyists," Muste noted, "this meant that the WP was ordered to enter the SP and the comrades were expected to see it that way, or at the very least to accept it and shut their mouths." While support for his stand evaporated, another piece of news presented itself. Muste picked up a copy of the *Daily Worker* and discovered that several of his own longtime associates, led by Louis Budenz and Arnold Johnson, had defected to the Communist Party. Betrayed by his lieutenants and outranked by the influence of the Old Man, he was defeated that day, and the defeat was ratified at another major meeting four months later.

For the time being Muste went along with the party which he nominally headed but could not control. Soon after the October meeting a statement issued over the names of Muste and eight other opponents of the "turn"[35] advised that "when the Party has formulated its position this must put a period to the discussion. It would be utterly indefensible to subject the Party to interminable and bitter internal conflict." Muste took out membership in the SP. Supposedly the WP-U.S.A. was dissolved as its members became socialists. But, Muste noted sardonically, "the politbureau of the Workers Party met as usual the Monday after we had ceased to exist and functioned as a manipulative faction within the SP." Thereafter in Trotskyist bulletins Muste was periodically accused of continuing to work at cross-purposes with Cannon. His future with the Trotskyists had grown dim.[36]

Several interpretations have been advanced as to why A. J. Muste fought the French Turn so vehemently. James Cannon attributed the vehemence to "organizational fetishism." Muste, he said, had made an ego-investment in the WP-U.S.A. and could not bear the thought of its disappearance. Max Schactman believed that the Musteites' longstanding prejudice against Socialist Party "reformism" had prevented their leader from supporting the "turn." A third Trotskyist, George Novack, agreed with Cannon but emphasized another factor, too—Muste's concern with the moral implications of infiltration.[37]

This concern is the one Muste stressed. He said that his opposition to the "turn" was opposition to the hypocrisy involved in "joining" those whom one actually despised. He quoted Cannon at some length to illustrate the disparaging image which Trotskyists held of socialists. Furthermore, Muste asserted, he opposed the deliberate demoralization of SP members by stirring up dissension among them.[38] Undoubtedly in later years these were criticisms which the then leading pacifist could honestly level against Trotskyist tactics. But it must be remembered that in the early and middle 1930s Muste had demonstrated his own capacity for stirring up dissension in the name of revolutionizing an organization. What may have happened during the French Turn controversy was that Muste suddenly found himself looking into a mirror. The Trotskyist maneuvers reflected there were his own tactics, magnified perhaps, but expressive of essentially the same intent that had driven him in the destruction of Brookwood and motivated his followers in their disruption of AFL policies in the coal, steel, textile, and auto industries. The mirror image of this intent to "radicalize" and "educate backward elements" was troubling.

Probably the most dominant feelings in A. J. Muste, in the fall of 1935 and the early months of 1936, were anger and some embarrassment over having been "taken." Cannon and company had effectively destroyed his organizational base by the same tactics that they now proposed to use on the socialists. And he had cooperated in eroding his own leadership. He was keenly disappointed that his grass-roots support had crumbled. Not a single new cadre was established after merger with the Trotskyists. The old unemployed leagues, left without guidance, merged in 1936 into a three-way alliance with the communists and socialists and, in Sidney Lens' description, "for all practical purposes were never heard of again."[39]

The warning that Fannia Cohn delivered when the CPLA first organized itself in 1929 had come true by 1935. She had told Musteites that they would write themselves out of the labor movement.[40] Now they had. The work of the CPLA and the parties which succeeded it were not without influence. But the Musteites' insistently leftward direction prevented their cultivation of that influence into political clout and recognition. While many of the progressive forces which Muste had helped to shape through Brookwood, and many of the workers which Musteite organizers and leagues had primed for radical action, assumed central roles in the exciting revival of unionism led by John L. Lewis, Muste himself was stranded on the sidelines.[41] He proclaimed the far-left line that CIO leaders were "class collaborationists" and warned that, however impressive their strike victories, the Lewis forces would not proceed into that "intransigent struggle" against "all agencies of the state" which was required to bring about revolution. In the long run Muste and other radicals were prescient in their assessment of the direction toward big unionism taken by Lewis and his followers. In some cases this direction would lead to corruption, racketeering, and exploitation of the rank and file.[42] But those he addressed did not listen. They were too absorbed in their successful offensives against the citadels of American industry, and too thrilled by the realization of a union movement bearing real clout.

After rubber workers at the Goodyear plant in Akron, Ohio, went on strike in February 1936, Muste put in an appearance on the strike scene. He must have been impressed by the sight of the largest rubber factory in the world shut down, and more than 10,000 workers refusing to work. The Goodyear walkout was "the first CIO strike" and its participants were pioneers in focusing public attention on the sit-down tactic which would be used so successfully in the auto industry in a few months.[43] Strike leaders did not appreciate criticism from far-left elements and took quick action to eliminate outside interference. They sent Muste packing, but only after one of them, Rose Pesotta, a Brookwood graduate, delivered a biting lecture. "You taught us to organize the mass production workers," Pesotta told Muste. "You laid stress on both the practical and ethical sides. And you never let us forget that when strikes are settled, they must be settled honorably. I won't fail your teaching now."[44]

Pesotta's appeal to a Muste whom she had known in earlier days was indicative of the affection which many former associates continued to hold for him despite the political disagreements which now separated them. Such lingering fondness on the part of old friends played a crucial role in keeping Muste and his family from destitution in these years.

Friends had provided rent-free shelter for the family in the first months after they left Katonah.[45] Their income then and for the next several years derived from "marginal maintenance pay" provided by the CPLA and its successor organizations. Although Muste alternately begged and threatened the directors of Brookwood for back pay which he claimed was due him, they ignored his claims.[46]

Despite their reduced and precarious circumstances Muste's family "was holding true through thick and thin," according to Ann Davis. Muste admitted that "the going is pretty hard and sometimes it is pretty trying for Mrs. Muste. She is, however, an awfully good sport." His daughters, he later recalled (Nancy was 17, Connie, 11, and their brother John, 6) were at first "desolated" by the experience of having to leave Brookwood. But no storm broke out within the family circle, "only mutual support against the storm we had run into."[47] Such support, fortified by outside aid, even kept alive the long-cherished hope of Anna Muste that her eldest child could attend Swarthmore College.

As valedictorian from Katonah High School, Nancy Muste secured admission and a scholarship while her father persuaded Elizabeth Glendower Evans to contribute toward expenses. The aging widow helped in this way (in concert with her friend Ethel P. Moors) for two years until Nancy transferred to Barnard, because "Nancy . . . and her mother have their hearts set on it," and despite the activities in which Nancy's father was engaged. Checks from Mrs. Evans were invariably accompanied by some critical comment on his recent activities. "I respect you from your head to your heels—leaving out your judgment!" she wrote in April 1935. Nine months later she phrased her disapproval more somberly: "I suppose, dear friend, you are going your own way and doing the deeds that seem to you right, but which seems to me such a strange way to proceed." She closed on a note that in retrospect would seem prophetic: "We grow very slowly, although now and then there are leaps and bounds. God help and guide you."[48]

Although Nancy's prospects were thus advanced, crises over health and money continued to plague her parents. In the spring of 1935 Muste wrote worriedly to Elizabeth Evans. Mrs. Muste had been ill. Promised funds from another friend in California had been tied up and were no longer forthcoming. They were one hundred dollars behind in their rent. The fifty-year-old man did not know "how the landlord can be stalled off beyond April 1" and added, "Mrs. Muste is not in condition to bear shocks of this kind as she used to be." Elizabeth Evans immediately sent fifty dollars and promised another installment if the additional rent money could not be found elsewhere. But, verging on her eightieth year, she was physically and financially coming to the end of her ability to help.[49]

Muste himself was felled by a severe attack of influenza only a few weeks before the October showdown over the French Turn. For some time after the worst effects wore off, he was limited to working only "a couple of hours a day."[50] As the year wore on and financial pressures failed to let up, he began writing articles and essays to augment the budget. He received a commission from the Christian Social Justice Fund to produce an analysis of "The Automobile Industry and Organized Labor." The assignment proved to be an interesting exercise in balancing the Marxist-Leninist line with objective reporting.[51]

As 1936 began, Muste's closest friends worried about his strained and straitened state. Cara Cook began to raise funds to give him a vacation. Others joined the effort, some pointing out that Anna Muste was equally in need of rest. The idea caught on more than Cook and her associates had dared hope. Money came in from publicly proclaimed foes as well as friends, validating the observation which George Novack once made that Muste "was trusted by many people who did not share his politics." The collection, according to author Milton Mayer, "overflowed with contributions from people who hated Musteism and loved Muste." The final sum was sufficient to send Anna Muste with her husband.[52]

On a June day in 1936, they boarded a ship at Hoboken pier. A group of well-wishers gathered to say farewell. As the ship pulled out to sea they saw A. J. Muste raise "his skinny arm in the clenched fist salute of the bloody revolution."[53]

Chapter V

Revelation and Renewal
"I Must Lead a Religious Life"

The Atlantic Ocean freed Anna and Abraham Muste from the immediate pressures of economic instability and social unrest in America. But conditions in Europe in 1936 allowed politically aware travelers no respite from
anxiety about the future. Governments were rearming. Nazi-inspired political
agitation was on the rise in Czechoslovakia. The inability of the League of
Nations to prevent aggression and maintain international peace had been
demonstrated during Mussolini's brutal and unimpeded attack on Ethiopia.
Soon the Spanish Civil War and Francisco Franco would provide Hitler and
Mussolini with a rehearsal stage for the weapons and tactics of World War II.

Against this backdrop the Mustes began their vacation. Their first stop
was the home of Konrad Knudsen in Vexhall, Norway, a village about thirty
miles north of Oslo. Knudsen was a Labor Party editor who had toured the
United States in the 1920s and had been a visiting lecturer at Brookwood Labor
College. In June of 1936, when Leon Trotsky was expelled from France and
admitted to Norway, Knudsen and his family invited the exile and his wife,
Natalya, to move into their spacious country home.[1]

The Trotskys had just settled into the tranquil atmosphere of the Knudsen estate when the Mustes arrived for a week's visit. The American Trotskyist
described their first meeting in a letter to Cara Cook:

> We drove out to the farm house, through a broad valley dotted with farms
> and, on either side, low wooded mountains, something like the foot hills
> of the Berkshires. As I turned around in the hall, after hanging my coat in
> the closet within two paces of me was Levidov (Trotsky) who in an in-
> stant, and before I could get a full look at his face, was by me and grasping
> my hand, and then with his left, Anne's. Immediately behind him was his
> wife Natasha [sic], equally cordial and gentle (yes, I think that *is* the
> word) in her greeting. Thus the (to me) great event had occurred—so
> casually and simply I had met Leon Trotsky.[2]

The warmth of the initial greeting set the tone for the entire visit. Muste declared himself and Anna "completely captivated" by their Russian hosts. Soon, he reported, the foursome came to feel as though they had known one another for years. Conversation ranged over a variety of subjects, including philosophy and literature. The "intellectual versatility and brilliance" with which Trotsky approached all topics greatly impressed his guests. Although later memories depicted the exile as humorless and sarcastic, Muste's impressions at the time were of a "simple, direct, utterly unassuming" man with "calm" and "utter lack of bitterness in his spirit." Muste remarked as well upon signs that Trotsky was "not in any sense a defeated man. His faith and courage are undiminished."[3] When the two men talked politics, disagreement over the French Turn inevitably figured in. According to Muste, Trotsky as much as admitted that the "turn" was not appropriate in the United States. He reportedly added, however, that since it had been executed there was little to be done about it and that Muste ought not "let it drive [him] out of the party to which [he] had too much to give."[4]

After leaving Vexhall the Mustes travelled to Paris, where a secret meeting took place among Trotskyist leaders from several countries. Muste recalled that "a considerable number" of the delegates shared his antipathy to the French Turn and reported that it was not working in their countries. But no one was willing to actively oppose it.[5]

When the meeting ended Mr. and Mrs. Muste moved on to Switzerland for uninterrupted relaxation. Toward the end of July they returned to Paris, still following a restful schedule of tourism and sightseeing. "When you go sightseeing in Europe," Muste later wrote, "you go to see churches even if you believe it would be better if there were no churches for anyone to visit."[6] Thus, the Trotskyist, while walking alone one day, entered the church of St. Sulpice. As historian Charles Chatfield has aptly noted, the edifice, located a few blocks from the Left Bank of the Seine, was an appropriate one for the former Christian-turned-revolutionary to visit. The medieval structure had once been converted, by a revolutionary movement in 1793, to a "Temple of Victory." In 1936, the building was under repair; scaffolding detracted from the altar and the whole church seemed "very much cluttered with statues." Yet when Muste stepped into the sanctuary these distractions receded and a "deep and . . . singing peace" came over him. Physically he heard and saw nothing unusual. But inwardly he experienced, he later said, what must have been meant by the biblical description of "the time 'when the morning stars sang together.' " The revolutionary took a seat facing the altar and the cross, both of which had been restored in 1802, when the Temple of Victory was reconverted to Christian worship. As he looked upon them an inner voice said, "This is where you belong, in the church, not outside it." He immediately determined that he must break with the Trotskyist movement and rededicate his life to Christianity.[7]

To exaggerate the importance of this moment in the life of Abraham John Muste is impossible. It is the point toward which all the forces of his formative years had pushed him, and the point from which all activities in the remaining thirty-one years of his life would emanate. Earlier mystical experiences had first brought to intense consciousness the religious passion within him, then had freed his mind from the dogmatism of his native church, and later had liberated his social conscience from the unquestioning patriotism of his immigrant upbringing. In this final moment of truth the demands of the passions, of the mind, and of the conscience were reconciled. The fifty-one-year-old man achieved emotional integration and equilibrium.

For all these years he had been seeking to improve, if not to replace, the provincial and often simplistic values upon which he had been raised. Now he found that the essence of those values—their religious nature—had so permeated what he called his "inner-most being" that it could not be eluded. His Trotskyist colleague, James Cannon, had been prophetic (if negative) in fearing that "the terrible background of the church" had marred Muste for life.

In the early days of his Newtonville pastorate someone among the Boston literati had introduced Muste to the poem, "The Hound of Heaven," by the British poet, Francis Thompson. The imagery of Thompson's work came back to him vividly as he reflected upon his illumination at St. Sulpice. "I fled Him down the arches of the years," the poet wrote. "I fled Him down the labyrinthine ways / Of my mind." Marxist-Leninist thought, Muste concluded, had been exactly such a labyrinthine way—"a labyrinth in which the next step is always so clear, so inevitable, so promising, but the goal is no nearer." Thompson depicted the fugitive from faith as being "shot, precipitated down Titanic glooms of chasmed fear." How aptly descriptive those Titanic glooms were of the Stalinist terror and, Muste added, of Trotskyism, which "would inevitably have ended in terror and dictatorship . . . if it had come to power." "All things betray thee, who betrayest Me," Thompson's heavenly messenger warned. The demise of Brookwood, the disintegration of the unemployed leagues, and the French Turn had betrayed Muste's best intentions. His espousal of the doctrines of secular revolution contradicted his most fundamental promptings.[8]

In obeying those promptings again the traveler returned home. Physical journeys in the future would take him through unexplored regions of modern war resistance and civil disobedience. They would carry him as far away as the continents of Africa and Asia. But the religious faith which A. J. Muste recovered in St. Sulpice endowed him with an inner serenity that became one of the hallmarks of his long pacifist career. His son, John Muste, once declared that "the basic thing" about his father was that "whether he's at a ball game or climbing over a fence into a missile base, he's always at peace within himself. He's the *happiest* man I've ever known. I can't believe a man can *be* that happy, but *he* is, he really is."[9]

The singing peace which characterized Muste's conversion in 1936 was evident in the explanations and analyses which he wrote immediately after it. As declarations of a return to familiar ground rather than a venture into the unknown, of reunion with old friends more than a rupture from present ties (Trotskyist philosophy had not encouraged great depths of personal comradeship), Muste's essays in the late summer and fall of 1936 were quietly confident in tone. Shortly before returning to the United States he mailed a sixteen-page, single-spaced paper to Cara Cook. It was his first formal announcement of his return to the Christian faith. The document made plain that Muste's Christianity was once again inseparable from pacifism. He was convinced that a second world war was coming. As at the dawn of World War I, his nature rebelled against the "creeping paralysis of the will" exhibited by his countrymen and Europeans alike. And he believed that the conversion of others to Christian nonviolence was imperative.

The sixteen-page analysis disposed of the alternatives. Present labor movements were no vehicle for salvation, he asserted. They were flawed by "narrowness, selfishness, bureaucratism [and] corruption." He extended his critique of working-class movements in general to Marxist-Leninist organizations in particular. "The Soviet Union," he declared, "and the official Communist movement throughout the world are but a broken reed for those who long to prevent war to lean upon." He decried communist glorification of "armed insurrection, civil war and terrorism," and argued that violence was reactionary. Far from being able to destroy exploitative political and economic systems, violence perpetuated them and was their foundation. As long as advocates of a new social order accepted that same foundation as their own, their every effort was doomed.[10]

To Cara Cook, and soon after to readers of the *Christian Century*, Muste explained that his experience at St. Sulpice had led him to say to himself, "What you have all along been seeking is what the Marxist calls 'the Party' and what the religious man calls the 'True Church,' and that is indeed the crucial question of our day: what is the instrument by which the revolution is to be achieved, the kingdom of God established? Where is The Party? Where is the True Church?" For an answer he returned to the faith that the "law of human existence is comradeship," that the universe is ruled by "Reason and Love," and that violence in any form is an unrealistic and fatal departure from these realities of life. Only the teachings of Jesus (interpreted by Muste as essentially pacifist) corresponded perfectly to "the real." The church founded in His name was the true church and the best guide to "what is real and fundamental, what is 'standard' in the moral and spiritual realm."[11] He recognized the difficulty that his former Marxist colleagues would have in understanding his position but suggested that "what is happening in Europe in respect of war preparation, . . . what is transpiring in Spain, what has just happened in Moscow [the Stalinist purges were under way], and what is symbolized by all these, at least warrants a thoughtful reconsideration by sincere revolutionists of their own position." As for himself, Muste sought membership in "a church, a religious communion of some kind," because "I hold a religious, essentially Christian philosophy and I must lead a religious life."[12]

When the Mustes returned from Europe at the end of August 1936, they rejoined their children in an apartment at 4010 Saxon Avenue in New York City. The family's financial status was still "pretty desperate." Back pay from Brookwood had never arrived and their rent was far in arrears. Muste secured a "small, temporary writing job" from the Christian Social Justice Fund to prepare a study on unionization in war industries. While working on that study, he continued to reexamine and amplify his freshly affirmed Christian pacifism.[13]

At the end of September he made his position public. The American Trotskyists were, by then, as Max Schactman described them, up to their "ear lobes in a violent faction fight" and had little time or attention to spend on Muste's resignation. Some among them expressed surprise. The group in Minneapolis who had fêted Muste and Cannon a few months earlier and had given them each a new suit of clothes were resentful. James Cannon reported that, while Vincent Dunne of the Minneapolis party was reading the letter conveying word of Muste's turnabout, he called to a colleague, Bill Brown: "Bill, what do you think? Muste has gone back to the church." Brown replied, "Well, I'll be damned." And a moment later: "Say . . . we ought to get that suit back!" Cannon, who spoke of the conversion with sarcasm, remarked that Brown "should have known better. Preachers never give anything back." Cannon's sarcasm had to be kept in check, however, for he had received a personal communication from Trotsky instructing him to do nothing that would "strike at Muste's prestige."[14]

To those Workers' Party followers, such as George Novack, who had worked most closely with Muste, "A. J.'s repudiation of Marxism . . . in the light of his background and personality . . . seemed natural." "A. J.," Novack continued, "was one 'ex-Trotskyist' whom we never ceased to respect and admire." Unlike such other defectors as Max Eastman, Eugene Lyons, and Sidney Hook, who came to be despised in far-left circles, Muste retained the respect of Marxists because he remained committed to social change and radical activism. In fact he continued to serve as "a sort of secular pastor" for Marxists who wished to be married, was generous with character references for former comrades who sought jobs or loans or welfare assistance, and was quick to spring to the defense when Workers' Party members fell victim to the Smith Act in the 1940s and fifties.[15]

Securing temporary work and making known his break with Marxism were Muste's first accomplishments after returning from Europe. Finding "a church or a religious communion of some kind" which would accept him became his next priority. For this purpose he turned to the Fellowship of Reconciliation and its leader, John Nevin Sayre. "I am again the unequivocal Christian and pacifist I was some years ago," Muste wrote Sayre. As such, he continued, he had reread the FOR declaration of principles, and now wished to renew his membership in the organization. "It is a joy to me to come back," Muste said. He praised Nevin Sayre for having held the Fellowship on a religious course: "The FOR must be and become revolutionary but out of *religious* experience and in a *religious* sense."[16]

In October 1936, Muste declared his recovered faith at an FOR annual meeting at Camp Northover in the hills above Boundbrook, New Jersey. His presentation, *Fellowship* reported, was the highlight of the conference. Muste manifested his "humble acknowledgment of God's leading" and at the same time provided a "keen analysis of the spiritual weakness of the strategy of hate and violence." The audience welcomed him back, elected him to their National Council, and approved his appointment to a paid staff position as chairman of the Committee on Industrial Relations.[17]

In his new job Muste lectured throughout the country and participated on the periphery of several labor episodes in 1936, including: a walkout by hosiery workers in the Berkshire Knitting Mills of Wyomissing, Pennsylvania; efforts by clergy in Detroit, Michigan, and Steubenville, Ohio, to support respectively the automobile strike and steel-organizing campaigns in those cities; and a union initiative of hotel employees in Chicago.[18]

Early in 1937, Presbyterian officials, seeking a director for Labor Temple in New York City, turned to Muste. The former director, Edmund B. Chaffee, had died suddenly in the fall of 1936. Muste suspected "the Hand of God" in the timing and circumstances of Chaffee's death. It had occurred as Muste was preparing to confer with him on the St. Sulpice experience and as Chaffee was speaking on the very theme which that conversion experience represented— Christian pacifism as an alternative to extreme ideologies of both Left and Right.[19]

The kinship which Muste felt with Chaffee made him confident that he would be effective as his successor. After a series of searching discussions the governing board of Labor Temple (the Labor Temple Committee) agreed. Early in May 1937, the Presbytery of New York validated his never-revoked credentials as a Congregational minister and called him to the post.[20] He accepted the call with profuse gratitude. "More perhaps than some who have not had the experience of separation from the Church and from the Christian faith," he declared, "I can understand the cry of the Psalmist: 'I had rather be a doorkeeper in the House of the Lord' than to dwell anywhere else on earth. Being back in the Church is to be 'back home.' "[21]

Not all Presbyterians welcomed him. *Time Magazine* reported that conservatives of the New York Presbytery "learned with consternation that they now were identified with" an ex-Trotskyist. The right-leaning church journal, the *Presbyterian*, editorialized unequivocally that "Mr. Muste is no man for the post." While expressing contrition and humility about his past errors, Muste rejected the *Presbyterian* argument that he should pay for his mistakes in "years of obscurity and humble service."[22]

When Labor Temple, at the corner of Second Avenue and East Fourteenth Street, opened in 1910 it had represented a pioneering effort by the institutionalized church to address itself to "the unchurched masses of the city." Always an object of controversy, Labor Temple provided an open forum for all points of view, along with social welfare programs, education classes, and religious services.[23] When Muste became director in 1937, he found himself serving two distinct "communities." On the one hand there were the people who lived in the neighborhood. The most recent immigrants, "Jews, Italians,

Poles and other Slavic groups," provided the participants for most Labor Temple programs, along with a "few of the older Germans unable or unwilling to leave the neighborhood." On the other hand there was the "community" who frequented the area known as Union Square, three blocks long and one block wide, the "Hyde Park of New York." "More discussion of economic, social and political issues from a liberal or radical viewpoint occurred in this section than in any other equal area in the United States, perhaps in the world."[24]

Soon Muste began to address yet a third "community"—"the intellectuals," as he called them. Seldom present physically, their influence was nonetheless pervasive, Muste felt; it set the tone of and established the context within which labor and leftist thought developed. In the writings of Ignazio Silone, Andre Gide, John Dos Passos, Sidney Hook, Edmund Wilson, Aldous Huxley, and Eugene Lyons, Muste found signs of a new moral awareness which he wanted to promote.[25] Between 1937 and 1940, Muste made certain that everyone within earshot of Labor Temple was acquainted with these writers. He hired the Reverend Laurence Hosie (a Baptist minister who had been Field and Industrial secretary at the FOR) to "mingle with the multitudes" in Union Square and draw them, through "outdoor evangelism," into discussions at Labor Temple.[26] To lead those discussions Muste brought in leading ex-Marxists as guest lecturers. He also added Morris Gordin to the Temple staff. To Muste this Russian-American's conversion from communism to Christianity seemed initially to be "a sort of 'first fruits' of a harvest that will be reaped by the Christian Church in this period." However, the convert turned out to be either "mentally unstable" or utterly lacking in "both Christian humility and ordinary good manners," and was fired.[27]

Muste was troubled by a similar lack of humility in other ex-Marxists, including Eugene Lyons, whose work, *Assignment in Utopia*, he greatly admired. Writing to Lyons some days after a stormy meeting at which the author had spoken, Muste commented, "I can hardly blame people for getting sore if a speaker informs them that they are utterly devoid of brains and sense."[28]

In his own lectures and sermons Muste maintained a tone of honesty and good will. His purpose was to persuade audiences that the Judeo-Christian tradition was a democratic workers' tradition. At the heart of Judaism, he taught, was the warning—not unlike more recent warnings from Karl Marx—that "those who buy the poor for silver and the needy for a pair of sandals and sell the refuse of the wheat" will be judged. Similarly, in the teachings of Jesus, he pointed to concern for the poor and disinherited, a concern that was present also in the manifestoes of Marxism.

But the message of Judaism and Christianity was, Muste continued, "not a theory, not an argument, not a manifesto or a program." Applied to contemporary struggles, this religious heritage called for nonviolent sacrifice on the part of labor and radical activists; that is, pacifism as a way of life governing all relationships, and not just as a political tactic. In this context Muste's strong support for labor rights was matched by a deep concern with labor ethics. "I do not want to create the false opinion that the labor movement as it now stands is the Messiah that will lead us into the promised land," he noted, "but it is here whether we like it or not and unless we infuse it with ethics and religion it may well be an evil and destructive force."[29]

In addition to his public ministry Muste also devoted considerable time to private counselling of individuals whose lives were in one way or another affected by the Marxist movements of the 1930s. Some, Muste wrote, were "young people . . . who had passed through the Communist movement" and were now seeking guidance "on problems of religion and life philosophy." Others who consulted Muste were relatives of communists, worried about the direction their loved ones were taking. If possible, Muste advised, direct the communist to read such critiques of the Marxist philosophy as H. B. Parke's *Marxism: An Autopsy*. But never, he urged, "withdraw affection from him. . . . Have faith in his sound qualities; and above all . . . have faith in God whose leading may at times seem strange to human eyes."[30] .

Muste felt that his efforts to combat Marxism and proclaim Christianity as a revolutionary doctrine were important. "It may well be," he predicted, "that human lives are more lastingly influenced in this way than by any other phase of our work."[31] Those associated with the Temple apparently agreed. Participation in lectures and classes grew, as did private financial contributions for his work. At the same time Muste was playing an active and respected role in wider Presbyterian circles. Appointed to the Committee on Social Education and Action of the Presbytery of New York, he became secretary of a subcommittee "on Strategy," charged with helping local churches increase their contact with community problems.

In the fall of 1937, he was asked to join a Presbyterian "preaching mission" which carried a message of Christian social responsibility across the country. "He's lived, that man," noted a journalist, reporting on a sermon Muste delivered in Iowa. "He knows economics, sociology and, yes, religion . . . , and he thinks the three go together. . . . He's got intellect. . . . It's something more too, . . . and that's what I'm wondering about, that look behind his eyes."[32] In 1938, Muste accepted a lectureship at Union Theological Seminary. In the same year he helped draft the Labor Sunday message which was read from pulpits across the country. The message extolled democracy, cited collective bargaining as a crucial exercise of democratic principles, and urged world peace.[33]

Muste's family life was relatively tranquil in this period. His contract provided an apartment above Labor Temple where they could live. For a year, Nancy and her new husband, John Baker (a Katonah High School classmate whom she married in September 1937), shared the apartment. As soon as they were able to manage the finances, however, Muste insisted that they take their own place. "Dad was a very strong person and didn't mollycoddle people," Nancy recalled. Yet with his younger daughter, Connie, he was protective. After a year at Hope College proved to be too lonely for her, she returned to her parents, completing her studies at Columbia University, and would continue to live with them until she married at the age of thirty-three. According to John Muste, who was ten years old when the Labor Temple job began, and who attended Friends' Seminary, a private Quaker school around the corner, their father supervised Connie's comings and goings "in subtle ways" as long as she lived at home.

Aside from their responsibilities as parents and their concern over Anna's health (a physician discovered that she had a serious heart ailment, stemming from rheumatic fever when she was a child), A. J. and Anna Muste were at last comfortably settled and enjoying the security of a $300 monthly salary.[34]

But this stable situation was not to last. With the thunder of the Second World War growing louder in the distance, Muste's pacifist vocation began drawing him away from his ministry to labor. The transition which he would make in 1940 from Labor Temple to the Fellowship of Reconciliation would not be as personally unsettling to family members as had been many earlier changes in their lives. It would entail neither a fundamental shift in beliefs and values nor a serious rupture of friendships. But it did indicate that Muste was not done with travelling. "I do not think I welcome change for the sake of being in motion," he mused toward the end of his life. "[But] where a decision is to be made, one's allegiance should be to . . . the experience ahead. The peril," he argued, "is *not* to move when the new situation becomes possible."[35] Muste's response to the new situation presented by Adolf Hitler and World War II was both activist and analytical in nature. While taking a leading role in anti-war activities, he would also develop an incisive analysis of world events.

Part Two
Peace: "The Seamless Garment"

If I am accused of being too ambitious
I shall plead guilty. If I am told
that my dream can never materialize,
I would answer "that is possible" and go my way.
I am a seasoned soldier of non-violence
and I have evidence enough to sustain my faith.
Whether, therefore, I have one comrade or more
or none, I must continue the experiment."

Mohandas Gandhi, 1940

Chapter VI

World War II and "The Number One U.S. Pacifist"

$\mathbf{A}$s an opponent of international war A. J. Muste never experienced widespread popular acceptance of his position. He missed each of the historical moments in his lifetime when "peace" briefly became a celebrated cause. The unprecedented burgeoning of peace societies and sentiment before World War I occurred prior to—and had given way to war fever by the time of—Muste's first pacifist awakening. Renewed support and organizing for peace in the 1920s and 1930s was fueled by general disillusionment over the outcome of World War I.[1] But in the years after that war Muste had moved toward accepting revolutionary violence and "wars of liberation." At the time of his return to pacifism in the summer of 1936, popular enthusiasm for peace had just about peaked. As events in Europe grew more ominous the interwar romance between public opinion and peace groups began to sour. Muste emerged as a leading opponent of war preparations just when the need for making such preparations began to seem increasingly obvious. Many contemporaries questioned the wisdom of his anti-war actions and declarations. In future years critics—including those who held him in highest personal esteem—remained skeptical. How, in the face of the madness of Hitler and of the Axis powers supporting him, could A. J. Muste (or anyone) have advocated pacifism?[2]

The answer Muste gave in sermons, articles, and lectures from 1936 to 1940, and in his first book, *Nonviolence in an Aggressive World* (published early in 1940), was specific in its analysis of why the new threat of war had occurred.

Paramount among the reasons which he delineated was the Treaty of Versailles, "a 'peace' of treason and revenge," which stripped the German economy, fragmented all of Europe, encouraged "suicidal" tariff policies, and thereby virtually guaranteed the failure of the peace-keeping instrument which it had created in the League of Nations.

A second major reason for world tensions, according to Muste, was United States policy in the Far East. He decried the Oriental Exclusion Act, the maintenance of American troops on Chinese soil, and the use of American naval ships to convoy "tankers of Standard Oil" in Pacific waters. These were policies of aggression and they robbed the United States of the moral right to speak for an authentic peace.[3]

Muste cited as a third cause economic anarchy in a world where "the 'have' nations. . . . control 3/5 of the earth's resources."[4] He effectively documented his discussion of this dangerous economic imbalance and of the dangers resulting from Western imperialism in the Far East and Allied vengeance in Europe. Identifying actions and policies of the Allies as primary stimulants for fascism, he focused his analysis of fascist regimes on the violence embodied in them and, from that vantage point, pressed the view that only nonviolent initiatives could effectively counter fascist forces. "The shocking abnormalities" of fascist societies reflected, he believed, the religious truth that humans "were made for freedom and love and the absence of these . . . drives them mad." Only gestures of humaneness—not further expressions of brutality in war—could call fascist societies back to a state of sanity and stability. However logical this may have been in the abstract, the concrete solutions which Muste proposed were not entirely persuasive.

He claimed that a series of Allied acts of repentance would undermine fascism, but did not explain how the Allied nations were to be convinced of their sins. He merely predicted that if the victors of the last war would admit their own lust for power and cease in their self-righteousness, and if military preparations and imperialist designs were abandoned, then the true nature of the struggle would become evident. "The war is not between angels and devils," Muste declared. "It is between, on one hand, a group of nations satisfied with a status quo which is vastly to their advantage, . . . and on the other hand, a group of nations . . . determined to smash the status quo and no longer accept an inferior status."[5]

In keeping with a number of other peace groups and spokespersons, Muste urged President Franklin Roosevelt to convene a world conference immediately, to begin disarmament, redistribution of raw materials, downward revision of tariffs, and adjustment of national currencies.[6] If other nations would not agree to such a conference, Muste was prepared to have a single country act alone and urged the United States to disarm. "I believe with all my soul," he wrote in *Nonviolence,*

> that the embattled peoples of the earth looking at each other like savage witch-dancers through gas masks are waiting for a nation that would have the sublime horse sense, the divine foolishness, to break the evil spell that is on mankind, lay down its arms and say: "Boys, this thing has gone too far; I'm going home to work and live and love; and the next time I get restless and want some excitement, I'm going fishing or to see the Marx Brothers in a movie or maybe even to church." Uncle Sam and his Yankees ought to be capable of that if anyone is![7]

To the fear that such action would leave the country open to fascist invasion, Muste replied that an invasion of the United States by European forces via the Atlantic Ocean or by Oriental forces via the Pacific was improbable but maintained that nonviolent resistance could foil a land invasion should one occur.[8]

To those who expressed solicitude for the weaker nations of the world that were falling before the Nazi juggernaut, Muste commended this same notion of nonviolent defense. Big power intervention on their behalf was no answer, he said. They would be far more secure if they organized their own resistance without arms and escaped from the role of pawns manipulated by the big nations, and if countries such as the United States "refused to sell munitions to anyone at any time."[9]

For the most part Muste seemed to entertain no illusions about the depth of the viciousness of Adolf Hitler. He acknowledged the agonizing challenge that the Führer represented for pacifists in a meditation offered one Sunday in 1940, during a Friends' meeting for worship: "If I can't love Hitler," Muste reflected, "I can't love at all."[10] When the German dictator sealed his world-shaking pact with Joseph Stalin in August 1939, Muste sought to face the implications squarely. Two outcomes seemed possible to him. Either Stalin, having double-crossed France and Britain, would now do the same to Hitler, or "the same forces which drew Hitler and Stalin into each other's arms . . . may keep them locked in that embrace . . . [until] from the Rhine to the Pacific . . . some form of 'communazism' . . . would reign."[11]

Other comments by Muste in the late thirties and in 1940, however, belied an optimism about Hitler's openness to reason which fewer and fewer anti-fascist observers could share. In 1938, Muste was still taking hope from the German leader's assertion that in modern war there are no victors. In his book of 1940, Muste continued to assume that public sentiment could force Hitler to accept an authentic peace offer.[12] Muste's understanding of mass psychology was surprisingly limited. As crowds roared approval of the Third Reich the pacifist still held the view that "there seems to be something elemental, deep-seated about the shrinking of the masses from war."[13]

While Muste grounded his views as much as possible in fact, logic, and common sense, the source of his pacifism was personal faith and a religious historical perspective. "Those who have taken the course of repentence, nonviolence, love of the enemy," he wrote, have always triumphed while those who have brought themselves "down to Caesar's level," using Caesar's weapons, have been overtaken by destruction. The ancient Jews survived while the great empires of their enemies perished, Muste said, "because the Remnant at least . . . centered Israel's life . . . in God, not in power." Similarly, the followers of Jesus survived while Rome crumbled.[14]

As war threatened to engulf the present world order, Muste devoted more and more time to shaping a program around which a war-resisting remnant might gather. In 1938, he founded the United Pacifist Committee (UPC) in New York City, which opposed naval expansion, mobilization of industry, withdrawal of the United States ambassador from Germany, proposals for conscription, and revision of neutrality laws to allow for the policy of "cash and carry."[15]

The UPC regularly met at Labor Temple, which Muste now regarded as "a pacifist center which could be very crucial if war breaks out." Longstanding ties between the Temple and the FOR also grew stronger with the instituting of joint FOR (New York chapter)–Labor Temple worship services and the election of Muste as chairman of the National Council of the Fellowship.[16]

Five months after the outbreak of war in Europe, Harold Fey, executive secretary of the FOR, resigned from that post. John Nevin Sayre, as Fey's temporary successor, asked Muste to take on the job. At first he resisted, citing his commitment to Labor Temple. When no one else came forth, Sayre, supported by regional secretaries Donovan Smucker and John Swomley, addressed an impassioned plea to Muste. "Now you can make a greater contribution to the Church and Christianity in this country through the Fellowship than would be possible through Labor Temple or by a division of time between the two."[17] The following month Muste resigned from Labor Temple. "After much painful as well as prayerful consideration," he had decided to accept the post of executive secretary of the FOR, effective April 1, 1940.[18]

While Muste's decision left his Labor Temple associates in distress, it was greeted in Fellowship circles with elation.[19] John Nevin Sayre prepared to "withdraw myself from the [FOR] picture entirely so that the decks would be cleared for A. J. to initiate a complete new deal." But Muste asked him to remain. Sayre and Muste, with their respective offer and refusal, indicated the depth of their commitment to the FOR and admiration for one another. The two men were strikingly different; Muste's penchant for activism and radical experimentation contrasted sharply with the circumspect Sayre's piety and moderation. But while profound disagreements would arise over matters of policy, they would keep their 1940 pledge to "work as equal partners on the FOR staff, each having full faith in the other" for the duration of the war, and their friendship endured to the end of their lives.[20]

In time of war, organizations such as the FOR have a special need to strengthen personal ties and foster "community" among their members. As early as 1935, the Fellowship had adopted a "crisis strategy" which included the organization of local "peace teams" wherein FOR members practiced self-study and religious discipline while seeking to perform humanitarian service in the world around them. In 1940, Muste encouraged further development of these teams (or "cells" as he more often termed them) and urged each group to look immediately "into the question of probable future needs of members and families who may be prosecuted for conscience's sake."[21]

Within the FOR staff he promoted a vision of spiritual fellowship arising among those who lived by their convictions. "A power will come upon us," he promised. It "may work havoc with the outer framework of our lives [but] . . . it will enable us like men of faith in all ages to 'subdue kingdoms, work righteousness and obtain the promises.' "[22]

The vein of evangelism running through his responses to earlier crises was surfacing once again. But while the perils of this new situation were as grave or graver in their universal implications than any that had come before, American pacifists in 1940 faced lesser threats than Muste's visions of struggle sometimes implied.[23] The witness for peace in time of war was hardly applauded in the 1940s. But the naked repression of previous decades was no longer a threat. Still, pacifists faced complicated dilemmas arising from both external pressures on and internal disagreements within the peace movement.

Muste's devotion to the Fellowship in this era was perhaps the deepest loyalty to an institution that he ever held. And he exercised great vigilance against possible threats to the FOR from other peace groups. On occasion the War Resisters' League, which was in fact an offshoot of the FOR and included Muste on its executive committee, appeared to him to threaten the source from which it had sprung. In certain FOR-WRL endeavors Muste saw the Fellowship emphasis on "the religious basis of life" endangered by the secular philosophy of League members. He was careful to defend the right of the younger organization against interference with its activities and growth, but he was equally ready to withdraw from the Executive Committee of the League if agreements between the two organizations were not honored.[24]

Conflict between WRL and FOR was contained within the bounds of small confrontations and unpublicized exchanges. A clash of larger and more public proportions developed between the FOR and a very recent arrival on the peace front—the organization called Peace Now. The fundamental issue in this controversy was that of the usefulness and limits of an anti-war "united front." Before Pearl Harbor Muste had been rather liberal in the extent to which he permitted identification of his pacifism with the calls for peace of far more conservative individuals and groups. In 1938, he had shared the platform of a Keep America Out of War rally with Republican Congressman Hamilton Fish. When a correspondent expressed surprise, in October 1940, over the participation of FOR members, including Muste, at a recent meeting of the Emergency Peace Conference where Charles Lindbergh had been a featured and applauded speaker, Muste replied that "keeping America out of war at the present time is so important that I strongly incline toward the united front." He added, however, that the forces with which pacifists collaborated must not be allowed to obscure or hamper their own objectives and that there must be "some chance of success" for a united front to be attempted.[25]

But, by 1943, when Columbia University professor and well-known socialist lecturer George Hartman founded the Peace Now Movement (PNM), Muste had lost interest in united fronts. Hartman launched the organization independently and against the advice of all the established peace groups. He installed as spokesmen and organizers for PNM a succession of individuals whose integrity and stability were open to question. Muste learned from colleagues in the International FOR of rumors that PNM Secretary John Collet, a recent immigrant from Norway, had escaped after German occupation of that country by collaborating with the Nazis. Other sources reported that Collet was mentally unbalanced. When Collet did in fact suffer a breakdown and was removed from the PNM staff, Muste found his replacement, Bessie Simon, also objectionable. Her ties with America First isolationists complemented tendencies within PNM to court rightists who would, Muste predicted, stop the war only if their "reactionary interests were served." The tendency of the public and the press to link PNM to other peace groups, including the FOR, was Muste's overriding concern. He, Sayre, and Associate FOR Secretary John Swomley sent a memo to all field secretaries and local groups underlining the maverick and questionable nature of the PNM undertaking and the financial threat posed by "another organization having ostensibly the same objectives and . . . appealing chiefly to the same people for contributions."[26] PNM supporters interpreted the purpose of this and a subsequent "Personal Memorandum" which Muste sent out on his own as, in the words of FOR member Dorothy Hutchinson, "systematic persecution" of the Peace Now effort.[27]

The failure of valued FOR members to defend his stand against PNM troubled Muste. After a heated exchange over PNM between him and the *Christian Century*, Muste was startled to receive from one of his field workers a report that some "radicals" within the Fellowship regarded his insistence on separating their organization from the Peace Now group as an instance of "a bad case of institutionalitis." "I frankly can't understand," Muste retorted, "how you could feel critical of anything or anybody except the *Christian Century* in its attempt to cover its own confusion by attacking and misrepresenting pacifism." He made clear how personally stirred he was by this episode, declaring, "I am willing to stake my whole career in the pacifist movement on the issue" of the PNM.[28]

Hartman's organization did not last long enough to put Muste to such an extreme test but in another vastly more complex controversy—that over the issue of pacifist responsibilities regarding military conscription—his leadership was again seriously questioned. Provisions for conscientious objectors within the Selective Service Act of 1940 were the result of consultation between the Roosevelt administration and spokesmen for traditional pacifist churches and organizations. The arrangements for Alternative Service which they worked out involved the setting up of Civilian Public Service Camps to be directed and financed entirely by religious and pacifist sources. Initially Muste saw in this cooperation between peace-minded civilians and the Selective Service Administration "an interesting and in many ways encouraging and instructive example in human relationships." He encouraged all churches to put up money to support those from their own congregations whose consciences would lead them to the camps. At the same time the FOR became a full partner in, and made a substantial financial contribution to, the coordinating body for the camps, the National Service Board for Religious Objectors (NSBRO).[29]

Nonetheless, Muste was dissatisfied with the conscription law on three counts: the option of alternative service was limited to those who refused participation in war "by reason of religious training and belief"; automatic exemption from military service was provided for clergymen and theology students; no provision was made for those whose opposition to war was so extreme that they could not in conscience meet the requirement of registration. As conscientious objectors who could not demonstrate the requisite religious background went off to prison, and pacifist seminarians and ministers refused the exemptions that involuntarily set them apart, and while many of them, along with other war resisters, took the "absolutist" position of refusing to register and received substantial jail sentences in return, Muste grew more profoundly dissatisfied. But these were only the most obvious of the difficulties challenging him and the pacifist movement.[30]

By early 1941, turmoil began to overtake peace organizations as they sought to serve three distinct categories of war resisters with three sets of frequently conflicting needs: conscientious objectors from the Historic Peace Churches, committed to a role of thoroughgoing cooperation with the Selective Service Administration; men who saw in conscription the denial by the State of their inalienable right to direct their own lives, committed to the opposite position of thorough noncooperation with the law; other individuals who entered CPS camps or federal prison with cooperative intentions and evolved into noncooperators as the months and sometimes the years wore on.

Muste had foreseen that "some will be led to a more militant course, others to a quieter form of witness," and urged that "all must remain in . . . unity with each other, not thinking of themselves as more orthodox or honest or useful pacifists than those who put the emphasis in a different place."[31] The efforts which he expended in standing by this position and impressing it upon the spirits of his associates came to claim more of his time and energies than any other wartime endeavor.

The FOR secretary returned from visiting several CPS camps in the fall of 1941 with a foreboding sense of how difficult it would be for NSBRO to minister to the very diverse population of the camps. He recognized that for the most part the CPS setup reflected the values of the Quaker, Mennonite, and Brethren groups who bore the brunt of the financing. "From my point of view," he admitted, "there are grave limitations in these groups." But he conceded that their way of life "has had survival value both in a material and in a spiritual sense" and that embodied in this way of life was a centuries' long history of opposition to war and state regimentation. Many among the camps' populations were comfortable with the Historic Peace Church emphasis on "walking the second mile."[32] Yet Muste's own heart was with those who rejected that approach. In counselling men who refused to register for the draft he warned of the price they would be called upon to pay, including the bearing of responsibility for placing loved ones under duress by their actions. But against that price Muste placed the axiom that "in the moral universe great good always results when men stand unflinchingly by their convictions."[33] The FOR took special note of two cases resulting from registration refusals in October 1940—those of eight students at Union Theological Seminary who were sentenced a month later to prison for a year and a day, and five New York objectors who received jail terms of eighteen months to two years, and whose convictions were not only upheld when they appealed to New York District Court but were the basis for an ominous ruling that, even in time of peace and when no evidence that a national emergency exists, Congress has the power to conscript. In the wake of these cases Muste was moved to declare that, while he continued to see great value in the Civilian Public Service program, he was especially grateful for the steadfastness of the nonregistrants.[34]

Muste's backing of the absolutists occasioned considerable criticism from fellow clergymen, including Henry Sloan Coffin and Reinhold Niebuhr, both of whom had tried to persuade the Union students against their chosen course of action. Niebuhr described the young men as courters of martyrdom and proponents of anarchism. "There is no sense in getting decent provisions for conscientious objectors if the latter take the position that registration is itself cooperation with the war system," he lectured. But the real point at issue, as Muste defined it, was not the actions of the nonregistrants (which of course he did not consider in the same light as Niebuhr), but the stance of the state toward the matter of individual conscience. By failing to provide exemption from the draft for absolutists, the United States government was, in Muste's view, promoting the state as sovereign and denying the possibility of a higher loyalty. He warned religious leaders against being too grateful for Selective Service provisions for conscientious objectors. "Mortal men cannot do favors to conscience and to Almighty God," he said.[35]

On March 19, 1942, President Roosevelt issued a proclamation requiring that every male citizen between the ages of forty-five and sixty-five "on April 27, 1942, present himself for and submit to registration before a duly designated registration official or selective service local board." On April 3, Muste circulated a private memorandum within pacifist circles setting forth "Why I Cannot Register." For him to cooperate with conscription in America would be, he wrote, comparable to Fellowship members in Germany "saying 'Heil Hitler,' " and to early Christians burning the pinch of incense for Caesar. The view of registration as a harmless bookkeeping activity did not impress him. To register was to contribute to the war effort. Conversely, nonregistration was a fitting way to oppose it.[36]

"I feel as if I ought to be going to jail with them," Muste wrote of imprisoned war resisters and reflected, "I would have felt a deep contentment if the government had sent me to jail when . . . I refused to register." His persistent habit of placing his principles before the comfort of those directly dependent on him was at work again. Even the fact that Anna Muste's heart condition was growing worse did not deter him. Muste was never apologetic about the harsh implications of his position; he clearly felt that, because he was working for a greater good, the strains and uncertainties to which his work subjected his loved ones were justified. "The teaching is clear," he advised one man who was considering conscientious objection, "that situations may arise where we must 'hate' father, mother, wife, child—or we cannot be Christ's disciples."[37]

On the other hand, as John Muste has noted, his father never abdicated the parental role. In the same period when he was caught up in anti-war activities, Muste found time to make the long trip to Northfield, Massachusetts (five hours by train each way), to talk with John. The young man, after persuading his parents to let him transfer from Friends' Seminary to Mt. Herman prep school in Northfield, wanted to return to Friends' and Muste would not permit it. "We felt he ought to see it through since he had made his choice," said Muste. "He spent hours with me," remembered John. "I still don't know how he persuaded me since I was determined to leave, but he did, and made me feel glad that he had. But it was also during the two years that I spent at that school that he risked jail . . . and was clearly willing to trust to fate or the good Lord to feed his family."

As government policy developed, jail faded as a serious possibility for Muste and other older nonregistrants. He was arrested only long enough to be handed written charges and to have an official in the district attorney's office fill out and sign a registration card for him. His subsequent efforts to force the government to treat younger and older absolutists alike failed.[38]

He had limited success in trying to remain close to the men in jail. The majority of imprisoned conscientious objectors adopted a stance of cooperation with the regulations imposed upon them. But issues did arise—most notably the questions of racial segregation and censorship—that provoked some men to rebel. Out of this rebellion emerged a group of objectors who chose to stand against the entire prison regime, identifying it as another manifestation of the authoritarian, war-making, conscripting state.[39]

Stanley Murphy and Louis Taylor, two prisoners incarcerated at Danbury, Virginia, exemplified this position. They had walked out of a CPS camp and began after imprisonment a "fast unto death" (which ended, short of death, 82 days later) against the Selective Service system. Muste visited the men in March of 1943 and reported that he was "profoundly moved" by their sincerity. The FOR petitioned President Roosevelt to release the men and take immediate steps to correct the abuses in CPS camps which had inspired their action. But his intervention in the case availed nothing and, throughout, he questioned the "likely effects of the particular form of witness . . . which these men have . . . adopted."[40]

Protest against segregation in the federal prison system evoked a more active and positive response from him. When officials refused to allow a black inmate to sit with his white counterparts in the dining hall at Lewisburg, thirteen conscientious objectors initiated a work strike. Muste went to Lewisburg, spoke with the strikers, and sent his analysis of the situation to the director of the Bureau of Prisons, James V. Bennett, urging reform. Recalcitrant at first, Bennett eventually took steps to desegregate the prisons. But this did not end his problems with political prisoners such as the Lewisburg men who added censorship of mail to their list of grievances and whose protest against both censorship and Jim Crow evolved into a hunger strike. Muste declared his determination to stand by the men and his agreement that censorship and segregation should be abolished. But he doubted the effectiveness of the hunger strike and urged that it be dropped. He suspected that witness had given way to a decidedly non-pacifist test of wills and enjoined the rebels to think clearly about their position.[41]

Their line of reasoning was flawed, he claimed, when they equated conscription or totalitarianism with the prison system. Prisons had existed before totalitarian states, he pointed out. They were not simply part of the draft and, he argued, note should be taken of modern efforts at penal reform before the system was branded as totally evil. The historical and political tradition illustrated by "virtually all prophets and revolutionists in history," including the contemporary Gandhi, of cooperation for the most part during imprisonment weighed heavily with Muste. "Personally I have always felt that [cooperation] would be my position if I were imprisoned under the Selective Service Act," he stated.[42]

In December 1943, James Bennett directed a revision of the rules governing correspondence and literature; the thirteen Lewisburg prisoners then concluded their fast. This and similar episodes led Muste to observe that the pacifist movement was "being educated as well as trying to educate others." He was anxious that "the movement be given a chance to catch up with" the men who forged ahead so boldly in confronting the bureaucracies of federal prisons and Selective Service.[43]

Patience, however, was not the order of the day. Resentment over pacifist cooperation with Selective Service smoldered among absolutists in prison and in the CPS camps. When flare-ups over this issue first occurred Muste tried to put out the fire. As time went on, however, he began to carefully fan the flames. At moments the unity of the organization he led and the movement of which it was part seemed about to go up in smoke. He was able, however, to keep that from happening but not without sustaining some personal damage.

In the first two to three years of the camps' existence Muste tended more toward criticism of rather than sympathy for CPS men who grew restive and expressed disillusionment over their work assignments, living conditions, and lack of pay.[44] He reminded them that in accepting alternative service they had in effect "made some sort of contract with the Government." As late as January 1943, the FOR secretary advised against the walkouts which had begun to occur from CPS camps and urged that dissidents give the government a chance to correct the defects of alternative service.[45]

Yet reports of increased government intervention in the camps and acquiescence in government censorship by the head of the NSBRO had troubled Muste as early as the summer of 1942. Regulations which prevented men from access to news about events outside their camps and which prohibited their making direct contact with government officials struck him as legitimate objects of protest. Though opposing the walkout as a general tactic he proposed "in various camps a program of non-cooperation if the situation is not checked." The fact was growing on him, too, that in their preoccupation with winning the war federal officials were only slightly interested in the problems of conscientious objectors.[46]

By the spring of 1943, Muste was ready for an organizational parting of the ways between the government and pacifist groups. In March, he urged that the NSBRO refuse to accept men who did not want CPS assignments but were sent to the camps anyway. In May, he stunned the National Council of the FOR with a memorandum calling for the Fellowship to withdraw from NSBRO. "Had I known what I now know in the summer of 1940, I would have been more free and outspoken than I was in stating my opposition to conscription and regimentation," he told the Council. Now he knew that the promise of meaningful work projects for conscientious objectors was a hollow one and that pacifist direction of the camps was nominal only, with government and military personnel really in charge.[47]

The upshot of Council deliberations on Muste's memorandum seemed ironic to opponents of NSBRO. When the Council convened again in December to vote on the proposal for withdrawing from the organization, Muste himself voted to continue the relationship, thereby opening himself to the most bitter criticisms of his career as a pacifist leader. The position to which he held over the next tumultuous year was that, until a Quaker-style "sense of the meeting" could be achieved among FOR members, a change of policy was not appropriate. He expressed concern as well that precipitous action would leave the impression that participants in alternative service were "Grade B" pacifists while those who rejected the service were "Grade A." "There are certain issues where . . . each [side] . . . must believe that he is right. . . . But . . . no one need regard himself as more righteous than the other," he counselled. This proved impossible for some of his absolutist associates to accept.[48]

In February 1944, Muste received a scorching letter condemning FOR support of the CPS arrangement signed by sixteen war resisters at Lewisburg Prison. While scoring the organization for its policies they singled out Muste as the biggest source of their disappointment. In reply Muste took the Lewisburg men to task for the hostile spirit of their letter and argued that instead of either the cowardly compromise with which they charged him or the solution of political sectarianism which he inferred from their position, "a third method is possible," a method of fellowship in which the search for truth "carries the group as a whole forward to true heights." It was this method which he continued to seek.[49]

After another Council vote was taken in the summer of 1944 and the tally was thirty to twenty-four for staying with NSBRO, Muste admitted disappointment but maintained that a "tremendous advance" had been made over the previous position of the Council. His colleagues in Lewisburg disagreed. On June 3, eight FOR members in that prison submitted a collective statement of resignation, with four "non-member sympathizers" also signing. Again they zeroed in on Muste, inviting him with his "revolutionary past" to shake free of the FOR and its "social bankruptcy" and move forward with them in a "working-class, revolutionary, socialist movement which will be true to the best emphases of religious pacifism." The Lewisburg writers' final bow to religious pacifism notwithstanding, Muste found in their letter portentous signs of the state of mind that had caused disonances in his own life in the era of the

American Workers' Party and the WP-U.S.A.[50] "I am convinced," he said,

> that most if not all of you if you maintain your present attitudes and pursue your intended course will end up where I did when I left the FOR, i.e.—
>
>> You will lose your religious faith and adopt a purely secular outlook.
>>
>> You will cease being pacifists and find justification for certain kinds of war.
>>
>> You will try to build a secular revolutionary party rather than a religious pacifist fellowship.
>>
>> You will espouse revolutionary violence.[51]

Muste's dire prediction was more an index of how deeply the issue of alternative service was agitating pacifist circles than a valid description of the future. As he moved to forestall these and other resignations, he held doggedly to his faith that a sense of the meeting would emerge. It did, in December of 1944, when a poll of the membership revealed majority sentiment against the FOR continuing in the NSBRO. Members of the Council who personally favored continuation were now moved to propose a severing of the relationship in deference to the prevailing corporate feeling. They agreed that the FOR would cease to be a voting member, but would continue in a consultative capacity, and would maintain responsibility for counselling with the CPS registrants who were its members.[52]

For the most part Muste was satisfied. Nevin Sayre (who had consistently opposed withdrawal from NSBRO and who had a son in a CPS camp) and he agreed that they had "proceeded as a fellowship rather than a political party," and had thereby remained true to the spirit of Christian pacifism.[53] Still, some absolutists and some NSBRO supporters were not reconciled to the decision. Joining the ranks of those who had already resigned over the issue were individuals who withdrew from the Fellowship because it no longer fully supported alternative service. Others, whom Muste expected to rejoin, maintained their resignations on the grounds that the FOR was still tainted by the consultative membership in NSBRO. His close friend Evan Thomas was among them. In remonstrating with him Muste made an interesting observation: "I think I do not have the degree of confidence in the isolated individual witness that you do," he told Thomas. "I do believe that the truth comes to individuals, . . . but even more I believe truth comes to a true fellowship. . . . We are trying to make mankind into a fellowship or community. I believe that we have to make use of fellowship and community in order to achieve that end."[54]

Muste's stern resolve to have a "sense of the meeting" prevail over factional impulses, his striving to help all young men face the complexities of conscription with clear heads and without self-righteousness, and his personal sense of outrage at the draft and its many ramifications were signs of more than a pacifist leader doing his job. As his letters to Lewisburg plainly showed, memories of the Trotskyist interlude were still fresh and stinging. A different and more recent disappointment also weighed on him. "John Muste applied a short time ago for the naval training program," A. J. Muste wrote a friend in May 1944. When he made the same announcement to the New York staff he stressed that "there is complete freedom in the Muste family." But his tone, recalled one colleague, was so defensive that the staff restrained their impulses to tease him. "It is pretty tough to see [seventeen-year-old John] take this position," Muste wrote. "My own feelings about having pacifists and pacifist organizations in any way tied up with the administration of conscription have certainly not been reduced or softened by having the business come as close [to] home as this."[55]

With the draft bringing pressures to bear on his own family ("About the only comfort . . . Anne and I, and Connie, have . . . is that we have not subjected John to . . . undue emotional pressure," he wrote),[56] Muste carried an extra measure of interest into another wartime campaign, that against permanent military conscription. In the summer of 1942, reports appeared in the *New York Times* of efforts on Capitol Hill to frame a bill to establish permanent, compulsory military service. Following closely upon these reports was a directive from President Roosevelt for "the formulation of a National War Service Bill" to mobilize "the total manpower of the country" and involving "the registration of women between the ages of 18 and 65." Muste and the FOR staff immediately set about warning their membership of these portents and directed a strong letter of objection to Roosevelt. A new organization, the Committee to Oppose the Conscription of Women, took shape, headed by Mildred Scott Olmstead with A. J. Muste as treasurer. "While we do not distinguish in principle between conscription of persons of one sex versus another, it seems nevertheless clear," Muste cautioned, "that total conscription of women is a more direct threat to the home and is likely to interfere more drastically and swiftly with the process of education which centers in the home, than the conscription of men."[57]

Roosevelt's enthusiasm for a national service bill was not shared by enough congressmen to win its passage. But the chances looked better for the bill which would establish permanent universal military training introduced in Congress in 1943 by Representative James Wadsworth. Muste denounced Wadsworth's proposal as "contrary to a tradition of over 150 years" of freedom from peacetime conscription. In November 1944, the FOR joined four other major peace organizations in a two-day parley in Washington for laying plans to combat this new draft threat. In this and other conferences with fellow pacifists Muste rejected any thought of negotiating with the state for conscientious objector provisions in proposed draft bills. He was adamant that the goal should be to stop conscription "period."

The Wadsworth Bill failed to pass but, in 1945, efforts to renew the Selective Service Act were successful in May and again in September. In October, President Harry Truman requested that Congress replace Selective Service with universal military training, inspiring opponents to gear up for another energetic campaign. Washington, D.C., was the center of action where, by 1947, opponents had organized under the direction of the National Council against Conscription, headed by FOR staff member John Swomley. Muste's role, in New York City, was a supporting one.[58]

At the same time he worked out a far-reaching critique of the major arguments advanced on behalf of systems of permanent conscription. The arguments which most annoyed him were that the drafting of youth was beneficial to the young people themselves, gave the less advantaged access to needed physical and mental health care, imparted "discipline," and fostered a sense of the responsibilities of citizenship. Rejecting all of this out of hand, Muste described as "reprehensible" the "awful decision with which young men were confronted by selective service" and which, in his view, "they were not mature enough to face." Furthermore, he argued, "at an impressionable age they are subjected to training based . . . on a philosophy of mechanical unquestioning obedience which is bound to unfit them for responsible citizenship in a democracy." Other arguments alleging that a democratic levelling of social and class barriers occurred within the armed services and that maintenance of military forces would solve problems of unemployment seemed equally outrageous to the pacifist. He pointed to organizational hierarchy and Jim Crow policies in the armed forces, noting as well that, after military service, men returned to their own social strata. As for unemployment, Muste declared, "If we cannot put our unemployed to work it would be better to admit it and set about honestly solving the problem rather than rationalizing ourselves into the adoption of conscription by evading the real issue."

The question with which Muste wrestled most was that of whether or not to fight conscription by supporting the idea of a volunteer army. "I confess to having made use of such arguments," he wrote in 1947, when he had decided for good against them and advocated that pacifists adopt "a very clean-cut and unequivocal program" against the maintenance of military forces, "whether manned voluntarily or by draftees."[59]

Universal Military Training was rejected by Congress, which voted instead, in June 1948, to resume the Selective Service system for two more years. This outcome reflected conflicting pressures faced by the legislators. UMT had been opposed by "almost every major religious, labor, farm, and educational organization in the nation," yet public opinion polls repeatedly revealed "more than 60% in support of UMT." As his co-worker, John Swomley, had observed to Muste, the peace groups were failing to reach "the common man" on the draft issue. Muste was justified in predicting that once any draft legislation for peacetime was enacted, "pressures to extend it . . . will be terrific." But he also had reason to rejoice that "the cooperation in connection with the campaign against peace-time conscription has undoubtedly been more complete than has ever happened before in the history of the modern pacifist movement in this country."[60]

Similar cooperation was evident in the postwar undertaking to obtain amnesty for all violators of Selective Service regulations. Three months after the surrender of Japan, Muste, writing for the Executive Committee of the FOR, appealed to President Truman for amnesty for war resisters in prison and the release of those in CPS camps at a rate comparable to that of the demobilization of men in the armed services. In making the same appeal to Senator Robert Wagner, Muste pointed out that those conscientious objectors working at hospital and similar jobs would be taking employment away from returning veterans and others seeking work if they were not released.

The hope for speedy release of men from CPS camps (and the related desire for parole for imprisoned conscientious objectors) was never fulfilled. Instead, a glaring discrepancy between the proportion of men leaving military ranks and the much smaller proportion of war resisters being released plagued the peace movement to the end of the 1940s and gave added impetus to the call for a general amnesty.[61]

By 1946, a Committee for Amnesty had been established with Muste serving as "temporary chairman." Committee representatives picketed the White House and Justice Department, met with federal officials, and corresponded with President Truman and Attorney General Tom Clark.[62] Two days before Christmas the president appointed a three-man Amnesty Board whose deliberations lasted nearly a year. After a review of 15,805 cases the Board recommended and Truman issued pardons for 1,523 men. Muste issued a strong protest. Not only was the number of pardons miniscule but also those receiving them—according to Muste's review of the list—tended to be "draft violators who did not claim conscientious grounds" and a tiny minority of individuals who had "ecclesiastical connections or who had inherited a pacifist creed." Muste's appeal for "prompt further action" fell on deaf ears. Twenty-two years later a war resister would write, "President Truman did not declare an amnesty in the usual sense. . . . He simply pardoned a few people, about ten percent of the cases. The other 90 percent are still criminals today."[63]

Such callous treatment of war resisters by the government left pacifist organizations with sole responsibility for helping conscientious objectors make the transition into the postwar world. To this end Muste was instrumental in trying to raise funds for a pacifist equivalent of the G.I. Bill. A short-lived Committee on Educational Aid for men released from prison or CPS camps who wished to continue their education was begun, with Wallace Hamilton as executive secretary. Of more significance was the founding, in 1948, of the Central Committee for Conscientious Objectors, a counselling and legal referral service for any persons at any stage of draft resistance.[64]

Muste's unending involvement in the problems and struggles of conscientious objectors was a drain on time and energies that might have been spent on other issues. When John Haynes Holmes raised this matter, Muste recognized it as a "danger" but denied that he had succumbed to it. Nonetheless, his pursuit of other wartime issues was limited.

John Nevin Sayre, John Swomley, and FOR field workers on the west coast were much more attuned to the nature and implications of government evacuation of Japanese-Americans than was Muste.[65] He took the position that while it "was all wrong to evacuate the Japanese from their homes, it does not follow . . . that we insist that the only thing to do is to put them all back where they came from." He viewed the relocation camps as "a step in the direction of bringing the Japanese back into normal society." If he concerned himself with questions of restitution for damage and loss of property, the record does not show it. Indeed, he wrote, in October of 1944, that "after the initial mistake of evacuating the Japanese from the West Coast the WRA adopted a sound and liberal policy of relocation." After visiting the Tule Lake and Manzanar detention camps in July of 1943, he wrote a letter to Dillon Meyer of the War Relocation Authority commending the WRA staff for their humane "attitudes" and "methods."[66]

At least a few Japanese-Americans thought of themselves as pacifists and, according to Nevin Sayre, "in every center a small but active group of FOR residents were organized." The level of organization was generally that of unobtrusive study groups. However, when federal policy directly challenged pacifist rights of conscience, the FOR intervened. The requirement, in 1943, that all detention center residents complete "Form no. 126," which included questions as to whether the person signing the form was loyal to the United States and willing to serve in the nation's defense, occasioned a strong plea to Dillon Meyer from Muste that the WRA conform with Selective Service in making clear provisions for conscientious objection. Muste took a considerably stronger position against the attempt to remove a Japanese war resister, George K. Yamada, from a CPS camp in Oregon to an WRA internment center. He advised Yamada's fellow war resisters to strike if the young man was removed from their camp. However, when transfer to another CPS camp (outside the West Coast Military Zone) was effected, Muste acquiesced. The authorities' action, he said, was "evasive and tortuous," and it left him "somewhat uncomfortable and yet not profoundly disturbed." The impression persists that, in contrast to the intensity of Muste's involvement in the CPS controversy, his feelings were never comparably engaged by the struggle of interned Japanese-Americans.[67]

Other wartime, homefront concerns received varying measures of Muste's attention. Briefly, in the immediate aftermath of Pearl Harbor, he turned over in his mind the options open to pacifists should the United States mainland be bombed. He rejected any thought of pacifist involvement with civilian defense operations but was disposed toward pacifists acquiring first-aid instruction. On a few occasions Muste felt it important to address the question of sabotage, opposing it as a method for pacifists.[68] More than any other side issue, free speech attracted Muste's concern. He was quick to support the pacifist recipients of National Youth Administration grants in their protest against the tying of their appropriations to a loyalty oath. Reports out of Denver that an army commander had declared the churches of pacifist ministers "out of bounds" for enlisted men inspired a heated defense of "freedom of worship and Separation of Church and State" from Muste in the *Christian Century*. When representatives of the First Methodist Church of Evanston, Illinois, refused to permit an FOR conference in their building, he sent them a lengthy letter on freedom of conscience and the special responsibility of Christians for its defense. Throughout the war this vigilance continued, marginal in the amount of time consumed, but critical in the perceptions of a leader responsible for a minority of dissenters.[69]

The pacifist minority in the United States had little opportunity to affect the war in Europe and Asia. For the most part they could only keep as well informed as possible and exchange views among themselves on military and diplomatic events. John Nevin Sayre had built up and worked hard to sustain pacifist contacts in European countries, including those under Axis control. Through his efforts financial support from the FOR and other sources was channeled to churchmen struggling to help refugees and save Jews from extinction. Muste repeatedly memorialized the White House on the plight of European Jews, calling for expansion of U.S. immigrant quotas and stepped-up efforts to bring threatened refugees to this country. He warned President Roosevelt and other federal officials, in September 1943, that "unless something is done soon virtually none of the Jews native to Poland and Germany and who are still there or in other Axis-held territory will survive the winter." No reply was recorded.[70]

FOR protests against the practice of obliteration bombing received more attention. Muste vigorously promoted the pamphlet *Massacre by Bombing* by English author Vera Brittain. Twenty-eight leading religious figures lent their signatures to an accompanying plea for an end to such inhumanity. The campaign, in Muste's view, was an opportunity which the pacifist movement had not had since the beginning of the war "to reach non-pacifists with our message." The nonpacifist response was far from what Muste had hoped, however. Brittain reported that she and her pamphlet were "attacked in some 200 articles [in the U.S. press] which went all the way from expostulation to furious denunciation."[71] Among hostile critics was Bishop G. Bromley Oxnam, chairperson of the Federal Council of Churches, who denied that obliteration bombing had occurred and complained to Muste that "in these days the statements that you issue . . . assume that Americans sin above others; in fact, you indicate, are criminals above others and for some reason when you turn to the Germans and Japanese you find it hard to locate a word of condemnation." Muste was able to reply with some authority, since he had recently spoken with Visser 't Hooft of the World Council of Churches, who not only confirmed the bombings and quoted the president of the International Red Cross to the effect that in one night a quarter of a million people had died in Dresden, but also reported that "the effect of the Allied bombing is to cancel to quite an extent the German sense of guilt for the Nazi atrocities." Muste also reminded Oxnam that pacifists had opposed militarism, including the German and Japanese varieties, in times when "people who later went to war against Germany and Japan were in one way or another supporting these systems or at least not offering opposition to them." Finally, the FOR secretary cited the "good Biblical doctrine" that repentance of one's own sins should precede condemnation of the evils of others. When U.S. atomic bombs fell a short time later on cities in Japan, Oxnam publicly called for a suspension of "air attacks on the Japanese homeland."[72]

While trying to gain hearing and support for the pacifist views on Jewish refugees and obliteration bombing, Muste also carried on a steady campaign for the clarification of Allied war aims. He insisted that a credible promise of peace terms, formulated to insure "not a victory of one people over another but a victory for humanity," was a more potent weapon against fascist forces than any military device. Once hostilities had ended in Europe pacifists pleaded more vigorously that the Allies offer a concrete and humane peace to Japan. In the spring of 1945, the FOR circulated a petition to be forwarded to President Truman imploring him "to take the lead in a movement for a proclamation of specific terms of settlement with Japan." At the same time Muste was probing in Congress and the State Department for confirmation of and action upon rumors that peace feelers had been received from Japan. The State Department denied the rumors and was unreceptive to Muste's suggestion that, if the alleged peace offers were "phony," the United States should counter with genuine proposals for ending the war. Events of August 6 and 9, 1945, made any further discussion along these lines irrelevant.[73]

Muste was in Canada serving as a guest lecturer for the Alberta School of Religion in a backwood camping retreat in Calgary when rumors of the use of atomic weapons first reached him. An urgent ride to and purchase of newspapers from the nearest town verified events in Hiroshima and Nagasaki. Stunned, tempted to rush back to New York, but at a loss as to "what to do or say when I get there," Muste spent a few more days in Calgary. When he returned to the United States his thoughts centered on one terrible fact: "It was the United States, 'Christian America' which perpetrated the atrocities. It was we and not the Nazi swine as they were called, the Fascist devils, the Japanese militarists or the Russian communists." This fact, he recalled, set the direction for his work in the years that followed.

In the months immediately after the war, letters about international affairs from the FOR to Washington concentrated on appeals for relief for all victims of war, demilitarization activities such as the giving up of bases in Cuba, and the release of German prisoners of war in Europe.[74] At the same time, Muste gave increasing attention to proposals for the restructuring of international politics.

At the outset of World War II he had predicted the collapse of world order and advised fellow pacifists that their role in the uncertain future would either be as "islands of safety and sanity" in the midst of a new Dark Age, or as the forgers of a "mass instrumentality" by which the majority of humankind would be guided into a revolutionary pacifist order of life, with militarism, armed conflict, and exploitation relegated permanently to the past. In either case, Muste urged pacifists to work during the war for the trust and respect of the masses and for the spiritual and physical enhancement of their own move-ment. His strictures against careless alliances (as with Peace Now) stemmed in part from this outlook, as did suggestions he repeatedly offered to Fellowship groups that they seek ways of "organizing economic life now along lines that are consonant with pacifist philosophy and that give human beings bread and fellowship here and now." For Muste this meant increased pacifist involvement in farm and labor unions as well as experiments with cooperatives and " 'decen-tralist' enterprises."[75]

Peace-oriented research was another objective which Muste urged paci-fist groups to support. In writing the prospectus for a Pacifist Research Com-mission he warned that "pacifists will be ignored as dealers in abstract and impractical theories unless they demonstrate that they can give concrete answers to certain questions such as what substitutes they propose . . . for military force in a disorganized world." Out of the proposed commission grew the Pacifist Research Bureau, headed by attorney and legal scholar Harrop Freeman. The PRB had offices in Philadelphia and published a number of pamphlets on such topics as coercion in international affairs, peacetime con-scription, and the political theories of pacifism.[76]

Instead of falling apart as a result of mass fighting and bloodshed, the economic and political institutions of Europe and Asia experienced rearrange-ments, not of the revolutionary proportions envisioned by Muste, but along old-fashioned lines of power politics. The pacifist studiously followed the pro-cess of realignment. More often and earlier than most analysts of the time he saw behind the facade of Allied unity and foretold postwar tensions. Correctly, he sensed resentment of the United States' economic involvement in the war and predicted an international reaction against "Uncle Shylock." Brushing aside wartime propaganda extolling the virtues of America's Russian allies, Muste assumed an imminent Western-Soviet split and was highly critical of Soviet policies in Poland and the Soviet position taken at Yalta and other major Allied conferences. As occupying forces replaced fascist dictatorships in such countries as Greece, Italy, and Algeria, Muste pointed out how each victor na-tion was establishing its own sphere of influence, often accommodating local rightist forces in return for behind-the-scenes political and economic domi-nation.[77]

In the blueprint for a United Nations organization which emerged from the meeting at Dumbarton Oaks, Muste saw the gravest of mistakes. "The shape of the postwar world is being determined" at Dumbarton Oaks, he wrote, and in the name of peace the winners of World War II were, in his view, forging a military alliance that could only lead again to war. He noted that within the U.N. structure the Big Three (the U.S., Great Britain, and the Soviet Union) would dominate the Security Council while "practically every measure that could be conceived of would "limit the power of the General Assembly" (the only place where small nations would have a voice). Of telling significance, too, he observed, was the minimal attention paid to disarmament provi-sions.[78]

In the months between Dumbarton Oaks and the signing of the U.N. Charter in San Francisco, Muste worked to create an influential opposition to the U.N. proposal, concentrating his efforts on the Federal Council of Churches, where serious study of the matter had already begun. A conference in Cleveland in January 1945 of a Federal Council subcommittee headed by William E. Hocking evaluated the U.N. proposal. The evaluation was critical on grounds that coincided with Muste's critique and offered a list of substantial amendments to the Dumbarton Oaks plan. But the Hocking Commission ended with an appeal for Church support of the U.N. even if it was established without amendment. They argued that any form of united nations was better than chaos. This, Muste retorted, was tantamount to saying that the choices are between "chaos and chaos," when, in fact, the option of going back to the drawing board and creating a democratic and genuinely peace-oriented international body was still open. Among the few religious allies whom Muste found in the debate were seven Roman Catholic archbishops and three bishops who issued a statement on the eve of the San Francisco Conference declaring that "a sound world organization is not a Utopian dream" and calling for such an organization to replace the badly flawed plans from Dumbarton Oaks. Since, in Muste's view, "the Catholic Church as a political institution is one of the most dangerous elements" in the modern world, this stand by members of the Catholic hierarchy struck him as ironic in the extreme. He held it up before Hocking and others as a great rebuke and implored them to issue a Protestant statement as "straight-forward, dignified and clearly religious" as that of the Roman Catholics.[79]

The San Francisco Charter was signed without benefit of strong Protestant objections, in spite of Roman Catholic strictures and without reference to the incisive criticisms of A. J. Muste. In other ways the "essentials of peace," as he had identified them, were failing to materialize.[80] Against his hope for "no occupation of Axis territory" moved Allied occupying forces. In contrast to his opinion that "each nation should be left to deal with its own 'war criminals' " rose the Nuremburg Tribunal. The establishment of puppet regimes throughout Europe and Asia flew in the face of his conviction "that we shall have to deal with de facto governments and organs of the popular will as and where we find them." Muste's expectation that "revulsion against war will set in almost immediately" and that in an atomic age there could be no "basis left for the non-pacifist position" also went unfulfilled. Although for some scientists and advocates of world government the threat of atomic power became an issue, pacifist ranks did not swell with war-weary masses. For the most part atomic weapons heightened rather than removed the spirit of war.[81]

The course of World War II, then, was affected not at all by A. J. Muste. Immediate political results of the war bore little resemblance to his visions of a new Dark Age. Economic dislocation in Europe did tally with the destruction he predicted, but ways of remedying the problem never included the peace movement acting as "receiver of an exhausted and bankrupt world."

Yet, whenever he turned from generalized prophecy to specific observation, Muste hit the mark. His perceptions of the effect of war-making upon the Allied nations—while occasionally exaggerated when phrased as a vision of total fascist transformation—were essentially accurate. The victor nations did take on some of the worst characteristics of their enemies. The United States experienced increased militarization, as reflected in gargantuan growth of military bureaucracies, exorbitant defense budgets, and the establishment of permanent conscription. Dresden and Hiroshima became modern symbols of a lack of moral and humanitarian scruple that would carry over into later American wars. Civil liberties and free speech were eroded in the witch hunt atmosphere that gripped the country at the height of the Cold War.

Muste's understanding of the implications of the imperialism of the big powers was also sound. Their greed fueled the resentments and recurrent upheavals within "third world" countries as he repeatedly warned it would. Allied rivalries, especially between the United States and the Soviet Union, developed along lines that he had predicted. The general ineffectiveness of the United Nations in the face of one world crisis after another bore out his criticisms of that body. The degree to which power politics and nationalism have continually undermined efforts to achieve disarmament may still validate his predictions of universal catastrophe.[82]

However acute his observations of its causes and consequences, Muste's deepest personal involvement in World War II was in the internal affairs of the pacifist movement. This was a natural outgrowth of the meagre opportunities open for pacifists to exercise influence in a wider sphere. In addition, residual influences from the Trotskyist experiences of opportunism and schism were still at work within him. His strenuous defense of the FOR as an organization, his anxiety when younger war resisters failed to blend into their language of revolution a large enough dose of nonviolence, and his tempering of personal inclinations toward radicalism in deference to group strivings for consensus reveal the extent to which his values, perceptions, and priorities were still affected by traumas of the 1930s.

In the postwar era Muste would shake off these restraining forces from the past and edge away from wholehearted devotion to organizational forms of fellowship. The watershed was Hiroshima. In January 1945, Muste could still question the confidence of Evan Thomas in "the isolated individual witness." After August 1945, his guiding theme became "the individual conscience against the atomic bomb? Yes, there is no other way."[83]

The urgency engendered by atomic weapons directed Muste, still the Traveler, toward new terrain where he would make bold experiments with individual resistance and direct action.[84] He did not abdicate his role as mediator of internal disputes within pacifist ranks, nor cease trying to avoid factionalism, nor depart from a fundamental allegiance to religious pacifism. But a shift in priorities did occur. Alliances with non-religious pacifists grew stronger, and new organizations with a direct-action emphasis received his full support. His activities and objectives in the Cold War era took on a new dimension which he personally defined in the apt phrase, "Holy Disobedience."

Chapter VII

The Pacifist and
Civil Liberties

Although Muste sought a major social and economic transformation of modern society and often used the language of nonviolent revolution, he never challenged the constitutional foundations of the American political system. Indeed, he regularly invoked the United States Constitution as a source of his radical dissent from United States policies. The rights of conscience as guaranteed by the First Amendment were essential to the causes which he championed. Defense of those rights was an unavoidable and recurring part of his work.

In the years following World War II both historical developments and changes in his personal life encouraged Muste to sharpen his commitment to civil liberties and exercise it in bolder ways. United States use of the atomic bomb, production of the even more threatening hydrogen bomb, McCarthyite repression, and the war in Korea convinced Muste of the need for stepped-up protest. Restraints on his movement toward more drastic forms of civil disobedience would be minimized in the fifties by his retirement from the FOR and the death of Anna Muste.

In the summer of 1945, Muste began to write an autobiography and was anticipating, as the end of World War II approached, the kind of work schedule at the FOR which would leave him time for the contemplation and composition necessary to finish his life story. But the atomic obliteration of two Japanese cities in August abruptly changed his plans. "So far as writing is concerned," he later recalled, "[the atomic bomb] pushed the autobiography . . . in the background. The book which I was driven to write was one which dealt with Christian pacifism in the atomic age, published by Harper's in 1947, under the title, *Not by Might*." An impassioned "tract for the times," *Not by Might* was partly jeremiad, partly a critique of prevailing political and religious beliefs, and partly a guide for pacifist action.[1]

Fully in the thick of such action when the book was published, Muste became, a year later, one of the founders of a new organization, the Peacemakers. As the only group at that time to unequivocally advocate nonregistration for the draft, tax refusal, and civil disobedience,[2] Peacemakers drew its members largely from the Midwest and New York, organized them into cells, published a newsletter, and advocated grass-roots action directed against militarism and injustice. Muste helped to organize and oversee the Mt. Morris House cell in New York City and headed a research committee.[3] This involvement in Peacemakers was a departure from his practice of identifying the FOR as the sole most vital center of religious pacifism. Even more significantly, it indicated a change in his thinking about payment of federal income taxes.

In 1944, he answered an inquiry about whether pacifists should pay taxes by saying that "if the individual has a definite concrete leading" to refuse payment "he should obey the inner voice." For himself, Muste wrote, "I have not felt that way about taxes." He emphasized "the complicated character of modern life" which made it possible for the government to collect by levies against salaries, bank accounts, and personal property. Only individuals who were willing to endure poverty indefinitely could escape the long arm of the IRS, he observed. His conclusion was that tax refusal would be "effective for pacifists only if a very considerable number of people were prepared to engage in it."[4]

When Peacemakers established a Tax Refusal Committee, Muste apparently saw hope for recruiting a sufficient number of tax resisters. A memo drafted by his lawyer, Harrop Freeman, to the IRS in 1956 recorded that "in the year 1948 under Divine Guidance the taxpayer reached the conclusion that the payment of taxes for purposes of war . . . was contrary to his belief in nonparticipation in war." Muste's own statement on his failure to pay federal taxes for the years 1948 through 1952 emphasized weapons production as his chief motive: "I first took this stand," he declared, "when it became clear that the government would move from producing atomic bombs to the production of H-bombs."[5] After refusing to pay his 1948 taxes Muste adopted the practice of refusing even to file a return. Each year he issued a public statement and wrote a personal letter to IRS officials explaining his position. Typical of these statements was his letter to the Director of Internal Revenue in 1951 which he concluded by urging the director and his colleagues to "deal with this situation as persons and not merely officials who 'have no choice.' " As "supporting material" Muste enclosed copies of the Gospels and Thoreau's "Essay on Civil Disobedience."[6]

The federal government took Muste to court in March 1960, where Harrop Freeman defended his refusal to pay federal taxes as a probable constitutional right under the First Amendment and made a case for Muste's innocence of fraud, arguing that the defendant's motive stemmed entirely from his conscience and that he honestly sought to test the constitutionality of the tax law.[7]

A year later the court ruled against Muste on all counts except for dismissing the charges of fraud. Muste and Freeman put a positive construction on the outcome, regarding it as "an important legal precedent that fraud cannot be charged to people who openly and on conscientious grounds refuse to pay taxes."[8]

Muste could also take satisfaction in knowing that the federal treasury would never collect his back taxes. As Freeman's introductory statement to the court made clear, "Taxpayer has no funds. He has voluntarily lived for years at a subsistence level."[9] By 1961, Muste's income consisted of a small pension from the FOR, to which the government could not lay claim, since the fund from which it was drawn was based upon contributions of others (rather than on withholding from Muste's previous salary) and payments were legally defined as gifts. With no money to be seized and a favorable judgment regarding the charge of fraud, Muste's and Freeman's decision against taking the case to a higher court was undoubtedly sound. The judge, Craig S. Atkins, had touched the crux of the matter when he quoted from a Supreme Court judgment: "The power to tax is the one great power upon which the whole national fabric is based. It is as necessary to the existence and prosperity of a nation as is the air he breathes to a natural man." Muste made the same point from a different angle of vision: "The two decisive powers of government with respect to war are the power to conscript and the power to tax." Whatever else it may have done, his confrontation with the IRS had not visibly diminished the power to tax.[10]

Other Peacemakers who resisted that power (their total seems seldom to have reached more than 100 in any given year until the Vietnam era, when the numbers neared 400) were usually ignored by the U.S. Treasury Department, although a Peacemaker leaflet in the 1960s reported past instances where taxes had been removed from bank accounts and automobiles sold at public auction.[11]

Two tax refusers who faced government charges and suffered severe penalties were especially admired by Muste, and he involved himself personally in their cases. Chicago social worker and former track star Eroseanna ("Sis") Robinson had ceased filing statements of income in the early 1950s. In January 1960, she was sent to jail and told that she would be kept there until she filed a return. She began a fast. In February, she was formally sentenced to a year and a day. Her fast continued and the authorities began force-feeding. Muste and fellow Peacemakers, Marjorie and Robert Swann, appealed to the Justice Department on Robinson's behalf. In May, she was suddenly released. Save for demands for payment which periodically arrived in her mail, no further action was taken against her.[12]

The outcome of the even more dramatic tax protest by the Reverend Maurice McCrackin was far less favorable. Minister to an interracial congregation in Cincinnati, sponsored jointly by the Presbyterian and Episcopalian churches, the Presbyterian clergyman was well known as a man of strong convictions. Arrested for tax refusal in September of 1958, McCrackin would not cooperate in any way with the proceedings against him. He had to be carried to and from the courtroom and remained silent when addressed. This behavior, more than the issues, attracted widespread notice and stirred powerful feelings of antagonism and admiration among opponents and supporters.

The antagonists included District Judge John H. Druffel, who first imposed an indeterminate sentence upon him for contempt and then, after the tax trial (during which the judge described the FOR, to whom McCrackin had contributed in lieu of paying taxes, as "notorious" and as having "overwhelming Soviet Sympathies"), sentenced him to six months and a fine of $250. On top of these penalties the Presbytery of Cincinnati laid further punishment. In June 1962, McCrackin lost his pulpit and salary and was ousted from the manse where he lived.[13]

Muste supported a campaign to lift the sentence imposed by Judge Druffel and protested the actions of the Presbyterians. In the process his own appreciation of extreme noncooperation grew stronger. In contrast to the ambivalent note he had struck in defending such actions by World War II conscientious objectors, Muste was more forthright in interpreting McCrackin's deeds. He described Maurice McCrackin as "the very best of . . . all" the Peacemakers and added, "he comes very close to being a saint."[14]

Tax cases continued to engage Muste's attention in the 1960s. He supported the FOR staff in successfully resisting IRS efforts to revoke the tax-exempt status of that organization. As chairman of the Committee for Nonviolent Action he refused to cooperate with a federal garnishee of the wages of CNVA worker Neil Haworth. He retained membership on the Peacemaker's Tax Refusal Committee for the rest of his life.[15]

Just as atomic and hydrogen weaponry had inspired Muste to write *Not by Might* and to extend the range of his dissent to the point of income tax refusal, so the widespread postwar red scare, the peacetime draft, and the heating up of the Cold War in Korea prompted him to compose a minor pacifist classic which pushed the rationale for nonviolent protest to its furthest limits. *Of Holy Disobedience*, first published as a Pendle Hill pamphlet in 1952, was primarily concerned with identifying conscription as a taproot of war and with persuading the peace movement to adopt a thoroughgoing commitment to draft resistance and to the young men of service age who would bear the heaviest burdens of military refusal. But the implications of Muste's essay were wider still. *Of Holy Disobedience* brought war resisters face to face with the ultimate challenge and stark loneliness of their vocation: "The human being, the child of God, must assert his humanity and his sonship again. . . . He must understand that this naked human being is the one *real* thing in the face of the mechanics and the mechanized institutions of our age. He, by the grace of God, is the seed of all the human life there will be on earth in the future, though he may have to die to make that possible."[16]

Muste's own call to the path of Holy Disobedience was soon affected by changes in his personal life. Throughout 1952, the Muste family was beset by health crises. Muste was hospitalized for several weeks in the spring for a prostate operation, the near-invalid condition of Anna Muste continued, and their son, who had contracted polio while living in Mexico, returned home to recuperate.[17] By the time Muste recovered and John Muste's condition improved, the elder Mustes were facing a major transition. At the age of sixty-eight it was time for Muste, according to FOR guidelines, to turn over his administrative responsibilities. In October 1953, John Swomley became executive secretary and Muste was designated secretary emeritus. He was free to participate in all

FOR programs, was named staff representative for the Fellowship in New York City, provided with a secretary, and guaranteed a small pension for the rest of his life.[18]

Eleven months after the new arrangement was struck Anna Muste died. Her heart condition had taken a serious turn in 1944. Her husband put the best light on it which he could. "Anne . . . has to live at an exceedingly moderate pace," he explained to a friend in the spring of 1945. "When she does that she is well and cheerful pretty much of the time." Yet he recognized the gravity of her illness and worried about "taking long trips and trips which take me a good while to get back in [an] emergency."[19] He did not drastically restrain his activities, however. In 1947 and again in 1954, he travelled to Europe, leaving the care of Anna to their daughter Nancy Baker, into whose home at Thornwood, New York, the Mustes had moved in 1954. But anxiety about his wife's condition weighed upon him. While on the second European trip he learned from John Swomley that the Internal Revenue Service was threatening to issue "a warrant of distraint" against his pension because of his refusal to pay income taxes. Clearly fearful that Anna Muste would be upset by this, Muste instructed Swomley that she was not to be told and requested that an advance on his pension payments be transmitted to her before the IRS would have a chance to act. "Just tell [her] I'll explain . . . on my return," he wrote. Upon arrival in New York he forewent a trip directly to his office in the city to pick up his mail because such a trip would be out of the way, "and I know Anne will come to meet me if she possibly can and I don't want to lengthen the trip for her."[20]

When she died in September 1954, Muste outwardly bore the loss with composure. His younger daughter, Connie Hamilton, recalled: "I know of course that he felt it when Mother died, but he showed his feelings so little that his behavior fitted in with my older idea that he could handle such things with the ease and dexterity of a magician." While a case could be made that Muste's habit of always putting his principles and his work before the physical well-being of his family had, at the least, exacerbated the breakdown of Anna Muste's health, there is no doubt of their great love for one another, and no reason for Muste not to have taken comfort from a belief to which he clung long after her death—that "the doctors always said she must have been loved very much to have survived as long as she did."[21]

All the most important ties of emotional dependence in Muste's life were now broken. His parents—toward whom he had remained surprisingly deferential in small ways (taking care never to incur his mother's displeasure by smoking in her presence and avoiding upsetting his father by concealing from him Anna's and his habit of playing gin rummy)—had died during World War II. Now Anna was gone, his children were grown and on their own, and his place in the FOR—the one other object of long-term and intense devotion in his life—had changed.[22] He was, if not shaken, at least a little wounded, as a tender passage in his autobiography later showed. Harking back to an earlier period when "I was not yet sixty," he observed that "I did not know in my bones that people reach retirement age and younger men take their place. I did not know either that, when this happens, you just keep on. I did not know in my bones that a being you love and have loved for years on end can die, and that a home can cease to be. I did not know in my bones that it is possible—just possible—that some day one's own vital powers may fail. Such things are all just talk until they are experienced."[23] Family and co-workers sensed that Muste was lonely after Anna Muste died. He continued to live for a time with the Bakers, but when John Baker's career took them abroad for awhile, Muste began to live alone in New York City, as he would for the rest of his life, choosing to remain close to the offices and meeting places where he worked. He first took a place in an apartment hotel on Riverside Drive and later (in the mid-sixties) moved to an apartment in the home of co-workers Robert and Joyce Gilmore on Twelfth Street. His longing for the companionship which his marriage had provided surfaced when he considered remarriage to a close family friend. While this did not work out, he took care to stay in close touch with his children, to arrange time for visiting their homes and enjoying his grandchildren.[24] But, most of all, deepening involvement in radical peace action kept him related to an "extended family" of like-minded workers whose admiration and affection were as important for him as his clear thinking about and firm hold on the principles of pacifism and civil disobedience were for them.

In practicing and supporting others in civil disobedience Muste saw himself as claiming rights of conscience guaranteed by the First Amendment. He pressed the same claim for other forms of dissent, many distinctly contrary to his personal political views. In defending allies and opponents alike in their right to question establishment policies and voice anti-establishment alternatives, Muste assumed that civil liberties required a climate of respect and toleration in which all points of view could be freely put forward and as freely criticized.

The anti-communist mania which plagued postwar America put Muste's insistence on untrammeled speech and thought to many tests. He recorded for *Fellowship* readers in 1948 the "ominous" symptoms of spreading hysteria: riots in upstate New York following a concert by Paul Robeson; loyalty-oath requirements for teachers, college professors, and other civil servants; prosecution of Communist Party members under the Smith Act; and deportation of "politically suspect" immigrants. These measures, he wrote, would not phase dedicated communists, who could easily evade them. But, he warned, the boomerang effect of such repression would seriously damage American society by reducing democracy to the very "illusion" and "farce" that the communists claimed it already was.

Muste's admonitions were directed toward government-condoned witch hunters and right wing vigilantes but were not reserved for them. In his opinion, the American Left was culpable too. For example Stalinists who were pained when the Smith Act was used against them, but who supported the prosecution of Trotskyists under the same law, contributed very little to the cause of toleration. Muste saw that failure to control the hysteria of anti-communism was rooted not just in the United States–Soviet antagonisms, but in the fragmentation of the left-Progressive forces which had traditionally functioned as guardians of free speech and which were now both victims and perpetrators of repression. The tendency which developed in the Truman era for Democratic "New Deal Liberals" to identify with harsh anti-communist policies, the anti-communist purges which occurred in major labor unions in the same era, and the universal acceptance of red-baiting as a legitimate political tactic among the non-communist left contributed to the climate of intolerance in the 1950s just as surely as did such right wing forces as the House Committee on Un-American Activities, the Senate Subcommittee on Internal Security, or the Federal Bureau of Investigation.[25] Muste advised fellow pacifists to be resolute in resisting all repression and hysteria, even though such resistance might entail imprisonment, as it already had for violators of the Ober loyalty oath law in Maryland.[26] Yet while he encouraged pacifist support of individuals who fell victim to such laws, he emphasized that when such victims were communists, defense of their rights need not muffle criticism of their philosophy.

That Soviet communism and the international communist movement must undergo profound humanizing transformation was as firm a belief in Muste's mind as was his conviction that the Western capitalist nations must be brought to "repentance." A series of events in the mid-fifties—Nikita Khrushchev's denunciation of Stalin, the breakaway of certain "satellite countries" from the Soviet Union, signs of a "thaw" in relations between the United States and Russia, the growth of dissent within the Communist Party-U.S.A. against the "official line"—encouraged Muste to believe that totalitarian rule might begin to give way to democratic socialism in Russia if "the right kind of democratic socialist support from without" could be marshalled. If the "split between Socialists and Communists could be healed" and a "united world socialist and labor movement" emerged, he believed that a new world order might take shape which would be free of the bitterness and anxieties of the Cold War and in which the rights of conscience would again be cherished.[27]

In May 1956, he persuaded the FOR to sponsor a public exchange among various types of socialists and pacifists at Carnegie Hall. Five months later he was instrumental in promoting a similar meeting in Chicago, where a four-man panel—a trade unionist, a socialist, a member of the Communist Party, and Muste—explored the question of "What Lies Ahead for the American Left?" That meeting attracted 700 people and was, he estimated, "by far the largest . . . meeting in which unorthodox views were expressed in a good many years." He was further cheered by the fact that "the meeting went off without interference or untoward incident, which meant registering a gain for civil liberties."[28]

In December 1956, Muste invited thirty-five men and women from all parts of the Left-spectrum to a meeting in New York to explore the pressing political issues of the day and to consider a "tentative structure" for promoting such discussion on a wider basis.[29] Out of these experiences emerged the American Forum for Socialist Education, which would, in the years 1957 and 1958, hold numerous open meetings in various cities on issues of interest to radical social activists.

Before the Forum ever held a meeting, however, its chief promoter found himself under attack by the FBI. Moved by the same spirit that inspired the American Forum, Muste had arranged for impartial, non-communist observers, including himself, to attend a convention of the Communist Party-U.S.A. in February 1957. "That the security of this country is actually threatened by anything that may have happened at the convention of the drastically weakened CP is an idea which it is not possible to take seriously," the observers concluded.

But J. Edgar Hoover disagreed, and shortly after the CP convention he issued the report in which Muste was described as having "long fronted for Communists." When the report was quoted in the *New York Post*, Muste sent Hoover a detailed reply, emphasizing his long history of "analyzing and exposing the dangers and fraudulent character of united fronts." An aide in Hoover's office reported that a "barrage of mail" was received in Muste's defense, but "we frankly concluded that no purpose would be served in acknowledging Muste's letter." On his side, Muste saw no purpose in being deterred by Hoover. "In insisting that all views should be publicly heard I am true to one of the most basic of American traditions," he told the FBI director.[30]

The American Forum, which held its first meeting in May 1957, was able to survive for only two years. From the outset the new undertaking was beset by the very intolerance which it was, in part, designed to erase. The Forum was not only investigated by the Senate Internal Security Committee and attacked by the press (a particularly virulent broadside was published against it in the *Saturday Evening Post*),[31] but it was also denounced by some elements of the Left. Providing a platform from which communists could speak and including a communist on the National Committee of the Forum provoked strong criticism from certain socialists. Muste viewed their reactions as far more damaging than the witch hunt tactics of federal and media agents.[32]

In retrospect, however, labor activist Sidney Lens, who worked closely with Muste in establishing the Forum, did not recall anti-communism as a major problem. He believed that the Forum foundered because it did not attract enough "third camp" figures (radicals who identified with neither the Soviets nor their red-baiting opposition), and because the Communist Party of the United States did not undergo the transformation which Muste had hoped would occur when some CP members, led by John Gates, had begun to challenge party dogma and old-line leadership. Instead of wresting control from the leadership, however, Gates and others like him simply left the Party. Disintegration, rather than regroupment and revitalization, had taken place.[33]

Two other weaknesses in the Forum undertaking may have contributed to its demise. Muste entertained the hope that the Forum would eventually have a full-time organizer (preferably Sidney Lens), who would provide the man-hours and persistence required to bring longtime foes to really communicate with one another. But this never happened. Also, Muste never stated the purposes of the Forum well enough for them to be easily understood by observers. The gap between the long-range objective of "regrouping" and the immediate goal of initiating dialogue caused considerable confusion. Not only were his descriptions of goals vague but also such descriptions usually failed to emphasize the international context in which he had originally conceived the Forum.[34]

The American Forum had represented Muste's hope that, after twenty years of bloodletting and schism, forces of the Left could reunify and resume their struggle for a new world order, and that progressive forces in America could show the way. By 1959, however, he had to report that the Forum had fallen into a state of "suspended animation." He did not mask his disappointment, describing the Left as "people who are holding their heads in bewilderment and outrage and who are fumbling for a clue to guide them out of the dark tunnel in which they find themselves. I do not for a moment suggest," he continued, "that this does not apply to myself."[35]

While the American Forum drew special attention to Muste's concern with freedom of speech and political dialogue, he was always ready to struggle for the cause of civil liberties. His own rights of expression were recurrently subject to attack. Mention of his name in hearings of the House Committee on Un-American Activities during the Seventy-fifth Congress in 1942 had led to great embarrassment in Baptist circles when Muste was invited to address the Northern Baptist Convention in 1942, only to have the invitation rescinded when supporters of HUAC in the fundamentalist wing of the denomination threatened a floor fight over Muste's presence.[36] Hoover's "communist fronter" label trailed the pacifist through the rest of his life. Wherever the charge popped up a Muste fan would usually rise to answer it. "Muste," wrote Kenneth Rexroth in the *San Francisco Examiner*, "is one of the oldest anti-Communist radicals in America. . . . I could put together a book of clippings the size of a Britannica volume of nothing but Stalinist abuse and vituperation directed at poor Muste."[37]

The alleged communist fronter was largely unruffled by these episodes. As John Nevin Sayre noted, "Muste can stand it because his record in opposing the Stalinist and Communist line . . . is so very well known and his livelihood not affected."[38] The same could not be said for many victims of anti-communist slander, including individuals subpoenaed by the Senate Subcommittee on Internal Security and the House Committee on Un-American Activities. Muste supported political opposition to both Senate and House investigating committees but was generally careful about joining opposition groups with united front overtones.[39]

When the HUAC subpoenaed members of the Women Strike for Peace in 1962, Muste appealed to liberal educators and opinion leaders to protest

what he viewed as an "inquisition" and an "attack on the whole peace movement and on the cause of *Peace* itself." He warned that "if the label 'Communist' and the label 'peace' become synonyms in the thinking of the American
people, . . . chances for a real peace" would be jeopardized if not destroyed.[40]

No episode had done more to reinforce Muste's point of view on this
matter than the controversy which had swirled about the National Committee
for a Sane Nuclear Policy (SANE) when its reputation was publicly disfigured
by Senator Thomas Dodd, vice-chairman of the Senate subcommittee on
Internal Security. SANE dated from June 1957, when a rough tripartite division
of labor within the peace movement had taken shape. While established peace
organizations continued their programs, two new, ad hoc, groups were begun—
the Committee for Nonviolent Action (CNVA), to which radical pacifists interested in direct action and civil disobedience rallied, and SANE, whose emphasis on nuclear weapons testing attracted liberals and moderate pacifists who
preferred traditional methods for educating public opinion to the methods of
civil disobedience.

Muste was a participant in the meetings which led up to this new align-
ment but he did not play the major role that might have been expected. His
efforts to create lines of communication between the communist and the non-
communist Left not only were absorbing much of his energy at that time but
also undermined his credibility among some peace people. Once the ad hoc
groups took shape Muste worked much more closely with CNVA than SANE,
though he was a member of the board of the New York SANE chapter and was
featured with Norman Thomas at a major SANE rally in New York City in
1959.[41]

SANE's troubles began in the spring of 1960, when Senator Thomas
Dodd informed the group's leader, Norman Cousins, that one of the organizers
of a forthcoming rally, Henry Abrams, was a member of the Communist Party.
Dodd agreed to Cousins' request that the allegation not be made public until
after the rally. According to a later statement by Dodd on the floor of the
Senate, Cousins "asked for the subcommittee's assistance in ridding the Committee for a Sane Nuclear Policy of whatever communist infiltration does exist." Cousins, continued Dodd, "offered to open the books of the organization to
the Subcommittee and to cooperate with it in every way." Norman Cousins
denied ever having made such an offer and the executive board of SANE replied
to the Dodd investigation by asserting that "as a matter of democratic principle
and practice we resent the intrusion of a Congressional Committee into the
affairs of an organization which during its entire life has acted only in accordance with its declared principles." At the same time the leaders of SANE instituted measures designed to rid their organization of communists.[42]

Dodd's action drew a predictable protest from Muste; SANE's acquiescence to Dodd evoked a more intense response. Muste summarized Dodd's
move as "an obvious attempt . . . to weaken peace organizations by scaring
people from joining them." Instead of bowing to that policy, Muste argued,
SANE should have denounced Dodd's interference at the outset and defended
Abrams against congressional investigation.

Muste wrote Cousins, in September 1960, "that the SANE Board must immediately break off its relations with the Eastland-Dodd Committee. If it fails to do so," he warned, "I shall not be able to maintain silence." His warning was based on some exaggeration of the extent to which Cousins and Dodd had collaborated, and it was also out of sequence, since he had already (three months earlier) written an article for the small newsletter *Survival* in which he con-demned SANE's "grave mistake." At the same time, in private correspondence, Muste uncharacteristically succumbed to passing along gossip which impugned Cousins' motives and could not be substantiated. Nonetheless his overall as-sessment of the SANE-Dodd situation was well argued. In subsequent articles in *Liberation* and in correspondence with various individuals Muste laid out his position.[43]

While reiterating his personal opposition to totalitarianism and his firm resistance to united front cooperation with communist groups, he was most anxious to press a distinction between "the Dodd problem" and questions about the objectives of the Communist Party. Cousins and his defenders inevitably used the latter as an explanation for SANE's handling of the former. Muste urged on them the view that "HUAC and the Senate Committee are a much more appalling danger to a sound U.S. peace movement then [sic] what com-munists in this country at this time are able to do to such a movement."

The SANE-Dodd affair, following on the heels of Muste's efforts on behalf of the American Forum, also brought to the surface his very personal concern with opening channels of political expression for genuine ex-communists. Some of the old hope that he had expressed in the years imme-diately following his own turnabout—that widespread conversions from com-munism to other philosophies more congenial to pacifism would provide fresh troops for peace—was evident again. "There are a good many 'Leftists' who are not looking for another 'front' but for a genuine anti-war movement in which they would like to work hard," he declared, adding that such "people ought not to be branded forever, should have a fair chance to prove themselves and be judged on their actual conduct."[44]

Muste's criticisms of SANE and Cousins elicited a mixed response. In a conversation some nineteen years later Norman Cousins complained that, at the time, Muste had not tried to talk with him personally about the problem, had drawn unwarranted conclusions, and had neglected to appreciate the im-portance of Dodd's having honored his promise not to release the names of SANE members which the Committee had wanted to investigate, thereby pro-tecting many innocent individuals from being publicly pilloried.[45] On the ques-tion of alleged communist influence in the peace movement, an old and dear friend, Tracy Mygatt, wrote Muste of her puzzlement after reading his articles in *Liberation*: "The curious thing to me is that it was in part some of your very own words . . . some years ago that have made me anxious to keep myself from any cooperation with communists." Another valued comrade, John Swomley, wrote Muste of his impression that "you were leading some kind of attack, that a new movement was in the offing that was to some degree CP influenced and that you had not yet decided whether to go along with it." Even a colleague close at hand, Alfred Hassler, who attended the same meeting Muste had attended, in December 1960, of opponents to and exiles from SANE (including Abrams, socialist author Corliss Lamont and scientist Linus Pauling), was unsure of whither Muste was tending. "I did have the impression," Hassler wrote Muste, "that you were keeping the door open to the possibility of support for the kind of organization that was being discussed there" and that would, in Hassler's view, only intensify internal peace movement rivalries.

As in debates over the American Forum, Muste was confronted with a need to reconcile short-term tactics with long-range goals. He told Hassler that he did not mean to support a new organization, but "I did and do want the door left open for discussion with these people about fundamental questions."[46]

To avoid united fronts *and* to shun collaboration with investigators representing cold war values, to support sound programs for peace wherever they might originate, to judge the actions of individual peace workers by present conduct rather than past mistakes, "to be as canny as possible in tactical matters [but] not to cut off communication"—these were Muste's prescriptions to the peace movement for maintaining internal soundness and warding off external attacks. The dose was too big for many fellow peace workers to swallow, including the leadership of SANE. But Muste's view carried the day with most local SANE chapters and with the young people and students who had contributed such large numbers to SANE rallies and demonstrations, many of whom would later help to build a non-exclusionary, coalition movement against the war in Vietnam.[47]

Peace groups and anti-war activists were only one category of dissenters that aroused the interest of congressional investigating committees. Non-pacifist dissenters were equally if not more subject to attack. In whatever ways seemed open to him, Muste rose to their defense.

When, in 1953, Julius and Ethel Rosenberg were tried, convicted, and sentenced to death on charges of spying and passing atomic information to the Soviet Union, the International Committee to Secure Justice in the Rosenberg Case was formed in an effort to save their lives. The FOR, with Muste at its head, remained aloof from the Committee because of its communist overtones. This position, while politically prudent, cut pacifists off from first-hand familiarity with the case and from a full sense of the patent injustices which had occurred in the Rosenberg trials. Consequently the FOR response was framed in terms that history would show to be unduly respectful of the judicial system and the authorities that sent the couple to their deaths.

A petition to President Truman in December of 1952 was circulated by the FOR and received 157 signatures. The petitioners stated their assumption that the trial had been fair, carefully dissociated themselves from any sympathy with the actions charged against the accused, and based their case for clemency on general opposition to the death penalty. They focused on the special unfairness of its imposition in a case where other defendants, and defendants in related cases (for example, Klaus Fuchs), received much lighter punishments, and a desire that the United States avoid emulation of totalitarian ruthlessness toward those regarded as enemies of the state.[48]

Seven years after the accused couple died in the gas chamber of Sing Sing Prison, a manuscript raising, in Muste's words, "the most serious questions" about the Rosenberg case was submitted by author Irwin Edelman to *Liberation*, whose editorial board included Muste. Muste sent summaries of Edelman's work to Morris Rubin at *Progressive* magazine, Sidney Lens, and Norman Thomas, suggesting that "maybe the things Edelman brings out ought to be made public." However, the readers to whom Muste sent the manuscript, as well as others on the *Liberation* board, found it to be uneven, convincing in some places, highly questionable in others. Edelman's past associations with the International Committee also called his reliability into question for Muste. The board decided against using Edelman's material. The "most serious questions" which Edelman raised would re-emerge in the 1960s, brought to attention by a new generation of activists, including Michael and Robert Meeropol, who had been only ten and six years old, respectively, when their parents were executed.[49]

The dual tugs of caution and conscience which Muste felt regarding the Rosenberg case were present also in his response to the actions of four Puerto Rican nationalists who gunned down five congressmen in the House of Representatives on March 1, 1954. American pacifists had shown serious interest in the Puerto Rican struggle for independence. A Peacemaker team had travelled to the island in 1951 to advocate nonresistance as a means toward liberation. Longtime Peacemaker Ruth Reynolds headed the American League for the Independence of Puerto Rico and was imprisoned by Puerto Rican authorities for her support of nationalist leader Pedro Albizu Campos. At one time Campos had been seen in American peace circles as "the Gandhi of Puerto Rico," but by 1954, Muste reported that Don Pedro had frankly "dismissed non-violence as impractical in the Puerto Rican situation."[50]

After the Washington shootings and the arrest of the assailants, Muste organized a small committee to disseminate information about the Puerto Rican struggle against U.S. colonialism, and to advocate "as good a defence as our legal system can provide" for the four terrorists. Muste admitted that "there is something peculiarly shocking and horrible about the kind of random attack" that had occurred in the Congress (and earlier, in 1950, when an attempt on the life of Harry Truman had resulted in the deaths of a U.S. guard and a Puerto Rican gunman). But, while condemning such violence, he urged individuals to address its causes, political repression and economic exploitation. The Puerto Rican yearning for independence, Muste argued, was broad-based, authentic, and reflected "heroism, commitment to an ideal and capacity for sacrifice" which Americans must appreciate.

Several years later Muste joined in appeals for clemency for the imprisoned Puerto Ricans. To commute their sentences, he reasoned, would be a "humanitarian act" and also an affirmative gesture by the United States which would be welcomed by peoples throughout Latin America who identify with the Puerto Rican struggle for independence.[51]

Muste also spearheaded a petition on behalf of eleven U.S. communists who had been convicted in 1949 of violating the Smith Act provision against advocating "the overthrow and destruction of the government." Signed by Eleanor Roosevelt, Norman Thomas, and others, the petition asked that amnesty be granted to the eleven persons already in jail and that further prosecutions be suspended pending Supreme Court review of the law. Although that review upheld the Act, subsequent decisions modified the effect of the law by distinguishing between statements and overt acts and extended First Amendment protection to statements. While some persons indicted under the original act had won dismissals by 1958, seven accused communists faced a retrial in Denver and two others, Gilbert Green and Henry Winston, remained in jail. Muste led campaigns for the freedom of all these individuals.[52]

By 1962 the Smith Act had become a dead letter and its victims were left at least the freedom to try to piece together and carry on with what was left of their personal lives. Morton Sobell, another casualty of anti-communist zeal, and for whose liberty Muste worked, was still in jail at Muste's death. A single witness in the trials of Julius and Ethel Rosenberg had linked Sobell to the treason with which they were associated and no other person testified against him. On his lawyer's advice, Sobell declined to testify on his own behalf. The trial judge, after noting that "evidence in the case did not point to any activity on your part in connection with the atomic bomb project," sentenced Sobell to thirty years.

Muste shared the view of the sizeable group of persons who appealed to President John F. Kennedy for amnesty in this case that the punishment was out of all proportion to the alleged crime of espionage, that, by 1961, Sobell had served more than a long enough sentence, and that the evidence adduced against him was questionable in many respects.[53]

In the last months of his life, Muste sallied forth into other controversies on behalf of civil liberties. In March 1966, he posted a letter to the Union of Soviet Writers protesting the recent trials and prison sentencings of dissident authors Yuri Daniel and Andrei Sinyavski. Signed by forty American writers and peace workers, the letter was written, Muste said in his covering statement, "in a spirit of goodwill and not of carping criticism." He added that "the signers are without exception persons who desire good relations between your country and ours and who have contended against McCarthyism . . . in this country."[54] As if to underscore his point Muste, in that same month, departed from his usual caution toward united front activities and his longstanding refusal to participate in electoral politics to become involved in Herbert Aptheker's campaign to be included on the ballot as a candidate in the 1966 congressional elections, running from the Twelfth District of New York. The well-known Marxist historian made no secret of his membership in the Communist Party and this was precisely why it was possible and necessary, Muste explained, to give Aptheker public backing. Anti-communism was still afoot, critics of the war in Vietnam were being branded as reds, and ugly attacks on peace organizations and individuals were occurring. In such times it seemed to Muste that "the right of the CP and of Communists to function in American political life" and the right of the Vietnamese people to function without U.S. military intervention were related and undeniable imperatives which he was obligated to champion.[55]

Muste's position suggested the strain which the war in Southeast Asia placed on him and the nonviolent movement. From a distance it would be possible to wonder about the advisability of this close identification of nonviolent anti-war objectives with defense of communist individuals and regimes. But Muste's commitment to civil liberties, freedom of speech, and self-determination for all people could not be properly served by statements of principle from the sidelines. He always found it necessary, whatever the risks, to stand directly with those whose freedom was threatened or denied.

Chapter VIII

The Pacifist and Civil Rights

The same consistency which characterized Muste's record on civil liberties is found as well in his life-long commitment to civil rights and to racial equality for Americans of African and other non-European origins. Resistance to union discrimination against Negroes was a central feature of Musteism in the thirties.[1] During World War II he supported the struggle of conscientious objectors to end segregation in federal prisons and civilian public service camps. By the end of that war he had clarified his own convictions to the point of publicly advocating far-reaching action and had begun to view the FOR as an instrument for initiating and guiding such action. He came to believe that America had reached one of those "periods in history when forces that have been operating for a long time, and injustices and inequities which have gone uncorrected, suddenly come to a head." At such times, he noted, "the pace of history is . . . stepped up. God no longer permits us to delay." He admonished whites who feared racial violence that "postponement of change simply makes it certain that a greater harvest of violence is stored up." Personally he admitted to having "on a good many occasions in the South . . . conformed to Jim Crow practices. Whenever I have done so," he said, " . . . I feel that if I really saw the situation as a whole, including what it means for the Negroes and for people of color throughout the world, it would be impossible for me to conform." After describing token gestures of protest that he had made, such as entering a Jim Crow train car and voicing disapproval before acquiescing in being sent back to the "White" section, he concluded, "I feel pretty certain that it will not be possible for me in the future to content myself with such measures."[2]

In 1943, the FOR published a Muste pamphlet titled *What the Bible Teaches about Freedom*; the first edition included the subtitle, *A Message to the Negro Churches*. Writing in sermon form, Muste repeated certain biblical stories, adding interpretative flourishes. He wrote of Moses as the leader of a mass movement who organized his enslaved people into "Bricklayers Union Number One" and then led them, with great travail, out of bondage.

In another Old Testament story, that of the priest Ezra, who, centuries after Moses, led a small group of Jewish exiles back to their homeland, Muste found an instructive example of the combined power of faith and nonviolence, for Ezra resisted the temptation to ask for armed protection. The central protagonist of Muste's pamphlet was Jesus, who lived in an age of terror and dictatorship that bore many resemblances, as Muste drew them, to the twentieth century. Jesus resisted the evils of his time by active nonviolence and by exemplifying, through his "capacity to suffer unto death, . . . the real power that makes human life possible." At some length Muste expounded on Jesus' rebuke of the "good and respectable" pharisees.

To the good and respectable reader of *What the Bible Teaches*, Muste emphasized that "in Christian teaching and in democratic concepts there is *no moral basis for Jim Crow.* . . . The attitude of the Christians and of Christian people, North and South, smells of the same hypocrisy that Jesus was constantly exposing in his contemporaries." Toward the end of his essay Muste proposed that black people, particularly the leadership and membership of black churches, take the initiative in nonviolent resistance to segregation. Black Americans, he advised, must "find ways to keep consciences in those who impose discrimination on Negroes, awake and hurt, with the hurt that heals in the end because it makes the oppressor whole and unites him with those he has injured."[3]

Black reaction to the sermon was favorable. Muste reported that he had given "the substance of it in a dozen addresses, before audiences containing both Whites and Negroes. . . . In each instance," he recalled, "publication was strongly urged." After publication the pamphlet was reportedly distributed by the NAACP, Negro women's groups, and the March On Washington Movement.[4] Not all white reaction was so positive. The Executive Committee of the Nashville FOR saw the pamphlet as both "an incitement to conduct that will lead to violence" and as a move by Muste to foist responsibility for a nonviolent direct action campaign on the national FOR without consent of the membership.

Although they drew inferences from Muste's piece that were not supportable, the Nashville dissenters were quite right that *What the Bible Teaches* stressed the idea of resistance more emphatically than the linking of such resistance to nonviolence. Although Muste was troubled by the charge that he was trying to " 'put over' the non-violent direct action technique" on the membership of the FOR, he was in fact pointing the organization toward major involvement in the struggle for equality.[5]

By 1942, the concept of a mass movement for the liberation of Negro Americans had gripped the imagination of key persons in and around the American peace movement. Conscientious objectors, inspired by their experiences and some real achievements in changing racial policies of the federal prison system, and by a growing awareness of how intertwined were war, racial oppression, and other injustices, began to articulate a philosophy of far-reaching social revolution. The example of the Gandhian movement in India counted heavily with them, as it did with other individuals who were moving from such diverse orientations as the Methodist youth movement and the Young Communist League toward the concept of dynamic, disciplined, pacifist action.

In the FOR Muste encouraged programs that would speak to this band of rising revolutionaries and took pride in the claim that the Fellowship "has been by far the most important channel for . . . disseminating information about and popularizing the ideas of nonviolent direct action."[6] Shortly after Muste became executive secretary, the FOR opened a southern office. In 1942, an FOR Department of Race Relations was established and several members of the staff began to organize around the issue of racial equality.[7]

Most crucial to the future of nonviolent civil rights protest were staff persons James Farmer, George Houser, and Bayard Rustin. Farmer and Houser had worked in the Methodist student movement during the 1930s. In 1941, Farmer received a Bachelor of Divinity degree from Howard University and then rejected ordination because he could not "honestly preach the Gospel of Christ in a church that practiced discrimination." Houser's studies at Union Theological Seminary were interrupted by imprisonment when he refused to register for the draft. Following a year at Danbury Penitentiary he resumed his religious program at the University of Chicago. Both men worked in the Chicago office of the FOR. Rustin was a Quaker by upbringing whose inner leadings had taken him into and out of the Young Communist League. Under the combined influences of the crisis of the war and the counsel of A. J. Muste, Rustin became a pacifist in 1941 and spent twenty-eight months in prison for resisting the draft. A fourth figure whose influence was notable but short-lived was Jay Holmes Smith, who, after the transition from being a street gang worker to becoming a religious pacifist, had worked with Gandhi in India and was, in 1941, the founder of an interracial Gandhian Ashram (cooperative) in Harlem. Smith saw it as a center from which trained pacifist volunteers would launch direct action campaigns for civil rights, civil liberties, and economic justice.[8] But, as historian Lawrence Wittner has written, "Smith's expectations far exceeded his leadership qualities" and the Harlem Ashram "came to naught."[9]

The FOR became involved in another and more dramatic false start in 1942, when A. Philip Randolph signaled his interest in Gandhian techniques as they might be applied to his March on Washington Movement (MOWM). Randolph had secured a striking victory in 1941, when the threat of a MOWM mass demonstration in the nation's capital prodded President Roosevelt to issue his executive order creating a Fair Employment Practices Committee. Bayard Rustin, who had joined both the FOR staff and the youth division of MOWM, was among those who felt that Randolph had not pressed his point far enough when he called off the march after the appearance of Roosevelt's order. Rustin also questioned (as did Muste and other members of the FOR) the MOWM policy excluding whites from membership and demonstrations.[10]

But Randolph's speeches in subsequent months calling attention to events in India filled Rustin with hope. After a Randolph speech in Ohio in early 1943, Rustin reported to Muste, "A. Philip Randolph spoke in a way that convinced me that he is really concerned to develop an understanding and use of nonviolence by the American Negro." Rustin and Farmer, with the full encouragement of Muste, assisted Randolph in carrying the message of nonviolent direct action to the membership of MOWM. Randolph asked Muste to address the first annual MOWM Conference in Detroit in the summer of 1943. A longstanding previous engagement forced the pacifist to decline but he assured the MOWM leader that Farmer and Rustin would be there, and sent copies of *What the Bible Teaches* to Randolph, whose thank-you letter in return announced, "we are making a great drive among Negro ministers to win them over to the philosophy of nonviolent solutions."

Twelve hundred persons attended the Detroit gathering, where Randolph's keynote address challenged them to adopt "nonviolent goodwill direct action" as organizational policy. Other parts of the program reinforced this appeal. According to Jay Holmes Smith, who was an observer, Rustin greatly moved the audience by a talk on the power of nonviolence, "climaxing with a deep and searching note asking us to bow our heads and breaking out with 'It's Me O Lord Standing in the Need of Prayer'." In historian Wittner's words, "the delegates had been taken by storm; the decision to adopt nonviolent direct action tactics was unanimous. Projects were scheduled in the twenty-six cities of the nation with MOWM chapters." No projects materialized, however. They were aborted by hostility from the black press and by repercussions from the riot which had shaken Detroit only a few months earlier, the white postmortem on which blamed "so-called responsible Negro leaders" for exhorting their people to militance.[11]

While Rustin had placed great faith in the Randolph movement, his FOR colleague James Farmer had been concentrating his efforts along somewhat different lines.[12] Farmer outlined his own idea for a "Brotherhood Mobilization" in two lengthy memos to A. J. Muste early in 1942. According to Farmer's scheme, a nonviolent direct action organizing movement would develop out of FOR cells, would eventually become autonomous, include nonpacifists in its ranks, and possibly reach the proportions of a mass movement within ten years. Farmer's thinking was perfectly in tune with the direction in which an FOR cell (founded in 1941) at the University of Chicago was tending. As he later recalled, "While I was drafting a memo they had already begun formulating action projects. So that when I was authorized by the FOR to set up a pilot project in Chicago we had only to stretch out our hands to one another and a movement was created." Farmer's memos were the foundation from which the Congress of Racial Equality (CORE) evolved.[13] Despite the skeletal and wobbly figure it cut in the forties, this organization would become, as historians August Meier and

Elliott Rudwick have documented in their thorough study, *CORE,* one of the three major sources of the Negro revolution of the 1960s. The achievements of the early CORE consisted in demonstrating that nonviolent techniques could be used to challenge racial injustice in the United States and in working out guidelines for the future.

Following in the essentials, though not in every detail, the steps outlined by Gandhi for awakening and converting the conscience of the oppressor,[14] CORE groups carried on throughout the 1940s numerous forays against segregation and discrimination in housing, public accommodations, and employment. The only two nationally directed projects of any substance were the Houser-inspired summer workshops, which began in Chicago in 1945 and ran annually in Washington, D.C., from 1947 to 1954 (with the exception of a Los Angeles workshop in 1948), and the Journey of Reconciliation in the spring of 1947.[15]

The workshops, whose participants studied and tested nonviolent action techniques, drew public attention to CORE, contributed to the desegregation of the nation's capital, and helped to further interest in nonviolent action. The Journey of Reconciliation took sixteen men, eight of each race, on a bus trip through the upper South to test new federal laws prohibiting segregated services in interstate transportation. Few incidents occurred but those few were ugly. One, in a mill town outside Chapel Hill, resulted in the trial and conviction of four riders: Rustin, law student Andrew Johnson, a representative of the Workers' Defense League Joe Felmet, and New York printer Igal Roodenko. They were sentenced to thirty days on the road gang and all but Johnson served twenty-two days with "time off for good behavior." The legal expenses incurred in the case were borne largely by the FOR.[16]

Indeed, CORE's survival throughout this period was heavily dependent on funds and staff time tendered by the Fellowship. This dependence was the source of many tensions. At the outset, according to the recollections of James Farmer, Muste urged that CORE be established as an entity completely separate from the FOR while CORE organizers, including Farmer, preferred that it be a part of the pacifist organization. Once CORE picked up some momentum, however, the organizers and Muste exchanged positions. He was becoming more and more committed to the idea of the Fellowship as the fulcrum of an emerging revolutionary movement, and was anxious to identify it with the black revolutionary potential of CORE, while Farmer, Houser, and other CORE workers had concluded that the pacifism of the FOR would not appeal to the black masses and that it was necessary to maintain a separation. Dialogue on these questions became quite heated at times[17] and revealed Muste's continuing anxiety about revolutionary violence. "I see no place for a nvda [nonviolent direct action] movement to grow effectively and to be healthy, except within the general religious pacifist movement," he wrote Houser. "If it does not have the spiritual connection I am sure," he worried, "that it will go wrong, . . . either . . . by progressively under-emphasizing the religious basis and inspiration . . . or by going off the deep end on the use of violence."

Fund raising was another sensitive question with Muste. When advocates of autonomy for CORE proposed a drive to raise money specifically for their work, Muste, according to Farmer, opposed it immediately. He reportedly argued that the sources to which CORE would appeal were FOR sources and that the results of such an appeal would be detrimental to the Fellowship.[18] On their side, CORE activists were troubled by the unfavorable image which religious pacifism had in circles from which CORE wanted to recruit. "I am not as optimistic as you about the FOR developing into a disciplined nonviolent group," Houser told Muste. "Most of the membership . . . are not trying to think in political terms or in terms of strategy. . . . Most are too individualistic," he observed. Farmer, whose commitments to CORE and FOR became increasingly incompatible, shared the view of other Chicago CORE volunteers that their group ought to avoid close association in the public view with pacifism and the Fellowship.

This urge to keep the FOR in the background rankled with Muste but did not prevent him from extending considerable support to CORE. As Meier and Rudwick note, "By permitting Farmer, Rustin, Houser and Houser's secretary to spend considerable time on CORE affairs the FOR in effect subsidized a part-time secretariat for CORE. . . . CORE's national projects were jointly sponsored by the FOR with the Fellowship providing a major part of the financing." Without this support CORE would not have survived. Without A. J. Muste, the FOR would not have provided this support. Its more traditional and moderate members were not easily reconciled to the increasingly radical actions of the new civil rights group. Some FOR members and staff resented CORE as a distraction from the greater problem of war. Muste disagreed, maintaining that "it is utterly unsound to isolate war from racialism, capitalism, etc." A more common objection to CORE was that its participants were stirring up forces that they would ultimately be unable to control. Muste did not share this fear, he explained, "because my experience in the labor and radical movement has taught me that you cannot create movements of this kind by a tour de force. If there is not a real need for it, which is bound to find expression in some way or other anyway, no amount of work by the so-called outside agitator gets any results."[19]

Complaints from within the FOR staff, especially from Muste's associate secretary, John Swomley, about lapses on the part of both Rustin and Farmer in their administrative responsibilities to the FOR, Muste met with sympathy for all parties involved. Without denying their weaknesses, Muste would remind Swomley of the strength and potential in Farmer and Rustin. "Jim . . . does a great job speaking," he noted. Into his comments on Rustin entered a special note of personal affection and concern. "Administration and follow-up is not one of his strong points," Muste wrote of Rustin, "but I am hesitant to relieve him too early in life of a certain amount of administrative responsibility and experience—just for the good of his soul, among other things." A southern FOR member who was disturbed by the militant edge in Rustin's style was answered by Muste that "he's nearer to what you would call a universal Christian base than you would seem to think. . . . He has demonstrated a very sweet, generous, courageous and devoted spirit in many situations . . . and probably has an unusually significant future before him." In a later letter to the same person Muste declared, "I have great faith in Rustin and pray fervently that he may grow in grace."[20]

Rustin again served as a link among CORE, FOR, and A. Philip Randolph when, in 1947, in the face of pending draft legislation which contained no guarantee against segregation in the armed forces, Randolph formed the Committee against Jim Crow in Military Service and Training. A year later the committee was expanded in the League for Nonviolent Civil Disobedience against Military Segregation, with Rustin as executive secretary.

However, the excitement generated by Randolph's adoption and linking of two causes dear to the hearts of militant pacifists (opposing the draft and opposing racism) died aborning. President Truman issued Executive Order 9981 directing that discrimination in the military end "as rapidly as possible" and Randolph, after obtaining assurances that the order included segregation, called off his direct action campaign.[21]

Rustin reflected the dismay of radical pacifists when he refused to accept Randolph's action. The presidential order was neither sufficiently clear nor strong, in his judgment, and civil disobedience should continue until a better guarantee was achieved. Though Randolph officially dissolved the League, Rustin and his supporters continued to send out correspondence on League stationery. In October, while Rustin was in India, Randolph and Grant Reynolds (commissioner of correction for New York State and a close associate in establishing the original Committee against Jim Crow) issued a statement attacking both Rustin and Muste, charging that they represented a "pacifist nucleus which engaged in 'unethical' practices and had used the League for 'ulterior' purposes!" Muste answered Randolph that the timing of the attack—"when Bayard is out of the country and will be for several months"—was unjustified and that the charges were unfounded.[22]

A certain wariness toward Randolph had appeared previously in Muste's dealings with the man. They worked together on the National Committee for Winfred Lynn (a black man imprisoned for his refusal to serve in a segregated armed services) where Muste sensed and resisted a seeming trend toward takeover of the campaign by MOWM. Similarly when plans for the first CORE summer workshop in Washington were discussed, the minutes of the meeting reported that "Randolph raised the question whether the project should not be almost exclusively a Negro one and suggested that the MOWM take it on," a suggestion that was rejected. That Muste had sensed reciprocal wariness in Randolph circles toward the constellation of activities around FOR is reflected in careful instructions he gave the FOR membership secretary who took minutes at their meetings. "Some matters ought to be omitted altogether or ought to be very carefully phrased," he advised. "For example, . . . the question was raised as to George and Bayard 'becoming *leaders* in the Anti-Jim Crow Committee.' That term would . . . be subject to misinterpretation if it got into certain hands."[23]

Yet Muste was undoubtedly sincere when he wrote Randolph that "nothing in life is more saddening than disappointment in those one had treasured and still wants to treasure as friends." Their friendship did continue beyond this rift. The political realities of their relationship made misunderstanding hard to avoid but worth surviving. Randolph had a predominantly black constituency while Muste and the pacifists were predominantly white. Randolph was hostile to the existing political system only to the degree that it did not serve his people. The militant pacifists were much more alienated from that system and considered nonviolent resistance to it as a way of life. Yet Randolph and Muste were important to one another. Muste was anxious to broaden the appeal of pacifism and establish links to non-pacifists. "I tend strongly these days in the direction of making the Fellowship more of an organization to bring the pacifists' message to those who are on the fringe than an organization for those who are already pacifists," he had confided to John Swomley. Randolph was anxious for whatever help he could get to exploit the potential of Gandhian techniques. In one sense or another each side probably did incline to "use" the other, but the integrity of both leaders kept that inclination in check.[24]

A similar analysis may be made of the tensions between CORE and FOR. Both sides in this case were also in a sense "using" each other—CORE surviving on Fellowship resources while publicly declaring autonomy, Muste permitting the near-deception and continuing to hope that in nurturing this civil rights project the FOR would eventually become an agent of nonviolent direct action in its own right.[25]

The Fellowship failed to rise to Muste's expectations and CORE chapters and programs entered a serious decline in the late forties. James Farmer left both the FOR and CORE in 1945 to devote his energies to union organizing. The civil rights organization continued to be torn by questions regarding its relationship to the pacifist movement; membership declined, and weak chapters died and were not replaced by new ones. In 1953, personal problems related to Rustin's homosexuality led him to leave the FOR and in the same year Muste retired as executive secretary. Shortly thereafter, George Houser also resigned from both groups to organize the American Committee on Africa. The Fellowship governing committees—with Muste's concurrence—voted to phase out staff commitments to CORE "as rapidly as possible." Meier and Rudwick note that "in the very year [1954] that the NAACP won its landmark school desegregation decision from the Supreme Court, CORE was at its lowest ebb." Nevertheless, they add, "by the end of the decade growing public acceptance of both racial equality and nvda enabled CORE to enjoy a substantial revival that laid the groundwork for its flowering in the 1960's."[26]

In later years Muste liked to describe himself as "a kind of grandfather" to CORE. As some grandfathers are, Muste was faced with conflict between the parent (FOR) and the child (CORE). His concern for both was great. But finally it became clear that religious pacifism as embodied in the elder FOR was not ready for nonviolent action as it was germinating in the youthful Congress of Racial Equality. By the time of Muste's retirement from the FOR the bonds which he had nurtured between it and the offspring CORE had dissolved. Muste remained close to both of them as the pattern of his "retirement years" reveals. He kept a special place in his heart for the activism of CORE and its operations at the cutting edge of social change.[27]

The historic ruling against "separate but equal" by the Supreme Court in *Brown* vs. *Board of Education* in 1954, was a fitting prelude to the equally historic black boycott of public buses which began the following year in Montgomery, Alabama, when the unassuming, but immovable Rosa Parks declined to yield her seat to a white passenger on the city bus line. The influence of A. J. Muste on the events that followed was by most accounts important and real, yet not entirely easy either to document or measure. Martin Luther King, Jr., who emerged as the leader of the Montgomery Movement and subsequently became a momentous force in the annals of social protest, encountered, and was to some degree affected by, the pacifism of Muste. The very first encounter, a lecture by Muste at Crozer Seminary, where King was a student in 1949, left a mixed impression. The pacifist's objections to war struck King as unrealistic. Yet, he recalled, "I was deeply moved by Mr. Muste's talk." When other influences, most notably the firsthand account by Mordecai Johnson of the Gandhian movement in India, led King to study further in nonviolence, he included Muste's books in his reading.[28]

At the height of the crisis in Montgomery two of Muste's associates, Bayard Rustin and FOR National Field Secretary Glenn Smiley, lent their services to the boycott. The decision for Rustin to enter the Montgomery situation was reached at a meeting of influential social activists who gathered at the offices of A. Philip Randolph in New York and included Randolph, Muste, Norman Thomas, James Farmer, and a representative from the Jewish Labor Committee. As Rustin later remembered this meeting, Randolph and Muste overcame the objections of the others to Rustin's taking on this task so soon after the public embarrassment which had prompted his departure from the FOR. The two older men argued that Rustin could work in the background and be trusted not to permit personal questions to become a public issue again. Through no fault of his own, however, such questions were raised by reporters covering the Montgomery story. Rustin had to withdraw, though he kept in close touch and continued to advise King. In the meantime the FOR had sent staff representative and native Southerner Glenn Smiley to work with Martin Luther King. Smiley's arrival in Montgomery preceded Rustin's departure by one day. The two men conferred and were in frequent contact thereafter. "The degree of influence exerted by Rustin, Smiley, and the FOR on the Montgomery Bus Boycott and Martin Luther King is hard to assess," Smiley has said. "In my opinion," he added, "Rustin stands alone in this respect, for certainly no one had as great an impact on King personally as did he through the many contacts outside Montgomery in the years following 1956."[29] For his part, Rustin, who continued to serve as one of King's principal advisors, has reported that "during all my work with Martin King, . . . I never made a difficult decision without talking the problem over with A. J. first."[30]

While Muste's involvement in the Montgomery Bus Boycott and later campaigns directed by King was chiefly through Bayard Rustin (and also James Lawson, as discussed below), he did from time to time personally confer with King and directly participate in civil rights programs. King and Muste were formally introduced by Glenn Smiley at a meeting of FOR and Montgomery Improvement Association people in Atlanta during the bus boycott.[31] From that time forward King and Muste periodically called upon one another as speakers for their respective causes. At King's urging Muste was present at a conference of the Southern Christian Leadership Conference (SCLC) in Norfolk, Virginia, in 1958. The following year he was invited to speak to an SCLC meeting in Tallahassee. His initial acceptance prompted King to write "we are thrilled," but, when the dates of the meeting were changed, Muste was unable to attend. He did participate in a number of other SCLC functions, however, a contribution he somewhat embarrassedly tried to capitalize on when pressuring King to accept a speaking engagement for an American Friends' Service Committee (AFSC) function in 1961. "I don't know quite how to put this," Muste wrote the busy black leader, "but if in any sense you may feel that you owe me something in exchange for engagements I have filled for the Southern Christian Leadership Conference or in connection with the needs of students up here, then I would consider that your accepting the invitation to the New England AFSC . . . would be ample repayment." The reference to "the needs of students up here" was to black youth who had been expelled from schools in the South for protest activities and were attending New York University on scholarships from the SCLC. When funds did not arrive to cover the students' expenses, Muste vouched for the SCLC and assured university officials that the bills would be paid. Nearly a month later the money was still due. Muste prodded King, adding, "I trust that you people will make it clear that I do not have any financial responsibility in the matter!" The misunderstanding, which involved SCLC having revoked one student's scholarship "for reasons best known to him," was finally settled and Muste absolved of any accountability.[32]

The integration struggle received strong stimulus from student sit-ins early in 1960. The student movement began at a Greensboro, North Carolina, lunch counter in 1960 and rapidly spread to cities across the South. An FOR account in comic book form of the Montgomery movement which reportedly inspired some of the early student action and FOR Southern Secretary James Lawson's expulsion from Vanderbilt University School of Religion for participating in sit-ins in Nashville, quickly implicated the Fellowship. Appeals from student leaders to Martin Luther King for his support resulted in SCLC involvement. A three-man team from the FOR travelled among action sites, training local leaders in nonviolent techniques and tactics. In April 1960, Lawson and King were the principal speakers at a conference at Shaw University out of which the Student Nonviolent Coordinating Committee (SNCC) was born.[33]

While the record of Muste's efforts to relate to this unfolding drama is sketchy, it does include clear indications that he found the student movement inspirational and politically very significant. "Negro youth," he declared, "are teaching their elders . . . how freedom is won." He sent notes of admiration and encouragement to individual student protestors, though they were probably too young and too unfamiliar with history to know who their correspondent was or to see the touching humility in this gesture of appreciation from one who had weathered battles similar to theirs before they were born. To five CORE volunteers from Tallahassee who went to jail, he sent a dollar bill as a token "of my great admiration for the courage and dignity which all of you have displayed." To another young protestor he wrote:

> I have just read the reprint from *Look* magazine of January 3 containing the statement you made in connection with your participation in a sit-in in New Orleans, and I cannot refrain from writing you.
>
> I am a kind of grandfather of CORE, I suppose, and I have certainly never experienced a deeper emotional satisfaction about any share I may have had in its work greater than your action and your statement about it have given me.
>
> There is about what you have done something which suggests coolness, which is not at all the same thing as coldness, like a healing wind in the midst of almost unbearable heat. Simplicity and cleanness are other characteristics of your attitude and action.
>
> These things also characterize your statement. It is seldom that one's action and one's words about it are in such complete accord, and when this happens, it is an event.
>
> I want to express special appreciation of your characterization of people who "just automatically think about themselves" and who call that "judgment". How right you are in pointing out that people with this kind of good "judgment" aren't doing anything at all.[34]

Beyond these overtures to the youthful protestors, Muste's role in the drama they had created was an advisory one. Through the channel of *Liberation*, a magazine which he helped establish in 1956, dialogue was encouraged between the peace movement and the rapidly developing civil rights struggle. Proceeding from the assumption that the pacifist contribution lay "in supporting and commending nonviolence in popular struggles rather than in developing struggles ourselves,"[35] Muste, as an editor of *Liberation*, encouraged reports and reflections from the field of action and beamed back messages intended to bolster and extend the nonviolent force of that action.

Liberation had carried some of the earliest firsthand accounts from King and Rustin of the Montgomery struggle.[36] Three months after the sit-ins began, and in the weeks following the founding of SNCC, Muste and his fellow editors at *Liberation* (David Dellinger, Roy Finch, Sidney Lens, and Bayard

Rustin) prepared a major statement on "Fundamentals of Strategy for the Struggle for Integration." The student movement, they argued, had lifted the integration struggle out of "the doldrums" into which it had settled in the late fifties. While leaders of SCLC or other groups could take no direct credit for them, "the sit-ins have conferred," the editors maintained, "a fresh importance on such men as Roy Wilkins of the NAACP and Martin Luther King, Jr."

The editorial included some pointed advice to these public figures. Circumstances demand, the editors said, that civil rights leadership be "southern and a leadership of masses of people in motion." Such mass action, they added, made mass arrests inevitable and "the thesis that mass action leads to jail applies to leaders as well as to the rank and file." The *Liberation* group inveighed against possible attempts to change the essential, "church-centered and preacher-led" character of the southern movement and warned against employing the tactics of guerilla warfare.

In the *Liberation* description of changes which would occur if the southern, nonviolent, church-centered movement was successful, signs of Muste's pen were especially evident, as in the prediction that "liberation of Negroes in the South . . . will bring with it a great release of moral energy . . . which will greatly affect the whole of American life, including our attitude toward war and our relations with the rest of the world."[37]

It was on this issue of war and American relationships in the world that Muste was most anxious to influence Martin Luther King. He had written another editorial for *Liberation* in 1959 when the black leader travelled to India. King "is indeed a fitting 'ambassador' from the United States to the land of Gandhi," he said. By his journey, Muste went on, King would become "in some degree a world figure." As such, the pacifist advised, it would not be "possible to separate the struggle for basic social justice and the practice of nonviolence from the struggle to prevent and end war."[38]

King, having returned to the United States in March, wrote a brief comment in October for *Liberation*:

> Repeatedly in public addresses and in my writings I have unequivocally declared my hatred for this most colossal of all evils [war] and I have condemned any organizer of war, regardless of his rank or nationality. I have signed numerous statements with other Americans condemning nuclear testing and have authorized publication of my name in advertisements appearing in the largest circulation newspapers in the country, without concern that it was then 'unpopular' to speak out.[39]

For several years to come, however, Muste would remain on edge about King's stance on foreign policy. When a group of churchmen wrote Muste about the advisability of inviting the SCLC leader to an international conference on "the cause of peace and the church" Muste warned them to make it clear "to him that he is not being asked to make a speech about the integration movement in the South." Inviting him was a good idea, Muste said, because "he should be thinking more than he probably is about the peace issue and if he does put his mind and heart to it he would have a significant contribution to make." Answering the question of an American Friends' Service Committee secretary as to which black leader would make the best speaker for a meeting the AFSC was organizing, Muste wrote that neither of the three SCLC aides which the secretary had suggested (Ralph Abernathy, Fred Shuttlesworth, and Wyatt Walker), or "Martin himself will really do an . . . analytical and sound job on the relation of the peace issue to the social problem. . . . They are so absorbed in the integration struggle that they do not find time to look with real concentration at other aspects of nonviolence."[40]

Muste's editorial for *Liberation* on the awarding of the Nobel Peace Prize to Martin Luther King hailed the moment as " 'an event' in the history of nonviolence" but took King to task for giving an acceptance speech which failed "to make as specific and ringing an appeal for the renunciation of violence and the concrete application of nonviolence to contemporary war and war preparation as we would have thought appropriate."[41]

Muste hoped that these wider implications of nonviolence might receive more of King's attention and take deeper root within the SCLC if a stronger pacifist presence was added to the SCLC staff. His candidate for maintaining that presence was James Lawson who had worked in the FOR as southern secretary and was deeply committed to pacifist activism. For Lawson, Muste had been a seminal influence since that "unforgettable moment" when the pacifist had spoken to his history class at Baldwin-Wallace College in 1947, Lawson's freshman year. From that time he incorporated into his studies and his political activities the works and values to which Muste had introduced him. His jail sentence for conscientious objection and his expulsion from Vanderbilt were a logical consequence of acknowledging Muste as "a major teacher."

In 1960, at an Easter weekend meeting in Raleigh, North Carolina, of King, Lawson, and Douglas Moore (later a councilman in the District of Columbia), Lawson and Moore made plans to join the SCLC staff. Although King reportedly called their decision "the best news I've ever heard in my life," he soon retracted the offer. Muste was asked to explain to Lawson and personally visited him to do so. As Lawson recalled the episode, Roy Wilkins of the NAACP had threatened to cut off ties between his organization and the SCLC if the Lawson and Moore appointments were made. Apparently Lawson's outspoken criticisms of leaders such as Wilkins for being too much concerned with "the middle class comfort process," and of organizations such as the NAACP for being too much akin to "social clubs" were at the bottom of this threat. Muste, Lawson remembered, "was very clear that [deciding against Lawson and Moore] was not what he would have done but he was very understanding of King's position." Muste and Lawson were agreed that "in potential and in power . . . and in the eyes of the world," Martin Luther King was "the real leader" of the civil rights struggle in the United States, "and nobody could rival that." They felt he could have afforded to have stood up to Wilkins on this question of staff, but clearly he was not prepared to do so." Shortly thereafter, however, Lawson did become the SCLC 'Director of Nonviolent Education,' a part-time position.[42]

King's unwillingness to do battle on such issues also injured Bayard Rustin, in whom Muste continued to take a deep personal interest. In 1962, Congressman Adam Clayton Powell Jr. insisted that Rustin be dismissed from the SCLC. He threatened to have Rustin's one-time association with the Young Communist League investigated by the House Un-American Activities Committee and implied, as Rustin understood it, that King would be labeled a homosexual if he did not proceed with the dismissal. Rustin insisted on resigning for the sake of the organization, but nonetheless felt that Martin Luther King had not supported him adequately. Muste, who was privy to the affair, concurred. In his view, King should not have succumbed to Powell and was at the very least derelict in his manner of handling the situation by sending a committee to receive Rustin's resignation rather than dealing with him personally. Muste wrote that he was "personally ashamed of Martin and a couple of other Negro clergy who were involved" for not standing up to Powell—"perhaps," by Muste's description, "the most unsavory of Negro politicians." Nonetheless, as Rustin reminded him, Muste's own record in matters of this kind was not perfect. He had succumbed to outside pressures in 1953 when Rustin had had to leave the FOR. As Rustin recalled, Muste's response to this reminder was, "I was wrong then; times have changed; history has since shown your trustworthiness; and that is what redemption means."[43]

Muste's disappointment in King in this instance was clearly deepened by his belief that Rustin was immensely important to the King movement. "Bayard," he worried in a letter defending Rustin to a detractor, "is working terribly hard and in a situation where he has to handle an immense amount of detail, thus saving much wear and tear on Martin while putting his own spirit in jeopardy."[44] Shortly before the Powell attack, Rustin's involvement in a lawsuit stemming from his organization and administration of the Committee to Defend Martin Luther King had put his legal person temporarily in at least as much jeopardy as his spirit. The Committee was organized when King was put through a series of court trials stemming from an innocent and minor infraction of the law (neglecting to renew his out of state driver's license in Georgia), trumped-up charges of submitting fraudulent income tax returns, and participation in a student sit-in that technically violated the probation under which he had been released in the case over the expired driver's license. The Defense Committee was international in scope and drew on support from many prominent persons including Eleanor Roosevelt. An ad placed in the *New York Times* by the Committee created new litigation when charges were brought that information in the ad was fallacious. Rustin, who had used the careless (though not really untrue) wording which eyewitnesses of the episode in question had provided, took the legal responsibility for the mistake. When the story cropped up two years later as an argument against trusting Bayard Rustin, Muste spoke out in his behalf. "I was on the Defense Committee and in constant touch, attending committee meetings, etc.," he wrote a Rustin critic, and "the true facts are a testimony to Bayard's integrity, rather than otherwise." Rustin and all those on the protestors' side of the litigation were vindicated in 1964 by a Supreme Court ruling in their favor.[45]

As Muste remained in Rustin's corner through the various public and personal struggles which engaged the younger man over the years, he also renewed his contacts with and interest in CORE. As a member of the organization's National Advisory Committee, he wrote Jackie Robinson in February 1960 to thank him for a column he had recently written on CORE activities. "I used to get my kicks out of seeing you play baseball," and Muste added, "it is delightful to get kicks fairly frequently now out of your column in the *New York Post*." When James Farmer returned to CORE as national director in 1961, Muste extended his congratulations. "I do not think that CORE ever would have 'gotten off the ground' had it not been for your initial interest back in 1941," Farmer wrote in reply, promising to be in touch soon to discuss "CORE plans" with Muste. The older man did not figure prominently in the direction of CORE in the ensuing years. But when only one or two advisory people were coming to CORE meetings in the sixties, Muste was always there and his support still counted. Even after the departure of Farmer and organizational espousal of "Black Power" in 1966, Muste held his place on the National Advisory Committee. Less than a month before his death he attended a Committee meeting, where a statement of congratulations was drafted in recognition of CORE's twenty-fifth anniversary. "Reverend Muste said he approved," the minutes report, "but that, considering the financial crisis it should include a plea for funds." Muste's own scratchings on the margin of his agenda included a note to himself to make up "lists of people to whom to appeal for CORE."[46]

A variety of other civil rights–related causes received Muste's attention during this period. He lent his name to an unsuccessful protest against efforts by Tennessee authorities to close down the controversial Highlander Folk School. He was a moving force behind a mass appeal on behalf of a black activist Asbury Howard in Bessemer, Alabama. According to Muste's "Statement on the Case of Asbury Howard," the man was vice-president of the local NAACP and president of a black voters' league. He had hired a sign painter to reproduce a cartoon to be hung in the league's meeting hall. The picture was of a Negro in chains saying "Lord help all Americans to see that you intend human beings to have the same rights." For placing this order Howard was arrested, tried, and found guilty of publishing "intemperate matter." While leaving the courtroom he was reportedly attacked by a mob of some forty or fifty white males as "15 or more policemen" looked on. His son, who tried to go to his father's aid, was arrested and charged with disorderly conduct and resisting arrest. Along with the American Civil Liberties Union, signers of the appeal which Muste circulated called for the Department of Justice to immediately investigate. Muste was disturbed during this campaign by labor leader Victor Reuther's refusal to give his signature because Howard was an officer in a rival union. "It seems to me extremely important," Muste chided, "that the issue of civil liberties should never be obscured or blunted because of political or other such differences among people."[47]

Muste followed the battles in Congress over civil rights legislation and at one point was moved to personally and publicly upbraid Senator William Fulbright, not only for making "a major foreign policy speech as part of the Southern filibuster against the civil rights act, which was," Muste said, "shocking," but also for quoting from the Bible inaccurately.[48] While Fulbright worked to forestall change, Muste continued to work in defense of those who could not wait for new laws. When a group of prominent Negro activists in Monroe, North Carolina, were sentenced on a variety of false charges, Muste worked vigorously with the FOR to raise money for their defense committee.[49]

In Mississippi another civil rights initiative began with the organizing in 1963 of the Council of Federated Organizations (COFO). A state-wide coalition of groups dominated by CORE and SNCC, COFO, as Meier and Rudwick have noted, "remained viable and effective for more than two years and was a unique phenomenon in the history of the civil rights movement." That uniqueness was highlighted in the COFO-sponsored Mississippi Summer Project of 1964 which brought a thousand or more northern volunteers into the state to assist with voter registration drives and to organize community centers and "freedom schools." The potential for massive violence was recognized and widely discussed when the plans for the summer project were made known. Within the civil rights movement many important figures, including James Farmer, urged that the federal government provide protection for the volunteers. Muste (who lent his name to the project as a sponsor) offered his thoughts on this suggestion and on the state of the movement as he saw it, in a May 1964 essay for *Liberation*.[50]

The attitude taken by many that "Negroes have a peculiar obligation to be non-violent" was, in view of the decided violence of the entire society, hypocritical, Muste observed at the outset. Nonetheless, he argued, leaders have to make choices, and in his mind their best choice was to stick with nonviolence and improve its application. He suggested the direction which such improvements might take: more work among the "depressed and poverty-stricken elements in the Ghettos" of the North, more attention to training for nonviolent action, and more efforts to tap the "great force of moral revulsion" against racism which a growing number of whites were experiencing. Speaking to the growing phenomenon of racial nationalism Muste stated his belief that, while "the desire of Negroes to control their own movement and not have it run by whites is legitimate, . . . Negroes as a people want to live in the United States, they don't want to migrate and they don't seriously want to live in a Negro nation-state in some corner of American soil."

Remaining nonviolent meant resisting federal intervention into situations such as Mississippi. The connotations of reliance on troops for protection clearly bothered Muste but in this case he argued politics rather than morality. "The civil rights movement cannot expect the support of the very federal agency that is supposed to hold society together," he pointed out, "and at the same time itself work for the (temporary?) breakdown of the society, or more accurately, accept it as inevitable." After all, he reminded, "those who have been denied freedom and equality have to . . . struggle for them in a way that will 'disturb' society. . . . This involves 'social dislocation.' "[51]

Copies of Muste's essay were stacked on the literature table at the Ohio College campus where summer volunteers gathered in June for "orientation" before setting out to play their part in the "social dislocation" of the state of Mississippi. Three young men who participated in the first orientation were reported "missing" shortly after the second wave of volunteers had begun their week of training. Near the end of the summer the bodies of James Chaney, Andrew Goodman, and Michael Schwerner were found. Public pressure generated by fears for the missing youths and for the remaining volunteers forced President Johnson to increase the federal presence in Mississippi, though troops were not employed.

The mental state of tense and besieged civil rights workers grew increasingly uncongenial to nonviolence. Their ambivalent feelings toward the main black nonviolent symbol, Martin Luther King, became ever more critical. King's 1963 campaign in Birmingham was seen as ending in a "sell-out," made all the more unpalatable by the epilogue in which four small girls were killed in the dynamite-bombing of a black Birmingham Church.[52]

Muste's worry over these developments was evident in a memorandum he wrote in July 1964, which was later reprinted by *Liberation* for distribution as a pamphlet. It was, he admitted, "an appeal . . . that in considering how to deal with the agonizing and complicated problems which now beset us the emphasis should be on nonviolence." The agony was exemplified in the cruel fact that "three young men . . . have simply disappeared." The complications, as Muste defined them, went beyond tension in Mississippi, even beyond the struggle for integration. Pressures bearing down upon human society required profound changes—in social relations, yes, but also in economic organization and in habitual human ways of responding to conflict. For civil rights workers to shoulder arms and assume the posture of conventional revolutionaries was, Muste instructed, either to assume a " 'revolutionary' situation which we do not have in the U.S." or to express "psychological frustration which should not determine the political policy of a movement." On the other hand, Muste wrote critically of the pattern King had followed in Birmingham and suggested that once a campaign is begun "the struggle should be maintained until some specific steps toward integration are assured."[53]

Muste had in mind as a specific instance of such continuing struggle, the example of "Peace Walkers" who had recently spent forty-nine days in the Albany, Georgia, jail and whose perseverance had resulted in a modest but specific breakthrough toward integration. The Quebec to Guantanamo Peace Walk grew out of a concern in the Committee for Nonviolent Action (CNVA) over hostility between the United States and Cuba, which had erupted twice in recent years—at the Bay of Pigs and in the near-lethal missile crisis. "The

walk was to be a journey of friendship and understanding between peoples,"
explained a CNVA supporter. "Its primary message carried directly to the peoples of three countries along its route would be the advocacy of non-violence;
and . . . the presentation of peaceful alternatives to the hostile acts that had
dragged the world to the abyss of nuclear war." Begun in Toronto in late May of
1963, the walk's primary message was soon and repeatedly overshadowed by
"secondary" struggles for civil liberties and civil rights that arose along the way.
The most difficult struggles occurred in Georgia.[54]

The integrated walking team of twenty-three persons (three black men,
fourteen white men, six white women) was arrested in Griffin, Georgia, on
November 7, for violating an ordinance against distributing leaflets in certain
sections of town. They were manhandled and assaulted with an electric cattle
prod by local police and representatives of the "GBI" (Georgia Bureau of Investigation). The Griffin sheriff who was, as the walkers perceived him, deeply
upset by such brutality, arranged for their release. Ten days later the walkers
were arrested in Macon, Georgia, again for alleged illegal distribution of leaflets; they were given sentences ranging from three to thirteen days (depending
on whether or not they cooperated in their arrests) and began fasting. The
assassination of President Kennedy prompted local officials to release the
walkers. "Authorities felt," according to David Dellinger, "that they could not
be responsible for their continued safety in view of the notion, current in Macon
at the time, that both the assassin and the walkers were 'pro-Castro Communists.' " The Negro minister who had extended hospitality to the walkers
feared that their continued presence posed a threat to the safety of his church
and family. They moved to Atlanta and were put up in a Mennonite house
there. Muste arrived to consult with them about the next steps. He was promptly treated to a firsthand experience with "southern-style" law enforcement
when police entered the house uninvited, lined the walkers up, and gave them
three choices. They could demonstrate and be arrested, get out of town, or get
jobs to avoid arrest for vagrancy. Instead, Muste arranged for the pacifists to
participate in a Thanksgiving service at Mount Moriah Baptist Church where
Martin Luther King preached the sermon and where apparently officials were
unwilling to risk the bad publicity of interfering. After two weeks of discussion
and evaluation in Atlanta, and the departure of six walkers from the march, the
band proceeded to Albany where the most harrowing experience yet awaited
them.[55]

Albany had been the site of a serious setback for Martin Luther King in
1962. Police Chief Laurie Pritchett, who claimed to believe in nonviolence, liked
to boast that he had beaten King. While Pritchett avoided public displays of
open brutality, he and the city power structure enforced a rigid pattern of segregation in Albany. Oglethorpe Avenue was the racial dividing line. The south
side of that street was the limit beyond which blacks were not to go without
permission. City authorities sought to impose the same limit on the Peace

Walkers who refused to obey and were jailed. Many of the walkers adopted a stance of complete non-cooperation, forcing police to carry them to and from court and to their cells where they refused all food. Those who fasted throughout the episode went for a total of forty-nine days without eating, with an eleven-day interval between the two consecutive sentences which they served. Two walkers were hospitalized; in the last days, prison officials began vitamin injections and forced feeding.

Muste worked in Albany during the last two weeks of the walkers' imprisonment. He and David Dellinger, with the temporary assistance of James Bristol and Calhoun Geiger of the American Friends' Service Committee, carried on negotiations between Albany authorities and the walkers. They worked closely with leaders of the black Albany Movement, including attorney C. B. King who had defended some of the walkers in court, and Movement Secretary Marion Page. Muste stayed at the home of the attorney's brother, Slater King, the director of the movement. The movement leader's experiences with nonviolence were embittering; his pregnant wife was kicked into unconsciousness by a sheriff's deputy during the Martin Luther King campaign in Albany and subsequently lost her child. He told his pacifist guest, "White people understand no language but the language of force."

These leaders were not at first overwhelmingly happy about the arrival and activities of the walkers. Certainly the pacifists' campaign seemed to go beyond the earlier *Liberation* philosophy of supporting nonviolence in struggles that develop rather than taking the initiative to develop such struggles. But, as the days of imprisonment and fasting went on, new stirrings within the Negro community were evident. At about the time when the walkers were on the verge of giving up, their resolve was bolstered by word from the Albany Movement of their declaration that if the walkers were defeated, "it's a defeat for us again." Barbara Deming reported that Movement Secretary Marion Page, "as old as he is and in ill health, . . . has personally committed himself to go to jail if necessary."[56]

In negotiations, Police Chief Pritchett and City Manager Stephen Roos represented the city. Roos, Muste felt, was more flexible than Pritchett, who unblushingly informed Muste after his first private meeting with the prisoners that the room where they met had been bugged. Through the good offices of Bristol and Geiger, religious leaders in the community were also brought into the negotiation process. The level of hostility toward the walkers was clearly reflected in the outcome of a request by Bristol for Bibles for the prisoners. The minister of the Christian Church turned the request over to the Gideon Society, whose workers refused to fill it. The minister, whose own feelings toward the walkers were unsympathetic, was taken aback: "That's the first time I ever knew the Gideons to refuse the Bible to anyone."

While the intransigence of the white racist power structure was the greatest impediment to a settlement, instances of poor judgment on the part of walkers also presented serious problems. Dellinger recalled the note which was smuggled to Muste and him from the jail advising that the black leadership of

Albany should prepare for action, arrest, and fasting while in jail. "We never issued that prophetic call to righteousness," Dellinger said, adding that "A. J. said to me (only half facetiously, I think) 'Burn that note before it falls into the wrong hands.' " An interview that a walker had with the press in which she was quoted as saying, "If we can only break Pritchett on this one issue," made the Muste-Dellinger negotiating job no easier. "This was the wrong way of putting it," Muste noted. At the very moment when an acceptable settlement was within reach, a recent arrival from Canada who came to support the walkers insisted on initiating his own leafletting campaign and was arrested. "A. J. was most unhappy with this development," James Bristol reported.[57]

The gravity of the Albany conflict, with very real danger to the health of some of the walkers should their fast continue, weighed heavily upon Muste. Barbara Deming, who shared part of the imprisonment, described Muste on his first visit to the Albany jail. He was, she penned, "an anxious figure. . . . His long knobby-knuckled hands, moving against the bars as though to remove them, as though to touch us, are trembling. His voice trembles a little, too. . . . Behind his glasses his eyes, which can sometimes light up like a fire, are dull." The septuagenarian was once described as not "the sort of man you'd slap on the back, . . . very few people get familiar with A. J. . . . There's a detachment in most of his personal relations." Yet he was clearly not detached in Albany. Behind those bars, in addition to Deming, was Edie Snyder, a young woman drawn to pacifism and activism by working in New York as Muste's secretary. Deming related how, during the prison visits, "by thrusting their faces between the bars" Muste and Snyder "manage to kiss," and how, on one occasion, he "took Edie's hand and then burst out 'Oh, I want to get you all out of here so much!' "[58]

The agreement which finally made their release possible came about after the AFSC representative stumbled on the fact that local clergymen did not know that the walkers had been restricted to the south side of Oglethorpe Avenue. They were persuaded that it might be possible to have that restriction lifted. In the protracted and tortured discussions which followed, a formula was finally devised whereby five walkers (one less than the six which a city ordinance defined as a "parade") were permitted to walk around the entire block (four sides) of the previously restricted area, after which all the walkers would proceed up the north side of Oglethorpe for one block and then leave town. The pacifists thus gained entry to the forbidden ground while Albany laws were still nominally honored. Some CNVA people who were not in jail were reportedly displeased with the settlement. But local black leaders, James Bristol said, saw it as "more than they had dreamed possible," and felt that it "was a distinct victory for the walkers and . . . represented real progress in increasing the area of freedom in Albany." On the morning of the release of the walkers (Saturday, February 22), the Albany Movement held a "Freedom Day," picketing and leafletting north of Oglethorpe in front of the courthouse and city hall. No arrests occurred. The following Monday, after the walkers rested at Koinonia Farm in Americus, five of them, including one member of the Albany Movement, carried signs and distributed leaflets through downtown Albany while their comrades "demonstrated north of Oglethorpe Avenue in the 'white' business area. The 'impossible' had happened," wrote exultant walk coordinator Bradford Lyttle.[59]

Muste was cautious but pleased in his assessment of the Albany experience. "It would be fatuous to think that it was more than a beginning," he wrote. But at the conclusion of his assessment (in which he considered mistakes that had been made and intergroup tensions which had detracted from the walkers' cause), he offered the walkers' stand in Albany as a viable alternative to the violent strategies associated with "Malcolm X and others of his tendency." The walkers, he further argued, pointed the way to "a more dynamic fundamental and viable strategy and spirit" than advocates of nonviolence had developed so far. "I am certain," he maintained, "that their argument-by-action for nonviolence has caused a good many people to reflect again."

Muste's impressions were at least partly borne out by a report that *Liberation* received from Albany two years later. Marion Page wrote of widespread public desegregation, the hiring of black bus operators, and black policemen. "The real big story," according to Page, was that "all these changes have been made without rancor, without bitterness and without incident. . . . Coming from me," he added, "the man whom one of the walkers described as the 'most bitter' he had ever seen, this would indicate quite a change." Page concluded with a testimonial: "Deep down within me is the knowledge that the protracted stand of your group for their fundamental freedom created the first crack in the wall of repression and intimidation. . . . To all of that group who did so much, . . . our heartfelt thanks and friendship."[60]

Two of the peace walkers, Katherine Havice and Edith Snyder, returned to Albany in the summer of 1964, staying into the fall and trying to communicate with representatives of the white citizenry of Albany. "It is a terrible mistake to dismiss the entire white community . . . as monolithic," David Dellinger had written. Havice and Snyder agreed. No one in Albany would openly sponsor their "project," but with the backing of Muste and other supporters to whom he had appealed on their behalf, they acquired money for rent and subsistence. Muste kept in close touch with them, and although he had a letter from Mayor James V. Davis (assuring him of "my highest personal regard in spite of our differences") which emphasized that "the efforts of persons from outside our community usually create far more problems than they solve," Muste believed that a significant number of whites were secretly glad that the women came, and others, though perhaps not glad, were prepared "to vouch for their sincerity and defend them in one way or another if this should prove necessary." The violence which erupted in St. Augustine, Florida, and swept Mississippi that summer confirmed, he felt, "the importance and timeliness of the kind of thing they were trying to do in Albany."

The tensions and frustrations involved in "that kind of thing" were recorded by Snyder and Havice in their "Albany Log." No dramatic or quantifiable results appeared in their record. But they perceived that "spiritually the

Negro is no longer the underdog [and, therefore,] our compassion, our sympathy must now be for the white, perhaps even more than for the Negro." This was a reminder that nonviolence disturbs in order to reconcile and that all persons caught up in the racial conflicts of their age still partake of a common humanity. Muste once likened the period to "a world upheaval which is 'happening' to all of us . . . like a hurricane or tidal wave, . . . making no distinctions based on character, color or anything else."[61]

If it was important not to lose sight of the humanity of whites who resisted integration in America, it was at least equally important in Muste's view, to keep in focus the humanity of the non-white peoples whose culture and society this nation was destroying in other parts of the globe. "I sometimes think," he told audiences in the 1960s, "that the gulf between the peoples who have experienced humiliation as a people and those who have not is the deepest and most significant that we have to face. . . . When one undertakes to do that," he continued, "one comes to see that most people are on one side . . . and that almost alone . . . on the other side are the white Americans."

In the bold and chilling statements of black poet LeRoi Jones (later known as Imamu Amiri Baraka) and Muslim leader Malcolm X about America as, in Jones' words, "the source of Western Culture, . . . whose time has come and which is rotting at the roots," Muste heard truths that most of his countrymen did not want to accept, but which he predicted, were "bound to command . . . influence . . . in most of the rest of the world." The conclusion in favor of violent revolution or black nationalism to which a Jones or a Malcolm X pointed, Muste naturally did not share. But he warned that, if Americans did not quickly "build a bridge of reconciliation" across the gulf between them and the humiliated peoples, the only result could be a "bridge of retaliation" constructed from the other side.

Muste held that should they remain "indifferent to the abject inequality of the non-white part of the world," Negro Americans, and by extension, their Caucasian supporters would lose their integrity. To remain true to themselves and their cause they had, he admonished, to withdraw support "from the violence of one's own country which is an instrument of oppression" and extend the movement for "Freedom Now" to "subjugated and humiliated people everywhere." Muste publicly urged Roy Wilkins, Whitney Young, Martin Luther King, James Farmer, Bayard Rustin, and the leaders of SNCC to assess their own position vis-à-vis American foreign policy. President Johnson, Muste anticipated, would exact from black leaders a quid pro quo for protecting their workers or otherwise extending his patronage to their movement. The president would expect their support for his misadventures abroad, especially as the crisis in South East Asia deepened.[62]

In 1965, Muste singled out James Farmer as an example of black leadership being co-opted by establishment politics. An announcement of Farmer's trip that year to nine African countries triggered fifteen pages of reflection by

Muste on "The Civil Rights Movement and the American Establishment." In this polemic, which appeared in the February issue of *Liberation*, Muste, inferred more from Farmer's pre-journey press conference than the facts justified. He portrayed Farmer as an emissary of the White House and the State Department, eager to convey a positive image of the United States to Africa. What Farmer demonstrated in reality, however, was "the extent to which the civil rights movement, except for its left and/or fringe elements, is tied in with the current American regime and is in no small measure its tool."

Although, as his writings on King illustrate, Muste was accustomed to making public his disagreements with civil rights leaders, he usually was in personal contact with the leaders as well. In this instance, however, he seems to have made no effort to call Farmer. The article was published when Farmer was already abroad (the timing was ironically reminiscent of the Randolph-Reynolds attack on Rustin and Muste in 1948), and copies were soon circulated among CORE groups throughout the United States at a time when Farmer's leadership was being challenged. Farmer has flatly declared that Muste's approach in this case left him "furious."

The story took a strange turn when later revelations (two years after Muste's death) established that Farmer's trip had in fact been financed by the CIA. Farmer remained firm in his contention, however, that he did not know that this was the source of funding for the group which sponsored him. Furthermore, he had spoken frankly and critically throughout the trip against U.S. support of apartheid and the use of U.S. arms against African liberation struggles.

On balance it would seem that Muste strayed from the ground of fair play in his assault on Farmer. Yet, his basic perception that civil rights leaders were sometimes inclined to more political accommodation than was healthy for the integrity of their movement was valid, especially by the lights of radical pacifism. Farmer had never fully met Muste's expectations under these lights. In the early CORE years Muste and Rustin both chastised him for "hiding his pacifism." Now, in a period when Muste was turning these lights more relentlessly than ever upon national and global affairs, non-radicals such as Farmer were bound to be diminished in his view until or unless they broke entirely with the United States government which was, as Muste described it in the essay on Farmer, a "regime which has the equipment to wipe out the human race several times over and which is waging a 'dirty' war in South Vietnam."[63]

By 1965, with his own increasing outrage against that "dirty war," Muste was more insistent than ever that Negroes, as American citizens, had a responsibility to take a stand on Vietnam, and on the foreign policy assumptions which generated and fueled that conflict. But he argued not only from the responsibilities of citizenship but also from dictates of the self-interest of minorities. Issues of economic inequality and denial of civil rights would never be resolved in the context of war, he insisted. The threat of nuclear war gave his argument additional force. What will the struggle for civil rights avail, he asked, if it ends with "equality in extinction"? Muste had the impression that by the mid-sixties some Negroes were ready to expand their horizons beyond their own immediate struggle. "Being drawn into broader activities is stimulating . . . for young Negroes," he wrote.[64]

Some firsthand contact between Muste and these young black leaders developed as the tie between civil rights and peace grew stronger. Robert Parris (who in 1964 as Robert Moses had been the director of the Mississippi Summer Project and whom Muste rightly viewed as a "spiritual leader of the Student Nonviolent Coordinating Committee") was one of the young persons who worked to strengthen that tie. In August 1965, with considerable organizing and fund-raising support from Muste, a four-day program of anti-war activities was carried out by an estimated two-thousand protestors in Washington, D.C. The climax of that program, which had begun on Hiroshima Day, was the August 9 convening of "the Assembly of Unrepresented People" on the grounds of the United States Capitol building. Among the thousand members of that Assembly were a group of Mississippi Negroes whom Robert Parris had accompanied from the South and the money for whose travel and accommodations had been raised by Muste. Parris was among the first signers of the anti-war movement's "Declaration of Conscience against the War in Vietnam." From the ranks of the Mississippi Freedom Democratic Party, of which he was a part, had recently come a call (which was not officially sanctioned by the Party) for Negroes to refuse induction into the armed services. Parris openly supported that call, remarking that "Negroes better than anyone else are in a position to question the war—not because they understand the war better but because they better understand the United States."[65]

Here was the kind of straightforward, unqualified identification of racist transgressions in the United States with national transgressions in foreign lands for which Muste had been looking in the American civil rights movement. Parris was not alone in coming forward with such a position. The entire SNCC organization, under the leadership of John Lewis, adopted an anti-war posture. When news of this action reached Muste he "rejoiced" and immediately contacted Lewis for the complete SNCC statement on the war. Shortly after, he sought a meeting with Lewis. "I am very eager," he wrote, "to have a chance for real discussion with people like yourself . . . who have a commitment both to revolution and to nonviolence." Julian Bond, the first black person to be elected to the Georgia state legislature since Reconstruction, was ousted from that body when he publicly declared against the war. Muste wrote of the "great satisfaction" he took in the young man's "strong stand."[66]

Within Martin Luther King's SCLC, anti-war sentiment was also rising. At the SCLC convention in Birmingham in 1965, James Bevel, a product of the Nashville student movement and the influence of James Lawson, had spoken up strongly for cooperation between the struggles against war and against racial injustice, and had reportedly described the Johnson policy in Vietnam as "foolishness and a fallacy." King himself came out in support of Julian Bond and told the 1965 SCLC meeting, "It is worthless to talk about integration if there is no world to integrate . . . . The war in Vietnam must be stopped."

The board of the Southern Christian Leadership Conference responded with a reminder that "the primary function of our organization is to secure full leadership rights for the Negro citizens of this country" and to confine organizational efforts "to the quest for racial brotherhood." However, the board added, should there occur "perilous escalation of the Vietnam conflict we respect the right of Dr. King and the administrative committee to alter this course and turn the full resources of the organization to the cessation of bloodshed and war."[67]

Most black leaders, with the exception of SNCC people, greeted King's statement on the war with extreme hostility. His call for the war to stop "brought such criticism," Coretta King has written, "that Martin said no more, rather than risk creating disunity among his people." He did not, however, maintain total silence. In November 1965, Dr. Benjamin Spock spoke to Mrs. King about the possibility of a joint peace campaign initiated by King and him. The notion appealed to Mrs. King. When Muste heard of it (or a similar proposal involving King and Spock which was being talked of in peace circles) he urged Martin King to consider it seriously.

News reports of King's speech in Paris during a European tour in 1966 raised Muste's spirits, for the civil rights leader had reportedly declared "his intention to broaden the civil rights campaign to include opposition to the Vietnam War." In May of the same year, King sent a statement to an anti-war rally in Washington. It was read by William Sloan Coffin to 15,000 protestors: "The pursuit of widened war," he declared, "has narrowed domestic welfare programs, making the poor, white and Negro, bear the heaviest burdens at the front and at home." In the same period King lent his name, as co-chairman, to the Clergy and Laymen Concerned about the War in Vietnam.[68]

Whenever an opportunity presented itself Muste encouraged King down this path. *Liberation* reprinted a "Letter to Martin Luther King" from Buddhist monk Thich Nhat Hanh (originally published in Saigon in a collection of Hanh's essays). After explaining the philosophy behind the self-immolation of Buddhist monks and nuns ("To burn oneself by fire is to prove that what one is saying is of the utmost importance"), Hanh addressed the conscience of King on the subject of "this unnecessary war." "You know," the monk stressed, "that war is never necessary. . . . I am sure that since you have been engaged in one of the hardest struggles for equality and human rights you are among those who understand fully, and who share with all their hearts, the indescribable suffering of the Vietnamese people. The world's greatest humanists would not remain silent. You yourself cannot remain silent." When Hanh came to the United States in 1966, Muste arranged a public meeting of the black American preacher and the South Vietnamese monk. "There is a lynching going on in Vietnam," Muste wrote King; "all of us must be deeply aware of that and must do everything we can to stop it." As plans were laid for the trip which Muste and others made to Saigon in April 1966, he invited King to accompany them. But his prediction that "this idea may just be completely out of the question because of other responsibilities" proved valid. Muste persisted however. As he worked on preparations for what would prove to be his last trip abroad—to Hanoi in January 1967—the eighty-one year old activist wrote Mrs. King: "It would be a great event if by any chance you and Martin could make a visit to that country."[69]

While King moved more slowly than Muste wished toward an all-out attack on the war, his SCLC aide, James Bevel, plunged ahead into the thick of the anti-war movement. Only a few days before Muste's death Bevel assumed the post of national director of the Spring Mobilization against the War, which Muste had been instrumental in organizing. Securing Bevel for this position— an achievement on which James Lawson had worked and which had the approval of King—represented to Muste "an important coup. . . . This obviously opens up," he observed, "the possibility of a much more elaborate participation on the part of the Negro community and organizations than we have ever had before." Bevel's explanation of why he took leave from his civil rights commitments to work full time in the peace movement was simple. "White Americans are not going to deal in the problems of colored people when they're exterminating a whole nation of colored people," he told a *New York Times* reporter.[70]

W hile King was moving along a line that finally converged with Muste's position on the war in Vietnam, their mutual associate Bayard Rustin took a different tack. The result left him on the opposite side of a cleavage that rent the civil rights movement in the mid-sixties. An early sign of the coming division appeared at Atlantic City in the late summer of 1964. There, during the Democratic National Convention, delegates from the Mississippi Freedom Democratic Party (MFDP) attempted to unseat the official Mississippi delegation. When party leaders refused to support the total MFDP objective and offered a compromise instead (the regular Mississippi democrats were to sign a "loyalty oath" to the party platform and two MFDP delegates were to join the regular delegation), Rustin urged the compromise and persuaded King to do likewise. MFDP forces rejected their advice which many considered to be the equivalent of "selling out." Rustin (the same Rustin who only two years earlier had, as Muste saw it, done battle with Congressman Powell in an effort to keep the civil rights movement out of the clutches of the Democratic establishment) defended the compromise strategy he had proposed in Atlantic City and revealed the larger rationale behind it in his soon famous essay, "From Protest to Politics, the Future of the Civil Rights Movement." Printed in the February 1965 issue of *Commentary*, the article called for black Americans to drop what Rustin described as a "no-win" moralistic adherence to the tactic of trying "to change hearts by [traumatizing] them" and to forge a political coalition with trade unions, liberals, and religious leaders. Muste's position on the MFDP in Atlantic City went unrecorded but he took a keen interest in the debate which Rustin's article churned up. "Bayard . . . is undergoing a very grave inward struggle," Muste concluded. He saw the individual struggle as part of "what the civil rights movement is going through" and predicted that the outcome

would have a major impact on not only civil rights but also the anti-war movement and American society.[71]

Rustin's leaning toward coalition politics may not have evoked such a
strong reaction had one factor not been present—the war in Vietnam. To call
for a coalition with labor and liberals was to sanction cooperation with the
mainstay of the very Democratic administration that was waging and widening
the war. That was the consideration that most angered Rustin's critics. Articles
by David Dellinger and Staughton Lynd in *Liberation* made this clear. Their
highly critical evaluations of Rustin (which spread the breach between his coalitionism and their radical activism so wide that it was never closed again) were
written after the April 1965 anti-war rally in Washington, D.C. That rally had
been organized by the Students for a Democratic Society (SDS), whose opening
of the rally to people of all political persuasions and whose occasional failure to
distinguish clearly between policies governing the rally and policies intended
only for SDS led eleven older figures in the anti-war movement (including
Bayard Rustin and A. J. Muste) to issue a statement on the eve of the demonstration announcing disagreement with "particular positions expressed by
some of the elements in the March" and calling for "an independent peace
movement, not committed to any form of totalitarianism nor drawing inspiration or direction from the foreign policy of any government." Dellinger, Lynd,
and others interpreted the statement as an effort to sabotage the rally. They
regarded Muste's signature on the statement as an unusual slip on the part of an
old friend while seeing in Rustin's name final proof of their worst suspicions.
Their denunciation of Rustin—ranging over his behavior in Atlantic City, his
coalition article, and the peace rally statement—was so vigorous that another
longtime peace worker, David McReynolds, was prompted to ask "whether
Liberation had declared open season on Rustin." Lynd's use of the epithet,
"labor lieutenant of capitalism" to describe Bayard Rustin was particularly objectionable to critics such as McReynolds.[72] Muste said nothing in public print
during the debate which Dellinger and Lynd had triggered. Presumably he assented to the statement from "The Editors" of *Liberation* which maintained
that Lynd's article ought not be viewed "as in any sense constituting 'character
assassination' of Bayard Rustin. . . . We stand back of it as a serious and deeply felt contribution to the crucial discussion of coalition politics, nonviolent
revolution and related matters." The May-June 1966 issue of *Liberation* carried
a notice of Rustin's resignation from the editorial board. He was quoted as
saying that "involvement in the civil rights movement does not give me time to
struggle for the point of view I hold on a number of matters that really differs
with the other Editors."[73]

Muste, as one of those editors, could not have been other than perturbed
at the swipes which Rustin took at the anti-establishment politics that had so
long engaged radical pacifist energies: Rustin's dismissal of the "strong moralistic strain in the civil rights movement which would remind us that power
corrupts, forgetting that the absence of power also corrupts"; his charge that
the leader who "shrinks" from entering coalitions "reveals not his purity but

his lack of political sense"; and his sarcastic observation that without coalitions "the Negro is left in majestic isolation, except for a tiny band of fervent white initiates." Rustin's mild reaction to the war in Vietnam, his view of it as a "vexing problem" which might engage the interest of some Negroes but which for most black Americans would rightly remain peripheral, must have been even more aggravating to Muste. And given the long history of Muste's concern with and support for Negro struggles, and the involvement of peace organizations in those same struggles, Rustin's assertion that "peace workers" have failed to realize "that the peace movement must give a large part of its energy to the struggle to secure the social and economic uplift of the Negro community" was nearly incomprehensible and surely insulting.[74] On the other hand, the language employed by Lynd was also insulting, and the *Liberation* attack on Rustin hardly met the standards of personal nonviolence upon which Muste usually insisted.

Privately he expressed his feeling that the Lynd article was necessary and had said what he personally believed. He dismissed Rustin's reaction as "much too personal." Not surprisingly, efforts at dialogue with Rustin failed. He had passed up a chance to include a statement of his own in the same issue of *Liberation* where the Lynd statement was published. Subsequent plans for a meeting between him and a small number of peace people were thwarted by Rustin's always having other commitments. Yet at the personal level the long-term friendship exerted its pull. "I still very much want to have a talk," Muste wrote Rustin in October 1965. In the months that followed the two friends did have several talks. "A. J. believed," Rustin has said, "that war is the most pressing danger of our times. My answer was that people have to divide their various functions." But, Rustin continued, "A. J. felt that I had let down the movement. He saw me as one of the more brilliant communicators of pacifism. There were all kinds of people who could do what I was doing in the civil rights movement but so few who could communicate the pacifist message." At the end of their conversations, Rustin recalled, "A. J. would do what he did with few people— put his arm around me and say he hoped that we could talk further. He kept thinking," Rustin smiled, "right up to his death that if he talked enough he could convince me." So, while the political barrier that now separated them was never crossed, the personal affection between A. J. Muste and Bayard Rustin survived. "A. J.," observed Rustin, "was very hard on political questions but very soft with people."[75]

Muste's unwavering commitment to justice and equality for America's minorities, particularly Negroes, was a major part of his life. He was not himself a "civil rights leader" but the support and counsel which he gave those who did lead were of critical importance in helping to start, shape, and sustain major black organizations and to forge and maintain the link between their struggles and the struggle for nonviolence and peace. Few other white Americans matched Muste's contributions in this regard. Perhaps no other white American could have earned the tribute which Martin Luther King paid the pacifist on his eightieth birthday:

You have climbed the mountain and have seen the great and abiding truth to which you have dedicated your life. Throughout the world you are honored as our most effective exponent of pacifism. You have been a great friend and inspiration to me and the whole nonviolent movement. Without you the American Negro might never have caught the meaning of true love for humanity.[76]

Chapter IX

The Pacifist in an Age of Cold War and Megadeath
Dialogue and Persuasion

$\mathbf{W}$hile domestic struggles revolving around the civil rights and civil liberties of minorities in the United States absorbed a significant amount of A. J. Muste's time and energy, the search for world peace remained at the center of his attention. The atomic bombs which destroyed Hiroshima and Nagasaki shattered the main predictions and strategies which had governed his actions since the onset of World War II. He had predicted that at the end of that war only two outcomes were possible. Either there would be a new Dark Age in which "small groups of pacifists might serve as little islands of safety and security and faith in a black sea of barbarism" or a period of rebirth in which the "bankrupt western world" would be "taken over" by a "receivership" of pacifist forces.[1]

But the abrupt onset of the atomic age made references to islands of sanity in an age of darkness irrelevant—the darkness which atomic weapons could produce might envelope the entire human race. The western powers whose exhaustion and war-weariness once seemed certain now competed for possession of the most powerful weapon in human history and displayed little interest in the surcease from violence which the pacifist movement offered.

Yet the Cold War did not come as a total surprise to Muste. As early as 1944 he had seen signs of a growing rift between the Western powers and their war-ally, the Soviet Union. It may well be, he predicted, "that before many years or even months we may have to work even more vigorously for tolerance toward the Russians, for an appreciation of what is sound in Russia, than we have had to contend for an objective Christian attitude to the Germans and Japanese!"[2]

By 1947, when the sternly anti-Soviet Truman Doctrine was announced, Muste's prediction had been validated. He was highly skeptical of Truman's claim then that a state of emergency existed in Greece, requiring immediate American military aid to prevent a Communist takeover. Sensing that Truman had exaggerated the peril, he protested the emphasis on military aid rather than humanitarian relief. Moreover, despite his lack of faith in the United Nations, he saw in the bypassing of it by the United States an alarming disregard for international cooperation. When, to forestall such criticism, Senator Vandenberg introduced amendments to provide for future U.N. review of U.S. actions Muste waxed sardonic. "Through these amendments," he wrote, "the United States government is now saying, in effect: 'We are embarking on a radically new foreign policy, establishing a Monroe Doctrine for the entire earth, the doctrine that the United States security sphere extends all over the world. We are going to act on that doctrine now in Greece and Turkey and no one is going to be permitted to stop us. But if in a month or six months from now the U.N. should vote that this doctrine was wrong or unnecessary we shall promptly abandon it.' "[3]

Although the European Recovery Program (ERP) announced by Secretary of State George Marshall, also in 1947, held more promise than the Truman Doctrine of meeting human needs, Muste doubted that it was as great an act of generosity as the government made it out to be. Rather, Muste suggested, the ERP was an extension of the anti-communist offensive to which Truman had committed the United States. "Pacifists have a primary responsibility in not permitting people to believe there is peace when there is no peace," he urged. The peace movement in his judgment, should "insist on adequate relief and reconstruction aid . . . but not directly support ERP" unless "actual changes such as abandonment of UMT [Universal Military Training] and of the production of atomic weapons by the U.S. are instituted."[4]

As the Cold War suddenly flamed into heated conflict in Korea, and as the attendant arms race spiralled after the 1949 announcement of a Russian atomic weapon, existing arguments and analyses by which pacifist forces sought to break the grip of anti-communism on American thought and action needed to be revamped and sharpened. Muste made several contributions in this area, including an essay on the Korean War and a pamphlet on "how to deal with a dictator." In the essay on Korea, published as a pamphlet by the FOR in 1950, Muste argued against the notion that we were preventing a war there by "applying force in time." Not only did the sending of U.S. troops to Asia not prevent war, he maintained, but, with the U.S. government viewing the Korean conflict as part of the "power struggle between Russia [and itself]," it could mean the beginning of World War III.[5] The futility of military action was also the theme of his incisive and witty pamphlet, *How to Deal with a Dictator*, which appeared in 1954. In this piece Muste showed how, since 1914, one dictator after another had appeared on the stage of western history and in each case the response to him had been premised on "the mad dog theory"; "Anybody knows what you have to do with a mad dog," Muste summarized. "You shoot him." After that theory put the Kaiser out of the way Hitler and Tojo emerged. They "were [no sooner] licked," than Stalin became the next mad dog. "Two World Wars, war under the guise of 'police action' in Korea, Cold War, and still we face a bigger and more powerful dictatorship than ever," Muste declared. Furthermore, the newest preparations for shooting down the Stalinist dog involved "super-atom bombs, . . . the risk of mass suicide and the certainty of spiritual degradation that go with atomic war." Muste concluded that "if we start out with the idea of killing a mad dog and end up with all mankind leading a mad dog's life, . . . it could be that the mad dog theory was wrong all the time."[6]

In these and other writings and speeches of the 1950s and early sixties, Muste advised anti-communists to reckon with the fact that the origins of communism were in their own culture. "The philosophies of secularism, atheism, and materialism upon which Marxism and Leninism have drawn did not come from Russia, Asia, or Africa. They came from Western Europe and the United States," he argued. The traits of enforced conformity and unscrupulous resort to violence for which communists were vilified were present as well in Western states, Muste pointed out. Before attributing "hysterical nationalism and antiforeignism" solely to countries behind the Iron Curtain, Muste suggested, people should think of the importance which "McCarthyism loyalty oaths, etc." were coming to assume in the United States. And before condemning nations for brutality, remember, he said, that "in the development of the obscene technology of atomic war . . . it was not the Communists who led the way."

The alacrity with which Soviet communists had adopted the worst Western traits and the zeal with which they pursued, however belatedly, "the obscene technology of atomic war" were also the subject of Muste's condemnation. "The policy makers, generals, scientists and opinion makers . . . know the nature of modern weapons and the character of the war in which they are to be used," he noted, concluding that "*in this crucial respect* there is no difference between the leaders in the two rival blocs." By the same token there was no difference in the grave danger to which the peoples of both blocs were exposed. "The operative concept today," Muste stressed repeatedly, "is no longer mutual conflict but rather mutual entrapment."[7]

Many reformers who championed the notion of alternatives to the power politics of Cold War and the arms race tended, in Muste's view, to miss the dire nature of the crisis confronting them. The flaws that he had pinpointed in the United Nations Organization at its inception continued, in his judgment, to enervate even the most noble of U.N. programs.[8] And, as the U.N. foundered, so too did world government efforts. "World government cannot be established by legal or constitutional fiat," he maintained. "Community creates government and there is no world community." For the same reason proposals for an international police force seemed naive to Muste. "So long as nations depend upon military force," he argued, "I do not see that under conditions of modern warfare any of them would give such [forces] . . . the slightest opportunity to operate."[9]

U.S. and Russian proposals for international control of atomic weapons and materials (the so-called Baruch and Gromyko proposals), seemed to

Muste to suffer from all the weaknesses of other international efforts. "Each nation is in effect saying to the other," Muste observed, " 'I don't trust you and will not take any chances but I ask you to trust me and take the chances which that involves.' "[10] Dismissing as impractical international efforts which stopped short of obliterating nationalistic and militaristic rivalries, Muste also dismissed proposals for piecemeal change within the United States. In his view the movement to create a new cabinet level "Department of Peace," which was spearheaded by Senator Ludlow in 1945, was essentially sentimental. "The State Department ought to be the Department of Peace," he argued, "and it will be if we get rid of conscription and the national military establishment."[11]

Nor could Muste ever involve himself on one side or the other of national elections even where issues of peace and war were supposedly at stake. The postwar foreign policy of the United States was, he believed, fundamentally bipartisan and the effort of one candidate or another to appear to stand for a new policy was always at bottom a sham. Thus when Henry Wallace emerged in the late 1940s as a critic of the Cold War policies of Harry Truman, Muste admonished pacifists to recognize that, though the deposed cabinet member "uttered many important truths about the present situation, . . . he was a devoted supporter of the war policies of President Roosevelt and was now an advocate of a world divided into spheres of influence."

While many Cold War critics, including some radical pacifists, tended toward the Wallace camp in the Presidential election of 1948, Muste maintained his longtime practice of casting no vote. Heavy Communist influence in Wallace's campaign, combined with the candidate's "traditional power politics view of the world" discredited him, by Muste's standards, as a genuine peace candidate. Three years later Senator Robert Taft stirred considerable political speculation by his open attack upon the military and diplomatic strategies of the Truman administration. Muste again hastened to disabuse his cohorts of "any idea that Taft may be a sort of leader of a peace movement in this country." Both Truman and Taft, Muste asserted, had made plain their commitment to "global war against Russia and Communism." The difference between them had to do only with tactics.[12]

Such political analysis by Muste impressed few observers in the postwar world. Even fewer could make sense of the repeated urging that some nation or some world leader should unilaterally repent of reliance on military power and show the way to sanity and the salvation of humankind. Although Muste sincerely believed in this possibility and held firm to a personal faith that far-reaching miracles could occur,[13] his sense that humans must take a major hand in creating the conditions by which their prayers would be answered was very strong. He combined his faith with unceasing efforts to organize a strong movement for peace, and attempted to develop peace constituencies among certain key groups of people—scientists, church people, social scientists, and other academics. His first overtures were to the scientific establishment.

In the fall of 1945, Muste learned that scientists at Clinton Laboratories, Oak Ridge, Tennessee, and at the University of Chicago had organized efforts to, as a Chicago professor explained, "convince the people of the country that a continuing monopoly of the atomic bomb by the United States is impossible and that the future security of the nation requires that information and facilities this country controls be placed under the jurisdiction of an international authority." Muste began to follow the new scientists' organizations very carefully and urged FOR staff to "establish contact . . . with atomic scientists in their respective localities. . . . Many [scientists'] utterances," he observed "border closely on the pacifist position."[14]

That scientists were not likely to cross the pacifist border soon became evident, however. Muste's efforts to enlist atomic experts in the anti-conscription cause were rebuffed. His argument that international cooperation would depend upon the elimination of national military establishments and their conscripting powers did not register with the scientists. The anti-draft issue, they replied, was of "secondary importance" and not a cause to which they wished to divert their attention.[15]

Scientific concern over atomic danger seemed to Muste to be surprisingly shallow. He was nonplussed in the spring of 1946 to learn that some of the very physicists who had expressed dissent from U.S. atomic policies accepted Medals of Merit from the Truman administration for their role in helping to create the bomb. "When people see you accepting medals for and presumably taking some pride in the production of the bomb, some of the edge is certain to be taken off your warning about the horrible nature of the weapon," Muste wrote them. The medal recipients responded in various ways.

No reply from Enrico Fermi is on file. Harold Urey of the University of Chicago felt the weight of Muste's criticism and confided that he had "personally thought of the advisability of declining the Medal of Merit." He was quite frank, however, in describing the exposed position he felt himself and fellow atomic critics to be in. "We have been afraid of being accused of being Communists or something of that sort," he noted. "This Medal of Merit button protects us, and I personally am using it that way." Urey sadly concluded, "I . . . have received many medals and honors, and I have never received one that gave me so little pleasure." By contrast Urey's colleague Cyril Stanley Smith defended his role in helping to develop the bomb. "Nazi philosophy was so abhorrent and the growth of the Nazi system seemed so inevitable that I was glad to play my small part in combatting it," he wrote.[16]

The scientists who seemed to express the greatest sense of urgency about atomic dangers belonged to the Emergency Committee of Atomic Scientists founded by Albert Einstein in the spring of 1946. But Muste soon felt let down even by them. The Einstein group wanted to launch a campaign to educate the nation to the dangers of the atomic age and to encourage a new type of thinking about international relations. But nowhere in their appeal did they mention wanting to cease making atomic weapons. In an impassioned public letter to Einstein, Muste wrote: "Meetings, printed propaganda and lobbying [are] not the proper first step in such a campaign. [They are] indeed, in the absence of a prior personal and moral act on the part of the scientists, a trivial and in effect—though not in intention—a dishonest thing to do."

Muste circulated his letter among scientists in all parts of the country. He exchanged lengthy letters with men at the Randall Morgan Laboratory of Physics at the University of Pennsylvania, the Laboratory of Nuclear Studies at Cornell, the Institute for Nuclear Studies and the Institute for the Study of Metals at the University of Chicago, the Northern California Association of Scientists, and the Federation of American Scientists. Most scientists whom Muste contacted found reasons for why they could not become conscientious objectors to atom weapons manufacturing. One common reason was that it would endanger national security for stockpiling to stop before international controls were achieved. This was Einstein's line of thinking, to which Muste replied, "This position means that if international control is not established scientists in all countries will just go on making more and more diabolical weapons, even though according to their own warnings this means the complete destruction of the human race." He added, "This simply represents the abandonment of all moral standards."

The other common reason was that a refusal of scientists to continue making bombs without a clear mandate from the public would be undemocratic. That did not impress Muste, who reminded his correspondents that the bomb had been built without a public mandate and without public knowledge of how billions of their tax dollars were being spent. "Is it not the fact," he asked, "that if leading scientists will continue to work under conditions of secrecy on atomic and biological weapons without consulting the people, . . . all possibility of the survival of any kind of democratic life will be removed?"[17]

A few scientists welcomed Muste's challenge, including Victor Paschkis, a specialist in the field of heat transfer who was on the Mechanical Engineering Faculty at Columbia. A German emigré whose pacifist philosophy had been deeply influenced by the German FOR worker Sigmund-Schultze, Paschkis belonged to the American FOR and the Society of Friends. As the result of an article he wrote in the *Friends' Intelligencer* of August 1947, commending Muste's "open letter," Muste contacted Paschkis and together they prepared a conference for scientists which took place on the Haverford College campus in the summer of 1948. After that initial meeting an organizing conference was planned, and, in September 1949, the Paschkis group assembled again at Haverford to found the Society for Social Responsibility in Science (SSRS). From a charter membership of thirty-five Americans the Society grew modestly but internationally to an estimated membership of 700 persons by the 1960s. The SSRS encouraged its members to employ their expertness in constructive service to humankind and to heed their consciences when deciding what work was congruent with such service. The group also attempted to help its members find jobs that were free of destructive potential. Included in the total list of seven Nobel Prize recipients who became members of the SSRS were two residents of America, Linus Pauling and Albert Einstein.[18]

Muste had kept after Einstein, following his first "Open Letter" to the physicist, with a personal letter in the summer of 1946, and a second open letter in September 1947. Although he did not expect a response, joking about his "imaginary correspondence with Albert Einstein," he did, as time went on, establish a dialogue with the physicist. Once the SSRS was underway Muste talked with Paschkis about sending a deputation from the new group to Einstein. Although the latter had written Muste that little was to be gained from organizing scientists, since the problem was "political and economic rather than technical", Paschkis and chemist James Vail saw Einstein in 1950 and persuaded him to join the SSRS. At Muste's prompting Einstein published an open letter in July of that year announcing his membership in the group and endorsing its objectives.[19]

Subsequent exchanges between Muste and Einstein followed the pattern of the scientist praising the pacifist's objectives while rebuffing his approach. Refusing to sign a statement in the fall of 1950 against Japanese rearmament, Einstein likened it to "sending a bottle of sugar water to a chronic alcoholic." Similarly, in 1954, he shrugged off an appeal for his signature on a petition to President Eisenhower concerning Cold War tensions with the observation that "such a small scale effort by a few private persons will not have the slightest influence. Only powerful political agencies can influence the course of events." Still, shortly before his death in 1955, Einstein agreed to join Bertrand Russell in a public declaration (endorsed by nine other eminent scientists) posing, as the stark alternatives of the nuclear age, an end to the human race or renunciation of war. Paschkis and SSRS President Franklin Miller spoke with Einstein when this statement was being prepared. They believed, as *Fellowship* later reported, that their encouragement "may have had an important influence on his [Einstein's] decision to issue the statement." Minimal though his own influence had been Muste took satisfaction from the evolution toward pacifism which Einstein had made.[20]

Muste's direct involvement in the SSRS did not continue beyond the initial organizing phases. He did not again become involved organizationally with scientific or technical experts until some fourteen years later when he surprised and, in some cases, dismayed his pacifist colleagues by becoming a public member of the Hudson Institute, founded by Herman Kahn, the expert on the probabilities of thermonuclear war. In the early 1960s, Kahn expressed an interest in current pacifist thought and attended some institutes on international affairs sponsored by the American Friends' Service Committee. As he later recalled, he also "read several things which [Muste] had written and heard him speak several times and found this profitable." When Kahn established his Hudson Institute study center in upstate New York, the acting president of the Institute, Max Singer, invited Muste to become a public member. Muste accepted election which carried a term of seven years and gave him equal billing with leading figures of the academic and scientific worlds, including persons such as Sidney Hook and Reinhold Niebuhr whom he regarded as great antagonists of pacifism. Because the Institute held research contracts with many military and corporate organizations, and because of Kahn's own reputation for making chilling estimates of the millions of lives a country could afford to lose in a nuclear attack, some of Muste's friends questioned the pacifist's judgment. Muste was certain, however, that Kahn "is not [a] special kind of demon." Rather he said, Kahn's knowledge and forthrightness made him a source from which the peace movement must learn. "Both sides benefitted from the dialogue," Kahn observed. Yet there is little evidence that Muste made much use of his Hudson appointment or that he left a significant impression on the weapons-centered mentality that prevailed at the Institute.[21]

Muste worked much harder at establishing communication between pacifists and nonpacifists in the realm of organized religion. At the end of World War II, he urged on fellow pacifists the need to "go to the churches and put [the pacifist challenge] to them. A good many people still do find the basis for their thinking in the church," he argued. "We cannot influence the government as such as directly as the churches. If the churches are willing to accept the challenge then perhaps," he hoped, "the miracle of the nation following will happen."

A major obstacle to this development in Protestant churches was the strong influence of "neo-orthodox theology." The most famous American advocate of the neo-orthodox point of view was Reinhold Niebuhr. Muste, who usually avoided looking upon those with whom he disagreed as adversaries, mounted a strikingly militant challenge against Niebuhr and what he saw as the "phenomenal prestige of Niebuhr among . . . liberals and ex-liberals" since the late 1930s.[22]

At first glance the early pastoral career of Reinhold Niebuhr parallelled that of A. J. Muste. The effect of World War I on both men was that of making them declare for pacifism. They were colleagues in the Fellowship of Reconciliation in the early 1920s. Their respective experiences in trying to combat economic and social injustice led each toward Marxism and away from pacifism in the 1930s. On closer examination, however, these parallels are more apparent than real. Niebuhr's devotion to pacifism was always experimental. His involvement in the social movements of the 1930s, including the Socialist Party, was intense at the level of theory but peripheral in terms of field work and street activism, in sharp contrast to the direct plunge which Muste took into the labor struggles of that era. In the understanding of the two men regarding the relationship of Christian teachings to secular politics lay the most profound difference of all. Niebuhr in his Marxist phase adapted religious ethics to socialist doctrine, hesitating very little over possible incompatibilities between the two. Muste, on the other hand, felt that, in assuming a position which included the concept of violent revolution, Niebuhr had disavowed all ties to Christian teaching, which as he read them, included an unbending pacifist ethic.

In the light of these earlier differences the wide gap which prevailed between Muste and Niebuhr in later years is easier to understand. When they broke with their respective Marxist organizations—Muste leaving the Trotskyists in 1936, Niebuhr resigning from the Socialist Party in 1940—the former Trotskyist could return to a pacifist community which he had previously served with deep devotion and whose values he now reaffirmed in the light of extensive experience in secular revolutionary struggles. Niebuhr having been more tentative in his pacifism and less involved in the grass-roots struggles of socialism was readier to dismiss both and place his allegiance in the socio-political system to which they had posed alternatives and which, as World War II loomed in Europe, the theologian came to value more and more. Just as he had previously found it possible to fuse Christian teachings with Marxist theories, now Niebuhr found in neo-orthodox theory moral dictates that complemented the national and allied effort to combat fascism.[23]

The intellectuals and politicians who made up the substantial following which he had acquired by the end of the 1940s applauded Niebuhr for providing an antidote of clear-minded realism to the fuzzy thinking which supposedly had characterized liberal politics since the First World War. His realist point of view stressed that the moral context in which humans function is blurred and equivocal and renders even the purest of human motives imperfect in their application. Liberals, according to this view, oversimplify the difficulties inherent in making moral decisions. They assume that reason and love will always overcome irrationality and evil. The terrible rise of Hitler, which, by Niebuhr's account, had been facilitated and encouraged by liberal naiveté, proved once and for all the fallaciousness of the liberal position. Stalinist tyranny and subsequent exponents of "international communism" merely reinforced the point. Historian Paul Merkley has observed that "Niebuhr to some degree prepared the minds of many intellectuals and policy makers with arguments and with language . . . which proved appropriate to the preparation of the case for 'realism' in political theory," and by extension in American Cold War foreign policy.[24]

To the critics of that foreign policy and of the Niebuhrian sources which were frequently invoked in its behalf it seemed clear that the authority which Niebuhr's views took on was at least in part a result of his saying—albeit in very sophisticated and forceful ways—what many tired and anxious political leaders, opinion shapers, and intellectuals wanted to hear. To these critics it seemed equally clear that Niebuhr's blanket condemnation of earlier liberalism, of which he offered pacifism as the worst possible product, never adequately or fairly met the strongest contentions of radical Christian pacifists.

Niebuhr's assumption, for example, that he could dispose of pacifism by citing the Munich Agreement as a classic instance of naive pacifist faith in compromise failed to take into account the strong opposition to Munich voiced by leading peace workers, including Henri Roser of the French FOR and A. J. Muste, who had denounced Munich as "giving away what does not belong to you and then hurrying home to speed up your armament program so that you can take it back in six months, or at least avoid giving away anything of your own." This, he had concluded, "never did spell appeasement or peace in the intelligent pacifist's dictionary."

Muste's efforts to clear up such misunderstandings seldom succeeded, and the dialogue between pacifism and neo-orthodoxy for which he pressed remained heavily one-sided. Muste and Niebuhr "did argue with each other," John Howard Yoder has observed, and "although one can object to Niebuhr's not continuing the conversation in true ecumenical openness," yet, Yoder adds, "it is possible to understand that he didn't have anything more to say."[25] Whatever the case, Niebuhr never responded to the public challenges which Muste laid down in *Not By Might*, and in such essays as "Pacifism and Perfectionism" and "Theology of Despair," which appeared in *Fellowship* in the late 1940s.

In these writings Muste acknowledged that liberal Christianity owed a limited debt to Niebuhr and the neo-orthodox school for pointing out the oversimplification and undue optimism with which the liberal religious tradition was sometimes flawed. But having said that, the pacifist stressed that the pervasive pessimism in neo-orthodox thought could "dry up the springs of individual responsibility" by overwhelming the individual with such a sense of personal sinfulness that all encouragement to assert one's own dignity would be gone.

This notion of sin, along with other biblical notions of nonresistance, forgiveness, and grace were the focal points of theological disagreement between Muste and Niebuhr. In the Niebuhrian view the worst social evils, including war, were rooted in the ineradicable sinfulness of human nature and were themselves ineradicable. According to the theologian, Christian injunctions to practice love toward one's neighbor and to overcome evil with good stand as norms "outside history" by which imperfect humans know themselves to be judged and by which they are ever reminded of their limitations. For Muste, however, Christian scripture provided more than "an extended commentary on the single text, 'vanity, vanities, all is vanity.' " He preferred in his repeated calls for unilateral disarmament to emphasize "the commandment 'be ye perfect as your heavenly Father is perfect,' and the promise 'Behold I make all things new.' Even Paul declared," Muste noted, " 'I can do all things in him that strengthens me.' "

Muste assured Niebuhr that "I am as pessimistic as you are about what man in himself and by himself can do." But for the pacifist the whole point of laying stress upon the pervasiveness of sin was to demonstrate the need for and the limitless possibilities in repentance and redemption. The ethic of perfectionism which Niebuhr located outside the context of history seemed to Muste to lie at the very heart of the meaning of the historical existence of human beings. Beyond reminding humans of their limitations, the Christian injunction to be perfect, as Muste read it, called on them to emulate the example of Jesus and model their own lives after him.[26]

Another area of disagreement between Niebuhr and Muste focused on their views of the historical Jesus. Niebuhr's Jesus had not involved himself in the political and social struggles of his time. He advocated a doctrine of nonresistance; the principles of loving behavior which he set down were intended for individuals and had no direct application to larger social units. Muste's Jesus, in contrast, was deeply concerned with contemporary politics, and far from advocating nonresistance, he enjoined his followers to "overcome" the evils of their time "with good." Niebuhr's suggestion, then, that pacifists could perform a valuable service by withdrawing from the stage of history and practicing their pacifism as a personal, nonpolitical vocation, found no acceptance with Muste.

Neither did the clergymen agree on the political implications of biblical promises of divine forgiveness and grace. "Niebuhr regards grace as forgiveness," Muste observed, "rather than as power [or] as 'enabling grace.' " In his discussions of forgiveness Niebuhr emphasized that even the individual who experiences grace remains capable of sinning again and of becoming self-righteous about having been forgiven. Muste conceded that the "temptation to pride and self-righteousness is real and pervasive," but he believed that "the temptation to adapt the Gospel demand to circumstance and to abandon the hard effort to mold one's own life and the world according to that imperious demand is no less subtle and pervasive." He also felt, as a result of his own experience, that God-given grace was empowering and that such power could seize not only individuals but nations, that a new Pentecost was possible and that it was the vocation of Christians to prepare themselves for that Pentecost.[27]

While the institutionalized church showed few signs of adopting this vocation, from time to time ecclesiastical convocations and commissions took note of pacifist concerns and Muste in turn paid close attention to church pronouncements on war and peace. Delegates to the protestant World Conference of 1937 at Oxford, while finding themselves divided on the question of participation in war, declared their unwillingness to "rest in permanent acquiescence in continuance of these differences" and agreed that "the Universal Church . . . must pronounce a condemnation of war unqualified and unrestricted." While no such condemnation was forthcoming during World War II, at the founding conference of the World Council of Churches in Amsterdam in 1948, religious leaders recognized that the nature of modern war called into question all traditional arguments for "just war", but that Christian thinkers remained unable to speak with "one clear voice" to this issue. They described three general trends of thought within the church—a trend toward accepting war as a possible duty but never an act of justice; a tendency to insist that the possibility of war must be understood as the "ultimate sanction of the rule of law"; and the third position amounting to absolute refusal to participate in war. In this "third position of Amsterdam," as Muste understood it, pacifists were acknowledged as belonging "in the main body of the church, not outside as 'sects'."

Although he sensed in fellow pacifists a profound pessimism over the chances of their values being widely adopted in church circles, Muste himself was "not quite that pessimistic." He was eager in the wake of Amsterdam to press for discussion among churchmen of the implications of the diminished status of concepts of just war and was instrumental in drafting an appeal to the Federal Council of Churches that this issue receive serious attention at the FCC Study Conference to be held in Cleveland in March of 1949. The tone of this conference was set, however, by keynote addresses from John Foster Dulles and Reinhold Niebuhr, which, as Muste summed them up, left Protestant leaders in support of "a foreign policy which they profoundly mistrust [and which allows] for resort to war while pronouncing war to be diabolical and suicidal."[28]

The notion of a major conference of pacifist theologians where church-state relationships and peace-war questions might be examined in a less nationalistic framework had been in the air in pacifist circles since at least the Amsterdam convocation. Lending impetus to it was a felt need among pacifists with strong commitments to institutional churches for a peace witness that would reaffirm the Christian foundations of pacifism. Many such church-related pacifists were dissatisfied with the FOR in this area. Thus, Muste directed his attentions to organizing such a gathering. Slated for May 8 through 11, 1950 in the Detroit Church where the veteran pacifist Henry Hitt Crane was then pastor, the projected Conference on Church and War "ought," Muste declared, "to prove an epoch making occasion in the post–World War II history of the Christian church." He placed it "in the same category as Oxford and Amsterdam. And it might prove even more important than either of them," he predicted.[29]

Four hundred invited delegates and another four hundred or more observers appeared at the Detroit Central Methodist Church for opening services and keynote addresses by Clarence Pickett of the American Friends' Service Committee and Henry Hitt Crane. With three hundred to four hundred persons in regular attendance for three days, the conferees directed their prayers and study to three areas of pacifist concern: the theological basis of pacifist teachings; their political and social implications; and "practical instrumentalities" for implementing a far-reaching program of peace.

The theological discussions, which were moderated by Baptist scholar Culbert Rutenber, involved a written exchange between A. J. Muste and Alexander Miller, an assistant to Reinhold Niebuhr at Union Theological Seminary. In an informal essay distributed to the delegates, Miller wrote of the need to break "new ground . . . in the old debate between the Niebuhrs and the Mustes" because "the atom bomb is a new thing." But beyond agreeing that in trying to end war it might be better to stress practical questions rather than theological differences, the two sides found little in common in their exchange.

Another paper authored by Muste on "Pacifist Strategy" was included in the conference study materials. Its influence was evident in the "Affirmation and Appeal" which the delegates issued at the end of their deliberations and which, over the signatures of respected scholars from several parts of the world, received wide distribution in the months following the conference. Calling upon the church "to speak a distinctive and steadying word, drawn not from the judgments of the secular world but from its own gospel," the statement identified renunciation of war not with "impractical perfectionism" but with "simple devotion to morality in loyalty to Christ." It denounced the policy of containment of Communism as "contrary to Christian principles" and urged that "a policy of active goodwill" replace it. The pacifist gathering also recommended that an "informal mission" be carried on until Christmas to spread their message and lay the ground for its implementation. The convocation ended on a note of hope and satisfaction. "We lived a real and vital fellowship as we worshipped and worked together," delegate Harold Chance reported to the American Friends' Service Committee. "At last," he sighed, "the pacifists in the Protestant churches have spoken with a united voice."[30]

In the course of two "post-conference committee" meetings held immediately after the Church and War convocation, Muste's often expressed belief that "a great mission to the churches must be organized" became a reality. Originally conceived as a six-month project, the Church Peace Mission (CPM) gathered enough momentum to justify repeated extensions of its existence over a period of twelve years. In the beginning, administrative responsibilities were shared between Muste, who was given released time from the FOR to become "Missioner," and a director (Lutheran Pastor Robert Weiskotten until the spring of 1951; Martin England from September 1951 to the end of 1952). From 1953 (when Muste turned over the executive office of the FOR to John Swomley) until 1962, the Missioner carried the main administrative burden of the CPM. The organization was funded primarily by other pacifist sources, with the FOR, the American Friends' Service Committee, and the Brethren Service Committee making the most substantial contribution.[31] Setting forth a two-fold purpose—to raise the level of pacifist commitment within the historic peace churches and to change the theological climate in the United States—the CPM sponsored local conferences and numerous colloquies to promote discussion of war and of Christian teachings among theologians, seminarians, and other Christian teachers and students.

In the early 1950s, attendance at CPM meetings was restricted by the climate of fear which prevailed in the face of McCarthyite accusations and the outbreak of war in Korea. "The word 'peace' was nearly everywhere being given a sinister inflection," director Robert Weiskotten reported. Still, the mission tallied up an "overall attendance of about 6500" persons at their large meetings during its first year of operation. Concentration thereafter was more on small gatherings. While the many colloquies which CPM initiated in seminaries and universities throughout the United States did not have the revolutionary impact for which Muste had hoped, they did encourage pacifist-nonpacifist dialogue and seemingly fostered a new level of appreciation among nonpacifists for anti-war arguments.[32]

That appreciation was fostered as well by the drafting and wide circulation of peace-oriented pronouncements endorsed by major church figures. The first such statement which the CPM produced was formulated in response to a report issued in 1950 by a National Council of Churches Commission on "The Christian Conscience and Weapons of Mass Destruction." Under the leadership of Angus Dunn of the Protestant Episcopal Diocese of Washington, the Protestant commission had concluded that the use of atomic weapons by other nations against "us or our friends in Europe or Asia" could justify "our government to use them in retaliation with all possible restraint." Three days after the Dunn report was made public, President Truman announced that use of atomic weapons in Korea had been and continued to be under consideration. Pacifists charged that the Dunn Commission had given "moral backing to the secular authority in contemplating resort for the third time in this generation to atomic bombing by the armed forces of the United States in Asia."

"The Christian Conscience and War," as the CPM response was entitled, was two years in preparation and unbending in its position that "the Church and Christians must stand over against the world, not conformed to it," and that "for the Christian conscience the basic issue is not what it means to die but what it means to inflict death on another." The thirty-four clergymen who signed the statement called on the church "to break with modern absolutized war . . . ; the church should be to culture what the pacifist is to the church," they declared.

Roughly 17,000 copies of "The Christian Conscience and War" were distributed. Many went to delegates who attended the World Council of Churches Assembly in Evanston, Illinois, in 1954 and some delegates reportedly wrote to the CPM "indicating that they are deeply impressed by the study." It was appreciatively reviewed in the Niebuhrian journal, *Christianity and Crisis*, as "a call that has long been needed which ought not to go unheeded."[33] But it generated considerably less interest than the pronouncement which the CPM distributed in nearly 40,000 copies at the dawn of the next decade. That statement, "A Christian Approach to Nuclear War," originated outside the CPM with nonpacifist theologians Harold DeWolf of Boston University School of Theology and Norman Gottwald of Andover Newton. The two professors' critique of a study document by a World Council of Churches Commission on "Christians and Prevention of War in an Atomic Age" aroused the interest of CPM workers when they learned that most faculty members of the authors' schools and some additional faculty from Harvard and Cambridge theological seminaries had signed the critique which was sent to the Study Commission of the World Council.

Under the auspices of the CPM and with the permission of Gottwald and DeWolf, Muste reworked the critique into a statement to be distributed widely in, as the pacifist explained, "an effort to determine how many Christian spokesmen are now prepared to adopt what is sometimes called 'the nuclear pacifist position.' " "A Christian Approach to Nuclear War" was published in 1960 with the endorsement of Gottwald, DeWolf, and nine other churchmen. Within five months, Muste reported, signatures of approval from churchmen in the United States numbered "several hundred." The CPM circulated an abbreviated version of the statement in 1962 over the signatures of "more than 500 clerical and lay Christians" and received fairly extensive and sympathetic press coverage.

Although Muste said he had "defined somewhat more sharply the political conclusions" reached in the original critique, his unilaterialism and absolutist pacifism were muted in "The Christian Approach." The statement advocated "controlled multilateral disarmament" while suggesting that American leaders should "not persist in piling up nuclear weapons, even if other nations are not prepared to agree to the same course." The strongest affirmation was embodied in the claim that "as Christians . . . we cannot under any circumstances sanction the use of nuclear and other mass destruction weapons nor can we sanction using the threat of massive retaliation by these weapons for so-called deterrence." "The Christian Approach" urged "serious study" by political and educational leaders of "the possibility of nonviolent resistance to possible aggression and injustice."[34]

While such statements circulated beyond the borders of the U.S., the CPM was involved in other attempts to influence international opinion. Beginning in the mid-fifties, CPM personnel, and especially Muste, became involved in efforts to encourage dialogue between pacifist and nonpacifist churchmen in Western Europe and in bringing religious leaders of the Eastern European community into communication with their counterparts in the West. "On the continent of Europe," Muste noted in 1955, "there has hitherto been virtually no theological discussion between theologians and pastors of the large Lutheran and Reformed bodies on the one hand, and those of the Historic Peace Churches on the other." This communication gap, dating from the Reformation, was bridged in August of that year at a conference held in Puidoux, Switzerland, an outgrowth of earlier meetings between pacifist churchmen and the World Council of Churches' leadership. Muste played an active role in the preliminary planning and also attended the Puidoux meeting. The conference, involving twenty-seven persons from seven nations, found themselves "unanimous in affirming that our Lord expects from us today action for justice and peace among men . . . by every means compatible with the Gospel and therefore without recourse to war." "Not an inconsiderable number of continental theologians," Muste concluded, "have arrived at or are approaching a pacifist position."[35]

In even such an influential figure as Karl Barth, Muste saw this happening. He spoke with Barth in the latter's home town of Basel, Switzerland, in March 1955. Having for a long time viewed the Swiss theologian as an arch opponent of pacifism and being aware of current speculation that Barth's political allegiances were running toward the Soviets, Muste was pleased to report that their conversation confirmed neither view. He recalled Barth as saying, "I detest [communism] from my heart. But it's too easy here to talk against Communism and for Western policies. My belief is that on both sides Christians must swim against the stream . . . , protest against the present regimes . . . , at least not become instruments of the regimes." The Swiss theologian was reportedly highly critical of Reinhold Niebuhr for his support of American policy. When Muste inquired about Barth's attitude toward nuclear weapons he replied, "In a way the trouble is that the truth is so simple, so clear. Atomic war is madness. So what shall we do—stand on the street corner and cry 'Madness, madness, madness'?" When Muste reminded him that "perhaps that is what the Old Testament prophets did," the theologian agreed, "yes, I suppose so." However, when Muste pressed him that "it would mean a great deal if you would speak or write about these things," Barth demurred. "Politics is really not my line," he said. Though rebuffed Muste was not disheartened. He concluded his report on this talk with the reminder that a Barth student, American Mennonite John Howard Yoder, was convinced that "an analysis of Barth's writings in so far as they derive from *Biblical* revelation, as distinct from political judgment, all tend to support pacifism as the truly Christian attitude."[36]

The desire among European religious leaders to further examine the ethical dilemmas posed by modern war led to three further "Puidoux" gatherings—in Iserlohn, Germany, in 1957, at Bievres, France, three years later, and at Oud Poelgeest, the Netherlands, in 1962. Muste was in attendance only at Bievres where he again saw evidence of religious thinkers turning toward "nuclear pacifism." Of most significance to him, however, was "attendance for the first time at a Puidoux Conference of Eastern Churchmen."[37]

Dialogue across East-West boundaries in the era of the Cold War was difficult both to begin and to sustain. In the early 1950s, Muste refrained from attempting it. He turned aside overtures from the Soviet-dominated World Peace Council (WPC). "The official line of the W.C.P. [sic] has been," he observed, "that Soviet foreign policy is a peace policy, that wars in which Communist countries engage are 'defensive' and/or 'Progressive' in character and that the military establishments of these countries are a force for peace. I do not believe these things any more than I consider U.S. foreign policy to be a peace policy," he declared. In an article for the *Ecumenical Review* in 1954, Muste described religious thought "on both sides of the Iron Curtain as . . . distorted and confused. The churches of East and West alike are," he lamented, "unable to . . . pass judgment on the culture and nation with which their life is deeply enmeshed." However, shortly after the WPC collected 300 million signatures against atomic weapons, and the influential nuclear pacifist convert Pastor Martin Niemoller of Germany told an American FOR meeting that the Kremlin-sponsored petition showed that "even the Communist system has to serve the will and aims of God," Muste became engaged in informal talks with peace spokesmen from communist regimes. Representatives of the International Fellowship of Reconciliation, including Muste, met with WPC members in Stockholm in March 1955. While the Marxists seemed unmoved by the pacifists' insistence that, as IFOR leader Andre Trocme put it, "Christians are above nationalist pattern [sic] of thought", and the IFOR group remained firm in their refusal to participate in the WPC mass meetings, both sides felt the benefit of a frank exchange of views.[38]

Some three years later, a separate group of Eastern European Churchmen, under the leadership of Czech theologian Joseph Hromadka, organized the "Prague Conference" and called for a world conference of Christians on peace. Muste and a variety of other pacifist and nuclear pacifist American and

Western European leaders met with some of these figures at Buckeburg, Germany, in August of 1958. "All of us got a very deep and in a sense painful realization of the extent to which those in the East and West live in different milieus, different 'universes of discourse' and how important it is that each should understand the other's position and condition in order that genuine discussion of controversial questions may take place," Muste reported.[39]

Muste's own efforts to understand the Eastern Europeans' "condition" were cautious. He divided members of the Prague Conference into three categories: "some who must definitely be regarded as politically suspect; others who definitely are not politically suspect and still others who fall somewhere in between." He approached dealings with the first and third categories very warily. In the judgment of Milton Mayer, a longtime friend who had lived in Czechoslovakia for a time and was acquainted with many of the churchmen from that part of the world, Muste's caution was excessive and might "weaken what already appears to be a generally weak will among American Christians to deal with their brethren in the East."[40]

Even so, increased contact with leaders of Eastern European peace groups did decrease the distance from them which Muste had previously maintained. In 1959 he concluded that, while collaboration between Western peace forces and groups dominated by the Soviets was still unacceptable, "FOR members should not put up a 'curtain' of their own, isolating them from contact with people of Communist countries." He recommended to the IFOR that it send observers to WPC gatherings. He personally served as such an observer at the Stockholm World Peace Council meeting in 1961, but found the outcome disappointing. Too much time was spent in posturing and polemics he indicated, and too little time was devoted to discussing further cooperation among peace forces.[41]

More satisfying were small East-West gatherings of churchmen which occurred periodically beginning in the late 1950s. A few days before Puidoux III "a private unpublicized meeting took place in Paris," involving Muste (representing the CPM) and other Western pacifists, and a group of Eastern churchmen. The main topic was the call for a "World Christian Peace Conference" which members of the Prague Conference continued to press. The Westerners were chary of such a meeting, with its obvious usefulness to Soviet propaganda, and promised no more than participation as observers. The idea of a smaller meeting, involving truly representative and influential leaders from both sides was also explored then and in subsequent correspondence. While Muste contributed time and organizing effort and took a keen interest in later developments, American Quaker Douglas Steere became the facilitator for this smaller meeting, which occurred in Karlovy Vary, Czechoslovakia, in January of 1962. The participants reportedly managed to transcend nationalism and found a common ground of mutual concerns.

Muste was gratified by the positive reports which the American churchmen brought home from Karlovy Vary. "This outcome has been very significant to me," he wrote Hromadka. "The Karlsbad [the German name for the Czech city] meeting is a significant contribution to . . . the effort to develop understanding at a deep level among Christian leaders." "Remember," conference participant John C. Bennett later noted, Karlovy Vary was near "the height of the cold war and any human contacts across the divide made some difference."[42] Yet how much difference and what political or spiritual effect it had is impossible to measure.

The same difficulty of measurement applied to all of Muste's work with the CPM and related activities in the church. He and pacifist colleagues were convinced that within their own ranks they had experienced increasing unity since World War II, and that their position had become "more solidly theological" than at any previous time in this century. The ability of the Historic Peace Churches along with the FOR to sustain the CPM for more than twelve years, and the high level of theological discourse which occurred in the CPM colloquies and conferences supported this view. Their further contention that they had effectively exposed the neo-orthodox position as being more political than theological was less easy to document, but dialogue with thinkers who identified with that position revealed that at least serious questioning and reappraisal had begun in circles where neo-orthodoxy had once held undisputed sway. At the same time pacifism was receiving increasing consideration. When the *Ecumenical Review* printed Muste's article on "War, Politics and the Normative Principle," and asked a leading Danish theologian to write a critique, John Howard Yoder commented that not since "the patristic period" of church history had the question of pacifism received such attention. While the traditional pacifist position won new respect, "nuclear pacifism" nudged previously adamant nonpacifists toward a peace-centered stand. "What seems to me to give power to your statement ["The Christian Conscience and Nuclear War"] at the present time," wrote Dean Francis B. Sayre of the Washington Cathedral, "is the fact that the alternative which we are now pursuing obviously does not work, and so the risk you propose is probably the lesser one, since at the same time it has the advantage of being based on principle." "For the first time," declared Niebuhrian John C. Bennett, "I agree with you that if the USA did take the initiative along your lines this would probably be a better policy in terms of prudence as well as in terms of ethical sensitivity". But for all the change in attitude that such concessions implied, there was no comparable change in actions.[43]

"I cannot avoid looking at the question in terms of what is politically and psychologically possible for the American government," Bennett had added. "I am still hung up," he said, "by the realization [that] the USA will not do this [unilaterally disarm]." Even Paul Tillich—whose vision Muste had repeatedly quoted, of "a people [becoming] the church . . . seized in an unexpected historical moment . . . by the transcendental idea and for its sake [renouncing] power"—had become similarly skeptical. "The idea still has much attraction for me," he wrote Muste. "but my doubts have increased." Many other clergy and theologians also had their doubts. The response to a *Christian Century* article on the horror of atomic weapons indicated clearly, editor Harold Fey wrote Muste, that ministers were not "waiting to be mobilized on a unilateral disarmament platform."

Muste's hopes for converting the church into a center of advocacy for pacifism went unrealized. Churchmen valued his influence but did not follow his lead. "I am not sorry you are pushing," John Bennett told him. Bennett later reflected that Muste had done "much of the best thinking about the theological and ethical bases of pacifism." Others expressed appreciation for his "vision, wisdom, challenge, and inspiration." A common response to the CPM call for a prophetic stance on modern war was neatly expressed by the Congregational minister who wrote, "You did not convert me but surely [you] brought me under the conviction of sin." By 1962, Muste was ready to lay down his responsibilities as chief missioner, pleading advancing age and attendant strains on his health. Such considerations, however, did not prevent him from immersing himself in the many and demanding programs of other groups such as the War Resisters' League, the Committee for Nonviolent Action, and the World Peace Brigade. A warning Muste delivered in 1966 pretty well summed up his final conclusions about the church. To expect that institution to live up to its teachings and its prophetic function "might lead to great disappointment," he said.[44]

In the same period of the 1950s and early sixties that Muste was seeking to persuade churchmen of their prophetic obligations, he was also urging the academic and intellectual community to face up to their responsibilities in finding and championing alternatives to the Cold War and the stockpiling of nuclear arms. Throughout his career Muste regularly turned to academic institutions as potential sources of support for the causes which he championed. He scoured the work of eminent scholars for information and themes that seemed applicable to his work and exerted continuing pressure on those engaged in research and teaching to address the critical issues of their times. While usually disappointed by their response, Muste continued to value academe. He was genuinely pleased to receive appointments as visiting lecturer at New Brunswick and Union Theological seminaries. He enjoyed setting up and participating in short-term seminars with professors and experts. He was a voracious reader and remained abreast of the most current and most serious work in a wide variety of disciplines, though occasionally he would toss off an aside about his own "lack of expert standing."

Most of all Muste harbored a strong impression of mutual need between the world of scholars and the world of activism. He knew that movements for social change needed creative ideas and responsible research and believed that researchers and thinkers, in order to achieve creativity and responsibility, needed to align themselves with movements for social change. "Intellectual exchange . . . is an essential part of the nonviolent way of life," Muste declared. Contrary to the impression which debunkers such as Oscar Handlin held, that Muste's "call to action was a substitute for thought," Muste rebuked fellow activists who denigrated the life of the mind. He reminded them that "there could have been no revolutionary movement, no socialism, no communism . . . without Marx," and added that "no movement which really expects to make history and assume responsibility for the reorganization of society can get along without its philosophical commitments." He knew, as Nathan Glazer once observed, that pacifists have a reputation for being "wooly-minded." Muste was anxious to be rid of that reputation and promoted, as he put it, "research, not propaganda."

At the same time he noted the way in which professional thinkers tend to compartmentalize their lives; how, for example, psychologists and educators might practice sound principles of nonviolence in their offices and classrooms and yet fail to see any application of those principles to the society beyond their work place. Muste was concerned, also, to encourage a reordering of research priorities. We need people to study how to improve the quality of human life, he argued, rather than people who first work on making men fight better and then on rehabilitating the survivors of the better fight.[45]

With these considerations in mind Muste helped to launch a number of projects oriented toward research and intellectual exchange. He had worked on two such projects in the years immediately following World War II—a Pacifist Research Bureau and a research committee attached to the Peacemakers' organization. But inadequate funding and a general tendency among peace workers to put other endeavors ahead of research weakened them seriously, and they produced limited results. Still, the Pacifist Research Bureau did publish a series of pamphlet-length studies on such topics as coercion in international affairs, peacetime conscription, and the political theories of pacifism, which were well-documented and thought-provoking.[46]

In the early fifties Muste's writings began to appear in journals such as the *Progressive*, which were widely read by politically minded intellectuals. The *Progressive's* editors found his arguments for nonviolence in their May 1951 issue cogent enough to merit analysis by Arthur M. Schlesinger, Jr., who did not share Muste's opinion that "so long as the government spends tens of billions on war but not even a million in a study of what Gandhi called the science of nonviolence, . . . the case for nonviolent means to resist and overcome the menace of Stalin has not been scientifically disposed of."[47] Later, editors of the *Progressive* devoted most of their October 1955 issue to the nonviolent point of view when they printed a condensed version of the controversial Quaker statement, *Speak Truth to Power*.

Muste was part of the working party appointed and directed by the American Friends' Service Committee which formulated that statement. According to Stephen Cary, who chaired the group, Muste helped to "carry the political argument" in the process of formulating *Speak Truth*. "His forte was in dissecting Soviet-U.S. relationships. Muste and [Bayard] Rustin established the common ground on which pro- and anti-Soviet points of view represented by others in the group could meet." The heart of *Speak Truth* was its third chapter, entitled "The Enemy Redefined," which began with a quotation from eighteenth-century Quaker John Woolman: "To consider mankind otherwise than brethren, to think favors are peculiar to one nation and exclude others, plainly supposes a darkness in the understanding. "Drawing partly on arguments which Muste had made in *How to Deal with a Dictator*, the authors discredited the "devil theory in history," and contended that "the real evils that have driven the world to its present impasse, and which we must struggle to overcome, spring from the false values by which man has lived in East and West alike"—the lust for power, denial of human dignity, atheism, and above all, the cult of violence. Subsequent parts of *Speak Truth* prescribed nonviolent methods for overcoming these evils. The statement ended with the reminder that "there is a politics of time, but there is also a politics of eternity that man would ignore but cannot," and with an invocation of the spirit of the early Quakers who "realized only too clearly that the Kingdom of God had not come but they had an inward sense that it *would never come* until somebody believed in its principles enough to try them in actual operation."[48]

"Those who saw [*Speak Truth to Power*] in proof, men like Robert M. Hutchins, Lewis Mumford, Erich Fromm, Norbert Wiener, and Hans J. Morgenthau, pleaded at once for the widest possible discussion and debate," the *Progressive*'s editorial introduction explained. "We believe," added the editors, "that this is the most significant symposium it has been our privilege to publish in many years." Of the five figures chosen to respond to it (Karl Menninger, Reinhold Niebuhr, George Kennan, Norman Thomas, and Dwight MacDonald), all but Menninger found *Speak Truth* to be "unrealistic" and "irresponsible." Yet they all acknowledged a debt to the pacifists for raising the issue in such bold and clear form. As James Reston had recently editorialized, "For perhaps the first time in history reflective men have had to grapple with the pacifists' question: can national interests and human values really be served by waging a war with atomic and hydrogen weapons?"[49]

Anxious to press these questions further, Muste became increasingly interested in creating new channels for pacifist and radical publication. With Sidney Lens he explored the possibilities for establishing an outlet tentatively named "the Living Politics Publishing Association, which would publish pamphlets "to help in clarifying American thinking on the basic economic and political issues of the day." The LPPA did not survive its gestation period, but another publishing venture did materialize and proved to be of some moment in the history of the American pacifist Left: Volume One, Issue One of *Liberation* magazine appeared in March 1956. The lead editorial, "A Tract for the Times," defined the politics for which *Liberation* would stand—the "politics of the future, . . . [a] creative synthesis of the individual ethical insights of the great religious leaders and the collective social concern of the great revolutionists." With this combination of ethics and revolution, *Liberation*, its editors promised, "will seek to inspire its readers not only to fresh thinking but to *action now*, . . . day to day support of movements to abolish colonialism, and racism and for the freedom of all individuals from domination." *Liberation* soon became the most comprehensive and widely read source of information on such movements, providing the earliest firsthand reporting of landmark episodes in social action—the Montgomery Bus Boycott in 1954, the sailing of ships into forbidden waters to protest atomic testing in 1955, and the genesis of an African anti-nuclear movement in 1959.[50]

Liberation editors David Dellinger, Roy Finch, Bayard Rustin, and A. J. Muste consciously challenged the standards of conventional reporting, calling to the attention of their readers such lapses in the establishment press as that involving the withholding of information on the Project Argus nuclear tests in 1958. For Muste the new magazine soon became his chief public forum, the one place where his writings would appear regularly throughout the last decade of his life. The seminal Muste essays of that period—"Rifle Squads or the Beloved Community"; "Who Has the Spiritual Atom Bomb?"; "The Movement to Stop the War in Vietnam"—were written for *Liberation*. His most memorable exchanges with the establishment experts, as, for example, that with George Kennan on American policy in Asia, were reprinted in that journal. In Muste's opinion it was the only periodical, "except for professional and pacifist publications," which advocated nonviolence and interpreted it "to those not ordinarily touched by this point of view." In fact, however, much of the readership of *Liberation* came from leftist, pacifist backgrounds. "Those not ordinarily touched by this point of view" had to be reached in other ways.[51]

In helping to establish the Council for Correspondence in the early 1960s and in serving for a time as an editor of the Council newsletter, the *Correspondent*, Muste explored one way. The Council developed out of the deliberations of a small group of individuals who met in San Antonio in 1959, and at Bear Mountain, New York, in March 1960 to discuss ways to encourage intellectuals to address the critical issues of the nuclear arms race. "We risk a great deal in reliance on nuclear arms," they concluded at Bear Mountain, and "we must be willing to take risks in pursuit of peace." This group, which included sociologist David Riesman, American Friends' Service Committee Secretary Robert Gilmore, and historian H. Stuart Hughes, called on "the university communities to make their concern for survival an integral part of their concern as professional thinkers."

David Riesman, who was the central figure in guiding and sustaining the Council, stressed the idea of "unilateral *steps* toward disarmament." In his view, resisting the federal fallout shelter program was such a unilateral step. The *Correspondent* addressed itself fully to this issue and in retrospect Riesman saw the anti-shelter campaign waged in its pages as the newsletter's "most successful battle."[52] Muste was in full accord with the campaign, having played a major role since 1955 in annual civil defense protests in New York City. Yet the difference in approach between the *Correspondent* campaign and the New York demonstrations was significant. While the Riesman group concentrated on presenting the case against shelters in practical terms that policy makers and public opinion might understand, Muste and other New York protestors pitted themselves squarely against prevailing mores and many, Muste included, wound up in jail. Muste was thus never entirely comfortable with the orientation of the Council of Correspondence whose advocates sought to work within the existing political framework. "It seems to me," he wrote Riesman, "that it would be more fruitful, if a serious attempt were made . . . to examine the profound changes that would necessarily be implied in the achievement of the world without war, . . . and then ask what is the image of the future and how is it to be translated into political reality." He looked hopefully for signs that participants in the Committee of Correspondence were "ready to make a new move, cross a new line." He thought he detected stirrings in that direction. "The kind of anguish which is expressed in Riesman's letters shows," Muste confided to a pacifist friend, "that he and other key people in the Committee of Correspondence [are engaged in] the mental struggle which might conceivably lead eventually to taking a new position." But he and his scholarly friends continued to view their respective work in distinctly different lights. For the pacifist, thought and research remained preludes to action; for the academics, scholarship was a kind of action in its own right. Not only, then, did the cluster of thinkers around the *Correspondent* not accept the conclusions which Muste put forward as most practical ("The idea that one could have unilateral disarmament" or that " only a radical peace movement' could 'bring peace' seemed to me," Riesman reported, "a view that was useful to have in the spectrum but that was useless in terms of what could be done politically"), they also backed off from the activism to which he called them. Muste "was always trying to get me to do things for which I had no time," recalled H. Stuart Hughes. "While this used to embarrass me," Hughes added, "he took it in good grace. I found him a curious combination of stubborn and insistent Dutchman and a man sensitive to the different life style of a person like myself." Riesman also observed the good grace which Muste showed in urging his radicalism on others. "Other critics" of the Council of Correspondence, Riesman felt, "liked the idea of sounding radical." Some of Muste's colleagues from *Liberation* who discounted the Council were, in Riesman's judgment, "beginning the tactic that became more familiar in the late 1960's of being 'more Left than thou.' " But, Riesman added, "I felt in A. J. Muste a religious element which held him to a vision."[53]

In addition to their academic involvements and obligations (for which there would have been no time had they followed Muste's lead), scholars had other reasons to evade Muste's challenge. Not the least of these was the assurance of perennial poverty for the writer, teacher, or thinker who would shun the usual avenues to job security, research grants, publishing opportunities, and the like. The *Correspondent* was only kept alive by funds which Riesman and Erich Fromm took from their own pockets. Muste knew this problem and never resolved the dilemma which it posed. At one point he who denied the viability of existing political institutions and processes participated in the drafting and submitting of a memo to President-Elect John F. Kennedy. The memo suggested creation of "an agency specifically for the purpose of research on possible ways of conducting U.S. foreign policy without resort to violence or threats of violence," the said agency to have at its disposal "all necessary funds, resources skills and intelligence."[54]

Not only did the New Frontier prove unready for that proposal, but, with the entry of Kennedy into the White House, there occurred what author Irving Horowitz has described as a "proliferation" of "the new civilian militarists [on] the Washington scene," whose outlook and advice resulted in a full scale Asian war. Muste continued to encourage "serious writing and discussion . . . about what are 'the agencies of change' in our time and in our society, though," he observed, "we necessarily have to occupy ourselves with the immediate issues having to do with Vietnam." The *Correspondent* served, in the words of Horowitz, as a "beacon light, . . . providing a forum for the early opponents of U.S. military involvement in Southeast Asia."[55] But when Muste withdrew from the editorial board of the newsletter in 1965, direct action and civil disobedience against the war far outweighed his interest in a forum for dissenting intellectuals.

Chapter X

The Pacifist in an Age of Cold War and Megadeath

Protest and Resistance

Muste's work with scientists, churchmen, and intellectuals stemmed partly from his concern to maintain cooperative ties between peace-minded moderates and pacifist radicals. "Moderates and radicals are not going to get rid of each other or be able to avoid each other," he pointed out and urged that "various sections of the peace movement should work together when they can." But "when they cannot," he was quick to add, "it is better that each section work hard in carrying out its own programs, rather than trying to accommodate it to some other emphasis." While he was interested in the emphasis of moderates on finding issues which would have the most immediate appeal to the general public, he was more interested in experimenting with efforts directed toward enlarging and sensitizing the public consciousness. "We must not be tempted to let up on protest," he argued; "It is essential now to create a 'climate' for living which will result in making nuclear war seem preposterous and horrible. . . . So long as people can *stomach* what is going on there will be no fundamental progress toward peace." His faith in prophetism remained intact: "Assume that [protest] is only the cry of a prophet in a political wilderness. Are prophets not needed in this age? Should prophets keep silence if they are unpopular and unheeded?"[1]

Gandhism provided the basic model for the protest efforts made by Muste and other radical pacifists against preparations for nuclear war. Viewing the Indian leader as having been "an experimental scientist of strategy as well as an inspired saint," the American pacifist nonetheless made clear that he did not "take Gandhi as infallible and certainly not as having provided formulas to be applied to all future times in every country."[2] Muste sought to give nonviolent protest in America organizational continuity while leaving ample room for spontaneity and openness to the "leading of the spirit." In the summer of 1955, noncooperation with civil defense drills was organized jointly by the WRL, the New York City FOR, and the Catholic Worker. On June 15, the governments of the United States, Canada, and Mexico engaged in "Operation Alert." During a mock air raid top government officials fled to secret sanctuaries while private citizens were asked to take shelter in publicly designated areas of safety. Twenty-eight such citizens, including Muste, remained seated on benches in City Hall Park in New York City, holding signs that declared "End War . . . the Only Defense against Atomic Weapons." They were arrested, charged with violating the New York State Emergency Act, labeled "murderers" by the Night Court magistrate, Louis Kaplan (who dramatically concluded that "these people . . . contributed to the utter destruction of those 3 million theoretically killed in our city," and held in jail for two days while bail ($1,500 for each defendant) was raised.

At their trial in November of the same year, Muste was chief witness for the defense. His testimony and that of the codefendants stressed that the June defense drill misled the public. In the event of atomic attack shelters would, at best, "facilitate mass burial." The protestors were certain that "such drills serve primarily to condition the public to accept and expect war, instead of demanding peace and working for it." The judge, Hyman Bushnel, who proved as hostile as his counterpart in Night Court, found the pacifists guilty but gave them suspended sentences, in order, as he explained, not to make martyrs of them. *New York Post* writer Murray Kempton was quick to observe that "a man cannot be a martyr unless his cause is just. . . . Poor Judge Bushnel," Kempton suggested, "feared not [the protestors'] sin but their virtue."[3]

While civil defense drills occasioned some public skepticism and brought increasingly large numbers of protestors to City Hall Park during subsequent demonstrations,[4] the issue of atmospheric nuclear testing raised more public clamor. Muste had been eager to take action against such tests since their inception.[5] Not until 1957, however—in the same period when leading scientists and humanitarians were gaining the headlines with their warnings and protests against nuclear weapons building and testing—did Muste's emphasis prevail. At a spring meeting called by longtime peace and civil rights worker Lawrence Scott, a committee devoted to "Nonviolent Action against Nuclear Weapons" was established. On a motion from Muste the committee took as its first project a demonstration against Atomic Energy Commission tests scheduled for Nevada in the summer.

The weekend before the appointed tests (whose occurrence coincided with the twelfth anniversary of Hiroshima), Muste and other representatives of the new committee worked in Las Vegas to arouse community support and provide training in nonviolence for those who would join them in the protest at the test site. "Despite the intense heat," recalled veteran activist Jim Peck, "A. J. . . . worked day and night, visiting local ministers and community leaders, negotiating with the state and local police . . . and attending the last minute . . . committee meetings on logistics. Then, when the vigil started at dawn, A. J. was there. And he was there all through the torrid day and the long night until the next morning when the nightmarish bomb exploded and the vigil ended." The seventy-two-year-old Muste was also among the eleven of an estimated forty vigilers who had purposely walked into the restricted testing area, been arrested, and were subsequently found guilty and given suspended sentences.[6]

The symbolic act of voluntarily risking death to focus the attention of their fellow citizens on the perils of nuclear weapons received more dramatic expression the following spring in the voyage of the *Golden Rule* from San Pedro, California, toward the Eniwetok atoll where the United States government was planning to conduct H-bomb tests. Sponsored by the Nonviolent Action against Nuclear Weapons group, the voyage was undertaken by four Quakers, including the *Golden Rule* commander, Albert Bigelow. Halted in Honolulu, first by a federal restraining order which they ignored, then arrested and placed on probation which they broke, the crew was finally sentenced to sixty days in a Honolulu jail. Muste, who had been working on the mainland to attract public support for the sailors, flew to Hawaii after they had received probation to persuade them to sail again. He was present to counsel with them through the next critical junctures. In June the crew of a second ship, the *Phoenix*, took up the thwarted protest voyage. *Phoenix* skipper Earl Reynolds managed—with a crew of his wife and two children—to sail his vessel into the forbidden area, for which he was later sentenced to a two-year prison term. The *Golden Rule* and *Phoenix* actions received world-wide media coverage and considerable public support.[7]

Encouraged by this experiment the ad hoc committee on Nonviolent Action reorganized themselves in the fall of 1958 into an ongoing Committee of Nonviolent Action (CNVA).[8] Their next projects were not, however, as clearly fruitful as the sailings had been. On behalf of the new committee Muste put his fund-raising talents to work to send the crews of the *Golden Rule* and *Phoenix* to nuclear test-ban talks in Geneva, Switzerland, among Great Britain, the United States, and the Soviet Union. Although CNVA spent considerable effort on this project, the results were unappreciable.[9]

Controversy and bad feeling among pacifists characterized the other CNVA project of 1958—nonviolent action against the Cheyenne, Wyoming, missile base, which began in August and involved pacifist efforts to halt construction of an intercontinental ballistic missile (ICBM) base. In addition to distributing leaflets on federal property some CNVA demonstrators obstructed the passage of construction trucks into the base by lying in the road. One demonstrator, Ken Calkins, was purposely run over, suffering a broken pelvis. Five protestors, including Calkins, were given jail sentences of one hundred days each. Their actions disturbed some peace workers almost as much as they upset federal authorities and missile base employees. The shift of emphasis away from nuclear testing to missile building struck some peace workers as unfortunate and holding little chance for arousing public sympathy. Even more unfortunate, in their estimation, were the tactics of "nonviolent obstruction" which, they argued, created such fury in the opponent that all basis of communication was undermined.[10] Muste had some doubts about some of the specific decisions taken by pacifists in Cheyenne. But he welcomed the focus on missile building and defended continuing experiments with nonviolent noncooperation.[11]

The full weight of Muste's influence was brought to bear on behalf of this focus when he personally committed civil disobedience at Mead Air Force Base, Omaha, Nebraska, in 1959. At age seventy-four, with multiple responsibilities to the many organizations of which he was a part, and a pressing invitation from the international FOR to take part in nonviolent training sessions and a pacifist youth festival in Vienna in the summer of 1959, Muste at first hesitated to commit himself to full involvement in the Omaha project. But, as resistance within peace circles grew stronger, Muste became absorbed in building support for the project. In an appeal to longtime backers of more conventional peace action, he exhibited his unfailing willingness to travel down new pathways when he addressed the central issue: "Some of those who come to Omaha may take action which will seem to you unusual or extreme," he wrote. "Well, the times in which we live are unusual and we can hardly think that the threat of nuclear holocaust will be averted unless we find new ways of bearing a witness, summon fresh courage, and are ready for sacrifice beyond what we have thus far offered." Muste's efforts notwithstanding, intramovement controversy continued, and, less than a month before the project was scheduled to begin, two influential officers of the FOR withdrew their support from the action. At this point one of the leading organizers of the effort, Theodore Olson, urged Muste to assume leadership. "Certainly," he pleaded, "you are the one man who is equally trusted and respected by all these [different] friends." Omaha Action got underway in mid-June with A. J. Muste as "Co-Coordinator" and chief spokesman.[12]

His overtures in late May to community leaders and local clergymen had been curtly received. The Omaha *World Herald* editorialized against the project, emphasizing Muste's Trotskyist past. The climate was not friendly, therefore, when thirty CNVA workers began a week long vigil on June 22. Hecklers picketed with signs reading, "Your hammer and sickle are showing," and derisive comments were jeered at the demonstrators. On June 29, Muste wrote President Eisenhower for permission to enter the missile site "to speak with our fellows who are building the missile base . . . , part of a military program which we believe to be both profoundly evil and practically suicidal." In the same letter Muste articulated the position that "we cannot recognize the right of government to take over . . . more and more land and equipment of all kinds for mass destruction . . . the land," he avowed, "is a trust committed to each generation." On July 1, with permission to enter forthcoming from neither Washington nor on-site authorities, three vigilers prepared to enter the base. Muste, as Nat Hentoff later reported, "spoke to the crowd of the curious, the hostile, the converted, the police and the press." "I have heard . . . many sermons," recalled his fellow-vigiler Wilmer Young, "but none I think more impressive." After quoting from Isaiah ("In returning and rest shall ye be saved; in quietness and confidence shall be your strength"), Muste hoisted his frail frame over a four and one-half foot fence, was presented with a letter from the base commander requesting him to leave and escorted out the gate. "Muste read the letter, stepped to the fence, climbed over once more and was placed under arrest." He spent eight days in jail and received a suspended sentence of six months, a $500 fine, plus one year probation.[13]

The Omaha arrests (Muste's was followed that day by two more and, thereafter, pacifists continued to attempt to enter the base and be arrested until the close of the project on August 10) stirred deep thankfulness and prophecy among project supporters. The first five demonstrators imprisoned prompted one backer to hope that "perhaps God will spare us for the sake of five! Perhaps more of us will be involved in genuine witness. One can feel it coming." Even some who disapproved of civil disobedience made gestures of sympathy. Congressman William Meyer, whose son was among those arrested, preferred an "approach through reason and law" but conceded that he "would join a movement of 'On to Omaha' if I thought it might bring sanity to this crazy world. Perhaps I should anyhow!" And Norman Thomas, long and far removed from the pacifism he had shared with Muste in their younger days, sent a check for the defense of those Omaha activists who pleaded not guilty. "Under present conditions in America I would not choose for myself or recommend to others civil disobedience as practiced in Omaha Action," the socialist wrote. "Nevertheless I deeply respect the sincerity and dedication of those who have practiced it."

Muste was particularly pleased that the judge who tried the Omaha cases let it be known in private that he was "fully sympathetic with [the] aims" of the project, "but had no choice than to enforce the law or resign." Heartening, too, were observations that the local press and T.V. reaction "got more favorable as time went on."[14] But for such small victories Muste paid a substantial emotional and physical price. Traces of the heavy strain which the project imposed on him appear in his correspondence with Omaha residents. Something other than his usual personal reserve poured forth when the head of the local Council of Churches rebuffed his best effort "to get . . . especially from our fellow Christians an understanding of our plans and confidence in our integrity."

Countering the rebuff in an unusually emotional reply, Muste quoted to the Omaha minister from a letter written by Connie Muste Hamilton in which she spoke of bursting into tears at the thought of the peril awaiting her children in a world increasingly contaminated and devoted to preparations for mass destruction. She mentioned especially her daughter Anne, his only granddaughter, the pacifist stressed, and named "after her grandmother, my wife whom I lost nearly five years ago after forty-five years of a deeply blessed marriage." Of the child, Connie had written, according to Muste, "Imagine what the world will be like when she grows up—assuming anybody gets that far! . . . It is very hard for me to keep back the tears, as I write this." Muste continued, turning again to family details—his experience in World War I, and son John's in World War II. "My oldest grandson . . . is now . . . of the 'right age' for war. But of course," he added, "everybody is of the 'right' or 'wrong' age as one chooses to think of it, for nuclear war. We have to make these things personal, dear friend and brother in the ministry," he implored.

After Muste's struggle to reach a level of personal communication with those present at Mead landed him in jail, his young fellow activist Bradford Lyttle reported that "he had a hard time":

> It was hot and the jail was a real hole. The food was terrible. A. J. was allowed no exercise; and only relatives were allowed to visit, but he had none there. By the end of his time he was exhausted. I've never seen him so tired. Yet he remained unemotional. He betrayed how worn out he was only by the fact that his hands, which shake anyway, were shaking much more than usual. His pallor was marked, but his spirit was whole even though the guards had treated him with curt disrespect.

That such disrespectful treatment rankled was indicated in another letter Muste wrote after he returned to New York. Addressing himself to the head of the Omaha YMCA, Muste commented on that organization's denial of the CNVA request to meet in their building and took special exception that a representative of the "Y" had not attempted to confer with him personally. His assertion of his integrity—mild and accurate though it was—was an uncharacteristic gesture for him: "There surely were people at the YMCA who knew enough about me to realize that, however they might differ with my views, I had standing in the church and in the nation as a sincere interpreter of the Gospel and worker for peace over many years."[15]

But whatever the strains to his health and psyche of the Omaha endeavor, Muste did not dwell on them. He assured co-workers that he did not expect to violate his probation "in the next few months" but was "not at all sure" he could "conform to it for an entire year! We shall see and wait on the leading of the spirit in that respect," he commented.[16] For the duration of his probation Muste took his usual active part in the radical pacifist community, showing special interest in the CNVA Polaris Project in New London, Connecticut. Direct action initiatives there toward the employees of the Electric Boat Company, manufacturer of nuclear submarines, included leafletting, the sailing along the New England coast of a yacht named the *Satyagraha*, and the boarding of nuclear submarines by pacifist demonstrators. Muste's backing was instrumental in the decision to go forward with the Polaris Project. His visits to New London, involving meetings with community leaders and clergy, and his fund-raising support strengthened the project, which enjoyed wide news coverage and gained increasing local support. He did not, however, participate in the civil disobedience phases of the undertaking.[17] In addition to being on probation Muste was too involved in other experiments to tie himself down to one single situation.

One such experiment, an outgrowth partly of the Polaris project and partly of seeds sown in earlier years, was the San Francisco-Moscow Peace March. Conceived as a peace movement response to the frequent challenge from critics to "go tell it to the Russians," the march was attempted when a march volunteer contributed $6,000 toward expenses and when Muste made clear his "own personal firm conviction . . . that strategically this is the next major job, though by no means the only one for CNVA."[18]

Muste had visited the USSR in 1958 as a discussion leader with a tour group consisting mostly of clergy and teachers. The trip was disrupted during a visit to the U.S. Embassy when the tourists ran into marchers protesting the U.S. Marines' landing in Lebanon. According to eyewitness Cara Cook, "Some of our group grew a bit anxious and thought we better get away. However, this was all meat and gravy to A. J. . . . . He and Anna [the tour guide] were surrounded and began to answer the questions fired at him from all sides."[19] That ability to take fire from all sides would be taxed to the fullest in his negotiations with the Soviets in clearing the way for the 1960–61 Peace Walk.

A team of ten walkers left San Francisco on the first of December 1960, picking up and leaving off members as they travelled across the United States. The walkers declared themselves "equally opposed to armaments in East and West," and were prepared to call "on the Governments of *each* of the countries" through which they planned to pass "to abandon unconditionally nuclear weapons and all other weapons of mass destruction."

The American team was joined by nationals from eight other countries as they walked across Europe. Thirty strong, they entered communist terrain in August through Poland, crossing the Polish border into the Soviet Union on September 15. While covering the next 660 miles, through the Russian countryside enroute to Moscow, they spoke almost nightly at meetings to substantial crowds of Soviet citizens who came out to hear their message. On the outskirts of Moscow they stopped to demonstrate against a Soviet radar base and, once in Red Square, they mounted a two-hour picket line of silent protest against Russian war preparations. The effort ended October 8, 1961.[20] The bare statistics reflect the prodigious weight of the undertaking: 310 days, 6,000 miles, the crossing of six national borders, and the distribution of hundreds of thousands of leaflets (80,000 in Russia alone). The behind-the-scenes record indicates how much of that weight was borne by Muste.

In addition to working with walk coordinators (Bradford Lyttle, a key figure in the conception of the march, was the chief coordinator on U.S. soil; April Carter of Great Britain worked with Bayard Rustin, on loan from the WRL, preparing the way in England and Europe) on endless details of organization, interpersonal relations and finances, he personally visited the U.S. State Department and Soviet Embassy to explain the march to officials and wrote a personal letter to Nikita Khrushchev. Throughout it all, Muste's enthusiasm and sense of anticipation were keen. "I expect to do a few miles myself as [the walkers] get to New York," he confided to journalist Nat Hentoff. " 'Of course,' he barely suppressed a grin, 'we don't expect to walk across the water at that point.' "[21] His determination to do all in his power to prevent the walk from failing was intense to the point of painfulness. Such failure seemed imminent when officials in France (in turmoil over a recently aborted right-wing coup) refused to let the walkers enter that country, and when the governments of

East and West Germany (at a peak of confrontation over the Berlin Wall) similarly refused them passage. During the stand-off in Germany Muste wrote IFOR representative Heinz Kloppenberg, "It is possible, that I might feel compelled to make a supreme effort, such as a fast after the example of Gandhi, in order to try to work through this grave situation."[22]

Muste's powers as negotiator and reconciler were taxed to their fullest in trying to remain sensitive to the feelings of the European pacifist committees, being firm with government officials, and maintaining credibility with the walkers. At critical junctures members of the march rejected his advice. Some jumped into the English Channel to try to swim to France; most voted to enter East Berlin without permission.[23] Even more trying than these disagreements over tactics, however, were his struggles to work out satisfactory guidelines for the march into Russia. In June, Muste had come from a visit to Moscow with an agreement that seemed to give the walkers free speech and a visit of several weeks' duration. After the Soviets resumed nuclear testing Muste received a cable from the Soviet Peace Committee indicating that the original arrangements were to be altered. He hurried to Moscow where the committee received his statement taking their government to task for resuming the nuclear tests. After hearing him out, the Committee reduced the time the walkers could spend in their country and indicated that their activities would be restricted. In the eyes of the walkers Muste "had failed." A few marchers, reported Brad Lyttle, "felt that A. J. had let them down. . . . I suspect he returned downcast to New York."[24]

"This is taking a lot out of A. J.," worried his friends. After the last disappointing visit to Moscow Muste spent about a week in London, meeting with pacifists and observing a massive civil disobedience demonstration there, of the kind which, along with its most famous advocate, Bertrand Russell, was attracting world-wide attention. But on the day of the protest the American pacifist was so weary that, after walking "among the crowds in the early evening" around Trafalgar Square, he was "not able to stay up until the finish," even though he later told *Peace News*, "I was extremely curious as to how things were going to end." He flew back to New York on September 19. Except when he returned to the states at the end of August "to report and rest" for eight days, he had spent the entire period since June 1 in Europe, working for the march. "That you lived through your journeying back and forth and the delicate and skillful negotiations involved with alien cultures and variant values is nothing short of miraculous," wrote Marcia Lyttle (mother of Brad Lyttle) to Muste.[25] Even more miraculous, from his point of view, was the fact that the marchers did get to Moscow; their message was heard in Red Square. Tiredness aside, his spirits soared. "Stupendous," "providential," "fantastic"—no superlative was strong enough to encompass his satisfaction. Agreeing for once with a Republican mouthpiece, Muste quoted the *New York Herald Tribune*: "The peace marchers . . . have raised a little candle of dissent in the vast, gray conformity of the Soviet Union. . . . Through this tiny chink in the Iron Curtain a few seminal ideas may have been penetrated. They will not affect the current crisis, but they may grow." Muste added another analogy: "Like . . . a scientist's taking hold of what seems a foolish approach to a problem after all the traditional sensible approaches have finally led to an impasse, . . . the Peace March has been," he declared, "an Experiment in Truth and Nonviolence in the Gandhian tradition."[26]

Muste hoped that, along with other developments, the Soviet public's reception of the San Francisco to Moscow Walk indicated a growing spirit of independence within communist countries and a strengthening impulse on the part of peace workers there to reach out to forces in the West which were critical of both sides in the Cold War. This hope flickered toward extinction, however, when the crew of another protest ship, the *Everyman III*, sailing from London to Leningrad, was prevented from landing on Russian soil and speaking with the Soviet population about nuclear testing. Muste's letters to the Soviet Peace Committee availed nothing.[27] But the flame grew a little brighter when that peace committee and a comparable group in Poland pursued an invitation for the walkers to send a return delegation to the United States. Despite continuing Soviet-U.S. tensions over such issues as Berlin, Cuba, and weapons testing, the Eastern peace committees persisted. Off and on through 1962 and into 1963, Muste and the committees corresponded. Suddenly in the summer of 1963, the chairman and general secretary of the All-Soviet Peace Committee cabled Muste, "We are ready to send six, seven member delegation of public figures in October November at invitation Committee for Nonviolent Action." Urging them to include some non-public figures and asking that they give Americans more time to prepare, Muste and his colleagues began final arrangements to receive the Soviets and Poles in January 1964. A last minute denial of visas by the State Department nearly ended the whole episode, but the denial was reversed—"chiefly if not solely due to the efforts of A. J. Muste," according to *Fellowship*. For a fortnight the visitors, including a surgeon, a writer, a journalist, a trade unionist, and two peace committee representatives toured the United States. They visited New York, Philadelphia, Washington, Atlanta, San Francisco, and Chicago, met Americans in both small private discussions as well as large public meetings, and communicated their views to the press and over American airways.

Efforts to communicate the message of nonviolence to the Soviets were but one example of Muste's deepening commitment to transnational action. Antedating his involvement in the San Francisco-Moscow walk, and continuing well after the episode was concluded, were Muste's contributions toward cultivating the seeds of pacifism in African soil. Those seeds had been germinating for many years. As Bill Sutherland, a black American with a long history of involvement in African liberation movements, has noted, "The 1952 Defiance against unjust laws campaign in South Africa predates by several years the Montgomery bus boycott. . . . The Positive Action Campaign in Ghana's independence struggle—1948 to 1952—was definitely inspired by India and the Gandhi movement."[28]

When French authorities announced plans in the summer of 1959 to soon test the first French Atomic Bomb in the Sahara desert, American and British anti-nuclear activists, some of whom had contacts with African leaders, began to explore the possibility of mounting a resistance movement against the French tests. The resulting Sahara project was an historical "first," as Muste pointed out: "This project protesting against the proposed explosion of an atomic bomb at Reggan in the Sahara Desert" is the "first *international* direct action program against nuclear war . . . in which West European and American pacifists had sought to enlist and train people of other continents . . . in 'positive non-violent action.' " In the words of the Finance Minister of Ghana, project participants came to "represent an international team traveling to the Sahara as a mission for all mankind."

The goal of the project was to send a team from some major African center to the Sahara test site, raising African awareness en route as to the implications of the proposed bomb explosion and demanding, once at the site, that the test be cancelled. By so doing, pacifists hoped "to arouse the conscience of the French people and the people of other nuclear powers; to stimulate further active opposition in Africa; and to halt the bomb tests—or at least to embarrass the French Government." As Africans within fallout distance of the testing site observed, "If [the test is] harmless why not hold it in the country outside Paris, so all the French people can see the wonder?"[29]

Headquarters for the protest were located in Accra, Ghana. While the Ghanaian government of Kwame Nkrumah took great pains to dissociate itself officially from the protest, many members of the government lent their support as private citizens. Nkrumah himself contributed over $1,000 to the project fund and Ghanaian Finance Minister K. A. Gbedemah became a stalwart backer of the Sahara project. "Whatever country you may come from and whatever your color may be, you are now a part of Africa," he told the Sahara project team. As the project took form other indigenous forces rallied to its support. The secretary general of the Ghanaian Trades Union Congress (who was also secretary of the All-African Trade Union Federation) called on "all African workers . . . to demonstrate against the French tests." Ntsu Mokhehle, president of the Basutoland National Congress Party, personally joined the protest team. Traditional African leaders, including the chief of the Ashanti people (who donated $150) and local chieftains whom the protestors met enroute to the French testing site, demonstrated their sympathies.

Three attempts were made to enter French territory and find a way to Reggan, where the tests were to occur. On December 6, 1959, nineteen people (twelve volunteers from Ghana, one from Nigeria, the president of Basutoland, one French pacifist, three British anti-nuclear activists including Michael Scott, who was an extremely popular figure in Ghana because of his work on behalf of Africa at the U.N., and two Americans) began the journey in two land rovers and a truck toward the Algerian border one thousand miles away. As they travelled they were joined by another Ghanaian and another French citizen. They were stopped three days later as they attempted to cross the border from Ghana into Upper Volta, which was under French control. After five days of unsuccessful effort to persuade the French soldiers to let them pass, the team made "a strategic withdrawal" to the Ghanaian village of Bolgatanga.

A smaller team of seven people (four from Ghana, two from England, and one from the United States) crossed again into Upper Volta on December 17; again they were stopped by French military officers. They vigiled, leafletted (the leaflets explained the team's purpose in four languages—Arabic, Hausa, French, and English), and sent their appeal through the countryside by loud speaker and finally, on January 3, 1960, attempted to pass the military barrier on foot. Arrests occurred promptly, team vehicles were confiscated, and the protestors were once again returned to Ghana. When enough money had been raised to buy a new jeep the team made one last unsuccessful attempt on January 17. "All possible routes in Upper Volta now under close twenty-four hour guard," cabled team member Michael Randle to the Council for Nuclear Disarmament (CND) office in London. "Team and Ghanaian Council estimate further confrontations on Volta border ineffective following eight weeks spent there already."[30]

For four weeks, until about December 20, Muste was in Africa, working with the team as a coordinator. In addition to bringing his experience and insight to bear on pressing questions of strategy (where to attempt the border crossings, how to relate to the French military officers, what degree of resistance to employ when arrested, etc.), he had, in the words of team member Michael Scott, "an important steadying effect. . . . Our team was quite mixed," Scott explained, "and many of its members differed widely in their motivations and expectations. . . . A. J.'s internal strength of purpose and his ability to communicate clearly did much to keep the team from losing its bearings." It was physically a strenuous time for Muste, but his enthusiasm for the project and his "delight" (a word he used several times in reports back to New York) in being introduced to a new culture overrode the discomforts he faced. "It was extraordinarily hot all the time A. J. was there," remembered Bayard Rustin, who also played a key role in organizing the team and was part of its first entry into French territory. "I was fearful for him the first couple of days, but he quickly adjusted to the climate and plunged into a rigorous schedule that left him little sleep." Team members began their activities in the early and relatively cool morning hours. Muste "was used to rising later," noted Michael Scott from England. "But he didn't at all complain at our hours, though I must admit he was grateful for the tea I brought him each morning when he awoke." Scott recalled that Muste became "exercised about his hat. He was looking for a particular quality of Panama hat and searched through many long hot streets in the markets of Accra before he was satisfied. Otherwise," Scott concluded, "he was quite content with working conditions."[31]

The surroundings and customs were largely unfamiliar to Muste. Even the British-made land rovers were new to his vocabulary and came out as "land-rollers" in his first report for *Liberation*. "My education in African ways . . . was on the whole a very delightful experience," he wrote. He watched with fascination when African hosts chanted and poured measures of beer into the ground, "an offering," he surmised, "to the soil or motherland itself, to the gods and to ancestors." "Lovely" was his word for a dance improvised by Ghanaian women at a demonstration of support for the Sahara team. Muste's travels through the "back country" were intriguing; native huts and stores, dress styles which, he could not refrain from mentioning, "in many cases means no clothing from the waist up" all caught his eye. Certain individual Africans left a special impression with him: the chief of the village of Bawku who made a present to the team of two baskets of canned goods in a manner which was, Muste observed, "truly touching"; the young Ghanaian official who served as a government representative in the area around and including Bawku—"trim, handsome, completely unassuming . . . , idealistic and quietly efficient"; and the child of a Ghanaian who had helped the team. Once back in the states Muste sent the father "a pound for your boy Cornelius. . . . I found him a very bright and promising child and would like him to know of my goodwill."[32]

In this satisfying personal adventure Muste saw a promising development for pacifism. Although the French exploded their bomb (on February 13, 1960), they failed, it seemed to Muste, to win approval from the world. "With the single and sinister exception of West Germany and Adenauer," he observed, "no western government and no leading western statesman has expressed any enthusiasm on France's achievement." Although disheartened by the failure of the governments of the French-speaking states in Africa to speak out against the test, he gladly listed the areas where "the Sahara Test has met with outraged protest—many other parts of Africa, the middle East, India, Indonesia, and Japan—and quoted *Ghanaian Times* columnist Mabel Dove as a fair sample of Third World feeling. The French bomb shows Africa, Dove wrote, that "western civilization is a sham, totally bankrupt and bereft of Christian values, a 'whited sepulchre full of dead bones.' " The French did not continue their testing in the Sahara very long. According to Bill Sutherland, "The Algerian war certainly had a great deal to do with this but the protest was a real factor, both in galvanizing world opinion against the testing and incidentally promoting the cause of justice in Algeria."[33]

Whatever blow may have been dealt the French government, Muste was more keenly interested in the possible consequences of the "immense propaganda job for the idea of nonviolence" which the Sahara team had carried out in Africa. Their influence was, he noted, "by no means confined to Ghana—we have had letters from important organizations [in] Kenya, the East and Central African countries, Nigeria, the Cameroons, Guinea and Basutoland." The impact of nonviolent training on individual Africans was epitomized for Muste "in one of our training sessions shortly before the team left Accra"; there, the pacifist recalled, "a Ghanaian volunteer suddenly got up with his face alight and said: 'Now I know what nonviolence is. It means that if Ghana shall decide to test an atomic bomb, I'd have to oppose that most of all.' " Muste also heard in government pronouncements "a new note which Ghana had learned mainly from the Sahara Project." Before the Ghanaian Parliament in December 1959, the Foreign Minister corrected a colleague who had called their nation's foreign policy anti-French. "This," he said, "is not true. We are against French atomic policy—against nuclear testing by whomsoever carried on." Here were signs, Muste believed, "that the sights of large masses of Africans had been raised above concern about independence and the building of new regimes to concern about the world struggle against nuclear war."

Seemingly a way was open by which the Sahara initiative could be carried on. About two months after the team was disbanded, Michael Scott suggested to President Nkrumah that "a conference should be called with emphasis on methods of continuing nonviolent action against Sahara bomb tests at all levels." Nkrumah agreed and asked that Michael Randle begin to work on such a conference. The resulting All-African Conference on Positive Action for the Peace and Security of Africa took place in Accra on April 7–10, 1960. In the judgment of Bill Sutherland, "This conference represented not only the height of influence of the world pacifist movement on the African liberation struggle; it was a joining of the world pacifist movement, the African liberation movements and the American civil rights movement." Pacifist representatives included Asadevi Aryanayyakam, close associate of Gandhi, Madam Tomi Kora of Japan, Muste and a sizeable contingent of other Western peace workers, and Martin Luther King's top aide, Ralph Abernathy. Pacifists hoped, because of their entree to Nkrumah, that the conference would reflect their primary objectives. Nkrumah reinforced these hopes at the beginning of the proceedings when, according to Sutherland, he called pacifists together to say, " 'This is your conference. What is the nonviolent answer to the French explosion of the bomb in the Sahara and the Sharpville [massacre] (which had just occurred)?' A. J. was ecstatic and incredulous," Sutherland said. "He remarked that no revolutionary movement had such access to power before." But Sutherland, aware of powerful counter forces, cautioned against over-optimism. Advocates of armed struggle, including the eloquent Franz Fanon, who had seen firsthand how viciously nonviolent methods had been suppressed in Algeria, strongly influenced the tone and outcome of the conference. In Sutherland's view pacifists' suggestions "were quite inadequate to meet the problems discussed and the Congo crisis which followed." Muste had "labored mightily" on a document expressing the pacifist point of view, but that document was drastically cut and became a very small part of the final communiqué.[34]

Yet Muste's report when he returned from Accra to the United States bordered on the euphoric. The outcome of the conference was, he declared, "gratifying beyond any expectation." He described as highly significant the facts that the conference had directed protest statements to the U.S. and to French West African governments regarding French bomb tests, and that the whole Conference had unanimously recognized the contribution made by the nonviolent Sahara Protest Team to the liberation of Africa, and called for "the development of much larger-scale action against French tests . . . and . . . the establishment of training centers for 'positive action' in Africa." At the conference's conclusion Nkrumah held a special meeting with Muste and other pacifists to plan for the future. According to Muste the Ghanaian leader promised to "make 10,000 pounds, about $28,000 immediately available" for the enlarged protest project and training center.[35]

Over the next three months, however, these plans and promises languished. Nkrumah's time was taken up in meetings with other heads of state. The "Congo" crisis in the area to become Zaire became the focus of African attention, while French preparations for further atomic tests and the planting of missiles in the Sahara received less and less official notice. Bill Sutherland met with Nkrumah in mid-July to discuss the training center, and he took the opportunity to propose that a nonviolent positive action team go into the Congo "for purposes of recruitment and assessment. The interview," he wrote Muste, "was not encouraging—obviously the centre and non-violent positive action have been relegated to a remote corner of his [Nkrumah's] mind."

When the public announcement was made that the Kwame Nkrumah Institute would be set up at Winnego College, thirty miles from Accra, details further disheartened the pacifists. The institute was to have two sections, one for training ruling Party and trade union members, the other for instruction in "positive action." Neither Muste in New York nor his co-workers in Ghana could see how a truly nonviolent program could be so closely associated with government forces. In the first place, some aspects of the Ghana government were directed by people who were, in British activist April Carter's words, "bitterly opposed to nonviolence and might try to divert the Centre to specifically violent action related to Algeria or South Africa." Indeed, though Muste had chosen not to stress it, the same Accra conference which passed resolutions for nonviolence had also voted to send a military brigade into Algeria. Secondly, nonviolent commitments to civil liberties and nonviolent interest in decentralizing power as much as possible were bound to conflict with policies adopted by a new nation state struggling to survive. Nkrumah's domestic actions, which included press censorship, preventive detention, and police harassment against his political opponents, became increasingly desperate.[36] Yet Muste remained convinced (and twenty years later Bill Sutherland was still convinced) that Nkrumah was "deeply interested in nonviolence, [and does not] think of it as completely irrelevant in the way that top Western political leaders do." Muste did agree, however, with the decision of Randle and Scott to leave Ghana, and for the time being, to leave at rest the idea of a training center for nonviolence.[37]

As April Carter has noted, pacifist influence in Ghana had waxed and waned in accordance with how well pacifist goals coincided with government policy. The initial Sahara protest, as a well-focused, single issue project which served the purposes of the government yet remained technically independent of it and was of limited duration, proved more fruitful than the less-focused notion of a training center dependent on the government and of indefinite longevity. Once the partisans of nonviolence "moved away from the realm of direct action . . . to the realm of conference politics and bidding for long-term official support," they were, Carter observed, "likely to lose out to the rivalries governing that level of political activity. The team," she pointed out, "could no longer inject their own moral and political concepts into the situation. . . . The element of daring and simplicity which is appropriate to direct action is quite inappropriate to conventional political maneuvering," she concluded.[38]

Whatever the lessons learned in Ghana, veterans of the Sahara Protest were not deterred from trying to bring pacifist influence to bear in other nations of Africa. With the formation of a World Peace Brigade (WPB) in January 1962, Muste and his co-workers initiated projects in Tanganyika (later Tanzania) and Northern Rhodesia. The idea of an international nonviolent brigade or "peace army" had been suggested by Gandhi in South Africa in 1906. The idea was periodically revived across the years and had received some attention from Muste when he attended a world pacifist meeting in India shortly after Gandhi's death in 1949. There an International Liaison Committee was set up to work out plans for a brigade but nothing came of it. National peace movements were "not far enough along," Muste explained, and "the general situation wasn't right for it." When Charles Walker, a Quaker and longtime American peace activist, proposed in late 1959 that a "World Conference on Nonviolence" be convened in 1961 to explore the international dimensions of pacifism, Muste vacillated in his reactions. His enthusiasm reached its lowest point in July 1960, when he wrote Walker, "It seems to me extremely doubtful whether in the midst of the very intense activity going on all over Africa, . . . it is going to be possible to get such a conference called and held." Walker persisted, however, and the notion was finally taken up by the War Resisters' International meeting in India in January 1961; they scheduled a world conference for Beirut in the following year. Again Muste reacted with skepticism and originally planned not to attend. "You may list me as a sponsor, he told conference organizers, but "it still seems to me that it is going to be extremely difficult to work out a plan which could be both creative and practical." By the fall of 1961, however, he had decided to go, though he was still ambivalent. "My hunch is," he remarked, "that Beirut may just end up in our being 'confused at a deeper level and about more things.' "[39]

The conference experience swept away all his hesitation. Delegates heard agonizing reports from Indian representatives about their government's invasion of Goa; they considered the manifold crisis in Africa and pondered Muste's apprehension, which had been growing over the past months, that nuclear war was closer that it had ever been. Assuming his characteristic role of synthesizing divergent tendencies and striking the note of inspiration around which all participants could rally, Muste was elected one of the three co-chairmen of the World Peace Brigade which they founded. Delegates to the conference went away with his concluding challenge in their minds: "If we were going to wait to build . . . [an international] movement until we were all perfect satyagrahas we would never begin at all; and we ought to begin where we are and with what we have and go on from there."[40]

The new Brigade, led by Muste, Michael Scott, and the influential Gandhian, Jayaprakash Narayan, was seen by its founders as "the first *instrument for international* (eventually perhaps global) *action*." Muste's interpretation of this initiative suggested that he was verging on a significant departure from his longtime emphasis on "Holy Disobedience" and the importance of the lone individual conscience. In the aftermath of Beirut, he contended that "the essentially individualistic moral or religious pacifism, characteristically expressing itself in conscientious objection to war is no longer a sufficient basis for the organizing center of the movement. . . . The nonviolent revolutionary movement," he said, "must somehow affect the centers of power in contemporary society." His hopes were high that in the WPB a way could be found. "Even from a very sober and objective standpoint," he wrote an Indian colleague, "there is a real hope now that the whole movement of nonviolence may become something of a world force."

The aims defined for the WPB included organizing, training, and maintaining "a brigade for nonviolent action in situations of potential or actual conflict, internal and international [and] against all war, preparations for war and the continuing development of weapons of mass destruction." Brigade founders also proposed "to revolutionize the concept of revolution itself by infusing into the methods of resisting injustice the qualities which ensure the preservation of human life and dignity and to create the conditions necessary for peace."[41]

A concrete opportunity for putting these aims into practice presented itself when four WPB delegates secured permission to participate as observers in the Fourth Annual Conference of the Pan Africa Freedom Movements of East and Central Africa (PAFMECA) at Addis Ababa, February 21, 1962. Michael Scott, Bayard Rustin, Bill Sutherland, and Siddharaj Dhadda of India were able to cooperate with African leaders who favored nonviolence in securing a conference resolution that did not rule out pacifist strategies but approved the use of "many methods" in the struggle for liberation. Of most value to the aspirations of the WPB was the election of Kenneth Kaunda (leader of the United Independent Party of Northern Rhodesia [UNIP]), as president of PAFMECA. An unusually outspoken advocate for nonviolence who had declared in May 1960, "Violence I condemn without reserve and very strongly no matter where it comes from. . . . No circumstances can be so trying as to justify violence!" Kaunda had earlier appealed to the American peace movement to publish an inexpensive edition of the pacifist classic, *Power of Nonviolence*, by Richard Gregg, so that he could make it available to his followers. He sympathized with the Sahara protest and was viewed by pacifists who knew Africa as "the one person who is an African leader who . . . understands and is willing to go all-out on nonviolence."[42]

Kaunda and the UNIP were locked in a struggle with Sir Roy Wilensky, prime minister of the Central African Federation which had been imposed upon Northern Rhodesia, Southern Rhodesia, and Nyasaland by the British government. Kaunda contemplated calling a general strike if forthcoming elections were not held on the basis of universal suffrage (which would oust the Wilensky regime and create an African majority). The WPB suggested that an international freedom march from Tanganyika into Northern Rhodesia be organized to complement the strike and demonstrate international solidarity with the struggle for independence. Kaunda agreed. A working committee called African Freedom Action (AFA) was set up to work on the strike and march. UNIP, PAFMECA, the WPB, and the Tanganyika African National Union (TANU—Tanganyika's leading political party) were represented in the AFA.

This group's energetic preparations for nonviolent direct action by the AFA were slowed when authorities in London brought pressure to bear on Wilensky to modify the discriminatory political set-up in Northern Rhodesia. The constitution was revised sufficiently for Kaunda to see a chance for fair elections. He held off on the general strike and the freedom march in order to test the new constitutional provisions.[43]

Muste, who had recently promised his friend Alfred Hassler at the FOR that he would cut back on his activities and start to write his memoirs, travelled to Dar es Salaam in May for meetings with the AFA and the chairmen of the WPB. He wrote Hassler: "I am embarrassed whenever I think of my running off to Tanganyika just after you had labored with me so persuasively in favor of sitting down." At Dar es Salaam, Kaunda requested that AFA plans be held in readiness until African Majority rule had become a reality. Muste, who, it was reported, "has been instrumental in raising most of the funds to support the overseas aspect of the march, . . . has now accepted primary responsibility for its overall direction." Primed for action, and feeling, as he wrote Michael Scott, "that the occasion for truly significant work in Africa for which you have in a sense been waiting a good many years has opened up," the pacifist was nonetheless left in limbo. Without qualification he and other Brigade members accepted Kaunda's decision to hold direct action in abeyance until the election provisions had been tested. But this placed them in an awkward position, having raised funds and recruited volunteers for a march that might never (and in fact never did) occur. They were cheered by reports from African leaders and from their contacts in London that the threat of the march had been influential in moving the British toward constitutional reform, but this did not constitute the kind of visible achievement which well publicized and widely supported nonviolent action might have brought for the WPB.[44] Similarly, however effective their contribution to the UNIP election campaign—which ended in October in a clear victory for Kaunda—the spotlight had shifted from protest, where the pacifists could take some of the initiative, to politics where their public role was minimized.

Another way that nonviolent direct action was kept alive and visible in the African setting was by the establishment of another "positive action" training center, similar to the one that had been attempted in Ghana. Strong statements of support for this endeavor were provided by Kaunda and another African leader who was given to public advocacy of nonviolence, Julius Nyerere, president of Tanganika. Set up on a small scale in Dar es Salaam in March 1962, such a center materialized, staffed by four workers from the UNIP along with Bill Sutherland and a veteran Gandhian, Suresh Ram. They gave typing lessons, held discussions, supported nearby self-help projects, took in political refugees from other parts of Africa, and explored with them possibilities for extending nonviolence to their struggles. At the peak of the election campaign these activities gave way to working for the UNIP victory. In the wake of that victory steps were taken, again with the express backing of Kaunda and Nyerere, to find a larger and permanent site for the center. The UNIP even offered a plot of ground, but Muste and other WPB leaders failed to drum up adequate financial support. As Charles Walker observed, "Without a dramatic project at hand money was hard to come by." In June of 1963, Muste reported that the center had been closed.[45]

Other initiatives taken by the WPB in relation to Africa had limited import. During the election campaign the Special Committee on Colonialism of the United Nations held hearings in Dar es Salaam. World Peace Brigade workers testified at these hearings and worked with the UNIP preparing documentation for the committee about the obstacles—including alleged harassment and murder—faced by Kaunda's Party. Several months later, and just prior to the October elections, Muste and Michael Scott met with U.N. Secretary U Thant who was, Muste said, "most cordial and frank." He heard their reports of WPB efforts with interest and indicated that other nonviolent overtures which they were considering in Africa might be useful to the U.N. But the means for translating these overtures from paper to action were not found. Nor did the "Poster Walks" which Muste was instrumental in setting up around the South African Consulate in New York City, calling attention to the racist and repressive practices of the Republic of South Africa, have visible effect on the policies of that government.[46]

On the face of it, pacifist effort in Africa was, as a critical supporter phrased it, "an expensive experiment—or failure." Like most of Muste's endeavors, there was no practical justification for ever expecting it to turn out otherwise; the Sahara protest and WPB projects were acts of faith. The fiscal resources on which they could rely were pitifully weak by any modern political standards and entirely inadequate to support them in the contest for influence which they had to wage against other forces attempting to affect events on the African continent.[47] Both to bring in money and to attract the attention of the multitudes to whom nonviolence was virtually unknown, the pacifists needed opportunities for dramatic action. "To Africans action from Dar [es Salaam] directed at Southern and Central Africa must seem somewhat remote," Muste observed to Bill Sutherland. "We ought to find some more dramatic way to organize the program than we have yet hit upon." But as non-Africans they were never fully free to experiment.[48]

The World Peace Brigade was also up against the hard problem of how to have a transforming effect on "centers of power" without being instead transformed by them. A Quaker observer who spoke from the perspective of considerable experience in Africa warned of the "heady wine of high places about WPB that needs watching—U.N. testimony, prime ministers as friends and patrons, etc. It is easy to get led down the primrose path by this heady wine," he noted. "Keep in mind that WPB is not and cannot be number one with any of these people, even Kaunda." The same observer worried that the WPB relied too heavily and uncritically upon Kaunda and his party for an understanding of African politics, that, for example, Brigade testimony before the U.N. committee had been too much based on hearsay from the UNIP and too incognizant of that party's own violations of personal liberty.[49]

Despite critics' complaints that the WPB claimed "too much too soon" for their role in the emergence of Kaunda's opportunity to win an election victory, there was reason to believe that the nonviolent presence strengthened Kaunda's efforts to restrain violent elements in Northern Rhodesia and that the prospect of nonviolent direct action encouraged British authorities to restrain Wilensky and permit the political reform on which Kaunda was able to capitalize. There was also reason to assume, despite subsequent developments toward domestic repression on the parts of both Kaunda and Nyerere, that these leaders were sincere in their interest in nonviolent methods. On the other hand, as a Brigade supporter pointed out in the case of Nyerere, he and Kaunda were each a head of state "responsible for the maintenance of military forces whose use [they did] not repudiate," and which, it should be added, the nature of the modern nation state made difficult if not impossible to repudiate.[50]

For whatever reasons, nonviolence did not become a force to reckon with in Africa. Muste mourned the lost opportunity. Noting the rising level of violence on the African continent by 1964, he wrote, "When one reflects upon the period where it looked as if there was a pretty good chance of getting nonviolent training schools underway in Ghana, one can only hold his breath." He also chafed at the sight of, on the one hand, Western black nationalists "who have ties with Eastern countries" gaining a foothold in Africa, and, on the other, of leaders such as James Farmer and Martin Luther King speaking too much, in his view, the language of the American establishment in their contacts with African nations. But what possible nonviolent alternative there was to these approaches remained obscure. "I certainly don't feel at home," Sutherland wrote from Dar es Salaam where he had a close view of the complexities confronting Nyerere and Kaunda as national leaders. "I just can't find room within modern statehood for basic nonviolence." Although Muste had been proud that through the WPB, "at least we gave evidence that . . . non-Africans were willing to come to the support of an African independence struggle," he had no answer to Sutherland's lament that "pacifists . . . have not been able to provide answers for the security of National Interests. . . . We do not have anything new to say to the Freedom Movements, although," he added with a glimmer of continuing hopefulness, "some are ready to listen." Lyle Tatum of the American Friends' Service Committee offered a useful perspective from which to view the WPB: "If it strives and dies but gives birth to the next step in the development of international cooperation in nonviolent attempts to correct injustice, . . . the WPB will not have been a failure."[51] Although the working out of that next step was not to occur in the lifetime of Muste, he did not brood over such disappointments. The World Peace Brigade was busy with other projects as well, including sponsorship of the *Everyman III* voyage from London to Stalingrad, to which he devoted considerable time trying to raise funds, negotiate with Russians, and generate expressions of international support.

Upon his return from Dar es Salaam in May 1962, Muste found a cable waiting from the Gandhi Peace Foundation; an Anti-Nuclear Arms Convention was planned for New Delhi in June and the American pacifist was urged to come. Though this allowed virtually no time to rest after the African trip, Muste accepted the invitation. "The fact that the Gandhi Peace Foundation is concerning itself with the problem of nuclear arms is a development of tremendous importance," he wrote Jayaprakash Narayan. "It would have been a matter of real grief to me if I had felt that I could not respond to this invitation," he told another Indian friend. At the New Delhi convention major Indian leaders went on record in support of unilateral disarmament.[52] But Muste's high hopes over this development were dashed four months later by the border dispute which erupted between India and China and the military response mounted by the Indians. As one of the few Gandhians who sought some response to this situation other than support of government actions, J. P. Narayan asked Muste to return to India in December 1962. The American's appraisal of Indian policies and attitudes, including a forthright critique of the failure of the Gandhian movement to rise above nationalism, was valued by many troubled public figures there but most were not ready to accept his conclusion that, "from a cold practical standpoint, unilateral disarmament would be the best and safest course for India to take."[53] The venerable disciple of Mohandas Gandhi, Vinobe Bhave, assumed the position that "India has not yet developed adequate strength to achieve all its ends through nonviolence." The claim that nonviolence "can face the enemy without an army . . . has not been proved yet." He concluded that until the change of hearts and minds required for such proof had occurred in their land, Indians should concentrate on creating national unity. In conversation with Bhave, Muste stressed the violent implications of national unity and the inevitable contradiction between conventional national defense and nonviolence. Having heard Muste out, Bhave concluded the interview with an evasive question: "What do you think? Does God want to destroy the world now?" Muste replied, "God wishes to save it, not destroy it. But . . . God has put in man's hands power to destroy the world" "I am quite sure in my mind," Bhave said, "that God is not going to destroy the world now. If he were, he would not let you and me and other pacifists think along these lines."

Muste smiled, "That is evidence," he agreed, adding, "and in the final analysis perhaps the only evidence."[54]

Before Muste left India he, Narayan, and other members of the WPB agreed to develop the idea of an international Friendship March from New Delhi to Peking. Proposed by CNVA worker Ed Lazar, the march idea appealed to Indian peace advocates as a means of "people-to-people communication expressing the friendship and unity of peoples, irrespective of the policies pursued by their governments." In consultation with the European advisors of the WPB in London in January, Muste helped hammer out details. The march would cover 4,000 to 5,000 miles at a rate of about ten miles a day, leaving time for communication with local people in each area through which it would pass. Marchers would not prescribe a specific political solution to the Sino-Indian dispute but would stress that "differences must be resolved without recourse to violence."[55]

Muste returned to New York after the London meeting, agreeing to work on personnel and funds for the march but he asked that more overseas travel not be required of him "on account of my age and for other fairly obvious reasons, . . . unless a visit from me seemed necessary and promised to be fruitful." He assured his Indian friends, on the other hand, that "if they did call me, I would do my utmost to respond." The call was only seven months in coming. Thirteen Friendship Marchers from five countries (the United States, Great Britain, Austria, Japan, and India) had started their trek in March from Rajghat where Gandhi was buried. An Indian correspondent for the *Christian Science Monitor* reported that it was impossible not to be moved by the serenity of these men and women from many lands and by their sense of purpose and dedication. Although they had met some hostility in their travels across India, their biggest difficulty became evident as they approached the border area. The route to China, via Burma, which they originally intended to follow was not permitted them by the Burmese government. An alternate route through the Indian-China (Tibet) border was reported "not negotiable except by highly skilled and well equipped mountain travelers." In addition, whatever route they might try, they were faced with a Peking regime that was unwilling to welcome them.

Indian peace leaders and Friendship Marchers prevailed on Muste in October to consult with them at Assam, on the Burmese border, 2,000 miles from their point of departure. Muste spent three weeks in India, including ten days with the marchers at Assam and then went on to London to confer with WPB advisors there. Although the strategy and philosophy governing the India-China undertaking was innocuous in comparison to that of other projects which he had helped direct—no civil disobedience was involved and the emphasis was on "love, persuasion and understanding," rather than on protest—Muste, the marchers, and their other advisors were unable to find a way out of the maze of world politics and to a position where they could be seen as "human beings, desiring to communicate with other human beings regardless of national boundaries." They were perceived by Indian nationalists as encouraging Chinese aggression, by partisans of China as playing into the hands of Western–Soviet attempts to isolate Peking, and by the Chinese themselves as partisans of India.[56] Muste proceeded on the belief that his own record, and that of the marchers, of resisting war preparations in all countries, including their own and the Soviet Union was esteemed by the Peking authorities. But after lengthy and futile efforts to get the marchers into Hong Kong and from there send them by boat to mainland China, Muste had to admit defeat. "It is now, short of a miracle, out of the question for the Friendship Marchers to be admitted to the Chinese People's Republic," he reported to a supporter in Japan in January 1964.[57] Although he had reminded the WPB all along that "we must not flinch if [the] time does come when we have to say we have done all we can and have to end the project," when the end did come, he felt it as "a source of very deep regret to me personally."

By the spring of 1965, he had concluded that continuation of the WPB was no longer possible. As he mentioned often in this period, and as Charles Walker observed in a later evaluation, the undertaking had depended heavily for financial support upon radical pacifist movements in the U.S., India, and England. As widely publicized nonviolent civil rights campaigns in the United States drew heavily on monetary sources, funds became less accessible for all peace projects, including the WPB. In India, Gandhian resources became more concentrated on the Sino-Indian dispute and no longer available for WPB work in Africa. Jayaprakash Narayan observed that in addition to the failure of funding the Brigade was critically impaired by inadequate "mechanisms to consult . . . at the international level." "The WPB was never formally laid down," wrote Charles Walker. "It fell into disuse, leaving an ambiguous legacy of what American activist Theodore Olson called 'vision and failure' but perhaps invaluable experience on which to build at a more propitious time."[58]

While WPB involvement took Muste to the Third World continents of Africa and Asia, rising alarm within CNVA and *Liberation* circles over developments in U.S. relations with Cuba required that he pay careful attention to that Latin American country. In the Castro overthrow of the U.S. supported Batista, which occurred on that small island in 1959, some radical pacifists saw a perfect example of, in the words of David Dellinger, "revolution against . . . American financial interests and corrupt [native] collaborationists" which was sweeping South and Central America. "There is no more point in quarreling with these revolts than in shaking one's fist at a hurricane," Muste declared. "Furthermore," he added, "it is impossible to quarrel with the basic aims of these revolts. They arise out of human dignity."[59] To make the Washington government understand this and shape policies to support rather than subvert leaders such as Fidel Castro became an increasingly urgent objective for the CNVA and its national chairman, Muste. He was quick to spot harbingers of a U.S. invasion plot in the press and equally quick to deplore any such prospect. When the *New York Times* reported that a Cuban exile who had recently announced that an invasion of his homeland was imminent was welcomed at the State Department, Muste wrote the newspaper to decry the implications. The Bay of Pigs fiasco, which occurred less than a week after Muste's letter, drew his disdain. The whole episode, he wrote in *Liberation*, was an "incredible series of miscalculations, blunders, goofs. . . . Everyone knows," he taunted, "that intellectuals, political amateurs, spies and cloak and dagger operations can make mistakes, but not that many in one week; they can be stupid, but *that* stupid?" An ad hoc Nonviolent Committee for Cuban Independence drafted an "Appeal to the American Conscience," calling attention not only to the recent humiliation in Cuba but also to the increasing power of that "cruel and ruthless secret agency, the Central Intelligence Agency," which had been responsible for preparing the invasion attempt. "The Appeal" called for a reversal of U.S. policy and for Castro and his followers to show forgiveness to the captured invaders.[60]

This appeal was issued by an ad hoc rather than an established pacifist group, because pacifists were divided over the question of how humane and compassionate the Cuban revolutionaries really were. Debate enlivened the pages of *Liberation*, and one member of its editorial board, Roy Finch, resigned because he was convinced that the Cuban revolution had become hopelessly totalitarian. While Muste showed interest in explorations by the FOR into possibilities for a nonviolent education project in Cuba and a conference on nonviolence for non-communist radicals in Latin America, he believed that American pacifists' primary responsibility lay in seeking to change the U.S. stance toward Cuba. That stance, he was certain, had driven Castro into the Soviet sphere of influence and was in important measure responsible for provoking the dictatorial and militaristic behavior exhibited by the Cuban government. Muste and others who agreed with his position appealed to U.S. officials to lift the embargo against Cuba. He was alarmed by signs that the American government might be planning another invasion attempt and feared that pacifists (like Finch) who spoke of engineering a nonviolent overthrow of Castro were merely reinforcing Washington imperialism. "I deeply want to struggle nonviolently to eliminate evils in the Castro regime," Muste maintained, and he was careful to avoid association with uncritically pro-Castro groups such as the Fair Play for Cuba Committee. But he concluded that no alternative to Castro could be implemented without the active military and political support of Washington. "Any regime which now replaces Castro will be as effectively dominated by the U.S. as we now charge that the Castro regime is dominated by the Soviet bloc. . . . The present Cold War mentality of both blocs," he argued, "[destroys] any hope for a basic change in Cuba."[61]

This wide-angle assessment of the Castro regime, placing it in the context of Cold War international rivalries, muted the sharpest contradictions between pacifism and Castroism. It suggested more of a convergence between them on the goal of economic reform than a commitment to nonviolent means could ever really permit. While Muste's interpretations of such phenomena as the Cuban Revolution were perceptive and thought-provoking, they were in the end mostly descriptive. He was so secure in his own pacifism that he could personally negotiate a stance of qualified support for a figure such as Castro. But he never prescribed an adequate strategy by which the entire nonviolent movement could enter into such relationships without some uncertainty and confusion.

Although the role of Cuba as a pawn in the game of Cold War power politics was plain for all to see, no one was quite prepared for the deadly turn that game took in the October 1962 crisis over the installation of Soviet missiles on Cuban soil. Muste, with the CNVA, put out "a policy statement" demonstrating that, for every Soviet act in Cuba condemned by John Kennedy as aggressive and deceptive, there was a "nearly identical" action taken against the Soviets for which the United States was responsible, and expressing the deepest fear that gripped so many during the crisis period: "We stand on the brink of thermonuclear war . . . knowing that 'the fruits of victory would be ashes in our mouth.' "[62]

The CNVA list of specific recommendations for actions that the governments of the United States, Cuba, and Russia might take to resolve the current crisis and avert similar confrontations in the future was, predictably, ignored. Nikita Khrushchev's decision to withdraw the Soviet missiles rather than call the American bluff did contain traces of self-sacrifice and appreciation for the larger good to which apostles of nonviolence could point. (Was it not interesting, Muste asked, how the American government could convince its people that the USSR was, on the one hand, "diabolical and yet, on the other hand, reasonable enough to back down before a U.S. challenge"?) But what struck Muste hardest was how quickly people were able to put behind them the terror at having looked World War III in the face, and how fast they were in turning that experience into a formula for reassurance. Seasoned as he was in the role of disregarded prophet, he was astounded at the popular arguments: "If we did get to the brink once and not go over, we could do it a second, a third— who knows how many times."[63]

To remind people of the grim implications of the Cuban crisis and to confront them with nonviolent alternatives to U.S.-Soviet competition over Cuba, the CNVA instituted new programs of nonviolent direct action. From mid-January to mid-February 1963, seven CNVA workers conducted a peace education campaign in Miami. In that city, with its considerable Cuban-exile population, the pacifists' leaflets—which asked "Do you really think that sabotage, arson, terrorism, invasion and the risk of nuclear war are appropriate ways for free men to fight for freedom?"—caused a substantial stir.[64] Meanwhile Muste was at work laying the foundations for another great international peace walk. Comparable to the San Francisco-Moscow venture, and with Bradford Lyttle again handling the most critical aspects of planning, coordinating, and day-to-day leadership, the Quebec to Guantanamo Walk was to traverse Canada, the United States, and Cuba. Departing in May 1963 from three points—Quebec, Boston, and Cleveland—eighteen walkers converged in Rome, New York. Their itinerary called for them to follow the full length of the U.S. east coast to the Florida keys from where they hoped to sail for Cuba. Except for internal problems unavoidable in such undertakings (personality clashes, differences over operating policy, etc.), the walk proceeded according to plans until it reached the deep South. There the walkers' racially integrated ranks outraged local mores and shifted the focus of the walk from foreign policy to civil rights. Stalled first by police brutality in Griffin, Georgia, in November, the walkers were next subjected to harrowing imprisonment in Albany from December 23, 1963 to February 24, 1964. After recuperating at Koinonia, Georgia, the walkers resumed their pilgrimage on March 15. Muste, who had worked so devotedly to find a morally acceptable resolution to the Albany impasse, preceded them to Florida, doing "advance work" for their accommodations and meetings.[65]

They arrived in Miami in mid-May, where the obstacle of U.S. State Department denial of visas stood between them and Cuba. Thirty-eight-year-old Kenneth Meister witnessed for the group's freedom of travel by fasting for over thirty-three days at the office of the Cuba division of the U.S. State Department in Miami. Other peace walkers, with the aid of local supporters, vigilled and lobbied at the same office. Meanwhile, Muste made personal appeals to the Department of State and to sympathetic congressmen who intervened in his behalf. New York Representative John Lindsay wrote Muste that the official who had denied the walkers' passports "said that he and his colleagues . . . have the highest regard for you and for the genuineness of your ideas and your purposes." However, the government found it impossible to make an exception for the pacifists to the prohibition on travel to Cuba.[66]

When all legal avenues had been exhausted CNVA decided to send their emissaries to Cuba without U.S. permission. Six walkers attempted on October 27, 1964, to sail a powerboat christened the *Spirit of Freedom* to Havana. U.S. authorities impounded the boat and a court case "aptly entitled," as Barbara Deming noted, *The United States of America* v. *The Spirit of Freedom* ensued.[67]

Thus, Muste had spent his "retirement years" crisscrossing the country and the globe; serving jail sentences passed down by uncomprehending magistrates in Omaha and New York City; struggling over racist viciousness in the Deep South; contending with dogmatic Cold War bureaucrats in Washington, Moscow, and Peking; and seeking to establish nonviolent channels for the nationalist passions seething in India and Africa and Latin America. Ceaselessly, he searched and pleaded for funds to sustain nonviolent projects. "This is his greatest burden—the strain of trying to meet one financial crisis after another," noted his secretary, Beverly Sterner. Always he was available to his fellow pacifists. "He is the leader, prophet, confessor and gadfly to us all," FOR staff member Glenn Smiley observed. To stress the extraordinary pace these activities held him to is to belabor the obvious. But he kept an even stride and, though occasionally complaining that "there is just no end to the damn meetings these days!" and reflecting that "something has gone wrong with time—peace movement activities have been stepped up beyond anything we have known hitherto," he was not overwhelmed.[68] The fine adjustment of his inner compass which had occurred in 1936 was lasting. His life-long cultivation of self-discipline gave him strength, and his never-failing sense of humor helped to keep temporal affairs in perspective. Yet inner security and firm self-control did not preclude his remaining open to new experiences and possibilities whether they involved scaling the missile base fence or joining a traditional African celebration. "One of . . . Muste's remarkable qualities the last years of his life," observed David Dellinger, "was his ability to learn from even the humblest, least experienced and most confused with whom he worked." He knew, Dellinger explained, how "to bring his own wisdom to [an] encounter, without being enslaved by it or intimidating others with it. There was seldom a strategy session of the organizations he headed, . . . in which most of the others did not speak before he did." For Bayard Rustin, Muste's capacity for joyous involvement in whatever the present moment offered was crystallized in a moment they shared in India, when Rustin roused the elderly Muste from his sleep to meet a band of gypsies who had come into the village where they were staying, with the result that Muste visited and danced until dawn with his new friends.[69]

Religious renewal remained important to Muste, though he did not be-labor his faith with his largely a-religious comrades. "I spend a good deal of time these days among those who are regarded as unbelievers," he confided to a Quaker audience in 1961, "and my thoughts constantly shuttle back and forth between the conviction that many of these are the true believers and the wish that I might give them an account of the faith that is in me." Ever dissatisfied with established churches, including the Friends (whom he reminded in the same talk, "the spirit has not invaded the houses where we meet. We are not on fire"), Muste yet sought ways to reaffirm and draw fresh power for his religious convictions. At the height of the Cuban crisis he was instrumental in calling for a week-long fast in Washington, D.C., to draw attention to the inhumane coex-istence of mass hunger in the Third World and mass expenditures for weapons of slaughter, and to make a statement about superpower intervention in Third World revolutions. But he intended the fast also as a means by which pacifists might seek "the practical wisdom which grows out of unhurried reflection and the strength which comes out of deep springs."[70] In the fall of 1964, at the prompting of FOR religious education director John Heidbrink, Muste joined a select group of peace workers in a retreat at the Trappist Monastery, Our Lady of Gethsemani, in Kentucky where Thomas Merton lived and worked. The Catholic Church, with its rigid hierarchy and strict demands of obedience, had never found comfortable acceptance in Muste's usually ecumenical world view. He respected Dorothy Day and the contributions of her Catholic Worker Movement; he had close relationships with some of the younger pacifists who created the Catholic Peace Fellowship within the FOR. But, for the most part, Catholic institutions remained beyond his ken. His visit to Gethsemani, therefore, took him into a setting that was unfamiliar and whose ritualistic routines and extreme reclusiveness were alien. "To my sorrow," remembered Tom Cornell of the Catholic Peace Fellowship, "[A.J.] never once went to hear the choir monks chant the Divine Office." But he did "walk in the woods to Merton's secluded hermitage over wet autumn leaves, dangerously slippery," with younger friends "hovering behind him as inconspicuously as possible to scoop him up if he fell, like angels commissioned lest he dash his foot against a stone." The retreat brethren searched together for the spiritual roots, sanctions, and dictates of their protests against war and other violence. They also socialized: "A Berrigan went for two cases of beer; and the Protestants, A.J. included, looked with bewildered condescension on the Catholics in the holy hermit's hut swilling down their beer, belly-laughing and running out to the trees for relief (Merton had neither electricity nor privy [Cornell explained])." Muste left the Abbey impressed with Merton's "really very brilliant mind" and called his visit "a very illuminating and encouraging experience. One feels no restraint in [the monk's] presence," he noted. But he found it "something of a mystery . . . how [Merton] manages to live in a Trappist Monastery."[71]

If the choices of celibacy and seclusion by one as earthy and politically sensitized as Merton left Muste puzzled, some of the choices confronting his secularized comrades were no less intriguing. Changing attitudes of and toward women in the larger society began to affect male-female relationships in the American peace movement in the 1960s. Muste had long worked with female colleagues on an egalitarian basis. During his labor education and organizing days the rights of women workers were clearly recognized by Musteites whose leader accorded strong figures such as Fannia Cohn, Elizabeth Gurley Flynn, Rose Pesotta, Cara Cook, and Josephine Colby the same professional regard he showed their male counterparts. On the other hand his own marriage had been patterned on the conventional model of husband-in-the-world with supportive wife-at-home. And he tended to assume that that would continue to be the norm for most families. That he had not had a chance to reckon with the increasingly large percentage of women who were permanently, and out of necessity, in the labor force was clear in the assessment he offered of the role women could play as peace activists. "Women can for a time take a more radical position than their men," he said, "because they do not have jobs or jobs that are immediately jeopardized, etc. But in the long run," he concluded, "the basic economic considerations weigh upon the family as such and a movement is solid only if it is based upon all persons." As some women activists began fusing pacifism and feminism, Muste voiced measured criticism. "The main consideration is that these activities should not develop into an anti-male movement or lead to any neglect of participation by men," he cautioned. And he complained, "When the on-going organizations, pacifist and peace, were trying to get some civil defense protest underway a good deal of energy had been drawn off because some group of women . . . had announced a 'strike' for the same or approximately the same time!" But his political instincts were alerted: "I don't myself think that the womens movement is going to bring peace by itself," he told *Peace News*. "But it is symptomatic nevertheless of something very important."[72]

Women who worked with the established pacifist groups—FOR, WRL, CNVA—received Muste's fellowship and support to the same degree as their male co-workers. In the most notable instance of internal conflict over the roles pacifist women would be permitted to assume—the debate over adding females to the crew of *Everyman III*—Muste was squarely on the side of the women who wanted to sail. In the flurry of letters between the U.S. and England that addressed this issue, the all-male planning committee for the voyage from London to Leningrad resisted the idea of women crew members on the grounds that inadequate privacy and sanitary facilities would make a coed situation extremely uncomfortable, while the presence of only one or two women would evoke high sexual tensions with the crew and adverse reactions in the press and even among many supporters. "Beverly [Henry's] striking physical attributes will be sheer dynamite in this respect," predicted an American pacifist. The women, on the other hand (twenty-two-year-old Beverly Henry who had worked on the Polaris Project and organized various women's peace demonstrations, and forty-five-year-old author Barbara Deming, with experience in the U.S. part of the San Francisco to Moscow Walk and many other CNVA projects), denied that the tensions and privations on board ship would be all that much more severe than those with which protestors had contended in the walk to Moscow, the Sahara project, and other efforts. To all the dire predictions of trouble arising from having only two women in a predominantly male crew, Henry responded that "perhaps what the project needs is a change of attitude regarding this, and perhaps, other issues." Muste agreed. To reject Henry and Deming as crew members would be, in his view "a grave mistake." Both were "mature and balanced people," he stressed, who "so far from adding to emotional problems on the boat, . . . will almost certainly do just the opposite." Given their contacts, especially Henry's, with women's groups who might help with fund raising, Muste saw the women as political and financial assets to the voyage. "I believe it will be considerably harder for the Soviet P[eace] C[ommittee] or Soviet authorities to turn the crew back at Leningrad if women of this calibre are on board," he concluded. The fact that neither woman possessed sailing skills or experience, Muste chose to ignore while he underlined that, if they were not taken on, "we shall have a problem on our hands with some of our best people, including fine young people." Neither Muste's practical weighing of political and strategic factors nor the women's arguments prevailed. *Everyman III* sailed without them.[73]

While Muste's support of Henry and Deming was in keeping with a lifelong ability to regard fellow workers as equals regardless of sex, other episodes in the sixties showed that some of his earlier views were changing. Faced with a sensitive "triangle" situation involving participants in another major peace undertaking, Muste championed the substance of love over the technicalities of propriety and law. A few months prior to the project in question, a married couple who were both peace activists separated when the wife and another activist found, as Muste put it, that "they loved each other and wished to be together." The man in the newly formed couple volunteered for the project and was enrolled on the assumption that he and his loved one would be apart for its duration. Sometime after the project began, however, he requested that the woman be allowed to join him. Extensive and impassioned discussion within pacifist circles took place. Not only did Muste advocate allowing the woman to join the project, but he also explained his position in two detailed "Not for Publication" memoranda. The unmarried couple, he noted, "consider themselves truly married but they have not been legally married by a representative of the State. . . . In a psychological and spiritual sense" he found nothing wrong in this. Far worse, he argued, were loveless situations where the conventions were strictly observed.

Muste's views were shared by the project participants themselves and by enough members of the project coordinating committee to permit the woman to join the group. Her estranged husband concurred in the decision but decried Muste's explicit memos. "Your mimeographed discussion of this sensitive issue is a caricature of openness," he wrote. While admitting some concern over the possible effect of having aired the issue in this way, Muste concluded that it had been necessary. "Our only recourse in a movement such as ours is to be quite open and frank with each other, however painful that may be," he argued. "We have to assume that somehow we are united in a bond of community, that if we were together we would talk frankly with each other and when we can't be together, we have to manage by correspondence, inadequate as that may be." Some three years later this episode reached its conclusion when the couple about whom so much controversy had swirled were finally married in a ceremony performed by Muste.[74]

Four years before his death Muste reported that he was "still occupied in trying to think through my attitudes on such matters as extra-marital sex relationships, homosexuality, etc." He rejected "judgmental and hateful" applications of old puritan standards and refused to regard unconventional sexual behavior as a "sin." He had read the British Friends' pamphlet, *Toward a Quaker View of Sex*, with interest and commended such reexamination of the question "in a religious spirit." By then he had had occasion to rise in defense of the soundness and integrity of his homosexual friend, Bayard Rustin, for whom he had urged psychological treatment in the fifties. And he had been a guest in the home of other close friends who were homosexuals. "He was perfectly at ease with us," reported one member of the couple, "and I never doubted that he was aware that we were lesbians."[75]

Although Muste could rise to the social and moral challenges of the changing times, physical limitations imposed by increasing age began to get in his way. In 1960, when he turned seventy-five, he began occasionally to refer to his mortality. He told readers of *Fellowship*, in July 1960, that pacifism had recently made so many gains (the Sahara project in Africa, the student sit-ins in

the Deep South, the signs of new awareness among theologians of their obligation to speak against nuclear war, and of intellectuals assuming a similar
obligation in the founding of the Council of Correspondence), that he felt almost as if the time had come to repeat "the utterance of another old man who
said: 'Now lettest though thy servant depart in peace, Lord, according to thy
word.' And if the departing comes," Muste added, "I think it would indeed be a
departing in peace." But he then shifted to a more characteristic tone: "I do not
feel like departing," he said, "and I probably don't know how to quit." He ended
the article with his favorite couplet from the "Battle Hymn of the Republic,"
"Be swift my soul to answer Him; be jubilant my feet."

Swiftness and jubilation gave way somewhat to overwork and fatigue in
the wake of the San Francisco to Moscow project. Through most of 1962, he was
troubled by a lingering virus and paid several visits to his doctor who told him
that his pulse "was too rapid by a good deal." Medication not only slowed the
pulse but, Muste complained, "has drained me of a good deal of strength." At
the same time his eyes were failing. "This is nothing really dangerous," he
assured friends. "The oculist says my eyes, such as they are, are good for another
twenty years. That ought to be enough." Nonetheless, he advised associates to
"remember that I am getting to be an old man."[76] While he made some token
gestures toward cutting back on his commitments, resigning as missioner of the
Church Peace Mission and turning down some speaking invitations, he plunged
ahead with the major international projects in Africa and India and continued
to be fully involved in many facets of the civil rights and peace movement
struggles in the United States.

A fall, in April 1963, slowed him up a little and left him temporarily lame.
Even more serious was the rapid development of cataracts over both eyes. Having decided to have an operation to remove the cataracts Muste wrote the FOR
office for the number of the insurance policy which was a part of his retirement
arrangement with the Fellowship. No sooner had he received the policy
number than he was called on to use it in the emergency room of St. Luke's
Hospital, having been mugged one evening about a block from where he was
then living in New York City. "I got off luckily, as such things go," he reported,
"one hard smack to the mouth without the slightest warning and the
perpetrators were scared off quickly by something or other so I lost nothing but
a cheap wrist watch." A split lower lip required stitches "and looked pretty
bad," he noted. "What has impressed me most about this somewhat bizarre
experience," he added, "is that it had no effect, so far as I am aware, on my
thinking or emotions but . . . I was both numb and achy for several days."
"You of all people," chided Milton Mayer. "The rest of us *deserve* it."[77]

The cataract operation, about which he had been most apprehensive ("I
don't think of anything else at the moment," he had admitted), took place in the
early fall of 1964 and was successful. After recuperating at his daughter Nancy's
home in Thornwood, New York, for a few weeks, he graduated from shaded
glasses to new prescription lenses and announced that his sight had undergone
a "wonderful transformation." In fact the joy he took in his restored sight is

what associates who accompanied him to the retreat with Thomas Merton remembered most about his presence there. "He was happy as a boy looking at everything to be seen as we drove from the airport at Lexington through the knobby Kentucky hills to the Abbey," recalled Tom Cornell. James Forest noted that in snapshots from the retreat Muste's "excitement with *seeing* is evident."[78]

Still, he retained the feeling that his powers were now limited and that he must choose more carefully among the jobs he was called to take on. "I am getting old and have to cut down," he wrote the Council of Correspondence in resigning from their editorial board in November 1964. "My age and physical condition . . . simply makes it impossible for me to undertake travels of this kind," he replied to an invitation to visit Japan in the spring of 1965. "I am simply not able to get as much done as I used to," he confided to an associate in the summer of that year.

By then his eightieth birthday had passed. In February 1965, admirers had gathered for a big celebration at the Midland Hotel in Chicago. The families of both John Muste and Connie Muste Hamilton attended. That was to be one of the last happy occasions he would share with his middle child. By the end of that year she was dying of an incurable liver ailment. According to John Muste, their father "spent as much time as he could in Indiana, doing whatever he could for [Connie]. She was in considerable pain much of the time, and I remember being there one day when he took her aside and assured her that none of the family would think any the less of her if she decided to end her own life. He was the only one who could have done this," the son stressed, "since she had always been especially close to him and would have found it very difficult to do anything she thought would make him think the less of her, and even though Connie chose not to do it, his talking with her must have been of considerable comfort." Muste felt his daughter's death keenly. She was the only one of his three children to become a pacifist and had worked with him in the FOR for many years. The only time that his FOR associate John Swomley ever knew Muste to cry was the night he called to report that Connie Hamilton had died.[79]

The note of optimism Muste had struck at the beginning of the decade—the nearly playful toying he could then do with the biblical notion of the servant departing in peace—was gone by 1966. Armed conflict in Africa, Black Power in the United States, acquiescence by churchmen and academics in the nuclear arms race mocked the belief which he had held that nonviolence had a chance to prevail. He continued to express strong faith, but with less joyfulness than in earlier times. In the summer of 1965, a correspondent asked him if he "retained a belief in an all-loving God." "I can say explicitly and unreservedly that I do," he replied. "Faith," he emphasized, "is significant in a situation which involves evil and tragedy not in a situation which presents no problems or obstacles." He then reminded his questioner of "the biblical saying: 'Tho' he slay me, yet will I trust him.' "[80] The loss of his daughter and a growing sense of his own frailty were also sobering. But most agonizing of all, for one whose life work was to eliminate violence and war from human society, was the escalation of slaughter and destruction in the Southeast Asian country of Vietnam. "I can't get it out of my head or my guts that Americans are away over there not only shooting at people but dropping bombs on them, roasting them with napalm and all the rest," he cried.[81] In the short time that was left to him Muste would direct his remaining political and spiritual resources toward bringing that war to an end.

Chapter XI

The Pacifist and Vietnam
The Final Years

Decades before most Americans even realized that Vietnam existed, Muste had worried about developments there. In 1946, he pointed out to the U.S. State Department that American declarations against colonialism were being flatly contradicted by Allied actions in Southeast Asia. Full restoration to power of the French in Vietnam—whose rule there had been temporarily upset by Japanese incursions during World War II—proved him right. Equally on target were his predictions that the French would not be able to maintain their position. Nearly a year before the 1954 victory of Vietnamese nationalist Ho Chi Minh over France at Dien Bien Phu, Muste warned fellow-pacifists that in Southeast Asia, "where the Dutch, the English and shortly, the French shall have been eliminated," the United States, with an investment in French colonialism totalling more than a billion dollars, would be left alone, trying to maintain a western, anti-communist presence "at a vast distance from its home base." A month before the routing of the French Muste noted sadly that the top priority of Americans in Vietnam remained that of trying "to defeat communism."[1]

This priority, critics observed, had long determined the role which the United States played in Asia. In an historical assessment written in 1964, Muste and his War Resisters' League colleague David McReynolds noted that, when the American-supported Chiang Kai-shek was defeated by the Communist Mao Tse-tung on mainland China in 1949, the United States had hastened to "contain" the Chinese Revolution by "building around it a ring of military bases and alliances." At the same time the United States followed a diplomatic policy of nonrecognition of Mao's government. "No settlement of the problem of Indo-China is possible as long as the United States refuses to face the reality of China," Muste and McReynolds declared.[2] For years, while acknowledging the repressive and militaristic nature of the Peking regime, Muste had championed U.S. recognition of the People's Republic of China, admission of that government to the U.N., and removal of the American military and monetary props supporting Chiang Kai-shek in Taiwan. Genuine progress in curtailing the arms race and beginning disarmament would never occur without these steps being taken, he argued, and the argument became more urgent by 1964 when the Chinese tested their first atomic bomb.[3]

He was convinced that American intervention in Vietnam stemmed directly from U.S.-China policy. As the Muste-McReynolds memo stressed, in the context of "containing" the Chinese Revolution, the French defeat in Indo-China had meant "that a huge 'hole' had suddenly appeared through which Chinese influence might flow into Southeast Asia." And Americans had taken it upon themselves to plug this hole. But their efforts, warned the pacifists, were doomed to failure. Seeing in 1964 what military experts would take a decade to admit about the U.S. struggle to shore up an artificially created government in South Vietnam, Muste and his colleague observed that sea power was useless in an Asian land war, that air power could destroy only civilians "because the Vietcong cannot be spotted," and that even extending the war to cut off supply lines from North Vietnam and/or China would be futile, since "enemy" forces in the South could keep going with arms and supplies captured from South Vietnamese troops. "We are trapped," the WRL evaluation concluded, "in a situation where no traditional military victory can be won in South Vietnam regardless of how many more troops and how much more equipment is [sic] poured in." (Belatedly this would be defined in experts' jargon, as "a no-win situation.")

In the pacifists' view, the fact that Vietnam was historically an enemy of China and that nationalistic Vietnamese were being driven toward alliance with that enemy by the very anti-communists who wanted to limit Chinese influence underscored the obtuseness of American policy-makers. Should the Americans come to their senses and withdraw from Southeast Asia, Muste and McReynolds thought it possible that Vietnam might evolve into an "Asian Yugoslavia," pursuing its own nationalist interests and remaining independent of Red China. But no one in a position to influence U.S. Asian policy shared this point of view. Even foreign policy specialist George F. Kennan, who would later be viewed as a "dove" on the question of Vietnam, upheld the containment view in a series of exchanges between Muste and him in 1964–65. Although he termed Muste's argument for U.S. withdrawal from Asia "a view I can respect as much as any other, even if it does imply an admission of complete failure and helplessness on our part," he insisted that such withdrawal would result in various Asian nations disappearing "behind an iron curtain no less cruel and unnatural than that from which the Eastern European peoples are beginning to emerge in this post-Stalin period." Muste's contention that containment—a concept closely associated with Professor Kennan's career in the State Department after World War II—had failed against the Soviets in Europe and would similarly fail against the Chinese in Asia ended the dialogue. Politely but definitively Kennan informed Muste that he would not "participate in any way in the coming period in the discussion of contemporary political matters."[4]

Muste's efforts to carry the discussion to other quarters were equally unsuccessful. In August 1964, he challenged the fateful Gulf of Tonkin Resolution which, with nearly unanimous Congressional approval, gave President Johnson "the functional equivalent" of a declaration of war. For most observers the circumstances prompting Congress to pass the resolution would not seem questionable until three years later when Senate Foreign Relations Committee investigations revealed that they had been fabricated, at least in part. But for Muste the Gulf of Tonkin episode rang false from the beginning. "It is surprising, and in a sense shocking to receive from the Department of State a version of the events of August 2 and 4 and related matters which is so far from the truth," he told a public affairs officer in Washington less than a month after the Resolution was passed.[5]

Consequently Muste did not view the presidential election of 1964 in the same light as did most liberals, many pacifists, and other opponents of war. Although the Republican candidacy of Barry Goldwater, with his reckless statements about "nukes," had tempted Muste "to depart from my long-time practice of not voting," he maintained his standard position and urged others in the peace movement to join him in staying away from the polls. "It is not Goldwater and Right extremists in this country who have built up our vast military establishment," he declared. His warning against putting too much faith in the Democrat Johnson would come back to haunt many of his peace-loving friends when, in defiance of campaign rhetoric and in only a matter of weeks after the election, that president irreparably intensified the war in Vietnam. Though horrified, Muste was never surprised; he had reminded his fellow citizens during the campaign of what Johnson and his running-mate Hubert Humphrey really represented: "The Establishment . . . which led the U.S. into World War II, which bombed Hiroshima and Nagaski, which took the initiative in developing the H-bomb, which is continuing to spend vast sums on research into weapons of mass destruction, . . . which assumes the role of policing the world on behalf of 'freedom' and against Communist advance, and daily boasts of its superiority in military capability, i.e., weapons of mass annihilation. This is a regime which has as one of its important arms the CIA with its unsavory record in relation to Cuba and other regions, . . . and which is carrying on a peculiarly senseless and cruel war in Vietnam."[6]

After the election Muste concentrated on building up an effective pacifist response to that war. "Public attention is again turning to problems of foreign relations," he observed, and if the peace movement were to capitalize on this attention, "the radical pacifist nonviolent revolutionary viewpoint . . . has to be somehow set forth and embodied in action." Despite freezing temperatures, and in pointed contrast to festivities of the approaching holiday season, Muste joined Norman Thomas and A. Philip Randolph as the featured speakers at an anti-war rally in New York on December 20, 1964, sponsored by the War Resisters' League, CNVA, the FOR, the Socialist Party, and the Student Peace Union. While 1,500 people braved the cold to hear their pleas for an immediate ceasefire and expeditious withdrawal of U.S. troops, smaller demonstrations occurred in ten other American cities. Though insignificant by later standards, these small crowds foreshadowed a nationwide peace movement of massive proportions.[7]

A major source of energy for this movement were the young people who, since the beginning of the sixties, had been showing increasing concern over their government's social policies at home and military actions abroad. The Student Peace Union (SPU), founded in 1959, sponsored one of the earliest post-McCarthy displays of dissent when its leaders brought some 5,000 college men and women to Washington in February 1962 to picket the Kennedy White House and the Soviet embassy, and to lobby Congress for a ban on nuclear testing. The Students for a Democratic Society (SDS), with their genesis in 1960 as a revitalized and renamed incarnation of the older Student League for Industrial Democracy, was also active in criticizing the Kennedy administration while organizing campus chapters and community projects to demonstrate their commitment to racial justice, full employment, and a return to sanity in foreign and military affairs.[8]

Muste looked hopefully upon these young people and took their part against authority figures who sought to penalize them for their political behavior. When students who joined the anti-fallout shelter protests in May 1960 were threatened with expulsion from Brooklyn, Hunter, and other New York area colleges, Muste interceded with college officials. The students' "frankness, solidarity and readiness to accept the penalties of nonviolent action . . . gave me a thrill," he wrote the college deans and urged them to respect their students' "high sense of civic responsibility . . . , commendable personal discipline and willing[ness] to make sacrifices in obedience to conscience."[9]

Both the SPU and SDS tapped Muste's experience with fund raising, and he did what he could to help them finance their projects and develop their own networks of contributors. His ability to cross the "generation gap" was demonstrated in June 1964 and 1965 when he addressed two annual SDS conferences. After receiving a resounding ovation for his first address, he was pleased and a little surprised that his pacifism could arouse such enthusiasm in young revolutionaries.[10] As SDS planned for a major anti-war rally in Washington in April 1965, Muste encouraged and helped with the organizing. But some of the policies and practices of his young friends gave him pause. They were careless, he believed, in allowing statements of other organizations to be confused with their own position on the war and were less than skillful in explaining and clarifying their commitment to open the march to participation by any individual, organization, and point of view.

A few days before the Washington demonstration Muste was drawn into a meeting called by Robert Gilmore with Norman Thomas, Bayard Rustin, H. Stuart Hughes, Alfred Hassler, and several other peace movement figures who were uneasy about the SDS approach. They expressed their uneasiness in a brief public statement which professed "interest and sympathy" for the upcoming march, but noted disagreement "with particular positions . . . [of] some of the elements in the March." When the statement was picked up almost immediately by the *New York Post* and given prominent editorial page coverage by James Wechsler, who implied that the student march was on the verge of becoming "a frenzied, one-sided anti-American show," SDS supporters charged the signers of the statement with attempted sabotage and Muste began to suspect that he was being used. "In another context [the statement] did not say anything that I could not go along with," he observed, but once distorted by the editorial ("there must have been something that is called 'planting' in connection with that editorial," he conjectured), and circulated by the avidly anticommunist Turn Toward Peace Organization (of which Gilmore was a prominent member and which as an organization had denounced the SDS March), the statement became an embarrassment.[11]

In his younger days Muste would probably have fired off a detailed, analytical, "not for publication" memo to clarify the problems of which this tangled situation was a symptom. But, as he said to one friend later, "The story of the meeting out of which the statement came is a long and complicated one"; and to another on the same topic: "It would take a lot of space to put down my summary of these events [and] I have just never found time to do so." He did take care to mend the relationship between himself and SDS. "The spirit of understanding and reconciliation with which you approached all parties concerned was instrumental in preventing a public rupture which would have served the interests of no one," wrote SDS leader Clark Kissinger to Muste in May. "And this we thank you for." From then on Muste remained on good terms with the SDS and did not again question their political soundness. "I am very committed to what the SDS is doing," he avowed. "There are extremely intelligent and deeply concerned young people among them. . . . It is simply inconceivable that in a showdown the SDS people would come down for totalitarianism or get involved as an organization in anything resembling a violent attempt to take power in the U.S. . . . My attitude on all these things is frankly an experimental one," he concluded. While he was not certain that the youth represented "a truly viable New Left or revolutionary movement," he was certain of one thing: "I don't want to be separated from these young elements at this stage."[12]

The angry questions and passionate promises of resistance which the SDS demonstrators (numbering between 15,000 to 20,000) had declaimed on April 17 still hung in the air in Washington, D.C., when a delegation of representatives from SDS, the SPU, the Student Nonviolent Coordinating Committee (SNCC), and the Congress of Racial Equality (CORE) arrived at the White House to present a Declaration of Conscience with the signatures of 4,500 persons promising to refuse to cooperate in the prosecution of the Vietnam war. Muste, who directed the attention of the editor of the *New York Times* to this event, pledged that "the campaign to secure adherents to this radical rejection of the American war policy in Vietnam will continue." The *Times* had just interviewed him on his recent trip to Stockholm where he attended an emergency session of the World Council of Peace. Vietnam was the main topic of deliberation, and the Chinese point of view calling for all-out support of the "Viet Cong" (as opposed to the Soviet position which included concern for "peaceful coexistence") had prevailed. While noting the ominous implications of this seeming ascendancy of Peking over Moscow, Muste emphasized that even more ominous was the course being followed by Americans in Vietnam, including by then the heavy bombing of the North.[13]

Preparations for confrontation with the decision-makers responsible for such American actions were soon underway. On June 16, 1965, 2,000 members and supporters of the CNVA (including a contingent of civil rights workers from Mississippi) converted the steps of the Pentagon into a platform for a "Speak Out" against the war and against recent U.S. Marine intervention in the Dominican Republic. For five hours one opponent of war after another condemned American foreign policy while others spread out to proselytize employees of the gargantuan military complex with 50,000 radical pacifist leaflets. "In a room dominated by a much-photographed map of Southeast Asia and a small arsenal of weapons captured in Vietnam," representatives of the demonstration—Muste, Sidney Lens, historian Staughton Lynd, former Congressman William Meyer and peace activist Mary Christiansen—met for thirty minutes with Secretary of Defense Robert McNamara. In his prepared remarks Muste quoted copiously from Anatol Rapoport of the University of Michigan whose 1964 work, *Strategy and Conscience*, dissected the failure of morality in the top echelons of policy-making. "Of you and the experts who work with you," Muste told McNamara, "Dr. Rapoport remarks: 'the monstrosity of their work carries little or no emotional meaning for them, not because they are mentally ill, but because they are more richly endowed than the rest of us with the most creative of human faculties, which becomes also the most dangerous one when coupled with a lack of extensional imagination—the faculty of abstraction.' " Muste added his own comment: "How difficult it is to relate what goes on in this huge but quiet structure on a beautiful day in spring with what goes on under its guidance in Vietnam." Afterward Muste reported that he had "no idea as to whether in any sense we got under his [McNamara's] skin." But the secretary "did say he respected [our] position . . . and would read our documents."[14]

At least one employee of the Pentagon was definitely touched by the CNVA effort. One day following the Speak Out, John M. Jones, a naval officer with ten years of service, sent Muste a check for five dollars and a note that he was resigning. Muste sent him more pacifist reading material and asked for further details. "Your visit to the Pentagon acted as a kind of catalyst to some rather basic moral values that had been smoldering inside of me for quite some time," the reply came. "I have been inwardly upset for several years now with the world and society in which my family and I live without troubling myself to look for answers, but now the search is on." Although that search did not take Mr. Jones into public peace advocacy or lead him anywhere near the radical pacifism which Muste represented, he would still remember, years later, watching Muste stand out in the rain on the Pentagon steps and reflecting on the depth of commitment which had brought the pacifist "right down into the lion's den so to speak."[15]

While CNVA workers continued to labor on a one-to-one basis with Pentagon and other government employees throughout the summer of 1965, plans went forward for yet another major demonstration in the capital city in August. "We choose August 6, 7, 8, and 9 for a new attempt to draw together the voices of nonviolent protest in America," read the "Call" for an "Assembly of Unrepresented People." Conceived immediately after the Pentagon Speak Out by a meeting of representatives from such groups as CNVA, SDS, SNCC, and Women Strike for Peace, the assembly drew an estimated 2,000 protestors to Washington and was supported by Muste's fund-raising efforts. After three days of workshops on community organizing and civil rights and their relationship to the war, members of the Assembly marched from the Washington Monument to the Capitol, where 350 persons were arrested for a sit-down demonstration.[16]

A coordinating committee was soon founded to maintain ties among the various groups that had participated in the assembly, and out of that committee came the notion of "Days of International Protest" which became a reality in October 1965. In New York City Muste immersed himself in endless meetings and discussions where all segments of the political spectrum, from moderate to Marxist, explored ways that they might participate together in the International Days. Out of these explorations emerged a remarkable new coalition—the Fifth Avenue Peace Parade Committee. Bringing together such liberal-respectable groups as SANE and Women Strike for Peace with such left-wing splinter elements as the Du Bois Clubs and the May Second Movement; including both the Communist Party and the Socialist Workers' Party along with the New Left as represented by the SDS; and also containing traditional pacifist organizations such as CNVA, WRL, AFSC, and the Catholic Worker Movement; the Parade Committee was an achievement and a challenge for Muste. "What made such a broad based coalition possible was the personality of A. J. Muste," peace movement chroniclers later wrote. "While few of the groups had ever agreed, worked with, or much less trusted one another, they were all united in their respect for A. J." They represented "the widest spread of viewpoints that has collaborated on any such activity in my memory," he exulted. But he also recognized "that this is a big experiment. . . . we are aware of the risks as well as the potentialities." Following the pattern established earlier by SDS—and handling the public relations aspect of it much more deftly than the students had in April—the Peace Parade coalition got up "an official leaflet which recognized the existence of political differences among the members of the ad hoc committee but stressed unity in the call for an immediate end to the war." They agreed that, at the October rally, speakers would represent various points of view on the question of how to end the war and that on that day each group would be free to distribute its own literature. On October 16, joined by a crowd of at least 25,000 supporters, the Committee conducted its parade up Fifth Avenue from Ninety-fifth Street to Sixty-fifth Street and could boast of having held what was probably the most successful of many protest actions that day in the country and the world.[17] Almost immediately thereafter, Muste was involved in making arrangements for the Committee to participate in a new series of demonstrations proposed for the spring of 1966. Setting their sites on doubling the October 16 crowd, he and his co-workers talked of holding the next meeting in Yankee Stadium.[18]

But as energy-consuming as these coalition building activities were, Muste did not limit his attention to them. The coalition had the potential for making a political impact by an impressive show of numbers. And Muste's vision—which he had articulated so clearly during his work with the World Peace Brigade—of a mass movement capable of "affecting the centers of power in contemporary society" continued to influence the course he took. But at the same time he held on to the belief that it was equally important for peace workers to address the moral issues of the war. And that became, in the final analysis, a job for the individual, in consultation with his or her own conscience. In the individual act of draft card burning lay one opportunity to make a clear statement against the immorality of conscripting men to kill. Since the moderate wing of the peace movement was disinclined to support such radical action and war opponents in the various Marxist camps did not share the pacifist convictions from which draft card burnings historically sprang, the impetus for these actions came from the traditional anti-war groups—WRL, CNVA, and the Catholic Worker.

In a small meeting, called in conjunction with the October Days of Protest but kept organizationally separate from the Fifth Avenue Peace Parade activities, Catholic Worker David Miller burned his draft card in lieu of giving a speech. Muste witnessed and applauded the action. Since Congress had recently passed a law making destruction of a draft card a felony, Miller's action created a furor. Partly in response to what pacifists perceived as a "massive public attack on those who have burned their draft cards," another card-burning ceremony was staged on October 28. Muste addressed the crowd in Foley Square in front of the New York City Court House, where the burnings were to occur. "Some young men here are about to burn their draft cards in public," he announced. "I am aware that if any considerable number of young men and other citizens were to take this stand the United States could not wage war. I think that would be a glorious day in the life of this nation and in the history of mankind." Less than two weeks later Muste spoke at yet another card-torching display, this one in Union Square, where he was joined on the speakers' platform by the Catholic Workers' indomitable sixty-eight-year-old Dorothy Day, and where a *New York Times* reporter came on stage to verify that what was burned was really a draft card.[19]

This November episode produced a federal grand jury inquiry to which Muste and other CNVA figures who had been involved were subpoenaed. Refusing to answer questions put by the jury, the witnesses issued a collective statement countering charges that they had engaged in lawless behavior. "The real lawlessness at loose in the world today," they contended, "is that of the

President and his advisors who violate international law and outrage the moral values of all mankind by their actions in Vietnam." Muste reiterated this position in his personal statement to the grand jury and asserted his belief that "to reverse [the present U.S. course] would perhaps be something of a miracle," but "it would surely be our honor to pioneer a new future for mankind by performing that miracle."[20]

Although visions of miracles and defiance of federal law seemed to most Americans an extreme response to the strange war so far away in Southeast Asia, for a tiny minority of U.S. citizens such responses were not extreme enough. Before 1965 was over, three Americans had dramatized their anguish over the war by burning themselves to death. On March 16 of that year eighty-two-year-old Alice Herz, a survivor of Nazi terror, set herself on fire in Detroit. She lingered in the hospital for ten days before dying. "I choose the illuminating death of a Buddhist to protest against a great country trying to wipe out a small country for no reason," she explained in a note. While generally dismissed as the act of an unbalanced mind, Herz's sacrifice was seen by Muste as "in harmony with [her] record and character. . . . It had what I would call integrity," he wrote. "If there is a question of 'sanity' here," he added, "or 'abnormality,' I find myself questioning more the sanity and normality of people who read about Vietnam and are not moved to any action and not deeply touched inwardly." Eight months later two other self-immolations occurred—Quaker Norman Morrison before the Pentagon on November 2 and Catholic Worker volunteer Roger La Porte (who had recently attended an anti-war rally where Muste was one of the speakers) in front of the U.N. in New York on November 9. Again Muste indicated acceptance of such extreme action. In a statement issued as chairman of CNVA, he made clear that he "would not encourage [the original draft read "would strongly discourage"] any to follow the example of Roger La Porte, Norman Morrison and Alice Herz," and urged instead that opponents of the war join in mass demonstrations and civil disobedience. However, he supported the spirit of irreconcilable grief which the three suicides expressed. Their actions would be open to criticism, he observed, if they had occurred in a society which valued human life. "But ours is a society composed of people who somehow feel that . . . the death of hundreds, thousands, millions in war is . . . somehow normal, human, civilized. . . . Even more," he continued, "this is a society in which people contemplate, for the most part calmly, the self-immolation of the whole of mankind in a nuclear holocaust."[21]

Although not as direct and dramatic as the approach of the self-immolants, Muste's own actions by this time—organizing, protesting, travelling, pushing his aging body far beyond its limits—were in keeping with their self-sacrifices, and his rejection of the war was no less final. His most compelling essay during the Vietnam period, "Who Has the Spiritual Atom Bomb?" made this clear. Published in November 1965, its title borrowed from Communist Chinese Minister of Defense Marshal Lin Piao (who wrote, "The spiritual atom bomb that the revolutionary people possess is a far more powerful and useful weapon than the physical atom bomb"), the essay flatly declared the United States to be the greatest obstacle to peace in the world. After reviewing the course of American foreign policy since World War I—a course which, as Muste described it, U.S. leaders pursued in a spirit of consistent self-justification and self-praise—the pacifist called on Americans to begin to see themselves as others saw them: as, in the words of the Chinese Defense Minister, "the most rabid aggressor in human history and the most ferocious common enemy of the people of the world." Once again Muste called on the American nation to repent by withdrawing from Vietnam, abdicating the role of superpower, and disarming at least to the level of nations such as the Scandinavian countries. Such a course, he avowed, would start a revolution in international relations and in "the behavior of peoples toward one another," and would help preserve humankind. It would truly be a "spiritual atom bomb."[22]

Muste was well aware that few readers would accept his apocalyptic analysis in total. But he believed that if radical pacifism could convince a sizeable body of opinion of the need for an American decision to withdraw from Vietnam, then the other steps for which he appealed might occur later. Yet, despite the great uneasiness over the war which was evident all across America, shaping such a body of anti-war opinion, keeping it firm and rooted in a commitment to unwavering protest, was extremely difficult. Against the minority view which Muste articulated stood a major tendency to give the United States and its government the benefit of the doubt. While he viewed the U.S. involvement in Vietnam as a logical outgrowth of U.S. addiction to violence and national chauvinism, most Americans saw the Vietnam War as at most an unfortunate mistake, an aberration from American traditions. When he insisted that the only way to change U.S. policy was for advocates of change to "clog [the war-making machine] with your whole weight," they preferred to express their opinions through ordinary political channels. Whereas he refused to be pacified by periodic statements of interest in negotiations from the White House, crying over and over again, "*but the slaughter goes on*," others were eager to trust those statements and use them to shift responsibility for ending the war to Hanoi.[23]

More than any other issue this tendency to expect peace to emanate first from Hanoi troubled Muste; it raised the perennial pacifist dilemma of how to reject all violence and at the same time distinguish the violence of the oppressor from that used by the oppressed. Although he did not define the problem as a dilemma, he became increasingly insistent that American pacifists' primary responsibility was to condemn and seek an end to the destructive forces unleashed in Vietnam by the United States. "As Westerners and especially as Americans," he argued, "we have no moral right to impose virtuous renunciation" of bombing, terror, etc., on the NLF or North Vietnam. "It is not that I am for torture, etc., or want to condone such practices by anyone," he explained. But he refused to be party to any implication that the United States was not obliged to end its war activities until so-called enemy forces became nonviolent. To pacifists who wanted to maintain a position of condemning the violence of both sides in the war Muste warned that "there is something about the way [such a position] comes out which makes it seem as if we are all on an equal footing. Before God? Yes. Before each other? Not so clear." What was clear to Muste was the culpability of America. As he put it to editor James Finn, "I think you have to be for the defeat of the United States in this war. I just don't see how anybody can be for anything except withdrawal and defeat." Not since the labor wars of the 1930s had Muste divided warring camps so explicitly into the right and the wrong, the good and the bad. Although he did not depart from his commitment to nonviolence as the method for transforming the United States, and although he did join with a small committee of distinguished opponents of war in writing Ho Chi Minh in January 1966 that "the time has come for a responsible proposal to be made by one side or the other," the care with which Muste avoided censuring the violence practiced by the victims of U.S. actions was striking.[24]

Through 1965 and early 1966, Muste appealed in the strongest possible language to those who, in his view, were simply failing to come to terms with the evils of U.S. foreign policy. Professors at the University of California at Berkeley who issued an "Open Letter" accusing radical protestors in the Berkeley Vietnam Day Committee of "exploiting" American misdeeds in Vietnam, heard promptly from Muste. "Those who do not want to see the nation's shame 'exploited' can disassociate themselves decisively from the moral scandal and summon their utmost efforts to terminate it," he observed. When *New York Times* commentator James Reston questioned the propriety of anti-war demonstrations after President Johnson declared his willingness to sit down at a conference table with North Vietnam, Muste wrote Reston a four-page reply. In it he argued that if demonstrations and other forces of dissent were to be given some credit for bringing the Johnson administration to the point of considering negotiations (and Reston had so credited them), then it was imperative to keep the pressure on to prevent further escalation, should Hanoi not immediately jump at Johnson's offer. Furthermore, Muste declared, "the idea of 'negotiating' about whether we shall or shall not further step up the killing of babies, women, men, even combatants in Vietnam is to me gruesome, repulsive, inhuman, dishonorable and a betrayal of the American Dream." Undaunted by Reston's parting thrust ("Your thoughts were stimulating—and I doubt they could have been presented from a picket line"), Muste continued to scold war critics who seemed to him more concerned with maintaining political moderation than with ending the war and to prod those public figures and opinion-shapers who seemed to be verging on a more radical position.[25]

In an exchange with *New York Post* columnist James Wechsler—who acknowledged the influence of Mustean arguments in his columns but felt stymied when he came to the question of "how the President of the United States . . . could follow the full course of your [Muste's] counsel"—Muste hammered away at Wechsler's observation that there must soon be "great new beginnings in the human adventure," and by implication a complete departure from prevailing power politics. Muste pursued the same theme with Senator J. William Fulbright, whose leadership of anti-war forces in Congress was coming to seem increasingly important to pacifists, and with major writers and scholars such as Anatol Rapoport and Herbert Marcuse who seemed to Muste to be at the very edge of the great flash of insight that might revolutionize the course of human history. His continuing deep respect for the power of ideas and the potential clout of radicalized intellectuals was evident in Muste's comments on and to such scholars and authors, and in his careful reading of Hannah Arendt, Martin Buber, and Albert Camus, among others whose quotations regularly found their way into his own essays, letters, and speeches.[26]

Similarly, his hopes for a public outcry great enough to change the direction taken by the American government in Vietnam were buoyed by an "Open Letter" from eminent scholars to the *New York Times* expressing strong dissent from the war. "The radical character of the statement and the prestigious character of the signers" encouraged Muste's belief "not only that the war in Vietnam may somehow be terminated but that a basic change in foreign policy and in orientation of American society might actually be possible." And when Muste joined the AFSC working party which prepared the study on *Peace in Vietnam* (urging an immediate end to escalation of the war and a commitment to withdrawal of U.S. troops as rapidly as possible), his optimism was high that the "brilliant Vietnamese experts" in that party would be able to create "something very useful" in the struggle against the war and against the assumptions about world politics from which the war had sprung. Interestingly, one simple declaration by Muste stood out from all the experts' technical arguments and became, as *Peace in Vietnam* Editor Charles Yarrow noted, "the motto of the whole work—'You can't burn a house and build it at the same time.' "[27]

As flames from the burning house continued to spread, Muste intensified his efforts to build a peace movement strong enough to put them out. "Every form of dissent and protest is valid now," he wrote in February 1966, "and ought to be pushed to the limit."[28] At the same time the coalition building which began with the emergence of the Fifth Avenue Peace Parade Committee in New York City and the National Coordinating Committee to End the War in Vietnam had to go forward. The drawing power of both groups seemed undiminished, yet not markedly on the increase. On the spur of the moment the Fifth Avenue Parade Committee brought out 5,000 pickets to oppose the presentation of a Freedom House Award to Lyndon Johnson in February 1966, and the following month between 20,000 and 25,000 marchers came together at its call to participate in another international protest action under the auspices of the National Committee. Led by a sizeable contingent of disillusioned American war veterans, joined by a group of Afro-Americans against the War, parade participants were a racially and politically variegated lot. "Bearded youths and matrons pushing children in strollers marched side by side," the *New York Times* reported. At a rally in Central Park Mall, Muste, Vietnam veteran Donald Duncan, and celebrated writer Norman Mailer were among the speakers. "By escalating our activity and protests we can deescalate the war," Muste declared. But in fact this demonstration ("the largest peace demonstration in the country since the protests began last year," according to the *Times*) and those around the country and world were not appreciably larger than their October predecessors while numerous reports of hecklers, egg-throwers, and other counter-demonstrators indicated that anti-peace forces were becoming more visible.[29] Although doing all anyone could do on American soil to help maintain and increase a still unpredictable peace movement, Muste was compelled to reach for other peace strategies. One such strategy involved his taking the cry for peace to the scene of the war itself.

Simultaneously with preparing for the March 1966 demonstration, Muste and others of the CNVA laid plans for a pacifist team to visit Saigon. This project was "above all [Muste's] idea," noted team member Barbara Deming. Muste's determination, precision, and sense of urgency pervaded the statements of purpose and the intricate planning which preceded the undertaking. The rationale behind the trip was not un-American, Muste emphasized. Rather it was "anti-war and pro-mankind." Shamed and outraged by the U.S. course in Vietnam, team members were nonetheless interested in communicating with American civilian and military personnel in Saigon and stressed that toward these people as individuals they felt no hostility. Above all, however, the pacifists sought to "know more at first hand" about the Vietnamese themselves and hoped to talk with representatives of all points of view among them. Aware that the journey would be seen as "impulsive" and "romantic" by some people in the peace movement, Muste maintained that by making the trip and taking the physical risks which it involved he and his comrades might be able to "establish an identity with the people of Vietnam . . . [which] in one way or another all of us are obligated to do. . . . We trust," he added, "that we are free of an emotional compulsion to engage in a melo-dramatic, spiritually shallow and fruitless action."[30]

In early April 1966, Muste, with veteran activists Barbara Deming, Bradford Lyttle, and Karl Meyer, outspoken anti-war scientist William Davidon, and a peace-movement novice Sherry Thurber, flew to Tokyo. After conferring with representatives of the Japanese Peace movement and receiving from them names to add to the list of peace contacts in South Vietnam which they had compiled before leaving the U.S., they continued on to Saigon. Allowed to enter South Vietnam on April 15 by authorities who showed little interest in carrying out their duties, the pacifists spent their first evening there at "the house of a friend on the other side of the river," in that section of the city which was a stronghold of the Viet Cong. Reminders that they had entered a nation at war were not long in coming. "We went to the fellow's house," Muste later said, "and were sitting around when suddenly there were two tremendous explosions and then small arms fire. Well, we all sat there on the floor in the courtyard and waited for things to calm down." The next morning they found that a police station down the block had been blown up. After the excitement, the visitors separated, men and women going to different hotels for the night. The men found accommodations in Saigon's best hotel, the Caravelle. While Brad Lyttle theorized that sympathizers on the hotel staff made this possible, journalist I. F. Stone, knowing well the difficulties of finding rooms in Saigon, thought that the CNVA delegation was able to acquire the Caravelle suite "because it was conveniently wired for sound by the police and they [the police] preferred to have the pacifists where they could keep a close watch on their comings and goings."[31]

During the next week team members spoke with American AID personnel, correspondents, Buddhist monks, Catholic priests, and university students. Muste was especially interested in what Karl Meyer learned from his conversations with the priests. An anti-war statement which twelve Saigon priests had recently smuggled out of the country was sent with the knowledge of the Bishop of Saigon and included among the signers the head of a parish of some 8,000 people, mostly refugees from North Vietnam and, according to their priest, at least eighty percent of these parishioners were in favor of his stand for peace. This information belied the image of Roman Catholics as universally hostile to the National Liberation Front and North Vietnam and as most supportive of U.S. intervention, and lent weight to the impression which the American pacifists received from many of their informants, that "the overwhelming majority of Vietnamese 'have no interest in ideology, whether pro-Communist or anti-Communist; they simply want to live.' "[32]

The liveliest encounter that the CNVA visitors had while in Vietnam came at a public press conference in Saigon City Hall. Attended by reporters and about fifty Vietnamese youth, the question and answer process proceeded smoothly for about an hour. "Then, almost at a signal one of these young fellows stood up and started to make a speech in Vietnamese," Muste reported. "When he sat down everyone cheered. Then another young fellow stood up and translated the whole speech into English and they all cheered again and the shouting all started. That's when the eggs and tomatoes were thrown." Toward the end of this melee one antagonist told Muste, "I will kill you with my own hands." Barbara Deming recalled that light bulbs were thrown against a wall, making a sound like gunfire. According to Brad Lyttle, U.S. newsmen who were present identified the instigators of the disturbance as South Vietnamese security agents. Muste assumed they had been "put up to it by the Chief of Police" and said that "some of them apologized to us the next day."[33]

The Saigon peace mission came to an end when the team attempted to hold a demonstration at the U.S. embassy on April 21. Walking from the Caravelle to the embassy (they knew, Brad Lyttle explained, that if they took a car they would definitely be involuntarily rerouted), they encountered half-hearted police efforts to stop them. Although these efforts temporarily subsided, Muste and company were finally arrested. As the police approached, a few brave sympathizers came forward to shake hands with the Americans. "I was very scared for A. J.—as well as for myself," Barbara Deming remembered. "For one thing we had decided not to cooperate with [South Vietnamese Prime Minister] Ky's police. . . . They would have to carry us or drag us. None of us had any idea how rough they might be; and A. J. looked so very frail. As it turned out they were gentle with us." Lifting the peace advocates into a paddy wagon (where they spent time "just sitting" under the broiling sun . . . "and that hadn't been easy for [A. J.]," Deming noted), the police eventually transported them to the airport. Held "in a kind of detention room," the pacifists waited for deportation. "I looked across the room at A. J. to see how he was doing," said Deming. ". . . He looked back with a sparkling smile and with that sudden lighting up of his eyes which so many of his friends will remember, he said, 'It's a good life!'. . . . He had done what he thought had to be done, . . . and he had done it as well as he knew how; and then—he was able to be happy." Carried to the plane by police, Muste and his friends were told by one officer, "I am sorry we have done this and we hope you will be able to come to Vietnam some other time."[34]

En route home the team made another stop in Tokyo, where Muste and Deming attended a Japanese Quaker Meeting for Worship and stayed after to talk about their experiences in Vietnam. The Friends who heard them were convinced by their report that the CNVA mission had been "a very worthy witness to make," and were moved by the "youthfulness" of A. J. Muste. "I shall never forget A. J. standing on one leg at a time to take off his shoes on entering our Japanese Meeting House," noted DeWitt Barnett. "I know some people a lot younger than 81 who find it difficult to stand stork-like to take their shoes off!"[35]

American reporters who met Muste at Kennedy Airport on his return on April 24 were also struck by his agility. Asked, "in deference to his age if he preferred to take the elevator to the second floor VIP Lounge, Muste said 'No, no we'll just walk,' " reported Pete Hamil in the New York Post. After a 12,000 mile plane ride, the reporter observed, "Muste's tweed coat was wrinkled and the gray suit gone baggy and he needed a shoe shine. . . . But the hand shake was firm, the voice was sure and he looked at you with eyes made clear by the almost forgotten practice of virtue." In the news conference, and in his subsequent speeches and articles, Muste expressed his satisfaction with the Saigon project. It had been important to show the people of Vietnam that there were Americans who opposed the war and were deeply committed to finding a way to end it.[36] It was equally important now to convey to the people of the United States the profound longing for peace—and for withdrawal of the U.S. military presence from that country—which permeated Vietnam. Fresh evidence of that longing reached CNVA three months after the team's visit to Saigon, when an American reporter brought back communications from Vietnamese students. The students denounced the disruption of the pacifists' news conference. Of the disrupters they wrote, "Although they speak Vietnamese, . . . we do not consider them Vietnamese. . . . They were tempted by money!" And to the pacifists they expressed "deep appreciation and gratefulness. . . . It was the first time our country had the great honour to welcome Americans who represent mankind's conscience," they declared.[37]

Sensitized by his Saigon experiences to feel more acutely than ever the urgency of shutting down the American war machine, Muste plunged back into the endless strategy sessions and on-going controversies of the American peace movement. The organizing of another major Fifth Avenue Peace Parade effort, scheduled for August 8, 1966, absorbed a good part of his time. Intended to give peace advocacy maximum visibility, this protest convened (on the twenty-first anniversary of Hiroshima) at twelve separate locations, from where marchers moved toward Times Square, giving residents all over New York an opportunity "to see the American peace movement 'live.' " Their route also purposely took them past the offices of corporations that manufactured napalm, that deadly chemical which left unspeakable horror wherever it was sprayed by the American military. Muste spoke at the Times Square Rally, emphasizing once again that holders of all the divergent views in the crowd were bound together, not by being "pro this government or that but [by] being anti-war and pro-mankind." He and other leaders of the Peace Parade Committee were not happy that numerous North Vietnamese flags were flown at the demonstration. But while they discussed the "inappropriateness" of unfurling such banners with those who carried them, they declined to either request the police to ban the flags or to enforce such a ban themselves. "I am pretty sure," Muste contended, "[though] it may not be apparent on the surface, that the procedure we have used teaches these people [those with the foreign flags] some lessons in nonviolence and the spirit of pacifism."[38] Applying friendly persuasion in relations with partisans of Hanoi, convincing traditional pacifists of the wisdom of this approach, laboring to find common ground with radical blacks, reaching out to uncertain and embittered enlisted men in the armed forces—all this activity, as one of Muste's fellow-organizers would soon observe, was akin to "climbing up a greased pole."[39] But the climb continued.

Reading of rising opposition to the war on the part of Congress and other federal authorities, Muste began to hope by the summer of 1966 that the Johnson administration would seriously explore new avenues to peace. At the same time he realized the terrible pressures under which the administration struggled: "I am convinced," Muste wrote to a friend in France, "that Washington wants to find a way out of Vietnam but how to do that without a terrific shakeup here is a very tough problem."[40] However tough the problem, the ramifications of leaving it unsolved were too grim to contemplate. The agony and terror generated by this American war were spreading beyond Vietnam. Muste called the attention of American peace workers to recent events in Indonesia where an estimated one million people were massacred in an anti-communist purge. No less circumspect a reporter than James Reston observed that "it is doubtful if the coup would ever have been attempted without the American show of strength in Vietnam or been sustained without the clandestine aid it has received indirectly from here." This "savage onslaught," as Muste described the Indonesian affair, provided yet one more reason for pressuring American opinion-makers to take a stand of unequivocal opposition to American foreign policy.[41] Thus he revived his correspondence with such figures as Reston, James Wechsler, George Kennan, and various congressional critics of the war. A common theme in this round of letters was the venality of the South Vietnamese leader, Marshal Ky, and Muste's conviction that only good could come from U.S. repudiation of him. He argued that so long as Washington backed this outrageous dictator (who declared that Adolf Hitler was his hero and who regularly contradicted White House and Pentagon statements of policy), the U.S. would have no moral leverage in its efforts to communicate with North Vietnam. To the American senators who had issued an appeal to Hanoi on behalf of the lives of captured American Air Force personnel, Muste protested that to create a furor over these airmen while making no response to Ky's call for escalating the war and his assertion that he would never negotiate with the NLF, was untenable. Similarly, Muste added, to plead for no retaliation by Hanoi would be useless unless an equally strong plea was made for Washington to stop bombing North Vietnam and for the American people to realize "that in the sight of God the death of a Vietnamese is as precious as that of an American and that the death of an American is as precious as that of a Vietnamese."[42] Another benefit the dumping of Ky would provide, according to Muste's analysis, would be the strengthening of nonviolent forces in Vietnam, especially that of the Buddhists. Though never clear as to how much political influence he expected these monks and nuns to acquire, Muste was keenly interested in and moved by the "nonmilitary form of struggle" which they had mounted against the Ky and preceding regimes.

In 1966, when no Americans were clear about their expectations for the future of Vietnam, Muste was at least certain that that future should be free of American military intervention, and in the view of one commentator, that certainty had come to mean a great deal. "On the basis of the record as of this moment, poor A. J. Muste, a lonely, abused iconoclast, has offered sounder counsel to our country than so skilled a product of our diplomatic system as Dean Rusk,"[43] wrote James Wechsler in the *New York Post*. However lonely and abused in the larger national context, within the American peace movement Muste remained a central figure, admired and looked up to by peace activists of every description, including representatives of the rebellious generation of youth who, by the mid-sixties, had reportedly ceased trusting anyone over thirty.

Wherever they met him, young activists were impressed by Muste. Having spoken his piece at a conference of "Non-Cooperaters" with the draft, Richard Schweid, a Boston University student, was approached by Muste. He "complimented me on the way I expressed myself," Schweid said, but then Muste added, " 'I'm afraid . . . that I must disagree with you. You are not radical enough. Not nearly enough.' " Schweid was intrigued. Muste, he concluded, had "refused to 'mellow' with age." At the same student conference Muste, though he spoke at none of the sessions, was at the end of each, according to Schweid, "immediately surrounded by groups of people soliciting his opinion, his support or his time." Another student, Joe Pilati, remembered how Muste's arrival on a "particularly listless picket line" outside an aircraft construction plant in Hartford, Connecticut, "suddenly, in some small way [made] the protest more visible."[44]

Young men such as these, and others both more and less radical, turned to Muste for direction. Michael Meeropol (son of the late Julius and Ethel Rosenberg) mailed him a position paper on peace movement strategies to which Muste responded with encouragement and the advice that Meeropol make his proposals "more concrete." Robert Watts, black leader in the left-wing youth group named for W. E. B. Du Bois, received Muste's immediate support when government charges were brought against him as a subversive. "It is of utmost importance that all citizens today should be unmolested in expressing their views on the tragic Vietnam War," Muste telegraphed President Johnson, "and [we] are determined, regardless of differences of opinion, to defend Robert Watts and any others in their exercise of that right and their duty."[45] As he rose to Watts' defense, while carefully distinguishing between his own views and those of the Du Bois Club, so Muste could sympathize with draft evaders who fled to Canada while making plain his own preference that men "face the [draft] situation at home." Asked to help raise money for these evaders, Muste responded that "there is nothing I can do about it financially." His fund-raising obligations were already overwhelming. But he also acknowledged that "what is happening is understandable. . . . If a lot of young Germans had refused to throw Jews in the ovens and had made their way to other countries we would all have regarded them as heroes. . . . Fellows who do not want to shoot Vietnamese peasants are probably in the same category."[46]

With another category of young war protestors, those reflecting "counter-culture" trends, Muste enjoyed good rapport. Seeing "themselves more in the bohemian-beat tradition . . . than in the pacifist tradition, . . . dissatisfied with the negative connotations of a peace movement that was *anti*war and in favor of *non*violence," these people called for "celebration of a new and different kind of life." With their interest in psychedelics, their advocacy of sexual liberation, and their ideas for organizing directed toward strewing the streets with flowers and balloons, and "launching" a Beatles-inspired "Yellow Submarine," such "peaceniks" were about as far-removed from Muste's Calvinist heritage and personal reserve as any group of individuals ever could be. But as they crowded into the CNVA-WRL offices to volunteer their services, and as they filled out the picket lines and vigils which were held nearly every week now, Muste beamed his approval. As he saw it, "a movement has true vitality when young people thus place talents and energy at its disposal." One consequence of this influx of talent and energy was the formation of the New York Workshop in Nonviolence, whose members—with fund-raising help and promotion from Muste—created a new, high-spirited, slightly outrageous movement publication, *WIN* magazine. Whenever the contents of the new magazine rubbed too sharply against the values of the CNVA traditionalists who had agreed to support it, Muste was called in to mediate. On one occasion, the editors recalled, they were about to print a piece using "words that hadn't appeared before in CNVA literature. . . . The work was read aloud and we all turned [to A. J.]. . . . He looked around the room at young, at middle-aged, at beards and jeans and suits and ties. 'Well to tell the truth,' he said at last, 'it didn't exactly arouse me . . . I kept waiting for the bad parts.' " Criticizing the work, then, by his own standards he left the final decision to them and they went ahead with publication.[47]

Attracted by programs such as those of the New York Workshop, draft-age students were turning in ever larger numbers to the CNVA and WRL. Some appeals came from young men raised in the historic peace churches. From Putney School in Vermont Tom Robbins, a Quaker youth, requested help from Muste in thinking through the most appropriate action for him to take regarding the draft. "The first consideration for a moral being," Muste noted in his reply, "has to be whether he is functioning morally, expressing what he is at that moment in his own life and history." But other advice seekers came, as Muste noted, "from families who have never been in touch with anti-war or pacifist activities before. . . . So that whole new sections of the population get drawn into the movement. In a growing number of instances," Muste continued, "young men already in the armed services . . . who . . . in conscience revolt against going to Vietnam to fight, have come to us."[48] John Morgan, for example, though explicitly nonpacifist, had walked away from the Marine Corps because of his revulsion against the carnage in Vietnam. "I developed a great respect and admiration for him," Muste said after conferring with Morgan over a period of several weeks, and he made a special effort to raise money for the legal services which defense of the AWOL Marine would require.[49]

Another case of defection from the U.S. military that received Muste's attention and developed into a celebrated cause for the American peace movement was that of "The Fort Hood Three." James Johnson, a black American; Dennis Mora, a Puerto Rican; and David Samos, of Lithuanian-Italian parentage, had all been opposed to the war in Vietnam before accepting induction into the Army, assuming that, despite their opposition, they could "go along with the program." During basic training, however, their alienation from "the program" increased. They observed that "Negroes and Puerto Ricans are being drafted and end up in the worst of the fighting all out of proportion to their numbers in the population." Furthermore, "no one used the word 'winning' anymore because in Vietnam it has no meaning. Our officers," the three men noted, "just talked about five to 10 more years of war with at least ½ million of our boys thrown into the grinder." Johnson, Mora, and Samos concluded that the "grinder" was not for them. "We have made our decision. We will not be a part of this unjust, immoral and illegal war." After receiving their orders to report on July 13, 1966, at the Oakland Army Terminal "for final processing and shipment to Vietnam," the G.I.'s arranged a press conference in their home city of New York on June 30 called by the Fifth Avenue Peace Parade Committee and supported by two radical black groups—the Student Nonviolent Coordinating Committee and the Congress of Racial Equality. Announcing their decision to refuse orders to board the ship for Vietnam, the draftees also pleaded with the peace movement to reach out to other enlisted men—the majority of soldiers, they contended, felt trapped and helpless. In organizing this press conference the Peace Parade Committee also established a Fort Hood Three Defense Committee, with Muste as "treasurer pro tem"; soon he became co-chairman with Staughton Lynd. Although the Fort Hood Three were not conscientious objectors of the sort Muste had historically supported—"We are not pacifists," they emphasized, "not nonviolent and . . . we will fight back"—they nonetheless expressed moral convictions with which he could easily empathize. "I've always believed," said Dennis Mora, "that if you act against your beliefs you die inside."[50]

Three days after the men made public their plan to disobey Army orders, "a senior legal expert at the Defense Department" told the *New York Times* that soldiers who refused to fight in Vietnam "might be prosecuted under existing laws and regulations and in extreme cases might be sentenced to death." Four days later the men were taken into custody by military police and held at Fort Dix. Their supporters demonstrated at that New Jersey army base on July 9. Photographers recorded Muste there peering steadily out from under the brim of his summer straw hat into the tense faces (eyes rigidly averted) of the military police assigned to restrain the demonstrators.[51]

Once the Army announced that court-martial proceedings would be held against the Fort Hood Three, Defense Committee efforts focused on generating world-wide publicity and establishing a strong legal case. The stand of the three men "constitutes a clear test as to whether the government, military or civil, can constitutionally and legally compel G.I.'s who are not pacifists but who refuse to fight in Vietnam to do so," wrote Muste. "It is a matter which involves the civil rights of all men in the armed services, their right to think for themselves, to discuss the issues raised by the War in Vietnam, and to refuse to obey orders to commit what they believe to be war crimes."[52]

When the military trials of the men opened on September 6, Muste was present to observe, along with the men's families and other supporters. Once the defense lawyers were denied their right to argue that the Vietnam War was illegal, the outcome was predictable. On September 9, Samos and Johnson were given maximum sentences of five years at Leavenworth, with Mora receiving a three-year sentence at the same penitentiary. All of the men received dishonorable discharges and forfeitures of their pay. Held in maximum security at Fort Meade, Maryland, while the sentences were reviewed, the Fort Hood Three were quarantined, denied library privileges, and forced to maintain a standing position from five A.M. until six P.M. each day. Muste and the Defense Committee protested these conditions as well as the sentences. On November 8, their sentences confirmed by the First U.S. Commanding General, the men were transferred to Fort Leavenworth. Muste's work with the Defense Committee continued. Not only had the case increased communications between the peace movement and G.I.'s and underlined the special price paid in the war by minorities and people of color, but also it brought home in an especially poignant way a point which James Wechsler had recently made: "In a sense we are all prisoners of this dead-end war."[53]

Though ready to establish supportive relationships with many nonpacifist elements during the Vietnam War, Muste avoided entanglements in situations where he could not guarantee that his own position would not be compromised or obscured. Uncertain about the health and mental stability of Lord Bertrand Russell, Muste turned down an invitation to participate in the British pacifist's War Crimes Tribunal.[54] He kept his attention focused instead on strengthening the American Mobilization against the War in Vietnam. Following a Mennonite "International Meeting for Peace" on the border between North Dakota and Manitoba on September 6, 1966, where he was one of two main speakers,[55] Muste prepared for a trip to Cleveland where on September 10 and 11, the demonstrations of August were assessed, the Coordinating Committee against the war was rechristened the November 8 Mobilization Committee, and plans were laid for intensive protests to precede and surround forthcoming national elections. The initiative for these plans came from college professors, (Douglas Dowd and Robert Greenblatt of Cornell and Sidney Peck of Western Reserve) who had mounted the first campus "teach-ins" against the war. But the mobilization effort was designed to continue the coalition-building of previous protests and to attract support from as many segments of American society as possible. An early press release stressed the cost which the war was exacting from minorities and people living in poverty, and warned of restrictions which unions might soon face on their right to bargain for higher wages and to engage in strikes.[56] As usual, however, the notion of a coalition proved troublesome, and many hours of Muste's time were taken in defending the idea and making it viable. He reminded those peace advocates who shied away from cooperation with extreme leftists that their moderation represented a coalitionism of another kind—the tacit condoning of the actions of Washington officials who could not or would not make a decision to end the war. At the same time he chided self-styled revolutionaries for their failure to recognize that nonviolence had become a necessity in the nuclear age. Muste tried to persuade both the "respectable" and the "fringe" elements of the American peace movement of the need to successfully execute a nonviolent revolution in foreign policy in this country before presuming to prescribe for or meddle in the foreign policy of other powers, such as North Vietnam.[57] Though agreement on these issues was hardly universal when November came, Mobilization achievements then were substantial; anti-war actions had occurred in at least eighty-six cities and "a great proliferation of peace groups" was evident.

Eager to capitalize on these gains the Mobilization Committee met again in Cleveland. One hundred and eighty activists representing seventy local and national groups assessed their strength and decided to aim for an even greater show of force in the nation's streets in April 1967. Now known as the Spring Mobilization against the War in Vietnam, the coalition was truly burgeoning. Increasing dissent from the war within the ranks of labor gave Muste and his fellow mobilizers extra reason for optimism. "There is no current evidence that millions could be brought into the streets at one time to demand an end to the U.S. role in the war. For that to happen a very large number of labor unionists would have to be involved," Muste reflected. "On the other hand," he estimated, "if it were to happen that tens or hundreds or thousands of labor unionists appeared in an anti-war demonstration, that would make an appreciable impact on the Administration."[58]

Keyed up by such visions, Muste pressed on with his multiple jobs of raising money, reviewing strategy, articulating objectives, and helping his diverse and frequently contentious co-workers find ways, as he regularly quoted from Martin Buber "to bear their differences in common." He also worked to infect others with his unassailable determination. "Johnson and the war machine are things to be faced, not to cringe before," he challenged. "Our task is to disarm them not to be morally and politically disarmed by them. Did we really think the job would be easy . . . [or] attained at a modest price?"[59]

There was nothing moderate about the wear and tear which his own health and well-being had already sustained in this battle against the war. And, as he approached his eighty-second birthday, Muste was clearly prepared to continue his pursuit of peace, whatever the physical risks, whatever the result, even if it be death. This became especially evident in his response to overtures which he received from Hanoi after the journey to Saigon. Shortly after the CNVA team returned from South Vietnam they received a message that a visit from American pacifists to the North would be welcomed. Several months later, in July 1967, Staughton Lynd attended a conference in Geneva where representatives of the North Vietnamese Peace Committee reaffirmed this suggestion, explicitly urged that Muste be among the visitors, and observed that September weather might be most comfortable for travelling. At this point Muste, having earlier announced that he would make no more long trips, told his friend David Dellinger, "but that didn't mean [I] wouldn't go to Hanoi." Then U.S. bombing raids over Hanoi and Haiphong were reported, and Muste, with Staughton Lynd and David Dellinger as probable companions, determined to make the trip immediately. But their hosts cabled, "We are not ready to receive you now." Surmising that an inability to guarantee the Americans' safety was behind the delay, Muste assured Hanoi that "we do not hesitate [to] assume any risk to ourselves" and urged that "first hand testimony by Americans to facts about civilian bombing would be most valuable." Nonetheless, a new invitation did not arrive, and, at the end of July, Muste and David McReynolds of the WRL, joined by other peace workers from France and Great Britain, presented a new proposal to Hanoi—that a team of up to twelve Western pacifists be received in North Vietnam. Carefully establishing the fact that the team would not identify itself with any political grouping there, the proposal also contained an assertion that if any harm came to team members it would be "the direct and sole responsibility of the American government." The idea, its authors declared, "is conceived in the spirit of Norman Morrison, in the belief that it is necessary for some individuals to make the most direct and total protest possible."[60] Twelve people proved to be more than Hanoi was able to accommodate, but further consultation with figures close to the North Vietnamese government revealed that, as British peace worker April Carter reported to Muste, "the North Vietnamese still have a Confucian veneration for the old; they would be most impressed by a group of men or women who have spent their lives in struggling for social justice, . . . and who also are now 'elder statesmen' of peace, civil rights, socialist . . . movements in their countries." Based on this intelligence, a revised proposal went out to Hanoi which was accepted: Muste, German pastor Martin Niemoller (aged seventy-five), Anglican Bishop Ambrose Reeves, and American Rabbi Abraham Feinberg, serving a congregation in Toronto (both aged sixty-seven), would spend ten days in Hanoi in January 1967.[61]

Although the U.S. State Department refused to validate his passport for North Vietnam, and although charges were outstanding against him from a recent anti-war demonstration at which he was arrested, Muste left for Paris on December 26, where visas for China and North Vietnam awaited him. With the three other "Volunteers for Peace in Vietnam" he participated in a press conference there on December 28 where their plans were made public for the first time. According to the Paris correspondent from the *New York Herald Tribune*, Muste expressed his desire to "convey the spirit of peace to the stricken people of Vietnam" and reportedly said, "If it is the last thing in my life that I am able to do, I shall be content."[62]

Between Paris and Hanoi Muste and his travelling companions endured one stressful episode after another. Their party now numbered three—Pastor Niemoller preceded them in Hanoi with a group of German clergy and was to rejoin them on January 5. From Paris they flew to London where their plane to Karachi, Pakistan, was late in leaving. Agitated throughout the flight by the fear of missing the one plane a week that connected Karachi with Canton, China, they saw their worst fear materialize as the Canton plane left them, standing breathless, a few feet from its take-off point. Temporarily stranded in Pakistan, they eventually discovered an alternate route by air to Hong Kong and then by train to Canton. The Canton train was crowded with "Red Guards engaged in singing, shouting slogans, receiving instructions." During a two-day layover in China the Westerners were restricted to their hotel and prevented from taking any pictures. But on rides to and from the airport they "got vivid and in some sense 'frightening' glimpses of marching Red Guards," and from an auditorium near the hotel they heard the sounds of an all-night rally— "singing, reading, slogan-chanting, it was clear that the hall was packed." It was also clear in Muste's report that the veteran organizer of labor and peace rallies was very impatient with the restrictions which kept him from seeing this production firsthand. At the airport, as they were leaving Canton, the visitors did have firsthand contact with the Red Guard—who appeared with "an orchestra . . . a dance troupe, singers . . . and young women to read from the little book of Mao's sayings. . . . They threw themselves with great . . . joy into their program and smilingly pinned Mao buttons on us," Muste remembered. He noted also that "Mao's image . . . was virtually omni-present" in all public places. A plane out of Canton carried them to Nanning, on the border of Vietnam, from where another plane (which carried a Chinese stewardess and Chinese passengers who read with her in unison from Mao's sayings) brought them at last to Hanoi—four days behind schedule, very weary, and unable to make contact with Niemoller who was returning home that day.[63]

For the next ten days (January 9-19, 1967) their North Vietnamese hosts surrounded them with hospitality and solicitude, while doing everything possible to meet their request "that every hour count for the achievement of our objective to find out all we could . . . about what was going on in North Vietnam." No fact was more obvious and anguishing than that the North Vietnamese were receiving brutal pounding from U.S. bombing raids. In flat contradiction to statements from the White House denying American air attacks in the vicinity of Hanoi, Muste wrote from that city to the CNVA that no more than three or four blocks from his hotel, which was in the center of town, there were civilian neighborhoods reduced to rubble. Further evidence that the Hanoi area was an American target presented itself when, on four different occasions during their ten-day stay, the visitors had to take refuge in the hotel bomb shelter, though none of these alerts involved a direct hit in the city. On the basis of what they were witnessing, Muste directed Americans back home to convey a message to Washington: "For God's sake stop lying! . . . Let us stop this bombing practice or else say honestly to our government, to the world and to ourselves, 'We are trying to bomb hell out of the Vietnamese people.' "[64]

If destruction in and around Hanoi was marked, devastation in the North Vietnamese countryside defied description. Muste learned, for example, of a work crew of twelve young women who operated "South of Hanoi toward the Seventeenth Parallel," repairing roads torn up by U.S. bombs. The women, who were forced to live underground, said that, in the course of two years, 2,690 bombs had fallen in their vicinity.[65] Equally instructive was the tour which Muste and his companions were given through the agricultural commune of Phuax-A about ten miles from Hanoi. Though plainly without military significance, the hamlet, whose population was Catholic, was bombed and strafed in August; most houses were destroyed, twenty people were killed and many others injured. One of the visitors' guides had seen her nine-month-old child die in the attack. A memorial building which stood where a family of nine had died housed relics of the bombs which had killed them. Muste examined part of an anti-personnel weapon, designed, as he bitterly noted, to release on explosion, "a hundred or more barbs . . . which cannot damage steel or even wood but only human beings."

During their visit to Phuax-A the three Westerners were taken to the village kindergarten. In a small, modern building "twenty-four round faced tots," as Muste saw them, sat on benches. The area for walking between the benches was extremely narrow "because in the middle of the building was . . . a trench," into which the children could dive in the event of a bombing alert; they might then crawl through the trench to a shelter behind the building. "These very children," Muste realized, were subject at any moment to the same fate which had killed their relatives and neighbors five months before. That realization bore down on him as "the children, led by the teacher, burst vociferously as well as melodiously into a song. We were told," he said, "they were enthusiastically welcoming 'the uncles' who had come to visit them." After other songs the uncles were given "little bags of sweets . . . and as is the custom . . . , I and my two colleagues passed along the benches and handed each child one of them." Having to watch his footing because of the narrow walkway, Muste also had to struggle with his emotions. "I almost remember each face," he recorded; "some were smiling, some demure, some seemingly bewildered by it all," and, he confessed, "the experience shook my composure as few things in a long life have."[66]

In addition to examining the evidence of human suffering and material destruction that American military actions were fostering in North Vietnam, Muste, Reeves, and Feinberg also met with two American pilots shot down by Vietnamese and received letters from three others. Also, the three men conferred with various North Vietnamese authorities, including the Mayor of Hanoi, the Minister of Health, and the director of the main hospital in the city.[67] Of greatest moment, however, were the two hours, on January 17, which they spent with North Vietnamese Premier Pham Van Dong, during thirty minutes of which they were joined by President Ho Chi Minh. Sitting on velvet-covered couches, under gilded ceilings in a palace reception room once used by the French Governor General, the three Western clergymen and two North Vietnamese dignitaries "ate petit fours and . . . had some sort of liquor." The hosts asked for their visitors' impressions of what they had seen in China; they talked about Saigon and then New York City. Ho Chi Minh "asked about Times Square," Muste said. "He seemed to know that we had demonstrations there. He also asked about Harlem; he said he'd spent a lot of time there." After each guest was given a walking stick, hand-carved by North Vietnamese artisans, the five men got down to business. President Ho, who relied on an interpreter for much of the meeting, made his main point in English. As Muste recorded them, the North Vietnamese leader's words were:

> Mr. Johnson has stated that he would talk to anyone, anytime, anywhere about peace.
> I invite Mr. Johnson to be our guest, sitting just as you are here, in the palace of the former French Governor General of Indochina.
> Let Mr. Johnson come with his wife and daughters, his secretary, his doctor, his cook, but let him not come with a gun at his hip. Let him not bring his admirals and generals.
> As an old revolutionary, I pledge my honor that Mr. Johnson will have complete security.[68]

Substantially the same message had been repeated to two other western visitors just a few days before the clergymen's visit, would be stressed in an interview that the foreign minister of North Vietnam held with war correspondent Wilfred Burchett in late January, and in the opinion both of those who heard it at the time & researchers who reviewed the evidence later, reflected a genuine interest on the part of the Ho Chi Minh government to coordinate with the United States a cessation of bombing attacks and a beginning of peace talks.[69] Never before had Muste been so close to the maneuverings of the powers of "the real world." But he and his colleagues were well aware that the North Vietnamese initiative could not succeed as long as American bombing missions continued. The statement which the three clerics issued at a press conference on their departure from Hanoi was calculated to disabuse the Washington administration of its stubborn faith in the efficacy of unending bombs. "We have every reason to think that the Government and the people of North Vietnam have an iron determination to fight for their independence and the eventual reunification of their country," the three declared. They conceded that "the people of Vietnam might perhaps be exterminated, were any nation capable of such a crime," but they predicted, "We do not believe that . . . they can be beaten into a surrender or submission by any foreign power."[70]

The long trip back to the West involved a few days in London, with more press conferences and a meeting at the House of Commons.[71] Muste arrived in New York on January 26, and soon thereafter drafted a letter to President Johnson. Underlining the fact that the "Volunteers for Peace" had gone to Vietnam as "simply private individuals, in no sense assuming any kind of representative function," and that "President Ho did not ask us to convey what he had said to you," Muste noted that the North Vietnamese leader had unreservedly given permission for his words to be quoted. After repeating the quotation, Muste concluded his letter to Johnson with his own comment on Ho's remarks. He would not and could not promise that "if the United States stops bombing then the Hanoi government will reciprocate by [meeting specific U.S. demands]," but he contended that "if bombing were stopped, a new climate would exist and the possibility of . . . a cease fire would be greatly enhanced." Similarly, Muste cautioned Johnson not to "regard President Ho's statement as an indication of weakening in the resolve of the government and people of North Vietnam," but added that "on the other hand, . . . it would be a mistake to discount the importance of Ho's statement. . . . I sensed only straightforwardness and no sarcasm in his 'invitation' to you," Muste concluded. He mailed the letter on January 31, 1967, sending an extra copy to the president's White House press secretary with an appeal that it "be called to [Johnson's] attention."[72]

As February began, Muste was fêted at the U.N. Church Center, where admirers gathered to welcome him home at a reception hosted by anti-war pediatrician Benjamin Spock. Muste then threw himself back into working on the Fort Hood Three and Spring Mobilization Campaigns, staying up the better part of one night with black activist James Bevel and others, helping to draft the "Call" for the April demonstration. On February 9, he spoke to the New York Lawyers' Guild, commenting briefly on the needs of Selective Service violators for legal aid, but concentrating primarily on his experiences in Hanoi. He was at work by then drafting reports on his trip for *Liberation* and *WIN* and preparing for a major public meeting on February 13, where he was scheduled to describe his visit to Hanoi and to officially announce the Spring Mobilization.[73]

He took time out on Friday, February 10, to see his physician, Dr. Eugene Mullen, about a sharp pain in his back and received a prescription for pain-killers. The discomfort became so acute that night that he was unable to sleep; early Saturday morning he phoned Robert and Joyce Gilmore in whose home Muste had an apartment and whose care and concern for him were warm and generous. When they came to his room they found him nauseated and very uncomfortable. Dr. Mullen was called, came to the house, gave Muste an injection for the pain, and arranged for an ambulance to pick him up later in the day. Though the doctor said there was no cause for alarm, he wanted Muste to undergo hospital tests. The Gilmores called Nancy Muste Baker in Thornwood, New York; she made plans to visit her father at the hospital. At 2:15 that afternoon an ambulance transported him, with Joyce Gilmore, to St. Luke's Hospital; about twenty minutes after arriving there he lost consciousness and his heart stopped. Medical staff were able to revive the heartbeat and for the next three hours he was ministered to in the intensive care area of the hospital; he did not regain consciousness. Doctors determined that he was suffering from an aneurism and were evaluating his condition, with a view toward possibly trying to make a surgical repair. Nancy Baker, delayed because the family car was not available when she first learned of the critical turn Muste had taken, arrived at the hospital about six p.m. Roughly half an hour later her father was pronounced dead.[74] "A. J.'s death is typical of him," a close friend later concluded; "he allocated eighty-two years to living but only one day for dying." Remembering a letter he wrote her a year before about a decision "not to go tramping about Europe" because it would "knock me out," his well-loved comrade Cara Cook observed, "Yet he did go tramping off to Europe again and to Asia—twice, and he was finally knocked out: he didn't quit."[75]

Announcements in the media of his passing drew small groups of friends and admirers to impromptu memorial gatherings all over the country. When the news was first broadcast in New York City, radio station WBAI invited listeners to come and share their thoughts and memories of Muste. The following morning was a Sunday, and what occurred in the Meeting for Worship at the Stony Run Quaker Meeting House in Baltimore undoubtedly took place in other religious services—out of the silence Friends whose lives were touched by Muste expressed what he meant to them.[76] On Monday, Muste's body was cremated—as had been Anna Muste's—in Ferncliff Cemetery, Ardsley, New York. A small private service for the Baker family and close friends was held there. That evening the meeting at the Community Church where he was to have officially launched the Spring Mobilization became instead a tribute to him by Mobilization colleagues as well as close comrades in CNVA and the WRL. One of these, David McReynolds, later recalled meeting Barbara Deming there—"We embraced and I held her very close and realized the death was real and all of us would have to go on now without A. J." Tom Cornell of the Catholic Peace Fellowship reminded the mourners that "we are all sons of A.J.," and one of Muste's peace movement "daughters," young Beverly Sterner, recalled their mentor's lifelong love for poetry by reading two of his favorite poems— "Prelude 24" and "The War God," both by Stephen Spender. Certain lines in "Prelude 24" conveyed especially well the feelings of Muste's followers about their fallen leader: "I think continually of those who were truly great," the Spender poem began and concluded with the image of "the names of those who in their lives fought for life, Who wore at their hearts the fire's centre. / Born of the sun, they travelled a short while toward the sun, / And left the vivid air signed with their honor."[77]

A week later the official commemoration of Muste's death was held at Friends' Meeting House on Rutherford Place in New York City. Over 700 people attended, representing every organization and movement he had influenced, every facet of the ecumenical faith he had embodied, and several generations of the radical activism for which he was a symbol. The eldest in the crowd—their public campaigns for justice dating back to the era of World War I—included Norman Thomas (now blind and crippled by arthritis) and his brother, Evan. Cara Cook, with Mark and Helen Norton Starr, were among those with vivid memories of the bitter struggles of the 1930s. No one from the generation who became conscientious objectors to World War II spoke more eloquently at the Meeting than Bayard Rustin. And no one caused a greater stir on his arrival than hair-laden poet Allen Ginsberg, symbol of both the disaffiliated "beat" generation and of the tie between them and the new "flower children" with whom Muste had enjoyed communion.[78]

This formal and largest gathering did not conclude the commemorations. In Chicago a few days later old comrades held a quiet memorial. Another occurred in San Francisco, at Howard Thurman's Church for the Fellowship of All Peoples. Musician Paul Knopf hurried to complete a jazz service—inspired by Muste and called "The Faith of a Radical"—on which he had been working at the time of the pacifist's death and which was performed on April 30 at Judson Memorial Church in New York City. Documentaries of Muste's life were produced on New York radio (WBAI, under the direction of Steve Post on April 29) and national television (CBS, for whom the script was written by Mortimer Frankel, on September 10). Congressman James H. Scheuer read a tribute to Muste into the *Congressional Record*. Liberal periodicals carried sympathetic reviews of his life. Special issues of *Liberation* and *WIN*—serious and detailed in the first instance, spirited and lovingly irreverent in the second—were published in his memory. *Fellowship* put out by the FOR in Nyack, carried a moving reminiscence by John Nevin Sayre. Into all the movement offices poured a steady stream of telegrams and letters from around the world paying final respects to Muste—from Hanoi, North Vietnam; Patna, India; Dar es Salaam,

Tanzania; Santiago, Chile; Tel Aviv, Israel; London and Paris; Pittsburgh, St. Petersburg, and Washington D.C. The tributes came from the famous (Ho Chi Minh, Robert F. Kennedy, Floyd McKissick, Erich Fromm) and the unknown, from organizations at the center of political action (the South West Africa People's Organization, the Japanese Peace for Vietnam Committee), and groups nurturing a spiritual life that was largely inward-looking (a commune of Doukhabors in British Columbia).[79]

Whatever their source and wherever they were received, the efforts of Muste's admirers to come to terms with his death revealed the intricacies and richness of his life. While most messages took note of the noble spirit, sharp mind, and passionate resolve which had characterized him, the comments of those who were closest to him disclosed personal traits rarely visible in his speeches, essays, or acts of protest and civil disobedience. Somehow, in the midst of carrying on all those strenuous projects for peace and justice, this old man had, for all these years, always kept up with his favorite sport of baseball. He was still hitting baseballs to his grandchildren at almost eighty, and, in the last season before his death, he and Ralph DiGia of the WRL had watched the Mets beat the Pirates in Shea Stadium. "A terrible start," DiGia recalled. "But A. J. stayed right in there cheering all the way and the Mets came on to win. . . . A. J. lost his hat several times during the excitement. At one point the Pirates put in a relief pitcher and A. J. immediately knew that he was a left-hander and what his win and lost [sic] record was!"[80] Somehow, all along, Muste had kept what Cara Cook called "his fun life, his relaxation, which he could pursue as intensively as his work." He rarely missed a Marx Brothers movie, found time to nurture a keen appreciation of ballet and modern dance and indulged with full pleasure in the extravagance of opera. Those used to the Mustean image of the erect, stern Dutchman might have trouble believing it, but, reportedly, amidst the brilliance of a New England fall he said he felt his "heart leap," and at the top of Mt. Washington gave himself completely to the breathtaking view.[81] While a good number of his family and friends knew these things, Cara Cook claimed "exclusive rights to his concentration at anagrams"; the Sidney Lens family treasured a private joke about his favorite breakfast (four pieces of crisp bacon, two pieces of whole wheat toast and one cup of coffee) and their rare experience of having one morning found Muste in his pajamas comforting a runaway cat ("Don't worry, Kitty, we'll get you home"). Muste's neighbor across the street from the Gilmores enjoyed the prerogative of having watched him tend the flower box which he kept outside his window. As one writer for WIN observed, Muste was "The True Foxy Granpa." The only way he lasted as long as he did, theorized Jackson Mac Low, "was by disguising himself as a skinny old preacher who couldn't (could he?) really be meaning what he said."[82]

All of these attempts to honor his life and define his humanity would have pleased and touched Muste. But, undoubtedly, the tributes which he would have most approved were those that came from the committee working on the Spring Mobilization. "A. J.'s not dead," announced Mobilization coordinator James Bevel. "People working together, people creating; people trying to get people together so we can end the war: that's A. J. He isn't dead. In the Old Testament language the prophets would say 'He walked away with God.' " The Mobilization newsletter made the point more forthrightly: "In lieu of flowers, friends are requested to get out and work—for peace, for human rights, for a better world."[83]

Without question, plenty of work remained to be done. The Mobilization turned out well enough. Muste's long campaign to bring the civil rights and peace movements into full cooperation with one another came to fruition about a month after his death, when Martin Luther King agreed to address the April 15 demonstration. On that day, before a rain-soaked but cheering throng estimated at between 300,000 and one-half million people in U.N. plaza, King delivered a moving denunciation of American policy in Vietnam. If, somehow, the souls of the dead continue to take an interest in the doings of the living, surely that event satisfied Muste's soul.[84]

But it did not end the war, which raged on for six more years, until a ceasefire was finally signed. Not until 1975, however, would the objective which Muste had sought—complete withdrawal of U.S. forces—be realized. By then the politics and culture of Southeast Asia were in such a state of chaos and disruption that no one could predict when, if ever, the decimated peoples of that area might experience peace. Meanwhile, the United States moved toward recognition of the People's Republic of China. Thirty years had passed and millions of lives had been lost since Muste first pointed out that such recognition was inevitable. In his own country violence also continued to take its toll. Martin King and Robert Kennedy were both assassinated in the year after Muste's death. Gains registered for civil rights, economic justice, and freedom of dissent in the early sixties shrank drastically in the next decade before war-fed inflation, resurgent racism, and the repressive policies of the administration of Richard Nixon. While the war continued the peace movement became "badly fractured into violent and non-violent factions." After the war ceased to be an issue the hazards of the nuclear arms race still loomed. Residents of Nevada—where Muste and his colleagues first protested U.S. nuclear testing—were dying in alarming numbers from cancer, believed to have been caused by fallout from those tests. Missiles, including many more swift and precise than the deadly ICBM's which Muste challenged in Omaha, were "in place" on both Soviet and American-controlled territory, promising instant death to millions of people at the push of a button. The technology for producing nuclear bombs was undergoing what columnist George F. Will termed "broad democratization"; the smallest countries, even a tiny band of terrorists, could now construct their own doomsday weapon. As Will pointed out, by 1978, the "nuclear age [was] the only age many people [had] known, . . . [and nuclear] weapons [were] part of the wallpaper of the age, unnoticed and, to almost everybody, uninteresting." By the late seventies Musteite peace organizations were again involved in a coalition—this time with environmental and consumer groups working against the powerful interests of utility companies and the perils of generating plants run by nuclear reactors. The outcome of this struggle was, at best, uncertain.[85]

During his life Muste saw some gains for the causes which he championed, especially where the rights of labor and the imperatives of racial justice were concerned. But, at the time of his death, counter-forces threatened these gains, as they threatened every program to defend civil liberties and promote world peace. Individuals and organizations influenced by Muste's example would carry on his work, but a verdict as to the feasibility of their objectives and the success of their efforts would have to wait for a future time. In the immediate present and by most measurable standards, Muste's labors to make a better world and to "create a climate" in which war and nuclear weapons would not be tolerated had largely failed. But measurable standards were never his sole criteria for action. The usual signs of personal success—wealth, fame, status, honors—were of only marginal importance to him. He was proud to have received the WRL Peace Award and a Gandhi Peace Award and chuckled heartily when W. H. Ferry of the Fund for the Republic promised him that upon Ferry's election to the White House, Muste would be appointed secretary of state. But when labor journalist Jerome Davis wanted to nominate him for the Nobel Peace Prize, Muste brushed the idea aside as improbable and not worth pursuing. In a similar spirit he cut short lamentations about the powerlessness of the peace movement. "I agree that there is a sense in which the so-called peace movement has failed," Muste told a querulous correspondent. "[I agree] that I have failed, as you suggest." But this, he concluded, was not "our real problem." The real problem was that too many human beings had lost touch with their own best instincts. "Joy and growth come from following our deepest impulses, however foolish they may seem to some, or dangerous, and even though the apparent outcome may be defeat".[86] This was the "light" by which A. J. Muste lived and died—this traveler from Zierikzee who "travelled a short while toward the sun, and left the vivid air signed with [his] honour." Whether that sign would be understood before time ran out for the humanity which it was intended to guide remained to be seen.

Notes, Bibliography, and Index

Notes

Abbreviations

AJM	A. J. Muste / Muste Papers	NCLB	National Civil Liberties Bureau
BC, WSU	Brookwood Collection, Wayne State University	NYPL	New York Public Library
CCCF	Central Congregational Church Files	PMMF	Providence Monthly Meeting of Friends
CCCR	Central Congregational Church Records	RCA	Reformed Church in America
FOR	Fellowship of Reconciliation Papers	SCPC	Swarthmore College Peace Collection

Complete citation for manuscript collections can be found in the Bibliographical Essay.

Introduction

1 *The World Tomorrow*, June 6, 1929, pp. 250–54.
2 CCCR, pp. 585, 587–88.
3 Edmund Wilson to John Dos Passos, June 24, 1931, in Edmund Wilson, *Letters in Literature and Politics, 1912–1972*, ed. Elena Wilson (New York, 1977), p. 218. See also Edmund Wilson, "Frank Keeney's Coal Diggers," *New Republic*, July 15, 1931, pp. 195–99, 229–31; "Sinclair Lewis Sees Unionism Urgent Need," *Brookwood Review* 8, no. 1 (Oct.–Nov. 1924); *Saturday Review*, June 29, 1935, p. 12.
4 *Time Magazine*, July 10, 1939, p. 37; clipping from *New York Post*, March 20, 1957; Kenneth Dole, "Senate Chaplain Decries 'Moral Flabbiness' among Clergy as Fostering 'Second Munich,' " unidentified clipping, n.d. [1959]; FOR Executive Committee Minutes, Dec. 15, 1959, p. 3 (SCPC), FOR Papers, Box 29; Martin Luther King and Coretta King, telegram to AJM, Feb. 5, 1965, AJM, Box 48, SCPC; Oscar Handlin, review of *The Essays of A. J. Muste* in the *Atlantic Monthly*, Jan. 1967, p. 120; Wallace C. Boyden, "Report of the Standing Committee to the Church, November 20, 1914 on a New Pastor," CCCR.

5 Donald B. Meyer, *The Protestant Search for Political Realism* (Berkeley and Los Angeles, 1961), pp. 368–69.

6 AJM to J. Edgar Hoover, April 2, 1957, AJM, Box 31, SCPC.

7 AJM, untitled manuscript, n.d. [1936], in AJM, Box 3a, SCPC.

8 Milton Mayer, "The Christer," *Fellowship*, Jan. 1952 p. 7; AJM, *Korea: Spark to Set a World Afire*, FOR pamphlet, 1950, reprinted in Nat Hentoff, ed., *The Essays of A. J. Muste (New York, 1967).*

9 Peter Stansky, "The Style of the 70's: History and Biography," *New York Times Book Review*, June 5, 1977, p. 10.

10 James Wechsler, "In the Twilight," clipping from *New York Post*, May 2, 1966, FOR, Box 29, SCPC.

11 AJM to David Riesman, March 11, 1963, AJM, Box 37, SCPC.

12 AJM, "Sketches for an Autobiography," in *The Essays of A. J. Muste*, ed. Nat Hentoff (New York, 1967), pp. 24, 25.

13 This quotation, often attributed to Muste, appears to have originated with Dr. Maurice Schwarz, who had been a leader of the French resistance during World War II. See AJM, "Peace Is the Way," *Fellowship*, Dec. 1976, pp. 3–5.

Chapter I

1 AJM to M. Weerheijm Muste, Oct. 18, 1946, AJM, Box 42, SCPC; Rev. Arthur C. Johnson (nephew of AJM) to the author, July 27, 1970.

2 AJM, Columbia Oral History Memoir No. 509 (hereafter Oral Memoir), the early 1950s, pp. 1–4, 7, Columbia University Library.

3 AJM, Autobiographical Lecture, New Brunswick Theological Seminary, Feb. 2, 1944, AJM, Box 2, SCPC (hereafter Autobiographical Lecture).

4 Oral Memoir, pp. 3–4, 9; AJM, "Sketches for an Autobiography" (hereafter "Sketches"), in *The Essays of A. J. Muste*, ed. Nat Hentoff (New York, 1967), pp. 15–16.

5 "Sketches," pp. 4, 16–17; "Labor Must Learn, A. J. Muste," in Devere Allen, *Adventurous Americans* (New York, 1932), p. 101.

6 "Sketches," p. 15.

7 Rev. Arthur C. Johnson to the author, Feb. 3, 1970; Oral Memoir, pp. 14–15.

8 "Sketches," p. 16; Oral Memoir, p. 14.

9 Ibid., pp. 9–11; "Sketches," p. 19.

10 "Sketches," pp. 20–22.

11 Ibid., p. 24.

12 Henry S. Lucas, *Netherlanders in America* (Ann Arbor, 1955), p. 3.

13 Ibid., p. 472. The original settlers were almost but not entirely Protestant Seceders, a small number of Dutch Catholics were among them.

14 Ibid., pp. 58–68, 87–150, 265–73, 642–43; Robert Benaway Brown, *The Netherlands and America* (Ann Arbor, 1947); Arnold Mulder, *Americans from Holland* (Philadelphia, 1947), pp. 109–19.

The seceders' need to seek freedom beyond the borders of their home country casts an interesting qualification over Holland's historical image as a haven of toleration. There is good evidence, recorded well by historian Henry Lucas, that they were persecuted there. The arrival of Dutch immigrants can be traced back to 1613 when "New Netherlanders" took up residence in the Hudson and Delaware River valleys (pp. 50–53). Yet the Netherlands was famous throughout this period for what sociologist Johan Gouds-blom calls a "social climate favorable to freedom of thought." Indeed Goudsblom implies that the "powerful counterweight to Calvinist dominance" which the "leading merchant regents" of the country wielded was the very basis of this climate. Had the stern and puritanical Seceders been in the ascendency, modern ideas, the entire heritage of the Enlightenment, may have become objects of persecution instead (Johan Goudsblom, *Dutch Society* [New York, 1967], p. 18). This probability does not diminish the irony that Dutch toleration for modern thought was partly dependent upon suppression of those seeking to return to what they believed were the pure doctrines of the past. The persecution which they experienced also contributes to the explanation of why they and their progeny, well down into Muste's generation, held with such tenacity to their beliefs and warded off change at every turn.

15   Lucas, *Netherlanders in America*, p. 492.

16   Ibid., pp. 506–11.

17   Ibid., pp. 511–13. A contemporary and opponent of the True Reformed seceders, William Van Eyck, satirized their position as one of opposition to "hymns, funerals, dead bodies in church during funerals, flowers on caskets, church organs, fire insurance, lightning rods, flowers on bonnets, white dresses, Sunday schools, the English language, the suffocating gas of Methodism, foreign missions, Christmas trees, vaccination and picnics" (quoted in Mulder, p. 193). More recently the student of Dutch society Johan Goudsblom has commented upon the schismatic tendencies which are still observable in the Dutch Reformed Church. "Awareness of such tendencies," he writes, "finds expression in the sally: 'One Dutchman a theologian, two Dutchmen a church, three Dutchmen a schism' " (*Dutch Society*, p. 54).

18   Lucas, *Netherlanders in America*, pp. 515–16.

19   Rev. Arthur C. Johnson to the author. Feb. 3, 1970.

20   Ibid. and July 27, 1970.

21   Oral Memoir, pp. 44–47.

22   Lucas, *Netherlanders in America*, pp. 516–17; Abraham Kuyper, *Calvinism, Six Lectures Delivered in the Theological Seminary at Princeton* (New York, 1898), p. 92.

23   "Sketches," pp. 59–87; Hentoff, *Peace Agitator*, p. 30. See also Lucas, *Netherlanders in America*, pp. 606–14, for the significant role of poetry in Dutch immigrant life. In his autobiography Muste said that Dutch was the only language used in the Christian Reformed school. And yet he never could remember "a time after arrival in Grand Rapids when [he] could not speak English." Perhaps extra-curricular play with English-speaking children sufficed to make him fluent in the new tongue. Or possibly his adult impressions of the church school as having been entirely Dutch-speaking were incorrect ("Sketches," pp. 29–30). The Mustes' relationship to the schoolmaster has been recalled by Rev. Arthur Johnson in his letter to me of Feb. 3, 1970. Abraham's recollections appear in the Oral Memoir, p. 59, and the "Sketches," p. 29. The exact number of years Muste attended the Christian School is not clear. He and the sister nearest him in age followed by the brother nearest her all attended the school—A. J. the longest, the third child "for less than a year" after which all the children were transferred to public school (Rev. Arthur C. Johnson to the author, July 27, 1970).

24   Hentoff, *Peace Agitator*, p. 27. In an earlier biographical sketch of Muste in Allen, *Adventurous Americans*, p. 102, Martin Muste's salary is put down as $6.25 per week.

25   "Sketches," p. 28.

26   Ibid., p. 30. I am indebted to Rev. Arthur C. Johnson for the name of the school, mentioned in his letter, July 27, 1970.

27   Cornelius Muste, quoted in Hentoff, *Peace Agitator*, p. 31. The descriptions of the houses in which the Muste family lived appear in the "Sketches," pp. 23, 30. The story of the friendship with Irving Quimby is also in the "Sketches," pp. 30–32.

28   "Sketches," p. 21.

29   Oral Memoir, p. 74. While Riley's verse is most notable for its extolling of rural simplicity and homely virtue, a strain of one-hundred percent Americanism also runs through it. See for example, "The Boy Patriot" and "Decoration Day on the Place" in *The Best Loved Poems and Ballads of James Whitcomb Riley* ed. Ethel F. Betts (New York, 1920), pp. 148, 256.

30   David D. Demarest, *The Reformed Church in America* (New York, 1889), pp. 117, 118–31, 156.

31   Autobiographical Lecture; Rev. Arthur C. Johnson to the author, Feb. 3, 1970; Oral Memoir, p. 62; "Sketches," pp. 5–6.

32   Synod of Dort (a church council which met in 1618–1619 to affirm and clarify Calvinist doctrine), quoted in Demarest, *Reformed Church in America*, p. 157; Rev. Arthur C. Johnson to the author, Feb. 3, 1970.

33   Autobiographical Lecture.

34   "Sketches," pp. 34–37.

35   Oral Memoir, p. 82; Autobiographical Lecture.

36   Oral Memoir, pp. 82–84; Hentoff, *Peace Agitator*, p. 30.

37   "Sketches," pp. 37–38; Hentoff, *Peace Agitator*, pp. 31–32; Oral Memoir, p. 76.

38   Oral Memoir, pp. 90–91; AJM, "Fragment of Autobiography," n.d. [probably 1939], p. 7, AJM, Box 2, SCPC.

39   Oral Memoir, pp. 90–91. Unfortunately, records to corroborate Muste's church membership have not been found. Rev. Arvin H. Wester, pastor in 1971 at the Fourth Reformed Church in Grand Rapids, Mich., was unable to locate them (Rev. Arthur H. Wester to the author, Oct. 1, 1971).

40   Oral Memoir and AJM to Mrs. Ethel Sweet, Feb. 1, 1944, AJM, Box 1, SCPC; Rev. Arthur C. Johnson to the author, July 27, 1970.

41   *Centennial of the Theological Seminary of the Reformed Church in America*, ed. D. D. Demarest et al. (New York, 1885), p. 253; Lucas, *Netherlanders in America*, p. 600.

42   "Sketches," p. 41.

43   Oral Memoir, p. 101.

44   Ibid., p. 95.

45   "Sketches," p. 41; Oral Memoir, p. 93. Hope College Catalogs, 1898–1904, list the annual fee as eighteen dollars. Dr. Paul Fried, Department of History, Hope College, to the author, Nov. 12, 1971.

46   Oral Memoir, pp. 98, 109.

47   Henry F. May, *Protestant Churches and Industrial America* (New York, 1963), pp. 47, 142; Dr. John W. Beardslee III (archivist, the Reformed Church in America) to the author, Nov. 8, 1971. See also Henry J. Ryskamp, "The Dutch in Western Michigan," (Ph.D. diss., University of Michigan, 1930), pp. 147–48.

48   Oral Memoir, pp. 99–100; "Sketches," p. 42; Joseph Le Conte, *Religion and Science* (New York, 1891), pp. 233, 237–38; Le Conte, *Evolution, Its Nature, Its Evidences and Its Relation to Religious Thought* (New York, 1901), pp. 280, 284.

49   Oral Memoir, p. 99; Philip Gilbert Hamerton, *The Intellectual Life* (Boston, 1882), pp. 210, 211.

50   Oral Memoir, pp. 134–35.

51   Dr. John W. Beardslee III to the author, Nov. 8, 1971; *World Who's Who in*

Science, 1968, s.v. "Mast, Samuel Ottmar"; Autobiographical Lecture; Oral Memoir, p. 112; Sophocles, *The Oedipus Cycle*, ed. and trans. Dudley Fitts and Robert Fitzgerald (New York, 1939, Harvest paperback ed.), pp. 211–18. Comments on Muste's performance in the student yearbook for 1905 included the observation that "all the world loves a lover, especially so ardent and youthful a lover as Muste. Dutch love is proverbially the Simon pure kind and Muste has it in him; at least he brought it out in his Haemon." The version enacted by his class was *Antiton b*, an adaptation for male players. *Hope Annual*, 1905, p. 152. Dr. Fried to the author, Nov. 12, 1971. Dr. John W. Beardslee III to the author, Nov. 8, 1971; Oral Memoir, p. 112; *Historical Directory of the Reformed Church in America*, ed. Peter N. Vandenberge (Grand Rapids, 1970), s.v. "James G. Sutphen."

52   Oral Memoir, pp. 103–4.

53   Ibid., p. 106; Hentoff, *Peace Agitator*, pp. 29–30, 36; Oral Memoir, p. 106; Allen, *Adventurous Americans*, p. 103.

54   Oral Memoir, p. 107.

55   G. J. Van Zoren to AJM, Christmas 1966, AJM, Box 48, SCPC.

56   Oral Memoir, p. 106.

57   Ibid., pp. 120–24; Rev. Arthur C. Johnson to the author, July 27, 1970.

58   Oral Memoir, pp. 129–33.

59   Oral Memoir, pp. 134–35; AJM to Rev. Paul Felt, Feb. 21, 1945, AJM, Box 7, SCPC; Oral Memoir, 118.

60   Hentoff, *Peace Agitator*, p. 32; Oral Memoir, pp. 112–18; See remarks by Professor F. N. Scott in Frank E. Bryant manuscript folder at University of Kansas.

61   Duplicated copy of the *Anchor*, Oct. 1904, attached to letter from G. J. Van Zoren to AJM, Christmas 1966, AJM, Box 48, SCPC; *The Oedipus Cycle*, pp. 211, 213; "The Problem of Discontent," *The Essays of A. J. Muste*, ed. Nat Hentoff, pp. 175–77.

62   "Sketches," p. 42; Oral Memoir, p. 138; Demarest, *Centennial of the Theological Seminary: The Reformed Church in America* p. 102; G. J. Van Zoren to AJM, Christmas 1966, AJM, Box 48, SCPC; Oral Memoir, pp. 138–41; Nelson Nieuwenhuis (curator, Dutch Heritage Collections, Northwestern College, Orange City, Iowa) to the author, Sept. 28, 1971.

63 "Sketches," p. 42; Hentoff, *Peace Agitator*, p. 36; Rev. Arthur C. Johnson to the author, July 27, 1970; Allen, *Adventurous Americans*, p. 103.

64   Allen, *Adventurous Americans*, p. 103; Oral Memoir, p. 143; AJM, quoted in Hentoff, *Peace Agitator*, p. 37.

65   Oral Memoir, p. 175; "Sketches," p. 42. Bush had been Muste's associate editor on the *Anchor* and a fellow orator on the debate team (*Historical Directory of RCA*, s.v. "Bush, Benjamin").

66   "Sketches," pp. 42–43.

67   Oral Memoir, pp. 150–54; John W. Beardslee to the author, Oct. 29, 1971; *Historical Directory of RCA*, s.v. "Gillespie, John," "Raven, John," "Schenck, Ferdinand S.," "Searle, John Preston."

68   Oral Memoir, pp. 150–54.

69   Ibid., p. 167. Lectures on ethics which Shaw delivered at New York University have been preserved in *The Value and Dignity of Human Life* (Boston, 1911).

70   Oral Memoir, pp. 164–71. Muste's record of enrollment and his transcript are available at the registrar's office at Columbia University. Andrew N. Greenwald, Columbia University registrar's office, to the author, Oct. 5, 1971; Montague's "Contemporary Philosophy" course, which in 1908–9 included a section on pragmatism, may have been the class that Muste remembered. Dr. John Randall, historian of the philos-

ophy department at Columbia, and Alice H. Bonnell, curator of the Columbiana Collection, verified the James lectures of 1907. Ms. Bonnell has suggested that Montague's course may have been the one to which Muste referred (Oral Memoir, p. 170).

71 Oral Memoir, p. 168; Frederick J. E. Woodbridge, "Confessions," *Nature and Mind* (New York, 1937), quotations from pp. 9, 15.

72 Oral Memoir, p. 176. No trace of those sermons has been found to date.

73 Ibid., pp. 178–79, 185. A search for records regarding Muste's work at the Middle Collegiate Church was fruitless; "Sketches," p. 44.

74 Oral Memoir, pp. 164, 180.

75 G. Campbell Morgan, *Christian Principles* (New York, 1908), p. 156. In 1924 Morgan's name was included among the top twenty-five "outstanding preachers of America" according to a poll taken by the *Christian Century*. See Robert Moats Miller, *American Protestantism and Social Issues*, 1919-1939 (North Carolina, 1958), pp. 45–46 fn.

76 Oral Memoir, pp. 153–54; Milton J. Hoffman to the author, Nov. 18, 1971; John W. Beardslee III to the author, Oct. 29, 1971.

77 Oral Memoir, p. 193; See also Demarest, *Reformed Church in America* p. 178, for explanation of the nature of the preaching license.

78 Oral Memoir, p. 193; Hentoff, *Peace Agitator*, p. 37.

79 Oral Memoir, pp. 193, 199.

80 "Sketches," p. 43; *Fort Washington Collegiate Church, 1907–1959*, pamphlet in my possession; *Yearbook of the Collegiate Church*, 1909, p. 841, in files of Fort Washington Collegiate Church, New York; *Yearbook of the Collegiate Church*, 1910, p. 129. Oral Memoir, pp. 189, 207.

81 Oral Memoir, p. 211; Paul U. Kellog, ed., *The Pittsburgh Survey* (New York, 1911), vol. 4, John A. Fitch, *The Steel Workers*. Fitch's research was conducted during 1907 and 1908. For Commons' recollections of his student, see John R. Commons, *Myself* (Madison, 1963), pp. 140–41; Raymond B. Fosdick, *Chronicle of a Generation* (New York, 1958).

82 Oral Memoir, p. 212; "Sketches," p. 43.

83 Oral Memoir, p. 212, 215, 245.

84 Ibid., pp. 245–47. Muste had at least been aware of national elections since 1896 when his father became a U.S. citizen in time to vote for William McKinley. The Muste family, following the practice of the majority of their Dutch neighbors, had supported Republican candidates regularly from that time on. There is no mention in any of Muste's recollections of whether he voted in the 1908 election. Having passed his twenty-first birthday the year before, he could have ("Sketches," p. 28).

85 Hentoff, *Peace Agitator*, pp. 38–39; Oral Memoir, p. 217. Record of the degree, magna cum laude, is on file in the office of the registrar at Union Theological Seminary. Muste was unimpressed by the degree itself. He had not enrolled, he said, to take a degree: "I was just interested in the courses." He did not realize that he had earned the B.D. "until they sent me a note."

86 Oral Memoir, pp. 229–34; Frame, *The Purpose of New Testament Theology* (New York, 1905) passim; Knox, *The Gospel of Jesus, the Son of God* (New York, 1909), pp. 55, 56, 69, 70, 72; *The Development of Religion in Japan, American Lectures on the History of Religion*, Sixth Series, 1905–1906 (New York, 1907), p. 7.

87 Oral Memoir, pp. 217–18.

88 Donald B. Meyer, *The Protestant Search for Political Realism, 1919–1941* (Berkeley, 1961), p. 48; William Adams Brown, *A Teacher and His Times* (New York, 1940), pp. 110–13.

89   Oral Memoir, pp. 246–47.
90   See Tolstoy, quoted in *The Pacifist Conscience*, ed. Peter Mayer (Chicago: Gateway paperback ed., 1967), p. 163. These are not necessarily the exact words of Tolstoy that Muste read in his gift book, which so far has not been found. But the gist of the argument is a familiar theme in the Count's writings. Oral Memoir, p. 232.
91   McGiffert, *A History of Christian Doctrine* (New York, 1932). According to Muste's Oral Memoir (p. 229), the substance of this book was the substance of the lectures he attended. "Sketches," p. 43; Oral Memoir, p. 236.
92   Oral Memoir, p. 219.
93   "Sketches," p. 44; Oral Memoir, p. 219.
94   For Muste's account of his decision to remain at Fort Washington, see Oral Memoir, pp. 248–51. See also Wallace C. Boyden, "Report of the Standing Committee to the Church, November 20, 1914 on a New Pastor," CCCR; and "Pastor Yields to Heavenly Vision," clipping from *Sunday New York Herald*, n.d., CCCR. The Minutes of the Executive Council of Hope College, Feb. 10, 1913, make note of Muste's interest in the history job and contain the offer of that job which was made to him. Dr. Fried of Hope College was good enough to pass a copy of the minutes on to me.
95   Oral Memoir, pp. 252–53; Boyden, "Report on a New Pastor," CCCR.
96   Oral Memoir, p. 221; "Sketches," p. 44; "Unable to Hold Church Doctrine, Pastor Muste Resign His Pulpit," unidentified news clipping, n.d. [Fall 1914], in the archives of New Brunswick Theological Seminary; AJM to the Executive Committee of the Fort Washington Reformed Church, Nov. 22, 1914, in files of that church, New York City; *Historical Directory of RCA*, s.v. "Muste, Abraham J."
97   "Pastor Yields to Heavenly Vision," CCCR; Dr. Cobb, quoted in Boyden, "Report on a New Pastor," CCCR.
98   Oral Memoir, p. 219; Rev. Arthur C. Johnson to the author, July 27, 1970. Years later Muste told a young friend whose two-day-old child had died that "Mrs. Muste and I can feel for you because we have had similar experiences," AJM to Elmer Cope, July 25, 1929, Box 2, Folder 6, Cope Papers.
99   "Pastor Yields to Heavenly Vision," CCCR.
100   Oral Memoir, p. 219; "Fragment of Autobiography," p. 8.
101   Oral Memoir, pp. 265–66.
102   Ibid., p. 237.

Chapter II

1   Wallace C. Boyden, "Report of the Standing Committee to the Church, November 20, 1914 on a New Pastor," CCCR.
2   AJM, Columbia Oral History Memoir No. 509 (hereafter Oral Memoir), the early 1950s, pp. 261–63, Columbia University Library.
3   Oral Memoir, pp. 260–62; AJM, "Sketches for an Autobiography," (hereafter "Sketches"), in *The Essays of A. J. Muste*, ed. Nat Hentoff (New York, 1967), p. 45; *Central Congregational Church of Newtonville, Centennial History*, p. 17. Anne Dorothy's full name is mentioned in AJM to Mrs. E. G. Evans, July 10, 1933, Evans Papers.
4   Oral Memoir, p. 262. For George A. Gordon's comments on this Ministers' Club of Boston, see his autobiography, *My Education and Religion* (Boston, 1925), pp. 320–21.
5   AJM, quoted in Nat Hentoff, *Peace Agitator* (New York, 1963), p. 190; "Sketches," p. 45.

6   "Sketches," p. 47. See also AJM, "What Shall Education Do about Pacifism?" *Religious Education* 19 (Oct. 1924): pp. 326–30.

7   Peace movements in and around Boston had a long history, as historians Merle Curti, David Sands Patterson, and others have pointed out. From the American Peace Society (the first such organization in the U.S.), founded in 1828, to the Association to Abolish War, which came into existence in 1915, the city had an impressive history of secular pacifism. The movement was still alive when Muste took up residence in Newtonville (David Sands Patterson, *Toward a Warless World* [Bloomington, 1976]. Charles De Benedetti, *The Peace Reform in American History* [Bloomington, 1980]; Merle Curti, *Peace or War* [Boston, 1936]); Oral Memoir, p. 263. Dole's name appears as Charles F. Dow in the manuscript of this memoir—obviously a typographical error. An image of Dole which complements Muste's description of the Unitarian leader is painted in Gordon, *My Education and Religion*, pp. 320–21. See also Dole's autobiography, *My Eighty Years* (New York, 1927); AJM to Sherwood Eddy, Dec. 27, 1940, AJM, SCPC, Box 1; Oral Memoir, p. 272. Later memories were unclear as to whether Bliss Perry also became a member of the FOR. It was Muste's impression that the Harvard professor had not been "political" enough to assume such an affiliation. For information on the FOR, see Vera Brittain, *The Rebel Passion* (New York, 1964), pp. 33–35, 37; John Nevin Sayre, "The Fellowship of Reconciliation 1915–1935," p. 3, unsorted FOR (SCPC); Charles Chatfield, "Pacifism in American Life 1914–1941," Ph.D. Vanderbilt University, 1965, pp. 204–5.

8   AJM, "The Opportunity of Lent," *Congregationalist*, April 13, 1916, pp. 501–3.

9   AJM, "Do Your Bit for Belgium," *Congregationalist*, Dec. 14, 1916, pp. 825–26. On the Ford "Peace Ship" see Charles Chatfield, *For Peace & Justice* (Knoxville, 1971) pp. 18–19.

10   "The Conscientious Objector" was excerpted in the *Congregationalist*, March 8, 1917, p. 318, and a summary of the sermon also appeared in the *Boston Transcript*, Feb. 19, 1917, clipping in CCCF.

11   AJM, "Sketches," pp. 51–52.

12   "Gift of Flags," unidentified news clipping, April 15, 1917, CCCR, p. 530.

13   "Sketches," pp. 48–49.

14   CCCR, pp. 531–32.

15   Ray Abrams, *Preachers Present Arms* (N.Y., 1933) pp. 139–85; *Survey Magazine*, June 9, 1917, p. 249.

16   "Sketches," p. 52.

17   AJM, quoted in Hentoff, *Peace Agitator*, pp. 44–45.

18   Clipping from the *Newton Graphic*, Friday, Jan. 4, 1918, CCCF.

19   CCCR, pp. 546–54.

20   The Dec. 28 meeting was announced in the back of the program for Sunday, Dec. 23. The Standing Committee Report was quoted in the *Graphic* clipping, CCCF.

21   AJM to Mr. Wallace C. Boyden, Dec. 27, 1917, CCCF; AJM to Wallace C. Boyden, March 31, 1918, CCCR, pp. 583–84; CCCR, pp. 585, 587–88, 593–95. Only a fragment of the Central Church membership seems to have outrightly rejected him because of his pacifist views. In the entire year of 1917, only fourteen persons transferred out of the church, while more than thirty new members were added to the congregation. The Newtonville parishioners as a whole tried earnestly to work out a compromise arrangement by which Muste could be retained. Their negotiations with him, in full church meetings and through the Standing Committee, were marked—as both his memoirs and the church records indicate—by deep mutual respect and affection. In addition to the

regard in which the minister himself was held, concern for his wife and infant daughter undoubtedly figured in the church's deliberations. The provision of a partial salary during the leave of absence and extension of salary for a month beyond the effective date of his resignation are partial reflections of this.

22   At least three and possibly five mystical and religious experiences had marked the development of A. J. Muste up to 1917: his conversion in adolescence, one or two events related to his break from Dutch Reformed moorings, and one or two experiences in Boston during the war. Only the "vision" just prior to his resignation from Fort Washington and the event on the day previous to his submitting a resignation to Central Church were recorded near the time of their occurrence. The other experiences were recalled after the passage of many years. Dates assigned to them could easily be inaccurate. The first experience is uncorroborated by primary materials. The other two episodes could be mistakenly dated versions of the ones on the contemporary records. It is somewhat puzzling that in December 1917, he claimed only one previous experience; but, perhaps, he was referring to his adult life and not counting the adolescent conversion.

23   For the report on the Socialist Party secretary, see NCLB, "War Time Prosecutions and Mob Violence," pamphlet 17 in vol. 3 (New York, 1918); of United States, *War Pamphlets.*

24   PMMF mins., First Month 26th, 1918, vol. 5, p. 255; Oral Memoir, pp. 321–25.

25   Ibid., p. 321; Harold Loukes, *The Quaker Contribution* (London, 1965), p. 15; Rufus Jones, *The Story of George Fox* (New York, 1919), pp. 6–7. Loukes, *The Quaker Contribution*, p. 40.

26   Mrs. Muste's expression of feeling to her sister-in-law has been reported in Arthur C. Johnson to the author, July 27, 1970. Her husband's comments on her position are quoted in Hentoff, *Peace Agitator*, pp. 44–46.

27   For Erik Erikson on Gandhi and his wife, see *Gandhi's Truth* (New York, 1960), p. 121; This loyalty was undoubtedly reinforced by the Dutch upbringing of Anna Muste which stressed the centrality of the family, the sacredness of matrimonial vows, and the acquiescent role of women in political affairs. On the traditional role of Dutch women see Henry S. Lucas, *Netherlanders in America* (Ann Arbor, 1955), pp. 577–78. See also Hentoff, *Peace Agitator*, p. 46.

28   "The Present Status of Conscientious Objectors," *The Congregationalist and Advance,* Jan. 10, 1918, pp. 49–50. For Muste's later memories of his work at Fort Devens, see his Oral Memoir, p. 325 and the "Sketches," p. 52. Details of the brutality encountered by numerous conscientious objectors in federal prisons may be found within several volumes of the *United States, War Pamphlets.* See the NCLB, "Conscription and the Conscientious Objector," pamphlet 1, vol. 1 (New York, 1917); NCLB, "Facts about Conscientious Objection in the United States," pamphlet 16, vol. 3 (New York, 1918); Judah L. Magnes, "Amnesty for Political Prisoners," pamphlet 7, vol. 3 (New York, 1919); and NCLB, "Political Prisoners in Federal Military Prisons," pamphlet 8 in vol. 8 (New York, 1918). Episodes involving Fort Devens objectors are noted in this last pamphlet, and also in Norman Thomas, *The Conscientious Objector in America* (New York, 1923), pp. 138–39.

29   "Sketches," p. 55–58. PMMF mins., Twelfth Month 28th, 1918. Records of the People's Book Room, including titles and names of those who donated or borrowed the materials, were xeroxed for me by Thyra Jane Foster, curator of the archives of New England Yearly Meeting. See also "Sketches," p. 24, and Devere Allen, *Adventurous Americans* (New York, 1932). On a sizeable list of titles in the book room was one

lonely work on "What is Quakerism." The tenor of the others may be gathered from a sampling: "Bolsheviks and Soviets," "Chapters from my Diary" by Leon Trotsky, "The Truth about the IWW"; "The Trial of Eugene Debs," "Lynchings of 1918," and "Is Freedom Dead?"

30 "Sketches," pp. 55–58; FOR National Council Minutes, Nov. 7, 1918, FOR Papers; Allen, *Adventurous Americans*, p. 106. Muste described Mrs. Evans as "part of the elite, . . . very active in peace and civil liberties activities, very courageous. Nobody dared touch what she was behind." Her friendship dating from this era and lasting until her death in 1938 became a source of not only moral support but also financial salvation. AJM, "Remarks at Meeting in Memory of Elizabeth Glendower Evans," n.d. [1938], Evans Papers; Oral Memoir, p. 327.

Muste's acquaintance with Roger Nash Baldwin is recalled as significant in the Muste autobiography. However, Baldwin did not, in 1970, remember a working relationship between his organization and Muste during the war. Muste's League for Democratic Control has been called a branch of the ACLU. Since Muste was relatively unknown on the reform scene at the time and since Baldwin's Bureau was just newly organized and subject to major harassment from its inception (Baldwin himself was imprisoned from the fall of 1918 until the following summer), perhaps Baldwin was too busy to take note of the obscure league and its then obscure executive. Oral Memoir, pp. 326–27; "Sketches," p. 52. On Baldwin, see Donald O. Johnson, *The Challenge to American Freedoms* (Lexington, 1963), and Roger Baldwin to the author, July 24, 1970. Reference to the League for Democratic Control as a branch of the ACLU appears in Robert H. Montgomery, *Sacco and Vanzetti, the Murder and the Myth*, (New York, 1960); "Sketches," pp. 55–56. On Bill Simpson, see "Brother Bill," the *Christian Century*, Sept. 20, 1928, pp. 1133–35 and Jan. 22, 1941, p. 130; "Sketches," pp. 55–66; and Oral Memoir, p. 358.

31 "Sketches," p. 57.

32 AJM, "Suggestions for Proposed New 'Preaching Order' to Disseminate Fellowship of Reconciliation Principles," typed manuscript, Dec. 31, 1918, FOR, Box 22, SCPC.

33 Ibid.

34 Muste emphasized the spirit of revolution in the air in his Oral Memoir, p. 360; the "Sketches," p. 85; and his address in memory of Elizabeth G. Evans. Jim Larkin's visit to Boston and his remarks on Russia are noted in Emmett Larkin, *James Larkin, Irish Labour Leader, 1876–1947* (Cambridge, Mass., 1967), p. 228.

35 See letter to AJM (signature indecipherable) on Yearly Meeting of Friends for New England letterhead, Feb. 4, 1919, BC, WSU, Box 42, Folder 1. See also "Sketches," p. 53.

36 The following account of the 1912 Lawrence strike draws heavily upon Patrick Renshaw, *The Wobblies* (New York, paperback ed., 1968), p. 98; "Sketches," p. 57.

37 Raquel Swing, quoted in Marion Dutton Savage, *Industrial Unionism in America* (New York, 1922), pp. 251–52.

38 Cole, *Immigrant City, Lawrence, Massachusetts 1845–1921* (Chapel Hill, 1963); Renshaw, *The Wobblies*, p. 101.

39 Renshaw, *The Wobblies*, pp. 97–112, quotations from pp. 102, 106.

40 Harvell [sic] L. Rotzel, "The Lawrence Textile Strike," *The American Labor Year Book, 1919–1920*, p. 172; Savage, *Industrial Unionism in America*, p. 253.

41 John Fitch, " '54–48' at Lawrence," *Survey*, March 8, 1919, p. 832; John Fitch, "Lawrence," *Survey*, April 5, 1919, pp. 42–46.

42 Rotzel, "Lawrence Textile Strike," pp. 172–73; AJM, "Sketches," p. 61; Fitch, "Lawrence," pp. 42–46.

43   "Sketches," p. 60.
44   Ibid., pp. 58–61; Allen, *Adventurous Americans*, p. 108.
45   Muste's letter to Sisson and meeting action thereon are recorded in PMMF Mins., Fourth Month 26th, 1919, p. 280.
46   AJM, "Christianity, the Only Hope of the World," in Haverford College Quaker Collection, Philadelphia Book Association of Friends, 1918; AJM, "Fellowship and Class Struggle," address at FOR conferences at Haverford, Sept. 15, 1929, unsorted FOR, SCPC.
47   The leadership provision for families in case of mishap is noted in "Sketches," p. 86.
48   Oral Memoir, pp. 454–55; "Sketches," pp. 62–63. The story of the police beatings of Long and Muste was reported by John Fitch in "Lawrence," April 5, 1919, pp. 42–46, and was repeated in 1938 by Muste in a letter to Bernard M. Allen, Jan. 26, 1938, Labor Temple Papers.
49   "Sketches," pp. 71–73; the *New York Times*, March 19, 1919, p. 20; April 29, 1919, p. 22; May 7, 1919, p. 11; May 9, 1919, p. 3.
50   Renshaw, *The Wobblies*, p. 103; John Fitch, "Lawrence," April 5, 1919, pp. 42–46.
51   Savage, *Industrial Unionism in America*, p. 254; Rotzel, "Lawrence Textile Strike," p. 173.
52   "Sketches," pp. 71–73. From this exploit stemmed the beating of Anthony Capraro who had helped transport Tresca, and Muste's narrow escape from a similar beating. AJM, "In Memory of Elizabeth Evans." Mrs. Evans' own memories of Lawrence appeared in the *Lafollette Magazine*, n.d. [August ?]. A copy of the article may be found in the Evans Papers.
53   Rotzel, "Lawrence Textile Strike;" "Sketches," pp. 74–75; *Survey*, May 31, 1919, p. 368; Rotzel, "Lawrence Textile Strike," p. 173.
54   Fitch, "Lawrence," April 5, 1919, pp. 42–46; William Crawford, "Three Months of Labor Turmoil in Lawrence, Massachusetts," *New York Times*, Sunday, May 25, 1919, sec. 4, p. 1; Cole, *Immigrant City* (Chapel Hill, 1963) pp. 200–1. On p. 201 AJM is incorrectly identified as a "Russian-born clergyman."
55   Savage, *Industrial Unionism in America*, pp. 255–58; Robert W. Dunn, "Unionism in the Textile Industry," *The American Labor Year Book, 1921–1922*, pp. 160–62.
     At the same time that Muste was plunging so deeply into the labor union movement, he may have been maintaining as well the peace-oriented League for Democratic Control which he and Rotzel had first announced in June 1917. The only publication of the League unearthed to date appeared apparently in the spring of 1919 when the Treaty of Versailles was first presented to the Germans. Bearing the League's name and an office address of Room 79, 2 Park Square, Boston (its initial address had been 120 Boylston Street), the 8 ½-by-11-inch broadside urged citizens to protest the discrepancy between "what was promised by America and the Allied governments and what they are now demanding of Germany." The discrepancy was so great, the League maintained, that it amounted to "the foundation for another world catastrophe." If Muste was behind the publication of this leaflet and still involved in the peace movement, he would only have been following the pattern of astounding activity and ability to juggle multiple causes at once that characterized later periods of his life. It is known that he became a member of the ACLU National Committee during his stint as ATW secretary (Donald Johnson, *The Challenge to American Freedom*, p. 147), and as other materials are uncovered, it will not be surprising to find his name on other organization rolls. Meanwhile, the League and Muste's relationship to it in 1919 have proven to be elusive

phenomena. See "The Peace Terms, Have We Kept Faith," Harvard University Library.
56   Savage, *Industrial Unionism in America*, pp. 261–63; Dunn, *Unionism in the Textile Industry*, pp. 156, 160; "Sketches," pp. 79–80; "Passaic-An American City," *The Christian Century*, Aug. 5, 1926, pp. 964–90; "Sketches," p. 79; Dunn, *Unionism in the Textile Industry*, pp. 156–57; Savage, *Industrial Unionism in America*, pp. 264–66; 256.
57   Savage, *Industrial Unionism in America*, pp. 269–70.

Chapter III

1   Sarah N. Cleghorn, *Threescore* (New York, 1936), pp. 225–46, quotations from pp. 226, 227; William M. Fincke, "How Brookwood Began," in *Brookwood Labor's Own School*, pp. 14–16, 1936; AJM, SCPC, Box 1a. See also "Report of Executive Board to Annual Meeting of Board of Directors and of Brookwood Corporation," section on "Historical Note," BC, WSU, Box 6, Folder 5.
2   Fincke, "How Brookwood Began," pp. 14–16; AJM, "Sketches for an Autobiography" (hereafter "Sketches"), in *The Essays of A. J. Muste*, ed. Nat Hentoff (New York, 1967), pp. 92–97; Cleghorn, *Threescore*, pp. 239–46.
3   "Sketches," p. 97; AJM, Columbia Oral History Memoir No. 509 (hereafter Oral Memoir), the early 1950s, pp. 442–43, 451, 454–55, Columbia University Library.
4   "Sketches," p. 86; Cleghorn, *Threescore*, pp. 240–41; "Sketches," pp. 86–87.
5   Cleghorn, *Threescore*, pp. 242–44; "Sketches," pp. 97–98. Reasons for the Finckes' abrupt departure from Brookwood are not clear. Muste attributed it to "personality conflicts" with another family, M. Toscan and Josephine Bennett, who also left the College about the time of the Finckes' departure. The Finckes went on to establish Manumit School in 1924 in Dutchess County, New York. See Cleghorn, *Threescore*, pp. 265–66; AJM to Rev. Edmund B. Chaffee, Jan. 21, 1926, Chaffee Papers; "Death of Brookwood Founder Great Loss," *Brookwood Review* 5, no. 5 (June–July 1927).
6   "Sketches," p. 104; Cleghorn, *Threescore*, p. 246; Fincke, "How Brookwood Began," pp. 14–16. Mark Starr was soon a notable long-term addition to the faculty, coming from the National Council of Labor Colleges of England and later becoming educational director of the International Ladies Garment Workers Union. On Starr, Saposs, and Muste as teachers, see James Morris, *Conflict within the AFL* (Ithaca, 1958), p. 96.
7   Len DeCaux, *Labor Radical* (Boston, 1970), p. 95.
8   "Sketches," pp. 99–102; Cleghorn, *Threescore*, pp. 244–45; Morris, *Conflict within the AFL*, p. 97.
9   "Brookwood's Sixth Year Commences Well," *Brookwood Review* 5, no. 2 (Oct.–Nov. 1926): 1; AJM, "The Year at Brookwood," *Brookwood Review* 4, no. 7 (May–June 1926): 1; "Two Millions for Brookwood Is Aim," *Brookwood Review* 4, no. 7 (May–June 1926): 14. The unions that gave Brookwood official endorsement were the United Textile Workers, Hosiery Workers, American Federation of Teachers, International Association of Machinists, Brewery Workers, Coopers, Maintenance-of-Way Employees, Railway Clerks, Railway Carmen, Painters, Hat and Cap Makers, International Ladies Garment Workers Union, and Amalgamated Clothing Workers (Morris, *Conflict within the AFL*, p. 94). DeCaux, *Labor Radical*, provides a vivid description of worker types (pp. 100–7). Scholarships for Negro students were provided by the National Association for the Advancement of Colored People and the Sleeping Car Porters. (correspondence in BC, WSU, Box 13, File 18).

10   "Brookwood's Sixth Year," 1; "New Garage," *Brookwood Review* 6 (Oct.–Nov. 1927): 2; "The New Swimmin' Hole," *Brookwood Review* 8, no. 1. (Oct.–Nov. 1929): 2; "Labor Sports," *Brookwood Review* 9, no. 1 (Dec. 1930): 2.

11   "Sketches," p. 86; Cara Cook MS., AJM, Box 1a, SCPC. The atmosphere and living conditions of Brookwood are highlighted vividly throughout this informal sketch of the college.

12   Anna H. Muste, "To the Faculty" (handwritten, n.d., [1924?]), BC, WSU, Box 7, Folder 10. Faculty minutes of Nov. 18, 1924, indicated that Mrs. Muste was paid seventy-five dollars per month as "housekeeper and head of the Commissary." BC, WSU, Box 7, Folder 11.

13   Cara Cook MS. Helen Norton Star has related that she spoke before a Katonah woman's club where great "tittering" occurred when she assured them that Brookwooders "were drearily respectable. All the faculty members lived with their own wives" (quoted in Nat Hentoff, *Peace Agitator* [New York, 1967], p. 65).

14   Cara Cook MS.; Hentoff, *Peace Agitator*, p. 64; *Brookwood Review* 10, no. 3: 2; "Marriage of Cook and Bellaver" on Muste's matrimonial services. DeCaux, *Labor Radical*, pp. 96–100, gives an entertaining account of his own love life and efforts of the Brookwood community to influence it.

15   "William Bloom Drowned," *Brookwood Review* 8, no. 3 (Sept. 1930): 17; "New Spring Styles in Babies," *Brookwood Review* 5, no. 3 (Dec. 1926–Jan. 1927): 1; "Yesterday, I became the father of a young gentleman whose name is John Martin Muste. . . . We are all of us doing very well, especially myself," reported AJM to Charles Reed, Jan. 22, 1927, BC, WSU, Box 50, Folder 5.

16   "Sketches," p. 86; Hentoff, *Peace Agitator*, p. 63; Cara Cook MS.; "Bums and Bolsheviks Cavort," *Brookwood Review* 4, no. 2 (Dec. 1925): 3. Readers too young to recognize the reference to Milt Gross would enjoy perusing his *Famous Fimmales witt Odder Ewents From Heestory* (New York, 1928). See BC, WSU, Box 8, Folder 2 for faculty skits, including one depicting Muste in something of a frenzy over financial problems; wife Anne needs to pay the ice man; daughter Connie needs a pencil; the college bank account is overdrawn; field workers are in jail calling for bail; and faculty member Mark Starr is stranded in Rye, New York, with a broken car. "Oh, hell," A. J. exclaims, "Tell him to hitch hike!"

17   Cara Cook to the author, Feb. 20, 1978. Cook added that Josephine Colby "had a background of choral training" and an "extensive collection of labor songs." See BC, WSU, Box 13, Folder 1 for *Brookwood Song Book*.

18   Cara Cook MS.; "Labor Sports," p. 2.

19   AJM, "What's It All About," *Labor Age* 13, no. 4 (May 1924): 1–4; "Sketches," p. 103; "Would-Be Speakers Receive Instruction," *Brookwood Review* 4, no. 3, (Jan. 1926): 1; AJM to Willard C. Mellin, Oct. 7, 1938, Labor Temple Papers, Box 1; Helen G. Norton, "Drama at Brookwood," *Labor Age* 15, no. 5 (May 1926): 18–19. It was rumored that when Colby took up residence in the Soviet Union, she became Stalin's English instructor. AJM, "Introducing Ourselves," *Brookwood Review* 3, no. 1 (Dec. 1924): 6. Another Brookwood publication of far less quality put out by faculty members' children with the help of some parents (Connie Muste, Donald Calhoun, and his father, Arthur, were most prominent in the effort) was called "The Holy Terror." It sold for a penny a copy and was an "in-house" gossip sheet. See Wayne State University vertical file on Brookwood, Oct. 1926–Jan. 1927.

20   *Brookwood Review* 1, no. 4 (April 15, 1923): 2; Marius Hansome, *World Workers' Education Movements* (New York, 1931), pp. 202–3, listed the Brookwood curriculum as it stood in 1927: First Year: How to study, training in speaking and writing, use of

English language, history of American labor movement, current events, sociology, social economics, labor dramatics. Second Year: sociology, statistics, public speaking, labor journalism, foreign labor movements, speaking and writing, trade union organization, structure, government and administration of trade unions, labor legislation and administration, seminar—workers' education, seminar—strategy of the labor movement. In Muste's course the reading requirements included John W. Gregory, *The Making of Earth*; Henry F. Osborn, *Men of the Old Stone Age*; and Franz Boas, *The Mind of Primitive Man*. The main texts were by "Breasted and Wells"—probably James Breasted's *Ancient Times* or *Conquest of Civilization* and H. G. Wells' *Outline of History*.

21   "Sinclair Lewis Sees Unionism Urgent Need," *Brookwood Review* 8, no. 1 (Oct.–Nov. 1929): 1. In the "Sketches," Muste listed as major visitors to Brookwood: Paxton Hibben, Harry F. Ward, Powers Hapgood, William Z. Foster, Henry R. Linville, Joseph Scholossberg, John Strachey, Andre Philip, J. F. Horrabin, Harry A. Overstreet, Everett Dean Martin, Harry Elmer Barnes, Horace Kallen, Reinhold Niebuhr, Sumner Slichter, Abraham Epstein, Father John A. Ryan, Norman Thomas, Roger Baldwin, Bertram Wolfe, J. B. S. Hardman, Oscar Ameringer, James H. Maurer, Phil Ziegler, Fannia Cohn, John Brophy, Abraham Lefkowitz, Robert Fechner, John Fitzpatrick. He mistakenly identified K. Knudsen as "J. Olson" ("Sketches," pp. 105–6). On Knudsen, see Isaac Deutscher, *The Prophet Outcast, Trotsky: 1929–1940* (New York, paperback ed., 1963), pp. 293–97.

22   Hansome, *World Workers' Education Movements*, pp. 202–3; AJM, "What's It All About?"; AJM, "Introducing Ourselves," p. 6; "Freedom in Labor Education," *Brookwood Review* 5, no. 4 (Feb.–Mar. 1927): 1; AJM, "The Purpose of Labor Education," *The World Tomorrow* 3, no. 7, (July 1925): 219; "Sketches," pp. 102–3.

23   Cleghorn, *Threescore*, p. 245. Interestingly, perhaps kindly, Muste overlooked or had forgotten Cleghorn's feelings on this score when he wrote his "Sketches," where her departure is attributed to ill health ("Sketches," p. 104); AJM, "Introducing Ourselves," p. 6; AJM to V. F. Calverton, April 24, 1926, Calverton Papers, NYPL. Calverton did visit Brookwood as a lecturer.

24   AJM to Ted Olson, Sept. 1962, AJM, Box 15, SCPC.

25   AJM, "The Purpose of Labor Education," p. 219; "What's It All About?" pp. 1–4; "Where It Counts the Most," *Brookwood Review* 5, no. 3 (Dec. 1926–Jan. 1927): 1; "The Outlook for Workers' Control," *The World Tomorrow* 8, no. 8 (Aug. 1925): 242–44; "Where it Counts the Most," p. 1.

26   AJM, "Birdseye View of European Workers' Education," *Labor Age* 12, no. 8 (Oct. 1923): 18–20; James Hudson Maurer, *It Can Be Done* (New York, 1938), pp. 308–9; Irving Bernstein, *The Lean Years* (Baltimore, paperback ed., 1966), p. 105. Green is quoted in Bernstein. *The American Labor Year Book, 1921–1922*, pp. 202–4, 238, 252, lists the numerous workers' education enterprises that were springing up. AJM, "Is Workers' Education Being Sold Out to Company Unionism?" *Brookwood Review* 7, no. 2 (Dec. 1928–Jan. 1929): 1–2.

27   "Conference of Labor College Teachers Called," *Labor Age* 13, no. 2 (Feb. 1924): 23. Succeeding conferences are noted in *The American Labor Year Book, 1927*, pp. 161–62; "Brookwood Labor Institute, Aug. 1–13, 1927," brochure in Chaffee Papers; " 'Negroes Can Organize' Is Conference Feature," *Brookwood Review* 5, no. 5 (June–July 1927): 1; "Negro Symposium Papers," BC, WSU, Box 44, File 11. In 1930 Brookwood sponsored a conference on "Workers' Education and the Negro" (correspondence in BC, WSU, Box 56, File 17); "Brookwood's 'Youth Institute,' " *Labor Age* 14, no. 12 (Dec. 1927): 11; "Brookwood Labor Institute" brochure; Morris, *Conflict within the AFL*, p. 101; Philip Taft, *The AF of L From the Death of Gompers to the Merger* (New York, 1959),

on Negroes, pp. 439–48; on indifference toward women, p. 8; "Brookwood Labor Institute" brochure.
28   Morris, *Conflict within the AFL*, pp. 106–10; Louis F. Budenz, *This Is My Story* (New York, 1947), pp. 61–71.
29   AJM, "Living Memorials," *Brookwood Review* 3, no. 2 (Jan. 1925): 1; "Lenin Memorial Meeting," *Brookwood Review* 3, no. 3 (Apr. 1925): 3; "Debs Eulogized at Memorial Meeting," *Brookwood Review*, 5, no. 2 (Oct.–Nov. 1926): 4.
30   AJM, "Sacco and Vanzetti," *Brookwood Review* 6, no. 1 (Sept. 1927): 1–2. For AFL hesitation and caution with regard to the Italians case, see Philip Taft, *The AFL*, pp. 7–8. On the case itself see Robert H. Montgomery, *Sacco and Vanzetti, the Murder and the Myth* (New York, 1960), Muste's involvement in the defense noted, p. 73; Cara Cook to the author, Feb. 20, 1978.
31   "May One Celebration," *Brookwood Review* 3, no. 4 (May 1925): 1; William Green, "More about Brookwood," Pamphlet in Chaffee papers; "Green's 'Irrefutable Charges' Answered," *Brookwood Review* 7, no. 2 (Dec. 1928–Jan. 1929): 1. Philip Taft discusses Green's outspoken anti-communism in this period (*The AFL*, p. 430).
32   AJM to James Maurer, Oct. 3, 1924; J. Brophy to AJM, Oct. 7, 1924; AJM to Brophy, Oct. 10, 1924; AJM to Maurer, Oct. 10, 1924, all in BC, WSU, Box 6, Folder 15; AJM, "Confidential to Polly, Arthur, Mildred," Sept. 26, 1924, BC, WSU, Box 7, Folder 7; AJM to Selma Borchardt, Jan. 19, 1925, Borchardt Papers, Box 87, Folder 18, WSU. F. G. Stecker, national secretary-treasurer of the American Federation of Teachers, wrote William Green about the allegations of Local 189's radicalism; Green confirmed that they were of concern (Stecker to Green, Feb. 2, 1925, and Green to Stecker, Feb. 12, 1925, Borchardt Papers, Box 87, Folder 18 WSU); Florence C. Thorne to AJM, May 18, 1925, BC, WSU, Box 16, Folder 7; Thorne to AJM, March 24, 1926; AJM to Thorne, March 16, 1926; and Thorne to AJM, March 18, 1926, all in BC, WSU, Box 16, Folder 9.
33   One of these students, James Boyd, also wrote an unflattering account of Brookwood for the *Illinois Miner*, which led to his censure by fellow students and the Brookwood faculty (BC, WSU, Box 7, Folder 2): BC, WSU, Box 19, Folder 6 for reference to a second statement sent by Boyd to the *Illinois Miner* to clear up errors in the first; George Creech to members of the Executive Committee, April 20, 1928; AJM to Brookwood student body, April 21, 1928; Spencer Miller to AJM, March 2, 1926; and AJM to Miller, March 16, 1926, in Borchardt Papers, WSU, Box 145, Folder 21; Morris, *Conflict within the AFL*, pp. 111–13. I am indebted to the careful and well-documented research of Morris for this account and have relied heavily upon his work. Morris lists the students who protested Brookwood's commemoration of May Day as R. M. Ware and Hector Daoust of the Railway Carmen, William Absolon of the Painters, P. E. Powers, a machinist, and James Boyd, a coal miner. Apparently, most of the information which the Woll report took from these sources came from Ware, Daoust, and Absolon (Morris, *Conflict within the AFL*, pp. 113, 115). AJM typescripts, "Mitten Management and the Street Railway Men, Some Questions," for *Labor Age*, April 4, 1928; and "Something New in Collective Bargaining," for *Nation*, April 24, 1928, in BC, WSU, Box 43, Folder 5. See BC, WSU, Box 41, Folder 1, for Brookwood conference on the agreement with "Department of Hindsight" notation by Helen Norton Starr, Aug. 16, 1954. The AFL-Brookwood controversy may be traced in detail in BC, WSU, Box 16, Folders 13–29, and all of Boxes 17 and 18. See in Box 18 especially Folder 18 for "Memorandum Containing Comments on Proceedings of Seventh Day of A.F. of L. Convention," n.d., n.a., Box 19, Folders 1–15. See also Box 6, Folder 7 for "Memorandum on Brookwood History and Policy," 1929, and Box 12, Folder 7.
34   "Brookwood Victim of Convention Lynching Bee," *Brookwood Review* 7, no. 1

(Oct.–Nov. 1928); *New York Times*, Aug. 18, 1928, cited in "Sketches," p. 126; Bernstein, *The Lean Years*, p. 106; "Proceedings of the Seventh Day," BC, WSU.

35   Green, "More About Brookwood." pp. 1–6; AJM "Still More About Brookwood," pp. 3–12; "Green's 'Irrefutable Charges.' " A cordial attitude toward the Soviet regime on the part of Brookwood staff was evident from the earliest years of the college. Muste sent eighty dollars raised by teachers and students who abstained from desserts for a month to contribute to Russian relief (AJM to Friends of Soviet Russia, Jan. 16, 1923, BC, WSU, Box 34, File 6). M. Naimark of Russian Red Cross to Brookwood, May 10, 1924, and Toscan-Bennett to Madame Krupskaia, Moscow, Jan. 12, 1924, BC, WSU, Box 50, Folder 10; AJM to G. Molnitchansky (USSR Central Council of Trade Unions), March 11, 1927, BC, WSU, Box 50, File 14; Bernstein, *The Lean Years*, p. 106; William Green, "More About Brookwood Labor College," and AJM, "Still More About Brookwood," pamphlets dated 1929 in Chaffee Papers.

Brookwood files on the Brophy movement provide strong documentation of a close relationship between the "rank and file" (Brophy) miners and Brookwood. (BC, WSU, Box 35, Folders 8–22, and Box 40, Folder 14, which includes a postscript [written in 1954] by Helen Norton Starr on Brookwood's "cordial relationship" with Brophy.) See also comments on the Brophy movement and the Brookwood involvement with it in Melvin Dubofsky and Warren Van Tine, *John L. Lewis, A Biography* (Chicago, 1977), pp. 127–28, 160–63. Other indictments of Brookwood which did not receive much public attention but which were reported to Muste as among the reasons for the AFL attack included the rumor that too much emphasis was placed on sex in the sociology curriculum and that the largely Roman Catholic Executive Committee of the AFL were upset by irreverent attitudes toward religion ("Pro Bono Publico" to AJM, Nov. 4, 1928, BC, WSU, Box 16, Folder 16; Anonymous to "Dear Bro. Muste," Sept. 26, 1928, BC, WSU, Box 16, Folder 14; and "Brookwood Fellowship" newsletter, Aug. 17, 1928, BC, WSU, Box 17, Folder 28).

36   Morris, *Conflict within the AFL*, pp. 107, 127; *The American Labor Year Book, 1930*, pp. 182–83; "Who Closed Door on Negotiations?" *Brookwood Review* 7, no. 3 (Feb.–Apr. 1929): 2; AJM to "Dear Friend," Jan. 22, 1929, BC, WSU, Box 7, Folder 3, gives the Muste version of events at the WEB meeting.

37   The lengthy list of alumni who sprang to Brookwood's defense included vice-presidents of the Massachusetts State Federation of Labor and the ILGWU, secretaries of the Philadelphia Dress and Waist Makers Local and the Organizing Council for Southern Virginia, and the president of Local 189, Brotherhood of Railway Clerks (AJM "Still More about Brookwood," in Edmund B. Chaffee Papers, pp. 10, 12); Morris, *Conflict within the AFL*, p. 119; "Convention Lynching Bee," p. 1; Morris, *Conflict within the AFL*, pp. 114–15; Excerpt from Mitchell letter, in John A. Fitch, "Workers' Education and the Spirit of Progress"; and "New York Teachers Protest AFL Action," all in *Brookwood Review* 7, no. 1 (Oct.–Nov. 1928): 3–4.

38   In February 1929 Muste commented on the desire of some Brookwood supporters to pursue a "militant progressive policy": "We are in all the stronger position for doing it because we have avoided at certain critical times forcing the situation and have rather permitted the situation to develop itself" (AJM to Cara Cook, Feb. 6, 1929; letter lent by Cook to the author).

39   "Still More About Brookwood." "Statement Issued by Board of Directors of Brookwood Labor College At Meeting Held June 9, 1929," Chaffee Papers; AJM to Willard C. Mellin, Oct. 7, 1938, Labor Temple Papers.

40   Morris, *Conflict within the AFL*, p. 115; "Sketches," pp. 128, 130; "Still More About Brookwood."

41   Bernstein, *The Lean Years*, pp. 105–6; John Dewey, "Labor Politics and Labor Education," *New Republic*, Jan. 9, 1929, pp. 211–13.

42   Morris, *Conflict within the AFL*, p. 96; Edwin Young, "The Split in the Labor Movement," in *Labor and the New Deal*, ed. Milton Derber and Edwin Young (Madison, 1957), p. 69. James Morris has penned an observation relevant to this point: "Brookwood and other labor colleges could not expect to get and keep the endorsement and financial support of conservative unions and, at the same time, cast doubt upon and advocate changes in the basic principles of these unions. Under these circumstances the doctrine of academic freedom would not appear to have been relevant. Nor is it likely that a public investigation or hearing would have changed the predicament in which Brookwood found itself" (*Conflict within the AFL*, p. 121).

43   "A. J. Muste's Address to 1928 Graduates," *Brookwood Review* 6, no. 6 (June-Aug. 1928): 1.

44   AJM to Fannia Cohn, Jan. 19, 1929, Cohn Papers. He added in the same letter, "Unless there is a definite change I shall have to withdraw from activity—or perhaps I ought to say Anne will drag me out." See also AJM to Fannia Cohn, May 14, 1929, and Jan. 10, 1929, Cohn Papers.

45   On the La Follette campaign see Kenneth C. MacKay, *The Progressive Movement of 1924* (New York, 1966), pp. 56–73, 75–78, 110, 115, 118–23, 230–38; "Sketches," p. 108, 111, 113, 114; Arthur Mann, *La Guardia, a Fighter against His Times, 1882–1933* (Philadelphia, 1959), pp. 170–71. On the League for Independent Political Action, see Donald B. Meyer, *The Protestant Search for Political Realism* (Berkeley, 1961), pp. 126–28, 179–80, 211, 231. Other founding members of the LIPA included Oswald Garrison Villard, James Weldon Johnson, Harry W. Laidler, Robert Moss Lovett, W. E. B. DuBois, Sherwood Eddy, Devere Allen, and Kirby Page. See also AJM, "Independent Political Action—Yes, But What Kind?" *Labor Age* 19, no. 6 (June 1930): 6–8; *New York Times*, Dec. 30, 1930, p. 3; and *The American Labor Year Book, 1931*, p. 158. On the Fellowship for a Christian Social Order, see Donald B. Meyer, "The Protestant Social Liberals in America, 1914–1941," pp. 86–92. This Ph.D. diss. (Harvard University, 1953) deals in more detail with the Fellowship than Meyer's later book, *The Protestant Search for Political Realism*, which also discusses it, pp. 48–50. Charles Chatfield, *For Peace and Justice* (Knoxville, Tenn., 1971), pp. 179–80, also provides information on the organization.

46   "School Ends First Decade," and "Muste Eulogized at New York Dinner," both in *Brookwood Review* 9, no. 2 (Feb. 1931): 1, 4. David Saposs reported to Fannia Cohn that Muste "outdid himself" in this speech (Saposs to Cohn, March 7, 1931, in Cohn Papers).

47   Morris, *Conflict within the AFL*, p. 125: "The Challenge to Progressives, An Editorial Statement," *Labor Age* 18, no. 2 (Feb. 1929): 3–7, reprinted in *The American Labor Year Book, 1930*, pp. 87–93.

48   Morris, *Conflict within the AFL*, pp. 126–27, quotations, p. 126. Muste had expressed similar sentiments in "Where to from Here?" *Brookwood Review* 7, no. 1 (Oct.–Nov. 1928): 1. A preliminary meeting which helped to set the stage for "The Challenge" and this meeting had occurred in December 1928 (AJM to "Dear Friends," Dec. 15, 1928; "Memorandum on Informal Conference Held at Katonah, New York at the Invitation of AJM," Dec. 30, 1928; "Notes on Conference Called by Mr. A. J. Muste," Dec. 30, 1928, all in BC, WSU, Box 12, Folder 1.

49   Morris, *Conflict within the AFL*, pp. 128–29. Other officers and executive committee members were Carl Holderman (UTW), second vice-president; A. J. Kennedy (Brookwood), treasurer; Leonard Bright (Bookkeepers and Stenographers Union), secretary; Justus Ebert (Lithographers journal); Israel Mufson (Philadelphia Labor

College); Clinton S. Golden (Brookwood fund-raiser); J. B. S. Hardman (author); Joseph Schwartz (Jewelry Workers); Nathaniel Spector (Cloth Hat and Cap Makers); Frank Crosswaith (Sleeping Car Porters); Henry R. Linville (AFT); Frank Manning (UTW); Winston Dancis (Postal Clerks); James O'Neal (socialist editor); and Norman Thomas. Andrew Vance, Frank Morris, Carl Johanntges, and Nellie Lithgow also sat on the executive committee; their affiliations are not known. When the CPLA letterhead appeared Brookwood student Walter Wilson was replaced by Ludwig Lore. Files on the CPLA are in BC, WSU, Box 28, Folders 1–30 and Box 29, Folders 1–11.

50 Quoted in Morris, *Conflict within the AFL*, p. 123. The statement of purpose was also reproduced on the new conference's letterhead. Donald McCoy, *Angry Voices* (p. 30), cites one instance of cooperation between this new Conference and the LIPA—a meeting of "political independents" in June 1933. But he does not indicate that anything came of the effort. AJM quoted in Morris, *Conflict within the AFL*, p. 128.

51 Morris, *Conflict within the AFL*, pp. 126–27; Fannia Cohn to AJM, Jan. 10, 1929, Cohn Papers. Another prominent labor figure on the Brookwood Board of Directors, Phil Ziegler, shared Cohn's sentiments (Ziegler to Fannia Cohn, Sept. 1, 1929, in BC, WSU, Box 16, Folder 25). The CPLA resolutions against Green are reported in *The American Labor Year Book, 1930*, p. 93. A similar complaint against Green was brought by the editors of *Revolutionary Age*. Benjamin Gitlow and Will Herberg denounced the labor leader for giving a speech at the Army Industrial College in 1930. The War Department denied that this speech occurred, but Gitlow and Herberg seem to have provided Muste with a copy of it (Gitlow to Cara Cook, n.d.; Cook to Gitlow, Oct. 29, 1930; Herberg to Cook, Nov. 19, 1930, all in BC, WSU, Box 16, File 12).

52 Quoted in Morris, *Conflict within the AFL*, p. 129.

53 "CPLA Criticism of Green-Hoover Pact," *Labor Age* 19, no. 1 (Jan. 1930): 21; AJM, "Who Shall Organize and How?" *Labor Age* 19, no. 9 (Sept. 1930): 9–11; AJM "The AFL, the CPLA and the Future," *Labor Age* 19, no. 10 (Oct. 1930): 16–17; AJM, "The AFL in 1931," published by the National Executive Committee of the CPLA, n.d., pamphlet found in Harvard College Library.

54 "The Challenge to Progressives," p. 3–7.

55 When the first reports from disillusioned visitors to Russia began to circulate, Muste did not deny their truth but continued to argue that even valid criticisms "must not . . . blind us to the essential significance of the overturn of the old regime in Russia and the importance of enabling the experiment that has been launched there to be carried through without molestation from without" ("Militant Progressivism?" *Modern Quarterly* 4, no. 4 [May–Aug. 1928]: 332–41); AJM, "Who Shall Organize and How?" pp. 9–11; *American Labor Year Book, 1930*, p. 94. On p. 93 of this volume it is reported that at their original organizing conference, CPLA members "overwhelmingly defeated . . . an amendment to strike out all reference to the communists in the statement of policy." Communist Party charges against Muste were summarized in a handout: "The Communist Party Challenges; A. J. Muste—'Little Brother of the Big Labor Fakers'—to Debate William Z. Foster" n.d. [1931?], BC, WSU, Box 43, Folder 14. For an eyewitness account of a Foster-Muste debate which was reportedly attended by a crowd of over 3,000, of whom "A.J. had about 150 supporters," see Walter Wilson to Arthur Calhoun, May 12, 1931, Calhoun Papers (unsorted).

56 For insight into the background of Calhoun's alienation from Brookwood, see Arthur Calhoun to AJM, Aug. 8, 1928; AJM to "Helen et al.," Nov. 13, 1928; Calhoun to AJM, n.d., Calhoun Papers. On the actual firing see Minutes of Faculty Meeting, June 2, 1929, BC, WSU, Box 7, Folder 13; "Statement Issued by Board of Directors of Brook-

wood Labor College at Meeting Held, June 9, 1924," BC, WSU, Box 16, Folder 20; AJM, "For Your Information," June 11, 1929; AJM to Len De Caux, June 11, 1929. Two years after Calhoun was fired, the directors of the college adopted the policy that "persons committed to the present line of the C.P. in the U.S." would not be admitted to Brookwood ("Annual Report, 1941–1942," BC, WSU, Box 6, File 9). Arthur Calhoun to Mrs. Florence C. Hanson, June 2, 1929, BC, WSU, Box 19, Folder 22; Hanson to the Executive Committee of the AFT, Aug. 28, 1931, BC, WSU, Box 20, Folder 19. The national executive council of the American Federation of Teachers reviewed the case at Calhoun's request and upheld the Brookwood position. "Charges by A. W. Calhoun against A. J. Muste before Brookwood Local 189," BC, WSU, Box 25, Folder 27; Len De Caux to AJM, June 6, 1929; "Caroline" [De Caux] to AJM, June 6, 1929; "Ainsworth" to "Dear Bro. Muste," June 8, 1929, BC, WSU, Box 25, Folder 24; "Ainsworth" to AJM, June 19, 1929, Box 25, File 24; David Berkingoff to AJM, July 5, 1929, BC, WSU, Box 25, Folder 26. See also Muste's letter to Fannia Cohn, reassuring her that Calhoun's charge that Brookwood was becoming "the seminary of a sect" was unfounded (AJM to Cohn, June 27, 1929, BC, WSU, Box 16, Folder 25). Fannia Cohn later wrote that Muste's release of a statement about the firing "to the capitalist press" occurred without prior knowledge or consent from the college Board of Directors (Cohn to Clint [Golden], April 20, 1933, Cohn Papers). Peggy Greenfield to "Dear Friend" indicates that Ms. Greenfield, a secretary at the college, also left because of the Calhoun affair, reportedly after Muste told her that if she sided so strongly with Calhoun, she should leave (BC, WSU, Box 26, Folder 11). For a retrospective analysis by Muste of the firing of Calhoun, see AJM to Arthur Calhoun, handwritten, n.d., Calhoun Papers, temporary Box 20, Folder 70).

57   Morris, *Conflict within the AFL*, pp. 133–34.

58   Morris, *Conflict within the AFL*, pp. 134–35. Fleeting references to CPLA work on racketeering appear in the Chaffee Papers (For example: AJM to Rev. Edmund B. Chaffee, March 1, 1933, and Chaffee to AJM, March 6, 1933). These letters corroborate Sidney Lens' suggestion that one of the main campaigns was against corrupt leadership in the New York Electrical Workers (Sidney Lens, *Left, Right and Center* [Hinsdale, Ill., 1949], p. 261).

59   AJM, "Local Reports," typescript, n.d.: "We have to take each situation as we find it. In some places we can work for independent political action; in others trade union organizing is the present job" (BC, WSU, Box 28, Folder 8). Lewis L. Lorwin, *The American Federation of Labor* (Washington, D.C., 1933), p. 268; *American Labor Year Book, 1932*, pp. 72–74; Editorial in the *New Republic*, Aug. 12, 1931, p. 326. On silk workers, see BC, WSU, Box 24, Folders 1–5.

60   On the strikes at Henderson and Elizabethton, see Bernstein, *The Lean Years*, pp. 12–20, and BC, WSU, Box 15.

61   Bernstein, *The Lean Years*, pp. 29–33; Sinclair Lewis, *Cheap and Contented Labor* (Philadelphia, 1929); Cara Cook MS. The quotation is Cook's. "Sketches," pp. 145–46; Tom Tippett, *When Southern Labor Stirs* (New York, 1931) pp. 109–55. For details on the Marion Strike, see BC, WSU, Box 53, Folders 18 and 19, Box 54, Folders 1 through 15. The funeral orations delivered by Muste, Tippet, and an AFL official were published by the CPLA as "Progressive Labor Library Pamphlet #2—the Marion Murder," 1929, Labadie Collection, University of Michigan. The death of the handcuffed victim is described therein. Muste also wrote about "The Marion Massacre," *Canadian Forum*, (Dec. 1929): 81–82; See also "Report of Extension Director [Tom Tippett], 1929–1930," BC, WSU, Box 6, File 7.

62   AJM, quoted in *American Labor Year Book, 1930*, p. 94. Cara Cook designated the strike as the CPLA's "first major undertaking" (Cook MS.).

63   Bernstein, *The Lean Years*, pp. 33–40; *American Labor Year Book, 1932*, p. 74; "Larry Hogan Killed in Motor Accident," *Brookwood Review* 14, no. 1 (Nov. 1935): 3.

64   Fine, ed. *American Labor Year Book, 1931*, pp. 115–23; *American Labor Year Book, 1932*, pp. 72–73; Lorwin, *The AFL*, pp. 266–68. See also the anonymous reports on the Reorganized Miners' gatherings in the Adolph Germer Papers; Edmund Wilson to John Dos Passos, June 24, 1931, in Edmund Wilson, *Letters on Literature and Politics, 1912–1972*, ed. Elena Wilson (New York, 1977), p. 218. See also in Wilson's *Letters*, Wilson to Sherwood Anderson, June 24, 1931, p. 217. Edmund Wilson, "Frank Keeney's Coal Diggers," *New Republic*, July 15, 1931, pp. 195–99, 229–31. Files on the Keeney Strike are in BC, WSU, Box 54, Folders 16–21. See also AJM to Elmer Cope, Cope Papers, Box 9, File 1; Bernstein, *The Lean Years*, pp. 382–85; *American Labor Year Book, 1932*, p. 73; Lorwin, *The AFL*, p. 268; AJM, Letter to the Editor, the *New Republic*, Feb. 17, 1932, p. 22; David A. Corbin, " 'Frank Keeney Is Our Leader and We shall Not Be Moved': Rank and File Leadership in the West Virginia Coal Fields," in *Essays in Southern Labor History: Selected Papers, Southern Labor History Conference, 1976*, Gary M. Fink and Merl E. Reed, eds. (Westport, Conn., 1977), pp. 144–56; Dubofsky and Van Tine, *John L. Lewis*, pp. 171–72. There is also discussion about the Keeney movement in the "Annual Report 1931–32" section on "Extension Department," BC, WSU, Box 6, File 8. See also Morris, *Conflict within the AFL*, p. 132.

65   *American Labor Year Book, 1932*, p. 74; Morris, *Conflict within the AFL*, p. 133; Thomas R. Brooks, *Toil and Trouble* (New York, 1964), p. 154. An extensive collection of papers belonging to Cope and relating to his work for the CPLA is housed at the Ohio Historical Society in Columbus. To sample Cope's detailed reports to Muste—which clearly show that the CPLA organizer was deeply engaged in "dual unionism" and promoting much of the very factionalism which Muste publicly decried, see AJM to Elmer Cope, July 19, 1930, Box 7, Folder 1; Cope to AJM, June 23, 1930, Box 7, Folder 5; Cope to AJM, Dec. 1, 1930, Box 7, Folder 1; Cope to AJM, March 11, 1931, Box 7, Folder 11; AJM to Cope, Oct. 2, 1931, Box 8, Folder 1; Cope to AJM, July 20, 1933, Box 10, Folder 4.

66   For Muste's early pacifist thinking, see AJM, "Labor's Fight against War," *The World Tomorrow* 5, no. 11 (Nov. 1922): 341; AJM, "American Labor and Peace," *The World Tomorrow* 7, no. 2 (Feb. 1924): 48–50; AJM, "Them Foreign Relations," *Labor Age* 16, no. 8 (Aug. 1927): 8–9; AJM, "Two Tests," *The World Tomorrow* 3, no. 7 (July 1920): 214; AJM, "A New and Different Fundamentalism," *The World Tomorrow* 8, no. 12 (Dec. 1925): 369–72.

67   His stepping down as vice-chairman of the FOR in 1931 signaled the weakening of close FOR-Brookwood ties. The FOR had funded scholarships for Brookwood students and John Nevin Sayre, a major force in the Fellowship, had made sizeable personal loans to the college (Brookwood Executive Committee Minutes, May 29, 1929, BC, WSU, Box 7, File 3, and correspondence with Sayre, BC, WSU, Box 8, File 8).

68   AJM, "Organizing and the Organizer," *Brookwood Review* 6, no. 1 (Sept. 1927): 3–4; AJM, "Workers' Education and the Depression," *Brookwood Review* 10, no. 1 (Nov. 1931): 2; AJM to Manford Ettinger, Dec. 29, 1931, BC, WSU, Box 28, Folder 14; AJM to J. B. Matthews, Jan. 1, 1932, in BC, WSU, Box 32, Folder 28.

69   *Brookwood Review* 7, no. 3 (Feb.–April 1929): 1; Katherine H. Pollak, "Our Labor Movement Today," *Brookwood Labor Pamphlets*, ed. David Saposs (March 1932). AJM to Elmer Cope, Nov. 2, 1932, Cope Papers, Box 9, Folder 3.

70   *American Labor Year Book, 1932*, p. 71; "Against the Launching of Another Reformist Party" n.d. [ca. June 1931]—petition with eight signers (presumably Brook-

wood students) against the new CPLA posture in BC, WSU, Box 29, Folder 1. Abraham Lefkowitz, chairman of the Brookwood Board of Directors, also opposed the new direction. (Lefkowitz to AJM, Nov. 16, 1931, BC, WSU, Box 28, Folder 14.) Faculty resignations from the CPLA did not occur until 1933. See statements of resignation by J. C. Kennedy, K. H. Pollak [Ellikson], David Saposs and a collective, "A More Detailed Statement of Our Reasons For Leaving the CPLA," all in Ellikson Papers, Box 3, File 7.
71   "Muste Quits in Rift Over CPLA," *Brookwood Review* 11, no. 2 (May 1933): 1.
72   "Muste Quits"; Brookwood Faculty Minutes, May 23, 1932, BC, WSU, Box 7, Folder 16.
73   "Sustaining Fund Drive Planned," *Brookwood Review* 9, no. 2 (May 1931): 2.
74   Ibid.; "Education Now Greatly Needed," *Brookwood Review* 11, No. 1 (Dec. 1932): 1; AJM to "Dear Friend," Feb. 25, 1930, Chaffee Papers; AJM to Rev. Edmund B. Chaffee, March 7, 1932, Chaffee papers; undated "Labor Endorsers, Brookwood Appeal for Funds," mimeographed list in Chaffee Papers; AJM to Mrs. E. G. Evans, Sept. 1, 1932, Evans Papers; "Brookwood's Reply to the Memorandum on Brookwood Labor College in Relation to the Release of the 1932–33 Appropriation of the American Fund for the Public Service Submitted by Robert W. Dunn and Clarina Michaelson," BC, WSU, Box 13, Folder 11; Robert W. Dunn to AJM, BC, WSU, Box 23, File 10; Clint Golden to AJM, Dec. 6, 1931, enclosed letter from head of the American Fund indicating his growing antagonism toward Brookwood for not being "left" enough, and AJM to Golden, Dec. 30, 1921, both in BC, WSU, Box 34, File 20; AJM to Robert Dunn, May 11, 1932, BC, WSU, Box 23, Folder 15; Roger Baldwin to AJM, June 13, 1932, BC, WSU, Box 23, File 16; Baldwin to AJM, March 2, 1933, BC, WSU, Box 23, File 18. All of Box 22, BC, WSU, has materials on the Brookwood-American Fund relationship, later headed by Roger Baldwin and Elizabeth G. Flynn.
75   "Speaking of Depressions," *Brookwood Review* 10, no. 3 (May 1932): 2; Hentoff, *Peace Agitator*, pp. 82–83, for Muste-faction statement.
76   "Muste Quits"; "Sketches," p. 151; Brookwood Faculty Minutes, Jan. 14, 1933, BC, WSU, Box 7, File 17. At a "Current Event Session" the previous month, Muste allegedly told students, "Don't get too excited about the way people act. You and I are made a certain way and we act accordingly and whether we like it or not we shouldn't get too excited about it" ("Comment of AJM at Current Event Session," Jan. 26, 1933, BC, WSU, Box 7, File 17). "Supplement to Statement Issued February 9 By Majority of Brookwood Faculty" n.d. [Feb. 1933], Ellikson Papers, Box 3, Folder 25; "Sketches," p. 151; Cook MS.; Hentoff, *Peace Agitator*, p. 82. See also "Dave" to "Dear Kitty" [Saposs to Pollack], n.d., Ellikson Papers, Box 3, Folder 21, in which Muste's remarks are described as "opera-comic boufee."
77   "Muste Quits," p. 1; "Sketches," pp. 149–52; AJM, "My Experience in the Labor and Radical Struggles of the Thirties," in *As We Saw the Thirties*, ed. Rita J. Simon (Urbana, Ill., 1967), pp. 123–50. The enrollment figure was reported in *Brookwood Review* 11, no. 1 (Dec. 1932): 4. Hentoff reports it as twenty-eight (*Peace Agitator*, p. 83). Cara Cook MS.; Secretary Doris Prenner complained to Fannia Cohn, "Last night Mark Starr took the key to the supply closet in the office and said 'if you want any supplies you'll have to ask Helen [Norton Starr]. We are running the office now' " (Prenner to Cohn, March 8, 1933, BC, WSU, Box 26, File 11); Hentoff, *Peace Agitator*, p. 82.
78   "Whither Brookwood," *Labor Age* 22, no. 2 (Feb.–March 1933): 14–15; "The Statement of Purpose Which Brookwood Repudiated," pp. 16–17; "Brookwood Turned Right and We Left," p. 17; "Muste Quits," p. 1; "Labor Director Refutes Attack," *Brookwood Review* 11, no. 2 (May 1933): 2.

79   Elizabeth G. Evans to Temporary Finance Committee, April 14, 1933, Evans Papers. References to the demise of Brookwood are scattered throughout the Labor Temple Papers. "The Future of the CPLA," *New Republic*, Feb. 8, 1933, pp. 353–54. Editorial Comment, *New Republic*, Mar. 22, 1933, p. 143. The latter contains the quotations.
80   AJM, "Militant Progressivism?" *Modern Quarterly* 4, no. 4 (May–Aug. 1928): 332–41; James Maurer to Fannia Cohn, Mar. 23, 1933, Cohn Papers. The charge of "exaggerated ego" had been made earlier—A supporter of Arthur Calhoun asked Muste in 1929, "Do you realize how much all your activity, both political and educational, is based on personality and how risky and ephemeral this is likely to be?" ("Ainsworth" to AJM, June 19, 1929, BC, WSU, Box 25, Folder 25). "Tony" to AJM, Nov. 26, 1931, had written regarding the reorganizing of the CPLA: "You are . . . looking upon yourself as the *it*, acquiring a messionic [sic] attitude" (BC, WSU, Box 28, File 14); Fannia Cohn to "Dear Phil [Ziegler]," Feb. 27, 1933; Cohn to David Saposs, March 7, 1933; Cohn to John Brophy, March 15, 1933; Cohn to Clint Golden, Apr. 20, 1933, all in the Cohn Papers. For other opinions see Phil Ziegler to J. C. Kennedy, March 14, 1933, BC, WSU, Box 57, File 21; James Maurer to Cohn, March 23, 1933, Cohn Papers; Martin Calhoun to Arthur Calhoun, March 15, 1933, Calhoun Papers (unsorted). Clint Golden to Cohn, Feb. 27, 1933, Cohn Papers. Cara Cook reported that, when she took up a collection to give the Mustes a vacation in 1936, contributors included some who had opposed him in the Brookwood split (Cook MS, AJM, Box 1a, SCPC.) Lefkowitz, "Labor Director Refutes Attack," p. 2; Helen Starr, quoted in Hentoff, *Peace Agitator*, p. 83. Parts of later cordial exchanges between Muste and Cohn are extant in Fannia Cohn's Papers: AJM to Cohn, Dec. 26, 1951, and AJM to Cohn, Dec. 23, 1952. For Muste on the disintegration of the community, see "Sketches," p. 148.
81   Ann Davis to Elizabeth G. Evans, Aug. 2 [1933], Evans Papers.
82   AJM to Willard C. Mellin, Oct. 7, 1938, Labor Temple Papers, Box 1.
83   "Sketches," p. 148.
84   AJM, "The Christian Employer," *Labor Age* 19, no. 7 (July 1930): 11–12; AJM, "The Battle of Brooklyn," *Common Sense* 1, no. 1 (Dec. 5, 1932): 14–15. AJM to Rev. Edmund B. Chaffee, Feb. 19, 1932, Chaffee Papers; Jerome Count, "Brooklyn Edison Against the Public," *Nation*, Jan. 18, 1933, pp. 56–57; AJM et al., Letter to the Editor, *Nation*, Feb. 8, 1933, p. 150. Muste's increasing hostility toward the church establishment is also evident in his letter to the *Nation*, Jan. 14, 1931, p. 248.
85   Ann Davis to Elizabeth G. Evans, Aug. 2 [1933], Evans Papers.

Chapter IV

1   Louis Adamic, *Dynamite: The Story of Class Violence in America* (New York, 1931), pp. 427–28. In November of the same year in which Adamic wrote, Muste observed, "The whole labor situation is pretty much up in the air. Anything may happen in the period just ahead" (AJM to Elmer Cope, Nov. 10, 1931, Cope Papers, Box 7, Folder 12).
2   Sherwood Eddy to "Dear Friend," May 6, 1933, Evans Papers. For details of the case see Haywood Patterson and Earl Conrad, *Scottsboro Boy* (New York, paperback ed., 1969).
    For a time the CPLA also worked with the People's Lobby, launched in the summer of 1931 with John Dewey at its head. The Lobby existed to pressure the federal government into combat against economic disintegration. In one of its first campaigns the Lobby sent a delegation to wait on President Hoover with their plea. Muste was a delegate. Little

came of the delegation efforts. See Edmund Wilson's report on this episode, quoted in Nat Hentoff, *Peace Agitator*, (New York, 1963), p. 80, and in "Two Protests," *New Republic*, Feb. 18, 1931, pp. 251–53. John Dewey, Letter to the Editor, *New Republic*, Aug. 28, 1931, and Joseph Dorfman, *The Economic Mind in American Civilization* (New York, 1949), pp. 172, 637, also discuss the People's Lobby.

3   In the 1960s Muste was still convinced that the language of war had fitted conditions in the thirties. In support of that view it might be noted that one depression-era survey revealed that one-fourth of the unemployed felt that "a revolution might be a very good thing for this country" (Bernard Karsh and Phillips L. Garman, "The Impact of the Political Left" in *Labor and the New Deal*, ed. Milton Derber and Edwin Young [Madison, Wis., 1957, pp. 83, 84, 88]). See also A. J. Muste, "Sketches for an Autobiography" (hereafter "Sketches"), in *The Essays of A. J. Muste*, ed. Nat Hentoff (New York, 1967), pp. 162, 155. For a period Muste also chaired the short-lived Committee on International Anti-Fascist Protest. The committee attracted some attention in January 1932, when bombs mailed to Italian diplomats and Italian residents in the United States were generally assumed to be the work of anti-fascists. Muste protested that fascist forces were not above mailing the devices to discredit their enemies, although even the liberal journal, *New Republic*, doubted his arguments (A. J. Muste, Letter to the Editor, *New Republic*, Jan. 27, 1932, p. 298).

4   Karsh and Garman, "The Impact of the Political Left," pp. 86–94. Elmer Cope to AJM, Aug. 3, 1933, Cope Papers, Box 10, Folder 4.

5   Sidney Lens, *Left, Right and Center* (Hinsdale, Ill., 1949), p. 258; Brian Glick, "The Thirties: Organizing the Unemployed," *Liberation*, Sept.–Oct. 1967, p. 13; Karsh and Garman, "The Impact of the Political Left," pp. 86, 92; Eleanor Nora Kahn, "Organizations of Unemployed Workers as a Factor in the American Labor Movement" (Master's thesis, University of Wisconsin, 1934), p. 27. This contemporary student asserted in 1934 that "probably somewhere in the neighborhood of a million men and women have at one time or another taken part in the movement." When, in 1936, the three kinds of unions combined into a united front effort, they claimed a total enrollment of 800,000. Labor analyst Sidney Lens has estimated that at their peak, the unions held, in total, 150,000 to 250,000 persons. Even the highest claims represent only a fraction of the total number of unemployed workers in the United States in these years. In 1933 the figure was set conservatively at 13 million unemployed; in 1936 it was still 9 million.

6   "Sketches," pp. 156–57; AJM to Mrs. E. G. Evans, July 10, 1933. Louis Budenz, *This Is My Story* (New York, 1947), p. 98; Kahn, "Organizations of Unemployed Workers," pp. 21, 107; Editorial in *New Republic*, July 20, 1933, p. 274. For background on CPLA thinking leading up to the Ohio convention, see Elmer Cope to AJM, May 9, 1932; AJM to Cope, May 10, 1932; Cope to AJM, May 25, 1932, all in the Cope Papers, Box 8, Folder 6. Also see Cope to AJM, Nov. 11, 1932, Box 9, Folder 3, and Cope to AJM, March 24, 1933, Box 9, Folder 8, both in Cope Papers.

7   For an overview of the Musteite Leagues, see Roy Rosenzweig, "Radicals and the Jobless: The Musteites and the Unemployed Leagues, 1932–1936, *Labor History* 16 (Winter 1975): 51–77. Many details of the day to day work of the unemployed leagues in Pennsylvania may be gleaned from the Elmer Cope Papers. Karsh and Garman, "The Impact of the Political Left," pp. 86–94; Lens, *Left, Right and Center* 258–59; David J. Leah, " 'United We Eat': The Creation and Organization of the Unemployed Councils in 1930," *Labor History* 8 (Fall, 1967), 300–15; Sam Pollock, "A. J., the Musteites and the Unions," *Liberation*, Sept.–Oct. 1967, p. 19, and John Dos Passos, *In All Countries* (New York, 1934), p. 251. The National Unemployed Leagues established units in small

towns in Ohio, Pennsylvania, and West Virginia; it claimed membership in only a few cities of which Columbus, Toledo, and Pittsburgh were the main representatives (Sarah Limbach, "The Tactics of the CPLA," *World Tomorrow*, Feb. 15, 1934, pp. 90–91; Ernest R. McKinney, "A Letter from Pittsburgh," *World Tomorrow*, March 29, 1934, pp. 163–64; Arnold Johnson, Letter to the Editor, *Nation*, Nov. 22, 1933, p. 598). "Museteite Paper," quoted in Lens, *Left, Right and Center*, p. 259.

8   Glick, "Organizing the Unemployed," p. 13; McKinney, "A Letter from Pittsburgh," pp. 163–64; Elmer Cope to AJM, Feb. 22, 1933, Cope Papers, Box 9, Folder 7. Cope had written at length in an earlier letter about Communist efforts to infiltrate CPLA unemployed organizations (Cope to AJM, Nov. 20, 1932, Cope Papers, Box 9, Folder 3). From Pittsburgh the chairman of the Unemployed League of Allegheny County wrote Muste, "Another problem which we have here is the problem of watching the Socialists and preventing them from gaining control and upsetting our organization. . . . In addition to these problems," he continued, "we are kept constantly on our toes by the Communists, who are trying to embarrass us at every point." For more detail see Limbach, "The Tactics of the CPLA," p. 90–91 and McKinney, "A Letter from Pittsburgh," pp. 163–64. Muste's thinking on the Socialist Party, as of 1931, is described in some detail in AJM to Leonard Bright, Oct. 20, 1931, BC, WSU, Box 38, Folder 13; "Sketches," p. 135; Earl Browder, *Communism in the United States* (New York, 1935), pp. 183–269.

9   John Gates, quoted in Hentoff, *Peace Agitator*, p. 86; Max Schactman, Columbia Oral History Memoir no. 254, 1962–1963, pp. 219–20; Lens, *Left, Right and Center*, p. 261. Louis Budenz claimed to have originated the concept of a purely American revolutionary group (Budenz, *This Is My Story*, p. 971). The Museteites were aware that the Communist experiment in Russia had many grave flaws (AJM to Elmer Cope, Oct. 21, 1930, Box 7, Folder 1, and Muste to "Dear Comrades," Box 10, Folder 5, both in Cope Papers); Browder, *Communism in the U.S.*, p. 149.

10   "Sketches," p. 162; AJM, "An American Revolutionary Party," *Modern Quarterly*, 7, no. 12 (Jan. 1934): 713–19; Editorial, *New Republic*, Dec. 27, 1933, p. 179; Review of AJM, "Toward an American Revolutionary Labor Movement, a Statement of Programmatic Orientation by the AWP," *New Republic*, May 2, 1934, pp. 344–45; Anthony Bimba, *History of the American Working Class* (New York, 1927), p. 331.

11   AJM, "An American Revolutionary Party," passim.

12   While the behavior of the American Communist Party in this era deserved the kind of criticism that the Museteites were levelling at it, there is reason to question whether their dismissal of the entire Socialist Party as hopelessly reformist was legitimate. The left wing of that party—which was in the ascendency by this time—would seem to have shared some common ground with the Museteites. Why that ground was never explored is not clear from the available evidence; "An American Revolutionary Party," passim.

13   "Sketches," 160–61; *New Republic*, July 4, 1934, p. 193; AJM, "In the Lincoln Country," *New Republic*, Sept. 19, 1934, pp. 155–56. Muste, in the "Sketches," said that bail was set at $40,000. The July *New Republic*, however, reported that he had been released on $25,000 bond. The *Nation*, June 20, 1934, pp. 688–89 reported the bail as $4,000.

14   AJM, "The Automobile Industry and Organized Labor" (Baltimore, 1935), pp. 37–39.

15   AJM, "The Battle of Toledo," *Nation*, June 6, 1934, pp. 639–40; Karsh and Garman, "The Impact of the Political Left," p. 98.

16   "Sketches," pp. 157–60; Pollock, "Museteites and the Unions," p. 19.

17   AJM, "The Automobile Industry," p. 38; AJM, Columbia Oral History Memoir, p. 468.

18   Budenz, *This Is My Story*, p. 96; AJM, "The Automobile Industry," passim.; Browder, *Communism in the U.S.*, p. 195, 249; Karsh and Garman, "The Impact of the Political Left," p. 98.

19   Karsh and Garman, "The Impact of the Political Left," p. 100; Lens, *Left, Right and Center*, p. 259; Irving Bernstein, *The Turbulent Years* (New York, 1970), pp. 218–27. For reference to another strike reportedly initiated by a Musteite unemployed league—this one a strike of garbage collectors in Pittsburgh, which resulted in a wage increase for the workers—see Elmer Cope to AJM, March 11, 1933, Cope Papers, Box 9, File 8.

20   Sidney Fine, "The Toledo Chevrolet Strike of 1935," *Ohio Historical Quarterly* 67 (Oct. 1958): 326–56; Jack Skeels, "The Background of UAW Factionalism," *Labor History* 2 (Spring, 1962): 158–81 (On p. 163 Skeels writes that the Toledo settlement of 1935 "represented the largest single gain hitherto made by the auto workers in collective bargaining."); AJM, "The Automobile Industry," pp. 40–48.

21   Fine, "The Toledo Strike" pp. 326–56; AJM, "The Automobile Industry," p. 48.

22   AJM, "The Automobile Industry," p. 48; *Brookwood Review*, 4, no. 4 (Feb. 1926): 2; Leon Trotsky, "On the Revolutionary Intellectuals, an Open Letter to V. F. Calverton," *Modern Quarterly*, 7, no. 2 (March 1933): 82–85.

23   Karsh and Garman, "The Impact of the Political Left," pp. 99–100; Max Schactman, "Radicalism: The Trotskyist View," in *As We Saw the Thirties*, ed. Rita James Simon (Urbana, Ill., 1967), pp. 27–28.

24   George Novack, "A. J. and American Trotskyism," *Liberation* Sept.–Oct. 1967, p. 22; Arne Swabeck to "Dear Comrades," May 10, 1934, and Leon Trotsky to Comrade Swabeck, March 29, 1934, Socialist Workers' Party Papers, Reel 1. In explaining how easy it was to influence the Musteite meeting, James Cannon described Muste's followers as including some YWCA girls, Bible students, assorted intellectuals, college professors, and some non-descripts who had just wandered in through the open door" (*History of American Trotskyism* (New York, 1944), p. 177).

25   AJM, "What Mean These Strikes?" *Modern Quarterly*, 8, no. 9 (Oct. 1934): 517–21.

26   Cannon, *History of American Trotskyism*, pp. 184, 171; Novack, "A. J. and American Trotskyism," p. 22; Secretary Swabeck to the International Secretariat, to L. D. Trotsky, and "Report on Negotiations with Musteites," all in Socialist Workers' Party Papers, Reel 1.

27   Swabeck report on negotiations; Memo to all POC members, Aug. 30, 1934; and AJM to Branches, Organizers, and Members of the American Workers' Party, Oct. 30, 1934, all in Socialist Workers' Party Papers, Reel 1; "Sketches," p. 163; Budenz, *This Is My Story*, p. 99; Novack, "A. J. and American Trotskyism," p. 22. While negotiations led closer to merger, opposition grew stronger in the ranks of both groups. For several months in the fall and winter of 1934, Cannon battled with that faction led by Hugo Oehler who opposed fusion with the AWP and maintained that Muste and company were insufficiently radical. In the same period, in the AWP, Louis Budenz and J. B. S. Hardman fought Muste's inclination toward union with the Communist League of America. The tremendous amount of energy expended in these struggles was an omen of things to come.

28   Novack, "A. J. and American Trotskyism," p. 22.

29   Philip Selznick, *The Organizational Weapon* (New York, 1952), p. 168; Cannon, *History of American Trotskyism*, pp. 181, 182.

30   "Declaration of Principles and Constitution of the Workers Party of the United States," 1935, Harvard College Library.

31   AJM, "Which Party for the American Worker?" (New York, 1935), Harvard Col-

lege Library. In another article in this same period, in which Muste repeated the same themes, he described the individualist as a "conscientious objector" and independent action as "civil disobedience." Such action, he argued "is for the most part futile,"—an ironic assertion from one who would later write a classic statement "Of Holy Disobedience" (AJM, "The American Approach," clippings from a four-part article in an unidentified newspaper, May 11, 1935, AJM, Box 15, SCPC; and AJM, *Of Holy Disobedience*, Pendle Hill pamphlet, Jan. 1952, reprinted in *Not by Might*, intro. Jo Ann Robinson (New York, 1971), pp. 1–34.

32 Cannon, *History of American Trotskyism*, p. 197.

33 Ibid., p. 230; "A Final Note: The Muste Group," *Internal Bulletin*, Feb. 1936, Socialist Workers' Party Papers, Reel 1. A sample of the approach which Muste was inclined to use in enforcing the party line appears in a letter he wrote to Elmer Cope before the CPLA had been transformed. After dressing down Cope for certain organizing failures, Muste quickly added, "You understand, of course, that in all this I am not for a single minute forgetting either your many qualifications, the swell jobs you have done in many instances and the terrific sacrifices which you are making for the cause. I am writing because now that we are a real organization and proceed in an organizational manner, we want to be entirely frank with each other in matters of this kind and furthermore must all of us toe the line and submit to discipline" (AJM to Cope, Sept. 28, 1933 [dictated Sept. 26, 1933], Cope Papers, Box 10, Folder 4).

34 Novack, "A. J. and American Trotskyism," p. 22; "Sketches," pp. 163–67; Schactman, Oral Memoir no. 254, p. 254; Isaac Deutscher, *The Prophet Outcast*, pp. 271–72; Hentoff, *Peace Agitator*, p. 92.

35 "Sketches," pp. 168–69; pp. 170–71; AJM, "Statement on Attitude of W.P. to S.P. and C.P.," *Internal Bulletin*, Jan. 10, 1936, Socialist Workers' Party Papers, Reel 1; Bulletin no. 5, Jan. 20, 1936, Socialist Workers' Party Papers, Reel 2. The cablegram from Trotsky may be the one quoted in a Workers' Party Bulletin of several months later, said to be addressed to Muste and conveying the message, "unanimous prompt entry seems best way." An earlier instance of Budenz's unpredictability may be glimpsed in Muste's report in 1931 on an episode where Budenz suddenly resigned from the CPLA and then resumed his work with that group (AJM to Elmer Cope, July 27, 1931; Cope to AJM, Aug. 2, 1931; and AJM to Cope, Sept. 29, 1931, all in Cope Papers, Box 7, Folder 12).

36 AJM, "My Experience in the Labor and Radical Struggles of the Thirties," in Simon, *As We Saw the Thirties*, p. 141; Bulletin no. 2, Jan. 17, 1936, Socialist Workers' Party Papers, Reel 2; Bulletin no. 5, Jan. 23, 1936, Socialist Workers' Party Papers, Reel 2.

37 Cannon, *History of American Trotskyism*, pp. 195–96; Schactman, Oral Memoir no. 254, p. 254; Novack, "A. J. and American Trotskyism," p. 22.

38 "Sketches," pp. 164–67.

39 Ibid., p. 164; Lens, *Left, Right and Center*, pp. 262–63.

40 James O. Morris, *Conflict within the AFL* (Ithaca, 1958), pp. 126–27.

41 Thomas R. Brooks has outlined Muste's contribution to the launching of the CIO in noting the "impressive number of people" trained at Brookwood "who played leading roles in the founding of the CIO and have since filled many positions of leadership in the unions. Among them were the two Reuther brothers, Victor and Roy, Julius Hochman, vice-president of the ILGWU, Rose Pesotta, an ILGWU organizer and Clinton S. Golden, who with other Brookwood graduates, was active in the founding of the steelworkers" (*Toil and Trouble* [New York, 1964], p. 154). Joseph Rayback in *A History of American Labor* (New York, 1966), p. 318, makes a similar assertion.

42   AJM, "The Automobile Industry," pp. 54–56; AJM, "Preface to the AF of L Convention," *Nation*, Oct. 16, 1935, pp. 440–41. For a scholarly assessment of the Lewis movement, see Melvin Dubofsky and Warren Van Tine, *John L. Lewis, a Biography* (Chicago, 1977).

43   "The Goodyear Tire and Rubber Company," *Monthly Labor Review*, 42 (June, 1936): 1288–93; Sidney Fine, *Sit-Down* (Ann Arbor, Mich., 1969), pp. 123–25; Edward Levinson, *Labor on the March* (New York, 1937), pp. 143–46; Rose Pesotta, *Bread upon the Waters* (New York, 1944), pp. 195–27; AJM to Mrs. E. G. Evans (from Akron), March 18, 1936, Evans Papers.

44   Pesotta, *Bread upon the Waters*, pp. 224–25, 226. See also Ruth McKenney, *Industrial Valley* (New York, 1939), p. 366, and the Workers' Party newsletter, the *Gum Miner*, March 19 and 23, 1936, Labadie Collection, in which the rubber strike and Muste's presence at Akron are discussed.

45   AJM to Mrs. E. G. Evans, July 10, 1933; AJM to Evans, July 24, 1933; AJM to Evans, Sept. 18, 1933; Nancy Muste to Evans, Sept. 14, 1933; AJM to Evans, Sept. 18, 1934, all in the Evans Papers.

46   Tucker Smith to AJM, Dec. 21, 1933; AJM to Smith, March 6, 1934; Smith to AJM, March 13, 1934; Smith to AJM, June 21, 1934, all in BC, WSU, Box 12, Folder 2; Tucker Smith to Abraham Lefkowitz, June 28, 1934, Box 37, Folder 26; AJM to Smith, July 10, 1934, Box 12, Folder 2; Smith to AJM, July 31, 1934, Box 51, Folder 11; AJM to Smith, Aug. 31, 1934, Box 51, Folder 12; AJM to Lefkowitz, Sept. 6, 1934, Box 51, Folder 12; Lefkowitz to AJM, July 24, 1934, Box 51, folder 11, all in BC, WSU. Some money may have also supplemented the Muste's finances as a result of a fund appeal made on their behalf by Sherwood Eddy, Reinhold Niebuhr, and W. B. Spofford in 1933 (Sherwood Eddy et al. to "Dear Friend," May 6, 1933, Evans Papers).

47   Ann Davis to Mrs. E. G. Evans, Aug. 2, [1933]; AJM to Evans, Sept. 18, 1933, both in Evans Papers; AJM, "Sketches," pp. 149–49; Hentoff, *Peace Agitator*, pp. 142–43.

48   AJM to Mrs. E. G. Evans, July 10, 1933, July 24, 1933, Sept. 18, 1933, Sept. 18, 1934, Sept. 21, 1934, Sept. 12, 1935, Sept. 24, 1935, Sept. 25, 1934, April 22, 1936, and April 30, 1936, all in Evans Papers; Nancy Muste to Evans, Sept. 14, 1933, and Jan. 3, 1936; Evans to AJM, Sept. 12, 1933, Sept. 20, 1934, Sept. 23, 1935, Jan. 9, 1936, Jan. 31, 1936, March 20, 1936, and April 24, 1936, Evans to Nancy Muste, Sept. 18, 1933, and Jan. 9, 1936; Ann Davis to Evans, Aug. 2, 1933; Evans to AJM, April 1, 1935, and Jan. 9, 1936, all in Evans Papers.

49   AJM to Mrs. E. G. Evans, March 27, 1935; Evans to AJM, April 1, 1935; and Evans to AJM, Sept. 24, 1935. On March 18, 1936, Muste wrote Mrs. Evans congratulating her on her recent eightieth birthday.

50   AJM to Mrs. E. G. Evans, Sept. 12, 1935.

51   AJM, "The Automobile Industry."

52   Cara Cook and Doris Prenner to "Dear [ ]," April [ ], 1936, Evans Papers; Cara Cook MS., AJM, Box 1a, SCPC; Novack, "A. J. and American Trotskyism," p. 22; AJM, "My Experience in the Struggles," p. 145; Milton Mayer, quoted in Hentoff, *Peace Agitator*, p. 94. The Muste children stayed beyind in the Bronx apartment. Nancy was working part time at Macy's. A family friend looked in on them from time to time through the summer and they, in the words of the eldest daughter, "spent a lot of time playing monopoly with some young men from . . . some Socialist faction" (Nancy Baker to the author, Nov. 19, 1971).

53   Milton Mayer, "The Christer," *Fellowship*, Jan. 1952, p. 7.

Chapter V

1   Isaac Deutscher, *The Prophet Outcast* (N.Y. Vintage ed., 1963), pp. 292–95; AJM, "Sketches for an Autobiography" (hereafter "Sketches"), in *The Essays of A. J. Muste*, ed. Nat Hentoff (New York, 1967), pp. 105, 168; AJM, "My Experience in the Labor and Radical Struggles of the Thirties," in Rita J. Simon, ed., *As We Saw the Thirties* (Urbana, 1967), p. 146.

2   Cara Cook MS., AJM, Box 1a, SCPC.

3   Cara Cook MS. For contrasting later impressions see AJM, quoted in Nat Hentoff, *Peace Agitator* (New York: 1963), p. 95.

4   AJM, "My Experience in the Struggles," p. 146. In this source Muste states that Trotsky did admit the wrongness of the French Turn. In Hentoff Muste says that the party leader said "perhaps" the Turn had been inappropriate in America (Hentoff, *Peace Agitator*, 95–96). "Sketches," p. 169.

5   AJM, "My Experience in the Struggles," p. 146.

6   Ibid.; AJM, "Fragment of Autobiography," typed manuscript, 1939, p. 4, AJM, SCPC.

7   AJM, "Fragment of Autobiography," n.d. [probably 1939], pp. 4–5, AJM, Box 2, SCPC. Hentoff, in *Peace Agitator*, tells this story in the plural, with Anna Muste present. The fragment relates that only A. J. Muste walked into St. Sulpice. Charles Chatfield, *For Peace and Justice* (Knoxville, 1971), p. 3.

8   "Fragment of Autobiography," pp. 6–7. The complete Thompson poem may be found in Oscar Williams, ed., *Immortal Poems of the English Language* (Pocket Library, paperback ed., 1957), pp. 476–81.

9   John Muste, quoted in Hentoff, p. 148. Quaker scholars Rufus Jones and Howard Brinton have both observed in their studies of mysticism how the mystic often emerges from his inward seeking with new powers and capabilities. He not only, as Jones said, "stands the world better but he becomes a better organ and bearer of spiritual forces" (Rufus Jones, *New Studies in Mystical Religion* [New York, 1928], p. 20). Also see Howard H. Brinton, *Ethical Mysticism in the Society of Friends*, Pendle Hill Pamphlet no. 156, 1967.

10   Untitled manuscript, n.d., AJM, Box 3a, SCPC; AJM to Kirby Page, Sept. 2, 1936, Page Papers.

11   Untitled MS., pp. 7, 8, 10, 13, 14. Muste's conclusion that Marxist organizations were unconscious and perverted expressions of a religious motive force was in keeping with the psycho-sociological hypotheses advanced by other observers, including the ex-Trotskyist Nicolai Berdaeyev and the leftist British authors J. Middleton Murray and Aldous Huxley, all of whose work Muste read around this time. How much his conversion may have been influenced by such reading cannot be determined, however, as it is not known whether he read these authors before or after his St. Sulpice experience; "The True International," *Christian Century*, May 24, 1939, reprinted in the *Essays of A. J. Muste*, pp. 207–14. Muste admitted that the church in its contemporary form was imperfect but he believed that it would evolve beyond its imperfections. He could not entertain similar hopes for Marxist institutions because they were not in harmony with "the essential nature, the heart of the universe." Untitled MS., p. 14.

12   Untitled MS., pp. 15–16.

13   See Doris Prenner to Tucker Smith, Sept. 27, 1934, BC, WSU, Box 51, Folder 12 for an indication that Muste and Smith had a personal meeting on this matter. In an angry letter to the Brookwood board after he returned, Muste wrote, "One of the first things I learned on getting back a couple days ago was that no check nor any other communication had been received by the children, that what I had promised Anne and them would

not happen (viz. duns for the rent being given them) had happened." He stressed that the family's financial situation was "pretty desperate." He was even faced with the prospect of having to hitch-hike to Michigan to visit his ailing eighty-year-old mother (AJM to Smith, Aug. 23, 1936, BC, WSU, Box 12, Folder 2; AJM to John Nevin Sayre, Sept. 16, 1936, in unsorted FOR: SCP; "Fragment of Autobiography," pp. 5–6; AJM to Kirby Page, Sept. 2, 1936, Page Papers).

14   Schactman, Columbia Oral History Memoir no. 254, 1962–1963, p. 256; George Novack, "A. J. and American Trotskyism," *Liberation*, Sept.–Oct. 1967, p. 24; James Cannon, *History of American Trotskyism*, (New York, 1944), pp. 198–99; AJM, "My Experience in the Struggles," p. 146; Novack, "A. J. and American Trotskyism," p. 24.

15   Novack, "A. J. and American Trotskyism," p. 24; George Novack, ed., *Their Morals and Ours: Marxist Versus Liberal Views on Morality* (New York, 1966) indicates the contempt in which Novack held other defectors from the Trotskyist ranks; Novack, Foreword to *Their Morals and Ours*; Novack, "A. J. and American Trotskyism," p. 24. Muste had been equally willing to speak out for the civil liberties of the leader whom he had repudiated, when Trotsky was made prime defendant, *in absentia*, in the Stalinist purge trials. In contrast, as Isaac Deutscher has shown, many American and European intellectuals (many of whom later became avid anti-communists) supported the trials and denounced defenses of Trotsky as unwarranted interference in the Soviet Union's affairs. Muste was one of the relatively few observers who could balance his distaste for Trotskyism with a judicious concern for the rights of Leon Trotsky (Deutscher, *The Prophet Outcast*, pp. 360–95; and AJM, "Is Leon Trotsky Guilty?" *Monthly Quarterly* 10, [March, 1937]: 4–7). Of the twelve persons polled for this article on Trotsky's guilt or non-guilt, four respondents were uncertain, three believed him guilty, and five, including Muste, declared his innocence. Muste's old colleague in liberal politics, John Dewey, chaired a Commission of Inquiry in Mexico City in 1937 which found Trotsky not guilty (Deutscher, *The Prophet Outcast*, pp. 360–82).

16   AJM to John Nevin Sayre, Sept. 17, 1936, in personal Sayre Papers.

17   "Northover Conference" *Fellowship*, Oct. 1936, p. 13.

18   On the Wyomising walkout see *New York Times*, Oct. 4, 1936, p. 39; and Oct. 5, 1936, p. 17; Herbert G. Bohn, "We Tried Non-violence," *Fellowship*, Jan. 1937, pp. 7–8; *New York Times*, Dec. 1, p. 5; Dec. 3, p. 4; Dec. 6, p. 12; and Dec. 10, p. 4, all in 1936; "Report of A. J. Muste, Field and Industrial Secretary," to the FOR conference, Sept. 10–12, 1937, FOR, SCPC; *New York Times*, Jan. 10, p. 35; Jan. 14, p. 14; Jan. 15, p. 5, all in 1937; AJM, "Sit Down and Lie Downs," *Fellowship*, March 1937, pp. 5–6, reprinted in the *Essays of A. J. Muste*, pp. 203–6; Reference to the other labor episodes may be found in AJM, "Report to FOR."

19   AJM, "Fragment of Autobiography," pp. 5–6; Edmund B. Chaffee, "Communism or Fascism: Must We Choose?," *Fellowship*, Nov. 1936, pp. 7–9.

20   Much of the information on Labor Temple included here was first published in the *Journal of Presbyterian History* 48, No. 1 (Spring 1970): 18–37. Norman Thomas to Theodore Savage, Nov. 30, 1936; Henry Sloan Coffin to Savage, Jan. 18, 1937; Savage to Coffin, Jan. 16, 1937, all in the Labor Temple Papers, Box 1.

21   AJM to Rev. Dr. E. Graham Wilson, Board of National Missions, May 26, 1937, Labor Temple Papers, Box 1.

22   "Muste to Labor Temple" *Time Magazine*, May 10, 1937, p. 49; Editorial in *Presbyterian*, June 17, 1937.

23   AJM, "A Survey of Labor Temple, New York," Dec. 1940, Labor Temple Papers, Box 3. On the founder of Labor Temple, Charles Stelzle, see his autobiography, *A Son of*

the Bowery (New York, 1926), pp. 117–33 deal with the Labor Temple. Also see George H. Nash III, "Charles Stelzle, Apostle to Labor," *Labor History*, 11 (Spring 1970): 151–174. Muste had been in contact with Labor Temple at least since 1926 (AJM to Charles Stelzle, Nov. 22, 1926, BC, WSU, Box 55, File 2). See also AJM, "A Survey of Labor Temple," Dec. 1940, for further discussion of the open forum tradition. Also see John M. Stuart, "The Presbyterian Church and Labor, 1900–1945" (Master's Thesis, Princeton, 1970).

24 AJM, "Does the Church Care?" *Pageant Magazine*, Oct. 1938.

25 Announcement of a lecture to be delivered at Labor Temple by AJM during 1937, entitled "Are the Intellectuals Getting Religion," Labor Temple Papers, Box 1; AJM, "The Future of Labor Temple," *Presbyterian Tribune*, Sept. 2, 1937; AJM, "The Situation and Program of Christianity," *Religion in Life*, Spring 1939, pp. 224–26; AJM, "Winning Industrial Workers to Christ and His Program," manuscript n.d. [probably 1937 or 1938], AJM, Box 3a, SCPC; AJM, "Beyond Marxism," *Fellowship*, Oct. 1937, pp. 9–13; AJM, "The Church and the Politico-Economic Situation," *The Church Faces the World*, ed. Samuel McCrea Cavert (New York, 1939), pp. 94–102.

26 AJM to Mrs. Andrew Carnegie, May 21, 1940, Labor Temple Papers, Box 3.

27 Announcement of courses to be offered at Labor Temple in 1938, Labor Temple Papers, Box 1; AJM, "Beyond Marxism," pp. 9–13; AJM to Morris Gordin, April 6, 1939; Gordin to Dr. William Adams Brown, March 11, 1939; AJM to Brown, March 24, 1939, all in Labor Temple Papers, Box 2.

28 AJM to Eugene Lyons, Dec. 15, 1937, Labor Temple Papers, Box 1; Lyons to AJM, Dec. 16, 1937, Labor Temple Papers, Box 1.

29 AJM, SCPC, Box 2; AJM, "Sermon on the Mount," manuscript lecture notes, March 20, 1938, AJM, Box 2, SCPC. The biblical reference to those who buy the poor for silver is from Amos 8:4–8; AJM, lecture notes: "Jesus as a Revolutionary," March 6, 1938; "Sloan House," March 6, 1938; "Sermon on the Mount," March 20, 1938, all in AJM, Box 2, SCPC; AJM, quoted in *Jamestown Post*, Jan. 19, 1939; AJM, "Sit Down," manuscript lecture notes, April 4, 1937, AJM, Box 2, SCPC; "Greetings by A. J. Muste, Director at Labor Temple, Candle Light and Carol Service, Dec. 26, 1947," manuscript, AJM, Box 1, SCPC.

30 AJM to Miss Lucy Pell, Greensboro, N.C., Feb. 2, 1940, Labor Temple Papers, Box 3.

31 "Report of Director to Labor Temple Committee for April 1940," p. 4, Labor Temple Papers, Box 3.

32 AJM to Miss Clarina Michaelson, Labor Temple Papers, Box 1; AJM to Theodore C. Speers, Jan. 17, 1940, Labor Temple Papers, Box 3. AJM to Mrs. Laura T. Huyck, Nov. 29, 1937; AJM to Dr. Jesse M. Bader, Dec. 8, 1937; AJM to William E. Sweet, Feb. 18, 1939, all in Labor Temple Papers, Box 1; AJM to Rev. Ralph N. Mould, Sept. 14, 1937, Labor Temple Papers, Box 1; AJM, "The Church and the Politico-Economic Situation," p. 94–102. For an unfavorable review of Muste and the Preaching Mission see Oscar L. Rousseau, executive secretary of the Central Patriotic Committee, Wichita, Kansas, "Radicalism in the Preaching Mission," clipping, n.d., n.p., AJM, SCPC Scrapbook. Merle Miller wrote the favorable report: "Around the Town," Iowa State newspaper clipping, AJM, SCPC Scrapbook.

33 AJM to Rev. Leon Rossen Land, Nov. 22, 1938, Labor Temple Papers, Box 2. During this period Muste also offered a course at the Central Community Training School of Union Theological Seminary and gave six-week courses on "The Christian in Our Present Day World" at Union Theological Seminary and Yale Divinity School. He also

appeared on a program with Paul Tillich and Walter Van Kirk at Crozier Theological Seminary, speaking on the topic of "The Gospel and the Economic Crisis" (James Myers to AJM, April 27, 1938, AJM, Box 1, SCPC).
34   AJM to Abraham Lefkowitz, Sept. 9, 1937, Labor Temple Papers, Box 1; AJM to Dr. Arthur W. Calhoun, Dec. 4, 1937, Labor Temple Papers, Box 1; Minutes of Labor Temple Committee, Dec. 14, 1937, Labor Temple Papers, Box 1; Nancy Muste Baker to the author, Feb. 8, 1979, and John Muste to the author, Feb. 6, 1979.
35   "Sketches," pp. 28–29.

Chapter VI

1   Merle Curti, *Peace or War, the American Struggle 1636–1946* (Boston, 1959), chaps. 7 and 9; Charles Chatfield, *For Peace and Justice* (Knoxville, Tenn., 1971), Part Two; Charles DeBenedetti, *Origins of the Modern American Peace Movement, 1915–1929* (New York, 1978), passim.
2   Later, in the era of the War in Vietnam, Muste saw (and contributed to) the beginnings of the massive movement of resistance which developed against U.S. involvement in that conflict, but he died before the movement reached its peak.
3   AJM, *Nonviolence in an Aggressive World* (New York, 1940), p. 143; Letter to the Editor, *New York Times*, typescript, Jan. 3, 1938, AJM, SCPC; AJM, "Another War to Save Democracy?" *Fellowship*, Jan. 1937 pp. 3–6; AJM et al., *Pacifism and Aggression*, FOR pamphlet, n.d. [1939?], AJM, Box 15, SCPC.
4   *Times* letter of Jan. 3, 1938.
5   AJM, *Nonviolence*, pp. 147–48, 129–30.
6   Clippings from the *New York Times*, Dec. 5, 1938, and April 18, 1938; and from *New Religious Frontiers*, Dec. 1, 1938, in AJM Scrapbook, SCPC. Also see proposal from United Pacifist Committee, Oct. 11, 1938, AJM, Box 1, SCPC.
7   AJM, *Nonviolence*, p. 157.
8   Ibid., pp. 136, 158.
9   AJM, *Nonviolence*, pp. 161–64. Muste developed this argument with reference especially to Spain where, he believed, the Loyalists should have opted for nonviolent non-cooperation rather than civil war. He also noted that "the little nation which happens to enlist our sympathies is never the stainless virgin we imagine her to be," offering Chiang Kai-shek in China as an example. (His use of the term "little" in this context was not quite accurate!) Muste further observed the inconsistency with which American sympathies could be raised or withheld: "If we should go to war to free Finland from Russia," he asked, "why not go to war to free 350 millions in India from British rule?"
10   Milton Mayer, "The Christer," *Fellowship*, Jan. 1952, pp. 1–10.
11   AJM, "Shadow over Europe," *Presbyterian Tribune*, Oct. 12, 1939; AJM, "Hitler-Stalin Pact, *Presbyterian Tribune*, Sept. 14, 1939; AJM, *Nonviolence*, pp. 135–37.
12   AJM, "Analysis of Hitler's Reply to Roosevelt," typescript, n.d. [1938?], AJM, Box 1, SCPC; AJM, *Nonviolence*, pp. 153–54.
13   AJM, *Nonviolence*, pp. 133, 62.
14   Ibid., pp. 28–29.
15   "Cash and carry" legislation in 1939 enabled Allied nations to buy war materials from the United States if they could pay cash and transport them in their own ships.

This represented a departure from previously strict neutrality policies. On the United Pacifist Committee see AJM to E. Raymond Wilson, Feb. 10, 1938, Labor Temple Papers, Box 1; AJM to Miss Ethel Jensen, May 25, 1939, Labor Temple Papers, Box 2; AJM Day Letter to FDR, Oct. 6, 1937, AJM, Box 16, SCPC; United Pacifist proposal; *New York Times*, Jan. 5, 1938; *New Religious Frontiers* clipping; and AJM, "Valley of Decision," *Presbyterian Tribune*, Sept. 28, 1939.

16   AJM to Mrs. Malcolm Forbes, Oct. 28, 1938, and "News Release," Sept. 15, 1938, both in Labor Temple Papers, Box 1; AJM to Miss Ethel Jensen, May 25, 1939, Labor Temple Papers, Box 2.

17   John Nevin Sayre to AJM, June [13 or 18 ?] 1940, AJM, Box 1, SCPC; Correspondence regarding the search for an FOR executive is extensive and divided between AJM, SCPC, Box 1, and Labor Temple Papers, Box 3. See also John Swomley, "John Nevin Sayre," *Fellowship*, June 1978, p. 9, and Jan.–Feb. 1979, p. 11. On salary arrangements, etc., see FOR Executive Committee minutes, July 16, 1940 (microfilm), SCPC.

The question was definitely one of where Muste would feel most effective in the coming years, rather than one of possible financial gain. By going to the FOR he would lose the rent-free apartment at Labor Temple and the privilege he had there of keeping all extra money he earned from lecturing and teaching. While the Fellowship offer would give him $400 a year more than his current $3,600 salary, it restricted his outside earnings to $500 and provided no living quarters.

18   Muste's letter of resignation pointed out that, while he continued to hold a positive attitude toward Labor Temple, his pacifist convictions now required a more single-minded devotion to anti-war work than he could pursue at the Temple. Undoubtedly memories of the unfortunate results of trying to balance his devotion to Brookwood with his activist commitment to the CPLA reinforced this decision. And while he did not regard his departure from Labor Temple as a departure from the Church ("I think of the [FOR] as, in essence, if not in outward form, an arm of the church," he wrote) he clearly was aware of the greater limitations he would have faced by staying within the Presbyterian bureaucracy rather than moving to an avowedly pacifist organization. Opportunities he had found in the late thirties to urge the establishment church in a pacifist direction were not many or major. He advocated war resistance in an address to the General Synod of the Reformed Church in America in 1937 ("The Church's Responsibility for Peace," June 17, 1937, AJM, Box 15, SCPC); wrote arguments against "increased armaments, conscription and industrial mobilization" into a Labor Sunday Message for the Federal Council of Churches which was read from pulpits around the country in 1938 (James Myers to AJM, April 28, 1938, AJM, Box 1, SCPC); and helped in this same period to oust an editor of the *Presbyterian Tribune* whose military bias was especially marked. Then Muste became part of the editorial board which temporarily took over the paper (AJM to J. A. MacCallum, Nov. 26, 1938; AJM to Phillips Elliott, Nov. 25, 1938; AJM to Rev. Roy F. Jenney, D.D., Nov. 29, 1938; and related correspondence, all in Labor Temple Papers, Box 2). But the stance of the new editorial board fell short of absolute pacifism.

On the resignation from Labor Temple see AJM "To Members of the Labor Temple Committee and of the Church Extension Committee, Presbytery of New York," July 19, 1940, and AJM to Theodore Savage, July 11, 1940, both in Labor Temple Papers, Box 3.

19   Some of his Temple associates declared themselves "shocked" at the resignation. Theodore Savage described Muste's departure as "tragic and pathetic." Telegram from George Richards to AJM, July 21, 1940, Labor Temple Papers, Box 3; Savage to AJM, June 1940, AJM, SCPC, Box 1; Abraham Stone to AJM, July 17, 1940, AJM, Box 1, SCPC.

Contrary to the impression under which Douglas Herron, "The Story of Labor Temple" (Master's thesis, Princeton, 1956) wrote and which is conveyed as well in "A New Proposal for Labor Temple," unsigned manuscript, n.d., in *Labor Temple Papers*, Box 3, Labor Temple was reported in "good shape" when Muste resigned. Herron and the manuscript assert, to quote from the latter, that Muste "had little response to the program he sought to promote." It is the impression of this author that, on the contrary, the period of Muste's directorship had been a period of growth, as is indicated in his final report, "A Survey of Labor Temple, New York. Prepared by A. J. Muste, Dec. 1940," Labor Temple Papers, Box 3. Prior to that report there were numerous reports and letters announcing new growth and strength. On the period immediately following Muste's departure, see "Report of Lawrence Hosie," Dec. 16, 1942, Labor Temple Papers, Box 1.

20   John Nevin Sayre, "A. J. Muste, Fighting Reconciler," *Fellowship*, March 1967, pp. 11–12; John Swomley, "John Nevin Sayre," pp. 6–9, 10–13. The dual secretaryship ended in October 1946 when Sayre became international secretary of the United States FOR.

21   Chatfield, *For Peace and Justice*, pp. 244–301; AJM, "Comments on General Perspective and Program," April 10, 1942, FOR, Box 16, SCPC.

22   FOR Executive Committee Minutes, July 16, 1940 (microfilm), SCPC.

23   In general historians seem warranted in comparing conditions for dissidents in World War II favorably to those that prevailed in World War I. Wartime hysteria and fervent patriotism did not flourish in the forties as they had in the teens. Nonetheless some excesses occurred. Two cases that became notable for Muste involved his young friend David Dellinger in the summer of 1942 and a young soldier not personally known to Muste stationed in Camp Roberts, California, in 1945. When Dellinger completed a year's sentence for refusing to register for the draft, he went before a Selective Service Appeal Board to be classified as a conscientious objector. The Board refused his claim and included in their ruling a remarkable diatribe against conscientious objection, in the spirit of what later generations would call "America—love it or leave it." Muste vigorously protested. Even more alarming was the case of Private Henry Weber at Camp Roberts who was court-martialed when he refused to participate in drill and was sentenced to hang. The sentence was subsequently commuted to life and then to five years. Again, Muste let his shock and objections be known (AJM to Francis Biddle, June 17, 1942, in Memorandum to National Council and Staff; AJM to Henry Stimson, Feb. 13, 1945; "Private Weber," clipping from the *San Francisco Chronicle*, Feb. 15, 1945, all in FOR, Box 16, SCPC).

On the other side of the coin was Muste's experience when—to forestall charges of subversion—he invited the FBI to monitor a conference of peace groups. The Bureau turned down the invitation, replying that its agents were thoroughly familiar with these groups and "would really prefer not to sit through the conference, thanks just the same" (SCPC, Consultative Peace Council, Box 1, "Snubbed by Golly," clipping from *Reporter*, Jan. 1, 1944).

24   On origins of the WRL see Chatfield, *For Peace and Justice*, pp. 106–7 and Lawrence Wittner, *Rebels against War* (New York, 1969), p. 12. For Muste's concerns see AJM to George Houser, June 6, 1942, FOR, Box 8, SCPC, and AJM to John Swomley, Aug. 12, 1944, FOR, Box 11, SCPC.

25   Clipping from Rochester *Times Union*, May 25, 1938, AJM, SCPC Scrapbook. AJM to Mrs. Lucille B. Milner, Oct. 30, 1940, FOR, Box 16, SCPC.

26   John Nevin Sayre to Frederick Libby, July 15, 1943, FOR, Box 21, SCPC; AJM to Frederick Libby, Aug. 31, 1943, FOR, Box 20, SCPC; AJM to Shirley Walowitz, Oct. 14,

1943, FOR, Box 20, SCPC; AJM to George Paine, March 21, 1944, FOR, Box 20, SCPC. The "reactionary interests" to whom Muste referred included Harrison Spangler, chairman of the National Republican Committee; General Wood, former president of America First; Clare Hoffman, "labor baiting Congressman," and "Patterson McCormick Press interests" (AJM, Personal Memorandum, Feb. 28, 1944, and AJM, John Nevin Sayre, and John Swomley to "Dear Friend," Aug. 20, 1943, both in FOR, Box 20, SCPC.

27 Dorothy Hutchinson to AJM, April 30, 1944; AJM to Hutchinson, May 11, 1944, FOR, Box 20, SCPC. A particularly hurtful rift over the Peace Now Movement issue developed between Muste and members of the Boston chapter of the FOR (Valerie H. Riggs et al. to AJM, April 6, 1944; AJM to Mrs. F. B. Riggs, April 14, 1944; and AJM to George Paine, March 21, 1944, all in FOR, Box 20, SCPC).

28 "Pacifists Want Peace, but When?" March 15, 1944; "Pacifists and Peace Now," April 19, 1944; "Pacifism Disintegrating," April 26, 1944; and "Mr. Muste Explains," May 17, 1944, all in *Christian Century*; AJM to Caleb Foote, May 9, 1944, FOR, Box 9, SCPC. In this letter Muste wrote, "In many ways I regard this issue as more fundamental and serious for the pacifist movement than the whole NSBRO [National Service Board for Religious Objectors] business. . . . We can recover from a lot of mistakes in connection with alternative service. We could not recover from once getting the pacifist movement identified in the public mind with appeasement, ultra-nationalism, imperialism, labor baiting etc."

29 See Wittner, *Rebels against War*, pp. 70–71; *Presbyterian Tribune*, March 1941.

30 See AJM's testimony before the Military Affairs Committee of the United States Senate, July 22, 1941, FOR, Box 11, SCPC.

31 AJM, *World Task of Pacifism*, Pendle Hill, 1941, pp. 30–31.

32 AJM, Report on Tour, Sept. 11–Oct. 18, 1941, FOR Executive Committee Minutes (microfilm), SCPC. AJM to Evan Thomas, Nov. 6, 1941, and AJM to Evan Thomas, Nov. 18, 1941, both in FOR, Box 11, SCPC.

33 AJM to James P. Alter, Oct. 17, 1940, AJM, Box 1, SCPC. When Muste felt that a draft-age youth was not mature enough to handle the strain of being a non-registrant, he counselled the youth to register (AJM to Mrs. Ernest G. Stillman, Dec. 10, 1940, AJM, Box 16, SCPC). He also noted in a letter to the *New York Times*, Dec. 3, 1940, that he never pressured young men to resist the draft: "Out of several hundred young men of draft age in the Fellowship who may have known my personal views, practically all registered and this includes all the young men who were on the employed staff of the Fellowship and who might have been most 'under the influence' of its secretaries."

34 FOR untitled pamphlet summarizing the Union cases, Nov. 19, 1940, FOR, Box 16, SCPC; "July 1–July 4, 1941," in *Fellowship*, July 1941, pp. 115–16.

35 AJM to the editor, *New York Times*, Dec. 3, 1940; Reinhold Niebuhr to DeWitte Wyckoff, Nov. 18, 1940; AJM to Niebuhr, Dec. 23, 1940; Niebuhr to AJM, Dec. 26, 1940; AJM to Niebuhr, Jan. 10, 1941; Niebuhr to AJM, Jan. 3, 1941, all in FOR, Box 18, SCPC.

36 AJM, "Why I Cannot Register," April 3, 1942, AJM, Box 9, SCPC. Muste wrote to Clarence Pickett of the American Friends' Service Committee (March 4, 1943, FOR, Box 10, SCPC): "The drawing of the distinction between religious and non-religious conscientious objector's was one of the reasons for my own personal stand against conforming at any point to the requirements of the law." Two years earlier Muste, Sayre, and Evan Thomas had issued a joint declaration that, had they been of draft age when the first national day of registration occurred, they would have refused to cooperate (John Swomley, "John Nevin Sayre," *Fellowship*, Jan.–Feb. 1979, p. 11).

37 AJM to Mrs. Helen Smiley, July 22, 1944, FOR, Box 10, SCPC; AJM to S. C. Morgan, May 13, 1942, FOR, Box 17, SCPC. John Muste to the author, Feb. 6, 1979; AJM to

Albert Livezey, March 12, 1942, FOR, Box 15, SCPC; AJM to Lloyd M. Crosgrave, Feb. 5, 1940, Labor Temple Papers, Box 3. With the latter correspondent he discussed "the incident of Jesus taking pains to insure the welfare of his mother by putting her in the care of John." The counterpoint to this, Muste noted, was that "in the garden . . . Jesus quite clearly indicated—when he told Peter to put up his sword—that he would not use the sword to defend those who were dependent on him any more than himself."

38   AJM to Werner C. Baum, Feb. 6, 1943, FOR, Box 7, SCPC. Writing to Arle Brooks (May 24, 1943, FOR, Box 17, SCPC) Muste said, "I have been carrying the card with the following written on the back: 'as a conscientious objector to war I refused to register voluntarily and received this card after having been registered under protest.' " He continued, "I felt completely . . . subject to the will of God in refusing to register. . . . I have not been able to feel the same compulsion" with regard to carrying the card. He added that the possibility of being detained for not carrying it while travelling might seriously interfere with his work for the FOR but he left open the chance of "circumstances arising where I might feel that I had to throw the card away."

39   AJM, "Reflections on Problems of c.o.'s in Prison," typescript for *Fellowship* issue, Dec. 1943, in AJM, Box 9, SCPC.

40   Murphy and Taylor were subsequently joined by a third resister, George Kingsley. See AJM to Franklin Roosevelt, March 9, 1943, AJM, Box 16, SCPC; Wittner, *Rebels against War*, pp. 86–87; AJM to Rufus Jones, March 14, 1943, FOR, Box 18, SCPC.

41   AJM to James V. Bennett, Sept. 24, 1943; Bennett to AJM, Oct. 1, 1943; AJM to Bennett, Oct. 14, 1943, all in FOR, Box 18, SCPC. See also Wittner, *Rebels against War*, pp. 87–89; AJM, "Thoughts on the CO Situation in Lewisburg," n.d., FOR, Box 19, SCPC; AJM to Mrs. Caroline B. Lovett, Nov. 24, 1943, FOR, Box 19, SCPC.

42   AJM, "Thoughts on the CO Situation"; AJM to Lovett, Nov. 24, 1943. Muste emphasized the importance of a scale of priorities: "No human being can take upon himself the righting of all the wrongs in the world," and he questioned whether censorship regulations should call forth the same kind of extreme action that might be warranted by such issues as "Indian independence, the extermination of the Jews, Jim Crow, the continuation of war itself."

43   "From Lewisburg Penitentiary," Dec. 5, 1943, FOR, Box 19, SCPC; AJM, "Thoughts on the CO Situation."

44   On the issue of pay Muste took the position that men who wanted it should be entitled to ask for the same compensation as soldiers received. However, he hoped that "large numbers of men . . . will not accept" a government salary and would thus remain, in respect to finances, free of federal control. He was adamant that the member organizations of NSBRO should not campaign for payment to CPS assignees from federal sources. On the other hand, Muste supported proposals for government support of the dependents of co's but stipulated that such support should come directly from the U.S. Treasury (as did army dependency allowances) and not from the wages of war resisters hired out to private employers. Muste vigorously objected to such employment of co's (AJM to Thomas E. Martin, Nov. 8, 1943, FOR, Box 13, SCPC; AJM to Werner C. Baum, Feb. 26, 1943, FOR, Box 7, SCPC; and AJM to Frank Olmstead, June 10, 1943, FOR, Box 10, SCPC. For discussion of the perspectives which wives of co's held on this issue see Heather T. Frazer and John O'Sullivan, "Forgotten Women of World War II: Wives of Conscientious Objectors in Civilian Public Service," *Peace and Change*, Fall 1978, pp. 46–51.

45   AJM to Philip Iseley, Sept. 4, 1942, FOR, Box 13, SCPC; AJM to John Haynes Holmes, Dec. 18, 1942, FOR, Box 8, SCPC; AJM to Donovan Smucker, June 2, 1944, FOR, Box 10, SCPC. In this letter Muste spoke of "the inner emptiness and frustration of many of the pacifists in CPS and in prison. . . . My heart has been

sometimes thrown almost into despair over some of their cases." See also AJM to W. H. Row, March 22, 1943, FOR, Box 13, SCPC. AJM to Karl Olsen, Dec. 23, 1942, FOR, Box 13, SCPC. Muste did back the walkouts of those men "who have come to hold the absolutist position and would not register if they had it to do over" (AJM to Caleb Foote, Dec. 12, 1942, FOR, Box 8, SCPC; and to Evan Thomas, Aug. 24, 1942, FOR, Box 11, SCPC). Muste was also quick to call for legal and other support for men once they had walked out. He expressed alarm when he learned that in Northern California the Service Board for Conscientious Objectors refused to allow its lawyers to represent "walkouts" even when the lawyers offered to do it as individuals and not in conjunction with the Board. "A situation where no pacifist agency exists to counsel with and help men who get involved with the law is fundamentally wrong," declared Muste to Philip Jacob, Sept. 2, 1943, FOR, Box 13, SCPC.

46   AJM to Evan Thomas, Aug. 11, 1942, FOR, Box 13, SCPC; AJM to Arthur Swift, Aug. 4, 1942, FOR, Box 13, SCPC; AJM to Edwin Brown, Dec. 4, 1942, FOR, Box 7, SCPC.

47   AJM, "Memorandum for May 1943 Council Meeting, on FOR Relationship to CPS, etc.," FOR, Box 13, SCPC. Efforts by pacifist groups to enrich CPS programs with special study groups, lecture series, etc., had by and large failed, adding, no doubt, to Muste's disillusionment with the camps. See Mulford Sibley and Philip Jacob, *Conscription of Conscience* (New York, 1952), p. 191; and FOR, Box 13, SCPC, regarding AJM at Powellsville, Maryland Camp, Spring 1944.

48   AJM, writing to Norman Whitney (June 6, 1944, FOR, Box 10, SCPC) noted: "I even drafted the motion for remaining in." A similar struggle was occurring within the American Friends' Service Committee from where Rufus Jones wrote to Muste (Jan. 9, 1944, FOR, Box 8, SCPC): "I should personally have preferred to have the AFSC break off its relations with NSBRO but it was plainly the judgement of the Executive Board of AFSC to continue for another year and there was nothing for me to do but acquiesce to that decision." See also AJM to Chris Ahrens, Jan. 13, 1944, FOR, Box 13, SCPC; AJM to Robert Morgan, June 15, 1944, FOR, Box 20, SCPC; and AJM to the editors, *Fellowship*, July 19, 1944, typescript, FOR, Box 19, SCPC.

49   David Dellinger et al. to "Dear Friends," Feb. 3, 1944, FOR, Box 19, SCPC; AJM to Dellinger, April 4, 1944, FOR, Box 9, SCPC.

50   AJM to Mrs. Ferner Nuhn, July 19, 1944, FOR, Box 9, SCPC; AJM to Denny Wilcher, Aug. 14, 1944, FOR, Box 20, SCPC, Dellinger et al. to "Dear Friends," June 3, 1944, FOR, Box 19, SCPC. Such sentiments were not unique to the men in Lewisburg. John Swomley wrote from Washington, D.C., that in some pacifist circles there the FOR position on NSBRO and related issues was being used to discredit the organization, and that "several times I have heard the comment that A. J. is becoming reactionary" (Swomley to Sayre, Jan. 31, 1945, unsorted FOR, SCPC).

51   AJM to David Dellinger, July 5, 1944, FOR, Box 9, SCPC.

52   AJM to Evan Thomas, Jan. 20, 1944, FOR, Box 11, SCPC; AJM to Caleb Foote, May 9, 1944, FOR, Box 9, SCPC; AJM to Evan Thomas, Sept. 26, 1944, FOR, Box 11, SCPC. This letter included Muste's comment that "if you ought to resign, presumably I ought to. . . . When I look at the matter objectively I cannot see that resignation is valid." See also AJM to B. Junker, July 15, 1944, Box 10, SCPC. While the later history of all the Lewisburg men is not known, those who did remain publicly active seem to have maintained a nonviolent orientation in the years after the war, some in the secular framework as illustrated by David Dellinger's long career in the WRL, and others continuing to identify with the action arms of the historic peace churches as did Bill Sutherland in his work with the American Friends' Service Committee.

53   AJM to Robert J. Leach, Dec. 21, 1944, FOR, Box 20, SCPC.

54   Evan Thomas to AJM, Sept. 13, 1944, and AJM to Thomas, Jan. 2, 1945, both in FOR, Box 11, SCPC.

55   AJM to Caleb Foote, May 9, 1944, FOR, Box 9, SCPC; Author's interview with John Swomley, June 19, 1978, New York City. Then and later Muste told a variety of people, including Lewis B. Hershey, that John "had been unduly influenced" by his peers at—ironically enough—Friends' Seminary. In an interval while enrolled at Mt. Hermon in Massachusetts, Muste related, his son "was a pacifist and active in a pacifist group." But all this had changed upon his return to Friends' School (AJM to Lewis B. Hershey, June 28, 1946, FOR, Box 14, SCPC). In retrospect, John Muste recalled that "the Quaker peace message was (to A. J., at any rate) lacking" at Friends' Seminary. "But the message was around me all the time at home, in the FOR office where I sometimes worked and in 'role models' like Bill Lovell and Dave Dellinger and Bayard [Rustin] and Al Hassler, . . . so it was not entirely fair of A. J. to blame Friends' Seminary for my 'weakness.' " Regarding peer pressure John Muste said: "All my friends were headed for the service and it would have taken more courage than I probably possessed to be a war resister, but in fact . . . the real reason was of the kind which A. J. said he could respect (and, in fact, did): by the time I was 17 I had recognized that I lacked A. J.'s religious faith, that I was not and probably could not hope to be a Christian in the only sense in which I had been raised to understand what being a Christian meant and that I lacked both the religious conviction that all wars are wrong and the political conviction that that particular war was wrong." John Muste concluded: "I have not changed my mind, nor do I regret what I did in 1944, even though there is a part of my mind which has always seen pacifism as the only logical response to war" John Muste to the author, August 10, 1977.

56   AJM to Caleb Foote, May 9, 1944, FOR, Box 9, SCPC.

57   AJM to Franklin D. Roosevelt, July 31, 1942; AJM to "Dear Friend," Jan. 14, 1947; and AJM to "Dear Friend," n.d., all in FOR, Box 13, SCPC. See also AJM, "Shall We Extend Conscription?" *Presbyterian Tribune*, Sept. 1942. Later proposals for the conscription of nurses drew similar objections from the FOR (Religious News Service Release, Jan. 11, 1945, FOR, Box 13, SCPC).

58   For details on draft legislation see John Whiteclay Chambers, *Draftees or Volunteers* (New York, 1975), pp. 359–71, 306–7. See also AJM to Andrew May, Feb. 6, 1949, FOR, Box 9, SCPC; Religious News Service Release, Oct. 25, 1944; AJM to Chamber Boss, Oct. 20, 1944; AJM to John Swomley, Nov. 7, 1944, all in FOR, Box 13, SCPC; and AJM to Paul French, Nov. 21, 1944, FOR, Box 20, SCPC.

Muste encouraged leaders in the black community and in his own Presbyterian denomination to publicly declare against a permanent draft, took the Department of War to task for sponsorship of a pro-draft campaign by the American Legion, questioned the propriety of Secretary of State Stimson's alleged efforts to pressure women's organizations to support a draft bill, sent an FOR representative to testify in Congressional hearings against Universal Military Training in May 1945, and complained loudly in 1946 when the Military Affairs Committee of the House of Representatives curtailed its hearings on the same topic, thus preventing many peace groups from giving adverse testimony. The struggle against UMT reached its highest point in February 1947 when between four hundred and five hundred persons returned their draft cards to the president or publicly burned them. Muste shared the speakers' platform with Dwight McDonald and David Dellinger in the New York City meeting where sixty-three draft cards were burned. Materials on these activities may be found in FOR, Box 13, SCPC. For an overview of the campaign against conscription, see John M. Swomley, Jr., *The Military Establishment* (Boston, 1964), chaps. 3 and 4.

59　AJM, *Conscription and Conscience* n.d. [1944?], AFSC pamphlet; AJM, *Not by Might* (1947; reprint ed., New York, 1971), pp. 141–42, 176, 207.

60　Chambers, *Draftees or Volunteers*, pp. 361–62; John Swomley to AJM, Jan. 3, 1945, FOR, Box 13, SCPC; AJM to Dr. Richard Present, Dec. 11, 1945, FOR, Box 10, SCPC; AJM to Ferner Nuhn, June 20, 1945, FOR, Box 13, SCPC.

61　AJM to Harry Truman, Nov. 27, 1954; AJM to Reinhold Niebuhr, Dec. 10, 1945, both in FOR, Box 12, SCPC; Sibley and Jacob, *Conscription of Conscience*, chap. 17.

62　Evan Thomas served as treasurer and, in June, Dorothy Canfield Fisher agreed to be honorary chairman. The committee was supported by an imposing list of influential "sponsors," including Arthur Garfield Hays, Sidney Hook, Max Lerner, Reinhold Niebuhr, T. H. McGiffert, Lillian Smith, and Henry VanDusen. Although not a sponsor, John Foster Dulles also lent support to the goals of the committee (Dulles to AJM, Dec. 13, 1946, FOR, Box 12, SCPC). "Report of Special Delegation Presenting Amnesty Appeal to the White House, May 11, 1946, FOR, Box 12, SCPC; Agnes Burns Wieck to "Dear Friend," June 7, 1946, FOR, Box 12, SCPC; includes discussion of the strikes at Danbury, Lewisburg, Springfield, and Sandstone prisons. AJM to "FOR staff et al.," May 10, 1946, refers to strikes at Glendora, Big Flats, and Gatlinburg, FOR, Box 12, SCPC. See also News Release, April 13, 1948, FOR, Box 2, SCPC; and Alfred Kuenzli, "No Amnesty in 1947," *War Resisters' League News*, Sept.–Oct. 1969; Sibley and Jacob, *Conscription of Conscience*, chap. 17.

63　Sibley and Jacob, *Conscription of Conscience*, Kuenzli, "No Amnesty in 1947," AJM to Hon. Owen J. Roberts, Dec. 12, 1947, FOR, Box 12, SCPC. Among those excluded from amnesty were 4,399 Jehovah's Witnesses.

64　Materials relating to the Committee on Educational Aid are in FOR, Box 13, SCPC; and materials about the CCCO can be found in FOR, Box 18, SCPC. Muste also considered a recruitment program for returning servicemen but did not pursue it beyond preliminary discussions (See correspondence with Urban L. Ogden, Spring 1945, in FOR, Box 10, SCPC). The CCCO continued to function in the 1980's; Muste served as a national chairman of the committee into the 1960s. The raison d'être of groups such as the CCCO was challenged by the courts in 1949 in the case of Bluffton College teacher, Larry Gara, who was sentenced to eighteen months in prison for having "counseled, aided and abetted" a Mennonite student who had (prior to consulting Gara) concluded that he could not register for the draft. Muste joined fellow pacifists in protesting "this interpretation of law which makes such a ministry to others a crime, which makes a man a felon for supporting another's obedience to conscience." Gara's case went to the Supreme Court and was lost by a four-to-four decision. The young pacifist, who had already served three years in prison during World War II, spent seven more months behind bars and then was paroled to graduate school ("The Larry Gara Case, Menace to Religious Liberty," unsorted FOR, SCPC; and Larry Gara to "Dear Friend" [Thomas E. Drake], July 26, 1961, Quaker Collection, Haverford College Library).

65　For information on FOR programs in this regard, see John Swomley's articles on John Nevin Sayre in *Fellowship*, June 1978, pp. 6–9 and Jan.–Feb. 1979, pp. 10–13; Sayre's summary of "The FOR and Japanese Americans in World War II," notes, n.d. [1945?], FOR, Box 19, SCPC; and Betty Lynn Barton, "The Fellowship of Reconciliation: Pacifism, Labor and Social Welfare, 1915–1960," (Ph.D. diss., Florida State, 1974), pp. 206–8. Relevant also is this comment by Richard Akagi in "East of the River," *Pacific Citizen*, March 3, 1961, AJM, SCPC, Box 36: "Thank God there are in this country oddballs like . . . A. J. Muste, Shorty Collins, John Thomas, Charlie Bell, C. B. Moseley, Allan Hunter, Norman Thomas. . . . Some of us owe to these men the faith we now have in the processes of a free society. The support they gave the Nisei during the period of evacuation and relocation helped to dissipate the skepticism we felt about the possibility of justice in 'a white man's society.' "

66 AJM to Caleb Foote, June 10, 1942, unsorted FOR, SCPC. Also see AJM to Dillon Meyer, July 26, 1943, unsorted FOR, SCPC; AJM to Harry Elmer Barnes, Oct. 23, 1944, FOR, Box 7, SCPC; and Caleb Foote to AJM, Aug. 6, 1942, FOR, Box 8, SCPC. The contrast between Muste's reaction to Manzanar and a memo on the same camp written a year earlier by Caleb Foote is instructive. Predicting (accurately, as later historical and sociological analysis would show) that "the dislocation of family life which [concentration camp] conditions create will be one of the most serious long-run consequences" of the evacuation for the Japanese-American community, Foote noted: "Manzanar is very subtle. . . . But if we fool ourselves thinking this isn't cruelty, we don't fool the Japanese."

67 Sayre, "The FOR and Japanese Americans"; AJM to Dillon Meyer, March 31, 1943, FOR, Box 19, SCPC; AJM to Charles Davis, July 31, 1942, FOR, Box 16, SCPC; AJM Night Letter to Paul French, July 6, 1942; AJM Day Letter to Henry Stimson, July 3, 1942, AJM to Charles Davis, July 31, 1942, both in FOR, Box 16, SCPC.

68 On first aide see AJM to Caleb Foote, Dec. 17, 1941, FOR, Box 8, SCPC. On sabotage see AJM to Y. H. Tomlinson, July 8, 1942, FOR, Box 11, SCPC, and AJM to *Christian Century*, typescript, n.d. [1942?].

69 See FOR, Box 20, SCPC on the National Youth Administration problem. On freedom of worwship see AJM to the editor of the *Christian Century*, Nov. 25, 1941; "D" folder in FOR, Box 7, SCPC; and AJM to Y. H. Tomlinson, July 8, 1942, FOR, Box 11, SCPC.

70 Message to Franklin D. Roosevelt printed in *New Religious Frontiers*, Dec. 1, 1938, AJM, SCPC Scrapbook. See also FOR Executive Committee minutes, Sept. 14, 1943 (microfilm), SCPC.

Evidence of Allied foot-dragging on, rather than supporting of, internal resistance to the Nazis was brought to Muste's attention by World Council of Churches Secretary Visser 't Hooft, who reported that the names of important German resistants (including many members of the Confessional Church) had been given in 1942 to the U.S. and British governments and that the governments offered "no encouragement whatever." Despite this the men had attempted a revolt in July of 1944; they needed, according to 't Hooft, military help which was never proffered (Untitled notes of off-the-record talk by Visser 't Hooft, May 14, 1945, FOR, Box 9, SCPC). On the related question of efforts to rescue the victims of the Nazis, see Henry L. Feingold, *The Politics of Rescue* (Rutgers, N.J., 1970).

71 Brittain, *The Rebel Passion* New York, 1964), p. 60; AJM to David Dellinger, April 4, 1944, FOR, Box 9, SCPC; Muste and Sayre changed the pamphlet title from *Seed of Chaos* and first published the piece as an article in *Fellowship*.

72 G. Bromley Oxnam to AJM, July 10, 1945, FOR, Box 9, SCPC; AJM to Oxnam, July 12, 1945; Untitled notes of off-the-record talk with Visser 't Hooft, May 14, 1945, FOR, Box 9, SCPC. *New York Times*, Aug. 10, 1945.

73 AJM to the editor of the *New York Times*, Dec. 14, 1941; AJM, *Wage Peace Now*, FOR pamphlet, n.d. [1942]; AJM to "Dear Friends," Jan. 10, 1944, FOR, Box 21, SCPC; AJM to Hugh C. Burr, April 12, 1946, FOR, Box 7, SCPC; AJM to Harry Truman, May 9, 1945; and "To the President of the United States," n.d. [May 1945], FOR, Box 12, SCPC; Communication with the State Department: Erle R. Dickover to AJM, June 15, 1945; AJM to Dickover, June 22, 1945, FOR, Box 12, SCPC. See also AJM to Jerry Voorhis, June 25, 1945, and Voorhis to AJM, June 16, 1945, FOR, Box 11, SCPC.

74 AJM to Harry Truman, Dec. 20, 1945, FOR, Box 12, SCPC; FOR petition to the

President, Senate, and House, April 1946; and AJM to James F. Byrnes, April 10, 1946, and Dec. 9, 1946, both in FOR, Box 7, SCPC; AJM, "Sketches for an Autobiography," in *The Essays of A. J. Muste*, ed. Nat Hentoff (New York, 1967), pp. 11–12.

75   AJM, *The World Task of Pacifism*; AJM, *Pacifism after the War*, 1941 pamphlet; AJM to James Farmer, Jan. 3, 1942, FOR, Box 7, SCPC.

76   AJM, "Unofficial and Provisional Memo on Pacifist Research Commission on the Organizing of Peace," Feb. 24, 1942; "Pacifism" typescript, n.d. [1944?]; SCPC folders on the Pacifist Research Bureau are in Box 20. These indicate increasing staff and organizational problems for the Bureau in the period 1944–46, with the Bureau entering into decline by the end of 1946.

77   AJM, *Where Are We Going?* 1941, FOR pamphlet; and *Wage Peace Now*. Also see AJM, "Footnote on Moscow," handwritten, n.d. [1943?]; AJM, "Holy Week 1943 Message," and "The Peace, A Nightmare, 1946," both typescripts in AJM, FOR, Box 9, SCPC.

78   AJM, "Is our Only Choice Dumbarton Oaks or Chaos?" *Fellowship*, April 1945, pp. 69–84; AJM to Malcolm W. Davis, Nov. 23, 1945; AJM to Lloyd J. Averill, Jr., Feb. 6, 1945; AJM to G. Shubert Frye, Feb. 20, 1945, all in FOR, Box 8, SCPC; No Author, "Brief Summary and Report, Seminar on Conscription, Coercion and Disarmament," Pendle Hill, October 16–22, 1943, Consultative Peace Council, Box 1, SCPC. Within the United States Muste saw the same absence of concern over military force. In the 1944 election he rejected Dewey and Roosevelt on the grounds that both "agree on . . . keeping peace by force; rule by the Big Powers" (AJM, "The Election, The War and the Peace," typescript, 1944, FOR, Box 9, SCPC).

79   AJM to Rev. Cameron P. Hall, Feb. 14, 1945, FOR, Box 79, SCPC; AJM to Walter Van Kirk, Dec. 26, 1944, FOR, Box 11, SCPC; AJM to Professor William E. Hocking, April 16, 1945, FOR, Box 8, SCPC; AJM to George Yamada, March 25, 1945, FOR, Box 28, SCPC; and AJM to Hocking, April 16, 1945. See also AJM to Hocking, April 16, 1945; AJM to Harry Emerson Fosdick, March 15, 1945, FOR, Box 8, SCPC; Fosdick to AJM, April 20, 1945, FOR, Box 8, SCPC; AJM to Reinhold Niebuhr, April 23, 1943, and Niebuhr to AJM, April 19, 1945, both in FOR, Box 9, SCPC. Muste's position on Dumbarton Oaks was fortified by the Pacifist Research Bureau pamphlet by Harrop Freeman, *Principles and Practice from Delaware to Dumbarton Oaks*, Dec. 1944, which was prepared expressly for use by the Hocking Commission.

80   AJM, "The Essentials of Peace," typescript, 1944, FOR, Box 9, SCPC; AJM, "What Lies Ahead", 1944. In the latter he predicted that a third world war would occur within twenty-five years if the essentials he was defining did not materialize. See also his rejection of the Socialist Party peace platform in 1944 because it pinned "sole guilt" on the Axis countries and set no specific timetable for disarmament (AJM to Norman Thomas, June 22, 1944, FOR, Box 1, SCPC).

81   AJM, "Memorandum on Some Aspects of the FOR Post-War Program," Oct. 15, 1945, FOR, Box 9, SCPC; untitled typescript, n.d. [1945?], a plea "for greatly increased support of the Fellowship and its activities," FOR, Box 9, SCPC.

82   Scholar and anti-war activist Noam Chomsky has argued, with careful attention to the historical events leading to and following Pearl Harbor, that Muste's analysis of U.S.-Japanese relations and the pacifist alternatives which he posed to military solutions were "eminently realistic and highly moral. Furthermore, even if we were to grant the claim that the United States simply acted in legitimate self-defense, subsequent events in Asia have amply, hideously confirmed Muste's basic premise that 'the means one uses inevitably incorporate themselves into his ends and, if evil, will defeat him' " ("The

Revolutionary Pacifism of A. J. Muste," in *American Power and the New Mandarins* (New York, Vintage Books, 1969, pp. 159–208, quotation, p. 208).
83   "The individual conscience . . . no other way" theme was used in an editorial, *Life Magazine*, Aug. 20, 1945. It became one of Muste's most frequent quotations.
84   Developments in the early forties in the area of civil rights also contributed to Muste's increasing interest in civil disobedience. See below, Chapter viii.

Chapter VII

1   AJM, "Sketches for an Autobiography" (hereafter "Sketches"), in *The Essays of A. J. Muste*, ed. Nat Hentoff (New York, 1967), pp. 4, 8–12; AJM, *Not by Might* (1947; reprint ed., New York, 1971), pp. ix–xiii, 1–227.
2   AJM to Arthur Springer, April 15, 1959, AJM, Box 36, SCPC.
3   Peacemakers, *Introducing Peacemakers* AJM, Box 7, SCPC: "Report of Chicago Conference on More Disciplined and Revolutionary Pacifism," *Fellowship*, May 1948, p. 26; "Summary of Proceedings and Discussion of National Conference of Peacemakers," May 30–June 1, 1952, AJM, Box 7, SCPC; "Discipline of Mt. Morris House Peace Cell" and "Release from A. J. Muste, Peacemakers' Research Committee," both in AJM, Box 7, SCPC.
4   AJM to Helen Corson, Aug. 18, 1944, FOR, Box 18, SCPC.
5   AJM to District Director, Internal Revenue Service, Nov. 1956, AJM, Box 3, SCPC. The typescript of this brief substituted for "Divine Guidance" the words "conscience and religious beliefs." AJM, "Why Tax Refusal?" March 1960, AJM, Box 3, SCPC.
6   AJM to Collector of IRS, March 1, 1951, AJM, Box 7, SCPC. Muste paid taxes to the state of New York (AJM to Don Kaufman, March 25, 1959, AJM, Box 26, SCPC).
7   "The Estate of Anna Muste Deceased and Abraham John Muste, Petitioners vs. Commissioner of Internal Revenue, Respondent. Brief for Petitioner," mimeographed by Central Committee for Conscientious Objectors, Aug. 1, 1960, AJM, Box 2, SCPC. A "Rights of Conscience Committee," headed by Quaker Lyle Tatum, raised funds to defray the legal expenses in this case (AJM to Tatum, Feb. 28, 1960, and Tatum to AJM, June 24, 1960, AJM, Box 3, SCPC). Along with the United States Constitution, Freeman invoked international rulings: the Kellogg-Briand Pact which outlawed war as an instrument of national policy and was to be fulfilled by the signatory nations "and the citizens thereof;" clauses of the Atlantic and United Nations Charters calling for the abandonment of force in world affairs; the "Opinion and Judgment" from Nuremburg regarding the "international duties [of individuals] which transcend the national obligations of obedience imposed by the individual State." In view of the impractibility of the Kellogg-Briand Pact and Muste's own rejection of the other documènts, Freeman was more than stretching a point in this part of his brief.
8   AJM to William Miller, April 6, 1961, and AJM to Franklin Zahn, May 25, 1961, both in AJM, Box 41, SCPC.
9   Brief for Petitioner to IRS.
10   "Tax Court Petition March 1961" [Judge's opinion], AJM, Box 3, SCPC; Muste's comment on the "two decisive powers" appeared in his letter to the IRS in 1948, quoted in the typescript draft of Freeman's brief, AJM, Box 3, SCPC; Alfred Hassler to AJM, May 11, 1961: "I confess I am not subtle enough to see quite how you interpreted [the court decision] as being a strong case for tax refusal" (FOR, Box 13, SCPC).

11   Press releases from the Tax Refusal Committee cited generally low numbers in the fifties (twenty-two in 1951, forty-three in 1954, twenty-seven in 1955) but then indicated a sharp rise in the sixties ("More than 400 Say 'No Tax for War' " in 1964). However, the sixties' figures may include types of tax resistance not counted in the fifties, such as payment of an estimated percentage that would hopefully not go to military purposes, keeping income below taxable level while still filing a return, etc. (Tax Refusal Committee of Peacemakers Press Releases, AJM, Box 3, SCPC). For a summary of some cases which did not directly involve Muste and of late sixties' developments in tax refusal see Robert Calvert, *Ain't Gonna Pay For War No More*, published by War Tax Resistance, 1971, 1972. Muste did not see the point of one idea which some pacifists promoted in the early sixties, that of a federal law guaranteeing pacifists that their taxes would not be used to support war. "Could this possibly be anything except a bookkeeping transaction?" he asked: "A would have a smaller part of his tax contributed to the defense budget but a larger part of B's tax will be shifted to make up for this" (AJM to Arthur Springer, Jan. 18, 1960, AJM, Box 3, SCPC). The War Resisters' League began to promote tax resistance during the Vietnam War era (Joan Baez et al. on WRL letterhead to Sidney Lens, Sept. 22, 1965, Lens Papers). The chance that government irritation over tax refusal would breed more serious consequences obviously weighed heavily with managers of the *New York Times* who refused a Peacemakers' ad in 1966. To run the message, "The Time Has Come [for tax resistance]," was to run the risk of conspiracy charges, *Times* personnel told Muste. On the proposed ad see AJM to Neal D. Newby, Jr., May 16, 1966, AJM, Box 3, SCPC.

12   File on conscientious objection in AJM, Box 26, SCPC; Calvert, *Ain't Gonna Pay*.

13   John Swomley mimeographed statement on McCrackin Case, Dec. 18, 1958, AJM, Box 34, SCPC; Mimeographed report, "To the Presbytery of Cincinnati Concerning the Judgment of the Synod of Ohio's Permanent Judicial Commission in the Appeal of the Rev. Maurice F. McCrackin vs. the Presbytery of Cincinnati," n.d. [Fall 1961], AJM, Box 34, SCPC; Vergie Bernhardt, "The McCrackin Verdict," *Christian Century*, June 5, 1961. Also see Calvert, *Ain't Gonna Pay*.

14   AJM to Margaret McCulloch, Jan. 16, 1961, AJM, Box 36, SCPC; Swomley statement on McCrackin Case; Walter Muelder, AJM, and Arthur Swift to "Dear Friend," Dec. 1, 1958; AJM to editor of *Cincinnati Inquirer*, Dec. 30, 1958, AJM, Box 34, SCPC. When Reinhold Niebuhr wrote that McCrackin's noncooperation was "in my vulgar view . . . nothing but exhibitionism," Muste shot back a barbed query: "The charge of exhibitionism can be made against quite a few of the prophets can it not?" (Niebuhr to AJM, Oct. 14, 1958, and AJM to Niebuhr, Nov. 5, 1958, both in AJM, Box 34, SCPC).

15   Neil Haworth to Donald F. McCaffrey, Jan. 23, 1963, and AJM to Anthony R. Marasco, April 23, 1963, both in AJM, Box 25, SCPC. See also AJM to Hon. Eugene Anderson, Sept. 3, 1964, and AJM to Thomas F. Scanlon, Nov. 18, 1964, AJM, Box 43, SCPC; AJM to Elmer Neufeld, May 17, 1961, and undated memo from Alfred Hassler reporting that the FOR would remain tax-exempt, but that the decision was based not upon First Amendment guarantees but rather upon legal technicalities about how the case had been handled, both in AJM, Box 28, SCPC. The FOR received political support in this struggle from Senator George McGovern who stated for the *Congressional Record* (May 13, 1963) his view that "it is absolutely fantastic that an agency of the U.S. Government should presume that working for world peace . . . is not a religious purpose. There have been many rebukes to the Prince of Peace," McGovern added, "but this must be the first time that the U.S. Government has officially declared that His message of peace and reconciliation is not religious" (AJM, Box 34, SCPC).

16   AJM, "Of Holy Disobedience," in *Not by Might*, quotation, p. 33.

17   AJM to Harold Gray, Dec. 19, 1952, Gray Papers, Box 3; Florence Horning to R. F. Christmann, March 19, 1952, FOR Papers, Box 1; John Muste to the author, Feb. 26, 1979.

18   John Swomley to the author, May 9, 1979; Nat Hentoff, *Peace Agitator* (New York, 1963), p. 149.

19   John Muste to the author, Feb. 6, 1979; AJM to Glenn Smiley, Nov. 29, 1944; and AJM to Helen Smiley, April 25, 1945, all in FOR, Box 10, SCPC; AJM to "Miss P. Muste," Sept. 22, 1947, AJM, Box 2, SCPC.

20   John Swomley to AJM, June 21, 1954; AJM to John Swomley, June 25, 1954; Peggy Wood to Nancy Baker, July 9, 1954, quotes from AJM letter about bypassing New York City office, all in unsorted FOR, SCPC. According to Muste's daughter, Nancy Baker, Anna Muste was aware of the tax refusal position that her husband had taken but probably did not know that his position involved legal liability on her part. "I think she would have been very upset if she knew," said Nancy Baker to the author, Sept. 12, 1979.

21   Hentoff, *Peace Agitator*, pp. 141, 143–44. John Muste has observed that the stressful years when their family was living at the Amalgamated apartments in a fourth floor walk-up apartment "may very well have helped to weaken [Anna Muste's] heart" (John Muste to the author, Feb. 6, 1979).

22   Connie Muste, who lived at home until her marriage at the age of thirty-three and worked with her father in the FOR, moved to the Midwest about 1954 with her social-worker husband, Doyt Hamilton. Her brother had not lived at home on a permanent basis since his seventeenth birthday, though he did stay with his parents for a year after graduation from college, while holding a job in New York, and again while recuperating from polio in 1952 (John Muste to the author, Feb. 6, 1979, and Nancy Muste Baker to the author, Feb. 8, 1979, and Sept. 12, 1979). On AJM's hiding his smoking and card-playing from his parents, sources are Hentoff, *Peace Agitator*, p. 148, and telephone conversation with John Muste, March 15, 1979.

23   "Sketches," p. 12–13.

24   John Muste to the author, Feb. 6, 1979, and Nancy Baker to the author, Sept. 12, 1979. Muste had eight grandchildren: Peter and Christopher, the sons of John Muste; John and Richard, the sons of Nancy Baker; Alan, Philip, Anne, and Dana, the children of Connie Hamilton. Philip Hamilton was killed in an accident.

25   AJM, "The Way Forward," *Fellowship*, Jan. 1948, p. 49.

26   The Ober Act in Maryland was one of several local loyalty laws passed in the McCarthy era. It stripped persons identified as subversives of their civil rights and involved heavy fines and prison sentences up to twenty years (R. E. Cushman, "American Civil Liberties in Mid-Twentieth Century," *Annals of the American Academy of Political and Social Science*, May 1951, pp. 1–8).

27   AJM, "Where Are We and What Is Ahead?" mimeographed "not for publication" memo, July 1956, AJM, Box 10, SCPC. His perception that significant changes might be expected within Communist circles and that these in turn would have an impact on other leftist forces was strongly shared by his friend Sidney Lens, whose European travels in 1957—including visits with laborites and socialists in such places as England, Ireland, Yugoslavia, and Poland—reinforced the impression of, in Lens' words, "a healthy optimism on the left" in non-communist countries and that "something is going on behind the [iron] curtain" (Lens to AJM, April 22, 1957, May 24, 1957, and July 2, 1957, Lens Papers). Lens' contacts with U.S. Communists also indicated forces working in the C.P.-USA for a break with Russia and a major overhaul of the Party (Lens to AJM, Sept. 21, 1956, Lens Papers). See also AJM, "Letter from the U.S.A.," AJM, Box 10, SCPC.

28   AJM to "Dear Friends," Aug. 13, 1956; AJM to Howard Mayhew, Sept. 21, 1956; AJM, "Letter from the U.S.A."

29   "For Immediate Release," n.d. [Dec. 1956]; "Where Are We?" and "Dialogue with Communists Today," February 1956, mimeographed, both in AJM, Box 10, SCPC.

Muste also believed that third-world nations in Asia, Africa, and Latin America would play a pivotal role in the revitalization of world socialism. He and his colleagues stressed, in the fifties, the need to encourage the growth of "a third force" of "peoples in between" the two dominant world power blocs. Finding organizational expression for this concept proved impossible, however. See AJM, *The Camp of Liberation*, (London, Peace News, 1954).

30   Those who attended the C.P. convention as observers were Muste, Dorothy Day, Roy Finch (WRL), Stringfellow Barr, Lyle Tatum (AFSC), Bayard Rustin, Alfred Hassler, George Willoughby (Central Committee for Conscientious Objectors), according to the "Statement by Observers at C.P. Convention, New York, February" (Statement issued over the date Sept. 12, 1957), AJM, Box 31, SCPC; AJM to Hon. J. Edgar Hoover, April 2, 1957; *New York Post* clipping, March 20, 1957, AJM, Box 31, SCPC; Copy, no signature (U.S. Department of Justice, F.B.I. typed at top), to Glenn D. Everett, Aug. 14, 1957, unsorted FOR, SCPC; John Nevin Sayre to Frederic Fox, April 15, 1957, unsorted FOR, SCPC.

31   AJM to the editor, *Saturday Evening Post*, March 11, 1958; Frederic Nelson to AJM, April 9, 1958, unsorted FOR, SCPC.

32   AJM to David McReynolds, July 15, 1957; AJM to the editor, *Saturday Evening Post*, March 11, 1958. One of Muste's fellow editors on *Liberation*, Roy Finch, opposed the Forum for its consorting with Communists "American Forum," *Liberation*, Sept., 1957, p. 3, and Roy Finch, "A Strange Mistake," *Liberation*, June 1957, pp. 13–14).

33   Sidney Lens to the author, Feb. 28, 1978.

34   Muste wrote to Irving Howe, for example, "it isn't simply a question of whether Socialist Jones will have a talk over a beer or coffee some day with ISLer or XYZer Brown. There is a process between touch and go talks on the one hand and unity negotiations, steps to form a program and organize a party or movement on the other hand. That step seems to me to be a continuous and serious discussion process" (Feb. 26, 1957, AJM, Box 15, SCPC).

35   AJM to Katherine Baker, Aug. 5, 1959, AJM, Box 17, SCPC; "Comment on Socialist Re-Thinking," typescript, n.d. [ca. 1960–61]. The merit of the American Forum attempt was viewed in widely different ways by members of the American Left. To Roger Baldwin it represented "romanticist nonsense." Norman Thomas dubbed it "premature." Supporters tended to emphasize its effect upon American Communists. For AFSC Peace Secretary Robert Gilmore the Forum did "establish the Communists as human beings" (Hentoff, *Peace Agitator*, pp. 165–66). Quaker Stephen Cary wrote Muste of his impression that many individuals who had severed their ties with the CP-U.S.A. had been influenced in doing so by the American Forum. Muste tended to agree (Stephen Cary to AJM, March 3, 1959, and AJM to Stephen Cary, March 10, 1959, both in AJM, Box 17, SCPC. See also AJM to Eugene Murphy, Feb. 2, 1962, AJM, Box 2, SCPC). A skeptic about the Forum, California pacifist Roy Kepler, quipped that the group should change its name to "The Christian Forum for Communist Rehabilitation," Letter to the Editor, *Liberation*, July–Aug. 1957, p. 31.

36   R. S. Beale to AJM, April 21, 1942; Rev. W. H. Freda to AJM, Oct. 21, 1941; AJM to Freda, Oct. 27, 1941; William A. Elliot to AJM, April 15, 1942; and D. R. Sharpe to AJM, May 20, 1942, all in AJM, Box 20, SCPC. In the last letter Sharpe, the executive secretary

of the Cleveland Baptist Association and biographer of Walter Rauschenbusch, wrote Muste in consternation: "I ask your forgiveness. We have committed a terrible sin in permitting a few Fundamentalists to have their way."

37   FOR Executive Committee Minutes, Dec. 15, 1959, FOR, Box 29, SCPC; "Anatomy of a Smear," *Fellowship*, Oct. 1956, pp. 22–27; *San Francisco Examiner*, April 2, 1961, AJM, Box 24, SCPC; Charles A. Wordworth to *San Francisco Examiner*, "Letters," AJM, Box 2, SCPC; Kenneth Dole "Senate Chaplain Decries 'Moral Flabbiness' among Clergy as Fostering Second Munich," unidentified clipping, n.d. [1959], AJM, Box 26, SCPC; "Ad Hoc Scheme Good for U.S., Communists Say," *Galesburg Register Mail*, March 6, 1964, clipping in possession of author.

38   John Nevin Sayre to Frederic Fox, April 15, 1957, unsorted FOR, SCPC.

39   Sidney Lens to AJM, Feb. 20, 1963, Lens Papers; AJM to O. K. Armstrong, March 29, 1962, AJM, Box 17, SCPC; AJM to James Roosevelt, Dec. 20, 1960, and AJM to William Fitts Ryan, Jan. 16, 1961, both in AJM, Box 31, SCPC. Muste declined to join the New York Council to Abolish House UnAmerican Activities Committee because "I cannot get involved in any more things" (AJM to Aubrey Williams, March 28, 1961, and AJM to Dr. Otto Nathan, Oct. 30, 1961, both in FOR, Box 31, SCPC). He told the May Day Committee in 1962 that his participation in a rally they planned to oppose the McCarran Internal Security Act "would be regarded as having political implications which I would not want it to have" (AJM to Joseph Brandt, April 13, 1962, AJM, Box 31, SCPC). On the other hand, he did permit use of his name on the list of sponsors for a rally against HUAC which included such pro-Soviet figures as W. E. B. DuBois, James Aronson, and Russ Nixon (John McCartney to AJM, April 17, 1961, and AJM to McCartney, April 24, 1961, both in FOR, Box 31, SCPC). See also the *Liberation* editorial on HUAC, "Government by Intimidation," April 1961, carbon of AJM's typescript in AJM, Box 11, SCPC.

40   AJM to editor of the *New York Times*, Dec. 7, 1962, and AJM to Nathan Pusey, Dec. 7, 1962, both in AJM, Box 31, SCPC.

41   Milton Katz, "Peace, Politics and Protest: SANE and the American Peace Movement, 1957–1972," (Ph.D. diss., St. Louis, 1973), pp. 69–71, 116. Muste and Lawrence Scott were the primary leaders in the Committee for Non-Violent Action while Robert Gilmore and Clarence Pickett, both of the AFSC, and Norman Cousins headed the Committee for a Sane Nuclear Policy.

42   Ibid., pp. 141–48; Lawrence Wittner, *Rebels against War* (New York, 1969), pp. 251–61; Hentoff, *Peace Agitator*, pp. 168–75.

43   "SANE and Abrams Case," typescript for *Survival*, June 23, 1960, and AJM to Norman Cousins, Sept. 24, 1960, both in AJM, Box 37, SCPC. The gossip—alleging that motives of professional and financial gain were behind Cousin's position—was discussed by Muste in a letter to John Swomley, Jan. 3, 1961, AJM, Box 37, SCPC. In a conversation with the author, Cousins said he was "frankly astounded" that Muste had "reflected on someone else's integrity" in this way and stressed that far from gaining materially from his work with SANE, he had contributed $400,000 to SANE's campaign for the test ban Treaty (Cousins to the author, telephone conversation, June 18, 1979). See also AJM, "Crisis in SANE," *Liberation*, July–Aug., 1960.

44   AJM to Alfred Hassler, Jan. 3, 1961, AJM, Box 37, SCPC. In the case of Henry Abrams, Muste was inclined to accept Abrams' contention that he was not acting under anyone else's orders, even though the alleged CP member had refused to answer a direct question as to his party affiliations. "I urge people not to take the Fifth," Muste noted, "but it is an important constitutional right and we cannot automatically assume

guilt on the part of those who take it" (AJM to Homer Jack, March 7, 1961, and AJM to John Swomley, Jan. 30, 1961, both in AJM, Box 37, SCPC).

45   Muste had written Cousins at least once (see n. 43), but in that letter he stated a firm position and did not invite dialogue. In June 1979 Cousins' assessment of Dodd was quite positive. The senator, he said, had "tried to be fair." He had a past record of resisting McCarthyism, as when he defended the United World Federalists against red-baiting; and eventually he even switched his position on the 1960 Test Ban Treaty, becoming one of its sponsors near the end of the Congressional debates on it (Cousins' call to the author, June 18, 1979).

46   Mygatt and her comrade Francis Witherspoon had taken part in founding the War Resisters' League and had worked with Muste in many peace-related causes over the years (Tracy Mygatt to AJM, Dec. 11, 1960, AJM, Box 37, SCPC); John Swomley to AJM, Feb. 28, 1961; Alfred Hassler to AJM, Dec. 23, 1960; and AJM to Alfred Hassler, Jan. 23, 1961, all in AJM, Box 37, SCPC. Muste told Swomley, "I have done everything possible . . . to spike the formation of a rival organization and have refused to spearhead any opposition inside SANE." He made the same claim to Homer Jack, March 7, 1961, AJM, Box 37, SCPC. Undoubtedly in the immediate short-run, he did oppose a new group, but, as his remarks to Hassler make clear, in the long-run he was looking forward to an organization that might include figures such as Abrams, Lamont, and Pauling.

47   Muste did believe, however, that Norman Cousins had come to wish that Muste's approach had been taken with Dodd. As Muste related a conversation between himself and Cousins, he told the SANE leader that if he "had stood up to Dodd in May, . . . the result might have been a rallying of liberal forces to SANE, a serious blow to the 'investigating' committees . . . making [SANE] a formidable mass force." Cousins, in Muste's telling, "lowered his head, paused for an appreciable time, and then looked at me and said . . . 'I think you are right, and this is what wrings my soul.' " Muste repeated this story at least twice: AJM to John Swomley, Jan. 30, 1961, and AJM to Homer Jack, March 7, 1961, both in AJM, Box 37, SCPC. Norman Cousins denied AJM's quotation when historian Milton Katz brought it to his attention. But Cousins said, "I love A. J. I still do"; and added "You always live in a state of anguish, always soul searching. I don't know if I did the right thing then, and if this thing happened now I still would not know what else to do" (Katz, "Peace, Politics and Protest," pp. 161–62). In the conversation of June 1979, Cousins again strongly denied Muste's story but said nothing about anguish or soul-searching.

Among the notable resignations from SANE were Robert Gilmore, Linus Pauling, and Stewart Meacham from the national board; Muste withdrew from the board of the Greater New York Chapter. In addition, about half of the local SANE chapters refused to comply with new anti-communist rulings by the national board and were expelled (Wittner, *Rebels against War*, p. 260). See also Nathan Glazer, "The Peace Movement in America, 1961," *Commentary*, (April, 1961), pp. 288–96.

48   AJM to Paul Krage et al., Feb. 24, 1953; AJM to "Dear Friend," Dec. 10, 1952; AJM to Harry Truman, n.d. [December 1952]; FOR Release, Dec. 31, 1952, "Non-Communists Ask Clemency in Rosenberg Case"; Cover letter to "Dear Friend" from AJM, June 16, 1953; AJM to President Eisenhower, June 16, 1953, all in unsorted FOR, SCPC. Muste's letter to President Eisenhower in June 1953 contained the same arguments as the earlier petition, adding the cautious observation that "there appear to be intelligent persons whose loyalty is not open to question who hold that [the Rosenbergs] may be innocent." He circulated the draft and urged others to write similar letters, noting "how deeply our people in Europe will grieve if the execution takes place."

49   Irwin Edelman, "The Suppressed Facts in the Rosenberg Case," MS. in AJM, Box 27, SCPC. See also in Box 27: AJM to Morris Rubin and Sidney Lens, Nov. 7, 1958; AJM to Norman Thomas, Nov. 10, 1958; and AJM to Rubin, Dec. 4, 1958; AJM to Fyke Farmer, July 27, 1959, AJM, Box 37, SCPC. Later studies on the Rosenberg case include Robert and Michael Meeropol, *We Are Your Sons* (Boston, 1975), and Walter and Miriam Schneir, *Invitation to an Inquest* (Baltimore, 1973).

50   Neil H. Katz, "Revolutionary Pacifism and the Contemporary American Peace Movement: The Committee for Nonviolent Action 1957–1967," (Ph.D. diss., University of Maryland, 1974), pp. 12–13; Federico Ribes Tovar, *Puerto Rican Revolutionary* (New York, 1971), on Ruth Reynolds see p. 157, on the shootings in the U.S. see pp. 113–15, 140–50.

51   AJM to Sidney Lens, April 15, 1954; Lens to AJM, April 7, 1954; Memo on Puerto Rico, March 8, 1954; and "A Petition to President Kennedy for Clemency for Puerto Rican Political Prisoners," typescript, n.d. [1960], all in AJM, Box 37, SCPC. Though his later appeals went unheeded, Muste believed that the initial handling of the Puerto Rican episode had been fair and restrained. The arrests, he pointed out, were made without excessive violence; competent and well-known lawyers were appointed as legal counsel for the defendants; press coverage, as he had seen it, was restrained. "It is," he emphasized, "a tremendous contrast to the way in which the Communist issue is currently handled."

52   "A Petition to the President of the United States on Amnesty for the Smith Act Victims and Postponements of Trials," Dec. 20, 1955; FOR, "Report on Civil Liberties," Dec. 1, 1950; "Complete Text of Letter Sent to President Eisenhower, September 23, 1958," (signed by Reinhold Niebuhr, Clarence Pickett, Aubrey Williams, Howard Fast, Alexander Meiklejohn, John Haynes Holmes, and Alan Knight Chalmers); AJM to John Nevin Sayre, n.d.; AJM to Hon. George Reed, Nov. 11, 1958; AJM to Arthur Swift, Oct. 28, 1959; AJM to Arnold Johnson, Feb. 18, 1960, all in AJM, Box 36, SCPC; AJM to Harris Wofford, May 5, 1961, AJM, Box 36, SCPC, Norman Thomas and AJM to "Dear Friend," Sept. 18, 1958; "Release: Educators and Religious Leaders Ask Dismissal of Denver Smith Act Cases," Dec. 18, 1958, AJM, Box 37, SCPC; Murray Kempton, "J. Edgar Hoover and the Industry of Fear," *Liberation*, April 1957, p. 8.

In this same period Muste joined Reinhold Niebuhr, Martin Luther King, Jr., Alexander Meiklejohn, Eleanor Roosevelt, and other noted liberals in defending the Highlander Folk School in Tennessee against efforts by the district attorney of Grundy County, Tennessee to shut it down for "subversive" activities (AJM to Myles Horton, Oct. 28, 1959, and Horton to "Dear Friend of Highlander," Nov. 10, 1959, both in AJM, Box 31, SCPC).

53   Beverly Sterner to Helen Sobell, Feb. 16, 1967, AJM, Box 49, SCPC; AJM to President Kennedy, Dec. 12, 1961, AJM, Box 38, SCPC; "An Urgent Public Issue: Freedom for Morton Sobell," *New York Times* Advertisement, Monday, June 20, 1960; legal memorandum re: *United States of America* vs. *Morton Sobell*, n.d. [1960], submitted by Donner, Perlin and Piel, and Benjamin Dreyfus, in AJM, Box 38, SCPC. See also Morton Sobell, *On Doing Time* (New York, 1974).

54   AJM to Union of Soviet Writers, March 16, 1966, AJM, Box 49, SCPC.

55   On the Aptheker Campaign (which ended in defeat for its candidate whose headquarters were at one point firebombed by right-wing "minutemen"), see Paul Hofman, "New Liberal-Radical Coalition Maps 'Good Society' Platform," *New York Times*, June 11, 1966, p. 12; "Bail Set for 19 Here in Alleged Fire Plot by Minutemen Unit," *New York Times*, Nov. 1, 1966, p. 1; Peter Kihss, "Derounian and Brennan Seeking Re-

counts in Nassau Defeat," *New York Times*, Nov. 10, 1966, p. 43. Earlier in the sixties Muste and Aptheker had debated on the topic, "Peace and United States Foreign Policy," at City College in New York (AJM, Box labeled '62–'63–'64, SCPC). As Professor Frank A. Warren of Queens College has reminded the author, Muste's support of Aptheker was in keeping with the mood of the anti-war movement in that period. For example, other leading peace advocates called on those of like mind to join the W. E. B. Du Bois Clubs when those Marxist groups came under U.S. government attack.

Chapter VIII

1   Muste was never involved after the thirties in sustained union activity, but he continued to make his views known to labor leaders. In 1941, for example, he took time, amidst the heavy pressures that war was bringing to bear on the FOR, to personally contact black leaders such as Walter White and A. Philip Randolph and urge them to get black workers on the CIO roles in Detroit where a drive to unionize Ford Motor Company was underway (AJM to Walter White, April 8, 1941, and Walter White to AJM, April 15 and 26, 1941, all in FOR, Box 19, SCPC).

2   AJM to S. C. Morgan, Oct. 6, 1942, FOR, Box 17, SCPC.

3   AJM, "What the Bible Teaches about Freedom," published by the FOR, 1943. In assessing the responsibility of religious forces to oppose racism, Muste had taken special note of what seemed to be dereliction on the part of the Society of Friends, with which he was still affiliated. "Some of our friends, both with a small and a capital "F" are in danger of weakening their testimony considerably," Muste wrote Constance Rumbough. He had recently been told, he continued, that there were "no interracial Quaker meetings . . . in the South . . . at all. If that is true," he declared, "Friends ought to examine their individual and corporate consciences in this matter" (AJM to Rumbough, May 16, 1942, FOR, Box 10, SCPC). Perhaps Muste's expectations in this regard were higher than the historical record justified. Quaker scholar Henry J. Cadbury had noted that, "At no period in history and in no part of America have Negroes ever become in large numbers members of the Society of Friends" (Cadbury, "Negro Membership in the Society of Friends," *Journal of Negro History*, 21, no. 2 [April, 1936]: 151).

4   AJM to Alfred D. Moore et al., Aug. 26, 1943, FOR, Box 9, SCPC; Interview by the author with Bayard Rustin, April 20, 1978, New York City.

5   James Best to AJM, Aug. 2, 1943; AJM to Alfred D. Moore et al., Aug. 26, 1943; and AJM to Margaret McCulloch, Aug. 17, 1943, all in FOR, Box 9, SCPC.

6   AJM to David Dellinger, July 5, 1944, FOR, Box 9, SCPC. The list of FOR commitments and initiatives in support of nonviolent direct action was an impressive one. The Fellowship made certain classic works, e.g., Shridharani's *War Without Violence*, easily and cheaply accessible to the public; it provided a substantial part of the financial support for the Pacifist Research Bureau. Wartime nonviolent demonstrations against conscription, the poll tax, and British imperialism were carried out always with the help of members of the FOR.

7   Although he frequently expressed the opinion that "so far as fundamental [racial] attitudes are concerned there is [not] a very great difference between sections of the country," Muste did take a special interest in the racial patterns and attitudes of the South. The FOR extended support to the Southern Tenant Farmers' Union, an organization concerned with the sharecroppers and tenant farmers who struggled to survive

at the lowest economic strata of southern society (FOR, Box 20, SCPC). The Fellowship also campaigned to end the poll tax which prevented so many southern Negroes from voting (Folder on poll tax in FOR, Box 20, SCPC). Muste personally visited in the South at least twice during the 1940s—in Greensboro, North Carolina, in the summer of 1944 and in Virginia and North Carolina again in 1946 (AJM to Constance Rumbough, June 23, 1944, and March 20, 1946, both in FOR, Box 10, SCPC). Of prime importance to Muste was the obvious need for fundamental changes in racial attitudes of white people. The examination of the corporate southern white conscience which Lillian Smith and Paula Snelling had been making in their unusual magazine, the *South Today*, seemed to him to be a model worth following. Years before she achieved national fame as author of *Strange Fruit* and *Killers of the Dream*, Muste hailed Smith as "a brilliant writer and speaker. I need not elaborate," he said, "on how effective it is to have a Southern woman go all the way down the line in opposition to segregation, etc" (AJM to H. J. Gibbons, April 22, 1943), SCPC for both.

8   James Farmer, *Freedom When?* (New York, 1965), 20–23; August Meier and Elliott Rudwick, *CORE, A Study in the Civil Rights Movement* (Urbana, 1975), p. 5; Bayard Rustin, *Down The Line* (New York, 1971), chap. ix–xv, Nat Hentoff, *Peace Agitator* (New York, 1963), 113–14. On Jay Holmes Smith see Lawrence Wittner, *Rebels against War* (New York, 1969), pp. 63–64. Wittner, *Rebels against War*, pp. 63–64.

10   Jervis Anderson, *A. Philip Randolph, A Biographical Portrait* (New York, 1972), p. 259; Rustin, "The Negro and Nonviolence," *Fellowship*, Oct. 1942, pp. 166–67.

11   Bayard Rustin to AJM, Feb. 22, 1943, FOR, Box 10, SCPC; A. Philip Randolph to AJM, April 30, 1943; AJM to Randolph, May 21, 1943; Randolph to AJM, May 25, 1943, all in FOR, Box 21, SCPC. Muste and Randolph had earlier exchanged letters regarding a recent statement by Eleanor Roosevelt urging Negroes to moderate their stance. "I agree with your interpretation of Mrs. Roosevelt's statement that Negroes 'ought not to do too much demanding,' these days," wrote Randolph. "If we don't demand now, when are we to demand?" (Oct. 18, 1943, FOR, Box 21, SCPC). Jay Holmes Smith to AJM, July 8, 1943, FOR, Box 21, SCPC. Rustin had supported himself in the 1930s while at the City College of New York by singing with Josh White and Leadbelly. The FOR later tapped his talent as a concert artist by having him cut a record which was sold to benefit the Fellowship. See also Wittner, *Rebels against War*, p. 65, and "March on Washington, Proceedings of Conference Held September 26–27, 1942," FOR, Box 21, SCPC; Garfinkel, *When Negroes March*, (N.Y. 1969) pp. 47–124, 135–37, 144–46, 208; and *New York Times*, July 4, 1943, pp. 7, 12.

12   Farmer's feelings toward MOWM were adversely affected by what he saw as the movement's "racial chauvinism," Meier and Rudwick, *CORE*, p. 21. He had lent his assistance to Randolph but not wholeheartedly. Jay Holmes Smith reported that "Farmer disappeared from the Detroit MOWM gathering before the last two days of the conference." When the conference ended Farmer correctly predicted that Randolph's new thrust toward civil disobedience would fail and that the MOWM would "practically fold up in a year" (Jay Holmes Smith to AJM, July 8, 1943, FOR, Box 21, SCPC).

13   James Farmer memo to AJM, "On Provisional Plan for Brotherhood Mobilization," Jan. 8, 1942, acknowledged by AJM, Jan. 1942, FOR, Box 7, SCPC. This memo, dated Feb. 19, 1942 (the later date is apparently when the memo became part of the FOR Executive Committee Minutes), and a subsequent "Additional Memorandum from James Farmer, March 9, 1942" are reprinted in Francis L. Broderick and August Meier, eds., *Negro Protest Thought in the Twentieth Century* (Indianapolis, 1966), pp. 211–19. See also Meier and Rudwick, *CORE*, p. 7.

14 Meier and Rudwick have summarized these steps: "Gandhi's method was to start with an attempt to convert the opponent through negotiations and then successively move on to more militant actions. . . . If negotiations failed, agitation was employed to arouse public opinion against the evil doer. If this did not succeed, there would be parades and other colorful demonstrations, and eventually an ultimatum threatening more radical actions. Finally, if all else failed, outright civil disobedience was employed" (*CORE*, pp. 12, 13). In condensing their summary I have omitted the Gandhian rituals that were not practiced by nonviolent actionists in the United States.

15 Ibid., chaps. 1 and 2.

16 Ibid., pp. 37–39. Johnson declared himself to be physically and mentally unfit to withstand the sentence.

17 AJM to George Houser, June 25, 1941, FOR, Box 17, SCPC; AJM to William Sutherland, Feb. 24, 1945, FOR, Box 10, SCPC; AJM to George Houser and James Farmer, June 4, 1943, and AJM to Caleb Foote, May 9, 1944, both in FOR, Box 8, SCPC; The author's interview with James Farmer, March 24, 1978, Washington, D.C.

18 AJM to George Houser and James Farmer, June 4, 1943, and AJM to George Houser, Jan. 11, 1944, both in FOR, Box 8, SCPC; Farmer interview, 1978.

19 AJM to George Houser, Jan. 25, 1944, FOR, Box 8, SCPC; Meier and Rudwick, *CORE*, p. 16; AJM to Norman Whitney, Jan. 13, 1944, FOR, Box 11, SCPC; AJM to Barnard Junker, July 31, 1944, FOR, Box 15, SCPC; AJM to Walter Sikes, March 9, 1945, FOR, Box 20, SCPC.

20 Farmer commented many years later that neither he nor Rustin were good administrators in their FOR days (Farmer interview, 1978). On Farmer as an administrator see Meier and Rudwick, *CORE*, pp. 145–46. See also AJM to John Swomley, Feb. 1, 1945, FOR, Box 7, SCPC; AJM to John Swomley, Nov. 9, 1949, unsorted FOR, SCPC; AJM to Margaret McCulloch, July 8, 1942, FOR, Box 9, SCPC; AJM to McCulloch, Aug. 5, 1942, FOR, Box 9, SCPC.

See Gunnar Peterson to AJM, Sept. 23, 1943, as a sample of good reports on Farmer as a speaker (FOR, Box 13, SCPC). It is possible that Muste's less intense involvement on Farmer's behalf was affected by antagonism between Farmer and Rustin. In a letter to AJM, July 11, 1945, FOR, Box 11, SCPC; John Swomley wrote, "Jim is suspicious of and distrusts Bayard. I know Bayard is disgusted with Jim's irresponsibility." In retrospect Farmer noted the "father-son" relationship between Muste and Rustin and said that he had always been uncomfortable in the FOR because of that relationship (Farmer interview, 1978). Rustin, Muste maintained, "comes nearer to working out imaginative techniques for dealing with the racial situation than anyone else we have" (AJM to Barnard Junker, July 16, 1942, FOR, Box 15, SCPC). An example of Muste's fatherly concern for Rustin appeared in a letter he sent Rustin, Sept. 29, 1943, FOR, Box 10, SCPC: "Watch your health. That includes your sleep. You are desperately needed; it is the responsibility of all of us at this critical time to discipline ourselves to keep 100% fit."

21 Anderson, *A. Philip Randolph*, pp. 274–82.

22 Ibid., p. 281, quoting the statement by Randolph and Reynolds; AJM to A. Philip Randolph, Oct. 18, 1948, unsorted FOR, SCPC.

23 Folder on Lynn Committee, FOR, Box 21, SCPC, see, for example, AJM to Lawrence M. Ervin, June 2, 1943; AJM to Wilfred Kerr, April 18, 1944; and AJM to Benjamin McLaurin, Oct. 11, 1943; "NVDA Committee Minutes," Feb. 15, 1945, signed by AJM as secretary; AJM to H. F. Hancox, June 19, 1948, unsorted FOR, SCPC.

24 Muste indicated in his letter that he and Randolph had just sent out a joint fund appeal (possibly for Winfred Lynn) and wondered about the effect of Randolph's

charges on that joint effort. See the exchange between Randolph and Muste, in their later years, on the occasion of Muste's seventy-fifth birthday. Randolph then wrote (to Sidney Lens, Jan. 19, 1960, AJM, Box 48, SCPC: "Brother Muste is one of the great liberals of our nation and has kept the torch of human dignity, racial and social justice, peace and plenty before the American public." Muste responded (AJM to Randolph, Jan. 27, 1960, AJM, Box 48, SCPC): "Your fellowship over these many years has been one of the precious things in my life." Looking back on the 1948 dispute, Bayard Rustin said that it had not hurt the friendship of the two men. "Both men were so full of goodwill." Rustin doubted ("I'd bet my bottom dollar") that Randolph answered Muste's letter. The MOWM leader would have taken the position, according to Rustin, that "we've both had our say and there is no need to prolong the discussion" (Rustin interview, 1978). The episode does provide an interesting example of how individual perceptions and positions change over time. Rather than remembering himself as an object of attack in 1948, Rustin spoke in the early seventies to Randolph's biographer of "feeling rotten about" his defiance of Randolph and expressing gratitude that when he saw Randolph again later for the first time the older man "never said a word about what I had done to him" (Anderson, A. Philip Randolph, p. 282).

25   AJM to George Houser, Jan. 11, 1944, FOR, Box 8, SCPC. Muste made his hopes very clear in this letter to Houser: "The Fellowship as a whole, as its life is deepened, and under given historical circumstances [may be] transformed into pretty much what you think of as a Nonviolent Direct Action movement." The realities of the FOR-CORE set-up were described in an unsigned "Memo on Core and its Relationship to the FOR," July 21, 1944, on FOR letterhead, FOR, Box 8, SCPC. According to the memo, "Core is organizationally completely independent of the F.O.R., . . . not either locally or nationally under the direction of the F.O.R. . . . The F.O.R. . . . does not take responsibility for CORE. . . . CORE's headquarters . . . in Chicago . . . operates without any national budget and except therefore as a means for creating a sort of bond of fellowship between local CORE groups the national organization exists pretty much on paper.

While F.O.R. has no organizational connections with CORE . . . it has been strongly sympathetic. . . . In practically every instance it is the F.O.R. members in a locality who have taken the initiative in forming CORE groups and in carrying forward CORE work."

26   Meier and Rudwick, CORE, pp. 69–71. Contrary to the impression left by Meier and Rudwick, who imply that "CORE's old critic John Swomley" was responsible for forcing the break between FOR and CORE, neither Farmer nor Swomley later remembered that to be the case. By 1954, as they recall, the opinion was shared by both sides that a division was necessary. Swomley has stressed that Muste concurred in this decision (Farmer interview, 1978, and the author's interview with John Swomley, June 10, 1978).

27   AJM to Miss Margaret Leonard, March 1, 1961, AJM, Box 38, SCPC; AJM to David Dellinger, July 5, 1944, FOR, Box 9, SCPC (the italics are the author's); AJM to George Houser, Jan. 11, 1944, and AJM to Caleb Foote, May 9, 1944, both in FOR, Box 8, SCPC.

28   Martin Luther King, Jr., Stride toward Freedom (New York, 1958), p. 95; Charles Walker, the FOR secretary in Philadelphia who had arranged for Muste to visit Crozer, reported that Muste had given "a mighty good talk" and had received "a fairly good reception, marred by the chilly attitude of the acting president of the seminary and the worst outburst of invective I have ever heard levelled at a person in public." Walker explained that the outburst came from a heckler, "a veteran who apparently

had a tough time during the war" (Charles Walker to Bayard Rustin, Nov. 14, 1949, Philadelphia FOR, Box 4, SCPC).

29   Farmer interview, 1978; Rustin interview, 1978; Glenn Smiley to the author, Feb. 13, 1979. Martin Luther King, Jr. joined the FOR in 1957.

30   Rustin, quoted in Hentoff, *Peace Agitator*, p. 17; Confirmed in Rustin interview, 1978.

31   Glenn Smiley to the author, Feb. 13, 1979.

32   A complete picture of the Muste-King relationship is difficult to reconstruct because of King's preference for the telephone over letters as a way of communication. Rustin, Farmer, Smiley, and James Lawson have all noted, in interviews with the author, that most Muste-King contacts would have occurred by telephone. For the cooperative efforts noted in the text, see AJM to King, March 8, 1961, AJM, Box 7, SCPC; King to AJM, May 4, 1959, and AJM to Ella Baker, May 11, 1959, both in AJM, Box 38, SCPC; AJM to King, Dec. 16, 1965, AJM, Box 38, SCPC, AJM to "Dear Sirs," and NYU, Jan. 27, 1961; AJM to King, Feb. 20, 1961; Wyatt Tee Walker to Bursar, NYU, Feb. 21, 1961, all in AJM, Box 38, SCPC.

33   Participants in the very first sit-in at the Woolworth's in Greensboro disavow any influence from the FOR comic book (Franklin McCain's oral transcript in Howell Raines, ed., *My Soul Is Rested* [New York, Bantam ed., 1978], p. 80). See also *Fellowship*, April 1, 1960, p. 5; and David Lewis, *King: A Critical Biography* (New York, 1970), p. 115.

34   "Methodists vs. Negro Youth," typescript, AJM, Box 11, SCPC, published in *Liberation*, March 1960, p. 3; AJM to Patricia Stephens, July 5, 1960, AJM, Box 25, SCPC; AJM to Margaret Leonard, March 1, 1961, AJM, Box 38, SCPC.

35   AJM to Robert Swann, May 13, 1963, AJM, Box 25, SCPC.

36   Martin Luther King, Jr., "Our Struggle," *Liberation*, April 1956, pp. 3–6; Bayard Rustin, "Montgomery Diary," *Liberation*, April 1956, pp. 7–10.

37   Editorial on civil rights strategy, typescript, AJM, Box 38, SCPC, published in *Liberation*, May 1960, pp. 5–9.

38   Editorial on Martin Luther King's journey to India, *Liberation*, February, 1959, p. 19.

39   Martin Luther King, Jr., "The Social Organization of Nonviolence," *Liberation*, Oct. 1959, pp. 6–7.

40   AJM to E. Philip Eastman, Jan. 24, 1961, AJM, Box 29, SCPC; AJM to Ken Kirkpatrick, June 10, 1963, AJM, Box 17, SCPC.

41   Editorial, typescript, AJM, Box 12, SCPC, published in *Liberation*, Jan. 1965, p. 28. King did link the struggle for racial justice with the struggle for peace in his address (as Muste noted in corresponding with author Kay Boyle, Dec. 16, 1964, AJM, Box 42, SCPC). Muste marked such passages as the following in his copy of the *New York Post* report on King's speech (Dec. 10, 1964, AJM, Box 42, SCPC): "I refuse to accept the view that mankind is so tragically bound to the starless midnight of racism and war that the bright daybreak of peace and brotherhood can never become reality. . . . I refuse to accept the cynical notion that nation after nation must spiral down a militaristic stairway into a hell of thermonuclear destruction. I believe that unarmed truth and unconditional love will have the final word in reality."

42   The author's telephone interview with James Lawson, May 11, 1979. Muste privately observed that Lawson "is in fact regarded by many as having more on the ball than Martin King himself" (AJM to Ken Kirkpatrick, June 10, 1963, AJM, Box 17, SCPC). For surviving samples of Muste's counsel to Lawson regarding SCLC, see AJM to Lawson, April 27, and May 24, 1960, both in AJM, Box 32, SCPC.

43   Rustin interview, 1978; AJM to Bradford Lyttle, May 9, 1962, AJM, Box 41, SCPC; Lewis, *King: A Critical Biography*, p. 131; William Robert Miller, *Martin Luther King* (New York, 1968), p. 87; James Baldwin, "The Dangerous Road Before Martin Luther King," *Harpers*, Feb. 1961, p. 42.

44   AJM to Howard Schomer, April 21, 1960, and Schomer to AJM, April 18, 1960, AJM, Box 36, SCPC. For other examples of Muste's concern for Rustin see AJM to Dorothy Day, July 21, 1964, and correspondence with Elliston Morris both in AJM, Box 2, SCPC.

45   *New York Times* ad, March 29, 1960; AJM to Bradford Lyttle, May 9, 1962, AJM, Box 41, SCPC; Rustin interview, 1978. See summaries of *New York Times Co., Petitioner* v. *L. B. Sullivan* and *Ralph D. Abernathy et al., Petitioners*, v. *L. D. Sullivan*, Argued Jan. 6, 1964, Decided March 9, 1964, in *Decisions of United States Supreme Court, 1963–1964 Term* (Rochester, N.Y., 1964), pp. 119–21.

46   AJM to Jackie Robinson, Feb. 18, 1960, AJM, Box 25, SCPC; AJM to James Farmer, Jan. 30, 1961; Farmer to AJM, Feb. 17, 1961; and AJM to Charles Oldham, Jan. 30, 1961, all in AJM, Box 25, SCPC.

The fact that Floyd McKissick, the new CORE director after Farmer, was outspokenly and actively opposed to the war in Vietnam was certainly important to Muste. It is also true that "McKissick himself was not an advocate of white exclusion" and while he remained director, the national advisory board on which Muste sat remained "nearly half-white" (Meier and Rudwick, *CORE*, pp. 415, 419). See also Minutes of National Advisory Committee Meeting [CORE], Jan. 26, 1967, AJM, Box 42, SCPC.

47   AJM to Myles Horton, Oct. 28, 1959, and Horton to "Dear Friend of Highlander," Nov. 10, 1959, AJM, Box 31, SCPC. John Egerton, "The Trial of Highlander," *Southern Exposure*, 6, no. 1 (Spring 1978), pp. 82–89; AJM to "Dear Friends," March 16, 1959, AJM, Box 31, SCPC; Victor Reuther to AJM, April 17, 1959, and AJM to Victor Reuther, May 1, 1959, both in AJM, Box 31, SCPC. The seventy-three signers were mostly educators and clergymen; Norman Thomas, Reinhold Niebuhr, Harry Emerson Fosdick, and Liston Pope headed the list with Muste.

48   AJM to Senator J. W. Fulbright, March 8, 1960, AJM, Box 38, SCPC: "I venture also to call to your attention the fact that in your reference to the President calling the people of this country to 'the hill of the Lord' you are evidently misinformed as to the passage in Isaiah 2 to which you refer and are giving a completely erroneous impression as to what that passage contains. The passage in Isaiah 2 tells how when the nations go to the mountain of the Lord's house, they will be taught His ways, He will do the judging between the nations and 'they shall beat their swords into ploughshares. . . . Neither shall they learn war any more.'

The well known New Testament passage about a high mountain refers to Satan taking Jesus there, showing him 'all the Kingdoms of the world and the glory of them' and telling Jesus they are his if he will bow the knee to Satan."

49   See folder on Monroe Cases in AJM, Box 34, SCPC.

50   Meier and Rudwick, *CORE*, p. 269; AJM to Mendy Samstein, April 6, 1964, AJM, Box labeled '62–'63–'64, SCPC; AJM, "Rifle Squads or the Beloved Community," *Liberation*, May 1964, pp. 1–6.

51   AJM, "Rifle Squads," pp. 1–6.

52   Lewis, *King: A Critical Biography*, chaps. 7 and 8.

53   AJM, "Nonviolence and Mississippi," July 1964, mimeographed, AJM, Box 23, SCPC.

54   Gordon Christiansen, "The Spirit of Freedom," *Liberation*, Nov. 1964, pp. 28–30.

55   "Nonviolence and Police Brutality: A Document," *Liberation*, Dec. 1963; "Cuba Walkers Arrested in Macon, Georgia," *Liberation*, Dec. 1963, p. 8; "Ten Days with the Cuba Walk," *Liberation*, Jan. 1964, p. 5–9, 30–31; AJM, "No Breakthrough of Peace," *Liberation*, Feb. 1964, pp. 12–15; CNVA *Bulletin*, Jan. 13, 1964, p. 3.
56   Lewis, *King: A Critical Biography*, chap. 6; Bradford Lyttle, "Walk Leader Describes Albany's Policy State," *Liberation*, Feb. 1964, p. 6; Leaflet, "We're Walking to Cuba," n.d.; Quebec-Washington-Guantanamo Walk For Peace, "Operating Policies and Discipline of Nonviolence," n.d.; "Biographies: Team Members, Quebec-Washington-Guantanamo Walk for Peace"; CNVA *Bulletin*, "Walk Arrested in Georgia," Jan. 13, 1964; AJM, " 'The Light of Courage and Love', An Appeal," March 14, 1964, all in AJM, Box 23, SCPC; Barbara Deming's *Prison Notes* (New York, 1966) first appeared in installments in *Liberation*, from Aug. 1964 through Jan. 1966; James Bristol, "Report on Visit to Albany Georgia," n.d. [February 1963], AJM, Box 23, SCPC; Lewis, *King: A Critical Biography*, p. 162; AJM to Lucy Montgomery, Jan. 8, 1964, AJM, Box 42, SCPC.
57   Deming, "Prison Notes," *Liberation*, Sept. 1965, pp. 21–25; Bristol, "Visit to Albany," David Dellinger, "A Plea for Understanding," *Liberation*, April 1964, pp. 22–23. Bristol commented on "a genuine inability on the part of several of the supporters of the Walk to understand people who disagreed with them and to be sensitive to these other people as fellow human beings. There was a good deal of self-righteousness which came close to being arrogance at times."
   The effect of the walkers' fasting upon their captors and upon the negotiation process was a matter of debate. Bradford Lyttle was convinced that fasting was a "powerful weapon." Barbara Deming's observations in *Prison Notes* indicated that the fasting did have the power to touch an opponent, at least momentarily, and that it also moved certain black observers. David Dellinger, on the other hand, wrote later that "the fast has no automatic power to reach people." Bristol noted that "there was so little clarity as to why the walkers were fasting. At least five reasons were given at various times and by a variety of people." The AFSC representative concluded that "the impact of fasting seemed to be negligible." Muste chose his words carefully in discussing the fast as a strategy. It had been known to move multitudes, he noted, but cases of imprisonment without fasting had also wrought fundamental changes (The historic imprisonment of socialist Eugene Debs, for example). Without really committing himself one way or the other on the Albany fast, Muste remarked that the "ascetic view" of life "is not mine" (Bradford Lyttle in *Liberation*, Feb. 1964, p. 7; David Dellinger, *Liberation*, April 1964: 22–23. Barbara Deming, *Prison Notes*, [Boston, 1966], pp. 1–181; Bristol, "Visit to Albany"; AJM, *Liberation*, April, 1964).
58   Deming, "Prison Notes," *Liberation*, Sept. 1965, pp. 21–25; Jan. 1966, pp. 24–27; Houser, quoted in Hentoff, *Peace Agitator*, p. 248.
59   Bristol, "Visit to Albany"; *CNVA Bulletin*, March 20, 1964. The black leaders with whom Muste conferred were, according to Bristol: C. B. King, Slater King, recording and executive secretaries of the Albany Movement—Mrs. Jackson and Marion Page, and Phil Davis of the Student Nonviolent Coordinating Committee. By chance, another AFSC person, Carl Zeitlow from Chicago, was in Albany and assisted Bristol and Geiger. It was Zeitlow who suggested sending five walkers into the restricted area.
60   AJM, "The Meaning of Albany," *Liberation*, April 1964, pp. 18–20. See also the assessments of Bradford Lyttle ("A Victory for Truth," pp. 20–21) and David Dellinger ("A Plea for Understanding" pp. 22–23), in *Liberation*, April, 1964; Marion S. Page, "Report from Albany Georgia," *Liberation*, Feb. 1966, p. 46.
61   Dellinger, "A Plea for Understanding," p. 23; James V. Davis to AJM, April 7, 1964, AJM, Box 43, SCPC; AJM to Farley Wheelwright, June 30, 1964, AJM, Box 42, SCPC;

AJM, untitled confidential memo, originally written April 1964, reprinted Aug. 3, 1964, AJM, Box 23, SCPC. While the project was ongoing Muste asked Slater King for an evaluation. In reply King noted that the Georgia Human Relations Council "feel that Kit and Edith made more of a breakthrough in Albany than they [the Council] have ever been able to make. So," King concluded, "though the gains are small, we hope that in time they will increase" (AJM to Slater King, Dec. 9, 1964, and King to AJM, Jan. 8, 1965, Slater King Collection). See also the "Albany Log," AJM, Box 23, SCPC, and AJM, "Rifle Squads," p. 1–6.

62   AJM, "The Civil Rights Movement and the American Establishment," *Liberation*, Feb. 1965, pp. 7–11; AJM, quoted by Grace Pruitt in mimeographed record of a conference in Elgin, Illinois, on the topic, "Beyond Civil Rights: The Peace Churches and Social Justice," n.d., AJM, Box 12, SCPC. See also AJM notes for a speech at Earlham, June 18, 1965, AJM, Box 12, SCPC.

63   AJM, "The Civil Rights Movement," p. 7–11; Farmer interview, 1978.

64   AJM to Robert Swann, May 13, 1963, AJM, Box 25, SCPC; AJM to William Morris, July 16, 1965, AJM, Box 46, SCPC; AJM notes for Earlham speech.

65   AJM, "Assembly of Unrepresented People: The Weekend That Was," *Liberation*, Sept., 1965, p. 8; AJM to William Vickrey, July 29, 1965, AJM, Box 46, SCPC; AJM to Mrs. Prathia Hall Wynn, Aug. 30, 1965, unsorted AJM, SCPC.

66   AJM to John Lewis, July 8, 1966, AJM, Box 46, SCPC; AJM to Lewis, n.d., AJM, Box 42, SCPC; AJM to Julian Bond, n.d., AJM, Box 42, SCPC.

67   Lawson, as Muste knew, was important in keeping before the Southern civil rights movement the total picture of nonviolence, including the witness against war. Lawson was an early opponent of the Vietnam war and had gone to South Vietnam with an interfaith team of the FOR in 1965. Others in the movement who actively opposed the war at an early stage were Bevel and Lewis (See Raines, *My Soul Is Rested*, p. 100, for Lawson's early influence on Lewis's nonviolent stance), Diane Nash Bevel, Bernard Lafayette, and C. T. Vivian (Lawson interview, 1979). See *New York Times* clipping, Aug. 14, 1965, AJM, Box 52, SCPC; AJM, "Assembly of Unrepresented People," p. 29; Coretta Scott King, *My Life with Martin Luther King* (New York, 1969), p. 291; and Lewis, *King: A Critical Biography*, p. 304.

68   Coretta Scott King, *My Life with MLK*, pp. 291, 293–94; AJM to Rev. Martin Luther King, Jr., Dec. 16, 1965, AJM, Box 38, SCPC. According to James Lawson, King had frequently denounced the war in mass meetings in the South, but these statements were overlooked by the press (Lawson interview, 1979). Coretta King wrote of her own desire to see Martin Luther King engage more fully in peace activities: "I remember saying to him so many times, especially after he received the Nobel Peace Prize, 'I think there is a role you must play in achieving world peace, and I will be so glad when the time comes when you can assume that role' " (*My Life with MLK*, p. 292). See also AJM to King, March 30, 1966, AJM, Box 43, SCPC; Miller, *Martin Luther King*, p. 239; memo from Clergy and Laity Concerned. The founding of CLC marked a cautious and—by Muste's lights—very belated recognition by religious leaders of the tragedy occurring in Vietnam. Muste had written Bishop Daniel Corrigan in November 1965 of his disappointment in religious leadership: "It seems to me . . . that Church forces—the National Council, the denominational agencies, Christian, especially Protestant, leaders to whom we are in the habit of looking for initiative—are not saying or doing anything of real significance in relation to the problem. I have the feeling that they are simply marking time and so contribute to the attitude of 'going along' with the Johnson Administration which is so wide-spread and, in my view, so dangerous. This represents of course, a great contrast to what happened among church people in relation to the race

situation during the past half dozen years or so" (AJM, Box labeled Corresp. 64–67, XYZ, SCPC). AJM to Bishop Daniel Corrigan, Nov. 15, 1965, AJM Box labeled Corresp. 64–67, XYZ, SCPC.

69   "A Letter to Martin Luther King from a Buddhist Monk," *Liberation*, Dec. 1965, pp. 18–19; AJM to Martin Luther King, Jr., March 17 and 30, 1966, both in AJM, Box 43, SCPC; AJM to Mrs. Coretta King, Dec. 5, 1966, AJM, Box 27, SCPC.

70   AJM to Claude Bourdet, Feb. 6, 1967, AJM, Box 46, SCPC; *New York Times*, Sunday, Feb. 26, 1967, p. 3, 5; Lawson interview, 1979. Muste's personal esteem for Bevel was reported by the pacifist's secretary: "Aside from A. J.'s feeling of confidence and admiration for Jim he really did 'enjoy' him. I remember, for example, A. J. sitting back in his chair listening to Jim 'preach a little' during a meeting and A. J. really chuckling over it" (Beverly Sterner to Hermene Evans, May 10, 1967, AJM, Box 48, SCPC). *New York Times* clipping, April 19, 1967, AJM, Box 48, SCPC.

71   Lewis, *King: A Critical Biography*, pp. 252–53; Miller, *Martin Luther King*, p. 197; *Commentary*, Feb. 1965; AJM to Staughton Lynd, April 20, 1965, AJM, Box 50, SCPC.

72   David Dellinger, "The March on Washington and Its Critics," *Liberation*, May 1965, pp. 6–7, 31; Staughton Lynd, "Coalition Politics or Nonviolent Revolution?" June–July 1965, *Liberation*, pp. 18–20; Mimeographed "Statement on Student March on Washington;" *New York Post* clipping, n.d. [April 1965], AJM, Box 47, SCPC; AJM to I. F. Stone, April 20, 1965, AJM, Box 47, SCPC; "Memorandum to Norman Thomas, A. J. Muste et al. from Mrs. Gardner Cox, et al., April 27, 1965," AJM, Box 50, SCPC; David McReynolds, "Transition: Personal and Political Notes," *Liberation*, Aug. 19, 1965, pp. 5–10.

73   *Liberation*, Oct. 1965, p. 29; *Liberation*, May–June, 1966, p. 2. There were interesting editorial deletions made in Muste's draft of a statement of appreciation for Rustin's services which accompanied the notice of his departure. The deleted words are bracketed in the transcription of that statement here: "We want to take this occasion to express the gratitude of the Editors for having had the [great] advantage of association [and cooperation] with Bayard through the past many years. We [deeply] regret the circumstances that have recently prevented discussion among us of diverging political views on current developments" (No author [presumably AJM], n.d., AJM, Box 33, SCPC).

74   Rustin, "From Protest to Politics," *Commentary*, Feb., 1965; Bayard Rustin, "Guns, Bread and Butter," and "Dr. King's Painful Dilemma," articles reprinted in *Down The Line*, (Chicago, 1971). Although these articles were published after Muste's death (March 1967), they reflected the position which Rustin had assumed months earlier and of which Muste was entirely aware.

75   AJM to Theodore Roszak, Sept. 23, 1965; AJM to Bayard Rustin, Oct. 5, 1965, AJM, Box 52, SCPC; Rustin interview, 1978.

76   Martin and Coretta King, telegram to AJM, Feb. 5, 1965, AJM, Box 48, SCPC. In discussing the possibility of hyperbole in this communication, Glenn Smiley, James Lawson, and James Farmer all said that King had a firm basis on which to have made these remarks. Farmer stressed that while Muste had not been in the thick of the civil rights struggle, he had played a crucial role in the early stages of CORE and that, through others, he had helped to strengthen the pacifism of King. Lawson cited the important Mustean influence on himself, Farmer, Rustin, Randolph, and the prominent black clergyman and philosopher, Howard Thurman. Thurman, a long-time member of the FOR, has credited Muste with having a role in Thurman's leaving Howard University in 1943 to head the Church of the Fellowship of All Peoples ("The First Footprints: Letters between Alfred Fisk and Howard Thurman, 1943–1944" [San Francisco, 1975], and the British Broadcasting documentary," Life and Thought of Howard Thurman").

Chapter IX

1   AJM, *Nonviolence in an Aggressive World* (New York, 1940), pp. 88–89. This book was selected as "One of fifty outstanding recent religious books by the American Library Association" in 1940 (See Eugene Exman to AJM, June 7, 1940, AJM, Box 1, SCPC; AJM, *The World Task of Pacifism*, Pendle Hill, 1941).

2   "Sixteen Seats at the Peacetable," typescript, 1944, FOR, Box 9, SCPC.

3   AJM to Charles A. Eaton, April 7, 1947, and AJM to Douglas Horton, April 9, 1947, both in FOR, Box 19, SCPC.

4   Muste, quoted in Minutes of the Consultative Peace Council, Dec. 13, 1947, Washington, D.C., FOR, Box 19, SCPC.

So eager was Muste to find an alternative to the Marshall Plan that he interpreted a *New York Times* story on the wealthy Joseph P. Kennedy, who reportedly had told Arthur Krock that the fight against communism could not be won militarily, as a sign that Kennedy might be ready to mobilize the American business community to develop a non-military program of foreign aid and wrote Kennedy to encourage this course. If the millionaire read Muste's letter there is no record of his response (AJM to Kennedy, March 13, 1947, FOR, Box 19, SCPC).

Muste tried also in this period to influence foreign policy by trying to persuade John Foster Dulles, who was assuming a key advisory role in the Truman administration, of the wisdom in dismantling the U.S. military establishment and foreswearing the atomic bomb. Dulles' totally distrustful view of the Soviets precluded any success for Muste in this effort (AJM to Dulles, June 10, June 11, and July 1, 1946; and Dulles to AJM, June 17, 1946 [two letters on this date], all in FOR, Box 7, SCPC).

5   *Korea: Spark to Set a World Afire?* FOR pamphlet, 1950. In this essay Muste also pointed out that in Korea the U.S. was: (1) at a military disadvantage; (2) interfering in a civil war; (3) symbolizing a "white" nation identified with Western conquest; (4) supporting a corrupt and repressive puppet regime. Also see the striking comparisons between these points and those made in a similar essay on the situation in Vietnam fourteen years later, in David McReynolds and AJM, "Memo on Vietnam," *War Resisters' League News*, July 15, 1964.

6   *How to Deal with a Dictator*, FOR, 1954.

7   Ibid.; AJM to Archbishop Lucy, Sept. 25, 1946, AJM, Box 9, SCPC. Muste developed these same arguments in a film which the FOR made about him ca. 1955, *Not by Might*, and in a pamphlet *Getting Rid of War*, published by the American Friends' Service Committee in 1959. See also Muste's pamphlet, *Challenge to Pacifism*, published by the Peace Pledge Union, n.d. [ca. 1950], in which he summarized his point of view: "The most important issue before the world, then, is not that of Communism versus capitalism, nationalism versus internationalism, Russia versus the United States. It is violence versus non-violence."

8   AJM to George V. Allen et al., Sept. 6, 1949, unsorted FOR, SCPC.

Muste's enthusiasm for the United Nations was always measured, but he did not actively oppose it once its existence was an established fact. He expressed a desire "not to alienate supporters of the UNO" and "to leave the way open . . . for progress through the UNO." However, he also hoped that peace workers would be ready, if United Nations channels proved useless, to "bypass" the world organization (AJM to Vernon Nash, Feb. 13, 1946, FOR, Box 9, SCPC). In later years Muste's stance toward the U.N. seemed to become more friendly. At least the letter which included his signature and the signatures of Robert Gilmore, Donald Harrington, Alfred Hassler, Orlie Pell, and Bayard Rustin would support this impression. "We consider it an honor that the U.N. is situated in our country," the signers said as they proceeded to deplore hostile demonstrations against Premier Khrushchev, Premier Castro, and other delegates to the U.N. assembly. In recent episodes of international tension, the letter continued, "the U.N. has exercised a constructive influence . . . and we are gratified by the vote of confidence recently given to Secretary Hammarskjold for the work done by himself and his colleagues [in the Belgian Congo]" (To the editor, *New York Times*, n.d. [ca. 1960], unsorted FOR, SCPC).

9   AJM, *Not By Might* (1947; Garland Library reprint ed., New York, 1971), pp. 33–34, 37–78; AJM to Vernon Nash, Oct. 1, 1946, FOR, Box 9, SCPC; AJM to John A. Folter, Jan. 16, 1945, FOR, Box 7, SCPC. World government projects by themselves, Muste pointed out, did nothing to halt the escalating testing and production of nuclear weapons (AJM to Thane Read, April 11, 1962, AJM, Box 37, SCPC).

10   Muste agreed with Norman Cousins and Thomas Finletter, who had written in the *Bulletin of Atomic Scientists*, July 1, 1946, that the substance of the Baruch plan "would be that of a most-favored-nation treaty—for the United States. All the nations in the world would be asked to surrender their sovereignty in the mining, processing, and manufacture of fissionable materials, but the United States would still be permitted to stockpile its own atomic bombs." Muste's opinion on this and his quote from Cousins and Finletter are in his letter to Dr. Felix Morley, August 1, 1946, AJM, Box 2, SCPC. See also his untitled memo on the International Red Cross which remarks upon the Baruch plan, n.d. [May 1950], AJM, Box 2, SCPC.

11   AJM to [indecipherable], Dec. 3, 1945, FOR, Box 9, SCPC.

12   "Statement on International Crisis," n.d. [ca. 1946], unsorted FOR, SCPC; "A Vote for Wallace Will be a Vote for the Communists," *Fellowship*, July 1948, pp. 5–9; "Taft and Truman: A Memo on the Crisis in Foreign Policy," Jan. 1951, unsorted FOR, SCPC.

13   The nations which Muste singled out as prime candidates for unilateral repentance were India, Japan, Germany, and the United States. (AJM to Mohandus K. Gandhi, September 27, 1946); FOR, Box 8, SCPC; Gandhi to "Dear Friend," Feb. 28, 1947, unsorted FOR, SCPC; AJM, "Report on the India Crisis 1962–63," n.d., condensed version in *Gandhi Marg*, April 1963; "Digest of A. J. Muste to Vinoba Bhave," and related materials, untitled manuscript on AFSC letterhead, Jan. 17, 1963, AJM, Box 40, SCPC; AJM, "Mid-Year Report, 1947," unsorted FOR, SCPC; AJM, "Germany, Summer 1947," in *The Essays of A. J. Muste*, ed. Nat Hentoff (New York, 1967), pp. 296–301; AJM, "A Visit to Germany," August 1947, AJM, Box 9, SCPC; AJM, "Problems of Non-Violent Revolution, Part II," *Peacemaker*, March 15, 1952; AJM, "Memo for IFOR Council, July 1953," dated June 6, 1953, unsorted FOR, SCPC; AJM, "From Berlin about Berlin," *Liberation*, August 1961; AJM, "Trends in Peace Movements Abroad," n.d., FOR, SCPC; AJM, "Berlin, Solomon, Kafka," *Liberation*, Sept. 1961, pp. 3–4; AJM, "A Time to Weep?" *Liberation*, Oct. 1961, pp. 5–8. On Muste's belief in miracles see *Not by Might*, pp. 117–18, 106–7. See also AJM, *How to Deal*, AJM to President Eisenhower, Sept. 24, 1959, and AJM to Christian Herter, Sept. 24, 1959, both in AJM, Box 1a, SCPC. A summary of his thinking on these subjects may be found in Jo Ann Robinson, "A. J. Muste and Ways to Peace," in *Peace Movements in America*, ed. Charles Chatfield (New York, 1973), pp. 81–94.

14   R. Redfield to Fred Eastman (copy sent to AJM), Oct. 9, 1945, and AJM to "Dear Friend," Jan. 15, 1946, both in FOR, Box 12, SCPC.

15   Joseph M. Keller to AJM, Dec. 21, 1945; AJM to Keller, Jan. 14, 1946; and AJM to J. Robert Oppenheimer, Nov. 20, 1945, all in FOR, Box 10, SCPC.

Muste also worked in this period to bring to public light a petition that had been signed by a reported sixty scientists advising President Truman against the use of the atomic bomb. The petition was probably that which had been circulated by Leo Szilard. Government officials whom Muste contacted admitted the existence of the petition but argued that it would have been a breach of national security to have made it public before Hiroshima, and that debate in the wake of the atomic bombings had covered all points raised in the petition and thereby made its issuance to the public unnecessary. Under further pressure from Muste federal officials suggested that the scientists should take the initiative in making it public. Muste was unable to persuade the scientists to do so (Austin Brues to AJM, March 20, 1946; AJM to Secretary of War Robert Patterson, April 1, 1946; and F. L. Parks to AJM, May 31, 1946, all in FOR, Box 12, SCPC; Martin J. Sherwin, *A World Destroyed* [New York, 1975], pp. 217–19).

16   AJM to Enrico Fermi, March 28, 1946 (similar letters went to the other medal recipients); Harold C. Urey to AJM, April 4, 1946; Cyril Stanley Smith to AJM, April 10, 1946, and AJM to Smith, April 18, 1946, all in FOR, Box 12, SCPC.

17   AJM, "Open Letter to Atomic Scientists and Others," March 12, 1946, and AJM "Letter to Dr. Albert Einstein on the Occasion of an Appeal for . . . a Campaign of Education on the Atomic Bomb," May 28, 1946, both in unsorted FOR, SCPC; AJM to Dr. Albert Einstein, June 28, 1946, FOR, Box 12, SCPC; AJM to Einstein, Sept. 15, 1947; Einstein to AJM, Aug. 11, 1947; and AJM to Einstein, Aug. 24, 1947, all in AJM, Box 2, SCPC. Muste's reference to his "imaginary correspondence" with Einstein was made in AJM to Don DeVault, Sept. 22, 1947, AJM, Box 2, SCPC. Harold C. Urey to AJM, June 10, 1946; AJM to Urey, June 17, 1947; Leo Breuer, Sept. 14, 1946; AJM to Breuer, Oct. 3, 1946; Hans Bethe to AJM, Dec. 16, 1946; AJM to Bethe, Dec. 18, 1946; Leo Szilard to AJM, Dec. 18, 1946; Louis N. Ridenour to AJM, Nov. 22, 1946; AJM to Ridenour, Dec. 18, 1946; Stanley Allison to AJM, May 12, 1947; and AJM to Allison, May 21, 1947, all in FOR, Box 12, SCPC.

Muste's dedication to leaving no possibility unexplored in the struggle against the bomb was evident in his letter to Jerry Siegel and Joe Shuster (Oct. 6, 1947, FOR, Box 7, SCPC), creators of the *Superman* comic strip. He praised an episode in which Superman cautioned scientists that "the atomic world cannot really afford more innovations it doesn't know how to use" and urged Siegel and Shuster to keep stressing that theme.

18   Victor Paschkis', "Double Standards," *Friends' Intelligencer*, Eighth Month 30, 1947, p. 463; AJM to Paschkis, Sept. 9, 1947, and AJM to Don DeVault, Sept. 22, 1947, both in FOR, Box 21, SCPC; Untitled memo, n.d., from AJM concerning Haverford conference plans in 1948, and AJM to members of the FOR staff, Sept. 7, 1949, unsorted FOR, SCPC.

The other three Nobel Prize winners in the Society for Social Responsibility in Science were S. E. Luria, Wolfgang Pauli, and Albert Szent-Gyorgi (SSRS pamphlet, 1969–1970). See also Paschkis, "A Review and Outlook," SSRS, July 9, 1970. Over the years the pacifist emphasis in SSRS lessened and the organization evolved into a more typical professional association (The author's interview with Victor Paschkis, Potts-town, Pa., April 13, 1978, and Paschkis' letter of resignation to Dr. Arthur Galston, April 4, 1974).

19   See Otto Nathan and Heinz Norden, eds., *Einstein on Peace* (New York, 1960), pp. 525, 537.

20   Nathan and Norden, *Einstein on Peace*, pp. 557, 604, 620; Pashkis interview, 1978; Victor Paschkis, "Conversations With Einstein," *Liberation*, May 1959, pp. 12–13; Albert Einstein to "Dear Fellow Scientists," *Science*, Dec. 22, 1950, pp. 760–61; "Einstein-Russell Statement," *Fellowship*, Sept. 1955, pp. 18–21. Other signers of the Einstein-

Russell Statement were Percy W. Bridgman, Hermann J. Muller, Linus Pauling (United States); Cecil F. Powell and Joseph Rotblat (Great Britain); Frederic Joliot-Curie (France); Leopold Infeld (Poland); Hideki Yukawa (Japan); Max Born (Germany). Only Rotblat and Infeld did not hold Nobel Prizes.

21   The author's interview with Stephen Cary, Haverford College, May 4, 1978; Herman Kahn to the author, June 23, 1978. In 1961 Muste corresponded with Kahn on the question of why "millions upon millions of dollars are spent on research into weapons systems" while studies of nonviolent alternatives were left "to people regarded perhaps as crack pots and who in any case have no money or facilities to speak of" (AJM to Kahn, Jan. 7, 1961, AJM, Box 22, SCPC); Max Singer to AJM, Jan. 6, 1962, and AJM to Singer, Jan. 12, 1962, AJM, Box 31, SCPC; Hudson Institute Brochure, n.d. [1961–62]; Herman Kahn, *On Thermonuclear War* (New York, 1960) pp. 1–668 passim; and *Thinking about the Unthinkable* (New York, 1962) pp. 1–254 passim; the author's interview with AJM at Lake Villa Ill., April 10, 1964. Earlier that year the author also interviewed associates of Muste at the FOR in Nyack, New York, who were incredulous that he had joined the Hudson Institute. The full list of Public Members for the Institute as of July 1, 1962, included: philosopher Raymond Aron; former ambassador to Belgium, William A. M. Burden; director of the Research Institute of America, Leo Cherne; philosopher Sidney Hook; then president of the Fund for the Republic, Robert M. Hutchins; lawyer John N. Irwin II; vice president of M.I.T., James McCormack; director of United Nuclear Corporation, John R. Menke; Muste; Vice-President Emeritus of Union Theological Seminary, Reinhold Niebuhr; president of Picker X-Ray Corporation, Harvey Picker; lawyer Oscar M. Reubhausen; the owner of Sprague Electric Co. in Massachusetts, Robert C. Sprague; member of the British Parliament John Strachey; labor leader Gus Tyler; International Business Machines representative, Thomas J. Watson, Jr.; and the New England Electric System representative, William Webster. In addition to the public members there were "fellow Members" who included nuclear physicist Hans Bethe, economists Kenneth Boulding and Milton Friedman, and historians H. Stuart Hughes and Henry A. Kissinger ("List of Members," Hudson Institute, July 1, 1962).

The only example of interest by Hudson people in Muste's ideas is a letter from Donald Brennan, president of the Board of Trustees, praising Muste's essay, "Who Has the Spiritual Atom Bomb?" Brennan wrote, "It is a pleasure to find a powerful, lucid and orderly mind brought to a discussion of these issues," then quickly added that "it will come as no surprise to hear that you have several opinions or views I do not share" (Brennan to AJM, Nov. 3, 1965, AJM, Box 42, SCPC).

22   FOR Executive Committee Minutes, 1946 or 1947 (before July 13, 1947), microfilm, FOR, SCPC; AJM, "Christian Pacifism Yesterday and Today," typescript, unsorted FOR, SCPC.

23   Alan Laurence Letts, "Peace and the Gospel: A Comparative Study of the Theological and Ethical Foundations of A. J. Muste's Radical Pacifism and Reinhold Niebuhr's 'Christian Realism'," (Ph.D., diss., Yale, 1975) pp. 1–225 passim; Paul Merkley, *Reinhold Niebuhr, a Political Account* (Montreal and London, 1975) chapter 15.

24   Letts, *Peace and the Gospel*, p. 180–218; Niebuhr, *Nature and Destiny of Man* (New York, 1941, 1943) chap. 9; Merkley, *Reinhold Niebuhr*, p. 206.

25   AJM, *Nonviolence*, p. 134; John Howard Yoder, tape-recorded comments to the author, January 1979.

26   "Theology of Despair," in *The Essays of A. J. Muste*, p. 307; AJM to Reinhold Niebuhr, July 2, 1945.

27   G. H. C. Macgregor, *The Relevance of an Impossible Ideal*, FOR, 1960 (first

published in 1941), p. 127; AJM, *Not By Might*, p. 157; Niebuhr, *Nature and Destiny*, chap. 4; AJM, *Saints for This Age*, Pendle Hill pamphlet, 1962.

28   The Second World War, following closely on the Oxford Conference, had all but reversed this leaning of the Church toward condemnation of war. See "The Relation of the Church to the War in the Light of Christian Faith," Federal Council of Churches, 1944; "Atomic Warfare and the Christian Faith," Federal Council of Churches, 1945; Muste's discussion of Oxford and these statements in *Not By Might*, pp. 159–63; and FOR Executive Committee Minutes, March 12, 1946, microfilm, FOR, SCPC.

The "third position of Amsterdam" was formulated for that Assembly in a statement bearing seventy-eight signatures of religious thinkers from fifteen nations, titled "The Church, the Christian and War," (FOR file on the Church Peace Mission, SCPC); Muste typescript, "Christian Pacifism Yesterday and Today"; the Executive Committee minutes of the FOR for Feb. 23, 1949; and a mimeographed statement by Muste, "The Dilemma of the Churches," 1949, all in unsorted FOR, SCPC.

29   Yoder comments on tape. FOR National Council Minutes, Dec. 3, 1948; "News Release", Jan. 23, 1950, with list of delegates expected to attend the conference; AJM to Harold Bosley, Oct. 25, 1949; FOR National Council Minutes, May 19–21, 1949, all in unsorted FOR, SCPC.

30   "Some Glimpses of an Historic Conference," n.d., [1950] AJM, Box 19, SCPC; Esther Holmes Jones, "The Church and War," *Friends' Intelligencer*, Fifth Month 27, 1950; Alexander Miller, "Theology and the Atom Bomb"; AJM, "Comment on Alexander Miller's Paper," xeroxed study materials, Conference on Church and War; AJM, "Pacifist Strategy," xeroxed study materials; Church Peace Mission, "An Affirmation and Appeal," and Harold Chance to "Dear Friends," May 16, 1950, both in AJM, Box 19, SCPC.

31   Minutes of "Post-Conference Committee," May 23 and 31, 1950; Minutes of CPM Committee, April 18, 1951, and October 31, 1950, all in FOR, CPM Records, SCPC.

32   Robert F. Weiskotten, "Report on CPM," Feb. 19, 1951; FOR National Council Minutes, Dec. 1–2, 1950, unsorted FOR, SCPC; Minutes of CPM Annual Meeting, May 9, 1960, AJM, Box 18, SCPC; J. Harold Sherk, "Summary of CPM Activities, 1950–1962," unsorted FOR, SCPC; "Consultation at Princeton Theological Seminary March 6, 1959," AJM, Box 36, SCPC.

33   Statement by National Council of the FOR, Dec. 1950, Dealing with the Dunn Commission Report, unsorted FOR, SCPC; "Commission on Christian Conscience and War Appointed by CPM," typescript, June 1951; "Draft Letter from Katherine C. Pierce and J. Harold Sherk to 'Dear Friend,' " typed, n.d. Another pacifist statement was also distributed at the assembly: "Peace is the Will of God," prepared by a committee of the Historic Peace Churches and the IFOR, calling the church to reject war but making no reference to the specifically modern nature of atomic and nuclear weapons, Oct. 1953, Haverford College Quaker Collection, pamphlet collection. See also "The Christian Conscience and War," CPM, 1953, 1958, and Edward LeRoy Long Jr., "The Recent Church Peace Mission Report," *Christianity and Crisis*. Long was himself a signer of the statement and had contributed to the drafting of it.

34   Faculty at the Presbyterian Seminary in Dubuque, Iowa, had issued a statement similar to that of the Andover theologians (Dubuque *Telegraph Herald* clipping, Jan. 13, 1960, p. 9, and W. H. DeWolf to AJM, March 2, 1960, both in AJM, Box 18, SCPC); AJM, "Annual Report of Missioner," May 9, 1960 AJM, Box 19, SCPC; AJM to George Buttrick, n.d. [1960], AJM, Box 7, SCPC; AJM to Robert McCrackin, Feb. 19, 1962, AJM, Box 18, SCPC.

AJM, "Christian Conscience and Nuclear War," typescript, n.d., first draft; AJM, "A Christian Approach to Nuclear War," typescript, n.d.; AJM to John O. Nelson, Nov. 30, 1960, unsorted FOR, SCPC; Cover letter for first issuance of "A Christian Approach," typescript, n.d.; AJM to sponsors of "A Christian Approach," Feb. 1, 1961. "A Christian Approach" was reprinted in *World View*, Feb. 1961; AJM to Paul Ramsey, Jan. 17, 1962, unsorted FOR, SCPC; "Draft of Proposed Release Based on 'A Christian Approach,' " n.d. [1962]; AJM to Harold Chance, April 24, 1962, in which he noted that "A Christian Approach" had been excerpted in the *New York Times* and *New York Herald Tribune*. "A Christian Approach" was eventually signed by over five hundred clerical and lay Christians, including Trappist Monk, Thomas Merton, civil rights leader Martin Luther King, Jr., and former National Council of Churches President E. Dahlberg. Enthusiastic commendation from leading Europeans was also reported, with specific references to historian Herbert L. Butterfield of Cambridge, the Very Reverend Sir George F. McLeod of Scotland, Professor Helmut Gollwitzer of the Free University of Berlin, and Dr. Martin Niemoller of the German Confessional Church who had been recently elected as president of the World Council of Churches.

35   "The Lordship of Christ over Church and State," Puidoux Theological Conference, August 15–19, 1955, xerox report, unsorted FOR, SCPC. Preliminary talks had been held in March 1955 between World Council leaders and representatives from the Brethren, the Mennonites, the Friends, the IFOR, and CPM (AJM, "Report on Meetings of European Continuation Committee of Historic Peace Churches and IFOR, Including Conference with Staff of Division of Studies, World Council of Churches, Geneva, March 22–23, 1955," AJM, Box 21, SCPC). Mimeographed report on Puidoux, AJM, Box 37, SCPC. See also Donald F. Durnbaugh, ed., *On Earth, Peace* (Elgin, Ill.: Brethren Press, 1978), pp. 122–45.

36   AJM, "Report on Conversation with Karl Barth at Basel, March 18, 1955," mimeographed, dated April 1, 1955. On Niebuhr, Barth allegedly said, "This is the man who accused me of having a theology which had nothing to say about our Christian responsibility to the social order and preached at us about our political duty."

37   AJM, "Report on Puidoux III Theological Conference, August 1960," mimeographed, AJM, Box 37, SCPC. See also Durnbaugh, *On Earth, Peace*, pp. 146–84, 196–222, 229–71, 319–28.

38   AJM to Joliet-Curie, Nov. 7, 1952, unsorted FOR, SCPC; AJM, "War, Politics and the Normative Principle," *Ecumenical Review*, April 1954, in AJM, Box 15, SCPC; Tape of speech by Martin Niemoller before the National Conference of the FOR, 1954, Michigan Historical Collection, Bentley Historical Library, University of Michigan; AJM, "Report on Discussion between Representatives of the World Peace Council and the IFOR in Stockholm, Sweden," March 16–17, 1955. AJM, Box 17, SCPC.

39   AJM report, "East-West Christian Leaders Conference, August 1–16, 1958," AJM, Box 17, SCPC.

40   AJM to Harold Row, Jan. 14, 1960, AJM, Box 19, SCPC; AJM to Milton Mayer, June 14, 1960; AJM to Norman Whitney and Milton Mayer, March 31, 1960; and Mayer to AJM, June 7 and 20, 1960, all in AJM, Box 36, SCPC.

Muste and Mayer were also in disagreement on the character of Prague Conference leader Joseph Hromadka. Muste's doubts about the Czechoslovakian stemmed from Hromadka's alleged failure to support pacifist churchmen during the Soviet takeover of that country after World War II. Later events, involving Communist moves against Hromadka which stripped him of his influence after the Soviet coup in Czechoslovakia in 1968, indicate the pressures under which the Czech leader had struggled (Heinz

Kloppenberg to AJM, March 1960; the author's interview with Douglas Steere, Haverford College, April 11, 1978; Yoder comments on tape; John C. Bennett to the author, Dec. 8, 1978).

41   AJM, "The IFOR in Relation to Communism and the Liberal World," mimeographed, n.d. [Summer 1959]; AJM to J. D. Bernal, Jan. 31, 1962; J. D. Bernal to Dr. Erich Fromm, Nov. 20, 1961; and AJM to J. D. Bernal, Nov. 28, 1961, all in AJM, Box 39, SCPC.

42   An earlier East-West meeting had taken place in Frankfort in July of 1959 which Muste was prevented from attending by a bout of flu (AJM to Heinz Kloppenberg, Jan. 8, 1959, AJM, Box 19, SCPC); Steere interview, 1978; AJM, "Report on Meeting of East-West Churchmen, August 1960," AJM, Box 36, SCPC; AJM to John Bennett, Aug. 30, 1960; AJM to James Gustafson, Oct. 5, 1960; "Minutes of Meeting on East-West Churchmen's Colloquy,"; Francis Sayre, Jr. to AJM, Feb. 17, 1961 (carbon copy); AJM to Dean Francis B. Sayre, Feb. 24, 1961; Copy of J. L. Hromadka to Douglas Steere, Feb. 19, 1962; AJM to Hromadka, March 9, 1962, all in AJM, Box 26, SCPC; John C. Bennett, to the author, Dec. 8, 1978.

43   Minutes of CPM "Consultation," May 7, 1962, unsorted FOR, SCPC; John Howard Yoder to Irvin Horst et al., April 22, 1954, unsorted FOR, SCPC. The companion piece to Muste's article was "War and the Commandment of Love," by N. H. SØe; Francis Sayre to AJM, June 1, 1961, and John C. Bennett to AJM, March 29, 1959, both in AJM, Box 20/21, SCPC.

44   John C. Bennett to AJM, March 29, 1959, AJM, Box 20/21, SCPC; Paul Tillich, *Interpretation of History*, quoted in AJM, *Not By Might*, pp. 106–7; Tillich to AJM, Aug. 23, 1963, AJM, Box 16, SCPC; Harold Fey to AJM, Oct. 17, 1960; Norman Gottwald to AJM, Sept. 17, 1965, AJM, Box 45, SCPC; Paul Peachey to AJM, May 15, 1962, AJM, Box 21, SCPC; Arthur Swift to AJM, March 22, 1962, AJM, Box 20, SCPC; Frank J. Scribner to AJM, May 2, 1950, AJM, Box 20/21, SCPC.

The meagerness of the results of CPM efforts is reflected in the comment of Ralph Potter in his *War and Moral Discourse* (Richmond, Va., 1969) p. 12: "Throughout the nuclear era virtually every major American denomination has issued statements or pronouncements pertaining to the use of armed violence in specific instances or to more general questions of the role of force in international relations. . . . It cannot be said that any of these materials made a fresh contribution to ethical reflection upon the dilemmas surrounding the use of violence. They seldom exhibit a profound appreciation or even awareness of the ethical tradition of the Christian churches." In a later assessment of the efforts of the Historic Peace Churches to promote dialogue on the peace issue, John Howard Yoder wrote, "If anything the discussants are farther from having a common vocabulary and common understanding at the end of the quarter century than they were at the beginning" (Yoder's "Epilogue," in *On Earth, Peace*). AJM, "Cleveland and After," *Mobilizer*, Dec. 19, 1966.

45   AJM to Erich Fromm, June 7, 1963, AJM, Box 30, SCPC; AJM, "Comment on Shankarras Deo's Points for Consideration by Sponsors and Sympathizers of the Friendship March," AJM, Box 41, SCPC; Oscar Handlin, review of *The Essays of A. J. Muste*, *Atlantic Monthly*, June 1967, p. 120; AJM to William Sutherland, Feb. 24, 1945, unsorted FOR, SCPC; Nathan Glazer, "The Peace Movement in America, 1961," *Commentary*, April 1961, p. 291; AJM, "Psychology and Pacifism," April 1950, mimeographed, AJM, Box 40, SCPC; Pendle Hill Lecture no. 8, April 1954, AJM, Box 5, SCPC.

46   "Unofficial and Provisional Memo of Pacifist Research Commission on the Organization of Peace (Name Tentative)," AJM, Box 36, SCPC. From this memo came the establishment of the Pacifist Research Bureau. See AJM to Harrop Freeman, FOR, Box

20, SCPC, on problems of financing the PRB. For Muste's comments on other proposals relating to research which came up across the years, see AJM, "Memorandum on Pickus Proposal for Pacifica Research Center," Aug. 26, 1958, unsorted FOR, SCPC; AJM to Ted Olson, Sept. 10, 1962, and AJM, "Memo Dealing with Lawrence Scott's 'A Desperate Appeal to American Pacifists,' " n.d., AJM, Box 37, SCPC.

47   AJM, "America Must Choose: Non-Violence, the True Revolution"; Arthur M. Schlesinger, Jr., "America Must Choose: Armed Resistance, Hope for Freedom"; AJM, "Mr. Muste's Final Comment", all in the *Progressive*, May 1951, pp. 10–14, 14–16.

48   Not only was Muste part of the working party which formulated that statement but he had also played a role in the internal politics of the American Friends' Service Committee leading to the appointment of that working party. The statement represented a departure from previous AFSC publications which had emphasized negotiations between the Soviet Union and the United States, and had taken the prevailing cold war framework as a given. In a memo to an AFSC conference in the fall of 1952, Muste challenged that approach. His memo was welcomed by peace secretaries in the New England and Chicago regions who had been urging the AFSC to emphasize pacifist alternatives in their programs dealing with foreign affairs. It was reported to Muste that after his memo was discussed at the Peace Secretarys' conference, they voted unanimously "to undertake . . . a serious job of analysis" of pacifist possibilities for foreign policy (AJM, "Memo to AFSC Peace Secretaries Round-Up", Oct. 1952, AJM, Box 17, SCPC); AJM to FOR staff, Oct. 13, 1952, unsorted FOR, SCPC; *Speak Truth to Power*, (Philadelphia, 1955), pp. 26–34, 67, 70. *Speak Truth to Power* was published over the names of Stephen Cary, James Bristol, Amiya Chakravarty, A. B. Chalmers, William B. Edgerton, Harrop A. Freeman, Robert Gilmore, Cecil Hinshaw, Milton Mayer, A. J. Muste, Clarence Pickett, Robert Pickus, and Norman J. Whitney. Although he played a very significant role, Bayard Rustin refused to have his name included, in view of his recent personal troubles and related withdrawal from public activity in the peace movement (Cary interview, 1978).

49   Editorial in *Progressive*, Oct. 1955, p. 5; Reston, quoted in *Speak Truth to Power*, page fronting page 1. For reactions to *Speak Truth to Power* see the *Progressive*, Dec. 1955, pp. 27–29. Muste wrote again on similar themes for the *Progressive*; see "Our Pro-Russian H. Bomb," Jan. 1956, pp. 15–18.

50   AJM to Sidney Lens, Dec. 16, 1954; AJM, "Proposed Letter to 'Dear Friend' " (attached to the above); "Living Politics Publication Association" (membership application attached to the above); Lens to Frank Marquart, Dec. 20, 1954; Lens to Harold Field, Nov. 2, 1954, all in Lens Papers; AJM, "Tract for the Times," *Liberation*, March 1956, pp. 3–6.

51   AJM to Harrison Butterworth, Feb. 26, 1960, AJM, Box 32, SCPC; Roy Finch, "The Liberation Poll," *Liberation*, Nov. 1959, pp. 14–16.

52   Nat Hentoff, *Peace Agitator* (New York, 1963), p. 183; David Riesman to the author, Feb. 9, 1978; *Correspondent*, Aug. 1960, p. 4. The *Correspondent* grew out of Riesman's "personal diary of foreign policy criticism." On the civil defense issue see the October 1961, fifty-five page issue of the *Correspondent*.

53   AJM to David Riesman, March 11, 1963, AJM, Box 37, SCPC; AJM to Barbara Deming, March 29, 1963, AJM, Box 34, SCPC; Riesman to the author, Feb. 9, 1978; H. Stuart Hughes to the author, Feb. 13, 1978. Riesman had written Muste in 1963 that he valued the pacifist's presence on the editorial board of the *Correspndent* for "the unique combination of shrewd judgment and detachment on the one side with passionate conviction and dedication on the other side" (Riesman to AJM, Feb. 26, 1963, AJM, Box 37, SCPC).

54   Riesman to the author, Feb. 9, 1978. The Pacifist Research Bureau of the 1940s had foundered, as Muste personally noted, because "research people have to eat" and supporting peace groups did not have adequate resources to feed them (AJM to Harrop Freeman, FOR, Box 20, SCPC.); AJM to James L. Morey, Sept. 15, 1964, AJM, Box 44, SCPC; AJM, Robert Gilmore, and Harold Taylor to Senator John F. Kennedy, Nov. 30, 1960, AJM, Box 25, SCPC.
55   AJM to Irving Louis Horowitz, Feb. 7, 1966, AJM, Box 45, SCPC; Horowitz to the author, Feb. 6, 1978.

Chapter X

1   AJM, "Memo Dealing with Lawrence Scott's 'A Desperate Appeal to American Pacifists,' " Dec. 1962, unsorted AJM, 1962–1964, SCPC.
2   AJM to Bradford Lyttle, Nov. 3, 1958, AJM, Box 35, SCPC.
3   *What Happened on June 15*, n.d. [1955], AJM, Box 37, SCPC. Kempton is quoted in this leaflet. The case was carried to the State Court of Appeals. In January 1960 that court upheld the convictions on a four to three vote. The dissenting opinion maintained that the case was not properly within the authority of the magistrate who tried it. The dissenting judges also questioned the constitutionality of applying the Defense Emergency Act to the defendants. Muste and his co-defendants decided to appeal to the U.S. Supreme Court (AJM to Rights of Conscience Committee, Jan. 14, 1960; AJM to Lyle Tatum, Feb. 9, 1960; AJM to Harrop Freeman, Feb. 9, 1960; and AJM to Kenneth Greenawalt, Feb. 9, 1960, all in AJM, Box 22, SCPC).
4   See, for example, Eleanor Roosevelt in her *McCall's* column, "If You Ask Me," Nov. 1960, where she described the building of bomb shelters as "nonsense," and the *New York Times* report, Nov. 25, 1960, about Senator Stephen M. Young of Ohio, who described the national civil defense program as a "billion dollar boon doggle." Historian Lawrence Wittner, who provides other examples of public figures and the public media deprecating civil defense concludes: "For a sizable constituency outside of pacifist ranks civil defense appeared worthless" (*Rebels against War* [New York, 1969], p. 266). On the expanding size of civil defense protests, see AJM to Commissioner Walter Arm, April 27, 1960, and Civil Defence Protest Committee to "Dear Friend," July 19, 1960, both in AJM, Box 37, SCPC; and Nat Hentoff, *Peace Agitator* (New York, 1963), pp. 4–5, 103, 157–58.
5   AJM to Consultative Peace Council Members and Friends, Dec. 15, 1947, FOR, Box 19, SCPC.
6   Jim Peck, "It's Ten Years since A. J. Died," *WRL News*, Jan.–Feb. 1977.
7   AJM, "Follow the Golden Rule," *Liberation*, June 1958, pp. 6–13; Earle Reynolds, *The Forbidden Voyage* (New York, 1961). Reynolds' prison sentence was later overturned. See also Hentoff, *Peace Agitator*, pp. 151–54, and Wittner, *Rebels against War*, pp. 247–48.
8   Minutes from Westtown Consultation on Direct Action, Sept. 17–18, 1958; and AJM to "Dear Friend," Nov. 20, 1958, both in AJM, Box 23, SCPC.
9   AJM, "Memo on Journey to Geneva," Nov. 28, 1958; AJM to "Dear Friend," Nov. 20, 1958; and CNVA, "A Journey in Hope to Encourage," Nov. 24, 1958, all in AJM, Box 23, SCPC.
10   Information Sheet, Report No. 1, Aug. 18, 1958; Report No. 2, Aug. 19, 1958; "Developments," Aug. 20, 1958; "News from Cheyenne," Aug. 28 and 29, 1958; and George Willoughby to "Dear Friend," Sept. 5, 1958, all in AJM, Box 23, SCPC.

11 AJM to Victor Paschkis, July 22, 1959, AJM, Box 35, SCPC; Bradford Lyttle to Lyle Tatum, Oct. 17, 1958, AJM, Box 23, SCPC; AJM to Lyttle, Nov. 3, 1958, AJM, Box 23, SCPC. See also AJM to Albert Bigelow, July 5, 1960, AJM, Box 17, SCPC, in which he wrote: "I am not much drawn to the literal blocking of the road technique. I think *very careful* deliberation should take place before it is practised and that it would usually be found that an alternative was available."

12 AJM to George Paine, May 29, 1959, and AJM to Hildegarde Goss Mayer, July 20, 1959, both in AJM, Box 35, SCPC. Because of the Omaha project Muste was unable to carry out the work which the IFOR had hoped he would do abroad for them that summer. See also AJM to Albert Bigelow, March 26, 1959, AJM, Box 35, SCPC. On the actual project see AJM to "Dear Friends," April 25, 1959, AJM, Box 35, SCPC; AJM to Bradford Lyttle, May 5, 1959; and AJM to Albert Bigelow, May 1, 1959, all in AJM, Box 35, SCPC; AJM, "Reflections on Nonviolent Intervention," AJM, Box 35, SCPC. He noted in these "Reflections" that reactions of hostility on the part of those to whom pacifists are trying to appeal are not necessarily signs of pacifist failure. He reminded readers that Paul had reacted with hostility to the Christians at first but later experienced a conversion to their religion. Also see Theodore Olson to AJM, May 7, 1959, AJM, Box 35, SCPC. Bradford Lyttle was the other coordinator of the project.

13 Omaha Action was preceded by public meetings, training sessions, and walks from Omaha and Lincoln to the Ft. Mead base (James Waltner, "Pacifist Witness," *Mennonite*, Aug. 11, 1959, pp. 483–84. AJM to President Eisenhower, June 29, 1959, AJM, Box 35, SCPC; Wilmer Young, *Visible Witness*, Pendle Hill pamphlet, Nov. 1961; Hentoff, *Peace Agitator*, pp. 156–57; Paul Goodman, "On A. J. Muste," *New York Review of Books*, Oct. 1963, pp. 12–17; "In the U.S. District Court for the District of Nebraska—*U.S. of A.* v. *A. J. Muste, Ross Anderson, and Karl Meyer*," AJM, Box 3, SCPC.

14 AJM to Members of New York FOR Council, Aug. 19, 1959, AJM, Box 35, SCPC; AJM to Victor Rabinowitz, Aug. 5, 1959, AJM, Box 17, SCPC; Francis D. Hale to AJM, July 9, 1959; Emily Scott to Ross Anderson, et al., July 9, 1959; Mildred Young to AJM, July 24, 1959; William Meyer to Karl H. Meyer, July 12, 1959; Norman Thomas to AJM, July 30, 1959; AJM to Francis Heisler, July 31, 1959; AJM to John W. Hewitt, Jr., Aug. 6, 1959; and Cecil Hinshaw to AJM, Oct. 2, 1959, all in AJM, Box 35, SCPC.

About a year after the project ended Muste was queried by an Omaha television station as to possible CNVA influence in reported construction delays at the Mead base. "It is flattering," Muste observed, "that people may actually believe that our nonviolent activity . . . might have the effect of reducing enthusiasm on the part of the workers for building missile sites. But," he concluded, "it is unlikely to put it mildly that we had any appreciable effect of that kind" (AJM to Max Fitch, Sept. 27, 1960, AJM, Box 23, SCPC).

15 AJM to Walter E. Daniels, June 2, 1959, AJM, Box 13, SCPC. When the trial of the three protestors who had pleaded not guilty was scheduled to take place, Daniels invited Muste back to Omaha to speak, but Muste was unable to do so (Daniels to AJM, Oct. 23, 1959, and AJM to Daniels, Nov. 3, 1959, both in AJM, Box 35, SCPC.); Bradford Lyttle, quoted in Hentoff, *Peace Agitator*, p. 157; AJM to Winslow M. Van Brunt, Aug. 6, 1959, AJM, Box 35, SCPC.

16 AJM to Clarence Bauman, Sept. 1, 1959, and AJM to Members of New York FOR Council, Aug. 19, 1959, both in AJM, Box 35, SCPC.

17 "Insofar as there was 'insistence' . . . that Polaris should be taken up," Muste wrote, "that 'insistence' [came from] me" (AJM to Albert Bigelow, July 5, 1960, AJM, Box 17, SCPC). One of the most grave results for CNVA of the controversy over

Polaris was the resignation of one of the Committee's most respected members, Albert Bigelow, who felt that the project lacked the "clarity [and] simplicity" of the *Golden Rule* efforts and that, unlike nuclear tests and civil defense, missiles were not "symbols of deep [public] dissatisfaction and uneasiness" (Bigelow to Bradford Lyttle, March 27, 1960; Bigelow to CNVA, June 15, 1960; AJM to Bigelow, July 5, 1960; Bigelow to AJM, July 6, 1960, all in AJM, Box 35, SCPC). AJM, "Visit to Polaris Project," n.d. [Summer 1960]; AJM to Mrs. Ruth Moore, Sept. 30, 1960, AJM, Box 36, SCPC; Barbara Deming, "The Peacemakers," *Nation*, Dec. 17, 1960, pp. 471–75; AJM to Alice Weber, AJM, Box 36, SCPC.

In this same period the FOR spearheaded a two-year vigil at Ft. Detrick, Maryland, where research on "germ warfare" was conducted. Although Muste was apprised of this project and encouraged by one of its leaders, Charles Walker, to visit it, his focus on it never went beyond words of encouragement (The author's conversations with Charles Walker).

18   AJM to Interested People in Europe and America, Oct. 20, 1960, AJM, Box 36, SCPC.

19   Letter written by Cara Cook, while on the Horizons Tour of July 1958, copy in the author's possession. According to Cook, Muste told the Soviet protestors "that many Americans, including us, thought our Government had made a mistake and the troops should be withdrawn 'as should occupying troops of all nations in similar circumstances,' aimed at Russia's tactics in the satellite countries. A reporter from Moscow's *Pravda* got this statement and two days later it was used, without the qualifying phrase!" Later that same evening the group was assembled by French pacifist Andre Trocmé, who thought that they should leave Russia immediately; he felt that "the situation was extremely dangerous." But, Cook remembered, "A. J. analyzed the situation to the effect that things just wouldn't move that rapidly and that nobody would want to hold us here anyway: also that Russia had only to sit tight—it was [the] U.S. which was out on a limb." Before leaving the Moscow area Muste and Cook had taken a sidetrip to a spectacular Russian air show. "It had no outward military aspects," Cook reported, "except that half of the Red Army must have been on policy duty—but a country which can fly like this, wow!"

20   "Outline of the Policy Position of San Francisco to Moscow Walk for Peace" n.d. [1961], AJM, Box 24, SCPC. According to Nat Hentoff the Soviet crowds numbered between 200 to 650 each night (*Peace Agitator*, p. 216). At the time Muste reported that the numbers reached to 1000 (AJM to George and Lois Hogle, Sept. 22, 1961, AJM, Box 33, SCPC). The walk is detailed in Bradford Lyttle, *You Come with Naked Hands: The Story of the San Francisco to Moscow March for Peace* (Raymond, N.H.: Greenleaf Books, 1966). See also Hentoff, *Peace Agitator*, pp. 213–20 and "They Made It to Moscow," *Liberation*, November 1961, p. 16. The other nationals who joined the march were British, French, Belgian, Dutch, Norwegian, West German, Swedish, and Finnish. A common leaflet was distributed at every opportunity along the way, conveying the March message in six languages: English, Dutch, French, German, Polish, and Russian.

21   AJM to Bradford Lyttle, Dec. 9, 1960; AJM to April Carter, Jan. 4, 1960; AJM to Bayard Rustin et al., April 13, 1961; AJM to Hon. Mikhail Menshikov, April 14, 1961; AJM to Thomas Taylor, April 20, 1961; AJM to Arthur M. Schlesinger, Jr., May 16, 1961; AJM to Premier Nikita Khrushchev, May 15, 1961; AJM to Bayard Rustin et al., May 24, 1961, all in AJM, Box 24, SCPC. See also Hentoff, *Peace Agitator*, p. 214.

22   See Hentoff, *Peace Agitator*, p. 214; and Lyttle, *You Come with Naked Hands*, pp. 127–49; AJM to Heinz Kloppenburg, May 9 and 18, 1961, AJM, Box 11, SCPC. As a link to East Germany, Kloppenburg was important to Muste's hopes for smoothing the

walkers' way in that area, but Kloppenburg opposed the walk. He was not alone among European pacifists in remaining aloof from the March. Some complained that they had not been involved at an early enough stage of the planning. Others, like Kloppenburg, warned that pacifists in Eastern Europe would suffer if they openly supported the walkers. The IFOR went so far as to instruct its staff not to devote time to the walk (AJM to Philip Eastman, March 20, 1961, AJM, Box 26, SCPC). Some of these problems are summarized in "European Part of Tour," typescript, n.d., AJM, Box 26, SCPC.

23 Hentoff, *Peace Agitator*, p. 215; Lyttle, *You Come with Naked Hands*, pp. 71–73.
24 "Statement of A. J. Muste to Soviet Peace Committee in Moscow, September 8, 1961," AJM, Box 26, SCPC. See also Lyttle, *You Come with Naked Hands*, p. 167, and Nikita Khrushchev, "Reply to a Letter from Professor John Bernal," n.d., AJM, Box 26, SCPC. In the letter the Soviet Premier defended Russian resumption of nuclear tests against "all the personalities who had appealed to the Soviet Government. . . . I mean Lord Russell, Canon Collins and other sincere champions of disarmament."
25 Minutes, New York FOR Council Retreat, AJM, Box 29, SCPC. These Minutes noted that Muste had asked George Willoughby to take his place as trouble-shooter for the last phases of the walk. See also AJM to Hugh Brock, Sept. 19, 1961, and AJM, "Comment on September 19 Demonstration" [for *Peace News*], typescript, both in AJM, Box 26, SCPC; and Marcia Lyttle to AJM, Oct. 22, 1961, AJM, Box 34, SCPC.
26 AJM to Elise Boulding, Oct. 9, 1961, and AJM to George and Lois Hogle, Sept. 22, 1961, both in AJM, Box 33, SCPC; AJM to Charles Pratt, Jan. 18, 1962, AJM, Box 22, SCPC; "They Made It to Moscow," *Liberation*, Nov. 1961, p. 16.

For other comments on the walk see Murray Kempton, "The Russell Thing," Oct. 20, 1960, unidentified clipping; clipping from *Time*, Oct. 13, 1961; p. 32 and Oleg Bykov to AJM, Dec. 13, 1961 (Bykov was a member of the Soviet Peace Committee), all in AJM, Box 24, SCPC. Peace Marcher Karl Meyer made a less positive analysis of the March: "The fact is that we have not touched the Soviet Union. We flicked in and out of the Soviet Union so fast that we hardly knew we were there" ("They Made It to Moscow," p. 16). In 1963, however, Muste was still convinced of the significance of the March. In a fund-raising letter that year he quoted reports from Indian Gandhians who had walked from New Delhi to Moscow to Washington recently and reported that "in every town and village on our way people remember and mention to us the 1961 San Francisco to Moscow March. The people have been greatly impressed by such individual actions against war and the arms race." He also quoted from the Vancouver *Sun* columnist, Elmore Philpott, who had written at the conclusion of the March: "Laugh if you like at those bearded youngsters who have the temerity to tell the great rulers of the earth that they, the rulers are marching all mankind down the road to hell, and that at least a few young people do not propose to go along like sheep to the slaughter. Some Russians jeered at these same pacifists, at first, exactly as it also happened in the U.S. But then those Russian scoffers fell silent and respectful when one young American told them he had gone to prison rather than serve in an army which has its rockets aimed at the very cities they were now visiting. 'How many of you have gone to jail for protesting the Russian rockets which are aimed at our home cities in the United States'? . . . Hats off to the brave young crusaders, who foot-slogged 8,000 long miles with their message to Moscow" (Quoted in AJM to "Dear Friend," June 5, 1963, AJM, Box 40, SCPC).
27 Another development which Muste noted with hope was a peace conference in London called by the Soviet-influenced World Peace Council and attended by Soviet delegates where a resolution against all nuclear testing was passed (AJM, untitled typescript, n.d., reporting on this conference, AJM, Box 40, SCPC). See also, "They Made It to Moscow," p. 16.

Everyman I, II, and *III* were all responses, in the tradition of the *Golden Rule* and *Phoenix,* to resumption by the U.S.A. and the Soviet Union of atmospheric nuclear testing. *Everyman I* and *II* were sponsored by the CNVA. The first made two attempts to sail in May and July 1962 from California to the testing site on Christmas Island. The crew responsible for the first attempt was jailed for thirty days; those responsible for the second attempt received sixty-day terms. *Everyman II* left Honolulu on June 23, reached the Johnston Island testing site on June 26, was seized by the Coast Guard on June 29 and its crew jailed for refusing to pay the imposed fine. In the *Everyman III* episode the crew attempted to sink their own ship when Russian authorities towed it out of Leningrad Harbor. The authorities prevented the sinking, kept the crew under arrest on the ship for eight days, then towed the vessel into international waters, from where the crew went on to Stockholm (Nikolai Tikhonov and Mikhail Kotov to "Dear Sir," Aug. 6, 1962; AJM to Kotov, Aug. 27, 1962; AJM to George and Lois Hogle, Sept. 5, 1962; Bertrand Russell to Soviet Peace Committee, Sept. 21, 1962; Russell to AJM, Sept. 21, 1962; "The Voyage of Everyman," *Peace News Supplement,* n.d., all in AJM, Box 23, SCPC; W. S. Merwin, "Act of Conscience: The Story of *Everyman,*" *Nation,* Dec. 29, 1962). See also AJM to Michael S. Grovlich, Nov. 12, 1962, and CNVA *Newsletter,* April 11, and May 12, 1962, all in AJM, Box 23, SCPC; AJM to Oleg Bykov, Sept. 25, 1961, AJM, Box 24, SCPC; CNVA Executive Committee Minutes, May 31, 1962, AJM, Box 23, SCPC; J. D. Berman to AJM, Oct. 2, 1962, AJM, 1962–64, SCPC.

28   AJM to Secretary Oleg Bykov, Jan. 31, 1962, AJM, Box 24, SCPC; AJM to Arthur Schlesinger, Jr., July 16, 1962, with enclosure of "Proposed Visit of Polish and Russian Peace Workers to U.S.," typescript, n.d., AJM, Box 24, SCPC; AJM to Tadeus Strzalkowski, Sept. 20, 1962, AJM, Box 23, SCPC; "Quaker Letter," typescript, n.d.; "Draft of Letter to Polish and Russian Secretaries, typescript, n.d.; AJM to Strzalkowski, Sept. 18, 1963; and AJM to Mikhail Kotov, Oct. 24, 1963, all in AJM, Box 24, SCPC; Frank Siscoe to AJM, Dec. 31, 1963, and AJM to Siscoe, Jan. 3, 1964, both in AJM, Box 25, SCPC; James Wechsler, in a *New York Post* article reprinted in *Liberation,* March 1964, reported that "the White House, I am informed, finally made the decision to sanction their [the Soviets and Poles] admission." See also the *New York Times,* Jan. 5, 1964, p. 2; "State Department Blocks Soviet Visit," *CNVA Bulletin,* Jan. 13, 1964, and *Fellowship Peace Information Edition,* Feb. 1964, pp. 1, 3. On the visitors' reaction to their trip to America, see Oleg Bykov, "Soviet and American Peace Dialogue," typescript, AJM, Box 24, SCPC; Bill Sutherland to the author, Aug. 23, 1979.

29   April Carter, "The Sahara Protest Team," in *Liberation without Violence,* eds. A. Paul Hare and Herbert H. Blumberg (London, 1977), p. 126; AJM, "Africa against the Bomb (II)," *Liberation,* Feb. 1960, p. 11; AJM, "Africa against the Bomb (I)," *Liberation* Jan. 1960, p. 4. Carter reported that the French government had falsely maintained that the test area was uninhabited and had even withdrawn all maps of the region from public access (Carter, "Sahara Protest," pp. 139–40). The idea of the protest was conceived by the activist wing of the British nuclear disarmament movement (Sutherland to the author, Aug. 23, 1979). On earlier contacts between American pacifists and Africa, see Bayard Rustin, "African Revolution," in *Fellowship,* Nov. 1952, pp. 1–6, and Constance Muste Hamilton, "South Africa Sows the Wind," *Fellowship,* Dec. 1952, pp. 5–10.

30   Quoted in Carter, "Sahara Protest," p. 138. This summary of events is taken from Carter and from Muste's *Liberation* articles cited in n. 29. Money for the Sahara Project was raised within Ghana by that nation's Council for Nuclear Disarmament. The existence of that Council, which had been formed in August, provided a further reason for the western pacifists to work out of Ghana. Other reasons included strong anti-French

sentiment among the people there and the fact that their struggle for independence (won in 1957) "had been based on Nkrumah's strategy of 'positive action' " which was closely akin to and easily associated with nonviolence. Moreover, Bill Sutherland had been living in Ghana, working as personal secretary to Finance Minister K. A. Gbedemah.

31   Quoted in Hentoff, *Peace Agitator*, pp. 204–5. Muste singled out as a particularly pressing concern the fact that the young Ghanaian volunteers had never before been exposed to nonviolence. "They had had," he said, "no experience of 'that other kind of force—patience,' as one of them put it to me later." The training which each volunteer had received before the team set out was sufficient preparation "for dramatic situations such as arrest and imprisonment." But "for the hard task of simply sticking it out day after day they were not as well prepared."

32   Typescript of *Liberation* report, Dec. 6, 1959, AJM, Box 37, SCPC (The error was corrected when the report was published); AJM to Alexander Aholu, Dec. 30, 1959, AJM, Box 37, SCPC.

33   AJM, "Africa against the Bomb (II)"; AJM to Abdoulaye Diallo, Dec. 30, 1959, AJM, Box 37, SCPC; AJM, "Comment on Sahara Protest Team," n.d., typescript [probably for *Liberation*]; Mabel Dove, quoted in the *Ghanaian Times*, Feb. 9, 1960, in "Africa: Bombs Away," *Liberation*, March 1960, pp. 3–4; Sutherland to the author, Aug. 23, 1979.

The Sahara project had generated a sizeable amount of protest in Africa. In addition to the large, supportive crowds that turned out for the Team throughout Ghana, project supporters staged other demonstrations. French pacifist Pierre Martin fasted for seven days before the French embassy in Accra; a Nigerian supporter, Hilary Arinze, conducted a three-day fast before the French Consulate at Lagos. The French Embassy in London, French Government Tourist Offices in New York City, and the French Consulate in Hamburg were picketed by project sympathizers. Other demonstrations, not directly related to the Sahara Project, occurred in the days immediately preceding the explosion. There were mass demonstrations in Tunis, Libya, and Morocco, as well as the gathering before State buildings in Paris of five hundred African students from French-speaking African territories. After the explosion Ghana froze the assets of French firms, receiving public congratulations from Julius Nyerere of Tanganyika for having done so. Efforts to stimulate protest in France had met with the biggest obstacles. But Esther Peter did successfully encourage the French Union of Teachers to take a position against the tests and was able to organize small demonstrations around Paris (Carter "Sahara Protest," pp. 140–41, and Muste's *Liberation Reports*.

34   AJM, "Africa against the Bomb, Parts I and II," and his typescript to *Liberation*, Dec. 6, 1959, AJM, Box 37, SCPC; Sutherland to the author, Aug. 23, 1979. Certain episodes during the protest indicate that this understanding of nonviolence was not universally profound. "Some of the Ghanaian youths found it difficult to understand how you could expect to gain anything by any kind of conversation with white French officers," Muste wrote. "They even harbored the absurd suspicion that the French woman who served as interpreter for the Team (Esther Peter) was somehow 'betraying' them when she conversed with the French" (AJM typescript for *Liberation*, Dec. 12, 1959); AJM, Box 37, SCPC.

35   Bill Sutherland to AJM, March 10, 1960, AJM, Box 37, SCPC; Carter, "Sahara Protest," pp. 140–41; "Our Editors in the Field," *Liberation* April 1960, p. 3; "Conference on Positive Action," mimeographed, hand-dated, March 11, 1960, AJM, Box 17, SCPC; Michael Randle, "Some Notes on the Positive Action Conference to Be Held in Accra, April 7th and 9th," March 20, 1960, AJM, Box 17, SCPC; AJM to Bill Sutherland,

n.d. [March 1960]; AJM to George and Lois Hogle, April 15, 1960; and AJM to Andre Trocmé, April 18, 1960, all in AJM, Box 17, SCPC.
36   Bill Sutherland to AJM, July 18, 1960, AJM, Box 37, SCPC. This impression was verified when in September of 1960 the French announced plans for a new series of atomic tests. Sutherland, with Michael Randle, proposed that another team try to make its way to the site, coordinating protest in African capitals with a charter flight of Africans to demonstrations in Paris. The proposals were left in limbo (Carter, "Sahara Protest," p. 143). On Muste's efforts in this period to raise funds and attract public support for peace work in Africa and related work in France, see AJM, Box 30, SCPC.
      Bill Sutherland has written, "I personally believe that Ghana *could*, under Nkrumah, have gone in a different direction and broken new ground in human organization and relations. . . . But it is intolerable for those who are 'secure' enough behind massive armies and modern weaponry to allow a degree of freedom commensurate with the safety of the State to criticize the leaders of the new nation-states who face destabilization by the intelligence operations of big powers as well as serious internal problems, all threatening their very existence and survival" (Sutherland to the author, Aug. 23, 1979).
37   Carter, "Sahara Protest," p. 142, n. 4. Michael Randle had foreseen these problems in "Notes on the Positive Action Conference." AJM to Harold Fey, Oct. 25, 1960. Hentoff found it necessary in his 1963 profile of Muste to note that Nkrumah was "hardly an apostle . . . of Muste's kind of nonviolence in his domestic conflicts" (*Peace Agitator,* p. 203).
38   Carter, "Sahara Protest," pp. 147–48.
39   AJM, "Satyagraha Units or the Peace Army," n.d. [Dec. 1949–Jan. 1950]; Charles Walker, "Nonviolence in Eastern Africa, 1962–64: The World Peace Brigade and Zambian Independence," in *Liberation without Violence,* p. 158; Barbara Deming, "International Peace Brigade," *Nation,* April 7, 1962, p. 303; AJM, "Internationalizing the Peace Movement," *Peace News,* Sept. 7, 1962, AJM, Box 11, SCPC; Minutes, Exploratory Committee for a World Conference on Nonviolence, Jan. 12, 1960, AJM, Box 17, SCPC; AJM to Milton Mayer, Jan. 28, 1960, AJM, Box 36, SCPC; AJM to Charles Walker, Jan. 28, 1960; Walker, "Assessment of the Proposal for a World Conference on Nonviolence," July 18, 1960; and AJM to Walker, July 26, 1960, all in AJM, Box 17, SCPC. Muste later noted the important contribution which Walker had made in keeping the idea alive (AJM to Arlo Tatum, Oct. 31, 1961, AJM, Box 39, SCPC). See also Arlo Tatum to AJM, and AJM to Tatum, both dated March 21, 1961; and "Information Sheet #1," World Peace Brigade Conference Preparatory Committee, May 2, 1961, both in AJM, Box 39, SCPC. Michael Scott seems to have been influential in convincing Muste to attend the conference (AJM to Scott, Oct. 20, 1961, and AJM to Arlo Tatum, Nov. 28, 1961, both in AJM, Box 39, SCPC); AJM to Art Springer, Dec. 13, 1961, AJM, Box 39, SCPC.
40   Barbara Deming, "International Peace Brigade," p. 303; AJM typescript, "Nonviolence and the World Movement, n.d. [1962], and "Some Meanings of the Beirut Conference," n.d. [1962], both in AJM, Box 40, SCPC; Bradford Lyttle, "Brummana Conference for a World Peace Brigade: Final Report," n.d. [1962], AJM, Box 40, SCPC.
41   AJM to G. Ramachandran, Jan. 17, 1962, and World Peace Brigade, "Statement of Principles and Aims," both in AJM, Box 39, SCPC.
42   Bayard Rustin to AJM, Feb. 22, 1962, AJM, Box 40, SCPC; Walker, "Nonviolence in Eastern Africa," pp. 159–60; "Statement of Kenneth Kaunda," May 13, 1960, AJM, Box 37, SCPC; AJM to *Friends' Journal,* Oct. 1, 1962, AJM, Box 40, SCPC; Bill Sutherland to Bayard Rustin, Jan. 20, 1959, AJM, Box 31, SCPC. See Kaunda to Bill Sutherland (postmarked Jan., 1959), AJM, Box 31, SCPC: "Bill your sincerity struck me so much I still

remember clearly the times we spent together discussing NONVIOLENCE and other matters. Your voice still rings deep in my ears and it will do so for a long time to come." See also *The New Africans*, (London, 1967), s.v. "Dr. Kenneth Kaunda," pp. 490–91, which describes his "political creed" as "faith in the common man and belief in nonviolence, based on a study of Gandhi and a visit to India. The life of Abraham Lincoln also inspired him."

43   Walker, "Nonviolence in Eastern Africa," pp. 160–63; Bayard Rustin to AJM, Feb. 22, 1962; and "Press Statement on the East African Situation, Feb. 2, 1962", both in AJM, Box 40, SCPC. This press release over the names of Kaunda and Tanganyika African National Union vice-president R. J. Kawawa welcomed the WPB as a part of the African Freedom Action. The Brigade, they noted, was composed of "members [who] have engaged in positive action in so many countries . . . [and now] add their experience to our own long efforts to achieve freedom in Africa through nonviolent resistance. . . . We are convinced, Kaunda and Kawawa declared, "that such action applied now in Northern Rhodesia may yet prove to be the key to the liberation of Central and Southern Africa." See also Bayard Rustin to AJM, March 8 and 16, 1962; and Rustin to Lyle Tatum et al., March 12, 1962, all in AJM, Box 40, SCPC.

44   AJM to Alfred Hassler, May 29, 1962; "Statement to the Press by the Three Chairmen of the World Peace Brigade for Nonviolent Action"; AJM to Michael Scott, June 2, 1962, all in AJM, Box 40, SCPC; Walker, "Nonviolence in Eastern Africa," pp. 166–67, 169, 175; Bayard Rustin to Lyle Tatum et al., March 8, 1962, AJM, Box 40, SCPC.

45   Walker, "Nonviolence in Eastern Africa," pp. 167–68, 171, 173; World Peace Brigade Positive Action Centre *Newsletter*, July 30, 1962; and R. M. Kawawa to Bill Sutherland, June 2, 1962, both in AJM, Box 40, SCPC. See also Muste's fund-raising letters for this project in AJM, Box 40, SCPC. The situation faced by the Centre staff was summed up by Bill Sutherland: "Our position is very bad because we have operated from the beginning far below the budget so that the small amounts coming in now are immediately eaten by the short term loans we have made to keep going" (Bill Sutherland to AJM, Oct. 30, 1962, AJM, Box 40, SCPC).

46   AJM to Bill Sutherland, Sept. 28, and Oct. 2, 1962; AJM to Colin Bell, Oct. 2, 1962, both in AJM, Box 40, SCPC. Other WPB ideas included a proposed journey of reconciliation by prominent westerners to "labor with" figures such as Wilensky and Verwoerd. Michael Scott had also worked on a proposal for a march into Southwest Africa, demanding the return of the lands from which Africans had been forcibly evicted and demanding that the territory be handed over to U.N. jurisdiction. On yet another front, Muste reported in October of 1962 that he, Scott, and Rustin had been in conference with "a considerable number of African leaders," including the leader of liberation struggles in Southern Rhodesia. While these leaders were not convinced of the usefulness of nonviolence, Muste said, they were "stymied as to what to do." The implication was strong that, had the pacifists developed a feasible suggestion, the Africans may have tried it. But, Muste admitted, "We . . . have not so far been able to come up with concrete ideas for nonviolent intervention in the situation" (AJM to Jayaprakash Narayan, Oct. 9, 1962, AJM, Box 40, SCPC). See also AJM to Bill Sutherland, Sept. 24, 1962, AJM, Box 40, SCPC; AJM to Hon. K. E. Pakendorf, Oct. 17, 1962; and James Farmer, George Houser, Muste, A. Philip Randolph, and Norman Thomas to Pakendorf, Oct. 22, 1962, both in AJM, Box 11, SCPC.

47   For the quotation on "an expensive experiment," see Anton Nelson to the Editor, *World Peace Brigade Reports*, n.d. [Summer 1965]. With regard to WPB competition with other forces, Muste noted in the summer of 1963 that when Kaunda visited the

United States, the "State Department had taken Kenneth in hand and was evidently keeping elements like ourselves away from him." A visit to the U.S. by Nyerere followed this same pattern (AJM to Lyle Tatum, June 13, and Aug. 7, 1963, both in AJM, Box 37, SCPC). Such maneuvering by governments of major nations of the world was but one force that the pacifists had to offset; a deep-rooted commitment to violence on the part of—as Muste viewed them, "multitudes of African nationalists"—presented the overwhelming challenge, as he knew. In a financial appeal to American Quakers he reminded them of violence in Southern Rhodesia . . . in Algeria, the Congo, Angola. . . . I think," he said, "of all that violence in Africa . . . and of how little has been done to experiment with nonviolence. . . . Then I think of the small, tentative effort of the World Peace Brigade. . . . Then I recall that the World Peace Brigade is behind in payments to keep the work in Dar es Salaam going and I am ashamed of myself. I am ashamed for all of us" (AJM to *Friends' Journal*, Oct. 1, 1962, AJM, Box 40, SCPC). In 1979, Bill Sutherland commented, "Those pacifists who condemn violence in the liberation movements in Africa today never put their money where their mouths were when called upon" (To the author, Aug. 23, 1979).

48   AJM to Bill Sutherland, Sept. 7, 1962, AJM, Box 40, SCPC. Bayard Rustin analyzed the problem precisely in his description of how African Freedom Action operated: "AFA is and must be run by a tightly knit working committee subject in most part to major political organizations. This . . . makes it somewhat impossible for the democratic and open approach most pacifists are used to in planning a project. . . . In regard to the march, . . . " Rustin pointed out, "we will be constantly subject to the veto of Nyerere and Kaunda. . . . They usually are inclined to take our view into full consideration and . . . are fully committed to nonviolence, . . . yet the working committee is the final authority" (Rustin to AJM, March 16, 1962, AJM, Box 40, SCPC).

49   Lyle Tatum to AJM and Bill Sutherland, July 19, 1962, AJM, Box 40, SCPC. In retrospect, Charles Walker has written, Tatum's "charge may have had some merit." Walker further points out, however, that Kaunda "was not averse to recognizing publicly the difficulty of restraining political workers even under harassment. Indeed, he [Kaunda] said the presence of the march idea was a restraining force in face of such problems" (Walker, "Nonviolence in Eastern Africa," p. 171).

50   On critics' complaints see Lyle Tatum to AJM and Bill Sutherland, July 19, 1962, and Anton Nelson to Editor, *World Peace Brigade Reports*, n.d. [Sept. 1963].

In the period before and during the WPB Kaunda repeatedly and unqualifiedly endorsed nonviolence in private exchanges and in public. The Brigade observers at Addis Ababa recorded a notable example of his public stance. As Bayard Rustin recalled, "When Kaunda was challenged by a delegate of Southwest Africa who said 'why nonviolence, which won't work. We should beat the drums and sharpen our spears,' Kaunda replied, 'Africa must not add to the violence of the West which already threatens the very existence of mankind. In principle we must find another way or perish.' " From his own personal conversations with the Zambian leader, Muste came away "firmly convinced that Kaunda was a 'devout Christian . . . seeking to apply Gandhian methods and spirit in his actions.' " Nyerere's appreciation for the values and goals which the WPB represented was also convincing. Having been directly challenged by Bill Sutherland on his policies of restricting civil liberties, Nyerere, in conversation with Bayard Rustin, "said it was a good thing for him [Nyerere] and others in his position to have Bill around." After the positive action center folded, Nyerere assisted Sutherland in finding a job working with refugees at Dar es Salaam (Rustin to Muste, Feb. 22, 1962; AJM to Robert S. Steinbock, AJM, Box 40, SCPC; AJM to Lyle Tatum, June 13, 1963, all in AJM,

Box 37, SCPC; and Anton Nelson to Editor, *World Peace Brigade Reports*, n.d. [Sept. 1963]).

Another sign of Kaunda's continuing interest in nonviolence was his agreement in August 1963 to have Lyle Tatum of the American Friends' Service Committee lay plans to set up a training center in nonviolence in Northern Rhodesia. This effort was interrupted, however, by the Unilateral Declaration of Independence by Southern Rhodesia (Walker, "Nonviolence in Eastern Africa," p. 176; Lyle Tatum to AJM, Aug. 2, 1963; AJM to Tatum, Aug. 7, 1963; and Memo from AJM to Stewart Meacham, Oct. 17, 1963, all in AJM, Box 40, SCPC).

51   AJM to Bill Sutherland, Sept. 8, 1964; AJM to Sutherland, June 6, 1965; and Sutherland to AJM, Sept. 21, 1964, all in AJM, Box 49, SCPC; Hentoff, *Peace Agitator*, p. 223; Sutherland to AJM, May 27, 1966, AJM, Box 42, SCPC; Lyle Tatum to AJM and Bill Sutherland, July 19, 1962, AJM, Box 40, SCPC.

Note might also be taken of Charles Walker's argument that "the fact that nonviolent actionists could work out practical strategies regarding resistance to colonialism, develop tactics applicable on a mass scale, and establish a cordial working relationship with a variety of independence groups is perhaps some indication of the potential of nonviolence, if more assiduously pursued [and he might have added financially supported] in its organizational and political aspects" (Walker, "Nonviolence in Eastern Africa," p. 176).

52   AJM to Harrison Butterworth, May 29, 1962, AJM, Box 40, SCPC; AJM to J. P. Narayan, May 29, 1962, and AJM to G. Ramachandran, May 28, 1962, both in AJM, Box 30, SCPC.

At the anti-nuclear arms convention in New Delhi in June of 1962, an unequivocal call to unilateral disarmament was delivered by former President Rajendra Prasad before Prime Minister Nehru, the then president, vice-president, and many dignitaries from the Indian Parliament (AJM, "Report on the India Crisis, 1962–63," n.d., condensed version in *Gandhi Marg*, April 1963, pp. 92–98).

53   AJM, "Report on the India Crisis," pp. 92–98; AJM to Michael Scott, Dec. 11, 1962, AJM, Box 30, SCPC. See also references to Narayan's call in "Proceedings of Joint Meeting of the World Peace Brigade Executive Committee and the World Peace Brigade European Regional Council," Jan. 9, 1963. One Gandhian wrote Muste, after reading the American's report on India, "You are as accurate as sincere. God bless you. I am overwhelmingly puzzled and am waiting for Divine help on clarifying my mind. Truth shines clear enough. But there is a roaring lion in between. I don't know where I am" (AJM, Box 37, SCPC). During a conversation with Gandhians in 1978, IFOR representative James Forest was told: "There are three groupings [of Gandhians in India]. There are the *establishment* Gandhians—the ones in the government—who take from Gandhi those things which will not be too disturbing to the government. There are the *official* Gandhians—who manage the institutions Gandhi founded, but try not to disturb the government. And there are the illegitimate children of Gandhi. . . . We are the ones who get in trouble just as Gandhi did." Very similar divisions appear to have existed in India when Muste was there in the sixties (James Forest, "Listening to Gandhi Again," *Sojourners*, Aug. 1978, p. 14).

54   Mimeographed digest of Vinoba Bhave's remarks as well as recent speeches by Bhave, compiled by Jim Bristol, Jan. 17, 1963.

55   Proceedings, Joint Meeting of the World Peace Brigade Executive Committee and the World Peace Brigade European Regional Council, Jan. 9, 1963; Carbon of "Friendship March: Delhi-Peking, Memorandum on Aims and Objectives," over signatures of the WPB Chairmen, all in AJM, Box 41, SCPC. While in London WPB representatives,

including Muste, met with the Secretary of the Communist Chinese Peace Committee and the head of the Chinese churches. They "seemed interested" and "A. J. judged that they would be open to further contact from the West." Meanwhile, in India, Narayan obtained Vinoba Bhave's support for the March and secured the participation of Shan-Karai Deo, described as "perhaps next in stature to Vinoba in the Indian peace movement" (Carbon of "Friendship March" Memo and Siddharaj Dhadda to AJM, Jan. 19, 1963, both in AJM, Box 41, SCPC).

56 *Christian Science Monitor,* March 20, 1963; AJM to Anna Louise Strong, Sept. 30, 1963, AJM, Box 41, SCPC. Western-Soviet cooperation against China seemed evident to Muste in the period following the U.S.-Soviet nuclear test ban agreement of 1963. He noted the statement of U.S. ambassador to the U.N., Adlai Stevenson, quoted in the *New York Times* on Oct. 16 of that year, who envisioned "a time when the Soviet Union 'may be an ally of the West' against an expansionist thrust from China." At the same time support for admission of China to the U.N. was forthcoming from neither the U.S. nor Russia. Muste vigorously protested these developments and felt that, by so doing, he could demonstrate to the Chinese that the Friendship Marchers rejected Soviet and U.S. policies on the same basis that they were appealing for a change in Chinese policies (AJM to Editor, *New York Times,* Oct. 2, 1963, carbon in AJM, Box 41, SCPC). A copy of the same letter was sent to Stevenson, Oct. 17, 1963, AJM, Box 41, SCPC. AJM to Mao Tse-tung, Aug. 27, 1963, AJM, Box 41, SCPC; AJM to Rev. Nichidatsu Fujii Guruji, Oct. 24, 1963, AJM, Box 1962–1964, SCPC.

57 On his assumption about the attitude of the Peking authorities, see Muste to Devi Prasad, Oct. 14, 1963, AJM, Box 41, SCPC. Correspondence relating to this March effort includes: AJM to Cho Pu-Cho, June 22, 1963; AJM to Rev. Nichidatsu Fujii Guruji, Aug. 19, 1963; AJM to Mao Tse-tung, Aug. 27, 1963; AJM to Bertrand Russell, Sept. 10, 1963; AJM to Anna Louise Strong, Sept. 30, 1963; AJM to Sinhjing Kotda-Sanghami Takhare Sahib, Oct. 1, 1963; Siddharaj Dhadda, Oct. 3 and 5, 1963; Copy of telegram from AJM to Martin Luther King, Jr. and A. Philip Randolph, Oct. 9, 1963; AJM to Siddharaj Dhadda, Oct. 14, 1963; AJM to Secretary Ho Ping Ta Hui, Nov. 19, 1963; and typescript "For Liberation News Service," all in AJM, Box 41, SCPC. On Muste's final admission of failure see AJM to Rev. Nichidatsu Fujii Guruji, Jan. 13, 1964, AJM, Box 41, SCPC.

58 AJM to Siddharaj Dhadda, Oct. 14, 1963; Rev. Nichidatsu Fujii Guruji, Aug. 19, 1963; AJM Memorandum on the World Peace Brigade, n.d. [Spring 1965]; AJM to Pearl Buck, March 7, 1963; and AJM to Harry Emerson Fosdick, March 7, 1963, all in AJM, Box 41, SCPC; Walker, "Nonviolence in Eastern Africa," pp. 174–75.

Specifically on the competition for funds in the U.S., see Muste to Mr. and Mrs. Charles Darlington, July 17, 1963, AJM, Box 24, SCPC: "Birmingham and the magnificent upsurge of the civil rights movement . . . knocked the financial props out from under us. Not only did the movement get the attention of the general public which we cannot yet reach anyway, but pacifists, Quakers and the people who CNVA helped educate in nonviolent direct action were besieged with appeals from the various civil rights organizations. Who are we to say they should not respond!" To Theodore Roszak, Sept. 17, 1965, AJM, Box 49, SCPC, Muste wrote in a similar vein: "Great amounts of money continue to go into the various civil rights organizations. A number of people I know, who but for the big sums for various civil rights projects to which they have committed themselves would send me $1000 every once in a while, now squeeze out $100 occasionally."

59 David Dellinger, *Revolutionary Nonviolence* (New York: Anchor ed., 1971), p. 129; AJM typescript on Cuban situation, AJM, Box 11, SCPC.

60 AJM to Editor, *New York Times*, April 11, 1961, copy in AJM, Box 32, SCPC; "Death of the Republic", *Liberation*, May 1961, pp. 13–15; CNVA, "An Appeal to the American Conscience," AJM, Box 26, SCPC.

61 "Cuba and *Liberation*", *Liberation*, May 1961, p. 5; Minutes, New York FOR Council Fall Retreat, Sept. 18, 1962, AJM, Box 29, SCPC; AJM, "Comment," *Liberation*, May 1961, p. 5; AJM to Richard Gibson, AJM, Box 27, SCPC, in which Muste declined to lend his name to the Fair Play for Cuba Committee but assured that committee that he would "go to bat" in defence of their civil liberties. See also, "Cuba: An Analysis of American and Soviet Policy, prepared by AJM for WRL," n.d. [Before Oct. 22, 1962],. AJM, Box 11, SCPC. A special flurry of protest over the report that the United States would ban the export of drugs, medicines, and food to the island is evident in an undated letter from James Baldwin, William Davidon, Dorothy Day, Dave Dellinger, Barbara Deming, Lawrence Ferlinghetti, Sidney Lens, Staughton Lynd, Kenneth Patchen, Bayard Rustin, Norman Thomas, William Worthy, and AJM to President Kennedy (AJM, Box 26, SCPC).

62 As the CNVA pamphlet described U.S.-Soviet actions, Soviet missiles in Cuba were parallelled by U.S. missiles in England and Turkey; Soviet secrecy in missile deployment complemented deployment of U.S. missile-launching submarines that was "as secret as the Navy can make it"; false statements by Soviet officials invited comparison with Adlai Stevenson's denial before the U.N. of U.S. involvement in the Bay of Pigs, and State Department denials during the Eisenhower era of the U-2 spy plane that was downed in Russian territory (CNVA, "The Cuba Crisis," Oct. 26, 1962).

63 AJM typescript, no title, n.d. [ca. 1962], AJM, Box 11, SCPC; AJM, "Love and Power in Today's Setting," *Christian Century*, May 15, 1963, p. 639; and AJM, "Accumulation of Peril," *Liberation*, Dec. 1962, pp. 14–18. The pacifists' alternative for U.S. policy in Cuba included: renouncing all intent to invade Cuba, withdrawing military forces from the area, closing the Guantanamo Base, ceasing to support "revanchist Cuban exiles", and instituting positive economic and technical assistance programs for the island. CNVA encouraged the Castro government to renounce military interventions, cease hate propaganda against the U.S., adopt nonviolent forms of resistance, and pursue cooperation with the U.N. For the Soviets CNVA recommended withdrawal of all military forces and technicians from the island and cooperation with the U.N.

64 CNVA *Newsletter*, Feb. 7, 1963, and CNVA leaflet, *Is This What We Really Want?* both in AJM, Box 43, SCPC.

65 "Biographies: Team Members of Quebec to Guantanamo Walk," n.d.; "We're Walking to Cuba," n.d.; AJM to Mrs. Lorna Scheide, Feb. 27, 1963; AJM to "Dear Friend," June 5, 1963; CNVA, "Operating Policies and Discipline of Nonviolence"; Memo from Irwin R. Hogenauer, Aug. 29, 1963; Memo from Neil Haworth, Sept. 3 and 4, 1963; AJM to Dr. Albert Sprague Coolidge, Nov. 20, 1963; and AJM to "Dear Friend," March 14, 1964, all in AJM, Box 43, SCPC.

66 AJM to "Dear Friend," May 1, 1964; AJM to Mrs. and Mrs. [sic] Halsey Hulbert, July 13, 1964; Bradford Lyttle to AJM et al., Aug. 18, 1964; and AJM, "Hurricane in Miami," mimeographed, Sept. 1, 1964, all in AJM, Box 43, SCPC.

  See also Abba P. Schwartz to AJM, May 6, 1964; John V. Lindsay to AJM, June 26, 1964; AJM to Schwartz, n.d.; and AJM to the Hulberts, July 13, 1964, all in AJM, Box 43, SCPC.

67 Deming, *Prison Notes* (Boston, 1966), p. 185; "The Spirit of Freedom," *Liberation* Nov. 1964, p. 28–31.

68 Eighty-Second Birthday Fund Appeal, and Glenn Smiley both in AJM, Box 48,

SCPC; AJM to Bill Sutherland, Nov. 9, 1962, AJM, Box 40, SCPC; AJM to Arlo Tatum, Feb. 6, 1962, AJM, Box 39, SCPC.

When Abba P. Schwartz, the State Department official with whom Muste dealt in this episode, later resigned from his post, Muste took time to express his respect for the official, both to the man himself and to his superiors. According to news reports Schwartz had been pushing all along for liberalized travel regulations and the lifting of bans on travel to such places as Cuba (AJM to Schwartz, March 11, 1966; AJM to Robert F. Kennedy, March 11, 1966; Schwartz to AJM, April 28, 1966, all in AJM, Box 49, SCPC). See also *New York Times*, March 7, 1966, p. 1, and March 8, 1966, p. 22.

69   David Dellinger, *More Power than We Know* (New York, 1975), p. 63; Bayard Rustin comments at Muste memorial service, reported by James A. Wechsler, "He Never Failed," *New York Post*, Feb. 22, 1967, p. 30.

70   AJM, *Saints for This Age*, Pendle Hill pamphlet, 1962. On the Washington fast see AJM to "Dear Friend," n.d. [Oct. 1962], AJM, Box 23, SCPC.

71   John C. Heidbrink to AJM, Nov. 6, 1964, unsorted AJM, 1963–1964, SCPC. Muste had made a case in *Not by Might* for the Catholic Church's assuming an unequivocal pacifist position (pp. 173–76). Gordon Zahn, ed., *Thomas Merton on Peace* (New York, 1974), p. 259–60, and see also p. xiv; Tom Cornell, review of *Thomas Merton, Fellowship*, Jan. 1974, p. 23; FOR Executive Committee minutes, Dec. 15, 1964, FOR microfilm, SCPC; AJM to Harrison Butterworth, Dec. 1, 1964; and AJM to Harold Fackert, Dec. 1, 1964, both in unsorted AJM, 1963–1964, SCPC. Participants in the retreat included John Howard Yoder, Daniel and Philip Berrigan, Robert Cunnane, James Forest, Tom Cornell, John Oliver Nelson, and Paul Peachey.

72   AJM to Mary Meigs, Feb. 4, 1961, AJM, Box 18, SCPC; AJM to Meigs and to Elise Boulding, both dated Jan. 18, 1961, both in AJM, Box 17, SCPC; AJM, "Internationalizing the Peace Movement," AJM, Box 11, SCPC.

73   Beverly Henry to Neil Haworth, Aug. 31, 1962; Barnaby Martin to AJM et al., Sept. 3, 1962, AJM, Box 13, SCPC; Beverly Henry to Project Committee, Sept. 14, 1962, AJM, Box labeled Misc. Reading Materials, SCPC; Henry and Barbara Deming to Inge Snipes, n.d.; Haworth to Henry et al., Sept. 16, 1962; AJM to Working Committee, Sept. 18, 1962; AJM to Earle Reynolds, Sept. 19, 1962, all in AJM, Box 23, SCPC; Reynolds to AJM, Sept. 28, 1962; Henry to Haworth, Oct. 31, 1962; and Marj Swann to Bradford Lyttle, Oct. 31, 1962, all in unsorted AJM, 1962–1964, SCPC.

74   AJM, Box 28, SCPC. Muste's son remembered his father as being sternly reserved about matters of sex: "We didn't talk about sex. Love in our family, as far as [AJM] was concerned was not a matter of physical touching, or of extended conversations about personal concerns. I was terrified rather than gratified when, as an adolescent, I put some (by today's standards very innocent) pinup pictures on the walls of my bedroom and he came in to get me to take them down. First he asked me if I was having any sexual problems (vehemently denied), then he told me to take the pictures down. . . . Before I was 14, I had . . . not the slightest inkling about where babies came from, and when I found out, it was not from my parents" (John Muste to the author, Feb. 6, 1979). It is possible, as Barbara Deming has pointed out, to see Muste's objection to the pinups as an objection to exploitation rather than as a sign of Victorian prudery (Telephone conversation with Deming, Jan. 18, 1980).

75   AJM, "Comments on Marjorie Swann's Memo of March 7, 1963," March 26, 1963, AJM, Box 34, SCPC; the author's interview with Bayard Rustin, April 20, 1978, New York City; Barbara Deming to the author, March 25, 1979.

76   AJM, "Pacifism Enters a New Phase," *Fellowship*, July 1, 1960, typescript,

AJM, Box 11, SCPC; AJM to Harold Row, May 2, 1962, AJM, Box 20, SCPC; AJM to Sidney Lens, April 23, 1962, AJM, Box 33, SCPC.

77   AJM to Thomas Atkins, April 24, 1963, AJM, Box 29, SCPC; AJM to Tracy Mygatt, April 26, 1963, AJM, Box 34, SCPC; AJM to Lillian Willoughby, April 23, 1963, AJM, Box 41, SCPC; Alfred Hassler to AJM, Aug. 4, 1964, and AJM to Hassler, Aug. 14, 1964, both in unsorted AJM, SCPC; AJM to Lindley Burton, Aug. 14, 1964, AJM, Misc. 1965–1967, SCPC; AJM to George Malloy, Aug. 21, 1964, unsorted AJM, SCPC; *Liberation*, Sept. 1964, p. 2; Milton Mayer to AJM, Aug. 16, 1964, AJM, Box 46, SCPC.

78   AJM to Glenn Smiley, July 30, 1964, AJM, Misc. 1965–1967, SCPC; Tom Cornell to AJM, Sept. 28, 1964, AJM, Box 42, SCPC; AJM to Neal (Rev. Cornelius Muste, a brother), Nov. 6, 1964, unsorted AJM, 1963–1967, SCPC; Tom Cornell, review of *Thomas Merton*, p. 23; Jim Forest, "Some Thoughts on the Resistance," *WIN*, Jan. 15, 1969, p. 4, Jim Forest to the author, Dec. 30, 1978.

79   AJM to Roger Hagan, Nov. 13, 1964, unsorted AJM, 1963–1967, SCPC; AJM to David Berkingoff, June 2, 1965, AJM, Misc. 1965–1967, SCPC; John Muste to the author, Feb. 6, 1979; AJM to Lucille Kohn, March 15, 1966, AJM, Box 46, SCPC; AJM to Ira Sandperl, Sept. 7, 1965, AJM, Box 49, SCPC; AJM to Tracy Mygatt, Sept. 22, 1965, AJM, Misc. 1965–1967, SCPC; the author's interview with John Swomley, June 10, 1978, New York City.

80   AJM to Mildred Romer, June 11, 1965, AJM, Box 49, SCPC.

81   AJM, "Who Has the Spiritual Atom Bomb?" *Liberation*, Nov. 1965, reprinted in *The Essays of A. J. Muste*, pp. 479–502.

Chapter XI

1   Francis H. Russell to AJM, Jan. 8, 1946, and AJM to Russell, Jan. 15, 1946, both in FOR, Box 10, SCPC; AJM, Memo to International FOR Council, July 1953, dated June 6, 1953, unsorted FOR, SCPC. AJM, Pendle Hill Lecture no. 2, April 7, 1954, Pendle Hill, SCPC.

2   David McReynolds and AJM, "Memo on Vietnam," *WRL News*, July 15, 1964.

3   AJM to Adlai Stevenson, Dec. 6, 1961, AJM, Box 38, SCPC; AJM to Mao Tse-tung, Aug. 27, 1963; AJM, to Editor, *New York Times*, Oct. 2, 1963; AJM to Stevenson, Oct. 17, 1963, all in AJM, Box 41, SCPC. AJM to Rev. Nichidatsu Fujii Guruji, Oct. 24, 1963, AJM, Box 1962–1964, SCPC.

Shortly after the Chinese bomb became a reality the FOR, over Muste's signature, sent letters to the heads of state of China, Russia, and the United States encouraging them to have a summit meeting to seek disarmament and world peace (Draft of Letter to Mao Tse-tung, Premier Mikoyan, and President Johnson, Jan. 1965, AJM, Misc. 1965–1967, SCPC. The same letter, translated into Chinese and Russian and dated Feb. 1, 1965, appears in AJM, Box 50, SCPC).

4   The division of Vietnam into North and South was instituted at the Geneva Conference of 1954 and conceived there as a temporary situation, pending national elections in 1956. The idea of those elections was scuttled by the American-backed Diem government in South Vietnam.

The term "Viet Cong" was an Americanism applied loosely to all forces fighting for North Vietnam. Later some anti-war spokespersons would object to the use of the term as demeaning to the Vietnamese, but Muste used it regularly and seemed unaware of this possible objection.

The Muste-Kennan exchange was published in *Liberation* April 1965, pp. 6–11, 24. It included a Nov. 24, 1964, Muste critique of Kennan's article in the *New York Times Magazine* of Sunday, Nov. 22, 1964, titled "A Fresh Look at our China Policy"; Kennan to AJM, Nov. 30, 1964; AJM to Kennan, Dec. 18, 1964; Kennan to AJM, Jan. 4, 1965; and AJM to Kennan, March 8, 1965. Not published was Kennan's final letter, Aug. 25, 1965, AJM, Box 46, SCPC. See also Norman Cousins to AJM, Jan. 27, 1965; carbon to AJM of Edmund Wilson to George Kennan ("In your controversy with A. J. Muste . . . I find myself rather on his side"), March 22, 1965; and Margaret Holt to AJM, April 6, 1965, all in AJM, Box 46, SCPC.

5   James L. Greenfield to AJM, Sept. 3, 1964, and AJM to Greenfield, Sept. 18, 1964, both in AJM, Box 43, SCPC.

The "functional equivalent" description of the Gulf of Tonkin Resolution was that of Undersecretary of State Nicholas Katzenbach, quoted in Ralph F. deBedts, *Recent American History, 1945 to the Present* (Homewood, Ill., 1973), p. 303. See also Anthony Austin, *The President's War: The Story of the Tonkin Gulf Resolution and How the Nation Was Trapped in Vietnam* (Philadelphia, 1971), p. 368, and I. F. Stone, "The Tonkin Bay Mystery," *New York Review of Books* (March 28, 1968), pp. 5–12.

6   AJM to Mary Eubanks, Aug. 19, 1964, and AJM, "Problems of the Radical Peace Movement," Sept. 10, 1964, mimeographed, both in unsorted AJM, 1963–1966, SCPC. In this same essay Muste noted that the Republican candidate's retrograde position on civil rights brought him "closest to sharing the alarm felt by my friends over the emergence of Goldwater." But he concluded that establishment politics did not hold the key to ridding America of racism any more than it held the key to peace, and that the Goldwater phenomenon "emphasizes . . . the urgency of finding more creative forms of nonviolent action than we have yet developed."

7   *New York Times*, Dec. 20, 1964, p. 52:2; Robert Cooney and Helen Michalowski, eds., *Power of the People* (Culver City, Calif., Peace Press, 1977), p. 183.

8   Irwin Unger, *The Movement* (New York, 1974), p. 83; Kirkpatrick Sale, *SDS* (New York, 1973), p. 3–172.

9   AJM to Dean Henry Stroup, May 4, 1960, and AJM to Dean Kathryn L. Hopwood, May 18, 1960, both in AJM, Box 22, SCPC.

10   SDS to AJM, May 7, 1964, unsorted AJM, 1963–1966, SCPC; AJM to Sidney Lens, March 16, 1965, Lens Papers; AJM to Gordon Christiansen, June 18, 1963, AJM, Box 22, SCPC.

11   "Memorandum for a March," *New York Post*, Apr. 16–17, 1965, clips in AJM, Box 50, SCPC; AJM to I. F. Stone, April 20, 1965, AJM, Box 47, SCPC.

12   "Statement on Student March on Washington," April 16, 1965, AJM, Box 50, SCPC. Other signers of the statement were Ed Clark, Roger Lockard, Emily Parker Simon, Alfred Hassler, Charles Bloomstein, and Harold Taylor. Muste stressed that "not a single point of view or basic position was held by all signers" (AJM to I. F. Stone, April 20, 1965, AJM, Box 47, SCPC). As he told Stone, Muste did not attend the March because he was not physically up to it. A statement criticizing the signers of the April 16 document was sent to all those signers by Mrs. Gardner Cox et al., April 27, 1965, AJM, Box 50, SCPC. See also AJM to Theodore Roszak, Sept. 23, 1965; Clark Kissinger to AJM, May 7, 1965; and AJM to Mel McDonald, Aug. 26, 1965, all in AJM, Box 49, SCPC. See also Kirkpatrick Sale, *SDS*, pp. 177–94.

About six weeks before the March (March 8, 1965) Muste had prepared a short memo on "Problems of Collaboration in Peace Activity" in which he found "the ideological basis of the SDS 'Call' on the whole satisfactory." He stressed, however, that pacifists must remain firm in "rejecting softness toward Soviet or Chinese militarism" and took to task those Americans who "operate as if they regard Moscow and/or Peking . . . as virtually pacifist." SDS carelessness later in keeping its position distinct in public announcements from such advocates of communist regimes apparently prompted Muste's signature on the Gilmore-signed statement (AJM, "Memo: On Problems of Collaboration in Peace Activity," March 8, 1965, AJM, Box 49, SCPC).

13 Draft of Resolution from the World Council of Peace, April 24–25, 1965, AJM, Box 52, SCPC; AJM to *New York Times*, April 30, 1965, AJM, Box 46, SCPC; AJM to Stewart Meacham, June 2, 1965, AJM, Box 52, SCPC.

14 "A Call to Speak Out at the Pentagon," and "For Immediate Release: Speak Out at the Pentagon," both in AJM, Box 49, SCPC; AJM to Robert McNamara, June 16, 1965, and AJM to W. H. Ferry, June 28, 1965, both in AJM, Box 46, SCPC. See also AJM, "Comment," *Liberation*, Aug. 1965, pp. 28–29. Fourteen years later Robert McNamara declined an invitation to comment on his memories and views of the Speak Out (Robert S. McNamara to the author, June 26, 1979).

15 To "Dear Rev. Muste" from John M. Jones, June 17, 1965, and Jones to AJM, July 6, 1965, both in AJM, Box 49, SCPC; the author's telephone interview with Jones, June 22, 1979. At the time of this interview, John M. Jones, a graduate of the Naval Academy, was employed there as a civilian. Muste had taken note of news reports of another dissatisfied Pentagon employee who had resigned from the Department of Research. But efforts to determine if the Speak Out had influenced his resignation were apparently unsuccessful (AJM to Eugene G. Fabini, July 19, 1965, AJM, Box 49, SCPC).

16 AJM to Irving Laucks, June 28, 1965, AJM, Box 46, SCPC; AJM to Sidney Lens, Aug. 13, 1965, Lens Papers. The importance attached by Muste to the Assembly's potential for furthering this link between peace and civil rights workers was evident in his appeal to one potential contributor: "I would be prepared to urge you to make a very substantial contribution now, even if that has to mean you forbid me to appeal to you again for quite awhile" (AJM to Harrison Butterworth, July 13, 1965, AJM, Box 36, SCPC).

17 Muste said his forces actually counted 25,000; the editors of *Power of the People* quote a figure of 50,000. See AJM to Sidney Lens, Sept. 16, 1965, Lens Papers; AJM to Arthur Miller, Sept. 30, 1965, AJM, Box 45, SCPC; AJM to Ray Brown, Oct. 7, 1965, AJM, Box 52, SCPC; AJM to Hermene Evans, Nov. 2, 1965, AJM, Box 49, SCPC; "Memo on Proposed Vietnam Peace Rally in New York City," Jan. 7, 1966, and AJM to Margaret Gardiner, Jan. 19, 1966, both in unsorted AJM, 1963–1966, SCPC.

Barbara Deming and others have observed that while Muste certainly was a key figure in the coalition-building described here, others also made major contributions which should be noted in the historical record. The work of Brad Lyttle and Norma Becker appear to be important in this regard, for example (The author's telephone conversation with Deming, Jan. 18, 1980).

18 AJM, "Proposed Peace Rally," unsorted AJM, 1965–1966, SCPC.

19 Cooney and Michalowski, *Power of the People*, p. 186. See photograph of AJM and Dorothy Day at this gathering in *WIN*, Feb. 24, 1967 special supplement, p. 14; Remarks by AJM at Draft Card Burning, Oct. 28, 1965, and AJM, "Statement of Support for Those Burning Their Draft Cards October 28," both in AJM, Box 44, SCPC.

20 "Statement of the Eight Persons Subpoenaed to Appear before the Federal Grand Jury, November 6, 1965," AJM, Box 44, SCPC; "Statement Made on December 21, 1965 by AJM to the Federal Grand Jury, reprinted in *The Essays of A. J. Muste*, ed. Nat Hentoff (New York, 1967), pp. 462–64.

21 Cooney and Michalowski, *Power of the People*, p. 184. On Alice Herz see AJM to Tony Ramirez, June 7, 1965, AJM, Box 49, SCPC. On all three deaths see AJM, "State-

ment on Self-Immolation," AJM, Box 49, SCPC. See also AJM to Long Clay Hill, Jan. 18, 1966, AJM, Box 49, SCPC. Even the *New York Times* editorialized with some sympathy on the suicides of Morrison and La Porte, concluding "confused and misdirected though they may have been, they may serve some useful purpose if their self-inflicted agony brings home—alongside the mounting casualty lists—the grisly cost of war" *New York Times*, Nov. 11, 1965, p. 46:2.

22 AJM, "Who Has the Spiritual Atom Bomb?" *Liberation*, Nov. 1965, reprinted in *The Essays of A. J. Muste*, pp. 479–502.

23 Ibid.

24 AJM to Alfred Hassler, Dec. 3, 1965; James Finn, ed., *Protest: Pacifism and Politics* (New York, 1967), pp. 193–205, AJM, quoted in interview, pp. 200–201; Benjamin Spock, AJM, Mildred Olmsted, Norman Thomas, and Gilbert F. White to Ho Chi Minh, Jan. 19, 1966, AJM, Box 50, SCPC. The letter was sent during a temporary lull in the fighting and after "peace feelers" had been extended by the Johnson administration. The letter included the argument that "the influence of the American peace movement will be greatly diminished in the absence of fresh initiatives from North Vietnam and the National Liberation Front."

25 AJM to James Reston, Oct. 18, 1965; Reston to AJM, Oct. 25, 1965; and AJM to Reston, Nov. 3, 1965, all in AJM, Box 49, SCPC. In this same period Muste sent a personal letter, representing no organization, to President Johnson appealing to his professions of religion (AJM to Johnson, Dec. 16, 1965, AJM, Box 46, SCPC).

26 AJM to James Wechsler, Dec. 28, 1965, AJM, Box 52, SCPC; James Wechsler to AJM, Dec. 30, 1965, and AJM to Wechsler, Jan. 7, 1966, both in AJM, 1964–1967, XYZ, SCPC; AJM to J. W. Fulbright, March 31, 1966, AJM, Box 44, SCPC. For AJM comments on Fulbright see AJM to Carl Landauer, Oct. 26, 1965, AJM, 1964–1967, XYZ, SCPC; and AJM to Sidney Lens, Feb. 15, 1966, Lens Papers. See also AJM to Anatol Rapoport Nov. 8 and 19, 1965, both in AJM, Box 49, SCPC; and AJM to Herbert Marcuse, Oct. 5, 1965, 1964–1967, XYZ.

27 AJM to Arthur Waskow, Feb. 15, 1966, AJM, Box 42, SCPC. See also AJM to Sidney Lens, Feb. 15, 1966, Lens Papers. Muste sent letters of commendation to all signers of the *New York Times* ad, AJM, Box 42, SCPC; See also the folder in AJM, Box 49, SCPC, containing Muste's letters to many people who wrote to or were published in the *Times* on Vietnam and/or the question of violence.

On American Friends' Senate Committee, *Peace in Vietnam* (Philadelphia, 1966), see Mike Yarrow to Vietnam Working Party, Dec. 7, 1965, AJM, Box 50, SCPC; AJM to Frederick J. Libby, and C. H. Yarrow to AJM, Feb. 4, 1966, both in AJM, Box 42, SCPC; AJM draft of a chapter for *Peace in Vietnam*, AJM, Box 48, SCPC. For a review which did in fact single out the Muste statement, see Warren Griffiths, "AFSC on Peace in Vietnam," April 15, 1966, copy in unsorted AJM, 1963–1967, SCPC. For a typical hostile review see Richard Eder, "Peace without Victory," *New York Times Book Review*, April 17, 1966, p. 10.

With regard to Muste's quote it is interesting to note that some three years later, in reference to the destruction of the village of Ben Tre, an American Air Force major told a reporter that "it became necessary to destroy the town to save it" (Quoted, among other places, in Alexander Kendrick, *The Wound Within* [New York, 1974], p. 251).

28 To Sidney Lens, Feb. 15, 1966, Lens Papers. See also Muste's editorial in *Liberation*, Feb. 1966, pp. 28–30, and March 1966, pp. 53–55. As his actions (and the narrative which follows) made clear, Muste was not on the brink of a new romance with revolutionary violence when he wrote these words. He saw a place for nonviolence

in "every form of dissent and protest" and maintained a continuous dialogue with activists who did not agree.

29   It was not always clear whether heightening protest and extending the coalition were compatible. Fearing that major military losses would drive moderate critics of the war into a position of supporting their beleaguered government, Sidney Lens advised Muste that "it is incumbent on us to devise means by which we can bring . . . the SANE forces, TTP [Turn Toward Peace], and similar groups towards us. We must drive a deeper wedge between them and the administration. . . . To put it in the terms of the 1930's we must extend the united front consciously, deliberately, carefully, effectively; and we must avoid the wild tactics that will isolate us. . . . Our more radical friends must continue to be active and sustained," Lens concluded, "but we must also recognize the major and primary need for consolidation." In achieving consolidation, Lens observed, Muste would be "the key figure . . . because you command everyone's respect" (Lens to AJM, Feb. 16, 1966, Lens Papers).

On the picketing of the Freedom House award to Johnson dinner, see AJM to Officers and Trustees, Freedom House, Feb. 18, 1966, and AJM to Robert Lowell, Feb. 28, 1966, both in AJM, Box 45, SCPC; *New York Times*, Feb. 24, 1966, clipping in AJM, Box 52, SCPC. While picketers walked outside Freedom House and held a rally where Julian Bond received their "Freedom Award," Jim Peck of the War Resisters' League entered the Awards dinner as a guest. He interrupted the ceremonies by baring a peace sign on the shirt under his dress clothes and shouting "Peace in Vietnam!" Present at the Freedom House dinner had also been TV commentator David Brinkley, who presided; black concert artist Leontyne Price, who sang the National Anthem; journalist Roscoe Drummond, NAACP leader Roy Wilkins, and cabinet officer Douglas Dillon, each of whom spoke. (AJM, Box 45, SCPC).

With regard to the peace march see the *New York Times*, March 27, 1966, p. 1; "News Release, Vietnam War Protestors to Parade on Fifth Avenue, March 1966"; Program for Fifth Avenue Peace Parade and Rally, March 26, 1966; and Fifth Avenue Peace Parade Committee pamphlet, n.d., all in AJM, Box 44, SCPC.

30   Barbara Deming, " 'It's a Good Life,' " *Liberation*, Sept.–Oct., 1967, p. 60; AJM, CNVA Asian Project and Related Proposals; DeWitt Barnett, "Report from Japan," May 10, 1966, and Gordon Christiansen, "The Southeast Asia Project: An Impressionistic Report," containing references to criticisms that had been made of the Saigon project, all in AJM, Box 43, SCPC.

31   Pete Hamil, "Muste, Unbowed Back from Saigon," *New York Post*, April 25, 1966, clipping in AJM, Box 43, SCPC; "Reports from Saigon," *Liberation*, May–June 1966, p. 11.

32   AJM, paraphrased in Barnett, "Report from Japan"; AJM, "A Visit to Saigon," *Liberation*, May–June 1966. The priests' statement had been published in *Commonweal* and *Viet Report*, copies in AJM, Box 43, SCPC.

33   Brad Lyttle in *Liberation* May–June 1966, pp. 11–17; AJM, quoted in Hamil, "Back from Saigon." See also "Statement of U.S. Peace Mission on Entry to South Vietnam," AJM, Box 43, SCPC. DeWitt Barnett, "Report from Japan"; Barbara Deming also recalled that when they first tried to hold the press conference at the Caravel, their lives were threatened (Telephone conversation with the author, Jan. 18, 1980).

34   Deming, " 'It's A Good Life,' " pp. 60–61 in *Liberation*, Sept.–Oct. 1967. Brad Lyttle in *Liberation*, May–June 1966, pp. 11–17, and AJM, pp. 7–10, in the same issue. As Deming later remembered, the pacifists, in full view of a guard, leafletted from the paddy wagon en route to the airport (Deming's phone conversation, Jan. 18, 1980).

35   "Report from Japan."

36   Hamil, "Back from Saigon,"

37   "Documents: Students and Student Organizations in Vietnam about Saigon Visit of Six American Pacifists," AJM, Box 45, SCPC; According to Muste the Buddhist Monk, Thich Nhat Hanh, told the team in April that these student communications had been mailed to New York, but they did not reach CNVA. Apparently the reporter received second copies of them.

38   News Release, "Vietnam Peace Parade Committee," Aug. 4, 1966, AJM, Box 45, SCPC; AJM to Peter Boehmer, Aug. 14, 1966, AJM, Box 42, SCPC. On the flag question Muste further explained to Boehmer, "The Parade Committee invariably takes the position that the only flag it sanctions is the American flag—this because it is legally required and not necessarily because we are typical flag wavers. . . . If I were to be fully consistent," he added, "I think I would have to refuse to march under the American flag or to submit to having it at a rally, when it is so thoroughly identified with the military and with atrocious conduct as it is today. In that context the Viet Cong flag seems to me not to be in what might be called an inferior position to the American. Certainly, the Vietnamese Viet Cong and their sympathizers have as much 'right' to carry their flag as the American soldiers and their sympathizers have to carry theirs."

39   Martin M. Goldsmith to AJM, Dec. 2, 1966, AJM, Box 45, SCPC.

40   AJM to Claude Bourdet, May 27, 1966, and expressing the same sentiment, AJM to Harrison Butterworth, June 6, 1966, both in AJM, Box 42, SCPC.

41   Reston, quoted from the N.Y. Times, June 19, 1966 in AJM, "What Is the Role of the White House, St. Department, CIA in the Indonesian Massacre?" unsorted AJM, 1963–1966, SCPC.

42   [CNVA] "Draft Memo on Ky Statement," n.d. [1966], AJM, Box 12, SCPC; AJM, "Reflections on U.S. Policy," mimeographed, July 27, 1966, AJM, Box 12, SCPC (This essay includes quotations from a recent letter which Muste sent to Frank Church and other senators). See also George M. McGovern to AJM, Aug. 1, 1966, and AJM to McGovern, Aug. 3, 1966, both in AJM, Box 46, SCPC; AJM to Reston, Aug. 1, 1966, AJM, Box 49, SCPC; AJM to George Kennan, June 23, 1966, AJM, Box 46, SCPC.

43   AJM, "Memorandum on Current Nonviolent Action in South Vietnam," June 15, 1966, AJM, Box 12, SCPC; James Wechsler, "In the Twilight," New York Post, May 2, 1966, AJM, 1964–1967, XYZ, SCPC.

44   The accounts of both Schweid and Pilati are reprinted in Liberation, Sept.–Oct. 1967, p. 59, originally published in the Boston University News, Feb. 15, 1967, p. 9.

45   Michael Meeropol to AJM, Nov. 1, 1966; AJM to Meeropol n.d. (draft of a night letter), AJM, Box 46, SCPC; Telegram sent Sept. 24, 1966, by AJM to President Johnson (mimeographed copy) AJM, Box 42, SCPC. As another example of a young person's response to Muste see this letter in AJM, Box 45, SCPC, dated April 15, 1966: "I am twenty eight years old and thoroughly disillusioned with the way the world is going. However, seeing someone your age still in there giving them all sorts of moral Hell is invigorating. It makes a young man . . . feel like no matter what he does, he isn't doing enough."

46   AJM to Don McKelvey, Oct. 5, 1966, AJM, Box 49, SCPC.

47   Cooney and Michalowski, Power of the People, p. 187; AJM to Honey Knopp, Oct. 6, 1966, AJM, Box 42, SCPC; "A. J. Muste, 1885–1967," WIN special supplement, Feb. 24, 1967, p. 12.

48   Tom Robbins to AJM, Dec. 17, 1966, and AJM to Tom Robbins, Dec. 29, 1966, both in AJM, Box 49, SCPC. AJM to Honey Knopp, Oct. 6, 1966, AJM, Box 42, SCPC.. Muste stressed in this letter, and later in a speech to the New York Lawyers Guild in February

1967 that the families of these new recruits to the peace movement tended to be much more supportive of their sons than families had often been in previous wars toward conscientious objectors. Text of that speech is in *Liberation*, Sept.–Oct. 1967, pp. 52–57; this particular point is addressed on p. 53.

49   AJM to Joan Nielsen, Aug. 2, 1966, AJM, Box 48, SCPC.

50   Fort Hood Three Defense Committee, *The Fort Hood Three*, pamphlet, July 1966, quotes from pp. 11, 16. Mora, quoted in James Wechsler, *New York Post*, clipping, Oct. 10, 1966, unsorted AJM, 1965–67, SCPC.

51   Quote from the *New York Times* on possible death sentence and picture of Muste at Ft. Dix, both in *Fort Hood Three* pamphlet, pp. 8, 27.

52   AJM to "Dear Friends," Aug. 26, 1966, unsorted AJM, 1963–1966, SCPC. News coverage of the case was quite extensive throughout the United States. David Dellinger reported in October, having returned from a trip to Cambodia, Thailand, South Vietnam, and Japan, that "the three soldiers are known everywhere in Asia" (Defense Committee to "Dear Friends," Oct. 18, 1966, unsorted AJM, 1965–67, SCPC).

53   Fort Hood Three Defense Committee to "Dear Friends," n.d. [ca. Sept. 1966]; Fort Hood Three Defense Committee to "Dear Friends," Oct. 18 and 25, 1966; AJM to "Dear Friends," Nov. 10, 1966; and "News Release," Nov. 9, 1966, all in unsorted AJM, 1965–1967, SCPC; James Wechsler, *New York Post*, clipping, Oct. 10, 1966, unsorted AJM, 1965–67, SCPC. New York Post columnist Wechsler commented on the "mysterious vagaries of military justice," by which the Mora sentence was less than the sentences of the others, though the offenses were identical. "One theory," reported Wechsler, "is that Mora was tried first and that the military authorities were distressed by his apparent lack of shock over the sentence."

54   See AJM to Pete Hamil, Aug. 12, 1966, and AJM to Russell Stetler, Aug. 23, 1966, both in AJM, Box 49, SCPC; AJM to Rev. John D. Langenes, Aug. 17, 1966, AJM, Box 42, SCPC.

55   See flier on the International Peace Meeting, unsorted AJM, 1965–1967, SCPC.

56   AJM to Hermene Evans, Sept. 27, 1966, AJM, Box 42, SCPC. See also two press releases, n.d., one over the name of Mortimer Frankel, one over that of AJM, and a "Flash Memo from A. J. Muste," also n.d., AJM, Box 42, SCPC. See also the folder on "National Leadership Conference, Cleveland, September 10, 1966," in AJM, Box 47, SCPC. Muste had participated in some of these teach-ins. See, for example, William O'Neill, *Coming Apart* (New York, 1975), p. 142.

57   AJM, "Is There a Way Out?" *Liberation*, Oct. 1966, pp. 19–22. In this editorial Muste wrote: "Our pacifist friends who are troubled over the presence in a 'coalition' to end the war in Vietnam of individuals and groups that are admittedly non-pacifist, . . . themselves are usually involved in joint activity with what may perhaps best be described as non-leftist . . . individuals and groups. . . . Quite often they devote more energy to criticizing what they regard as the mistakes of the more radical anti-war elements than in themselves doing their utmost to bring the war to an end." See also "Remarks by AJM at the Dinner of the National Guardian, November 4, 1966," AJM, Box 3, SCPC.

58   *New York Times*, clipping Nov. 6, 1966, p. 42; News Release, n.d., [ca. Nov. 26, 1966]; "Motions Passed at Evaluation Conference, Cleveland, November 26, 1966"; AJM, "Preliminary Mobilization Memorandum," all in unsorted AJM, 1965–1967, SCPC. AJM, "Mobilize for Peace," *Liberation*, Dec. 1966, pp. 21–25. Adding to Muste's optimism about trade union participation in anti-war work was a recent conference held by anti-war laborites in Chicago at which he gave an invocation that, according to

Sidney Lens, never mentioned God but was the best labor speech of the meeting (Lens in *Liberation*, Sept.–Oct., p. 7). Some indication of Muste's standing in at least some labor circles was given by Patrick Gorman, secretary-treasurer of the Amalgamated Meat Cutter and Butcher Workmen, who expressed skepticism about the anti-war effort but said that he would like to attend a Mobilization meeting "because I have a great admiration for A. J. Muste who will serve as Chairman of the gathering." (Nonetheless, Gorman had a previous engagement which kept him from attending the meeting.) See AJM to Frank Rosenblum, Dec. 26, 1966, and AJM to Rosenblum, May 27, 1966, AJM, Box 49, SCPC; AJM to Gorman, and AJM to Robert Greenblatt, both dated Nov. 22, 1966, and both in AJM, Box 48, SCPC.

59 AJM, "Cleveland and After," *Mobilizer*, Dec. 19, 1966; AJM, "Mobilize for Peace," *Liberation*, Dec. 1966, pp. 21–25.

60 Nguyen Duy Tinh to AJM et al., April 30, 1966, sent via Dr. John Takman in Sweden, whose cover letter was dated May 9, 1966, both in AJM, Box 45, SCPC. See also AJM to Takman, May 24, 1966, AJM, Box 45, SCPC, and Staughton Lynd "Comment" in *Liberation* Sept.–Oct. 1967, p. 57. The Takman letter expressed the appreciation felt by Swedish opponents of the war for Muste's activities. That appreciation had been evident in a Swedish radio program, "An American Revolutionary: A. J. Muste" broadcast July 26, 1965 (AJM to Bo Wimark, July 16, 1965, and Wimark to AJM, June 30, 1965, both in AJM, Misc. 1965–1967, SCPC. After the Saigon trip "Reverend Father A. J. Muste" had also received commendation from the National Liberation Front Mission of South Vietnam based in Algeria, n.d., AJM, Box 50, SCPC. On the final proposals for the Hanoi visit see AJM to Harrison Butterworth, July 1, 1966, AJM, labeled, unsorted 1965–67, SCPC; and AJM to John Takman, July 7, 1966 (includes transcript of cables between New York and Hanoi), AJM, Box 46, SCPC; David Dellinger, "The Death of A. J. Muste," *Liberation*, Jan. 1967, p. 3; AJM et al., "Draft to Hanoi," mimeographed, July 29, 1966, unsorted AJM, 1965–1967, SCPC.

61 April Carter to AJM, Aug. 25, 1966, AJM, Box 45, SCPC; "A Draft Letter for Hanoi," n.d., mimeograph, AJM, Box 45, SCPC. Other contacts between the American peace movement and Hanoi in this period included a letter from the Vietnam National Union of Students and the Vietnam Youth Federation calling on American youth "to step up your action" against the war (Oct. 30, 1966, AJM, Box 45, SCPC), and a cable from the Vietnam Peace Committee of Hanoi to Muste acclaiming the plans for the November Mobilization (Nov. 2, 1966, unsorted AJM, 1965–1967, SCPC).

Reeves had once been Anglican bishop of Johannesburg, South Africa, but was expelled by the white supremacist Verwoerd regime for his anti-apartheid activities. Feinberg had a background of activism in both the civil rights and peace movements in the United States before becoming rabbi (now rabbi emeritus) of Holy Blossom Temple in Toronto, where he also worked with the Canadian Campaign for Nuclear Disarmament. Niemoller, known for his resistance work in the Hitler era, was a president of the World Council of Churches and the War Resisters' International ("Press Release, Volunteers for Peace in Vietnam," Dec. 30, 1966, unsorted AJM, 1965–1967, SCPC).

62 AJM to Leonard Unger, Nov. 15, 1966; Philip B. Heymann to AJM, Nov. 29, 1966; and Beverly Sterner to Gerry Hunnius, Dec. 16, 1966, all in AJM, Box 46, SCPC. See also Dellinger, "The Death of A. J. Muste," p. 3. The press conference was also reported on Dec. 29 in *Le Figaro*, the *Washington Post, Le Monde*, the *London Times*, the *New York Times*, the *Montreal Gazette, La Croix*, and the *Manchester Guardian*. On December 28, the *Toronto Daily Star* carried a story on the four men, as did, on Dec. 30, the *Frankfurter Rundschau* (See clippings in AJM, unsorted 1965–1967, SCPC). The quotation is

from *New York Herald Tribune*, Dec. 29, 1966. According to Rabbi Feinberg, Muste mentioned the possibility that this "might be his last long journey on earth" and even indicated a willingness to spend the end of his life in North Vietnam. The relationship which Muste had with the people there, Feinberg noted, was very special. He was able to convey to them his deep desire that their country might have peace and they responded by "reverencing him" (Feinberg in *WIN*, Feb. 24, 1967, p. 20, and in WBAI documentary on Muste's life, April 29, 1966, tape recording in possession of the author). On Muste's outstanding court charges see "Warrant Out for Muste," for not appearing in court "yesterday on disorderly person charges," unidentified newsclipping, handwritten date on top, Jan. 4, 1967, AJM, Box 46, SCPC. The arrest is also mentioned in memorial tributes by Dellinger, "The Death of A. J. Muste," p. 3, and McReynolds in *WIN*, Feb. 24, 1967, p. 8–9.

63   AJM, "Draft of Report on Visit of Four Clergymen to the Democratic Republic of Vietnam (North) as Volunteers for Peace in Vietnam," typescript, Feb. 11, 1967. See also AJM, "Last Words," *Liberation*, Sept.–Oct. 1967, and AJM to Bev et al., Jan. 4, 1967, AJM, Box 46, SCPC.

64   CNVA, "2690 Bombs, A Report and Appeal from A. J. Muste," Jan. 16, 1967, AJM, Box 46, SCPC. Though known to give vent to an occasional "damn" or "hell" in private conversation, this may be the only instance of Muste's ever using profanity in print.

65   Ibid.

66   AJM, "An Episode during a Visit of American and British Clergymen to North Vietnam," Jan. 9–19, 1967, AJM, Box 12, SCPC. Written in longhand, this manuscript was never published, though part of the kindergarten story was told by Muste at a meeting on February 9 before the Lawyers' Guild AJM "Last Words" *Liberation*, Sept.–Oct. 1967, pp. 52–57.

67   AJM, "Visit to North Vietnam"; Marjorie Swann to Edouard Theis, Feb. 15, 1967, AJM, Box 32, SCPC.

68   David Kraslow and Stuart H. Loory, *The Secret Search for Peace in Vietnam* (New York, 1968); Murray Kempton interview with AJM, Jan. 31, 1967, AJM, Box 46, SCPC; AJM to President Johnson, Jan. 31, 1967, AJM, Box 7, SCPC.

69   Kraslow and Loory, *Secret Search*, pp. 160–62; Theodore Draper, "How Not to Negotiate," *New York Review of Books*, May 4, 1967, p. 17–29.

70   "Joint Statement on Conclusion of Clergy Visit to Hanoi," January 9–19, 1967," AJM, Box 46, SCPC. Kraslow and Loory report that when Robert F. Kennedy talked with Johnson on February 5 or 6, the president was still convinced that military pressure was the solution in Vietnam and was determined to get more from North Vietnam than a willingness to start talks before he halted the bombing (*Secret Search*, pp. 160–62).

71   These conferences and the meeting had been arranged on their first stop in London, en route (AJM to Bev et al., Jan. 4, 1967, AJM, Box 46, SCPC). Muste's mood of exhilaration was noted in Beverly Sterner to Nguyen Trung Kieu, Feb. 3, 1967, AJM, Box 46, SCPC; and Dellinger, "The Death of A. J. Muste," p. 3.

72   Handwritten draft to President Johnson, Jan. 31, 1967, AJM, Box 7, SCPC; AJM to George Christian, Jan. 31, 1967, AJM, Box 46, SCPC. Muste was told by the CBS television network that they had cabled Ho Chi Minh for confirmation of his message to Johnson, via Muste et al., and had received such confirmation. Muste mentioned this in his speech to the Lawyers' Guild (*Liberation* Sept.–Oct. 1967, p. 54). Rabbi Feinberg also conveyed Ho's message to various American officials. He was "debriefed" by the deputy chief of the U.S. Embassy in London, by a lieutenant colonel of the Air Force at the Pentagon, and by the head of the North Vietnamese section of the U.S. State Depart-

ment Bureau of Intelligence and Research. In addition Feinberg called Arthur Goldberg, U.S. representative to the U.N. and told him of Ho's statement (Kraslow and Loory, *Secret Search*, n. 2, pp. 162–63.

73   "Invitation: . . . To Welcome Back A. J. Muste . . . ," Feb. 1, 1967, AJM, Box 45, SCPC; James Bevel in *WIN*, February 24, 1967, p. 21. While stranded in Karachi Muste had begun to stew over the impossibility of keeping informed on these projects and wrote his secretary, Beverly Sterner, that he had been dreaming about them, which somewhat belies Rabbi Feinberg's impression that Muste would have liked to have stayed in Vietnam, even to have died there ("Minutes of Meeting of Working Committee of Spring Mobilization to End the War in Vietnam," Feb. 3, 1967, AJM, Box 47, SCPC; AJM to Bev et al., Jan. 4, 1967, AJM, Box 46, SCPC; and Lawyers' Guild speech in *Liberation*, Sept.–Oct. 1967, pp. 52–57).

74   Statement by Joyce Gilmore on the death of A. J. Muste, AJM, Box 48, SCPC; Nancy Baker to the author, Sept. 12, 1979. Both John Muste and Nancy Baker stressed the Gilmores' kindness toward their father (John Muste to the author, Sept. 22, 1979).

75   Quoted in "The Fellowship of Reconciliation Announces the Death of A. J. Muste," Feb. 11, 1967, AJM, Box 48, SCPC; Transcript of talk given by Cara Cook on the WBAI documentary, April 29, 1967, copy in the author's possession.

76   The author was an attender at that meeting. Then a graduate student who had been considering taking Muste's life as a topic for her doctoral thesis, she had nearly decided against the idea because, by traditional academic standards, he did not seem "significant" enough. She left the meeting with a new definition of significance and wrote a dissertation of Muste, which was the beginning of the present book.

77   McReynolds in *WIN*, Feb. 24, 1967, pp. 8–9. Spender's poems were reprinted in *Liberation*, Sept.–Oct. 1967, pp. 40–41 from *Selected Poems of Stephen Spender* (New York, 1961).

78   "Excerpts from Letter Written by Cara Cook to Several Brookwood Staff and Graduates At the Time of A. J. Muste's Death, 2/11/67," copy in the author's possession; James Wechsler, clipping "He Never Failed," *New York Post*, Feb. 22, 1967, AJM, Box 48, SCPC; "Attenders at the A. J. Muste Memorial Meeting," xerox from Rutherford Place Meeting House, courtesy of Elizabeth H. Moger, keeper of the Records, Haviland Records Room, New York Yearly Meeting, in the author's possession.

79   Shirley Lens to Beverly Sterner, Feb. 22, 1967, AJM, Box 48, SCPC; Tape recording of WBAI documentary; CBS "Man of Conscience," on the program "Look Up and Live," Sept. 10, 1967. Examples of tributes in the liberal press include those by Nat Hentoff in the *Village Voice*, Feb. 23, 1967, pp. 11, 22, and the *Saturday Review*, April 8, 1967, p. 35; and Norman Whitney, "Number One Pacifist," *Christian Century*, May 10, 1967, p. 622–24. *Liberation* special issue, Sept.–Oct. 1967; *WIN*, special supplement, Feb. 24, 1967; John Nevin Sayre, "A. J. Muste, Fighting Reconciler," *Fellowship*, March 1967, pp. 11–13. See also the poem by Edward Gottlieb in this issue. Samples of telegrams and letters on the occasion of Muste's death were printed in both the *Liberation* and *WIN* special issues.

80   John Muste to the author, Feb. 6, 1979; Ralph DiGia in *WIN* special supplement, p. 12.

81   Cook remarks in WBAI documentary. In contrast to such memories as these of Muste as a fun-loving and warm personality, see the impression of H. Stuart Hughes (who worked with him on the Council of Correspondence), that "to my knowledge Muste lacked a sense of humor" (Hughes to the author, Feb. 13, 1978); and the depiction of him by old associates as reported in Constance Ashton Myers' study of the

Trotskyist movement where he sometimes appears as an almost sinister figure (*The Prophet's Army* [Westport, Conn., 1977], pp. 233–34, n. 41, for example).

82   Shirley Lens to Beverly Sterner, Feb. 22, 1967, AJM, Box 48, SCPC; Sidney Lens "Humanistic Revolutionary" in *Liberation*, special supplement, Sept.–Oct. 1967, p. 8; Wechsler, clipping *New York Post*, "He Never Failed,"; and Jackson Maclow in *WIN*, Feb. 24, 1967, p. 7.

83   Bevel in *WIN*, Feb. 24, 1967, p. 15; *Mobilizer*, March 19, 1967, p. 6, copy in AJM, Box 48, SCPC.

84   *Mobilizer*, March 19, 1967; Coretta Scott King, *My Life with MLK* (New York, 1969), p. 295; *New York Times* clipping, April 19, 1967, AJM, Box 48, SCPC.

85   Cooney and Michalowski, *Power of the People*, p. 200; George F. Will, "Reflections in the Shadow of the Bomb," Baltimore *Sun*, Sunday, Dec. 31, 1978.

86   Frontispiece of AJM, *Getting Rid of War*, an American Friends' Service Committee pamphlet, n.d., mentions the WRL award. The Gandhi Award, from a foundation for "Promoting Enduring Peace Inc.," was presented to Muste in 1966. Previous recipients had included Eleanor Roosevelt and Linus Pauling. See "Hope Alumnus Lives Life Advocating Goals of Pacifism," *Anchor*, May 13, 1966, Hope College. On the Nobel Prize idea see AJM to Jerome Davis, April 26, 1963, AJM, Box 37, SCPC. On Ferry's notion see Beverly Sterner to W. H. Ferry, April 15, 1966, AJM, Box 44, SCPC. At the time of his death Muste had been nominated by the World Council of Peace for the Frederic Joliet-Curie Peace Gold Medal, but he was unable to comment on whether or not he would accept the nomination, news of which came while he was in North Vietnam and his response had not been made before he died (Beverly Sterner to International Institute for Peace, Jan. 20, and Feb. 15, 1967, AJM, Box 52, SCPC). Tom Brewer to AJM, n.d. [1964]; AJM to Tom Brewer, Sept. 18, 1964, AJM, Box 43, SCPC; AJM to Cara Cook, June 21, 1936, excerpted in a letter to the author from Cara Cook, 1978, in the author's possession.

Bibliography

Manuscript Sources

Primary source material pertaining to Muste's formative years is relatively scarce. Bits and pieces of evidence from his life before the era of World War I can be found in the Records of the Fourth Reformed Church in Grand Rapids, Michigan, and the archives of several of the schools which he attended: Hope College in Holland, Michigan; Northwestern College in Orange City, Iowa; and New Brunswick Theological Seminary in New Brunswick, New Jersey. The Registrar's Records at Columbia University and the Union Theological Seminary, both in New York City, also have material about Muste. The files kept by some of the churches which he served are another source of information; these include Fort Washington Collegiate Church in New York City and the Central Congregational Church in Newtonville, Massachusetts. Quaker archives—namely those of New England Yearly Meeting at the Rhode Island Historical Society Library in Providence, Rhode Island, and those of Chappaqua Monthly Meeting, housed in the Haviland Records Room of New York Yearly Meeting in New York City—include material on Muste.

A much more extensive collection of materials is available for the study of Muste's labor career. The papers of Elizabeth Glendower Evans in the Schlesinger Library at Radcliffe College in Cambridge, Massachusetts, refer to the Lawrence Strike of 1919. The years covering his work at Brookwood, with the Conference for Progressive Labor Action (CPLA) and through the Trotskyist interlude can be fully documented through the following collections: the Walter Reuther Archives at Wayne State University, specifically the papers of Brookwood Labor College, Arthur C. Calhoun, Katherine Pollack Ellikson and Selma Borchardt; the Labadie Collection at the University of Michigan Library; the papers of Harold Gray and Paul Blanshard at the Bentley Historical Library at the University of Michigan; the papers of Thyra Edwards and John Fitzpatrick at the Chicago Historical Society; the papers of Adolph Germer at the State Historical Society of Wisconsin in Madison; the papers of Elmer Cope at the Ohio Historical Society in Columbus; the papers of Fannia Cohn, Norman Thomas and V. F. Calverton at the New York City Public Library; and a few odd items in the papers of Oswald Garrison Villard at the Houghton Library of Harvard

University and the papers of Arthur L. Preis in the Special Collections of the Library at the University of Oregon.

Details about the merger between Musteites and Trotskyists and their stormy collaboration are available in the papers of the Socialist Workers Party, on microfilm at the State Historical Society of Wisconsin. Two of the key documents on this film, pamphlets written by Muste, are also available in the original published form at the Harvard College Library, Cambridge, Massachusetts. Papers from his work following the break with Trotskyism are housed in the Labor Temple Collection at the Presbyterian Historical Society in Philadelphia. Some materials from the Labor Temple period also appear in Muste's personal papers and the Fellowship of Reconciliation Papers at the Swarthmore College Peace Collection in Swarthmore, Pennsylvania, as well as in the papers of Edmund Chaffee at the Syracuse University Library in Syracuse, New York.

Documentary sources from Muste's efforts as a champion of civil liberties and civil rights are spread through his papers and those of the FOR at Swarthmore, and exist as well in the papers of Sidney Lens at the Chicago Historical Society. The Slater King Collection at Fisk University includes some correspondence between that civil rights activist and Muste. Most of the primary source material on Muste's pacifism is collected in the personal papers and FOR Papers at Swarthmore. Also in that library, evidence from Muste's pacifist career is filed among papers of the Women's Peace Union, the Consultative Peace Council, the Massachusetts Peace Society, and the papers of John Nevin Sayre. The papers of Kirby Page at the Southern California School of Theology in Claremont and those of Kermit Erby at the Chicago Historical Society are also relevant to this subject.

Writings by and about Muste

Muste was the author of two books—*Nonviolence in an Aggressive World* (New York, 1940) and *Not by Might* (1947; Garland Library reprint ed., New York, 1971, with introduction by Jo Ann Robinson). A good selection of the essays and articles that he wrote, dating from 1905 to 1966, was compiled by Nat Hentoff in *The Essays of A. J. Muste* (New York, 1967). Most of these, however, date from the late 1930s and after. Examples of his writings from the era of World War I through the thirties are available in several periodicals: *Survey Magazine*, the *New Textile Worker*, *Fellowship*, and the *World Tomorrow*. Letters to the editor and occasional articles from Muste also appeared in the *Nation*, the *New Republic*, and the *Christian Century*. These journals, along with *Fellowship*, continued to publish Muste's writings during World War II and thereafter. Letters to the editor, interviews, and running accounts of Muste's activities appear throughout his life span in the *New York Times*. Other periodicals to which Muste contributed between the eras of World War I and World War II include the *Congregationalist*, the *Annals of the American Academy of Political and Social Science*, *Religious Education*, the *Family*, *Pageant Magazine*, the *Presbyterian Tribune*, and *Religion in Life*. He also wrote two pamphlets in this period—*The Automobile Industry and Organized Labor* (Baltimore, 1935) and *Which Party for the American Worker?* (New York, 1935); and contributed essays to *Labor Speaks for Itself on Religion*, edited by Jerome Davis (New York, 1929), and *The Church Faces the World*, edited by Samuel McCrea Cavert (New York, 1939). In the years following World War II, Muste contributed prolifically to the pacifist press. His writings could be found regularly in the following: *Fellowship*, *War Resisters' League News*, the *Peacemaker*, *CNVA Bulletin*, *World Peace Brigade Report*, the

Correspondent, *WIN*, and, above all, *Liberation*. Less frequent contributions from him appeared in the *Progressive*, the *Friends' Intelligencer*, *Friends' Journal*, and *Gandhi Marg*. He contributed substantially to the writing of two statements from the American Friends' Service Committee: *Speak Truth to Power* (Philadelphia, 1955) and *Peace in Vietnam* (Philadelphia, 1966).

Five autobiographical essays were written by Muste—"A Fragment of Autobiography," 1939, is in his papers at Swarthmore and was also published in the magazine *Christendom* IV, no. 3 (Summer, 1939): 329–40; an autobiographical lecture that he gave at New Brunswick Theological Seminary in 1944, transcript at Swarthmore; an oral history interview in the early 1950s, transcribed as Oral Memoir 589 in the Oral History Office at Columbia University in New York; his memories in *As We Saw the Thirties: Essays on Social and Political Movements of a Decade*, edited by Rita J. Simon (Urbana, 1967); and, most extensive (and discursive) of all, the "Sketches for an Autobiography" in *The Essays of A. J. Muste*.

Biographical sketches include Devere Allen's in *Adventurous Americans* (New York, 1932), pp. 99–117; Milton Mayer, "The Christer," *Fellowship*, Jan. 1952, pp. 1–10, and Donald B. Meyer's reflections on Muste in *The Protestant Search for Political Realism, 1919–1941* (Berkeley, 1960). A short and uninformative description appears in George Thayer, *The Far Shores of Politics (New York, 1967)*. The only full-scale biography of Muste is Nat Hentoff's *Peace Agitator, the Story of A. J. Muste* (New York, 1963). Paul Goodman wrote a memorable review of Hentoff's book in the *New York Review of Books*, Oct. 1963, p. 14. Hentoff's introduction to *The Essays of A. J. Muste* includes valuable biographical observations, and a Muste-like character figures in this author's novel *Onwards!* (New York, 1968).

A variety of personal recollections, eulogies, and political essays related to Muste's beliefs and activities was collected by the pacifist press at his death—John Nevin Sayre, "Fighting Reconciler, A. J. Muste as I Knew Him," *Fellowship*, (March 1967), pp. 11–12; *Liberation* memorial issue, (Sept.–Oct. 1967); and *WIN* memorial issue, (Feb. 1967). Other memorials and obituaries of interest include: a documentary by New York City radio station WBAI; a CBS documentary, "Man of Conscience," written by Mort Frankel; an obituary by Nat Hentoff in the *Village Voice*, Feb. 23, 1967; reflections on Muste's death in the *Saturday Review*, April 8, 1967; and Norman Whitney's comments in the *Christian Century*, May 10, 1967.

Muste was included in the *Historical Directory of the Reformed Church in America*, edited by Peter N. Vandenberge (Grand Rapids, 1970), and was the subject, along with the FOR, of reflections by Edgar L. Jones, "There Is No Way to Peace, Peace Is the Way," Baltimore *Evening Sun*, Feb. 6, 1976. See also Jo Ann Robinson, "A. J. Muste and Ways to Peace," *Peace Movements in America*, edited by Charles Chatfield (New York, 1973), and Reinhold Niebuhr, "Christian Revolutionary," *New York Times Book Review*, April 16, 1967.

Oral and Living Sources

Through letters, telephone interviews, and some face-to-face conversations, a fairly representative sampling of Muste's associates were involved in providing information for this biography. But these sources represent only a fraction of those who are still living and who can be assumed to possess valuable memories of him.

Three family members participated: Muste's nephew Arthur Johnson and Muste's two surviving children, Nancy Muste Baker and John Muste. Muste's family friend, John Beardslee III, and his New Brunswick classmate Milton J. Hoffman recalled Muste in his seminary days. Roger Baldwin responded to questions about Muste in the World War I period. Cara Cook provided a wealth of information about the Brookwood era and about Muste's character and personality. Insights into his religious thought were offered by John Howard Yoder, Douglas Steere, John C. Bennett, and Norman Gottwald. His relationship to the civil rights movement was recalled by Bayard Rustin, James Farmer, James Lawson, and Glenn Smiley. No members of the Southern Christian Leadership Conference or the family of Martin Luther King, Jr., answered numerous requests for interviews. Collegues in the FOR whose memories were tapped include John Swomley, James Best, and James Forest. War Resister League (WRL) comrades who responded to questions were Ann Davidon, Barbara Deming, and Jim Peck. Among the various academic and scientific people who recalled Muste's work were Victor Paschkis, Irving L. Horowitz, Herman Kahn, David Riesman, H. Stuart Hughes, and Anatol Rapoport. Individuals who knew Muste through the American Friends' Service Committee and other contexts include Stephen Cary, Bill Sutherland, and Charles Walker. Sidney Lens was another co-worker on many projects. John M. Jones reported his reaction to Muste's pacifism as a Pentagon employee, and Edith Snyder, who worked as Muste's secretary for several years, shared some of her observations about him. Norman Cousins responded to questions on Muste and the Committee for a Sane Nuclear Policy (SANE). George Kennan and Robert McNamara each chose to let the record speak for itself when asked to comment on Muste's efforts to establish a dialogue with them. The author of this biography interviewed Muste in 1964 while working on an undergraduate honors' thesis about him and other pacifists.

Unpublished Theses
Several unpublished graduate level studies include Muste or information relevant to his background and work. Among these are: Henry J. Ryskamp, "The Dutch in Western Michigan" (Ph.D. diss., University of Michigan, 1930); Darrel E. Bigham, "American Christian Thinkers and the Function of War 1861–1920" (Ph.D. diss., University of Kansas, 1970); Emma E. Haas, "The Attitude of the Churches in the World War" (Master's thesis, University of Chicago, 1942); Eleanor Nora Kahn, "Organizations of Unemployed Workers as a Factor in the American Labor Movement" (Master's thesis, University of Wisconsin, 1934); Jon Bloom, "Brookwood Labor College" (Master's thesis, Rutgers, 1978); Glenn Zeitzer, "The American Peace Movement during the Second World War" (Master's thesis, Bryn Mawr, 1978); Alan Laurence Letts, "Pacifism and the Gospel: A Comparative Study of the Theological and Ethical Foundation of A. J. Muste's Radical Pacifism and Reinhold Niebuhr's 'Christian Realism' " (Ph.D. diss., Yale, 1975); Neil H. Katz, "Revolutionary Pacifism and the Contemporary American Peace Movement: The Committee for Nonviolent Action 1957–1967" (Ph.D. diss., University of Maryland, 1974); Milton Katz, "Pacifism, Politics and Protest: SANE and the American Peace Movement 1957–1972" (Ph.D. diss., St. Louis, 1973); William Batz, "Revolution and Peace: The Christian Pacifism of A. J. Muste 1885–1967 (Ph.D. diss., University of Minnesota, 1974); and Jo Ann Robinson, "The Traveler from Zierikzee" (Ph.D. diss., Johns Hopkins, 1972).

Scholarly Monographs and Articles
Works dealing with influences and institutions that were important to Muste in his formative stages include: W. H. Auden's comments on childhood and mysticism in Anne Fremantle, *The Protestant Mystics* (Philadelphia, 1964); Henry S. Lucas,

Netherlanders in America (Ann Arbor, Michigan, 1955); Gerald F. DeJong, *The Dutch in America, 1609–1974* (Boston, 1975); Albert Hyma, *Albertus C. Van Raalte and His Dutch Settlement in the United States* (Ann Arbor, Michigan, 1947); Wynand Wichers, *A Century of Hope* (Grand Rapids, 1968); E. T. Corwin, *The Reformed Church Dutch* in the *American Church.History Series*, vol. 8 (New York, 1894); David D. Demarest, *The Reformed Church in America* (New York, 1889); John Kromminga, *The Christian Reformed Churches* (Grand Rapids, Michigan, 1949); *The Heidelberg Catechism or Method of Instruction of the Christian Religion* (Hagerstown, 1830); and D. D. Demarest et al., eds., *Centennial of the Theological Seminary of the Reformed Church in America* (New York, 1885).

The intellectual and religious climate influencing Muste in the period through World War I may be better understood with reference to: Henry F. May, *Protestant Churches and Industrial America* (New York, 1963); John Hutchison, *We Are Not Divided* (New York, 1941); Robert Moats Miller, *American Protestantism and Social Issues, 1919–1939* (Chapel Hill, 1958); and Donald B. Meyer, *The Protestant Search for Political Realism, 1919–1941* (Berkeley, 1960). Relevant also is Ray H. Abrams, *Preachers Present Arms* (New York, 1933).

On the Quaker influence in Muste's life, several works are especially useful for background: Rufus M. Jones, *Studies in Mystical Religion* (New York, 1909), *The Story of George Fox* (New York, 1919), and *Spiritual Reformers of the Sixteenth and Seventeenth Centuries* (London, 1928); John Woolman, *The Journal and Plea for the Poor* (New York, paperback, 1961); Harold Loukes, *The Quaker Contribution* (London, 1965); and Jo Ann Robinson, *A. J. Muste, Pacifist and Prophet: His Relation to the Society of Friends* (Pendle Hill, 1980).

Works relating to Muste's labor career include Melvyn Dubofsky, *We Shall Be All: A History of the Industrial Workers of the World* (New York, 1972); Patrick Renshaw, *The Wobblies* (New York, 1961); and Donald B. Cole, *Immigrant City* (Chapel Hill, 1963). *The American Labor Year Books* include information on Muste's activities in most editions through the twenties and thirties. Also useful for the early twenties is Marion Dutton Savage, *Industrial Unionism in America* (New York, 1922). The philosophy and curriculum of Brookwood Labor College was discussed in Marius Hansome, *World Workers' Educational Movements, their Social Significance* (New York, 1931). Other memories of Brookwood can be found in Sarah N. Cleghorn, *Threescore* (New York, 1936); James H. Maurer, *It Can Be Done* (New York, 1938); and Louis Budenz, *This Is My Story* (New York, 1947). See also Charles F. Howlett, "Brookwood Labor College and Worker Commitment to Social Reform," *Mid-America*, 61, no. 1 (January 1979): 47–66.

On Muste's involvement with liberal undertakings in the twenties, the following are useful: Kenneth C. Mackay, *The Progressive Movement of 1924* (New York, 1966); Donald R. McCoy, *Angry Voices: Left-of-Center Politics in the New Deal Era* (Lawrence, Kans., 1958); and Arthur M. Schlesinger, Jr., *The Crisis of the Old Order* (Boston, 1957). On the rift which eventually occurred between Brookwood and the American Federation of Labor, see James O. Morris, *Conflict within the AFL* (Ithaca, 1958); and Irving Bernstein, *The Lean Years: A History of the American Worker, 1920–1933* (Baltimore, 1966).

For background on CPLA activities in industrial unionizing, see Melvyn Dubofsky and Warren Van Tine, *John L. Lewis: A Biography* (Chicago, 1977); Sidney Fine, "The Toledo Chevrolet Strike of 1935," *Ohio Historical Quarterly* 67 (October, 1958): 326–56; Sidney Fine, *Sit-Down: The General Motors Strike of 1936–1937* (Ann

Arbor, 1969); Irving Bernstein, *The Turbulent Years* (New York, 1970); Edmund Wilson, *Letters on Literature and Politics: 1912–1972*, Elena Wilson, ed. (New York, 1977); an essay on Frank Keeney by David Corbin in Gary M. Fink and Merl E. Reed, eds., *Essays in Southern Labor History: Selected Papers, Southern Labor History Conference, 1976* (Westport, 1977); Tom Tippett, *When Southern Labor Stirs* (New York, 1931); and Sinclair Lewis, *Cheap and Contented Labor: The Picture of a Southern Mill Town* (New York, 1929). Information about the unemployed leagues may be found in John Dos Passos, *In All Countries* (New York, 1934); Milton Derber and Edwin Young, eds., *Labor and the New Deal* (Madison, 1957); Sidney Lens, *Left, Right and Center* (Hinsdale, Ill., 1949); David J. Leah, " 'United We Eat': The Creation and Organization of the Unemployed Councils in 1930," *Labor History* 8 (Fall 1967): 300–315; and Roy Rosenzweig, "Radicals and the Jobless: The Museites and the Unemployed Leagues, 1932–1936," *Labor History* 16 (Winter 1975): 51–77. For communist attitudes toward the CPLA, see Earl Browder, *Communism in the United States* (New York, 1935), and Anthony Bimba, *History of the American Working Class* (New York, 1936). AFL attitudes toward the CPLA are dicussed in Jack Skeels, "The Background of UAW Factionalism," *Labor History* 2 (Spring 1962): 158–81; Walter Galenson, *The CIO Challenge to the A.F. of L.* (Cambridge, Mass., 1960); Philip Taft, *The A.F. of L. from the Death of Gompers to the Merger* (New York, 1959); Thomas R. Brooks, *Toil and Trouble* (New York, 1964); and Lewis Lorwin, *The American Federation of Labor* (Washington, D.C., 1933).

Information bearing upon Muste's experience as a Trotskyist may be found in Isaac Deutscher's *The Prophet Outcast: Trotsky, 1929–1940* (New York, 1963); Benjamin Gitlow, *I Confess* (New York, 1940); Max Schactman's *Oral Memoir 254* at Columbia University and his contribution to Rita J. Simon's *As We Saw the Thirties: Essays on Social and Political Movements of a Decade* (Urbana, 1967); and James P. Cannon's *History of American Trotskyism* (New York, 1944). Analyses of the merger between Museites and Trotskyists appear in Philip Selznick, *The Organizational Weapon: A Study of Bolshevik Strategy and Tactics* (New York, 1952); Sidney Lens, *Left, Right and Center* (Hinsdale, Ill., 1941); and Benjamin Gitlow, *I Confess* (New York, 1940). Brief reference to Muste's Trotskyist experience appears in Daniel Bell's essay on socialism in *Socialism and American Life*, edited by Stow Persons and Donald D. Egbert, 2 vols. (Princeton, 1952), vol. 1: 358–86. On the Goodyear rubber strike of 1936, see Edward Levinson, *Labor on the March* (New York, 1940), Rose Pesotta, *Bread Upon the Waters* (New York, 1944), and Ruth McKenney, *Industrial Valley* (New York, 1939). On differences between Trotsky and some of his critics, see George Novack, ed., *Their Morals and Ours: Marxist vs. Liberal Views on Morality* (New York, 1966).

Works relating to Muste's labor activities after his break from the Marxist movement include reports in *Fellowship* and the *New York Times*; Charles Stelzle, *Son of the Bowery: The Life Story of an East Side American* (New York, 1926); George H. Nash III, "Charles Stelzle, Apostle to Labor," *Labor History* 11, no. 2 (Spring 1970): 151–74; and Jo Ann Robinson, " 'Pharos of the East Side,' A. J. Muste and Labor Temple, 1936–1940," *Journal of Presbyterian History* 48, no. 1 (Spring 1970): 18–37.

Among the works which convey something of the mood of the times in which Muste was a labor radical are Louis Adamic, *Dynamite: The Story of Class Violence in America* (New York, 1931); Eric Goldman's *Rendezvous with Destiny: A History of Modern American Reform* (New York, 1962); Christopher Lasch, *The New Radicalism in America, 1889–1963* (New York, 1965). It may be useful to consult also the history of socialist programs in David A. Shannon, *The Socialist Party of America* (Chicago, 1967).

For some context in which to place Muste's activities as a civil liberties and civil rights advocate, see Donald O. Johnson, *The Challenge to American Freedoms* (Lexington, Ky., 1963); Paul Murphy, *World War I and the Origins of Civil Liberties in the United States* (New York, 1979); Richard H. Frost, *The Mooney Case* (Stanford, 1968); Robert H. Montgomery, *Sacco and Vanzetti, the Murder and the Myth* (New York, 1960); Haywood Patterson and Earl Conrad, *Scottsboro Boy* (New York, 1969); Robert W. Griffith, *The Politics of Fear: Joseph R. McCarthy and the Senate* (Lexington, Ky., 1971); Richard M. Freeland, *The Truman Doctrine and the Origins of McCarthyism: Foreign Policy, Domestic Politics, and Internal Security, 1946–1948* (New York, 1974); Walter and Miriam Schneir, *Invitation to an Inquest* (New York, 1978); Morton Sobell, *On Doing Time* (New York, 1974); Robert Calvert, *Ain't Gonna Pay for War No More* (New York, 1971, 1972); Harvard Sitkoff, *The Struggle for Black Equality, 1954–1980* (New York, 1981); James Farmer, *Freedom When?* (New York, 1965); August Meier and Elliott Rudwick, *CORE: A Study in the Civil Rights Movement, 1942–1968* (Urbana, Ill., 1975); Jervis Anderson, *A. Philip Randolph: A Biographical Portrait* (New York, 1972); Bayard Rustin, *Down the Line* (New York, 1971); Martin Luther King, Jr., *Stride Toward Freedom* (New York, 1958); David Lewis, *King: A Critical Biography* (New York, 1970); Coretta King, *My Life with Martin Luther King* (New York, 1969); Howell Raines, ed., *My Soul Is Rested: Movement Days in the Deep South Remembered* (New York, 1978); and Howard Zinn, *SNCC: The New Abolitionists* (Boston, 1964).

The unifying theme of pacifism in Muste's life can be examined in the context of general surveys of the American peace movement, such as: Peter Brock, *Pacifism in the United States: From the Colonial Era to the First World War* (New York, 1968); and *Twentieth Century Pacifism* (New York, 1970); Merle E. Curti, *Peace or War: The American Struggle, 1635–1936* (Boston, 1936); Lawrence S. Wittner, *Rebels against War: The American Peace Movement, 1941–1960* (New York, 1969); Robert Cooney and Helen Michalowski, *Power of the People: Active Nonviolence in the U.S.* (Culver City, Calif., 1977); David Sands Patterson, *Toward a Warless World: The Travail of the American Peace Movement, 1887–1914* (Bloomington, 1976); Charles deBenedetti, *The Peace Reform in American History* (Bloomington, 1980), and *Origins of the Modern American Peace Movement, 1915–1929* (New York, 1978); and Charles Chatfield, *For Peace and Justice: Pacifism in America, 1914–1941* (Knoxville, 1971). Studies of nonviolent direct action and reports on specific nonviolent actions are also relevant: Gene Sharp, *The Politics of Nonviolent Action* (Boston, 1973); Severyn T. Bruyn and Paula M. Rayman, eds., *Nonviolent Action and Social Change* (New York, 1979); Earle L. Reynolds, *Forbidden Voyage* (New York, 1961); Barbara Deming, *Prison Notes* (Boston, 1966), *Revolution and Equilibrium* (New York, 1971), and *We Can't Live without Our Lives* (New York, 1974); Bradford Lyttle, *You Come with Naked Hands: The Story of the San Francisco to Moscow March for Peace* (Weare, N.H., 1966); A. Paul Hare and Herbert H. Blumberg, eds., *Liberation without Violence: A Third Party Approach* (London, 1978); David Dellinger, *Revolutionary Nonviolence* (New York, 1971), and *More Power than We Know* (New York, 1975); and David McReynolds, *We Have Been Invaded by the Twenty-First Century* (New York, 1970).

Efforts to address the theological questions raised by Christian pacifism include: Reinhold Niebuhr, *The Nature and Destiny of Man*, 2 vols. (New York, 1941, 1943); Paul

Merkley, *Reinhold Niebuhr, a Political Account* (Montreal and London, 1975); Donald F. Durnbaugh, ed., *On Earth Peace* (Elgin, Ill., 1978); American Friends' Service Committee, *Speak Truth to Power* (Philadelphia, 1955); and Gordon Zahn, ed., *Thomas Merton on Peace* (New York, 1974).

The two major wars which brought Muste's pacifism into sharpest relief were the Second World War and the War in Vietnam. Works relative to the Second World War and pacifism include: Mulford Sibley and Philip Jacob, *Conscription of Conscience* (New York, 1952); John Whiteclay Chambers, *Draftees or Volunteers* (New York, 1975); Vera Brittain, *The Rebel Passion* (Nyack, New York, 1964); John M. Swomley, Jr., *The Military Establishment* (Boston, 1964); Henry L. Feingold, *The Politics of Rescue: The Roosevelt Administration and the Holocaust, 1938–1945* (New York, 1970); and Martin Sherwin, *A World Destroyed: The Atomic Bomb and the Grand Alliance* (New York, 1975). With regard to the Vietnam War and pacifist protest, see: Anthony Austin, *The President's War: The Story of the Tonkin Gulf Resolution* (Philadelphia, 1971); I. F. Stone, "The Tonkin Bay Mystery," *New York Review of Books*, March 28, 1968, pp. 5–12; Irwin Unger, *The Movement: A History of the American New Left, 1959–1972* (New York, 1974), p. 83; Kirkpatrick Sale, *SDS: Ten Years toward a Revolution* (New York, 1973); James Finn, ed., *Protest, Pacifism and Politics* (New York, 1967); American Friends' Service Committee, *Peace in Vietnam* (Philadelphia, 1966); Alexander Kendrick, *The Wound Within* (New York, 1974); David Kraslow and Stuart H. Loory, *The Secret Search for Peace in Vietnam* (New York, 1968); Frances Fitzgerald, *Fire in the Lake: The Vietnamese and the Americans in Vietnam* (Boston, 1972); Michael Charlton and Anthony Moncrieff, *Many Reasons Why: The American Involvement in Vietnam* (New York, 1978); and George C. Herring, *America's Largest War: The United States and Vietnam, 1950–1975* (New York, 1979).

Autobiographies and Biographies of Others

Memoirs and studies of other figures whose lives touched Muste's include: the sketch of Samuel Ottmar Mast in *World Who's Who in Science: From Antiquities to the Present* (Hannibal, Mo., 1968); William Adams Brown, *A Teacher and His Times* (New York, 1940); Raymond B. Fosdick, *Chronicle of a Generation* (New York, 1958); George A. Gordon, *My Education and Religion* (Boston, 1925); Bliss Perry, *And Gladly Teach* (Boston, 1935); Charles Dole, *My Eighty Years* (New York, 1927); Dores R. Sharpe, *Walter Rauschenbusch* (New York, 1942); John C. Farrell, *Beloved Lady* (Baltimore, 1967); Richard Drinnon, *Rebel in Paradise* (Chicago, 1961); W. A. Swanberg, *Norman Thomas: The Last Idealist* (New York, 1967); the profile of Elizabeth Glendower Evans in volume 1 of *Notable American Women 1607–1950: A Biographical Dictionary*, 3 vols., Edward T. James and Janet James, eds. (Cambridge, 1971); Emmett Larkin, *James Larkin, Irish Labour Leader, 1876–1947* (Cambridge, 1965); and D. Joy Humes, *Oswald Garrison Villard, Liberal of the 1920's* (New York, 1960). Erik Erikson's study of Mohandas Gandhi, the eastern leader of nonviolence (*Gandhi's Truth: On the Origins of Militant Nonviolence* [New York, 1969]) offers points of comparison and contrast to the background and character of Muste as a leading Western pacifist. See also Howard Thurman, *With Head and Heart: The Story of Howard Thurman*, (New York, 1979).

Index

D

O

About the Author

David E. Newton holds an associate's degree in science from Grand Rapids (Michigan) Junior College, a BA in chemistry (with high distinction), an MA in education from the University of Michigan, and an EdD in science education from Harvard University. He is the author of more than 400 textbooks, encyclopedias, resource books, research manuals, laboratory manuals, trade books, and other educational materials. He taught mathematics, chemistry, and physical science in Grand Rapids, Michigan, for 13 years; was professor of chemistry and physics at Salem State College in Massachusetts for 15 years; and was adjunct professor in the College of Professional Studies at the University of San Francisco for 10 years.

The author's previous books for ABC-CLIO include *Global Warming* (1993), *Gay and Lesbian Rights—A Resource Handbook* (1994, 2009), *The Ozone Dilemma* (1995), *Violence and the Mass Media* (1996), *Environmental Justice* (1996, 2009), *Encyclopedia of Cryptology* (1997), *Social Issues in Science and Technology: An Encyclopedia* (1999), *DNA Technology* (2009), *Sexual Health* (2010), *The Animal Experimentation Debate* (2013), *Marijuana* (2013), *World Energy Crisis* (2013), *Steroids and Doping in Sports* (2014), *GMO Food* (2014), *Science and Political Controversy* (2014), *Wind Energy* (2015), *Fracking* (2015), *Solar Energy* (2015), *Youth Substance Abuse* (2016), and *Global Water Crisis* (2016). His other recent books include *Physics: Oryx Frontiers of Science Series* (2000), *Sick!* (4 volumes; 2000), *Science, Technology, and Society: The Impact of Science in the 19th Century* (2 volumes; 2001), *Encyclopedia of Fire* (2002), *Molecular Nanotechnology: Oryx Frontiers of Science Series* (2002), *Encyclopedia of Water* (2003), *Encyclopedia of Air* (2004), *The New Chemistry* (6 volumes; 2007), *Nuclear Power* (2005), *Stem Cell Research* (2006), *Latinos in the Sciences, Math, and Professions* (2007), and *DNA Evidence and Forensic Science* (2008). He has also been an updating and consulting editor on a number of books and reference works, including *Chemical Compounds* (2005), *Chemical Elements* (2006), *Encyclopedia of Endangered Species* (2006), *World of Mathematics* (2006), *World of Chemistry* (2006), *World of Health* (2006), *UXL Encyclopedia of Science* (2007), *Alternative Medicine* (2008), *Grzimek's Animal Life Encyclopedia* (2009), *Community Health* (2009), *Genetic Medicine* (2009), *The Gale Encyclopedia of Medicine* (2010–2011), *The Gale Encyclopedia of Alternative Medicine* (2013), *Discoveries in Modern Science: Exploration, Invention, and Technology* (2013–2014), and *Science in Context* (2013–2014).